Proof
And the Difficulty of Meaning

Greg Heard

Copyright © 2015 Greg Heard

All rights reserved.

ISBN: 13: 978-1512178685

ACKNOWLEDGMENT

This book is dedicated to my son, Alex:

        Choose your beliefs wisely.

To my excellent friend Michael Kulas, you are my background of inspiration and many thanks to Sherree Felstead for her unfailing support and generous love.

CONTENTS

	Acknowledgments	i
	Message from the Author	iii
	Introduction	Pg. 1
5	Rose Glass	Pg. 13
6	This Way Up	Pg. 194
1	Ariadne's String	Pg. 306
2	In Such Manner Did I Dream	Pg. 387
3	Astrophysics, Astronomy, Biology and Beyond	Pg. 437
4	Alam Al Mithal	Pg. 528
7	No Guru	Pg. 591
	A Year of a Swollen Appendix	Pg. 602
	Glossary	Pg. 616
	About the Author	Pg. 622

MESSAGE FROM THE AUTHOR

Dear readers,

You will notice that the order of the chapters has been rearranged.

I felt that the fifth and sixth chapters represented a cleaner window into the meat of my argument, and that if I did not put these chapters first, the patience of you might be taxed to such an extent that these two chapters will not be read at all.

The development of the book, and the subsequent impact of my understanding of what it is I'm saying, reads better in the order of one through seven, and the book was always meant to be conceived in this way. But, as I re-worked the book, the *Rose Glass* and *Way Up* Chapters (5&6) became the hub of my unfolding insight. Also, my dim understanding of neuroscience unfolded and enhanced much inside my head. I'm not trying to be an artist and make some kind of grand statement that chapter orders are redundant *in my world*. I just want people to enjoy my work. I'm very proud of this book, but it is meaningless unless it has a chance to live in you, the reader.

   Thank you very much.

Greg

INTRODUCTION

"Philosophy never seems to me to have a better hand to play than when she battles against our presumptions and our vanity; when in good Faith she acknowledges her weakness, her ignorance and her inability to reach conclusions." – Montaigne on presumption

The thought to do a book about the nature of proof came into my head in about 2006. As a 'right brain' artist, I had the inkling to do more reading in the sciences, and over the course of my life, I have read quite a lot about psychology, religion and history. It dawned on me one afternoon that it would be interesting to look at the idea of scientific proof and then explore the larger implications of meaning as they relate to the different ways that we seek to construct and create our individual view of the world. Having meaning seems, to my mind, to be the key to enjoying a good life and meaning is pretty far from what the sciences-in general-can describe. What do we know, how do we know it and what does it mean when something is meaningful to us? If we believe we have found meaning in our life, what does it mean, exactly? Is it to believe in a belief system? A deity? Or, indeed, what does it mean to believe in ourselves or a concept like freedom? Renowned psychologist Carl Gustav Jung talks about the meaning of life as being an ongoing process that involves how *we* would wish to relate to the divine in its widest form, either out there or inside of ourselves. The process cannot be disentangled from the process. It is the process and all of the parts or the process entrenched in context. Coming to grips with the ambiguity of meaning, seems to me to be at the very root of how we begin creating a good life for ourselves.

But the real inception of writing this book was having heard an interview with a creationist, which-after my initial spurt of anger-lead me into thinking about the larger context of Darwinian thought, evolution and the role of the sciences in general. As I looked a little closer at some of what I believe is propaganda foisted by the creationist's movement, I heard that some creationist's have "used" the "scientific method" to create the appearance of a *proof*. (This is all succinctly laid out and even dogmatically chewed over by Richard Dawkins in *The Greatest Show on Earth*.)

The creationists have sought to create the appearance of validity in their arguments by adopting parts of the terminology of science, but not the rigorous distanced methodology. This can be seen in the creationist's efforts to confuse -or simply their inability to distinguish between- terms like theory and hypothesis in an effort to '*prove*' that their story or mythology of creation is a valid and therefore true and scientifically proven historical narrative.

Conversely, the more that I read in the sciences the more that I began to realize that many scientists are also stridently, and possibly unknowingly, defending their own created *belief* systems. Though, I would contend that they have other ways to hide a possibly more subtle set of myopic assumptions.

The main belief system in science seems to me to be the thought that, detached and rational thinking can supply the answer to all questions 'given enough time', or that abstraction and reductionism is a fairly universally applicable form of inquiry. This is based on an explicit belief in the "uniquely human" ability to represent reality by constructing models of understanding through our abstracted and therefore rational thinking. Thinking is an excellent tool in many ways but in many areas of inquiry -like all matters of relational value or the heart- it fumbles as the final word.

"The secrets of alchemy exist to transform mortals from a state of suffering and ignorance to a state of enlightenment and bliss."
- Deepak Chopra

Before we had chemistry, we had the God- infused art of alchemy. Alchemists believed that the world was animated by a ubiquitous substance called *phlogiston. Phlogiston was an active substance that filled all of the nooks and crannies up and did things like allow fire to burn. It was the animating substance or divine ether that surrounded us, which allowed the divine to move toward or away from us like fish in water. When an alchemist looked deeply into substances, they might see some forms of their own reflected presumptions about what it is that they might be looking at. Alchemists cast themselves into that which they studied and also found themselves reflected back into the universe that they were trying to unravel. Their reflected presumption might consist in believing that rubies were always linked to our heart and that having lost a loved one could -to a certain extent -be remedied by holding rubies near the breast. In the magical mind there is a confluence of energies based on correlation: rubies are red and blood is red so there must be some form of connection. The seat of our passions and intelligence is the heart, because the Egyptians believed it was so. Some ancient alchemist might have written down a very interesting description of his understanding of this correlation, and when I read this and suggested wearing a ruby to my dear friend after his wife died, I am amazed to find out that it seems to lift his spirit, and it actually does.

I met a fellow in Shimla in northern India and this fellow was convinced that he could heal people with Tibetan singing bowls, and that these bowls where infused with the song that reflects the beginning of the universe. Now, I'm a cocky westerner who has a really good understanding of the placebo effect and I challenged this fellow by telling him that these singing bowls are healing people, because they are set deeply within a situation in which people believe that they will gain benefit from the bowl because you believe that you can heal them and that really they are healing themselves because they need to believe that they can get healed. He happens to be a Cambridge University PhD in anthropology and he lives in Britain most of the time, but he heads to India to spend time with the Tibetan monks in eastern Kashmir. We talked for around six hours and he assured me that the bowls were part of the healing process. I assured him that this was magical thinking, but in the end I had nothing to prove my case and he had actually been healing people for years. He wasn't some stupid fool and we came to a draw after I threw all that I had at him. Ultimately, his humanity and gentle spirit was more interesting than my arrogant tirade, so I listened to him instead. He had also been invited to listen to the large Hadron Collider when they tried to fire it up for the first time, I hadn't.

India, like the unconscious, kind of gives you what you look for.
In the past it was also believed that bumps on the head where a reflection of different aspects of your personality and that if someone felt around your skull they could reveal aspects of yourself to you, because your personality was a reflection of this unique arrangement of bumps. These examples are indicative of bad science and it is presumed that we are now "smart" enough to see through this foolishness. It's my belief that we are always this foolishness. We have only tuned the screw one more twist.

Chomsky functioned under the implied assumption that there was a point-to-point correlation between linguistic construction and the inner architecture of the brain itself and that if we studied language we could gain a window into the actual mechanical functioning of the mind. In some sense we would be pressing our fingers through the skull and into the inner reaches of our mind. The behaviorists believed that we can never understand an animal's emotional landscape, because the animals will never be able to talk to us about how they feel about anything and so it is pointless to even ask questions that would drive us in this direction. All we can study is plotted reaction times in laboratory conditions and speculate about everything else, but of course, speculation is unscientific. So in the spirit of science we must restrict ourselves to being a passive detached eye in the world and this detachment is in perfect alignment with our thinking mind. B.F Skinner (the king of behaviorism), then wrote a book called: *"Walden Two"*–reflecting Thoreau's *"On Walden Pond"*- in which he lays out his vision of a behaviorist's utopia: in which humans will all get along, because their environment is so conducive to getting along. Like the communists, Skinner believed that if he could build a better mouse trap, the mice would line up and pay him to get caught.

Good science has now discovered the Higgs boson. The Higgs boson is a magical 'particle' and that by its simply being in the universe it has allowed everything else to have mass and substance. We have had great difficulty finding it, because it is almost mass-less. It is many different things that are beyond my ability to describe in a short introduction, but one thing that all scientists agree on is that it's not phlogiston, and there is no way that modern neuroscience is like phrenology and God is most certainly dead, because we have the large Hadron Collider to substitute in a particle that has been unfortunately dubbed the God particle. Animal's emotions are irrelevant, because they can't talk –and everyone knows for a fact that they have no soul- so we should eat that pig. Because we can talk and talk about our ability to talk it must be the most important thing that the brain does, it seems only logical that we should start there. The Higgs boson is the new animating spirit of the universe and we have gotten past our naive belief in crazy spirits, because science has found this wonder particle that really is something, although it's very difficult to actually say what it is.

My book is an attempt to peel back of onion skins of understanding to reveal what I believe is the fact that we end up looking at ourselves no matter where we go. We try so hard to eliminate ourselves from our exploration of the world and the way that we construct our vision of ourselves and the world around us; only to find that we walked in the back door and we need a shower, because we worked up such a sweat running around looking at our own back.

A large part of my book is concerned with the nature of thinking and how explicit thinking detaches us from our contact with both our body and the world in which our body lives. Science is about thinking and art is really not that much about thinking. I believe that scientists have developed a culture in which they have agreed that the mind is right and that thinking will lead us out of the shit pile that we constantly find ourselves in. I would argue that there are rubies in that shit pile and we should be up to our elbows in it. If you and everyone that you know think that thinking is the right answer, then you will all agree that thinking is the right answer. In my opinion thinking has a tendency to happen somewhere up in the clouds and the real world smacks you in the face at every other moment. We might become skinny as a rake and not really care about what clothes we wear, because thinking doesn't care about such trivial things. Thinking has found the God particle and we have it right where we want it.

The alchemists cast their own projections into substances by animating them with spiritual properties. Many where aware of elements of this psychological dimension, or some at least understood that they were studying themselves reflected in chemistry. We are in much the same position, but our projections are just that much more subtle. Chomsky developed his theories about the inner architecture of the brain, because one of the only models at hand was that of phrenology. Chomsky may have never encountered phrenology in his life, but these things float about the world casting influence without our ever having consciously recognized them. We kill our Gods and we invent the "God particle." Aren't we clever?

Science is by far and away the best model we have to gain an understanding of everything. I hope to show just how spectacular its rise has been, but I would also wish to highlight its limits and also try to illuminate why these limits have come about. Ultimately, I have come to believe that science, to a great extent, is a reflection of a mindset or it is a tool that is extremely useful but that the tool is a reflection of the tool maker. In this book, I try to take a really good look at the tool maker from the alternating perspectives of psychology, the arts, science and the incredible new vantage point of neuroscience. This is a book about how the brain both constructs and reflects the world and ourselves back to us and that we also construct and reflect the world of ourselves out and into everything. This does not mean that we can never know the truth about anything. It's just that we are that very truth. I try to champion context as opposed to analysis. Context cannot be held in the hand as easily as a tool. To gain context takes a different type of integrative, almost passive mindset that is more clearly reflected in the ambiguity of the arts than in the linear sciences. Both these entities dwell within our breast and we hold too tightly to either one at our own peril. The human mind is the sum total of being a human mind in the world all the time. We are never not this.

"It is always significant, Iris Murdoch has written, to ask of a philosopher; what is he afraid of!" - *The Paradoxes of Delusion* by Louis A. Sass - Pg. 74.

I am afraid we have driven God from the field only to reinstate ourselves as divine and that this assertion of hubris will draw to us, our deserved punishment. I see very clearly that this book is a reflection of many of my private concerns as I breathe in and out of my two conflicting standpoints in the world: that of trying to understand science and trying to assert the primacy of experiential or lived wisdom, each view point holds contradictions within it, but we are precisely those contradictions when we live them fully. Science is like a bully who has taken over the field and I want to kick a soccer ball a full arching fifty yards from out of the stands and hit it right in its disbelieving face. It took many hours of reading and kicking to develop the skill set needed and that's my point.

"I will play the swan and die in music" - Shakespeare's *Othello*

In science a naive worldview can be more easily proven wrong through open debate, but even so, as we've seen with climate change and evolution, some people can enter into the debate and continually spread mud around making it seem that no such definitive proof exists. (Exxon seriously attempted to prove through paying scientist to 'find evidence' that a lot of the oil that spilt on the Alaskan coast was naturally occurring) To the lay man these issues can appear to be largely unresolved, creationist still have a strangle hold over the school system in the United States and the Taliban still wants Afghanistan back. Cigarettes might not cause cancer. How much muddier can things get when we move out of science and into the softer areas of inquiry like psychology, religion, and anthropology or art criticism? Things get downright political and the easiest/most childish way to win an argument is to smear some mud on your opponent's fresh white shirt. No wonder people are disillusioned with politics, when will we grow up?

"When still young, the wise person should cultivate the virtues dear to the Divine. A human birth is difficult to obtain here on earth, and even though human life is fleeting, it is full of significance." - The Sage Prahlada in the *Bhagavata-Parana* (7.6.1)

These types of discussions were the main focus of this book and the building up of these themes occupied me for the first year of writing. I was quite content to prattle on in this way filling out my days in idle speculation and gazing abstractedly at the tapestry of my own inflated sense of self worth. Then I discovered Neuroscience and everything changed, literally everything. Neuroscience is creating a better understanding of the tool that we understand with and I immediately realized-thanks to Jung's prodding-that without an understanding of this root tool box that we have (the brain); much of our knowledge is fairly detached speculation Our understanding of the brain has lead to a recognition of the necessity of more context and a rightful embodiment of thinking. I will explain as we continue.

How can we presume to think about quantum mechanics if we don't even understand how thinking occurs within the brain of the person thinking about it? Many people cling to the idea that thinking is somehow separate from the brain and because we don't understand the brain perfectly, thinking becomes a magical result of our soul. For hundreds of years our thinking has been colored by this Cartesian philosophical premise and its implied assumption that there is a distinction between mind and other or that thinking and especially our representational self consciousness is a distinct almost godlike quality of the uniquely enabled human mind. We have believed in this particular duality for so long that we have assumed it to be true.

It took me a lot of reading to really pick my way through these presumptions but I feel that the Rose Glass chapter accurately represents most sides of these conceptions and also seeks to show the way toward some beautiful answers. This idea that thought is something special and distinct in humans has had vast ramifications in all disciplines, religious as well as scientific, and this thought is now understood to be at the very least misleading. The long and short of it is that the mind and your body and the world are all bound together in a much larger Meta frame work. This frame work of body/mind/world cannot be neatly disentangled from each other or even accurately represented in the intellect in a way that we can then say 'this is where I start and the other ends.' We must therefore constantly remind ourselves that WE are truly embedded *in* our body which is *in* the world.

Neuroscience is bringing change into many if not all areas of intellectual speculation. Being a new science, neuroscience has the advantage or disadvantage, that each of the viewpoints held by the various scientists hasn't had time to gain a lot of emotional investment yet, though squabbles are surfacing. Most of the people working in the neurosciences are so swept up in the explosion that they don't have time to quibble over insignificant details. The devil is in the details. This resulting exuberance of the dawning of a new scientific outlook was probably what it was like in the thirties after Einstein changed everything in physics. Though neuroscience by its very nature has to be multi-disciplinary and is being driven by psychology and philosophy as much as the stricter biological sciences. To my mind this revolution of Neuroscience, is at least as important as the changes that have occurred in theoretical physics over the last century and neuroscientists seem to be well aware of this. Theoretical physics has breathed out and neuroscience has breathed back in.

This inward breath is to my mind a reflection of the deep introspection that has been lacking in the scientific approach in the west. India has been lead to extremely profound religious truths through focused introspection in her millennia old practices of yoga and meditation. Neuroscience is confirming that root changes occur in the way that the mind works as a result of mediation/yoga practice. Many other things that the yogis have for eons asserted also given proper context seem to be true, and some of these assertions are now becoming relatively provable. The most important assertion -to this book- is that there is real improvement in personal outlook that results from these types of engagement with the body/mind. Some of these eastern insights have been built up and tested over time, but must be experienced individually because of their inherently introverted nature and there is no broad litmus test that we can apply to decide if three out of ten yogis have achieved an enlightened viewpoint with a error of one in twenty; five percent of the time. I won't dawdle on about eastern mysticism too much in the book, but it cuts to the quick much of what I'm driving at which is: we all carry representations of ourselves in the world and it takes effort to be reintroduced to the world and escape our neurotic attachment to ego-driven views. To a certain extent, we must take it on faith or at least view with detachment a personal testimony that there may be a profound experience to be had out there. We don't have to check our brains at the door when we approach religion and meaning though. To my mind religion trumps science as a world view worthy of investing time in but religion is not a logical beast and to gain real insight we must nurture a more artistic/associative metaphorical right brained mind set.

"You may ride to the temple on a donkey, but you don't ride the donkey inside" Author

    With the discovery of the unconscious we have come to realize that there is much going on in our house that is not directly under our nose. Modern psychology and neuroscience are showing us that in fact some 90% to 95% of our brains activity is completely unobserved and that the degrees of consciousness that we experience are really functioning on sets of presumptions that are being entrained in us by the unconscious. What if there is an underlying root experience within the mind that is pure bliss or a total absorption in God as thousands of Hindu, Buddhist, Muslim, Christian etc. seers testify. We will tease out some of these testimonies from different religious traditions as we move through this book. It is my naive hope that I will be able to put my understanding of these experiences into a frame work that the western scientific/philosophical community will not scoff at. Neuroscience is the first 'hard science' to be able to form a bridge over this gap between the religious arts and scientific reason.

    I have been lead to understand that the rift between science and religion–proof and meaning–is essentially a difference in ways of representing the world and that this split in viewpoints is embodied in the division of labor that are also represented in the two sides of our brain. Much of my ongoing understanding was crystallized within me as I read and reread The Master and His Emissary by Iain McGilchrist. It is an interesting thing to find a book that sets you on fire. Because of my extensive reading in history and psychology I immediately understood the import of this work and it has forced me to yet again rewrite my entire book. I will probably borrow too heavily from this work so I will now encourage everyone to read this work which is literally dripping with insight.

    Throughout this book we will inspect and dissect some small corners of thought and also try to explode these corners back up into a larger context again. I will chase some intellectual paradigms in an effort to expose underlying assumptions and try to nail down anything that is real and provable while trying to see if provability can be a final word. It is my contention that meaning as reflected in personal value is the really important issue in life, and what meaning we construct and invest our life time with, will make all of the difference for us. Meaning is essentially a creative act, we create meaning within ourselves but also meaning flows out of us and follows us around, if we are open to looking for it.

Along with discussions about current scientific thinking we will take a look at some fringe experiences such as ESP to see how these phenomena are understood. To try to work seriously in this area of "paranormal research" has been labeled a CLM or a career limiting move. To my mind the belief in ESP is part of the human experience and we should try to get to the bottom of it instead of assuming that there is no validity to it from the outset, science seems to easily prejudge and exclude much that is within the human experience, especially God. We shall try to filigree why it is that they stridently deny such phenomena or conversely try to understand what psychological mechanisms are in play that would make us believe that something like ESP exists. We shall take extended looks at the act and art of creation, both in the earlier chapters and later on. The arts and especially music are where my heart truly lays and I leave my brain behind when I go through that door, well not completely just the explicit side.

I have generously leavened the narrative with terms like, it seems to me or, I understand that, or I believe. These terms are put in very intentionally because this is where proof sits. There is nothing wrong with stating a belief system or being speculative, Black holes are a type of belief system, and no one has ever definitively found a black hole, though of course there is great consensus that they do exist. If something is stated clearly then it is my explicit understanding that it is so, I have left more than enough in the way of notes and I apologize in advance for any presumptive incorrectness. I have made great efforts to confirm 'facts' and any mistake made in presenting another's view point is completely my own. Much of what I am saying is a reflection of my own personal understanding and I have not shied away from presenting my understanding as a personal view point. I could have constructed a narrative that was completely quoted from other texts and simply pushed the burden of proof elsewhere, and that really is the point of my book. I have to stand for something at some point but I realize that because you *believe* something to be true, it doesn't mean that it *is* true in all situations and for all time or that you must leave your brain at the door and then defend you view point to the death. We can believe it's cold outside, because someone tells us it is and this doesn't present much of a problem.

    The mind/ body/world is subtle and nuanced and there is much terror and beauty to be found in its complexity, this complexity just might be a reflection of a single underlying unity that is difficult to grasp and embody. Many hands point in this singular direction and we shall endeavor to discern the Proof.

Faith

Faith is an island in the setting sun

But proof, yes

Proof is the bottom line for everyone

-Paul Simon, *The Rhythm of the Saints*

5 ROSE GLASS

Part One: The Theory of mind

It is my intention in this chapter is try to throw some light on where neuroscience has brought our understanding of the human condition and why this branch of science is so important. I will get to an overview of what I consider the most interesting aspects of neuroscience fairly soon, but I will rattle around discussing some of the predecessors to this branch of science that are collectively called the 'philosophy of the mind.' I will also try to explain some of the psychological models that have had an impact on neuroscience as well.

One of the great problems or leading paradigms that has worked its way into the study of our thoughts and has impacted our ongoing presumptions about the inner workings of the mind was introduced by Descartes. This is the notion of Cartesian duality, which has led us in the west -until recently- to believe that thought or how we think is something different from the brain that does the very thinking. Descartes was -in some sense- trying to separate humans clearly from the animals by wishing to establish that humans possessed a unique self-reflecting and rational consciousness. This vaguely implied that we also possessed a soul, because we alone could perceive it. This speculative division of the mind/body has come to us in the memorable statement 'cogito ergo sum': I think therefore I am.

This is considered to be one of the rock bottom statements in philosophy. Descartes has given us an absolutely self evident base in which to conduct a further survey of the relationship of our being in the world. The implication that has been drawn from this statement is that our self reflective thought is separate from; the mind that is doing that very thinking. Or that thought can be abstracted and reduced away from organic life or that thought would still be recognized as something even if we were a disembodied non- entity floating out in completely empty space. This is the essence and end point of radical abstraction and reductionism.

Descartes was expressing his idea that sentience (or reflective self-awareness) was of divine origin and was reflected to us in our 'unique' ability to introspect upon our own self-consciousness. Descartes believed that a split existed between the mind, body and soul and it has an incredibly long pedigree, dating at least back to the Egyptian concept of bodily resurrection, which has now re-established itself somewhat ambiguously in Christianity's current rapture movement (archetype). We have now grown accustomed to thinking that our soul or spirit is something vaguely detached from ourselves and that the soul/spirit keeps going after our bodily death (psychological fact). Descartes analogous presumption about the mind was that we can only definitively know that we exist and that this pristine realization is the result of our ability to represent our thinking in our mind. If self-reflective thought and abstract thinking are the only absolute road toward what is knowable, and if thought is separate from *you*, the individual brain that is doing the thinking, or restated; somehow our ability to think is above and separate or more than the sum of our mind (an epiphenomenon). This ability to reason is certainly a most precious commodity. I will argue that this very act of self-referential philosophizing is only a small and very specific aspect of the way the mind works and that this particular way of looking at things actually displaces us from the very reality we are thinking about. This is another more modern form of introverted Plutonic idealism, which is the separation and abstraction of real things from their idealized intellectual/divine forms or the separation of a thought from those things that we think about.

Descartes was driving at the idea that all of the input from our senses can be completely wrong, and we may be caught in a seemingly real matrix like illusion that we mistake for actual reality, and so he sought to establish the notion that the only thing we could know with absolute certainty was that we think. He was convinced that he had proved that he existed. Descartes goes on to say that people moving outside his window could be automatons and I have come to believe that this is the viewpoint that is overtly intellectual and a possibly unbalanced brain might seek to develop when it eliminates the wider symbolic context. If you sit alone in your room long enough you will begin to believe any number of things, but a brief walk outside will immediately place you back into the flesh and the smell of reality. How can you know love if you haven't been in love?

This path of thinking seems reasonable and above all it can conform to logical construction, but it is at the very least misleading for a number of reasons. I would argue that the very ground that this type of thinking is set upon has benefits, but also more than a few problems. Thought cannot be cleanly separated from the brain without introducing some form of speculative metaphysics (dualist verses materialist), and the brain did not simply evolve into a detached thinking thing. Thinking is a result of the complete and seamless integration within us, of our brain/body.

Unlike the movie the Matrix, if you put a billion computers together you will not get a form of artificial intelligence that contains any self representing awareness or even a twinkle of reflective consciousness. Self reflective consciousness is an aspect of our brain's ability to develop symbolic relationships, and along with this is the feeling that we have a sense of self direction or agency so that we will act in a way that will help to preserve ourselves. Thinking is not happening strictly -or even abstractly- in the brain; thinking is also not the result of a detached and soul-like mind that floats within the brain. The broad spectrum of thinking involves the whole of human being and is both the *result of* and in part the *creator of* the various experiences that you have *in the world*, along with your own internal ruminations on these *real world* experiences.

The brain functions through its ability to generate a constant feedback and feed forward of sensual information. This is happening all the time and your senses are the crucial link in this process and you cannot separate your thinking from your senses. Your various senses are collecting massive amounts of information and your brain is -mostly unconsciously- assessing and contextualizing this input, and constantly placing this information into symbolic contexts. Much of the brain's job is getting rid of irrelevant information so that consciousness is not overly cluttered. Most of your attachment *to* and experience *of* the exterior world is happening within you below the level of yourself consciousness or in fact any form of self-consciousness assessment. You cannot separate this bombardment of sensual information from the brain that is receiving it. As Eric Kandel said, *"Thinking is to the brain as walking is to the legs."* You cannot walk without legs and to speak of the fish as a walking creature is ridiculous.

The reason that we feel that thinking is distinct from our brain is because the mind makes us believe that this is so. This is largely a reflection of the brain's ability to create an ongoing narrative through its commonsense view of causality and our control of explicit language. When you really think about it for a moment, thinking must be a result of the brain and being embedded in this larger world ensemble (materialism). Why should we parcel thinking off into a separate realm from the brain? The brain's whole reason for being is to think in all of the manifold ways that we quite obviously do.

What does this have to do with proof? Well let me tell you. Descartes believed that he had reduced the world to something irrefutable. The only thing we can know for certain is that we think and we are alive. He unwittingly unleashed and then sought to validate a torrent of armchair thinking. This kind of self-absorbed thinking seeks to paradoxically establish you at the centre of everything while simultaneously removing everything into a nonexistent abstraction. This is what you get into when you spend way too much time alone in your room in a vaguely maudlin state, thinking 'deeply' about things and you cannot get away from your repressed Catholic upbringing. This strained introverted mind set can be seen reflected in our ever so modernist sarcasm and in the groundless hyper ironic outlook of American post modernism. The way that we know things is through the information gathered from our experience *in the world.* This information comes to us through our senses. The brain has evolved in the world, for this world.

"As a result of the work of Mountcastle, Hubel, and Wiesel, we can begin to discern the principles of cognitive psychology on the cellular level. These scientists confirmed the inferences of the gestalt psychologists by showing us that the belief that our perceptions are precise and direct is an illusion-a perceptual illusion. The brain does not simply take raw data that it receives through the senses and reproduce it faithfully. Instead, each sensory system first analyzes and deconstructs then reconstructs the raw, incoming information according to its own built –in connections and rules-shades of Immanuel Kant!" Eric R. Kandel - *In Search of Memory*

Conversely, good mental health is a reflection of our physical wellbeing and physical sickness can greatly affect our mental attitude, and I also believe that unhealthy thinking can affect the very foundations of not only our thinking, but how we organize and or construct our ongoing world view. If you are healthy and engaged in life, you probably wouldn't be sitting in a room alone and in the dark trying to reduce everything you experience to an extension of your precious and totally world-detached ego. Or you wouldn't be so heavily leavened with irony that you would seek to sell shit in bags as art; being shit, being art, etc. This is part of the folly that can flow from our being abstracted out of the all consuming context of the world. What is interesting is the amount of traction that this Cartesian belief system has had in the world, because it is -on the surface- logical and from the trembling ego's point of view, intellectually satisfying in that it asserts the egos primacy.

Thomas Metzinger in the *Ego Tunnel* delves deeply into the various aspects of the philosophy of the mind. One of the aspects of consciousness that seems to be unique to us as humans is this very act of attending to our own consciousness. (It's difficult to know if animals have this ability, because they can't use 'their words' to tell us though it seems that dolphins and some primates have a concept of self.) Not only are we conscious of ourselves, we can guide the spotlight of our own attention toward very specific aspects of our own self-consciousness. This means that we cannot only think about ourselves, we can think about ourselves, thinking about ourselves. He then goes on to point out that the brain is constantly constructing a version of the exterior world for us to witness, which can be thought of as a tunnel.

This tunnel that we witness is the result of everything that we are experiencing. We constantly travel down this tunnel and it extends forward from us in our anticipation of the future and it also extends backward to encompass our composed biographical history. As we move through the present, the tunnel displays the world all around us. This includes our brain's own construction and ongoing interpretation of external reality along with elements of our internal ruminations upon it. In some sense we can never escape this tunnel, because we are the tunnel itself, although we can develop a philosophical or explicit notion of the tunnel. In some sense this tunnel is science, but in many ways this argument is another more subtle form of Descartes displaced representation of the inherent alienation from the world that our ongoing abstraction forces us into.

The evolution of the human brain has seen fit to create an absolutely transparent version of the tunnel. This means that as far as we are concerned, we are the illusion that is the tunnel-the tunnel is unobservable or indistinguishable for us and our ongoing conception of the real world. We are never fully aware that our internal construction of events is in any way separate from the events themselves. We only end up creating this sense of displacement from the world and the subsequent attempts to pierce through our own sense of displacement, because we try to represent these thoughts in our mind. As we think about the mind, our thinking creates a representation of thinking, which automatically necessitates another. We have bitten the apple. We are at root never separate from the events that we are a part of, because we are exactly those events embodied (like walking with legs). This is why the book is called the Ego tunnel because without the displacement that the ego creates the illusion of the tunnel disappears.

Through our ability to displace ourselves we have been able to establish an external reference point outside of us. This is the mindset or the toolbox of the sciences, which allows us to confirm the more subtle and explicit dynamics of the externalized view of the world. The analogy that Mr. Metzinger uses to explain sciences empirical viewpoint is that: we see the world in the rainbow of colors that we are accustom to seeing and only those specific colors. Science tells us that the true reality of the world is that everything is brought to our senses by appearing to be made of solid stuff, but the reality is that everything is the vibrating appearance of energy spread across many frequencies. Some forms of energy are vibrating in the radio or even X-ray wavelength, which is beyond our capacity to actually see. Our vision has evolved to only see what is relevant to our situation and so we only witness the aspects of reality that are in our comparatively small visual range. Conversely, to call X-ray light, light at all is conceptually misleading and to say that the world only has the appearance of solidity may be logical correct but in many ways it is simply not true. Conversely to manically assert that everything has no solidity because science knows this as a fact is to bash your head into everything all day long as you seek to wander through the illusion of brick walls.

There are other animals on the planet that see more of the visual world than us; bees can see into the ultraviolet due to the evolutionary advantages of doing this. (Foxes may see elements of gravity waves) Snakes can see into the infrared spectrum to detect a mouse's body heat. We cannot see the world in the ultraviolet range but we can have this range interpreted for us by science, and we can be assured that there is something to see and that it is indeed so. This is a way that science allows us access beyond the tunnel of our own mind. By understanding how the mind works and looking at the actual nuts and bolts of our perception, we can peer beyond the limits of our own brain and pierce the casing of the tunnel a bit farther. This is the real nut of the argument that I will be developing in this chapter which is that by exposing the way in which the neurology of the brain both constructs the world and interprets the world we can gain insight into both ourselves and the actual world but we will need to be fairly explicit about the division between science and philosophy for a bit because both disciplines have impacted the way we approach the study of the mind, and we are always looking at the world through a mind.

Mr. Eric Kandel talks about two types of science; daytime and night time. Daytime science is the meticulous building up of real information 'facts' by doing experiments in the real world. This is the actual testing of a hypothesis against reality by constructing an experiment that will allow us to have independently verifiable results. This is analogous to Darwin travelling around the world collecting specimens with a vague sense in his mind of the over arching theory of evolution or at least a belief that there was a theory to be had; or within another discipline; collecting the facts of the various atomic weights of all the elements of the periodic table. Along with this daytime collection of facts-in the world-is the need to try to eliminate your preconceived notions about where you are going to end up. These prejudices and philosophical premises can influence and/or lead you toward what you may not have consciously understood are already anticipated results. (The question leads the answer) Night time science is the over arching theoretical speculation about the larger picture of what you are doing or more specifically the actual gestalt that gave us the arrangement of the periodic table. This is the creative aha moment when you can gain an understanding of a theory that explains the relevance of these bald facts in the real world; like the insight into natural selection as the driver of evolution. This type of night time thinking can also lead you to construct further experiments that will bring you closer to understanding aspects of the overall phenomena. This is the moment of grace that results from the pressure cooker of work.

In Mr. Kandel's case daytime science was the careful dissection of the nervous system of a sea worm called Aplysia. Looking for the electro-chemical basis of how neurons trigger and exactly how this electro chemical reaction works across a synapse and in between the axons of an animal's brain. He sought to understand how these electro chemical processes allow a biological animal to learn and retain information and how it constructs, stores and then subsequently accesses this memory. By reducing the scope of his investigation to trying to gain an understanding of the mechanics of the neuron systems at this elemental level, he could then begin to really understand the roots of learning and memory itself. This meticulous building up of facts is explicit sensate scientific thinking.

Night time science (largely unconscious) is trying to then understand how these individual electro chemical reactions could lead to the larger phenomena of something like episodic memory storage and retrieval, which may then lead us on to an understanding of the physical underpinnings of consciousness itself. From this we could then proceed on toward expressing our ability to create a personal biography of the mind: that *we* are. Through allowing this more free associative type of theoretical thinking a scientist can then further guide his experiments toward or away from a hypothesis; which in turn may uncover further aspects of the relationship between the facts that have been established and there by produce a theory that encompasses or reflects more closely reality.

One of the running themes of this book is to highlight how personal bias can interfere with understanding. Mr Kandel talks about a division in the early 1950's that happened in the neuroscience community itself. The essence of the division was between people who believed in an electrical method of synaptic transmission called 'sparkers' and those who believed in a chemical synaptic transmission system called 'soupers'. The reality of the situation was that the transmission of information along the axon to the synapse is a combination of both of these forms of communication. An electrical charge in the neuron initiates a further chemical interaction at the synapse which then initiates another electrical firing on down the line etc. When you focus too closely on a sectioned off element of reality you lose the larger context. My underlying thought on this will unfold slowly but I see that each of these ways of looking at the situation could be thought to engender an inherent archetypal belief system or thought structure.

If the ego/desire etc. is out of the equation we can learn to look at the reality of the world -and in this specific instance- see that the real situation is a combination of both ideologies at another higher and more integrated level. This is why Wolfgang Pauli wrote a book about the influence that archetypal ideas had on Johannes Kepler. Unless you can deconstruct your own explicit daytime bias, you will have difficulty exploding your work back out into actual reality or escaping from your questions implied direction.

Mr. Kandel goes on to tell an insightful story about a fellow researcher called John Eccles who had become quite embroiled in this soupers vs. sparkers debate. Eccles had firmly planted himself on to the sparker's side and it was becoming obvious to him that he may in fact be wrong. This fellow had the good luck to have been able to discuss this ongoing debate with the great philosopher of science Karl Popper, who helped him to understand that within the realm of science the validity of good research is not the problem, it is the further interpretation of the data that can be questionable. Popper encouraged Eccles to go back into the laboratory and further refine his ideas so that he could then actually disprove his own ideas, if that where necessary. I will quote Eccles himself from Mr. Kandel's book.

"I learned from Popper what for me is the essence of scientific investigation-how to be speculative and imaginative in the creation of hypotheses, and then to challenge them with the utmost rigor, both by utilizing all existing knowledge and by mounting the most searching experimental attacks. In fact I learned from him to rejoice in the refutation of a cherished hypothesis, because that too is a scientific achievement and because much is learned by the refutation.

"Through my association with Popper I experienced a great liberation in escaping from ridged conventions that are generally held with respect to scientific research... When one is liberated from these restrictive dogmas, scientific investigation becomes an exciting adventure opening up new visions; and this attitude has, I think, been reflected in my own scientific life since that time." - *In Search of Memory* Pg. 97

This is the essence of ongoing scientific proof, which is that we should be wary of our comfort with notions of what reality is and isn't. On the other hand, science sometimes seems to leap forward from a theoretical night time approach in spite of the rigorous collection of facts. Einstein came to realize a great many things by using his intuitive thought experiments; but he was, at no point in his life completely detached from the world. He was contemplating the world as he understood it, not as a completely abstract non-thing in his detached brain. Science seems to move forward by a combination of these two types of thinking and for a long time the night time aspect of science was not clearly acknowledged. In the realm of physics this split between conscious sensate work and unconscious casting can be illustrated by the almost complete division that exists between theoretical physics and practical physical research. It also seems that the physical world and its abstracted representation through mathematical expression is another form of this same division between introverted philosophical introspection and sensate fact collection as people grapple to represent reality.

Mathematical representation can only carry meaning to us if it has a relationship to us and it must also then bear a relationship to the world that it seeks to represent. Like the soul, mathematics seems to be mired in the world. Mathematics can also lead a scientist to make completely incorrect models of the universe and all mathematical speculation must be measured against the reality of nature, she has the last word. In other words Einstein still had to prove his theories with real experiments carried out in the real world, many of these experiments took years to verify. This is the same relationship that the mind has to thinking. The mind is constantly interpreting the sensual information that it receives and the mind is presenting a view of the world to us; the world that is presented to us is then being tested against the real world by pain, it is this modified construction of the real world that we are constantly presented with and we sometimes misinterpreted it. The brain has-over its evolutionary history-developed a number of interpretations of reality that are consensually correct in most instances; or more correctly our brain is the result of evolutionarily advantageous adaptations.

I have many seemingly random points to make in this chapter but assure you I will return in various ways back to certain key thoughts as we move along and I will seek to construct some over arching sense out if it for you, so please bare with me for a bit.

First off I should like to give a quick thumbnail sketch of the difference between the orientations of the right and left brain. I would encourage the interested reader to purchase: *The Master and His Emissary* by Iain McGilchrist Possibly the single best book I have ever read. This ensuing -brief analysis- of our brains bilateralization is largely based on my own ever increasing enlightenment, which is the direct result of having read and hopefully understood this phenomenal piece of work. I like to think that I have viewed this work from the advantage of a fairly dispassionate and well read context, but I wish to admit here that having read and reread this single book and my ongoing digestion of it on a trip to India has caused me to rewrite the whole of this book again.

The left brain is largely analytic and seeks to represent the world through a focused abstraction; it was thought for some time that language wholly resided in the left brain but this has been seen to be incorrect much of our language processing is in the left brain but not everything. That the structures involved in the act of speaking are mostly located around the ear on the left side and it seems fairly probable that the direct representation of words (denotative language: the one to one correlation of names for instance) is primarily a left brain concern. The left brain seeks to narrow the mind into thinking about and focusing on the particulars that exist in the now and its forte is representation and comparison of incoming reality to that which it has already developed a concept of. The left brain expresses itself through the ego and because it controls the denotative language which the ego speaks it has ample opportunity to reinforce this view. The left brain is also the tool maker and the ability to use tools is the stunning result of our ability to analyze and detach ourselves from the world to create a functional representation apart from ourselves. We literally grasp the world/ideas with the left brain as expressed in the right hand; regardless of which hand we use.

The right brain is less focused and tends to present us with a larger and more generalized wide angle viewing of the surroundings. The right brain brings the world into the mind and presents it to the left brain for analysis, categorization and further representation. The right brain is concerned with value and metaphor or the ambiguous poetry/music of speech. It is probable that the higher order context of speech analysis is passing through the right brain while the recognition of individual phonemes is a left brain operation. The right brain is more active in the act of dreaming and is more integrated with the fluid unconscious world. The right brain contains a preponderance of longer axons running from front of our heads to back which is thought to reflect its deeper integration with emotions and our episodic memory construction. The right brain is much more engaged in music although both sections are involved. The fuzzy non explicit metaphor -that is music- paints us a picture of what the right brain is about.

    Keep in mind that the right brain is in control of the left hand and eye etc. and the left brain controls the right side of your body. I will try to be clear as we move along and I will point out salient aspects of the right brain left brain division which have relevance but I wish to emphasize that this divide is never completely separate. The brain is always functioning as an integrated whole with each part and/or hemisphere only narrowly gaining preponderance over the other parts at any one time but none the less the division is real and has impact in the way in which we think and orient ourselves. Most of the understanding of this bilateralization is the result of studying people who have lost the ability to use one side of their brain through having had a stroke or they have had the corpus callosum-the mass of interconnections that integrate the hemispheres- severed to reduce or eliminate the severity of certain types of epileptic seizures.

    We can gain an understanding of the mind by looking at it with various tools like an fMRI machine. This machine focuses on the magnetic aspects of our blood flow, when a flush of blood occurs in different areas of the brain we can observe that increased flow and measure it. The parts of the brain that are receiving blood are presumed to be in use which it is thought indicates that we are using that part when we are thinking about an aspect of the world. To isolate a peek in blood flow you must focus on that peek and disregard other aspects. I will supply a metaphor: if you think of the brain as the continent of North America and you had a giant fMRI you could understand that politicians tend to cluster in Washington, Ottawa and Mexico City, but really they are all over the place serving their constituents at the same time as well though there is a higher percentage in the capitals. This is how the brain looks when we view it with our current technology. We tend to think that politics is all happening in Washington but to actually see this peek of activity we have to separate the noise of all of the other activity that's happening in all of the homes and constituents in America and everywhere else and focus our attention on Capitol Hill from this we can extrapolate meaning backward from the peek that we can witness in our fMRI.

So to dot the 'I's' here, no part of the brain are ever completely off line. They are always functioning below the level of consciousness. Even in a split brain patient-whose corpus callosum has been severed-there is still contact between the hemispheres through the less explicit limbic system and its connections to, and within the brain stem. So when I talk an fMRI will show increased blood flow in the left hemisphere around the ear, but this may be more of a reflection of the mechanics of my talking, as much as my thinking about what I'm saying. When I speak, there are many different parts of my brain all working in concert, but my mouth may need more energy to work the muscles involved in expressing my thoughts. It is difficult to tease these two processes apart although we can see some differences in thought process with an fMRI. My larger point is that speaking and thinking about speaking are virtually the same thing – t hey flow together from an integrated brain-like walking.

One of the greatest of our 19th century realizations has been the discovery of and explicit recognition of the unconscious. The philosophical problem that occurs in trying to represent the unconscious- as a strictly scientific postulate-was simply the fact that it is not conscious and you could dispute that it was real, because it was not in consciousness. How can we represent a concept in our consciousness that implies that there is stuff going on in our mind that we have no idea about? There is an unconscious in the sense that things go on in the brain that we are not directly conscious of, all of the time. At least three quarters of the brain energy (may be as much as 90 percent), are being used, assessing and dealing with our various perceptions and experiences, or regulating various systems within the body – life hormones, heart beat and body temperature. This all goes on below the level of explicit consciousness, and for the most part, this is the concern of so called older parts of the brain-the limbic system-near the spinal stem. Your heart does not stop beating, because you forget about it.

This is why we are not intimately aware of our feet when we walk, or why we don't have to consciously attend to every detail in our visual environment. Consciously attending to all of these procedures takes a lot of energy and we need to off load this type of mental baggage quickly, because it is expensive in terms of the brain's energy consumption. To be feeling, tasting and intently watching everything we do would-quite simply-be a sensory overload. The brain only bothers to pay attention when it's important, or our ongoing presumptions about the rules of the world are violated. Reality -as far as the brain apprehends it-is a rich and undulating mosaic and a focused and highly abstracted conscious perception. Higher consciousness, especially as it is expressed by the left hemisphere, works by an active nay-saying to this extraneous information.

We can learn to actively look into what isn't making it in our consciousness. This mysterious process is called learning. In the book *Blink* by Malcolm Gadwell, the author talks about the sense of intuition and how an expert can develop this sense into an explicit conscious recognition. For instance, some people can train themselves to study facial expressions. They can develop their ability to understand-with great accuracy- if someone is lying. (I just watched the CEO of Enron, Kenneth Lay lie on TV (*Smartest Guys in the Room* documentary. He briefly looked left at the exact moment he lied.) Other people can learn to isolate very subtle flavors in wine or other foods by directing the explicit spotlight of their consciousness toward their senses, though certain people have also been gifted a better set of taste buds in their tongues. What I wish to say here is that we all possess these abilities-to some degree-and they are reflected in our gut feelings (intuition) that someone is telling us a lie. This feeling is a reflection of your unconscious senses registering and interpreting these very subtle facial and bodily cues outside of the explicitly directed beam of consciousness. For instance, the right brain is concerned about the gestalt of full facial recognition. The left brain in isolation (after a debilitating right brain stroke), is almost completely incapable of assembling the face into a whole that is recognizable as someone. The left brain is primarily concerned with viewing the mouth only, because the left brain's concern is with speech analysis. We need both views to integrate into recognition.

What an expert does is make unconscious intuition relatively more explicit by consciously paying attention to the details in-what would otherwise be an unconscious- sensory environment. This is partially a matter of focusing the spotlight of conscious awareness, but also it is a matter of allowing information to come forward by dropping the narrow focus. We can all tell if we like a certain glass of wine over other ones, but an expert can isolate various distinct flavors and combinations, and discuss relative balances. They can articulate what it is that is good about *this* glass of wine in particular (although this type of thing is always highly subjective and can be influenced by other factors in the environment for example the label and price tag on the bottle). I will talk about a phenomenon called 'blind sight' later and this will help to explain how some of this subtle unconscious cuing works.

Dreaming is an unconscious process and I personally find the whole realm of dream interpretation extremely interesting. The brain can be studied in the dream state, but interpretation of dreams is an expert art like wine tasting, not a quantifiable science. Dream interpretation requires the belief in a hypothesis that dreams can in fact have meaning and this is extremely difficult to prove. An empirical study based on a theory that dreams are meaningful, will always be open to debate and the tyranny of formal logic, which will properly accuse it of being a belief system. To evaluate a dream's message implies that there is an exposable message in the dream content itself. Where would the meaning of an unconscious content come from? We will peck away at this nut as we move along.

The art of psychoanalysis is deep in the midst of a reassessment as it integrates the findings from the new science of neurobiology. Dream interpretation and things like the concept of consciousness itself are and will probably be for a long time threshold areas where the strict sciences have reached the limits of their ability to express any clear factual understanding. From here, we have to move into the realm of philosophy, socio- anthropology, history and the arts, (Jacques Barzun's 'ologies') to flush out the larger context of our humanity.

Jung spent an enormous amount of time reading about and talking to experts in the emerging fields of comparative mythology, religion and anthropological history, etc. He did this so that he could have some form of comparative cultural roadmap to use, as he tried to interpret the dreams coming to him from his patients. This idea of studying world mythology was based on the assumption that the world's mythologies are a reflection of the ongoing evolutionary expression of our collective unconscious. I only sight Jung in this instance, because I am so familiar with his work. Freud and many others were certainly as interested in all of these aspects of human culture too. What I am getting at -and this seems to be recognized within the neuroscience writers community-is that to truly understand the science of neuroscience and the brain, each researcher must be engaged in a vast multidisciplinary approach. The brain is not just biomechanics. It is quite obviously our culture as well and the borders between what are and isn't mind can be fairly arbitrary.

We are impoverished when we worship at the altar of explicit scientific facts.

    Jung sought to become an expert in understanding the metaphor that is the unconscious. In the same sense as Malcolm Gadwell's intuitive lie detectors or an expert wine taster. He looked about for all of the cultural manifestations of the unconscious in the world, so that he had some form of a yard stick to compare the individual unconscious to. He listened to thousands of dreams from his patients. (Look at a million paintings and you will know a good one every time.) We can fool experts, because of their own biased presumptions.

    I will lead this discussion back into the science of neuroscience after some other small discussions of philosophy and language, that we may see some of the winding roads that have led us to this point, and conversely, cast our net out for a wider context.

    I was listening to the *Philosophy Bites* podcast and a fellow by the name of Adrian Moore was discussing Immanuel Kant's *Critique of Pure Reason* (Sept. 14 2008). The part of the discussion that fascinated me was the idea of Kant's that we can only ever view the world as though it was presented to us through spectacles. For example, there is no way for us to view reality or the world in front of us without our eyes (reading spectacles). This viewpoint is itself an intellectual abstraction and I have reintroduced it to pursue a wider point.

What Kant had realized is that we can never know the world (as it is in and of itself distinct from us), without our eyes or our brains (he means discursive though) being in the way. (The view from nowhere) This is to some extent the same train of thought that led Descartes to reduce all knowledge down to the irrefutable Cogito Ergo Sum (I think therefore I am). I now understand that these are very subtle and reasonable, but I believe are mistaken notions, largely based on the analytic method itself.

Another example of this type of reasoning is reflected in a movement called 'scientific realism'. The main concern here is with the thought that when we do experiments-say in physics-such as winding up the Large Hadron Collider to smash together two atoms or create anti-particles–we are not actually 'seeing/ bearing witness to' the actual result of the experiment: we are not actually seeing these specific atoms collide with our own eyes. We have very sophisticated electronic gear that allows us to "see" and interpret the collision (spectacles), and in the ever-paradoxical quantum world, 'simply looking at something' changes the outcome. Therefore, we must forever be in a situation where we interpret scientific data through spectacles. It is scientific realism's contention that we really are experimenting with reality and that we are actually gaining insight, and building knowledge *into and about* the real world when we perform experiments on it. The real nut of these arguments comes down to a core assessment of what we really 'know' when we are using intellectual abstractions to describe these realities that we are trying to understand, etc.

The argument against whether we really know anything can be traced directly back to our earlier discussion about the ambiguous nature of light itself, which can in turn, be used as a metaphor or analogy for the whole way that we perceive reality. Depending on how we choose to view light or quanta (wave or particle), or how we conduct our experiments to look at either of them, the light will react for us-in these experiments-like a particle or a wave. So in a very real sense we cannot know the true reality of what light/reality is, because we simply cannot gain intellectual access into the thing itself. If we design an experiment to measure a light's wave-like qualities, we cannot view its particle like qualities and vice versa. We are tied to the representation that is our experimental data, and in some sense, we have not caught the ultimate essence of the real thing at all (the thing as it exists in its totality is called a 'qualia'). We only hold a vague mentally-constructed representation of it (an abstraction). By talking about the experiments, we are forced to change our understanding into a language, which to some extent, is compressing the already symbolic mental image into the even more narrow confines of a given linguistic structure (say English or math).

Some philosophers argue that we should always remain skeptical of observations in science like this, because if we look carefully at the history of science, we will see that everything that we have discovered so far has been over-turned by some subsequent scientific inquiry. This argument is used as a justification for the notion that the senses aren't the way to inquire into the nature of reality, because they have shown to be incorrect in many instances. For example, Einstein has improved on Newton; Darwin has improved on Genesis, etc. All of these understandings will be swept under the rug at some future point, and to some extent, they are already being swept away as we tinker with the story of science. (Neutrinos may travel faster than light.) Science is a representation of reality or a story about the map of facts. The ultimate and embedded context of reality eludes representation.

Now the scientific realist point is that we ARE in fact experimenting on reality and that we are gaining an understanding of things as they really are. The proof that they stand on is the fact that we have achieved so much in science that is of real value, and of pragmatic good use (we have created better metaphors), such as sending rockets out into space or plot the course of a ship. This to my mind seems blindingly obvious. How can I resist this artificial dichotomy-as represented by our spectacles-a reflex of abstract thinking? No one in the scientific world is prepared to state that they have uncovered the absolute final statement of physics or neuroscience, etc. If they did, we should rightfully be skeptical. The reality of the sciences is that the range of discoveries is so astounding and-like the way our brain builds reality for us-we can function more pragmatically within this scientific construct. If you are trying to gain access to the final bedrock of truth through scientific methodology, then you are really searching for some form of intellectual absolute and that this is really a religious attitude. I would argue that this absolute doesn't exist outside of the ever-present context which you seek to disentangle it from, or in psychological terms you've got stuck in a moment, and you can't get out of it. Context should always bring us back from this type of narrowing.

A rational panel of peers is the way that real science does things. Everyone has to put their science out into the world for a thorough viewing. (It takes a village to raise a child) Creationists already know what scientists will say about their hypothesis. The creationists are using the scientific mindset to try to pin their metaphor down into some form of abstracted quantifiable truth, simply to have an argument that appears to be on the sciences' playground. What neuroscience is helping us to see more clearly is the actual mechanics of our seeing and perceiving, which are much more interesting than this type of intellectual questioning would seek to assert.

This is the dynamic of the main argument that I will be developing in the first half of this chapter. The reality is that the brain is an actual witness to reality and it can be sharpened into an ever-more-accurate perceptual instrument through our ongoing learning process. This process includes both intellectually explicit learning, like being able to develop rational and logical discourse along with a more holistic or metaphorical approach that is more passively received into us through our really being in the world and our bodies – not simply thinking about the world as if it was an intellectual concept to be cracked open.

The preponderance of philosophers to elevate a logically consistent argument as though this where actually the way things are in the world is an example of the left brains view point. Obviously, there are good reasons for trying to put forward logically consistent arguments, in that they seem to accord with a representation of reality in the same way that mathematical facts also seem to accord with reality. We cannot build an argument, which anyone can really understand by willy-nilly grabbing at examples out of the sky. That maybe art it; is not philosophy or science (unfortunately, this willy-nilly thing is a little too close to my personal writing style).

I would point out that most philosophers are heavily invested in abstract thinking - within the Jungian realm anyway. This usually puts intuitive feeling in their shadow realm. I would suspect that this is really what is behind the ongoing intellectual disparaging of the emotions and feelings (and George Lukas's inability to create good female roles – Zing!) The relationship that overt thinkers have to feeling is usually poor, and therefore, easy to disparage. If the left brain is sectioned off from the right, it will go to great lengths to create a satisfactory narrative that suits its agenda. This narrative will be a reflection of the facts, as they are understood by the left brain and it will seek to create a logical and consistent worldview that it can represent. By doing this, it is involved in creating both the concept of an ego and allowing the ego to create the illusion of us having power in the world (Adam naming the animals). Because it owns the denotative tools of language, and because the right brain doesn't, it creates a closed self-referencing philosophical loop. This is really one of the great tricks of the brain. It creates a viewpoint within the world, and through this construction of personal biography and ongoing narrative, it convinces us that we are in control, but we cannot ever be outside of the brain, which is telling us this.

We all know that killing is wrong. We just feel it in our bones. Game theory is trying to put a logical verbal legalese polish onto these simple and highly relational value judgments that ultimately we all agree are self-evident (with the exception of lawyers). This prohibition against killing is not the ultimate point of most legal codes though. For the most part, legal codes are trying to articulate and grapple with much finer culturally- agreed upon distinctions like what is premeditated or first degree murder, or what constitutes third degree murder; or a working definition of the criminally insane. And really we will never be able to completely articulate and write down a legal system or life philosophy, or even create an accurate map of the world for that matter. We always need a human being, judging the ongoing subtleties of the actual crimes as they occurred in context (ugly people get longer prison sentences).

My larger point is that aspects of this moral sense of unfairness are-to a certain extent-hardwired into our brains and it becomes part of our behavioral patterning through both social queuing, and as a biological remnant of our evolutionary heritage. We instinctively function in the world in a fairly morally self-guided, though largely unconscious way. This is not to say that cheaters never prosper and I am also not saying that I won't cheat, because I am rationally self-aware and that I always know that it is in my enlightened self-interest not to. I think a very high percentage of us don't cheat all of the time, simply because-from an evolutionary and value standpoint-it has proven to be a poor life strategy, and we unconsciously feel this without having to become rationally self-enlightened. Though, I will seek to argue that a dose of rational self-enlightenment is probably the underlying drive of this book. If you lie and cheat all of the time, you have to develop an extremely long memory and the ability to shut out the extraneous noise of questioning. I think a large part of the exercise of exploring ethical philosophy or articulating a legal code, is to raise the ambiguity of context up and into our explicit conscious thought process so that we can articulate them with language. The Tibetans wish to train all monks in logical discourse in an effort to create self-awareness with the ultimate aim of creating better individuals. This thought process is a means to an end, not an end in itself and it is the western Socratic Method.

This idea of being rationally self-enlightened is in a sense another illusion or at least an ideal that thinking creates by displacing actions through the mill of self-reflection. You can build up the belief that thought is or can be separate from everything else. This overt rationalization of the thinking process can get lost in debating abstract concepts, like do we have free choice? Or what does empty space look like? Because our thought is expressed in words, we assume a reflective or implied substance to the words we use. What does empty space look like seems to be a rational question. Ultimately, we are only judged by our deeds. They are the final answer to who we are.

There was recently a strain of scientific thought, which sought to convince us we have no freewill because it was 'proved' that our actions are not directly linked to a quantifiable electrical brain signal (I will lay out the details later). If we displace and reduce our actions into this type of 'causal mental logic of evolution', then we develop a narrative that seems to agree with this set of intellectual assumptions (there is no freewill). We may go on to find more intellectual support for, and proof of, our assertion that we are 'simply automatons of nature', and from this, we can say we are 'nothing but' the will-less enacting of ridged, evolutionarily-adaptive electrochemical patterns. Descartes firmly believed his dog was an automaton or will-less biological machine. I believe that this was a reflection of Descartes' inability to empathize with his poor pooch.

I recently heard a critic say that the new David Bowie recording sounded like David Bowie trying to sound like David Bowie. I'm not sure that we can ascribe a motive to David Bowie making music that sounds like him. Ironically, he would do just that, given that he is actually David Bowie and this is intellectual tail-chasing that really doesn't say much. It is my contention that we are always on dodgy ground when we try to infer or ascribe a motive backward onto other people's actions. Even clearly understanding the level of conscious involvement in our own motivation can be extremely tricky. The world of a happy man is really much better than that of a sad one.

There is a certain magic that gets stuck to thinking when we try to discover and express what we believe are the underpinnings of our explicit conscious understanding, or what lies behind a behavioral pattern. We tend to feel that we own or grasp the idea that occurred to us and we assign an amount of certitude that ultimately only reflects the fact that we have isolated a part of something at the expense of its wider context. More than that, by exposing a perceived element of truth in nature, we feel that we have-to a certain extent-mastered the concept or the intellectual construct that *represents* this aspect of reality. Our ego is pleased by this reinforcement and we then feel that we own or have mastery over this idea, so further discussion is thought to be redundant. I will call this symbolic behavior 'land naming' after Otto Ranks concept of the same name.

Sex has evolved to feel good so that animals will seek it out and have it to further spread their genes about, but sex is only a small part of this genetic delivery system. When we reduce reality down into handy sound bites like 'genetic delivery systems', we really don't say much at all; it seems to us that we have said something. It's very difficult to talk about nature-in particular-without using phrases like 'the point of' or 'nature made this or that'. These linguistic constructs are shot through with implications that are a reflection of our own linguistic grappling. This is really a window into the way the brain has evolved to process the world through abstraction, and the accompanying assertion of mastery. We create a sense that we are willful creatures and it is embedded in our use of terms like *grasp*. We need an amount of certainty in the world and this is what Iain McGilchrist has called 'necessary distance' – when we seek to negotiate our way. The price of this intellectual distance is the pairing down of context, and like our own consciousness, there must be a pairing down simply to escape the constant noise of everything else. Or, the conceptual distance can only be created by removal of a part from the whole.

I am not trying to run down thinking. Obviously, thinking is heavily involved in the act of writing these ideas down. What I am driving at is the tendency that thinking has to displace us from reality simply because we are thinking about it. This is the circular loop that we get into when we explore the mind/brain. We can't think about the brain without using the brain, but what I should like to show is that neuroscience can actually tell us something about the real world outside of our internal introspection of it, especially the quagmire that is the theory of mind. Neuroscience does this by illuminating the processes that actually occur in our brain's apprehension of the world, while we are in it.

The brain is a thinking entity and one of its jobs is to create the illusion of independence and certitude of thinking, but as hammered home earlier, the brain/mind and body are all one package. The mind creates the illusion of our independence and freewill only if we displace our thinking into an abstracted observational mode. If we are engaged in life without the burden of self-observation, then we actually embody that very independence and freewill that the mind seeks to represent and/or create for us in our more abstracted thinking mode. When we are simply engaged in life, we function perfectly well under a transparent illusion that is in fact not illusory. Our thinking about thinking has an illusory feel to it when we stop and think about it. We create an intellectual displacement and then seek to assert that the displacement is a more accurate assessment than the actual experience, because we have a representation of it in our mind which we can 'own'. (This is largely a left brain tour de force.) In the same sense that the displacement of looking at art introduces us back into life. The right brain brings the world into us and the left brain seeks to inspect what is coming in and there is a tendency for this inspection to take us back out. We then need to come back in through an endless reintegration of being, which is the *in breath* of the right brain. Our ongoing apprehension continues in a never ending spiral, and when we are engaged in life, this loop is cut and we simply are.

The analytic process allows us to eliminate distractions and focus on representations of discrete aspects of our environment. The left brain allows us this abstraction and the ability to compare and then view objects symbolically, which has ultimately allowed us to become tool makers and develop language, etc. The problem with this is that tools are only useful, if they are in fact useful. They tend to embody a certain amount of ego-driven power, which attaches to them (weapons are a great example), and as Buckminster Fuller said, "If the only tool you have is a hammer, you will tend to treat everything as though it is a nail". Not only can you build a better house, you can short-cut that process and brain your neighbor and steal his. So if the brain is seen as something with which you can exercise power, then you will tend to conceive of the world as if it were something to be exploited, which is the down side of tool making.

    A quick metaphor: in England, scientists discovered great hoards of bronzed axe heads that were buried around 800 BCE. Bronze axe heads were not only religious items and tools, but they are believed to be one of the first forms of currency and collectable wealth. The reason that they were buried (some 400 were found together in one sight), is the arrival of iron-making. The next two hundred years rendered these mystical and probably revered items obsolete. (We, in our infinite modern wisdom, know that tools can't possibly hold a religious context in the world. That mindset is an illusion that held sway over these poor archaic fools.) Iron holds a vastly better cutting edge. It is much easier to work with, if you can achieve the high temperature needed to melt it and raw pig iron is literally found all over the place. This transition between ages perfectly represents the difference between the hemispheres. In the Bronze Age the right brain still had some sway and tools were sacred objects loaded with value for many reasons, but primarily because they embodied the difficulty that is involved in making and acquiring them. As stated earlier, the unconscious was cast about into the environment and this is probably a reflection of our symbolic mind cast. In the Iron Age, axes became tools and they stepped closer to the utility that they allowed. There is less extraneous psychic goo attached to them.

    I wish to make this thought explicit. The algorithms that were developed by Goldman Sacks and Merrill Lynch etc., to create derivative swaps were tools and they argued that they had no ongoing moral implications. These companies were simply trading the derivatives in a free and open market, even though they were betting against the collapse of that very market to gain a power advantage. Hitler himself never created the gas chambers that killed Jews. He was simply implying a direction from within his power structure. In his mind the Jewish race was a problem and everyone else took the cue. Monsanto overtly seeks to help to feed the world and they try to convince us that this implied direction is completely altruistic. This altruism is for a greater good, so supplying us with terrible fake science to backup their claims of altruism is for the best. They have no vested interest in peer review or the wider ramifications of insecticide use in the world; the world is not on the spreadsheet. This is how abstracted tool making plays out in the real world. Weapons help keep us safe; a free market is beneficial to everyone, the herbicide roundup helps us achieve higher crop yields, and if Zyklon gas is an efficient way to solve a problem, then let the eagles fly. We abstract at our own peril.

The View from Nowhere

As I was mentioning earlier in my brief look at Wittgenstein, what Wittgenstein was trying to understand was the nature of language itself. By understanding language, we can gain an understanding of the true nature of the world by disassembling what is implied in our linguistic construction. If you were to become a philosopher, one of your objectives is to create logically coherent arguments, and if you are analyzing someone else's argument, you would search for the point where their logic goes off the rails. (God would not create an evil world) Through this type of analysis you will hopefully find your way back into a higher integration or a more textured whole. I will give an example of a thought experiment that has come up endlessly in my reading that really drives me nuts. This thought experiment seeks to expose whether thinking is a physical reality or whether there is something extra, beyond the neuronal mechanics of thinking – an epiphenomenon.

Inside of a box that is painted only in black and white is a poor girl called Mary. Mary has a black and white TV and her books are only printed in black and white, and what Mary does all of the time is learn about colors, and in fact, she has learned everything there is to know about colors. She presumably has no mirror and can only see the black and white around her. Then, at some point she is allowed to go outside and she can finally see a rose and she now knows what red looks like. The thought experiment has probably unconsciously chosen a rose, because of its symbolic connection to Eros (silly romantic philosophers).

My simple understanding is that Mary now has a true understanding about the nature of a color. This understanding is deeper than her book-learned understanding, and therefore, may represent an extra layer of reality (qualia) that is experiential and beyond our ability to intellectually know (the dualist position. This new understanding is yet another level of her illusion of understanding represented by her glasses. She has not really experienced the rose in itself. She is trapped within her eyes, etc. Everything is an extension of the brain that experiences it and can be explained by increasingly complex mechanical and/or reductionist scientific explanations. (This is the materialist position, which is really talking about talking or an endless regress of abstraction.)

What drives me nuts about this thought experiment is that it implies we are discussing something real. The construction of this artificial environment and the naming of this creature Mary by a philosopher put an idea into my mind-by the use of language- that I should take this thought experiment seriously. On some level, I am meant to believe that Mary is possibly human, or that this idea I am thinking about is important. This is where language goes wrong, because thinking and experience flow out from and into our minds like legs that are walking. Where this thought experiment has gone right off the rails, is the abstract distanced nature of the whole thing itself, as though I should cherish someone called Mary. This thought experiment brings with it the implied context that we are engaged in valid philosophical inquiry. But in some sense we are simply moving words around and clinging to the idea that the words are actually valid signifiers of the associated ideas or an accurate representation of the reality we intend to expose.

Quickly: Mary could not understand the red of the rose, because her brain would not have developed the neural network to process this new color if she had never seen color in her life. Like someone blind at birth, she will simply not have the ability to understand it. Red does not exist outside of the context of red. People that are blind from birth do not suddenly gain sight at thirty years old. The brain would have already appropriated the space that would have been used for understanding the visual information that allows us to see color. The few people who have regained their sight-after a very long time-have to *learn* how to interpret this barrage of information almost from scratch, because they don't know what it means to have a visual impression of something. This is the difference between theoretical speculation and real observation in the real world. Interestingly though, there is a case of a girl in India born with no arms that suffers from phantom limb syndrome. See V.S. Ramachandran

Second: this is an argument about the term qualia, which is the intrinsic being of a thing 'in and of itself' beyond our intellectual displacement of that thing in the abstraction of our thinking. Mary has seen a rose and she now has an understanding of a rose beyond the abstraction of it that existed in her brain (all of her reading). She now is confronted with the thing 'in itself' which only exists as an individual thing unto itself beyond any category or mental construct. This is the raw sensual world that Monet sought to capture before it is compartmentalize into a place, likeness and category, or indeed, sentimentalized through reflection. Mary upon seeing a rose is engaged with the whole of the rose, hopefully in all its poetic and metaphoric beauty, as well as it's now-ness. This is partially what bothers me about this example, because the author has chosen a rose, which carries with it a massive symbolic background that is beyond our petty intellection. One would suppose that Mary has read a lot of poetry in which roses are used as a metaphor. What bearing does that have on the one rose she now sees?

And the sunlight clasps the earth
And the moonbeams kiss the sea
What are all these kisses worth –
If thou not kisses me? - Shelly

This is one kiss existing in time with a loved *one*, not a dry rumination on celestial astronomy, and inherent in this kiss, is value or a romantic reassertion of its singularity. This is the essence of symbolic thinking. It is a fully loaded Rose.

The fellow who developed this initially dualistic argument (Frank Jackson: listen to *Philosophy Bites*), has since recanted his position and embraced a logically satisfying, unified materialism. His initial position was that there was something beyond phenomena – epiphenomenalism. In this essentially dualistic view, it is presumed that the experience of reality is *more* than the reality itself, much like Descartes idea that the mind is more than the brain that contains it. Now it seems to be fairly well understood that the mind is the brain and I can see no way in which this cannot be so. But much of this argument is about the way that abstraction seems to present reality to us. There really are two positions: one is the displaced representation of reality that we can look closely at and discuss, theorize etc. This is largely the left brain's position. The other reality is the metaphor of the rose. This is the rose that every lover has ever given to anyone. It is a thousand different roses depending on what time of day it is, but it is both specific and heavy with the scent of every other rose that preceded it. It exists in the soft diffuse light that is reflected off the moon and into a calm lake. It is not too near to us and there is no hard relief of its edges. It embodies an associated symbolic relationship with the archetype and it always carries value into us. This is an inkling of the right brain's position, which ultimately defies the ridged rules of the left brain's linguistic constructs.

The world is brought to us as a series of specific items or index's (that oak tree over there). That specific tree can be related to other trees we have seen and we can compare them. This is known as an iconic process where we develop the idea of trees or forests, with each tree being a representative of the larger category of trees or we have the idea of trees as a separate iconic representation. Symbolic thinking allows us to combine the qualities of trees with our desire to build a house and we can use the wood in an abstracted way to create tools or houses by combining icon relationships. (That stone with this stick will make an axe, etc.) Symbolic thinking allows us to run different scenarios around in our mind in the abstract so that we can propel ourselves forward and into the future. The ability to combine icons and index or token relationships into symbolic webs of meaning is behind our language development. Language is a reflection or outward expression of this more abstracted process. But it is never removed from the world. It is always deeply embedded in these three levels. The word tree or rose in this case always implies a reference to trees not dogs, because our thinking is based upon these references back to real tokens. All thinking occurs within these set of indexes (tokens), which are a reflection of things in the real world. We have developed the ability to form a symbolic understanding of the world by creating distance through our rose-colored glasses, but not without a real world to refer it back to.

I would seek to blow this stagnant argument right over the top and go on to agree with Don Cupitt (again listen to *Philosophy Bites* podcast) and embrace the fact that we created God. This thought that God is our creation does not inevitably lead to the belief that God does not exist. God is not a concept by which we measure our pain; God is not properly a concept at all. The whole of this idea is deeply symbolic. Concepts must be subscribed by a limit. Chew on that and we will come back to it.

There is a newish movement within philosophy called 'experimental philosophy' that rejects abstract thought experiments (like the Mary argument) completely. They have a symbol for their movement, which is a flaming armchair to signify their rejection of idle and detached speculation. That's something I can get behind. (Again, listen to *Philosophy Bites* podcast)

I should like to take a further cut at this Gordian knot and express what I think Wittgenstein was also driving at. There is a world outside of our minds that we can and must consensually agree is real. We constantly discuss the real world with sets and definitions of words so that we don't have to constantly argue about (tokens) all of the time. We don't need to constantly speculate about what the precise definition of color might be. Colors-and the names signifying them-are vague (icons) and they must be referred back to the real colors that exist in the world. Surprisingly, they actually do. We are also constantly thinking symbolically or metaphorically and abstractly as well, and we transition seamlessly between these relationships all day long. All things in the world are both the things unto themselves and an ongoing comparison to all other things in the world. The real world is a wheel in which we travel from the hub of the 'thing unto itself' out through the various spokes of comparison and up through their symbolic relationships, and then back down into the qualia of the thing itself. Reality is both the hub and the spokes and the rim and the dirt on the road, etc. We all can and do regularly agree that something is being said about something real and we don't have to constantly issue a caveat or minutely describe the limit of our conceptual framework to communicate – a pipe is sometimes just a pipe.

I was working with an intellectually pretentious fellow once and I asked how he was doing. He replied 'what do you mean'? So I replied, 'what do you mean, what do I mean?' Then, I issued the very ambiguous rejoinder, 'never mind' and walked away. – The author's fascinating collection of true stories in the real world.

The consensual aspect of the real world is reinforced and made certain as we observe what other people are saying about the world to us, face to face. We understand very clearly what someone's intentions are while we are observe and absorb all of the subtle cues that pass across their face, and this is the right brain's unconscious tour de force. When we interact with others, we are embedded in the physical situation discussing a consensually real-world, using common speech. The written page doesn't talk into your mind with any type of subtle facial queuing. The face-unlike the written page-lends a phenomenal amount of further context and nuance to the words that are being used. You must abstract a lie or humor, or sarcasm out of the dull written page. This act of being embedded in a conversation is a result of our evolution with each other and much of the ensuing philosophical hair-splitting we have come to love so much is a result of the ambiguity of the displaced and written word. Hence, the philosophers' and lawyers' need to be articulate and specific (left brain forte), or the need for extensive commentaries, explaining the deep metaphors that are embedded in eastern philosophical texts. It seems that these old yogis were quite comfortable with ambiguity and metaphor, because these texts were not written to be separate from the physical bodies of yogis who were in the teaching environment. Such is the poverty of the modern world.

This brings us back to the idea that language can appear to be stating a truth. If I tell you that I am a liar, have I told you the truth? What I understand is that Wittgenstein sought to uncover that this type of word play as artificial and it is. The belief that we have asked some type of philosophically valid question about the nature of language or indeed lying, or that we have made a consensually understandable statement about the world-when we use this type of word play-is wrong. This type of lie/truth word play is part of humor, not logical debate. In this example, I made two logical statements and they are incongruous. When I say intentionally ambiguous things like, I am a liar, I am playing with implied meaning, which befuddles the strict one-to-one correlation in token language construction. This illusion of a statement about lying is implicit in the nature of our talking. We constantly take the words and statements we hear people say seriously. Of course, we should take words seriously and we do all day long as we listen to people talk or we read books, or whatever. Sarcasm is a dish best served face to face.

Sometimes people who have had a massive right brain stroke usually have trouble with the left hand. It is almost always the left hand that causes trouble. The left brain carries a representation of the right side of the body exclusively. The right brain contains a representation of the whole body. If the right brain is damaged, the left brain has no control and little ongoing integration with the left hand and body, which is specifically the purview of the right brain. The left brain will seek to concoct any number of fantastical tales in an effort to explain how this left hand is sitting beside them on the bed (It is my mother's hand; someone left it here), and sometimes the left hand will actually act up and fight with the person. (See Ramachandran and Sacks' *Phantoms in the Brain: Probing the Mysteries of the Human Mind.*) What I wish to point out is that the left brain will create a narrative story about what the facts are, and without the right brain's ongoing largely symbolic integration, it will seek to justify the narrative as if it were the truth, and it might as well be, because there is no internal censor to contradict it. It will construct a logical argument 'I'm a liar', but it will not re-contextualize the statement in the real world and it will instead, cling to its representation and adhere to its 'logic', because that is the left brain's tool box. This is important in that the left brain owns the token or denotative language and the ability to construct the architecture of sentences. I think that the determination to construct logical arguments is a reflection with this ownership over the tokens. This is the essence of the metaphor of the Gordian knot, which Alexander simply cut with his sword instead of trying to untie. The knot had proven to be impossible to untie and so it comes down to what does it mean to untie something? The sword untied it.

It is my contention that the token constituents of language removed from symbolic context are yet another form of the rose-colored glasses, but the rose-colored glasses are in fact both a representation of and the reality itself. The distinction is arbitrary in many ways. We are forced to express our thoughts with language, but we both do and don't think in language. We think with our brains and language is the way that we externalize and contextualize our thoughts. To a certain extent, language compresses and directs our thinking. This is because we pass through the filter of the left brain as we speak and this is also why it is so difficult to put our emotions or music (its direct representative) into words. They refuse to be placed into conceptual token boxes. I will come back to this as I try to put a lovely rose-colored bow on things.

So my problem with Mary in a box is the whole thought experiment itself. We will never have Mary in a box to really conduct the experiment, because it would be cruel and this thought experiment has led to apparently thousands of egg-head pages of discussion (mine included). When you actually conduct an experiment in the real world, you quite often get results that are unexpected. You have to submit your proposed experiment and the results to a peer review. I think that this type of thought experiment is intellectual knob pulling. It is actually not an experiment at all and again I will cut the Gordian knot and say that we will gain a better understanding of nature by trying to gain a better understanding of the brain's function itself and how it comprehends and represents the world.

To sum up: we cannot look at the world without our brains, and if we don't understand how the brain works, what the hell are we talking about? The brain makes millions of consensual assumptions about what we are looking at, based on what the world has been like for millions of years. This is how the world comes to us. These consensual assumptions are based on the weight of real world experience. Things simply don't fall up. We are the rose colored glasses. The intellectual distinction between us and the world is in many ways artificial. Indian philosophy has been pushing this thought for millennia. A real quote should be: "I am reality" or sum ergo sum.

What we talk' in bout

The art of psychology at the turn of the 20th century was largely dominated by Freud who was mostly concerned with what was understood as the talking cure or the thought that you could heal someone by bringing their various unconscious presumptions and issues forward and into their consciousness through unmasking them by discussion, elaboration and association etc., but really the cure consisted mostly of just talking. What I have come to understand is that Jung, and especially Freud, are like Sir Isaac Newton. Their understanding is not wrong. Neuroscience is creating a window into a new way to observe the underpinnings that lay behind strict psychological and largely phenomenological observations. As mentioned earlier, Jung developed a system that broke the human personality into various psychological types and I bring this up to highlight a point that I think is relevant to my further discussion of philosophy. Jung made much of the distinction between emotions and feeling, and I will highlight this distinction once more as this will be an insight worth milling around. It will have a much larger ramification later.

Jung conceived of the emotions as a somewhat more primitive or less reflective mental state, in that the emotions were more diffuse or less specific and usually associated with relatively unconscious thought processes. Emotions are essentially our form of instinct. We inherited them from our ancestors. For example, if I see a snake coming toward me, I probably would become very afraid and rightfully so. This is now understood to be a largely automatic and unconscious biological reflex. There could be an explicit intellectual assessment of the situation that happens later after the automatic biological reaction. If I had to go through all of the various explicit ramifications about what snakes could do to me and my ancestors, I would already be dead from a snake bite. It seems that we are hardwired to automatically become all of the physical manifestations of fear, especially toward snakes in particular.

For the interested reader, see Jaak Panksepp and Lucy Biven's: *The Archaeology of the Mind*

We have been evolutionarily wired in the oldest parts of our brain to fear snakes and this has been proven beyond a doubt. No one automatically fears flowers, but many people fear snakes, even if they have never seen one. Wallabies on the small island off the coast of Australia are afraid of predators, even though there hasn't been a predator on the island for nine and a half thousand years. These wallabies assume a defensive posture when shown a stuffed animal that represents a predator or snake. There are many very specific images that have been gifted to us through evolution and Jung chose the word 'archetypes' to try to explain what he saw in the psyche (see *Who's In Charge ?* by Michael S. Gazzaniga - Pg.43-44)

These emotions of fear or, for that matter, elements of being in love, seem to come from the collusion of "older" parts of the inner brain, but especially important, is the amygdale. The limbic system, which is closely allied with the amygdale along with the hypothalamus, hippocampus etc., have an evolutionarily adaptive ability to overwhelm all other things that are going on in the brain as they take control of the situation. Male philosophers have, throughout history, contrasted the emotional against the rational as if they were two distinctly diametrically opposed aspects. This argument is leveraged into ongoing sexist beliefs about women being overly emotional, etc. This has been one of the great patriarchal arguments that sought to elevate the rational logos-thinking mind over everything and it runs something like this: women are more emotional or less rational than men and so they are not fit to run governments or participate in serious thinking, etc. (ladies… it's time to get yours back, and I would suggest the term 'matronizing' as opposed to patronizing. This term could be used for anything that women are quite obviously better at than men. A woman could be matronizing to her husband by saying, everyone knows that you don't know the first thing about that baby's needs or how I feel at all etc. So of course, the man will buy his wife something to prove that he does know how she feels and she will not matronize him for this gesture even though his gift is an extension of the same matronizing problem. You matronize from the position of superior feeling.)

Jung tried to delineate the difference between feeling and emotion. Feeling is the relational aspect of the personality and it is also a rational function like thinking. When I talk about my wife, I don't need to construct an intellectual argument to explain why I love her. I just love her. I feel this to be true and I have a relationship with her that goes beyond any amount of temporary rational argument. Feelings can be deep and true; they are not the sensation that comes over you when you are drunk with your friends and you see an attractive person dancing. Feelings are always relational and value leavened; there is a certain amount of (whether I care about these things or not) that is involved in any feeling relation.

I can discuss music quite dispassionately, because my feeling relationship with music is quite rich. I have certain opinions about what I like and don't like, and I freely contradict myself, but the reality is that I feel very secure in my relationship *with* and appreciation *of* music. I can articulate the various contradictory notions I have about music, but this only happens when I run it through the intellectual grist mill. Like my wife, I have an extended meaningful relationship with music, which is full of diverse feelings and emotions, but it is based in, and cannot be removed from the experience of music. That is not to say that I can't get very steamy about music as well. If I feel that you as a musician-critic is completely off your nut, it wouldn't take much for me to get emotional about it, as you will see later in my discussion of dreaded modern art.

What I am trying to show here is the difference between feelings, which can be entirely accurate depending on their integration and emotions, and their effects, which are largely unconscious reactions to the world that have been built up over evolutionary history. Jung pointed out that French people will and do joke about the Catholic Church, because they have a very integrated and deep feeling relationship to their religion. I don't get as defensive about my opinions concerning music, because my relationship carries the weight of my experience, which is integrated. If you want to find someone's shadow or weak integration, you should look for an excess of emotion. Behind a fanatic is a secret doubter.

Emotions can also be accurate indicators of the world about us, but they have a tendency to be more easily side-railed and linked with irrational fears, which we see in such things as compulsion disorder or the mass hysterias that we have been unreasonably sucked into recently; for instance, going to war with Iraq or the SAR's "epidemic" here in Canada, or Y2K or the entire ass-dribble about the rapture and 2012. (We made it by the way) Emotions most closely reflect the underlying automatic unconscious and archetypal superstructures of the survival systems that come with us into the world at birth. They include primary drives like fear and a desire to seek everything from sexual partners to food. Emotions are extremely valuable and they are part of the tool box that we all have inherited. They should be embraced and integrated as an aspect of our humanity.

In one of my brain science podcast by Ginger Campbell there is a lovely German woman who was seeking to validate our emotions, by explaining that much of our experience of the world is rightly colored by emotional impact. What would be the point of music or falling in love, for instance, or the ongoing relationship to your children without your illogical emotional attachment? These are not irrational foolish things; they are-to my mind-some of the richest aspects of our life. We will see later that emotions and feelings are really the cornerstone of all symbolic thought. The point I should like to make here is that Campbell did not make a distinction between feeling and emotion. She constantly referred to emotions when-to my mind-she was talking sometimes about feeling and emotion. This is the thinking mind in action, and in the overtly thinking mind, this division between feeling and emotion is a more arbitrary distinction. I believe this lack of a clear distinction between the both of them is embedded in the social linguistic and cultural milieu of western society, and more specifically, flows from the intellect of the scientific communities themselves. (The west seriously under values the illogic of intuition) Few people seem to make this distinction between emotion and feeling and the terms are almost completely interchangeable to the extent that I feel compelled to try to explain the difference. (I am a left-handed feeler and I know of that which I speak, but I still can't pin it down.)

If you are a feeler, you can understand the many shades of your ongoing feeling relationships, but it is difficult to express the concepts through language and to really bear witness to them. They must be circled around endlessly. I cannot clearly express the beauty of a cord change and I find an endless string of adjectives describing such things fairly flat on the page. When we don't feel, we tend to flit about the surface and be content with hackneyed tropes instead of real insight. The ecology movement is more feeling based and that is why it is of no consequence to the industrial military machinery of say a Bush/Cheney/Halliburton axis of evil. You simply cannot sit at the table with thinkers and bleed your feelings on to them. They are not there with you.

Conversely, politicians in the west and especially in North America, constantly seek to blind side people with appeals to their base emotions through so-called rational arguments, because it is a large part of the collective blind side (shadow) of our culture. George Bush mentioned how he felt "born again" and Regan talked about his million spots of light. These are nebulous Bible based trigger ideas that feed into fundamentalists emotional superstructures. By appealing to our 'common sense' notion of the obvious simplicity of these things, you shut down any nuanced argument and imply that it is rational and apparent. One of the surest ways to spark emotions is to bring up abstract concepts like freedom or label something the Patriot Guard or Homeland Security of the fatherland. There is so much emotional baggage attached to this word 'freedom' that you can effectively shut everyone's brain off. Freedom is a relationship to the world and is embedded in experience, and because we are such poor feelers, we have to relate to freedom through the abstract intellectual grist mill where it doesn't belong. There is no discussion about what freedom is. We must have freedom at all costs. Who should get shot to preserve my freedom and the American way of life? If we have to wire tap everybody to preserve freedom, that's OK.

Hitler used the concept of the German people's relationship to their fatherland with a similar effect when he was talking to Germans. First, he would hammer on ideas with emotional triggers like ridding the world of the pestilential Jewish /Bolshevik conspiracy. Then, he would raise the pitch in his voice and go into a sort of divine trance when he really had the people's emotional ear. Hitler and Goebbels were masters at delivering their message to a mass audience. Hitler could easily speak for two hours and quite often four. He would do this at huge rallies in an effort to dumb everyone down into the collective mindset through mass emotional cuing. The total I.Q. or conscious awareness of a large crowd is exactly the same as one individual.

Jung watched Hitler very closely and he mentioned that Hitler would cast around ideas when he was addressing a new audience to gage their emotional response. Hitler was actively trying to discern where this particular crowd's collective shadow was. Once he found the shadow, he would hammer on this line of discussion to engage with their base emotions, especially anger which is mediated through the left and rational hemisphere, while lowering their explicit rational thinking. America in general has such a myopic inward looking worldview that it's easy to get everyone fired up and fighting, because of their poor relationships with almost every other country on earth (America does not apologize), and these relationships are largely based on power, which flows in one direction only.

If you were from a poor farming community with no land, then Hitler got you land from the subhuman communist slaves and Russians; they have lots. If you were a business man in debt, Hitler would run the Jews out of Germany for you. They hold all of the debt in Germany (this particular message of Jews holding all of the money proved especially effective in Viennese Austria). This naive belief in racial superiority was unfortunately floating around Europe in many different forms at this time for Hitler to grasp on to. We in the west in the 2000's have been collectively focused on Islam as our 'unique' version of the collective world shadow. If you were hopping mad about 9/11, it didn't take much to direct that anger on to Saddam Hussein. He must have weapons of mass destruction somewhere.. He is obviously evil. We connected this evil directly to Hitler by calling it an axis of evil. Islam now (thanks to the constant hammering of the western media) looks to us like it is living in the dark ages, especially the way that Islam treats women. They obviously hate our freedom so 'let the eagles fly' or 'bring the rain'. Saying 'bring the rain' is a way to create an intellectual barrier around the fact that you are indiscriminately killing human beings. They become 'collateral damage' as a result of 'personal disrupters' instead of somebody's dead babies. Hitler said if you are going to lie to people make the lie so big that people can't believe that you could be lying at all. The real key to public manipulation is to dumb your message down and let it ride into the room on the back of fear.

Fear and its highly contagious suite of emotional and hormonal cascades is the greatest intellectual leveler. We are all idiots when we are afraid. (The United States of America is now spending more money on 'homeland security' than all other forms of policing put together. It is literally a blank cheque. They now have the largest percentage of their population in jail of any country in the world.) Fear demands immediate action. I could say that the Bush Administration learned how to create the necessary psychic climate of fear so that we would believe that we should invade Iraq unconsciously or perhaps quite consciously, following the patterns realized by Hitler's propaganda machine. However, that is not what I am saying. That is conspiracy stuff. Observant or even stupid people learn these types of crowd control techniques from deep inside their own bones; is that being sufficiently vague and/or politically correct?

Babel on

I have become quite enamored with podcasts lately and have come to realize a number of things as a result of listening to them. I started listening to *A History of Rome* by Mike Duncan (which has somewhat influenced the style of this book). I was then led to a podcast called *Philosophy Bites,* and from there, I started listening to anything that I could find on the current state of neuroscience. The *Brain Science* podcast with Ginger Campbell is by far the best podcast that deals with neuroscience. Most of my ensuing discussion about neuroscience will be a reflection of her interviews and also of my having read through a number of the books that she has discussed or suggested; plus a few that I discovered myself. The *Brain Science* podcast (or BSP) is an excellent source of information and I highly recommend these podcasts to someone wishing to gain a foothold in their understanding of neuroscience.

I came to these podcasts after having written the initial parts of this book, except for this chapter. I subsequently found that many of the people working in the field of neuroscience have been addressing the questions that I am most interested in. Many authors I read recently came to a number of the same conclusions that I did and I was able to confirm some of my inklings, and greatly expand and re-conceptualize many of my earlier and very dim suspicions. I have also had to go back into the earlier chapters regularly and tweak a great number of things as a result of broadening my understanding. This book has really been a great unfolding process in my head, as I sought to cleanup and express my own naive thinking. My current re-reading in Indian philosophy is changing some of my ill-formed ideas yet again. I don't want anyone to think that Ginger Campbell is in any way responsible for my fuzzy thinking process. (She is virulently skeptical in a nice way and staunchly anti ESP etc.)

The big picture-for me-is that over the last six years, I have seriously re-evaluated much of what I was driving at in the initial viewing of this book. Now, feel that I have a better-though still dim understanding-of the real roots of the way that the brain works and how this, in turn, affects the way that we think. This is especially true when it comes to the ongoing discussions about feeling. I have long been a proponent of feeling as a rational function, largely due to my love of music and my own personality typology. I realized more explicitly that both feeling and its handmaiden music are far more important to us humans than I had ever imagined. I also realized that the benefits of art and music can actually be proven scientifically (if that means anything). I will try to tie many of the disparate strings of the earlier chapters together into this one, before I move on to discussing music and its relationship to the brain, culture, language and religion in the next chapter. This way up!

What's that you said?

Before I discovered the world of neuroscience, I was reading a lot about language and trying to understand how the brain works through this paradigm. I first came to the writings of Steven Pinker. His specialty is language and how the study of language can be a window into the inner workings of the mind. There are a number of things that he illuminates that will bring us closer to the realm of ideas that I have been circling around and through him. We will see some familiar themes from yet another angle. I will sidetrack this discussion for just a little bit longer, as we take a look at his work.

Pinker explains in *The Language Instinct* that the various rules of sentence construction are actually an instinct, but they are culturally flexible like the way that the French reverses the order of a noun and verb. He means that language is an instinct in the sense that some elements of the mind are pre-jiggered to receive language. This architecture in the brain is passed on to us through our genetic wiring to help us accept the existing forms of language into our brains. His main theme is that there is a genetic propensity in humans to accept and exploit the general structure of linguistic construction; but the full and real world genetic/linguistic expression of speaking is also environmentally conditioned. We will attempt to get behind what genetic expression is and its parallels with language, as we move along.

For instance, a literal translation of French doesn't work in English, because you end up with sentences like: 'he to the store goes'. This is not an inherent aspect of language. It is a culturally specific word order and the cultural aspect of language doesn't strictly affect the underlying meaning of sentences. We understand that someone has gone to a store.

What Mr. Pinker is driving at is that there are structures inside language that exist at a deeper level than the surface temporal word order and that these deeper orders seem to reflect an inherent aspect of the brain's inner workings. If we can unmask these basic structures as they appear in language, then we are-in some ways-looking at the fundamental building blocks of the mind itself. This is essentially the early leading insight of Noam Chomsky; which was that the underlying dynamics of language reflect the inner workings of the mind. Much of the real inner workings of the mind were unknown at the time Mr. Chomsky was studying language (fifties to late seventies), and so this was a new avenue into understanding the brain that wasn't as speculative as the field of psychology were at this time.

There are rules that a three year old learns that are extremely subtle. They don't learn them from hearing someone explicitly tell them what they are. We are peeking over the wall at the proof of archetypal forms, if we can find inherent structures within the mind or ideas that come with us into birth. Mr. Pinker is very clear and concise, so I will let him speak for himself in a fairly long quote.

"Evidence corroborating the claim that the mind contains blueprints for grammatical rules comes, once again, out of the mouths of babes and suckling's. Take the English agreement suffix, as in HE WALKS. Agreement is an important process in many languages, but in modern English it is superfluous, a remnant of a richer system that flourished in Old English. If it were to disappear entirely, we would not miss it, any more than we miss the similar –est. suffix in THOU SAYEST. But psychologically speaking, this frill does not come cheap. Any speaker committed to using it has to keep track of four details in every sentence uttered:

*Whether the subject is in the third person or not: He walks versus I walk

*Whether the subject is singular or plural: He walks versus They walk

*Whether the action is present tense or not: He walks versus He walked

*Whether the action is habitual or going on at the moment of speaking (its aspect): He walks to school versus He is walking to school.

"And all this work is needed just to use the suffix once one has learned it. To learn it in the first place, a child must (1) notice that verbs end in –s in some sentences but appear bare-ended in others, (2) begin a search for the grammatical causes of this variation (as opposed to just accepting it as part of the spice of life), and (3) not rest until those crucial factors-tense, aspect, and the number and person of the subject of the sentence- have been sifted out of the ocean of conceivable but irrelevant factors (like number of syllables of the final word in the sentence, whether the object of a preposition is natural or manmade, and how warm it is when the sentence was uttered). Why would anyone bother?

"But little children do bother. By the age of three and a half or earlier, they use the s-agreement suffix in more than ninety percent of the sentences that require it, and virtually never use it in the sentences that forbid it. This mastery is part of their grammar explosion, a period of several months in the third year of life during which children suddenly begin to speak in fluent sentences, respecting most of the fine points of their community's spoken language." The Language Instinct - Pg. 44

Mr. Pinker goes on to show some examples from a little girl's vocabulary where she is using this rule, but with words she could never have heard; showing that she is not simply imitating her mother's speech, but employing a larger pattern of understanding.

When she BE's in the kindergarten. She DO'S what her mother tells her.

He continues on to say that some dreaded scientists are looking for a specific language gene and specific areas of the brain that are used in the formation of language. This book was written in 1994. I have read three of his other works, which were all written after this book and it seems (surprise… surprise) that the whole picture is more complicated than finding a gene or synaptic ensemble or even a single definable place in the brain where language resides, though people were hung up on Broca's area in the left side of the brain for quite some time. Mr. Pinker sums this up quite nicely:

"The idea that the Human mind is designed to use abstract variables and data structures used to be, and in some circles still is, a shocking and revolutionary claim, because the structures have no direct

counterpart in the child's experience. Some of the organization of grammar would have to be there from the start, part of the language-learning mechanism that allows children to make sense out of noises they hear from their parents. The details of syntax have figured prominently in the history of psychology, because they are a case where complexity in the mind is not caused by learning; learning is caused by complexity in the mind. And that was real news." -The Language Instinct - Pg.125

He is saying that these elemental building blocks of sentence structure are a reflection of the inherent elemental building blocks of the architecture of the brain itself. Language reflects the inherent organizational aspects of the mind, passed on to us from our evolutionary heritage. I am now personally quite sure that there is not much evidence for a consistent argument for both of these ideas. It seems that the mind is inherently very complex, but that it is quite flexible in terms of how things are sorted out. Memory, for example, is stored all over the brain depending on which type of memory it is. The memory of a particular person's face is not stored in the same part of the brain that recognizes the face as being a constituent of a person. (See *The Man Who Mistook His Wife for a Hat* by Oliver Sacks.) Most of the face is recognized in the right hemisphere as a complete gestalt, which is related to everything else about the person. All of the various elements of language construction and speaking are parceled out across the whole of the brain. Although, it seems as though it flows out of the left hemisphere as it is packaged for consumption. Much of our ability to learn language happens well before we ever actually speak it. This idea that there is some form of grammar organization within the brain that our specific and/or elemental grammar structure reflects, is a chicken and the egg argument or a search for causality. Different parts of the brain are used for incoming sentences and outgoing communication and certain parts seem to be registering only very small elements of the sound while other parts are scanning the whole of the sentence to gain access to the wider implications or symbolic layers.

This theory of an inherent language architecture stems from the mistaken notion that language was completely the left brain's concern and it seems that explicit and direct denotative language is (denotative or indexical/token: that's a dog not a cat and, dog means dog, etc.) the left brain's forte. The right brain deals with the metaphorical, symbolic and poetic expressions that are implied. Though we are so embedded in this non-verbal context of facial cuing, that if there is a discrepancy between what is said with the mouth and what the body indicates (say I tell you to walk left, but point off to the right), we will always over-ride the spoken words and correctly assume the body is saying the right thing and we will be correct in that assumption. So the right brain is processing the world, language and communication as a whole ensemble that is set within context. Chomsky's model of an inherent linguistic/brain architecture is the type of model that the left brain seeks to construct. Communication is highly symbolic and extremely context driven, especially when we are learning it; and our spoken language is only one aspect of communication. I will expand upon this as we move along.

Mr. Pinker in the *Language Instinct* does an excellent job of showing how language is received into the mind and how the mind has evolved to accept the various forms of language that is brought to it. The mind is not a blank page nor is it a full floppy disc that contains sets of rules that only needs some external language source–say French-to stuff into pre-rigged pigeon holes. Learning to speak is the result of a flexible strategy -probably hijacked or coevolved along with the various brain structures that had originally evolved from music-making and mimicking bird songs (more later). Speaking is the result of accommodating the implied and or explicit rules of a language. The mind, or a collection of minds, can invent its own expression of a language like sign or a more basic pidgin, if need be. These two examples (Pidgin especially) seem to represent the most basic organizational levels of a language construct.

It has been speculated that a ribbon of music, like the way that whales communicate to each other, may be the most elementary non-declarative form. This way of communication is more concerned with the emotional expression of each part within the ribbon than with any strict correlation between symbol and object. More right than left brain. Nonetheless, we can catch the flavor of this by talking about music, and by looking at very young children as they build their symbolic understandings.

An open system like the brain can accommodate and allow an infinite amount of ongoing flexibility and nuance. For example, we can talk about anything that we have a word for, and if we don't have a word for it, we can make one up and use it instead. Language is a window into the way the mind constructs a view of reality, but it is a window that needs cleaning.

Mr. Pinker also talks about the way that language can be used to disguise intentions. For example, if you are on a date and you ask the person for coffee later on, there is probably a subtext involved in your request that you wish not to make too explicit, because it could prove socially awkward. We use coffee as a symbolic way of asking for sex. Freud saw and read much into this type of social subtext. Your subtext for the coffee is that you are offering to have sex without wishing to be explicit and this vague implied form of language is rooted in our expression of ongoing social interactions. This is part of the reason that non-European countries don't put prices on things that are for sale. This allows the seller to test your metal and take advantage of you, if you are sleepy. This affords the seller the best price he can get and it is part of the wider cultural context.

My friend Hugh and I quite often talk to each other using a veiled sarcastic/ironic threat to explicitly say something that could prove uncomfortable. This is part of our English and/or our self-indulgent 20th century heritage. We actually speak a form of intentionally uncomfortable straight truth to each other all of the time. These are the kinds of things that you don't say publically, and of course, we are much more subtle about it. But what we do is, say it as though we are using a very dry and ironic sarcasm to veil our brutal honesty. What is really going on is that we are trying to be so sly and brazenly honest to actually get a laugh out of each other. To say that our humor is dry doesn't quite capture the essence of it. Of course, the point of sarcasm and irony is that it shouldn't sound sarcastic; it should be delivered straight. We are trying to be as socially awkward as we can, delivered as a mildly sarcastic veiled threat (it's childish, I know). There is a larger
point I wish to make and I will get there.

Hugh and I had this fellow come and work with us who had part of his brain damaged in a climbing accident. This damage occurred in an area in the frontal lobe (I believe the right side), just above his eyes. This is the area that sends out the information that decides whether we should inhibit immediate physical action within an emotional environment or not. This part of the brain is crucial to many aspects of your mature social functioning, in that it stops or slows you down from instantly acting out things like aggression when you are threatened, or if you feel like punching people when you get mad. Now, Hugh and I were prattling on in the way that we do and I started to take my veiled sarcastic undertone out on this fellow who wasn't watching my face (he was reading a newspaper), and also I didn't realize that he had a very low tolerance for this type of veiled threat. Suffice to say, I nearly got my block knocked off. Because subtlety is the key to our childishness, this fellow easily misread what my intention. Or, in fact, he quite accurately assessed the threat behind the ironic self-indulgent veiled threat.

This is an excellent example of the dynamics of unconscious cues and the inherent ambiguity of speech when it is unmoored from context and our bodily expression. These more subtle social cues are completely eliminated when we use text messaging. In a text message, we must be very explicit and clear or constantly use emoticons to highlight our intent. If you have to write LOL in a text, you probably aren't that funny.

This idea that there is a specific area of the brain where language occurs has become associated with Noam Chomsky. My feeble understanding of Chomsky's work is that he believed that language was a result of explicit hardwired rules that probably related directly to an area of the brain. In other words, language was a good way to study the brain, because there was thought to be a direct correlation between the way we learn language and the way the brain is wired to receive it. This tied in very nicely to the realization that language resided primarily in the left brain. This has been the dominant paradigm in the field of linguistics for some 30 years. Up until the nineties, Chomsky had been an unassailable guru for most people working within linguistics. Some of this unassailability is a reflection of the fact that people don't or can't read his dense academic work, simply because it is extremely difficult to understand. Neuroscience has a very large problem with the leviathan that is Chomsky's work. I only bring this up, because it relates directly to the theme of scientific proof and our ongoing construction of belief systems within the sciences.

My understanding of this paradigm is that our brains are somehow ready to receive the building blocks of language. The evolution of our brain has made us ripe for receiving large chunks of language elements into specific language areas. There is some form of innate building block of language that locks itself directly in to a pre- prepared brain architecture is simply wrong. As we discussed earlier, and will continue to discuss as we go along, is the expression of language, and the symbolic way that we understand reality, is double coded (I will explain this in detail later), and firmly set within an emotional mind/body/environment. The brain doesn't receive language in an abstract intellectual or architecturally prepared way it receives and expresses language all over the brain and speaking reflects a cascade function which integrates many different forms of understanding. We both listen for simple phonemes so that we can then predict ongoing sentence structures and we draw back to observe large sentences within context in order to suss out implied meaning and relate symbols together. The more analytical elements of the 'left brain' seeks to compress language back into a causal way in an effort to express causality, partially because this is the way it comes out of the brain when we think about language in the abstract.

All of our experiences growing up are mixed together and language occurs as a result of many different parts of the brain initially developing an excess of connections within itself. The right brain dominates this process for the first two or three years, because we are simply listening to language; then the left catches up as we learn to speak it. Language has had to co-evolve with the development of the voice box, possibly because we sang so much. Our ability to understand intention through projecting ourselves symbolically into the act of empathy, language is rooted in context first and then it was written down and further abstracted later. (Much more later) Chinese people use more of the right brain when reading, because their highly symbolic writing is so inter-context driven.

Each symbol has a flexible meaning, which depends on a relationship to the surrounding context, like Arabic and Hebrew where the vowels aren't even written, but must be inferred backward from an understanding of the whole of the contextual gestalt. This represents a more archaic, probably more right brain level of written language, which were all initially written from the right side of the page to left belying the initial right brain prominence.

My understanding of language is that it is the result of many functions of the brain being co-opted into a 'higher unified expression'. There are at least two different types of memory systems available and a multitude of things going on below anything that starts to resemble the conscious construction of a sentence. I will give a quick example of double coding: if a baby touches something hot and hears the word hot, there is an explicit resulting linguistic and physical connection. This connection between the word and the pain is remembered, because of the resulting emotional impact of the situation, which along with the crying and subsequent use of the word 'hot' reinforces this ensemble into long term memory. The word 'hot' can be used as a trigger to bring back elements of this emotional memory and the word is now a functioning retrievable concept symbolized by the denotative word 'hot'. We can perhaps, always have it turned into a metaphor to describe the emotional impact of a good looking woman. The word pain is itself painful to speak, because it is much more than an abstract symbolic representation of pain: it is the pain remembered.

If we constantly express our anger instead of 'dealing with it', we actually *are that anger*: The distinction between me saying offensive things and actually *being them* is fairly arbitrary within the mind. We are the emotional environment that we express, and if we constantly express our anger, then we are actually angry all the time. Most of this symbolic emotional and metaphoric double coding happens around the age of two before the explosion of actual talking and language happen. When we study only language, we are working from the top down, but we don't get to the bottom.

Northrop Frye realized that the Bible's main form of expression is the repetition of metaphors expressed in words like: garden, mountain and snake, etc. There never is nor was one garden or mountain. All gardens and mountains point to the archetype of the garden or mountain, which exists outside of time. These words gain power as they become illuminated through repeated contextual evolution. We are constantly driven out of the garden (idealized naïve bliss, Israel) and up on to the mountain to ask God why. Then a leader emerges (messiah, Abraham Moses, Jesus, Mohammed, etc.), who brings us back into the metaphor. This is how the older forms of language are expressed. There is less of a one-to-one correlation and more of a context-driven gestalt that is developed within us through repetition and experience. We can then have a living experience of the truth of these metaphors by going to a real mountain or by being in the sacred geography, which is always spread out around us.

It seems that when children are learning to read, it helps to tie the words to physical objects that they can hold. For instance, if you are reading a story about a farm, you can have plastic farm animals around you on the floor and by putting them in to the child's hand, as you show them the words, you are establishing a multi-leveled (both right and left brain) ensemble that is easier to remember. *The Rosetta Stone* language learning system uses this same type of idea, which is tying the new words of another language to overt visual cuing to reinforce the words' impact into the various forms of memory. We lock our learning down by loading the word into multiple contexts and establishing it into different parts of the brain. Both the analytic denotative left and the metaphoric context- driven right become engaged. This multi-valence system of learning may work better than rote repetitive learning, because the brain stores memory in a number of different ways, and also by creating stronger emotional impact, it puts the things being learned into long-term (right brain oriented) memory. By tying words and pictures or ideas together, you have engaged different parts of the brain and you are accessing multiple areas of memory storage, and interconnecting them to build up what are known as entrained memory suites. Conversely, you may learn more easily with this type of system simply because it is more interesting and engaging than passively reading a book, which demands concentrated effort. The ability to sustain a focused effort is important for developing an ability to perform sustained analytic work, which usually happens around 18 years.

Mr. Pinker offers some wiggle room in this concept of a hard wired aspect of language learning and he is by no means dogmatic in his approach. We will discuss how early learning happens in more detail as we move along in the narrative. What I wish to draw from this tirade is yet another look at how science is done and how an academic strangle hold like Chomsky's or the behaviorist's ideology can and has put – specifically- brain science on to a narrow track of understanding. The Chomsky model of linguistic thinking (admittedly poorly represented by me) had-for sometime-dominated all other ways of thinking about the brain through its insistence on the relevance of viewing the mind through a linguistic model. Inherent in this model is a search for one-to-one correlation in the way that the left brain seeks to understand everything. The behaviorists also completely shut down any attempt at understanding feelings or emotions, or any discussion about the intentions behind consciousness, by insisting that emotions could not be quantified and that the study of emotions was therefore, unscientific. It was only relevant to study phenomena. This approach reflects a myopic analytic materialism, which seeks to eliminate human value out of the world.

I personally like Chomsky (as if that matters), but it seems that he is unwilling to relinquish his position that language reflects an underlying architecture of the brain against a literal landslide of dissention amongst neuroscientists. The brain must be understood as a vast ensemble of integrated systems within the human body that is set in the world. To really catch the flavor of how something like language could occur, you must seek to gain an understanding of communication set within the context of the whole of the world. You cannot view a small element of the workings of the mind like language construction and explode your understanding back up into general rules, etc. This is again the downside of analytic mental representation in that the model seeks to gain power over the thing that it represents. This is the comfort of land naming. Ginger Campbell credits Chomsky with holding back brain science for some 30 years. In such manner shall we dream the truth?

Dear reader you should also be wary of all of my Axe grinding in this. I have also constructed my narrative to reflect my agenda which is to expose the power drive behind the ego, really I am seeking to redress the balance in that I am constantly reminded how spectacular this drive in analysis really is.

I would like to explode this dichotomy again in to the argument of Nature versus Nurture because this is the real nut of the above mentioned argument. What I have come to understand is that the dichotomy of nature verses nurture is completely artificial and largely a result of our intellectual speculation. Nature has supplied us with a 'genetic' and/or evolutionary propensity toward certain ways of pattern expression-like the ability to learn language-but the actual process that occurs as we grow and learn are epigenetic in form, or they increases in complexity in an exponential way due to the ongoing influence of the environment as a result of real feedback both internal (nature) and external (nurture). When we trace things back toward the initial seed (reductionism) and try to convince ourselves that we have caught the essence of the phenomena we are setting ourselves up for mistakes due to our desire to hold/grasp/have power over a concept. The ongoing genetic expression of an individual is itself a feedback system and the process is constantly monitoring, assessing and influencing the environment and adjusting itself through the release of chemicals like hormones, etc. These integrated systems then trigger further adaptation into reality as it actually is not how we see it or how it should be. The whole of any phenomena cannot be seen 'out of context' nor can it be properly studied within context.

This was part of the discussion about biology earlier and elements of Rupert Sheldrake in particular. What I think he was trying to find out was how nature communicated aspects of the ongoing unfolding of form, and how much was hard written propensity. I now see that to think that things are genetically hardwired or that to construct a type of point-to-point growth, triggering ideology within an unfolding biological system is far too simplistic. My very brief discussion about Robert Wright and Darwinism was trying to show another related view of this same thing, in that, human evolution and sociological patterns are always based on a flexible strategy. But they also start with relatively unconscious elemental and long tested strategies that are supplied to us, or implied into context by nature. These initial strategies or starting points aren't necessarily passed on through the genes. Small children figure this stuff out unconsciously and very easily from a combination of social cuing (shame, etc.) and their own smart little brains but there are unconscious 'emotional' systems that reflect our more ancient biological underpinnings. Shame is an excellent teacher despite what anyone says. Not everyone should get a medal for simply showing up.

We don't need to explicitly or consciously understand that we should interact with other people in a tit for tat format; everything about our social environment is constantly reinforcing and double coding this and other modes of interaction. Learning goes on through a myriad of overt and subtle social cuing; along with the emotional reinforcement of that cuing, all of the time. Understanding literally becomes second nature or really it is just nature.

We see once again that Mother Nature has supplied us with an array of tools that allow the brain to absorb language or anything we need to learn. However there is also inherent structures (areas of the brain that encompass ways of functioning similarly to the brain's limbic system is the best example) or propensities toward structures within us that-as they manifest in the growth process- can assume flexible, culturally specific usages. These areas can also reorganize themselves completely and take on different usages, if the need arises. We will see later how this ability of the brain to rewire occurs in people who are blind from birth. This really is the nail in the coffin for the idea of a dedicated discrete and inherent section of the brain that is ready to receive language. Parts of linguistic representation (special mapping, etc.) are in more or less specific parts of the brain, but the brain isn't simply a collection of parts. Language is possibly a further refined and highly symbolic extension of music-as I will beat to death later-which happens simultaneously through our highly integrated brain.

Just to confuse the genetic plot a little more, I was re-listening to a *Brain Science* podcast on synapse evolution with Dr. Seth Grant (bps#51). He was saying that the next research he was going to do was on this very idea of how an idea or specific instincts can be passed on generationally. It sounds as though this type of specific information like instincts (inborn fear of snakes) or various evolutionary strategies, or even archetypal ideas can be passed on through a genetic expression, but the mechanics of it has more to do with how these genes express themselves around the synapses in the brain. I'm sorry that I am vague about this and I now suspect this fellow is chasing a bogey. What I wish to say is that like the Vatican, I have a man on this problem, so the answer is pending.

It is a certainty that some forms of information are being gifted to us at birth - fear of snakes is a fairly obvious example. What is emerging from the ongoing study of the brain is that we are the sum of our evolution, and the way that our brain functions, is the result of the selection of evolutionary strategies that have kept our ancestors alive. If you jump with fright when you hear something rustling in the grass and it turns out to be the wind, you will still be alive to laugh about it later (as the tension ebbs off). If it turns out to be a snake and you don't react, you will not live to pass on your passivity to another generation. Over time, all of our senses have become attuned to react to situations that have kept us alive.

I will return to the linguistic model for just a bit more, because it is a good place to start to understand some of the basic building blocks of the brain. Mr. Pinker in *How the Mind Works* explains that there seem to be four ways in which the mind represents ideas. The first seems to be a type of geometry template. If people are asked to press a button every time they see the same letter, for example A, they will consistently press it faster if they are looking for and then see an A (left brain template matching), as opposed to lower case a. When they see small case 'a' they are forced to recognize the letter as an equivalent, though not identical representation in a geometric sense. A quick visual template matching is no longer possible, so their reaction time slows down as this translation process takes place. We also slow down our reaction time when we are asked to press a button. If we see blue, but are presented with the word BLUE written in pink letters, we need to re-contextualize the question from the color to the written symbol.

The brain builds up the ensemble of our world viewing by sectioning off vertical, horizontal and curved line recognition into separate, though highly interconnected parts of the brain. It disassembles reality and then reassembles the overall scene we are witnessing from a feedback and feed-forward combination of this sectioning process. Chinese ideograms for instance, must all be read with a more explicit template-matching, and the way Chinese is comprehended in the mind, is completely different than the way that we process our western alphabet. As mentioned earlier, Chinese ideograms represent ensembles of ideas. They do not build a sentence piece meal. We build meaning through an assessment of fairly explicit (totally one-to-one in Greek) letter sound correlation. Also, blind people who have learned to echo locate construct geometric representations of the world (tree here; walkway there, etc.), using the same geometric representational regions that sighted people do, using clicks like bats to orient them.

Some of the visual assumptions that go on in the brain can be exposed through the use of visual tricks like a three-dimensional line drawing of a cube shape on a two-dimensional paper surface. The eyes and the brain are unsure how to interpret what exactly is the edge of the implied shape of this image and what the exact orientation of this object might be in space; so the mind flips this image back and forth trying to decipher the correct orientation of the object, or specifically which corner of the cube drawing is nearest to us. Another trick is the image of two faces in white looking at each other with a black vase in between. Again, the brain flips between the two images alternately. I think it was assumed that these types of drawing unmasked some ambiguous elements in our perception of the world in that we could so easily be drawn into the ambiguity of the renderings. To my mind this shows how well adapted our mind is to the real world. Illusions like this very rarely occur in nature and humans actually maneuver through our environment exceptionally well. We have no evolutionary need to pierce through these types of two-dimensional tricks and the brain is rightly miffed.

The second form of representation is a phonological representation, where we form sounds, using our mouth and imagine what the syllables sound like. This string-like representation is an important component in short-term memory retrieval. For example, saying a phone number long enough to yourself so that you can dial it, or repeating someone's name three times to remember it. We will see later that Bonobo monkeys also mouth words when reading and this belies the similarity between speaking and acting, or doing. Speaking is not as abstract as we might believe. It is very much embedded in us and the world. The letters in the Korean printed text represent what your tongue should be doing as you make the sound of the printed letter you are reading. This represents a stunning understanding of the embodied nature of speech. This written language was developed around the 16th century as a result of Korean frustration with the phenomenal amount of Chinese characters.

The third format is grammatical representation, where nouns, verbs, phrases and clauses, etc. are arranged into hierarchical trees like the example of the young girl we used earlier. We build up sentences with very complicated structures that we are in no way conscious of. This is the area where Chomsky spent a lot of time. He broke speaking and language down into their basic constituents, and recognized that these structures are so complex that he postulated an inherent language segment in the brain whereby its main purpose was to scaffold a type of linguistic architecture. We don't learn how to speak from just listening abstractly to what other people are saying to us. We are learning to express our embedded wants, needs and desires. We are constantly being reinforced in our expressed linguistic presumptions, because we are always observing the reactions of other people like our caregivers. We will come back to this.

The fourth format is-to my mind-the most interesting and it is known as Mentalese. This is the way that the brain understands conceptual knowledge. If you read a book, you don't need to tell someone the entire information to give them an understanding of what you read. You can summarize or provide 'the gist' of the work. Apparently, people confidently 'recognize' sentences that capture the meaning of something they have read even though these sentences are a paraphrase of what is really said. This is one of the problems involved in having a witness give a testimony many months after an event. What the witness remembers is really the overall feel and emotional impact of the situation. The details quickly get swallowed, as we construct a narrative.

These regurgitated impressions allow many subsequent presumptions or even alternate narrative compressions to influence and enter into the memory itself. These 'embellishments' may be reinforced by the witness reading about the case in the news or further elaborate on the narrative, as they construct the story to tell it to other people. There may have originally been four attackers and only one of them had a gun, but the witness remembers quite clearly being surrounded by five people and four of them had guns. Unless a witness is reminded of the facts constantly, a fish can grow to the size that would feed any amount of people, because we all love a good story. The brain extracts or re-composes the meaning of the world by using and manipulating what is relevant. A lie repeated takes on the shades of truth. Memory is yet another reflected layer of this extraction of what is relevant. As we later compose an event into a narrative, we unconsciously jostle details so that we can tell others about the experience. Explicit memory retrieval through the written word is a fairly new invention. All of our memories gain momentum from our subsequent emotional engagement with them. We don't relate boring stories.

Mentalese allows us to imagine what is described to us and carry out further instructions. It is the traffic of information among mental modules.

"This traffic can actually be seen in the anatomy of the brain. The hippocampus and connected structures, which put our memories into long-term storage, and the frontal lobes, which house the circuitry for decision making are not directly connected to the brain areas that

process raw sensory input (the mosaic of edges and colors and the ribbon of changing pitches). Instead, most of their input fibers carry what neuroscientists call, 'highly processed' input coming from regions one or more stops downstream from the first sensory areas. The input consists of codes for objects, words, and other complex concepts." (*How the Mind Works* –Pg. 90) The brain develops more refined and explicit connections between the various centers of the brain through the repeated firing of related neurons as we continue to build up our experience the world. Mentalese is the inherently abstract and largely unconscious symbolic mental activity. Language is our explicit translation or re-presentation of that raw flow into a medium. Music and visual arts are other less 'highly' abstracted forms of the translation of emotions.

    I have come to realize recently that this whole concept of mentalese is a bit of a bogey. I am currently reading Terrence Deacon's *Incomplete Nature* and he comments on this very concept of mentalese as described by Pinker. Mr. Deacon's contention is that to propose another abstract or hyper subjective and introspective layer behind language is to introduce a homunculus, which is another way of saying that you have only displaced the fact that you don't understand the phenomenon one level farther away from what you are observing, and that you really haven't explained anything. There is no proof that there is another more subjective layer behind language. The concept of mentalese clouds the issue by introducing what is called a grounding error or another layer, if introspection means something. (This turtle has the world on its back, but must be supported by another turtle, etc.) I would add that the route forward is to recognize that language is largely embodied and that concepts like mentalese are tools that we can use to represent our understanding in the same way that computer analogies are rife in neuroscience. Jaak Panksepp points out that scientists love to talk about the same thing, but only with their own terminology so that they infinitely cloud issues. Grounding error, homunculus, and turtles all the way down, are the same thing.

    "Its turtles all the way down."

Our ability to grasp a cup of coffee off of a table reflects a suite of very complex motor actions that do not have to go directly to some form of uber-comptroller to be checked out. Many brain functions can be dealt with at their own substation or through the already built up and existing interconnections that exist across many well oiled sub systems (read *Unconscious Old Brain*). Only the relevant or interesting bits of the experience get shuffled up stairs into the various spectrums of consciousness. Things like: *"did I put sugar in there or is the coffee still too hot to drink?"* These are some of the aspects of a situation that may need to be explicitly registered or just semi-consciously assessed. Even then, most things are only just barely paid attention to. We don't remember the temperature of our coffee later on in the day and we don't need to, so our mind enacts a number of presumptions about the raw world that the senses receive. Our consciousness is the result of a highly processed series of observations and assumptions about how the flow probably is, but more importantly, the brain infuses or extracts from the world its ongoing context and allows us to turn it into a symbol.

In my dream about crawling on black ice (the details are fuzzy), the overall feel/emotional impact and subsequent message that was extracted by me, are easily remembered and tied back to the image, because of the importance of the image itself and the overall context that I subsequently invested back into this image. I went through my journals and looked up dreams from 20 years ago and it is amazing how completely different the details are from my remembrance. The mind deals with the world in a more extracted symbolic manner, which as we will discuss shortly, is an extension of the double coding process that goes on between the abstracted information gathered by our senses, and our emotional/feeling relation.

The reason that the brain ultimately has no overly centralized uber-comptroller is the same reason that governments shouldn't. It is ultimately an inefficient use of very limited space and energy, which is inside of your head. I will use an analogy to illustrate: there was a massive famine in central Russia (Kazakhstan) in the fifties and part of the problem was that the communist government wanted to initiate the great leap forward, so they shipped off all kinds of 'state of the art' farm equipment to Kazakhstan. But they didn't send along anybody who knew how to repair it, if the equipment broke. Within five or eight years, all of it was rusting in the fields. The weather got very bad in the fifties and farmers could not go back to their old habits of manually planting, because the government forced them into industrialized farming with these heavy machines. This is what happens when directives are issued from an over-controlling central authority. China had many of these same problems and equally disastrous results in the fifties and sixties as well. Local problems need local solutions. The current economic crisis needs federal and global cooperation and a little wrathful retribution directed to Wall Street. (A fish rots from its head.)

The balance between global intervention and developing local solutions has been one of the great lessons learned in making foreign aid packages effective. It seems that natural systems are seeking balance between decentralization and hierarchical structures. Nature doesn't design systems abstractly and she never sticks manically to only hierarchal structures. Nature seems to practice redundancy and she always leaves room for flexibility. In the brain, there are plenty of ways for information to skip up the hierarchal queue or jump across many subsystems if necessary. For vital things like the fear response, shortcuts are built in to override everything and initiate a cascade of well-tested responses; this is both good and bad. This override is done through various trigger weighting of specific neurons. If a message coming from the limbic system is important, the axons travelling from this part of the brain have the capability of overriding everything else, because they can deliver messages with much more overall weight than say... a slight tickle on my back. There are many different types of connections in the brain and the 'emotionally driven' amygdale has an extensive override capability.

Enbrained

The brain is seen to be divided into a lot of specialized, though highly integrated areas, that takes care of some pretty specific tasks. These sub-sections are highly integrated with each other in both feedback and feed forward ways. For instance, the grey matter on the outside of the brain is really a folded sheet that is spread out across the entire brain. The thought is that different sections of the grey matter perform different tasks; for example, running along the centre ridge of both hemispheres is tactile body mapping. Underneath this grey matter is a large white mass that is thought to be all of the integrating connections that flow across and along the brain in all directions - although this part of the brain is very poorly understood. These are the brain's long axons and galila cells. At the end of each axon is a synaptic electro-chemical connection. This whole system is called a neuron and we have billions of them in our head. Each neuron is connected to some 10 thousand other neurons, which gives the mind a level of complexity that is way more intricate than a billion computers.

The right brain tends to have longer axons integrating the back and front of the brain, which possibly reflects the right brain's propensity to long term episodic and biographical memory. The left brain has a tendency toward shorter axons and is more involved in our procedural memory, which allows us the ability to focus on details and exclude irrelevant distractions.

When we look around at our environment, we are actually viewing two sets of two- dimensional images, one for each eye. These images are slightly offset from each other, because of the spread of our eyes. This small difference in perspective helps us to interpret relative depth and distance. All of the input from our eyes is constantly giggling while we walk, but we never 'see' it this way. Nor do we ever think that the world is two dimensional unless we suffer a massive right brain stroke.

If you close one of your eyes and look at a coin from the edge, but slightly offset, your mind doesn't see an ellipse. It understands and interprets that the coin is a round circle on its edge. Also, if you look at a rectangular table top from the corner of a room, you don't see a trapezoid, which is actually what you are looking at. You interpret the rectangular table top as it is, because your brain always assesses these objects as though they were in three dimensions. Surprisingly, we live in a three dimensional world-or maybe a 19 dimensional world. Anyway, as far as your brain is concerned, we live in a three-dimensional world and this assumption of it being so is valid, or consensually correct. You can also learn to assess relative distance quite accurately with only one eye, by learning how to gauge the relative movements between objects in the foreground and background. I don't know for sure, but I doubt you would have to explicitly learn this. Depending on the age that you lost an eye, you would simply develop a feel for distance in this way by being in the world.

It seems that different parts of the brain are used to determine all of the different and discreet aspects of the environment. The right eye is wired-for the most part-to the left hemisphere of the brain, but also to some extent, it is cross-wired to the right, and the same is true in reverse for the left eye. We are further reinforcing and gaining insight into our three-dimensional assumptions about the world when we bump into things as a youngster. This real feedback teaches us quickly about depth of field through our associations with pain (this is another example of emotional double coding). There is no time in our mental development where any kind of explicit mathematical calculation is going on between the focus and spread of our eyes, and the distance to a coffee cup. We learn about depth of field by our developing feel for our own body in space and through being in the world, which kindly offers us a continual feedback through trial and error.

As mentioned earlier, some parts of the brain handle geometric composition like letters while other specific areas register motions just outside of the narrow focus of the eye. All of these areas are collecting information and the brain is building a view of the world for us. Our brain is constantly making assumptions about how the world will unfold before us - a micro second in advance. The brain will assume that the tree on our right is not going to run away and so it puts it in the relevant area without our having to re-confirm and update its position. We can then concentrate on other things like a sudden movement. If the tree did run away, we would notice and even small babies will instinctively understand when the rules of gravity were violated.

It seems that nature has developed and chosen for us all of these abilities over evolutionary time, and she has equipped us with various tools that have proven most appropriate for the world we live in. As this human toolkit became more and more specialized, other things proved to be less important to us, like the ability to smell with the acuity of a dog. What we improved upon is our ability to remember an ongoing narrative, a biographical sense and the ability to reason or think, especially in the abstract and symbolically. This evolutionary adaptation seems to have been the result-in part-by our ability to be able to emotionally engage with others; to double code our experience, which has moved lockstep with our ability to form symbolic representation, possibly as a result of our fascination with storytelling and musical narrative. Terrence Deacon builds an excellent case for our symbolic ability as our single greatest achievement. Along with this, is our ability to read and anticipate, or empathize with other people's emotional and physical intentions, because we are able to form a conception of another's intentions by relating them to past actions.

We wouldn't learn to speak, if there was no reason to do it. Learning to speak allows us to ask for the food we want to eat. Children, who receive constant attention and care, sometimes don't bother to use their speech until 'late' in their development. The same is true for walking. Given this type of positive feedback, we then learn to articulate our needs using sets of much finer skills very quickly. Most important to us in our development, is the idea that when our mother/caregiver is feeding us we also get more or less uninterrupted face time. Very young children are much more right brain oriented, which is where our integrated ability to map faces is located. We cannot help, but revel in the attention and emotional feedback that occurs as we watch this other face to relate more and more. No wonder food is comfort. Children can also recognize their mother's voice from inside the womb.

So the way that we learn-even before we gain the ability to speak-is by watching things being done and also by doing things ourselves. The outcome of these actions gain reinforcement in our mind through double coding or associated directly with our feelings/value relation/emotions. The strength of many individual memories is probably a reflection of the initial and then repeated emotional intensity of viewing the particular event. This symbolic coding process also helps us to remove ourselves from the objects that we interact with or allows us to create an abstracted symbolic representation of both ourselves and other objects we encounter in the world. We thereby integrate and gain an understanding of the world in a symbolic and multi-leveled way. This is the left brain's abstraction and creation of a 'necessary distance'.

Speaking and language is way of expressing and adding another symbolic layer over top of our embedded or symbolically double coded reality. To call thinking an abstraction is mildly misleading. Thinking is highly symbolic or metaphorically double coded right from the get go, but this symbolism is embedded in us and is an extension of our being in the real world; it is not simply an abstraction. For us to speak of the world as being symbolically double coded is for us to analyze the process itself. We are *not the analysis* of the process. We are the process. This is another way of understanding that the inherent tendency of the mind is to create and/or impose meaning. We don't learn anything unless it carries a meaning for us, or we don't learn about things that hold no interest for us. The brain's main job is to suss out what is relevant - meaningful.

Terrence Deacon develops the argument in *The Symbolic Species* that symbolic thinking is a unique human ability, driven by our socialization. Symbolic thinking allows us to displace ourselves into another person's situation, because we need to be able to predict their behavior and this ability is driven by our single mate stratagem. We need to be fairly certain that our mate is being monogamous, so we created symbolic rituals to declare our intent, and this specific relationship we built, is both the result of past actions and being projected into the future. In fact, all of our relationships partake of this symbolic upgrading. People are never inert and to be looked at abstractly. What we think of them affects the way they are to us and the way we are to them. The actual act of partaking in a ritual helps to establish the symbolic relationship in the world. Puberty rituals allow youths to transition into adulthood by acknowledging this transition for both the youth and the wider society. Symbols are both the action you portray and the action itself embedded in the environment - you are both the dancer and the performance.

I was listening to my lovely CBC radio again and on the show *Quirks and Quarks* they had an interview with a neuroscientist/psychologist from here in Toronto called Dr. Adam Anderson. The segment was called '*This is your Brain on Rose Colored Glasses*'. What Anderson has done is wire people up to MRI or some such brain reading machine and showed them mildly depressing pictures or somewhat happy pictures (puppy dogs, etc.) He then tried to see how the brain processes information when it is happy or sad. Well guess what? It seems that your brain functions in a much more expansive and accepting way when you are happy. When people are prepped with happy thoughts, they notice more of the background details of the pictures they are looking at; in this specific case, a house behind the primary human figure in the picture. (Incidentally, it seems that Chinese people already notice more background than westerners. Where is the Tao/source of the big bang again? Oh yea... everywhere!

In another instance, when people were asked to look at and discuss the expression on a person's face in a picture, but they were first prepped to be mildly depressed by looking at mildly depressing pictures, They only registered the face in the picture and did not register the finer details of the face or background information of what they were looking at. I will speculate wildly here and say that this may be a result of the left brain's proclivity toward detailed attention and this depressive prepping is activating the left more than right or deactivating the right, etc – though the right does seem to be more involved in melancholy states. Mr. Anderson went on to say that the brain seems to be actually more creative or bi-associative when you are happy. In other words, if you were in love with someone, or yourself for that matter, you would be more willing to accept the world, or at the very least you would be more inclined to take in a larger swath of the immediate context of the world. (Read *The Right Brain*) If you witness two people kissing in a park, and you are also in love, you will enjoy seeing that kiss. If you are in a punk band and all pissed off about the future, you will tell them to get a room (but not offer up, even 20 bucks so that they actually could). So here we have a neuroscientist trying to construct a scientific proof that indicates that being happy is better and perhaps more fulfilling to experience the world. To my mind, this is a self-evident truth that the world's religions, especially Buddhism have been hammering home for years. However, I was greatly encouraged to listen to someone who was putting this realization on to a mildly scientific footing. I think only eggheads would need a scientific proof of this. Now you know why meeting new people can be so easy when you are on vacation: everyone is happy on vacation, or hopefully ready to be more open unless they are drunk and wasted.

Now here's what I see, and this fellow did imply it in his discussion: the essence of the creative mind is a reflection of a more positive outlook, or at least the ability to accept and embrace the world is greater when you are happy - not Pollyanna happy, but happy in the sense of being truly engaged and alive. There have been plenty of cynical and depressed writers/artists, but the interesting thing is that all of them worked on their art, or we wouldn't know about them at all. I would lay money on the fact that if you asked any one of them why they did the work they did, they would tell you that-on some level-they enjoyed it. In some way, their art work gives their life meaning, or they would have committed suicide and left us no record. What's the value of art?

For me, it was interesting to realize that the brain is wired to be more creative and accepting when you are happy, and of course, this makes perfect sense. It's hard to be depressed when you are having sex, and sex is good for evolution. This of course, relates to all aspects of further learning. Who could strive to continually generate an interest and be receptive to learning when they are in a classroom where the teacher is an ass and you simply don't want to be there? All thinking and learning is in its essence a creative act (though more or less unconsciously), and if you are engaged and happy, you brain is more willing to accept information. This acceptance allows learning to occur in a more integrated and emotionally impactful way. If a song brings you to tears the first time you hear it, I think that you would remember this. Multiplication tables are hard to learn, because they must be downloaded into memory only. They do not allow much in the way of fun participation. Multiplication tables can be learned much easier, if they are sung into the brain with a melody. If you are engaged in learning, it's not work at all. It is art.

Yoga is the art of creating sustained ecstasy.

Stop Making Sense

One of the features of the inner workings of the mind that really hit me was a phenomenon called 'blind sight'. This will help us to illuminate the huge role unconscious plays in the unfolding of our perception. Blind sight is a phenomenon that has been well documented and occurs in our brain like this: one of the subjects who were being studied assures the investigator that he cannot see a glass on the table in front of him. The subject's sight has been partially eliminated by some type of neural problem within the sets of optic nerves (for a full description and explanation of the neurology of this see V.S. Ramachandran), and as far as we can tell, he is describing the situation as he perceives it in front of him - or the reality as he perceives it. There is actually a glass placed in front of him. The doctor in the room tells the blind man to pick up the glass and he assures the doctor that he cannot, and yet when pressed by the doctor to move his hand forward, he goes on to pick it up flawlessly. He correctly estimates the distance, relative weight and shape of the glass, etc.

What is happening is that on the explicit self-representational conscious level, the man cannot actually see the glass in the centre of his visual field, but there is a part of the visual information bundle that he is not registering consciously and this unconscious part of his sight can coordinate the hands to reach forward and grab the glass flawlessly. Jung also talked about a colleague of his who was treating a woman who professed that she could not hear anything. She began singing a song to herself one day, and the clever doctor slipped on to a piano in the room and started to accompany this woman. The doctor did something particularly clever and changed the key of the song and she changed key along with his playing. We see that she could hear, but also couldn't hear. This is probably not an actual physiological problem like blind sight.

What is beginning to be understood is that there are not just five distinct senses. In fact, there are many more subdivisions of each sense and the brain organize them, like the different sensory input…say from the eyes, into a seamless coherent whole. There is thought to be 32 different sections of the brain that are integrating various aspects of sight alone. The creation of a cohesive and seamless world is a large part of the brain's main job. The brain has evolved to separate various types of information and direct it into the relevant and somewhat discrete, but also highly integrated segments of the brain. These different visual 'senses' are all put together within the visual cortex in the back of the brain and then combined with other relevant information before being shuffled upstairs, if need be, and into our consciousness.

The brain is constantly seeking to verify and interpret the incoming world through feedback, which is happening before we gain conscious access to anything like a 'complete' visual world. Some of the subtle unconscious verifications involve assessing other people's subtle body gestures so that we can infer the emotional gist of what is being said. As mentioned earlier, we are aware of the disconnection between what the body says and what the mouth is saying. By being able to register unconsciously the more delicate inflections in someone's tone of voice or the subtle cues that flit across someone's face, we get the impression (or intuition) that someone is lying to us or being sarcastic, or in love, etc. It seems that our vision has evolved to be most sensitive in the exact color range that is reflected back to us from human skin tones. This focused color acuity allows us to be able to perceive many of the subtle inflections in people's emotional states, as they are expressed through the changes in blood flow across their skin color. We are also very aware-although unconsciously-of the dilation of the pupils, which indicates engagement. (The pupils are regularly dilated on women-with an air brush-in photographs in print advertising. This indicates that the woman is engaged in looking at you.) The human brain is deftly wired to be aware of and interpret-largely unconsciously-all of these multiple double coded realities of human expression.

Children don't pick up on sarcasm or irony until they are about 10 years old, because it doesn't make sense that someone would intentionally misrepresent their words in a given situation. This subtle disconnect-that children can't grasp between the words and actions occurring in sarcasm-just doesn't make sense. Children are always on the lookout for explicit meaning. With some training, many of these subtle cues, like changes in skin tone or the micro movements in the eyebrows that we constantly unconsciously observe, becomes registered as explicit conscious information. It seems that women are much better at picking up on this type of subtle facial recognition than men are. They are much more concerned with the minutia of dress and style and the body in general than are men. Women need to be able to understand the various expressions going on in a baby's face and they seem to be oriented by nature to be much better at observing these empathetic subtleties than men. (Feeling... feeling right brain feeling)

Another excellent example of the intricate web of unconsciousness within the mind is playing sports or music, or anything that actually occurs in real time and not in the abstract self-reflective universe. When playing basketball, the brain is thought to be making thousands of special calculations, so that it can anticipate where the ball is going. Some people feel that there is a hyper-engagement occurring. The brain is not making specific mathematical calculations, because it takes far too long and the brain doesn't do math in nature. The brain is constantly assessing and distributing information instantaneously. It does this by integrating all of the sensory inputs such as balance, depth of field the shape, and weight of objects etc., so that we don't have to think about these things. (I think this is a large component of what Zen teachers are driving at.)

We don't need to calculate a ball's trajectory, because we are very adept at observing objects, as they move though space. We can then function on the assumption that a basketball will always react in the same way, because it and the court and the earth's gravity are standardized and well-known by feel. This anticipation of the uniformity of motion is so accurate that many of the players in the 2010 FIFA World Cup soccer match in South Africa complained about the new soccer balls reactions in the air, when kicked long.

When someone is playing basketball, their body mandala-their sense of their own body and an awareness of the external space that surrounds them (primarily right brain)-is extending out over the whole basketball court. I would say that when playing music or any sport, there is really very little time for thinking and many integrated moves can be accomplished by enacting suites of muscle movements, which are unconsciously fine- tuned as they flow out into the world through us. We make assumptions about where the ball will be in an arc of movement, based on previous imprinting that has been built up from playing basketball in the real world. Basketball *playing* is embedded in basketball *playing*. If you are not here, where are you? When *playing* music you become so immersed in the flow of the narrative that you don't need to think about what the next note will be. You can then be the piece that you *play*; much like a great actor is the character that they are *playing*. The guitar players in my band don't remember the chord progressions after they learn their part, because it is irrelevant.

Most of the aspects of spatial orientation involved in estimating distance or the sense of our personal body mapping, etc. are dealt with in a section of the brain just above the ears and along the top of the central ridge. Like our sight, each specific aspect of the environment, and each segment of our body are dealt with somewhat separately, but all of the spatial and 'geometric' information are flowing into the same general area above our ears. There is even a specific part of the brain that tells us that *we* are located in our bodies (the right angular gyrus). If this area gets shut off with an electrode, we literally feel as though we popped out of our bodies and we can-in an instant-pop back in when the stimulation from the electrode is shut off. This specific area of the brain is prone to overload, because it is near one of our major arteries and it can shut down in a life and death situation like a major stroke.

This is a literal biological explanation of why you may feel that you are out of your body when you have a near death experience. It doesn't explain where you may go, but there are some related and specific areas in the brain that create various perspectives that you may be looking at while you are 'out of your body'. It seems that most people see the room from a vantage point that is similar to their own projected body mandala and not from an uncommon vantage point, like from the floor looking up. We are rarely in that perspective in the real world. You might also feel that you are behind yourself or three feet above yourself. One of the most common seems to be about six to 10 feet above. Jung had a near death experience and he believed that he had floated up two miles above the earth and he was forced back into his body by someone who told him that he had more work to do. This is quite common and many people believed they were astral travelling great distances during these experiences. It seems that some people learn to project their consciousness or they consciously will themselves to be other places separate from their bodies. All of these experiences have more of the feeling of a dream, and of course, astral travelers cannot actively interact with other people while they are 'out of body'. Apparently, when astral travelling, we do not traverse the distance in between where we go to and where we came from. We simply appear where we wish to be. This is projection in all of its ambiguity, but we must remember that these are psychological facts.

We can explain the physical aspect of this type of experience, but we have not captured the experience itself. Like the discussion on auras earlier; there is a traceable physical reason why we feel when we are *in* or *out* of our bodies, or that there is a physiological reason why some people see colors projected around other people. We have not captured and explained away these phenomena. We cannot strictly say, well this out of body experience is an illusion, created by your right angular gyrus. You should best forget it. It's kind of like saying death is an illusion created by our right angular gyrus.

Although-in large part-that is exactly what it is going on. But I would counter that you could also infuse this type of occurrence with a symbolic meaning. If we presume a strict physical/literal and causal reductionism, this really just moves the question about what is really going on around the page, and it only answers some elements of the question. It only answers the parts that science wants to answer. In other words, we reduce the phenomena into something we can evaluate so that we can measure it. Always treat the patient not the disease.

I will give another quick example: it is now known that people who have mild cases of a form of epilepsy called 'temporal lobe epilepsy' are prone to religious writings and hearing voices inside their head. It is speculated that some religious visionaries like Joan of Arc, in particular, may have suffered from this specific form of epilepsy. Let's presume for one moment that all of the religious writing that has ever occurred in world history is 'simply' a result of a number of cases of temporal lobe epilepsy. By giving this scientific explanation, I'm not sure that we have actually said anything. Joan of Arc still went to the cross/pier, because she believed that the Lord spoke to *her*. It also would be very difficult to convince either me or a devout Muslim that the entire Koran is meaningless, because Muhammad had visions as a result of a fit of temporal lobe epilepsy. This diagnosis says nothing to us about the meaningful relevance of the content from the voices they heard, or the significance of what they went on to do in the world as a result of hearing the voices. Like the content of our dreams, meaning extends in both directions. I would be very careful to listen to the unconscious in whatever form is chooses to talk.

Jung's experience of floating above the world is an excellent reason not to stop at this patronizing intellectual 'nothing but' point of inquiry. (He actually believed –largely as a result of this experience-that he had been charged with trying to explain his work to a more general readership, and so he made an effort to write many of his main ideas into a more digestible form. (Read *Man's Search for Meaning*) There is or can be a symbolic aspect to his experience that we should also be aware of, which is scientifically quite un-provable and only realistic or indeed relevant as an unfolding commitment over time. If we wished to really fill out the symbolic aspect of an experience, we could make an effort to understand why someone like Jung felt that he was told to return to earth or why he had more work to do, and what it might be. This is the reassertion of context or value in the worldview.

Incidentally, there is a hospital in England that leaves a newspaper high up in the hospital room so that if someone has an out of body experience, they would be able to correctly identify the newspaper's headline that they see when floating around in the room; then we will have a proof. I personally doubt that they will get a proof this way. It seems that most out of body experiences do not put the viewer at a height of more than seven or eight feet. And they don't seem to be able to see through walls or witness the event in the next room, etc. The ability to astral travel is very similar to the ability to 'wake up' from within a dream and 'consciously' direct it. This ability is known as lucid dreaming.

With these so called scientific explanations, we are in the same situation as the fundamentalist Christian/Jew or Muslim, which is in part that they have a desire to reduce the world into a simple and clear-cut intellectual framework that can be more easily believed in (witness the current 'Tea Party' type anti-intellectual movement). They can hold up this simple representation as an absolute unclouded fact and or tool (where love is lacking, power will fill the vacuum), but the reality is that these reductions are always somewhat parceled and abstracted. Anti-intellectualism is an intellectual power drive, which strives to narrow everything down into a sound bite joke. This is like trying to deeply understand whirlpools without looking at the water in the rivers of which they are a part.

Many scientists are unforgiving atheists and they are doing science no great service in the public eye by antagonistically foisting this agenda. People who hate religion and or radical atheist/ scientists have decided to stop thinking very deeply about religion, which of course, is their prerogative. My counter would be that religion has deep psychological roots that have very little to do with rational inquiry and feeling, and thinking. Science and religion are not sitting at the same table. This is the tyranny of the rational brain as it seeks to impose strict causality with no room for meaning, and ultimately, it is trying to assert certainty into a world of confusion

I am going to beat up on Lawrence Krauss for a bit here in order to make a much larger point. Mr. Krauss and Richard Dawkins have seen fit to throw down the atheist gauntlet and I would like to pick it up. They have both approached the question of whether God exists from the rational logical/left brain/measuring/reducing side of things. John Lennon said God is a concept by which we measure our pain. This is how the left brain represents the world. It jams things into conceptual boxes and assures us that it has captured the thing in itself for all time. John Lennon is dead wrong on this one. God is not a concept at all. God is the experience of the symbol of God. The *concept* is the realization of a failure to embrace the limits of our minds. We are quite frankly being stupid.

How exactly do you measure anything? Laurence Krauss assures us that no one in the religious community can mount an adequate response to his arrogant tirade. Everybody in the audience laughs and they all pat themselves on the back for being so smart. What he has done is create a table (his intellect) on which he pulls God apart (a reverse Frankenstein), and then he requests that we use the same instruments of dissection to try and reassemble the corpse. I deny both the corpse and the table as being valid. How can you possibly disassemble an ongoing experience? The very act of analyzing it *kills it* then you pat yourself on the back for creating a corpse and challenge people to bring it back to life. Mary Shelly nailed it with Frankenstein. I firmly believe this is the same mistake Marshall McLuhan made when he said the medium is the message. He asserted that the message was embedded in the medium of its expression, but I would counter that the message only comes to life, if we are there to blow meaning into it. Unless we too are considered a part of the medium in which case he is correct. This one-to-one view seeks to deny that there is a symbolic and metaphoric way of understanding and yet this is the way that the world is constantly understood.

On the surface they are profound
But deep down they are really shallow – Oxford's quip about atheists

I would add that all of these statements can be reversed in the sense of a profound truth that is its opposite. Frantically religious people are not looking very deeply into science either. To hate something takes psychic energy and a certain amount of naïveté must be reinforced to keep you retaining your simplistic view of that which you spend time hating. And of course the same thing can be said about maintaining a religious attitude against the (black mud of the occult) land slide of scientific materialism. The refusal to inspect the concept of God or religious beliefs is also a reflex of left brain arrogance (its most powerful tool is comparison with that which it already knows) and this is why I think that the whole field is way too overheated.

People who have developed a particular sensitivity to other people's emotional states can be considered an expert, except they are more like musicians than scientists. They have developed a very rich feeling relationship that is hard for us to understand or represent in a logically constructed way. You literally have to feel it as well to really understand. The difference between a great carpenter and a college graduate is experience or the full battery of process. Blue is considered to be a particularly spiritual color when viewed from the symbolic world of understanding. This psychological interpretation of blue seems to hold sway across many cultures. (Krishna and Shiva are the deep blue/black of spiritual death the sky is blue and far away.) Aside: it is quite possible that all children are born as synesthete's. They can see auras around everyone, but that as they grow up, their brains develop and further delineate and articulate this combined sensory information into the more discrete set of senses that the rest of us come to know.

I don't mean to keep hammering on these types of fringe experiences. I fully understand that the meaning of an experience like auras or astral travel is outside the sphere of questions that science is prepared to ask. This really is my point. These types of experiences are human psychological experiences and neuroscience has uncovered some physiological substrate in which we can also contextualize this type of thing. But as Copernicus Science uncovered that the earth goes around the sun, they haven't proven that God doesn't exist. My contention here is that meaning extends forward, as well as backward and this ability to cast ourselves into symbolic understanding is both our greatest achievement and the root of our superstitions. Science teaches us that every whim should be verified against reality, but we constantly construct meaning and for good or ill this is an ever so human thing to do. The illusion or creation of meaning as an expression of ritual can, in turn, lead us to the real experience of meaning. The belief that meditation can help you improve your mind actually helps you to construct a healthier mind through the use of meditation. Belief is not simply illusion: *"the belief alters the world, but also alters me"*. Iain McGilchrist, *Master* - Pg.170

The belief in spirits could be seen to be detrimental or delusional. I'm smart enough to think that spirits are really a manifestation of the individual's own brain, exteriorized or projected on to the environment from within the psyche. In some sense, I have seen behind the illusion, but in another sense I have shifted words around on a page to displace this experience into a context that I prefer. I haven't changed the expression of the experience. I can also understand that there may be a reason why my unconscious is haunting me with spirits. I may want to take them seriously and listen to what they have to tell me as though they are real. I would argue that in many ways they are real. If the jungle starts to sing to you, I would advise trying to sing along. If you push that river, it will push back. I can place a value on my psyche as a manifestation of something beyond my ability to fully comprehend (we are the unconscious as well), and then I may stop trying to reduce everything into handy intellectual sound bites.

Who's Narrative? A Small Sentient Digression

As mentioned above, the left side of the brain is more concerned with developing a narrative that accords with its own agenda than the right side. (Whose hand is that?) This aspect of the left side of the mind has been labeled the interpreter module. It seems that there is an evolutionary advantage in having an ongoing constructed narrative for us, and I will come back to some of the larger ramifications of this ongoing narrative construction later. We are at heart storytellers. The various forms of memories are distributed all about the brain, so collected personal history and self-representation is a collaborative effort.

When someone is in outer space for an extended period of time, the brain stops registering information coming from the inner ear's balancing system. The brain quickly (over three or four days) realizes that this information makes no sense in a weightless environment, and stops paying attention to this noise. It then starts using only the visual information it receives to recognize what its spatial orientation is. When an astronaut comes back to earth, her brain can quite quickly reintegrate the sensible messages coming from the inner ear system. But until it does this, the astronaut will have a tendency to lose her balance and fall down, as soon as she closes her eyes.

Many of the postures in yoga can be performed in an inversion or upside down. When we turn ourselves upside down, the brain has to listen to the body again, because it is unaccustomed to this and so you actually pay closer attention to individual muscles as they fire into use. This is an overt stratagem to encourage higher order muscle mapping.

The brain can quite easily adapt to various forms of damage or ongoing integration that may occur over our life. It can more fully embody these various systems, though phantom limbs can continue to bother people for many years; rewiring isn't completely universal throughout the mind. The brain learns quickly to distinguish information that is inconsequential like a ticking clock or non-functioning ear balance information and stops paying attention. The mind also regularly color corrects objects in the environment to what the expected colors of the object should be. For instance, the mind sees a rose on the desk in front of you as the same color all day long, even though the light throughout the day is changing the actual tint of the rose considerably. This is why Monet painted 10 versions of the same hay stack. He trained himself to actually look at the world as it came to him and how it actually was in the light, *at that moment*.

There is a very short lag in your ability to consciously register your environment as it is given to you by your senses. The human brain compensates for this time lag by anticipating forward in time and constructing a probable version of how the world will be when we catch up to it. We are constantly anticipating environmental feedback and using our extended mapping system. Processing the world in the brain takes time (very small amounts, but time nonetheless), and so it has proven to be an evolutionary advantage to have an extended field of bodily consciousness that projects us forward into time. This extended sense of our surroundings is largely a right brain and unconscious process. This is also one of the leading factors in our conscious makeup that creates a sense of our being an individual in the world.

The brain has to have a self-referencing concept of what it is extending in order to have the ability to extend itself forwards or backwards in time. This is in part our sense of our own self-awareness or a self-referential model, which is intimately bound to our body and its surroundings. This representational aspect of ourselves can help us to create the sense of an individual ego that we will refer to. We are completely unaware of the fact that our brain is creating this 'illusion' and we feel as though we are here now. In a very real sense we both are and are not here now. (We are so, a split second ago) Meditation and various trance states and, or drug use like magic mushrooms may allow us to glimpse behind this 'illusion' and fully immerse us into the flow of the now, as it were. Magic mushrooms do this by shutting down areas inside the brain that seem to be concerned with self-image, not by 'turning us on man'. In India, you may wish to do a 10- day meditation retreat and the first thing you must embrace is no talking. Talking is the expression of left brain's linguistic mind chatter. If you wish to experience the right brain, you have to shut the left down and allow the right to emerge of its own accord. (See Thomas Metzinger *The Ego Tunnel* - Pg.32-4)

We are all quite aware of the personal space around u -all of the time- without having to consciously realize it or continually assert its tactile reality. This was the essence of the joke about the close talker on Seinfeld. We become very aware of our own space, if someone else's tolerance of personal space is less than ours. North Americans tend to have about a two-foot tolerance of personal space ownership. Other cultures can have considerably less. Sex obviously gains more intimacy, because you have completely surrendered your private space to another, or you actually become that other by having them encompassed within your personal body mandala. This also includes riding horses, where the horse extends its body map to you; hugging, handshaking and many other forms of social interaction. Willing to surrender your space is, of course, pleasurable and you are in some sense becoming the other person as your body maps mingle. People who ride horses understand this connection intimately.

The Chinese art of healing people without touching them now seems to have merit, because we are very aware-on many levels of consciousness or unconsciousness-when someone is near our body and inside of our personal space. The practitioners say that they are directing chi energy within the body and what I would say is that the constructed mental paradigm is relatively unimportant to the point I am making. The reality is that something is going on and these healers cannot only create a sense of wellbeing (possibly a placebo effect, which is a powerful effect nonetheless), they are actually affecting our psycho/physical space by simply being in it. The important idea I wish to convey here is that the brain has a very accurate understanding and mapping of the immediate space around you. In some sense, all of the space around you is also a part of you directly, depending on how in touch you are with it. And again, like auras and out-of-body experiences by using terms like 'chi energy', we have only assigned a term to indicate an aspect of the phenomenon. The actual phenomenon is undulating and wavelike and can be described with many reference points, but it is a real affect nonetheless.

What's the difference?

What is really happening now in this new light of neuroscience is that philosophy and psychology will have to reassess their positions, as we collectively get to know the instrument with which these viewpoints know anything (the brain). The best model that we have of the brain's inner physical workings is the one being constructed now by neuroscience. The brain's intimate relationship to the outside world seems to be getting moderately clearer as a result of the parallel advancements going on in cognitive and evolutionary psychology and biology. All of these sciences seem to be moving in a somewhat matched step and they have all gained some traction in the last 20-to-30 years (I will have to check their star charts). There are a lot of insights that are-to my mind-directly undercutting many of the prepositions that seemed self-evident, especially the various concepts that we have developed concerning the nature of our self- referential consciousness.

One of these 'self-evident' prepositions that gained a lot of traction politically is that all people were given the same tool box at birth. This is the idea that we are all born with a blank slate in our heads and that nature proceeded to fill us up. It seems to be born out of a definition of 'equal' in the sense of 'all men are created equal'. We greatly desired to be born the same, and so the dogma of the blank slate became so ideologically entrenched that it has been taken for granted. (Incidentally, the projected female anima and the left brain in general tend to speak in terms like, 'it is well known' or 'everyone understands that' just like her pompous intellectual male counterparts. The animus left brain tends to speak 'as though' the weight of the *collective opinion* is always behind it.) An artist in New York did an art installation on the side of a building that said: *"Raise boys and girls the same."* This fellow never had children or was tyrannically married to his myopic vision of the sameness in the sexes. Oh, the militant nineties!

    This idea of us inheriting a blank slate is not true for a number of reasons that should be embraced. By saying that we all don't think the same or that we are all not as smart as each other, or that women's brains are different from men's, I am not saying that we should start throwing babies over cliffs if we start to think that they might be stupid. Eugenics is immoral for any number of reasons and we don't need the Holy Scripture to concur or even help us understand what is wrong about it. Differences in humans are simply a statement of fact and are an extension of the myriad ways in which we experience the world. Women's brains are different from men's and some people aren't very intelligent. We all don't think the same and the culture we are born into further moulds and encourages elements of these differences. Generally, women tend to orient themselves in space, using specific and particular aspects of the environment (a specific red building, etc.). Men are more comfortable with an abstracted instruction manual (a map saying turn left, 50 yards that way). Nature likes to change it up and road test new things.

    When I was in school, I wasn't very good at math and I realized much later that I needed to understand how things related to the real world to really gain an understanding of them, or even to be remotely interested in them. (I'm left handed and very right brained) I don't have stunning memory retention when it comes to rote learning or detailed factoids, although I do remember the meaning of conversations -what I have been reading about most of the time. I certainly had a poor grasp on the minutia of details in many situations and I have had to train myself to pay attention to details in my work as a carpenter. I personally never need to calculate the correct trajectory that would send a rocket to the moon; therefore, I don't really need calculus or trigonometry. It seemed extremely abstract when I was taught math, and it is no less abstract to me now (though I understand the context much better now. This does not mean I could not understand it. Conversely, I may have a sudden religious conversion and embrace 'higher mathematics' wholesale. I am fascinated by higher math, because of its mystery).

On the other hand, I am a carpenter and I am forced to make calculations in the imperial system all day long. I have been constantly fascinated by geometry and Pythagoras specifically, and I am quite good at all of these types of elementary mathematics. But I've learned them out of necessity and interest, not under the duress of school. I actually enjoy geometry as an applied skill and some other aspects of math, as well and I can calculate in the imperial system quite a bit faster than a lot of my co-carpenters. What people really need-as far as mathematical skills-are the ability to understand their own finances and especially mortgages, and compound interest. This should be a number one real life job. (Did any one just go through the recent 2008 economic crisis?)

Conversely, some people are able to do mathematics with an unbelievable ease, as indeed some are able to naturally play basketball and music right out of the womb. Whether we want to admit this or not, mathematics seems to be the preview of the male mind. Before you crucify me, allow me to back this up, which I will be doing in a couple of paragraphs. This doesn't mean that people shouldn't or don't have to practice math or basketball, or anything. But some people do seem to have an innate leg up or at least a preponderance or inclination to do well at some things and others simply can't. (They have a leg up on me, for instance, and my un-masculine inability to do math.) This whole argument can degenerate into a nurture VS nature dichotomy, which I will and have repeatedly endeavored to show is also a false and simplistic view of how we learn.

There are probably aspects of the brain that are inborn or triggered by hormonal influence and these propensities seem to wire more easily, as the organism grows up. The very young brain sends out an excessive amount of axons, which seek to over connect with our neurons. Around the age of three, the brain starts actively pruning back this excessive connectivity, but at the same time, it starts to strengthen the connections that survive this pruning. Various 'innate' traits can either start to become established early on and then become elaborated on, or not as a result of successions of environmental cuing-being taught how to learn-in confluence with the epigenetic nature of the brain's ongoing construction. The idiot savant may be a result of the fact that they have a lot less noise in their brains and so they are spectacularly good at one thing.

This idea of the innateness of human ability is really the crucial-ideologically heated-essence of a lot of my ongoing arguments. I like to believe–sometimes, but not consistently-that innate sociological traits like certain various cultural tendencies are hard wired at birth. It is a very tricky thing to prove and I can find no shortage of "proof" that asserts the exact opposite. This is the founding element of what this book is trying to drive at and I will admit that it is very difficult to come up with any really hard evidence as to what exactly is culturally ingrained and what is biologically inherent. I have read repeatedly that a fear of snakes is hard wired and universal, though I still have no idea how. The drive toward sex seems to be an extremely elemental and primal urge that is most difficult to temper and this drive seems to be coming from a more basic-seeking urge that resides deep in the old brain. The ability to hear perfect pitch in music can be taught, but some people just have it from birth (10 percent of autistic children as opposed to one percent of the general population), or they acquire it at a very young pre-linguistic age. It's hard to imagine a strict evolutionary advantage to having perfect pitch. I've heard the same foolish thing said about female orgasm, but here we are. I'll take a run at how these things could have happened later. For now, let's agree that some people simply have a much more intuitive grasp of mathematics.

Anyone who has a brain can't deny that there are temperamental, and therefore, innate differences between breeds of dogs. Any dog breeder will tell you that these traits have been bred into the animals over many years. Sheep dogs seem to start herding animals straight away, and without sheep around, they will do an admirable job of keeping children in the backyard. Small dogs instinctively shake things, because it is the best way to break a small animal's (rats) back. Antelope seem to be able to walk seconds after dropping out of the womb. Some of these animals may be born with better temporal map-making abilities (blue jays, for instance) or other more developed brain anatomy that manifest in what we call 'a herding instinct' or inborn ability to walk. Sheep dogs have to be trained for the more specific aspects of their job, like where the door to the pen is and what the various verbal commands are -though certain tones and intonations are tied to specific types of commands that are somewhat universal and more embodied-so not everything can be inbred; although an innate ability toward herding and good spatial mapping skills seems to be within the evolutionarily inheritable tool box. This is probably what led Chomsky to assert an innate architecture that receives language.

This is the same as learning French or English. We are ready to learn how to speak, but the specifics of which language we will speak are ambiguous. People who have perfect pitch-the ability to know exactly which note they are hearing, as opposed to the relative harmony of that note)-don't know how to play piano or compose music without practice. I would suspect that they have to be acclimatized to certain harmonic structures as well. The interesting thing is that some people can identify the exact set of notes in a chord (because the same chord can be played using a number of different notes on a piano. This is particularly stunning). It seems that a lot of people with synaesthesia also have been gifted perfect pitch, but it is not known whether these two abilities are synonymous and have been gifted to them 'genetically'. Because of this gift, they can easily learn to bi-associate the emotional resonance of note tone with a color, or they may simply have perfect pitch and a corresponding color association straight out of the womb, which they learn to integrate, because they have always had it. (See *Musicophilia* by Oliver Sacks)

I am fully convinced that music is very deep in us and the related emotional tones of notes spontaneously occur as a result of our long evolutionary acclimatization to music. In a very real sense *we come to music* because it's already in us.

There is an example, which shows that very specific geographical spatial mapping techniques or geographic information seems to be passed on 'through the genes'. There are two distinct groups of the same breed of ducks in Europe. These ducks use two distinct migration routes around the Alps and down to Africa. One group uses the eastern route through Hungary and the other one uses the western route through France. If you take an egg from an eastern route duck and have it raised by a western route duck, the resulting chick will migrate along the eastern route even though every other duck that this eastern duck knows is flying down the western route. This seems to imply that an innate hardwired map of Europe is in this duck or at least some type of inheritable and possibly fixed temporal orientation.

Why do Kenyans and East Africans in general do well in the middle distance races at the Olympics? It seems that this distance of running has been highly prized in their culture, and in the past, the men who ran well received access to the best brides. It also seems that being too poor to buy shoes and running in your bare feet is the perfect way to train to be a middle distance runner. Ethiopian girls are positively encouraged to do it and they dominate this sport as well. If we spread this middle distance proclivity over hundreds of generations or even a few generations and also enshrine it into the cultural cannon, this type of thing will elevate your status. You tend to get Kenyans/Ethiopians dominating the middle distance running in the Olympics, and they do. Good runners will produce more children and these children will be good runners also. Is their body evolutionarily different from ours? Who knows? It seems that some of them have longer legs than our cultural median and it seems that moderately larger toes can actually give you a small advantage as well. I have no idea the relative toe size of Kenyans. Incredibly, nature has supplied us with the perfect thing to run on, which is the barefoot. Everyone may assume that I have some less than overt racist subtext I will be driving at and that is why I chose Kenyans. Is this also unfair that they have an evolutionary or even cultural advantage? Should we ban Kenyans from middle distance running, because they have such a proclivity towards it? Of course not! We should embrace this difference as part of the wonder of the diversity of our world. Equal, though different.

Jared Diamond makes excellent cases for the advantages and disadvantages of the environment that have directly impacted human socio-economic evolution and he highlights some of the specific reasons for the west's spectacular scientific rise. Many of the reasons why the west has sprung forward technologically can be traced to environmental and strictly geographical advantages. (See the excellent *Guns, Germs, and Steel*.) One of the greatest advantages that the west has is the access to all of the technologies of the other surrounding cultures that are connected through the similarity of our environment and long memory of the written word, dominance of left brain methodologies and a heated inter-cultural competition of Europe, etc. Europe is fortunate enough to be connected to the largest temperate climate zone consisting of the whole Eurasian land mass. There has always been a sense of competition between the independent European states, which the monolith of China, for instance, did not have the benefit of, though China has been technologically savvy for some time. In humans, individual cases will be a reflection of individual circumstances and random genetic mutations, but given enough time, evolution would shape us all into better middle distance runners, if this proves advantageous to us, for whatever reason.

The random element of genetics must be taken into account and it is hard to know exactly what is being directly passed on, and what can spontaneously arise through genetic drift. One of the genes that seemed to me to be ridiculous-but has been 'found' by scientists along with the gay gene and the alcoholic gene-is the smoker's gene. Tobacco is such a new product in the European world that I find it improbable that there is such a gene that arose and spread through the population and could be causing the descendents of white Europeans to become addicted to tobacco. Now we have probably mixed–to a greater or lesser extent-with the Native Americans who could have conceivably developed this gene over their longer exposure to tobacco. We in the west are really only talking about 500 hundred years of contact with tobacco, or at the most 25 to 30 generations of white European smokers. Maybe I am wrong and maybe these things can pop up quickly out of nowhere. Again, my understanding is that the genes are not an absolute A to B to C trigger that is set off, and once it starts, we have no way of turning it around, in the sense that I am pre-jiggered to become addicted to tobacco (I thankfully quit three years ago) . Genes only set up the possibility or probability of things happening and the genes then express themselves in an epigenetic way that is also using feedback from the environment. Maybe smoking tobacco is this environmental feedback? The highly addictive nature of tobacco and cocaine is a result of sets of chemicals set in motion - primarily our dopamine receptor system, which among many things, fires up our seeking system. Maybe there is a tomato gene as well.

Some genes seem to contain the information for a structural template that triggers the formation of more and more complex brain structures. While other genes initiate cascades that speed up and slow down in relationship to other environmental triggers, such as feedback messaging from hormones or the recognition of a limited food supply in the outside world; or the fact that I run every day in Ethiopia. Women stop menstruating under stress, because raising a baby in a famine doesn't make sense. I heard someone talking about a religious gene recently and I simply can't wrap my head around this thinking. This is bad science reflected in sound bite media. Although it does seem that the empathetic or communal aspect of archaic religious rights could be proven to be evolutionarily advantageous, this is yet another attempt to reason backward using utility as the yard stick.

There is most certainly a religious and or musical element in all societies, and nature is ruthless in eliminating non-adaptive behaviors, so they were definitely chosen. I have been lead to believe that our ability to be immersed in our emotions when listening to music is an evolutionary luxury–like female orgasm-and yet I now know that all cultures listen to music. I will come back to this point later. For now, it seems-from my vantage point-that the scientific community is not any clearer on the relative provability of inheritable behavioral instincts, or something called 'structural archetypes' either. I will apologize for the poverty of my own understanding of this and note that during my narrative, you may notice that I flip flop between vantage points. I will assure you that there is someone working on this and *we* will try to get there as well.

This thought about inborn ability extends into certain aspects of civil morality and its relationship to neuroscience as well. There is the thought that if we can reduce the brain and by analogy all thinking to neurological electro-chemistry, or if we can come up with some sort of electrical wiring diagram that represents the brain, we can then-with confidence-announce that there is no such thing as freewill, and that somehow all of the civil law codes that we have been functioning under for thousands of years, will be rendered invalid. We can start smashing deformed babies' heads against rocks. Some smartass lawyers have already tried to find ways to argue this type of strict genetic determinism in legal cases: *"your honor, my client seems to be hardwired by evolution to speed through red lights while he is drinking"*, but thankfully no judge is going to buy these arguments yet. (Watch any video of Rob Ford "explaining himself") This idea that our ongoing insight into the brain's architecture will allow us to dispense with the idea of freewill, or that freewill is 'simply' an illusion, created by our detached electrochemical brains is based on a number of incorrect ideas.

The first set of incorrect assumptions is the result of over-zealous reductive causality, which is the thought that, as you break things apart, you are somehow coming closer to understanding the essence of that thing you have analyzed. For example, small chemical reactions that we see in the brain seem to lead to the big ideas and resulting behavioral processes, which are the direct end result of the initial trigger reaction. This tracing of electro-molecular causality does not take into account the constant feeding back and feed forward dynamics between the different levels of the brain in the world. It seems that within the brain there is much more information going backward into the system, trying to verify what our senses are telling us than there is going forward into the final resulting formulation of our conscious view or even unconscious behavior. Causality is too constricted an idea to fit into integrated and dynamic systems like our brain or reality. Like looking at a whirlpool, you would never predict a whirlpool from studying water in a lab.

This type of strict reductive thinking goes something like this: if we could possibly reduce the mind into its smallest continuants and actually see synaptic firing, and then trace this firing directly to some event in the outside world; for example, a fire alarm going off that causes us to run out of our burning house. We may correctly assume that we have no freewill and we are just a bunch of highly organized electro-chemicals trained to react to the environment. There is a study that found that there is electro-chemical information occurring in our minds unconsciously and it precedes our physical action. This electro-chemical blip actually precedes any type of explicit awareness of physical action or the physical action itself. (Benjamin Libet 1983 at University of California) This seems to imply that we are-at some level-witless automatons. (I will untangle this specific illusion slowly.)

If I am an automaton and I hear a fire alarm, I will run from the fire and there is nothing to it but an overwhelming emotional urge to flee that is welling up from the unconscious; to stop is to reduce the mind to a state of idiocy. Or maybe my ongoing thinking about fleeing the fire is also 'just some' form of higher order behavioral template that I have fallen into that also allows self-referential thought as part of a larger automaton's inner workings. Or my thinking about thinking about fleeing from the fire is another higher order, etc...etc. (endless regressing, homunculus argument). The old brain/ limbic system is most certainly initiating a fight or flight reaction below any overt or even passive conscious assessment of the situation. However, this doesn't shut out all subsequent higher reasoning or ongoing conscious assessment, or any real and ongoing freewill. It is simply the most efficient way to deal with a fire. My later abstracted ruminations on the self or symbolic content of my constructed memory of the event are superfluous mind goo.

The mind, or really the brain, is an intricate feedback system and cannot be reduced into this type of simplistic reasoning. This was how the behaviorist tried to work. They restricted themselves to strictly observe the phenomenon taking place in front of them. Going back to my unfinished fire alarm metaphor: firstly, we denied that I took any conscious part in the decision to run from the fire alarm, but of course, I explicitly decided to run away, which was a reasonable course of action. There may have been any number of conscious or unconscious assessments that I made, as I was running. Should I check some other rooms for the cat? Where are my children?

Also, I have learned that the sound of a fire alarm indicates that there could be a fire somewhere and I should take note of that implied fact. (Pavlov's dog) I know that fire alarms have been designed to tell me that there is a fire and I accept that this system functions correctly, and I don't have to verify it - much like I don't need to check, if my leg muscles also agree that there is a fire. Maybe my running out of the house is strictly an emotional response to a situation coming from my amygdale? Slowly, my explicit consciousness will re-enter the situation and allow me to process the implications of the fire alarm and its double coded symbolic beauty within my mind. I react to the fire alarm, because the fire alarm is a symbolic representation of the fire in the house. I don't need to analyze this fire alarm to understand that it's telling me to get out of the house. The fire alarm represents both the emotional need to get out and the rational/symbolic understanding of why. Much like the door can represent the means for me to be outside playing-right brain ensemble-instead of a solid wooden object that swings (left brain lifeless and denuded). The fire alarm is embedded in a very complex sociological matrix that I don't have to analyze or even understand in an intellectual way to make proper use of. I don't need to be conscious of this response system and so nature has left it in the unconscious so that I can get on with my 'illusion' of freewill.

Incidentally, I have been in a car accident and I was amazed at how slow time seemed to move, and I was also astounded by the lucidity of my thinking, and the speed with which I had figured out my multiple plans of action. My first thought was to check if everyone in the car was safe and if that proved to be so. My next move was to run to the other car that hit us and see what the passengers' condition was. All of this happened as I spun around inside of our car, wondering how violent the stop was when we finally did stop. I also clearly remembered seeing that everyone had a seat belt on. All of this thinking probably represented a few seconds in normal time. I'm not sure.

I will re-digress momentarily and say that I think that this type of explicitly reductive thinking has a physiological and possibly left brain archetypal basis. When psychology first started in the mid 1800s, doctors were content to only diagnose patients. They could do very little to cure them and somehow naming the affliction was seen as a medical advancement. This naming of specific diseases was haggled over largely because of the complicated nature of schizophrenia, but for the most part, it was considered to be enough to correctly identify the problem. As mentioned above, Joseph Campbell calls this type of behavior 'land naming'. (I believe he borrowed this concept from Otto Rank: landnahme.) When people come into a new environment, the first thing they usually do is give names to everything in the environment that is the same or similar to the things or places they were accustomed to in their old environment, for, example, names like New England and New Amsterdam (New York). By naming things and places, and placing them into their symbolic inventory, they are able to gain a measure of psychological mastery through their created sense of familiarity. (Left brain owns the words) Or as another example: the Viking/English word 'walrus' is a composite of the Viking word for horse, 'Rus', as in Russia, and 'Wal' or whale; hence, whale horse or walrus (The unconscious is all around us and we cannot help but seek to create a self-referential narrative that makes it make sense). The left brain and humans in general, gain comfort by comparing things they already know.

By analogy, if I can correctly trace thinking down into its smallest identifiable constituents, I have somehow mastered an understanding of this or that aspect of thinking itself. Therefore, I gained an amount of mastery over the thing itself. I created a map that I can identify with.

Small children always desire to know the name of things and this reduces their anxiety in the world. Understanding the whole ensemble of the mind, as it is embedded in the ongoing flow of reality, is infinitely more complicated. There is a tendency to think that, because you have perceived the root of an event, you have somehow captured the essence of that 'thing in itself'. In fact, you have done little more than name it. This is-to my mind-the biggest problem with the analytical reductionist paradigm. Conversely, it has always proved worthwhile to understand an elementary aspect in the realm of the natural sciences, because it usually leads to a breakthrough farther up in the hierarchy of complexity. Simply identifying things is the beginning of raising them into consciousness

"The whole process is reminiscent of the wonderful image of Borges and Casares in their short story 'on exactitude in science", of a vast map, 1:1 scale, that is exactly co-extensive with the terrain it 'covers', both metaphorically and literally. The piece builds on an idea of Lewis Carroll's in Sylvie and Bruno Concluded, where a map is referred to as having 'the scale of a mile to a mile'. As one of Carroll's characters remarks, noting some practical difficulties with the map, 'we now use the country itself, as its own map and I assure you it does nearly as well." - The Master and his Emissary - Pg. 402

All the accidents that happen follow the dots
Coincidence makes sense, only with you

Then the riddle gets solved and you push me up to this

State of emergency

How beautiful to be

State of emergency

Is where I want to be - Bjork - *Joga*

The second problem with this stance of reducing us to sophisticated automatons is that it seeks to undermine the fact that the brain or the mind has a real ability to learn from its own past. It seeks to eliminate feedback and puts our memory only one step away from a passive waif-like existence. This ultimately leads us toward an upward spiritualizing of *the mind* out of the brain and body, and implies that our ability to think exists in some sort of separate duality in which thinking can be separate from the brain. The brain is just a complex of chemical reactions that creates the illusion of our independent reasoning. From this duality, comes the thinking that our ability to think is distinct from the body where it resides. This set of thoughts is-I believe-a carryover from our western Christian upbringing (archetype), in that we would like to postulate some form of distinct, God-given soul or mind that allows us to be unique and different from the world-and by implication-from all the other animals. Somehow God has decided that we should be the masters of the universe. This is a reflex of our analytical fear in the world.

Science has consistently undercut this idea of man's unique position in the universe. (I believe that this fear of change in our position in the universe is the root cause of the current anti-intellectual backlash, which is again a maniacal urge to displace reality into abstraction. Too bad, grow up and move on. (Foucault calls this transcendental narcissism) In reality, there is no real need to remove thinking from the brain or the brain from the body. The intricacy of the brain is so overwhelming and convoluted that in actual fact, it does possess freewill. And I would contend that in some ways the illusion of freewill (if it is an illusion) might as well be freewill itself. How am I to distinguish? I have been reading a bit about Systems theory and it seems that we can understand the construction of very intricate systems that represent certain aspects of the mind, including elements that could best be described as freewill. This is also a left brain attempt to reassert or reintegrate its dim awareness of the right brain's context-driven reality. This is quite an active field right now.

Briefly, the main thought-as I have come to understand it-seems to be that you can construct a system that is goal-directed or intelligent. We will use the thought that the system is looking for food. You allow the system to choose from a repertoire of actions and also allow it to screen itself from incorrect actions (negation and feedback). The right brain seems to be mainly concerned with limiting and screening the tyranny of the left, actively saying no to options more than creating a positive assertion. Then, you allow the system to reassess its larger goal in light of the actual situation it's in. If you add in an implied direction, say... the thought that animals that don't eat, won't live long enough to propagate (evolution). Then, you allow this system to represent a smaller embedded part of another identical structure, which is the same system over-lay again, which is then again a part of an even larger structure (the human being in the world). The resulting feedback and feed forward processes from all of these structures within structures can embody a form of intelligence. These systems can be arranged in both hierarchical and non-hierarchical ways, with feedback occurring across all levels; not just from the top down or bottom up. This type of multilayered feedback is called a 'nested hierarchy' like a bird's nest, within a bird's nest, within a bird's nest, etc. It seems that even single celled bacteria posses enough complicated proteins to allow them to read and discern various aspects of their environment. Some of these very same proteins are incorporated into our DNA and the resulting things that we call brains. Go figure… its bird's nests all the way down.

The other aspect of complicated systems like human beings is that, like traffic, humans exist at a meta- level of integration. Extremely complicated forms of behavior and feedback cannot be predicted from viewing each individual constituent of a human being, or even the relative understanding of any one segment of the mind. An arm or leg is meaningless unless it is understood that we can use them to interact and develop behavior in the real world environment or even among other humans. Behavior is incomprehensible without a cursory grasp of the extended environment, along with the complicated dynamics of human social interaction. Behavior is meaningless, if you strictly adhere to the behaviorist's agenda. Or behavior is meaningless to a behaviorist.

I want to give another quick example of how not recognizing feedback and the constriction of over reductionist thinking leads to absurdity. I was listening to CBC's *Quirks and Quarks* and there was a nice man explaining how tigers drink liquids. He built a machine that was a mock up of the tiger's tongue, which mimicked the motion of tiger's ability to lap up water. Tigers seem to use the flat of their tongue applied directly on to the surface of water and they allow the inherent surface tension of the liquid to adhere to it. Each animal that uses this method has adjusted their rate of water lapping to the specific surface size of their tongue and they have consistently struck the perfect balance between how fast they should move their tongue across the surface of the water in order to efficiently get the most water into their guts.

The scientist broke this ability down into its constituent parts and explained the dynamics of surface tension etc., so that we could marvel at the precise tuning to the environment that our abstracted nature has given these animals. It's incredible that nature has timed the rate of their lapping perfectly to fit into the abstract mathematical world of liquid dynamics. If you think about it for a minute, you will realize that animals can very quickly figure out that they aren't getting much water into their mouths by one method, and then, simply speed up or slow down, or flatten, or cup their tongue accordingly. This fantastical feedback process (called learning duh) was never mentioned on the show and-to my mind-any animal can watch another animal's technique (head down and near the water), and after a couple of tries, figure out easily the speed right. To bring liquid dynamics and surface tension flow rates into the discussion clouds up the issue. It's a tiger drinking water in the real world!

I recently heard yet another death knell to this type of strict causally reductive thinking. On the *Quirks and Quarks* podcast for Feb. 12, 2010, and again in April 6th 2012, there was a fellow discussing the discovery of the use of quantum mechanics in plant life. A plant needs to move the energy it received from the sun very quickly toward its processing centre so that it can-through photosynthesis-turn that energy into food. Plants convert almost 100 percent of the sun's energy they collect into food. There are a number of pathways that the cells can use to transport and extract energy from the sun. Instead of using a singular pathway, they use the inherent quantum properties of energy, which allow them to move energy across all of the pathways simultaneously. In an analogous way of thinking, light is both a wave and particle. The actual mechanics are complicated and occurring on, or beyond a strictly cellular level, but by doing this, the plant can use much more of the available energy. We would not be here, if plants weren't so efficient. What he is saying is that the plant is not a causal chain of events that moves energy around. This is too inefficient. This quantum exchange of energy is occurring within a biological sphere of reference at or below the cellular level. This is quite a stunning revelation. How do plants use Quantum Mechanics you might ask? They don't, because they ARE quantum mechanics. What is meaning of life? You are the meaning.

In the same vein one more time: I have been listening to my lovely *Philosophy Bites* podcast again and it is true that a little knowledge is a dangerous thing. There was an interview with a philosopher named Jennifer Hornsby and she was discussing human agency from June 1, 2008. Agency is a philosophical problem that has to do with trying to trace causal chains of action within human behavior. It encompasses things like the argument for, or against freewill etc., and I won't get to deeply into it except to say that Hornsby formulated the problem in the same way that I have been groping toward for the last couple of years, and I will paraphrase her beautiful insight. If you wish to understand why a woman crossed the road, you are almost immediately led astray by the question itself, because the question leads you into a causal reductionist framework. You displace her out of the world through the implied intellectual abstraction that is *the question itself*. She has crossed the road, because she decided to, using her freewill. Or, there was a physiological build up of electro-chemicals within her synapse that forced her to unconsciously proceed across the road, etc. You automatically search for a causal chain, because that is how physics has successfully represented the world to us. The reality is that you cannot separate the woman crossing the road from the woman crossing the road. She is a woman crossing the road, because she is a woman crossing the road. Only the question itself takes this embedded situation out of the world and into the realm of detached speculation, which leads us to try to impose or interpolate a causal chain back on to it. The appearance of a causal chain is a product of our imposition of perceived meaning and/or our intellectual discrimination back on to our detached and lifeless observations. This was ultimately where Ludwig Wittgenstein arrived while he sought to analyze thinking and language.

(I came to it too late to be integrated into the bones of this book, but I will mention again that this is spectacularly explained in *The Master and His Emissary* by Iain McGilchrist. My left brain would put this book in the top five books of my meager life.)

The very brief argument is that the right brain functions largely by restricting the left brain in a negative way, so as far as the right brain is concerned, it's not a question of whether we have freewill or not -this is the left brain's concern- it's more that we *don't* have freewill. Or it's not where you are that's important, it's more important that you are not here.

Way back there I made two points. The third point I would like to make is about the notion of causality itself. Causality as a concept seems to flow from our own perception of time moving in one direction, which in itself is a valid observation and we are justified in our consensual agreement that this is so. But the reality of the situation-from a physics perspective and ironically from many religious observations-just might be very different. We have seen earlier that the causal flow of time seems to be contradicted in certain aspects of modern physics. This has more to do with our inability to understand the true nature of quantum reality at these deep and elemental levels. Physicists rarely talk about 'now'. Time is so relative that depending on your observational vantage point, it is almost redundant to think of time in terms of an absolute now. This is especially true on the micro and macro levels of reality, which is again a reflection of the meta-relationships of scale. Our brain has been wired by nature-through its evolution-to understand reality as time bound and causal flow, and at our human scale it is. But also it feels true to us, because the mind seeks to fill in the blanks in our perception in order to construct a coherent seamless and predictive picture of reality, and we *are* embedded in our own perception of a biographical narrative. Over our evolution, the mind hasn't had a reason to revaluate the underlying concept of reality as a whole, because it is immersed in that very reality.

Let me illustrate this point by an analogy: Wittgenstein was talking to someone and the person said to him that they can understand why people thought the sun went around the earth. When you look into the heavens, it seems as though we are not moving and that the heavens are moving around us. Wittgenstein wanted to help this person understand what the validity of correct thinking is and he asked them what the sun would look like if the earth went around it instead. Of course, it would look exactly the same except for very small details of observation, and the reality is that one view is correct and the other is not. It was building proof through recognition of the contradictions inherent in these small details as they run up against our assumed perfection of the heavens that finally tipped the balance and brought the heavens down, putting God in his place.

We are putting our narrow expectations of causality on to the way we think the mind or universe should be, due to our perceived notion of what they could be. Trying to understand something as complicated as human consciousness is simply beyond the grasp of science as it stands right now and so the various aspects of it must be broken down into constituents so that we can actually know something about it. The big picture should be understood to be beyond our limited ability to understand. Conversely, I feel quite certain that if you ask any question deeply enough, you will find an answer that will-to some extent-satisfy your craving to know.

Here's my current tenuous metro-sexual stab at it: the right brain views the world holistically and it approaches the world from the widest angle and feeds forward information into the left brain for a more detailed analysis. This analysis is extremely important in that it allows us to represent the world, though displacing us from it or it from us. We need a sense of intellectual detachment in order to build any concept or tool, or even an image of ourselves. This strict conceptualization is given back to the right brain to reintegrate into a wider angle and then create an inclusive narrative that is our un-abstracted being in the world. The real world is a constant going between these two forms of representation. It is a constant-coming into the world-then going out, then going back into it at another level of the spiral.

This current sound bite of thinking outside of the box is not enough. We have to realize the relationship between the outside and the inside, and the stuff that the box is made of and its ongoing relationship.

"Love allows you to recreate the universe every moment. Love shuts down abstraction and fills us to overflowing with value and meaning making us really look at the world again. This is why art reintroduces us to life; it doesn't simply represent life in the abstracted sense of our being detached, art pulls us deeply into it which then puts us back into the world again."

Part Two Lavender Joga

After all that, we will get back to the brain

    This computer that I write on is a very complicated system, but it is insufficient to use as an analogy for our minds. We use computers as an analogy for the way the brain works, because we vaguely understand or at least somebody understands how computers work. It is also the closest thing that humans have made that is-in any way-like a brain. As I have hammered home, when we represent things with analogies to things that we have specifically constructed, we secure the lock on ownership and representational power. Read *Left Brain Interference*. One excellent reason not to use the computer analogy is that computers stop working when something goes wrong, largely because of the A-to-B-to-C construction. If the keyboard busts, I'm done. A is gone until I can get another. If, on the other hand I lose a finger, I and my sweet brain can relearn to type without it.

    A human being can continue functioning quite well with any number of deep problems in their brain, because different parts of it can-to varying extent-take over the old and new jobs, if the need arises (see *Astronauts and the Inner Ear Above*). I remember in the eighties-when holograms became popular-very soon after the invention of holograms, someone put forward the analogy that the human memory was like a hologram. Memory-in this analogy-was spread out all over the brain, but was also contained in discreet packets as well, similar to the way a holographic image is generated. The whole of the image is in all parts of the hologram. This is an excellent analogy in some ways, but like all analogies, it is also misleading. Scientists are constantly chasing better metaphors, but they continually grind to a halt, because they continually get caught using the analogy of a human constructed tool. (Maybe it is their deep rooted desire to really be poets that urges them to create metaphors.) The Babylonians saw their gods in the sky, the Dutch named the island of Manhattan, New Amsterdam. Memory is really not much like a hologram at all, although memory is spread out all over the brain. The brain isn't actually like a computer. This is both the beauty and the curse of expression. Everything that we express has to be turned into language and the left brain is a bit of a tyrant.

No single system has dominance over the entire brain. We cannot function *fully,* if we don't feel our suites of emotions and thoughts, or only understand color, but not depth of field; however, we can still function. The brain has an amazing ability to try to recover even after catastrophic damage late in life. This is partially because of the excess in redundancy. All of the subsystems and larger organizations in the brain are intimately connected to each other and the systems that are similar to each other will try to take up the slack, if one specific system is damaged. If someone suffers a minor stroke or a smallish concussion (a tear in the brain tissue), it can sometimes take very rigorous and specific testing to realize exactly which particular subsystem has been damaged.

The overall feeling we have inside of us is there is someone running the show. This is our perception of consciousness or sentience. There is sentience, but *someone* who is sensing their own consciousness is not separate and distinct from the show itself. The sense of sentience or our representational and guided attention is both ME watching the show and my involvement in the show itself. It is probably the combination of at least three separate sections functioning in concert. The idea that electrochemical reactions happen before we react or before we are aware that we react, as the proof of our lack of freewill seems to be tied to the idea that *we are* only the sentient or self-aware part of our consciousness. In fact, *we are* also the unconsciousness that constantly surrounds this light, and how could we not be? We are our personal biographical history that is retrievable from that very unconscious and also the largely unregistered awareness of our body in space. We both are and are not the ideas that pop into our mind unbidden. We rarely think deeply about these things and we rarely need to. I would argue that thinking deeply about consciousness causes this false representational distinction in the first place largely because we are tempted to then talk about it. The psycho-philosophy of Gurdjieff made much of this distinction between the watcher and the show-and in my mind-this was his leading philosophical error. A little more on this later.

Francis Crick (who helped discover DNA) and Christof Koch were very interested in this fact of sentient consciousness, and Mr. Crick worked on finding the underlying structure of referential sentience until the very day he died. These two had focused some of their research on a thin layer of the brain that has hardly been studied at all, called the 'claustrum'. The claustrum layer is spread in between the grey and white matter within the brain and it is intimately connected to most other parts of the brain. It appears to be a type of mediator between our explicit higher thinking-that occurs in the frontal lobes- and everything else. The claustrum carries the older limbic emotional sub-straight into consciousness and/or it acts as an interface between these emotions and our reasoning; so Crick and Koch seem to think that it could also be the creator of our feeling of sentience or self-consciousness. It may be this layer, which is allowing us to willfully concentrate the spotlight of our attention on to what we wish to think about. This inter-connected layer may also be the reason that we feel there is an ongoing unity within our consciousness. Crick was convinced that this layer held the key to understanding the phenomenon of our sense of self-consciousness. (See *In Search of Memory*)

This ability to hold and direct attention along with a long-term memory with which to form an ongoing concept of the self-through our ongoing historical biography-seems to be the essence of sentience or a self-reflective conscious awareness. Man seems to be the only animal to possess this ability. Other animals may possess it, but they cannot communicate their awareness of it to us. Sentience may also be a reflection of the ability to communicate, which is moving lock step with the construction of an explicit biographical or representative narrative. One cannot exist without the other. If you add a good external memory source (writing) into this mix, you quickly get the explosion of interconnected intelligence we are now witnessing, which includes the ability to try to understand the very process of self-awareness. Writing represents a massive contextual shift in our ability to externalize representation in the same sense -but much more fundamentally- as the enthronement of the heliocentric system.

In Robert Wright's work *Non-Zero*, he makes the point that writing was invented independently at least three times in the world. In Mesopotamia, China and in America, he points out that given enough time and a sufficient number of people in the world, writing is bound to occur and in fact it did - three times (possibly five). This could also be said about the brain. Given enough time and sufficient complexity-along with the simultaneous development of a sophisticated voice box, etc- consciousness or our being self-aware and the associated feeling of our own freewill is bound to arise. Conversely, we believe that animals possess no freewill or consciousness at all, which I think is a mistaken notion, based on our arrogant belief in the primacy of our own ability to express our self-consciousness through the left brain. Even simple bacteria 'choose' to swim toward food and away from noxious chemicals, but they don't go on and on about it at dinner parties though. Monkeys have proven that they possess the ability to think hours in advance of the present moment they are in and they most definitely prepare for a held concept of the future. Understanding the thoughts of a 400-year-old whale would be the final spike in this arrogance.

Chimpanzees and crows have proven that they can use a tool, which implies a form of abstracted thought and reasoning and also the ability to develop a skill set over time. These two notions come dangerously close to representing freedom of thought or self-reflective thought bound to a memory, which would be a prerequisite of sentient freewill. The big leap seems to be the emotional double coding involved in symbolic representation. The ability to empathize with others and also represent ourselves distinctly, allows us to externalized our sense of self, and by doing this, we can recognize other people's emotional situations through empathy, which sets us up for the greater leap towards an integrated metaphoric and denotative or declarative language, and tool construction; hence this focus on the claustrum as an interface between our deep emotions and our higher reasoning.

Conversely, the development of language has moved lockstep with the evolution of our emotional understanding and the abstracted, and representational symbolic nature of language. But none of this could have happened without the extension of range in the human voice box, which probably developed as a result of our ability and desire to sing. I will proceed into a full explanation of double coding and some clinching observations about the importance of representing the world with language that were made with bonobo monkeys in just a moment.

Double Code

As mentioned earlier, feeling and emotions are an intrinsic aspect of the way we learn. A considerable amount of how we understand our environment, and especially the way that we relate and empathize with other people, is a result of our ability to double code information and our ability to create detached symbolic meaning. This idea of the relevance of feeling was an idea that I had been groping toward and it has been brought home to me and elaborated on by the absolutely fascinating book: *The First Idea*. I will come back to this idea again and again, so here is a brief synopsis of emotional double coding as seen in this book.

When a child is first learning about the world, everything worth remembering is being imprinted in the mind and remembered, because it has an emotional or relational value. (Right brain... I will stop putting these hints in for some time but keep this in mind) If mommy brings me food, I feel good, and every time she brings me food, she says here's your food and smiles at me as she puts it down. All of these experiences are intertwined and can be represented symbolically by the word *food*. (Left) I will feel good about eating, because it is entwined with so many other positive emotional reinforcements like my mother's approval or her smiling face as I eat, or not. What is important in learning is not the abstract term *food* or my ability to elevate or remove this term into the abstract realm of thought. It is the whole ensemble, including the emotional aspect and the reality of my mother coming into my personal space and patting me on the head, etc. My mother is not an abstract quantity, she is the total sum of my emotional experiences of her and I can symbolize her with the term 'mother', but this term carries with it all of the feeling and past history of my experience of her in the world.

This or learning by developing a symbolic relationship with the world, but these symbols are embedded in emotional or feeling/relational environments. These symbols and the past experience (memory) are not initially neutral and passive objects for us to contemplate or learn by rote. Very powerful memories or heavily reinforced messages always carry an intense emotional kick. This is why we remember them. Shame and pain are excellent teachers. Embrace them. - Me

In my roundabout way, I will explain how all this comes about, but we will need to ramble about in some context first. One of the most interesting realizations that came out of the study of neurobiology is the discovery of a type of neuron called a 'mirror neuron'. This type of system of neurons resides in a larger system that is located near the same parts of the brain that became associated with both language and motor skills in both hemispheres. Before I discuss this, I wish to point out that the term mirror neuron is a bit misleading. Mirror neuron implies a very small area of the brain doing a fairly specific task and I hope by now that you have realized that the brain doesn't work that way. Mirror neurons-as though they are specific types of detached things-are now constantly referenced in literature about neuroscience, but the idea of a mirror neuron is similar to muscle memory in that 'mirror neuron' is a phrase that in many ways represents both an ideal and an integrated brain function, not a discreet and strictly identifiable thing. Mirror neurons should be thought of as a highly integrated system within the brain.

The mirror neuron system's job is to accurately perceive the nuances of someone performing a motion or series of motions, which then-as it gets kicked upstairs into the whole brain-allows us to determine the ongoing *intent* of that action. This system allows individuals watching tasks being performed to perform the task mentally along with the individual who is being watched. So if I was watching you play baseball or twirling spaghetti on to your fork, the mirror neuron system-to a certain extent-allows me to perform this same set of actions along with you, in my head. (Tigers drinking water) This set of neurons doesn't strictly distinguish between *you* doing the action and me doing it along with you. They mirror the exterior content being observed within my brain.

This doesn't mean that we can immediately do anything that we see happening outside. We quite obviously can't, but it does open a window on to how we learn to do things. The inhibitors that stop us from acting out things we see going on in the frontal lobes-that didn't work so well in my friend who wanted to punch me in the face- are the same or similar to the ones that stop you from constantly physically repeating the actions that you are watching being performed. These inhibitors are a specific 'higher' function within the frontal lobes of the neo-cortex working as naysayers. There seems to be an explicit feedback function within our consciousness that allows us to realize that we aren't doing the things we are watching. This is again an example of the feedback and feed forward functions of nested hierarchies that allows the brain to sort through its constant surveillance of relevant information.

Mirror neurons are most heavily inter-connected to the areas of the brain that control our fine motor skills and they are especially prevalent in the areas that are dedicated to control our hands and mouth, hence the reason that they are so closely integrated with our language centers. This heavy interconnection to the mouth is probably why children automatically pick things up and put them into their mouths and also why we talk with our hands. The hand and face are quite close to each other on the brain's mapping of the body (see Wilder Penfield). Most of our initial tactile information about the world and the ongoing integration of our physical sensations are through our fingers and mouth. In other words, we have much finer feeling acuity in our hands and mouth than say, our mid-back. People can quite easily read Braille with their fingertips, but not so easily with their bum. Whales can't tell us about the ocean, because they don't have hands.

The concept of the mirror neuron system brings us closer to an understanding and appreciation of some of the dynamic that is our set of fine motor skills. In some very real sense we are doing the things that we watch other people do. This appreciation of other people's skills is even more acute when we already possess some knowledge of how to do the thing we are watching. For instance, we can appreciate a great hockey player or jazz drummer, if we play hockey or a musical instrument ourselves because this subset of neurons and the whole of the mind has a more refined acuity when you have also developed a certain amount of skill in the action that you are witnessing. Like most other things about humans, the brain gets better at skills through observation and reinforcement. For example, people who watch people dance all of the time-even without having danced themselves-can become very skilled observers of movement. Just listen to someone discussing ice skating or synchronized diving at the Olympics and you quickly gain an appreciation for the minutia of observation that is involved in being an expert .(Degas was crazy for ballet and became-through constant skilled observation - an excellent observer of the human body.)

It would be nice to think that this set of mirror neurons allowed us to build our concept of empathy and to some extent, it does force us to be empathetic, but of course, the brain is a very complex system and this is not the whole picture. The feeling of empathy specifically seems to be tied with the production of oxytocin, which is a largely female hormone and predominantly of right brain orientation. The production of hormones like oxytocin and the other various mood enhancers we experience(testosterone and dopamine), are happening within and around the brain stem through the interaction of complicated feedback systems that involve many things like the amygdale, hypothalamus and penal gland (limbic system), etc. The development of empathy is not simply the mechanistic result of arbitrary hormone production in the mind. Testosterone is not the reason we start wars. Empathy can be nurtured by a sustained and conscious effort directed toward the understanding of other people's emotional states. This effort *may* result in the increased production of oxytocin, along with many other benefits. It certainly won't hurt you to try to nurture your ability to understand nuance no matter what is going on. Mirror neurons seem to be closely allied with observing the function of the motor systems in others, but it is important to realize that the function cannot be removed from the appraisal of the intention of others as well. The generation of empathy can never be completely separated from the process.

Mirror neurons seem to be involved in a number of interrelated faculties. They seem to be involved in the development of fine motor skills and appraising the shape of various objects, and in the construction of our understanding of how those objects are oriented in space. (Interestingly… pre-linguistic babies seem to show surprise when objects don't conform to the laws of logic or gravity, so there seems to be elements of our ongoing construction of the environment that are gifted to us from birth, or taken for granted very quickly.)

As you reach out toward a cup on the table in front of you, your hand is already taking on the shape of the cup in anticipation. Part of this motor system-which includes your eyes-is busy assessing the distance of the cup relative to your arm's length, and forming an approximation of the weight of the cup (blind sight). There are two sets of optic pathways from each eye that travel to the back of the brain: one is more directly conscious than the other. These types of functions quickly become standardized through practice in the real world and we will tend to hold a fork or coffee cup the same way without having to think about it every time. Both my son and I always use a drinking straw, pushed into the side of our mouths as opposed to held in the centre. He has probably seen me do this and now it is wired in to his procedural behavior. He can relearn how to perform simple actions just as I could completely relearn my technique on the drum set by flipping the drum set into its mirror image. This ability to relearn is due to neuroplasticity and our ability to rewire our body's mandala, which we will look at in a bit. My son's original imprint for drinking with a straw probably got into the system-as it were-on the back of his mirror neurons. My son has no need to develop a new technique for drinking out of a straw. He has seen my thoughtful expert straw drinking technique and realized that it works perfectly - job well done.

Any number of habits can be quickly imprinted in this way. The way that Rap singers' hunch-over and swing their arms or constantly try to shoot me with their fingers has become a nurtured cultural cliché; or the distinctly different way that hippies dance at outdoor concerts is most likely due to mirror neurons and the overt emotional double coding associated with the music that is behind the posturing. This is how we develop a sense of ourselves when we are young and we actually are the resulting cultural ensembles that we are a part of. Like the way that teenagers constantly say *like* all of the time as they reset their minds, it's like I was like dancing like. It was like a Grateful Dead concert, like in 1969. We take little bits of everything we witness and construct ourselves. To say that young white kids are mimicking black rap kids is to misunderstand how embedded the cultural memes are in the world and also to misunderstand what mimicking means by presuming that it is a conscious and willed process. We are born to mimic. English and Scottish pop singers are indistinguishable from American singers. We all sing with a mid-Atlantic accent, or more recently, the ebonics of modern black slang.

When the natives of Central America first encountered white people in the 18th century, there were many things they did that the natives could not understand. This was in part due to the natives' ingrained social behaviors being so different from the Europeans' ingrained behaviors. Native Americans in the mid-west were shocked by the seeming avarice and self-directed arrogance and greed of the rapacious white people. This initial assessment was reinforced in them constantly, as they repeatedly bore witness to everything that white people did. For instance, white people would walk right up to them while staring directly into their eyes. This was such an overtly aggressive act to the natives that they thought the white men must be completely crazy to be so brazen. Unfortunately, for the natives, they were reading the white people correctly and the white men were and still are crazy, and full of empty avarice and greed for power, especially at Goldman Sacks. Most animals interpret a direct stare as overtly confrontational.

All of these more subtle aspects of our collective social cuing are going on around us all day long-like eye contact and body posture. These cues are being reinforced for us by everyone else around us; constantly, though largely unconsciously. While a child is growing up, these social cues are being reinforced through the emotional double coding of the environment and their unconscious use of the mirror neuron system. Our initial exposure to social cuing is being loaded into our long-term memory by ongoing unconscious reinforcement (pain). It is then later refined and made more explicit through overt conscious social cuing that comes directly from our peers through explicit verbal chastisement or social shunning, or the explicit overt reinforcement of social and religious taboos (incest prohibition or not eating pork etc.) that is understood by larger social groups.

Personally, I think one of the main problems of the 21st century is our ongoing disconnection from the mid-size social networks of unconscious shunning and chastisement. This is in part a result of our extra large social networks. The secluded nuclear family is a hot bed of reinforced neurosis. Having to be in an intimate relationship with about 20 to 40 people all of the time seems to promote just about the right amount of social chastisement. Boys should regularly be with men in social environments so that they get the right amount of lifting up and letting down, etc.

The mirror neurons part of this socializing process is that it allows us to 'participate' in everything that we see all of the time. Everything else in our brain is reinforcing-either positively or negatively-our interpretation of these events through a constant internal feedback and reassessment. The small children in any society may be taught at a very young age that overt eye contact is either acceptable or not, depending on the social environment they are born into. Like the act of walking, children would never question the correctness of their social cuing unless they were later confronted by crazy white people. Men from Northern India have a very hard time addressing women face-to-face, because there is a very strict social taboo involved in this type of brazen act and it is considered rude or aggressive, or simply disrespectful of women's personal space. India has developed strategies for coping with extremely tight communities and the vast amounts of people living close together. People only become overtly conscious of the fact that they conform to these more subtle social taboos when they see someone else blatantly not conforming, or they are removed from their social environment. (Hijab) There are, however, a series of universal facial expressions that are understood in all cultures. These include: anger, contempt and happiness, and they probably represent deep emotional structures that we are gifted by evolution, inside of the older brain.

As an interesting side note, there is evidence that many psychological disorders can also be culturally conditioned; for instance, anorexia became more known in the west after Karen Carpenter died from it. It is not believed that it just wasn't being diagnosed before she died. It is thought that this disorder actually became more prevalent–culturally-as a physiological condition. I will give another example: fainting doesn't seem to happen anymore in social environments. It seems that in the Victorian era, women were fainting all over the place. This may have to do with their over-tightened corsets, but I would suspect that there was also unconscious social cuing going on as well. Women would see other women fainting and it most certainly would be an attention getter. The really interesting aspect is that as a social phenomenon you rarely see women fainting anymore. It is rarely portrayed in modern films, because it doesn't ring true for modern observers. The large pharmaceutical companies don't have a drug to counter the discomfort of public fainting, because there's no money in it and we just don't seem to swoon as much anymore, although Beatle-mania might be an exception.

Schizophrenia seems to be a largely modern disease that has only been recognized explicitly in the last 300 years. It seems fairly certain that it probably didn't exist before western industrialization, much like ADHD. Though manic depression and melancholia have very ancient pedigrees, the so called spectrum of disorders, such as Asperger, autism and possibly anorexia, all seem to be post-industrial revolution diseases. Why this is so, is a very open question and I won't discuss this here, but all of the disorders involve an over emphasis on the left brain's functioning, which may be that the left has accreted too much power or that the right brain has lost some equalizing power.

One of the main purposes of mirror neurons and the brain in general, is that it and they seem to be primarily concerned with our understanding of intentions. How you are doing an action is registered very accurately, but the literal muscular interpretation of the way in which your body performs the action doesn't seem to be the mirror neurons main concern. This may be due to the fact that some of the mirror neuron research is going on in fMRI units where the subjects are completely immobile and they have to either watch actions being performed or imagine themselves doing them. Because of their relative immobility, the subjects are not fully engaged in the process. Only some parts of the process are attracting the blood flow necessary to be registered by an fMRI.

The mirror neuron system allows us to develop an understanding and contextualize other people's actions as they are being performed around us. We observe other people doing things and gain an understanding of what the actions *mean* within the environment, and what will happen as they unfold over time in the real world. This is being loaded into the long term memory, based on the strength of its initial emotional impact or its subsequent internal or external reinforcement. This is a beautiful analogy of the difference between thinking about something and actually doing it.

It is my understanding that children of schizophrenic parents have a hard time in the world, because they are used to watching their parents perform actions that don't necessarily make sense to them. When observed actions are placed into the overall context of children's upbringing, this can cause an emotional disconnect for them, between the parents' physical actions and the emotional inference drawn by the children as they watch the gesturing. Schizophrenics tend to ritualize their environment and this emotional disconnect between intention and action is difficult for their children to decipher when they are young, and in the process of developing their understanding of their environment. The parent may repeatedly wake them in the middle of the night or constantly perform rituals that are hard for them to contextualize and understand, or conversely, they will not understand why everyone else doesn't ritualize their environment the way their parents do. Emotional coherence in childhood is very important in establishing comfort in the world. The inability to understand the larger context of emotional values and how they relate to physical actions can cause stress and possibly preponderance toward schizophrenia, although it is a very complicated problem.

Schizophrenia breaks up the individual ego within the psyche or the larger psyche, and divides, fairly discrete separate compartments so that there is a lack of emotional continuity within the individual. This in turn seems to be the result of the patient's continued immersion in the reflective abstraction within the left brain. Now, with the recognition of mirror neurons and the realization of how important they are in our development of sussing out meaning within emotional context through the observation of actions, this disconnect in schizophrenics makes a bit more sense. As mentioned above, schizophrenia and autism are largely 20th century diseases and they both seem to be the result of a disconnection between the left brain's representational world and a larger emotional context of the right brain. How schizophrenia starts is a question of aetiology or whether the ensuing chemical imbalance associated with having schizophrenia is inborn and leads to the disease or develops later as a result of exposure to an emotional disconnect, or whether this disease is the result of a reflection of cultural pressure, or genetic predisposition.

There is some evidence mounting that a genetic preponderance to having schizophrenia may be the result of three specific genes that may be reacting to other environmental cues. These environmental cues might even be specific chemical triggers, along with tumultuous changes that happen just after puberty. This ailment may also be aggravated and or triggered as a result of smoking marijuana. Conversely, there is a thought that smoking marijuana may be one of the few things that actually gives schizophrenics a measure of relief. The absolute root cause of Schizophrenia is extremely hard to pin down, if there is a single root cause at all. It is known that children of an immigrant minority are more likely to have schizophrenia, especially if the children are significantly alienated from the host community like the early Irish immigrants in 19th century America. So there may be a sociological component, but how that works would be pure speculation.

"Thus there is no single gene for schizophrenia, just as there is no single gene for anxiety disorders, depression, or most other mental illnesses. Instead, the genetic components of these diseases arise from the interaction of several genes with the environment. Each gene exerts a relatively small effect, but together they create a genetic predisposition (a potential) for disorder. Most psychiatric disorders are caused by a combination of these genetic predispositions and some additional environmental factors. For example, Identical twins have identical genes. If one twin has Huntington's disease, so will the other. But if one twin has schizophrenia, the other has only a 50 percent chance of developing the disease. To trigger schizophrenia, some other, non-genetic factors in early life-such as intrauterine infection, malnutrition, stress, or the sperm of an elderly father-are required" Eric R. Kandel, In Search of Memory - Pg.338

Understanding intent and its relationship to our emotions seems to be one of the intrinsic advantages of the mirror neuron system. Mirror neurons help us to register, understand and contextualize our emotions as they relate to the actions that we witness, such as emotions like disgust and joy. Mirror neurons allow infants to understand what facial expressions-like disgust-indicate, by building up context between the observed action and its expression - both verbal and facial, etc. This of course would be advantageous in an evolutionary sense in that we need to understand not to touch a dead corpse or human feces at a very young age, and so we have an accurate understanding of what disgust is. This-for a number of reasons I will discuss later-is quite possibly the large part of our great evolutionary advancement.

Involved in this recognition of disgust are several things that, when looked at closely, lead to some surprising ideas. Contextualizing the look of disgust involves the observer framing a concept of what has happened, after we watched what actually happens and then possibly testing the actual results against our ongoing understanding. This all occurs largely unconsciously as we participate in the facial expressions of disgust or joy, through our observation of other people. We only need to see these actions occur within the context of their associate emotions once or twice, and we automatically understand their import. Because of the impact of the emotional environment-being chastised for touching poop-we build up a very strong multi-leveled memory. This is why the idea of a holographic memory became prevalent, because this poop touching memory is associated with many different areas of the brain. We remember the shape and smell of the poop and our father slapping our hand, and the emotions of him yelling at us, etc. These individual aspects of the memory are located in different areas of the brain, but they are all part of a memory ensemble.

Even before we speak, we are trying to build a coherent picture of the world by participating in people's actions and trying to suss out their intentions through being in the emotional states that we both are and observe. We can be literally blind with anger, etc. When we hear the elevated pitch and volume of our mother's voice addressing us, we know that she wants our attention and that something good or bad will usually come from the tone of her voice. So we pay attention, watch, listen and then participate in whatever action is going on. Explicit experiences are remembered, because the human memory functions by gauging emotional thresholds; the stronger the input, the longer the input is remembered. Neurons work in the same way in that certain neuronal systems have a higher activation threshold and if the required threshold is reached, this high threshold system will override everything else and a powerful memory will be installed and reinforced. Conversely, if our mother is feeding us, this whole ensemble of getting food, the calm sing-song tones in her voice and our mother's pleasant facial expressions can create such a repeatedly satisfying experience that we enjoy a good meal more. This type of positive memory reinforcement is less articulated, but still carries a lot of weight, because it has been repeatedly reinforced over time. We will talk about people who don't enjoy eating in a bit.

Just as it is very difficult to be happy, if your face is physically wearing a frown, it is also difficult to be happy when you are watching someone else wear a frown. To some extent, you are wearing the frown that you are looking at in another person's face. fMRI studies confirm that some of the parts of your brain involved in frowning, anger or fear are activated when you see even the briefest glimpse of a picture of a person with those expressions. These emotions are registered unconsciously in us and affect our mood whether we like it or not. All of the less articulated emotions like fear and joy really are contagious. (This is why using 'constant yellow alerts' as a political tool or talking about being tough on crime even though the crime rate is going down, is so particularly cunning. The climate of fear renders life barely worth living. We are all ready to hate our own shadow.) It seems that young female babies spend a lot more time concentrating on people's faces than young boys do - at least twice as much time. There are very good reasons for this that I will get to.

Not only is it advantageous for us to quickly recognize and understand the import of disgust, alarm or surprise in another's face. This faculty is being integrated into the parts of our brain that are concerned with expressing this outwardly, which is also intimately connected to the language centers. There is some speculation that language is actually an extension of physical motion, and again, it is best not to think of the different sections of the brain as being too rigidly separate. So if language is tied to physical motion, this would mean that the earliest forms of communication are intimately connected to certain gestures, possibly linked to those ejaculate words we talked of earlier. It is known that if there is a disconnect between the observed gesture, and what is being said, the brain will go with the physical gesture 100 percent of the time, and it will be right. (See *Master*) This is why lying is so difficult. The body will strive to tell the truth every time.

The alarm calls of animals would be an obvious example and starting point to observe connected body talking. Things like the barking of a dog and our amygdale- wired swear words like 'shit' have very specific physical motions that occur in the mouth and face that must go along with the utterance. (You literally expel the word shit out from your gut.) So early language development is probably closely allied with our root- and therefore most important-basic emotional intentions (surprise, aggression, disgust, anger, etc.), and these resulting root-linguistic expressions are in turn tied back to the body's movements and facial expressions that they literally embody. They form a complete emotional/mind/body ensemble.

Just say 'blaah' without sticking your tongue out, or force yourself to wear a frown all day and see if you don't get depressed. This embodiment allows us to understand the emotional value of other people's actions. We can suss out the future intent of the person embodying the emotion we are watching, which in turn, leads us into an understanding of the emotional double coded nature of symbolic language. Swearing always carries an emotion atmosphere with it, and interestingly, your pain levels actually decrease, if you swear after you have been struck. This is what language really is: a symbolic representation of our embodiment. Conversely, we can influence -in a positive way- how we feel by forcing ourselves to smile or simply by standing up straight with our chest out. We can embody that positive outlook we wish to project and influence the system backwards through the right brain. Fake it until you make it.

If you watch nature shows, you will know that monkeys have very specific alarm calls. Some signify danger on the ground like snakes or danger from above like eagles, etc. Everyone knows exactly what to do when they hear this call. They don't need to think about it. So each call has a specific meaning, and when my mother raises the pitch of her voice, I immediately understand from subtle inflections in the tone whether I am in danger or she is going to feed me, etc. All of this vocal and linguistic representation is embedded in the larger context of the world and makes no sense outside of it. There would be no meaningful cry for danger from a snake, if snakes didn't exist. We immediately understand that this is a snake's call, because everybody else understands that it is a snake's call and we are with everybody else. We don't look up into the sky for snakes, because no one else is looking into the sky and snakes don't fly. These types of alarm calls and swearing seem to be deeply wired into our archaic limbic system.

The very archaic level of linguistic development may also reside in the beginnings of our music making. For example, killer whales organize very specific group activities, using the ribbon of song/speech and this all seems to occur without the use of explicit declarative words like now or turn, etc. (Again, see *Master*) I suspect that this is what language is like in the right brain and I will illustrate with another example. I was watching a show about doctors who were trying to inoculate a village for a disease and this very tall doctor asked the headman to gather everyone that lived in the village to come in from the fields. The headman got on to a drum and told everyone that the tallest man in the world was here, and they should come and see him. Everyone came to see him, and they all came in expecting to see the tallest man in the world.

Elvin Jones, the drummer of John Coltrane, talks about being in Africa and watching a young man tell the story of how he killed a lion through dance and drumming. One more example: my friend Hugh's father was working in a mine in South Africa and there was an accident in which a miner was killed. He drove immediately to the family's house to tell them the bad news, but they already had received it through drumming. This was both a specific series of events being narrated and an emotionally charged performance. It is my belief that this musical element is at the root of our language, before it actually became explicit. People understand the message being performed in these situations by also performing the intent of the message *along with* the drummer who may be two miles away. In the same way that a hunter becomes the animal when they hunt or an aboriginal becomes the dream time in Australia.

The performance is a right brain and embodied poetic metaphor, using the ribbon and varying intensities of rhythm to communicate. Only later could we reformulate it into a specific and declarative narrative where we might explicitly say something like 'the tallest man in the world is here' etc. It could be said that 'embodied poetic metaphor' is a verbal phrase that actually says nothing. However, the real issue is that I'm trying to represent a right brain function on the written page, and I firmly believe that we in the west have completely divorced ourselves from this form of communication, but the road back is through the beautiful ambiguity of music, without actually trying to translate it into words. Simply listening to music helps us to understand how this form of communication works well beyond my ability-or stunning lack of-to describe it. I can listen to someone singing in Arabic or Spanish and I have a pretty good idea what the emotional intent of the music is. The initial linguistic impetus or form is probably right brain, musical and physically embedded, and it later becomes declarative, abstracted and then written down. I will discuss this again and more fully in the next chapter.

I realized an even more explicit language connection the other day. When chimpanzees are showing their respect to the alpha male, they do so by cupping his testicles. This seems to go on at every meeting. I also know that the words testament and testify is rooted in the Greek word testicles and I had been led to understand that if you made a sacred vow to someone else in pre-classical Greece, you would show your serious intent by holding their testicles. I presume that they would also hold yours. This is probably urban myth. I thought that this was a show of vulnerability on each party's part, much like an opened palm and the resulting handshake, which signifies to someone else that you have no weapons. Now I see that it is a much older display and that these words directly relate to an ensemble of visual and sociological cuing that has to do with 'testing' each other, which is from the same linguistic root. The alpha male is testing the other males every time they meet, and if they don't cup his testicles, something is up. His power has been threatened. So the higher more abstract symbolism of words can sometimes be traced back directly to a physical act and a larger sociological matrix that is at the root of the concept. The word 'focus' can be understood in a similar way. The original Greek word 'foci' meant fireplace or hearth – sit around and focus on the fire. So language slowly became more abstracted from its root (to Google). The symbol and understanding of the etymology of a word re-links you backward and more deeply into a fuller and sometimes more physical understanding (religion).

So when a woman came to Jung with a dream about a black snake coiled around the bottom of her spine, Jung confidently placed this dream into a wider and related context of Kundalini yoga. This is the metaphoric mind aligning itself and we don't have to say that these images are identical, though they are equivalent and related. Like the cupping of testicles, we may have lost the original meaning, but we can still understand that an open palm means friendly intentions, and an Indian yogi would be able to talk about Kundalini snakes for days – even I can go on much too long about them. We can raise these images into our explicit consciousness by comparing them to similar symbols and then actively expanding the overall context and then further analyze them again for ourselves. Through this process we can both deepen our personal understanding of them and place them back into a wider context of our expanding consciousness. This is where science will not go and it is not science it is the humanities. We can also allow these images to remain un-analyzed and I think they are still food for the soul.

This universal ability to recognize the emotional intent of several of the most basic facial expressions like contempt and happiness explains why. If I was dropped off in the -almost non-existent-rain forests of Borneo, I would understand with some acuity that a native fellow may be aggressive to me and wanted to cut my head off or that the whole tribe was welcoming me into their village (probably more likely). These larger more basic types of facial expression and some basic physical gestures truly are universal, and intuitively understood by every human. They are also probably hardwired, in the sense that they may have an archetypal/emotional underpinning that is a result of our evolutionary repertoire. Whether they are genetically hardwired, I suspect, but don't know – regardless they really are universal. Smiling-as in a fake smile/grimace-at someone without the associated passivity of laughter is ironically considered aggressive and belied deep in the mind body connection.

Some of the much finer shades of emotions and certain types of specific body movements are culturally determined, and like the form of language that you speak, it develops unconsciously and the intent may not be immediately apparent to untrained observers. For instance, some people (mostly Mediterranean) beckon or request that you come near with the palm of the hand facing down. Flipping the bird (raising the index finger) to someone seems to have been invented in northern Europe. The story is that English long bowmen taunted their French adversaries by waving the bow finger at them on the battle field. The first thing that the French did if they caught a bowman was to chop off his middle finger. I don't know why it is called the 'bird' - probably a cute enantiodromia. It also seems that white Europeans gifted schizophrenia to Africa as Africans collected in urban centers trying to get jobs.

The ability to register and display emotion-especially on the face- seems to have been evolutionarily selected, to such an extent, that we now have the ability within our eye color receptors to see more accurately the color ranges of our human skin tones. This has probably been selected by evolution, because of our trying to suss out the emotions that are connected to the various movements of our blood as it flows across our facial flesh tone. Our eyes are especially accurate at perception across the specific range of the human flesh tones- from jaundiced yellow to blood flushed red-because of an extra receptor cone in our eye that occurs only in primates. This receptor may have developed as a result of, or developed in lock step, with becoming hairless, especially on our face. (See Mark Changizi's *The Vision Revolution*) It seems to me that we have initiated and achieved this evolutionary advantage, because it has proven to be advantageous for us to hone this ability to understand each other. We can quite accurately garner all manner of both reading into and the portraying of the outward display of emotions, and we can easily uncover the underlying intent that is being portrayed. This occurred and has been reinforced in us on many levels, from detecting subtle changes in the hue on our skin to the overt alarm calls, or the sussing out meaning of strong emotions-like disgust-through the use of mirror neurons, etc.

Steven Pinker notes that when we try to remember a set of numbers or a mathematical formula, or someone's name, it helps to physically repeat the numbers or words out loud. This may be yet another reflection of this mirror neuron systems proclivity toward physical mimicking and it also reflects this explicit relationship that mirror neurons seem to have with language. I would speculate that by physically repeating something out loud, you are probably involving two or more memory systems simultaneously in the brain and therefore, you are establishing or at least reinforcing the import of the memory into more than one place. I would suggest creating a song as a memory device and I will guarantee you will remember it. Also the physical actions embedded in the use of the abacus seem to help students to learn and do math.

I heard a lawyer speaking on the radio and he noted that when English/British people speak in the simple block-like structure of Anglo-Saxon, they are usually not lying, but the moment that they switch into the more flowery French-based Norman English, they are usually trying to disguise their intentions. The example he used was from Churchill's speech, *"We will fight on the beaches; we will never surrender."* The whole speech is in the blockish almost monosyllabic Anglo-Saxon, except for one word 'surrender'. He could have said 'give up' which is Anglo-Saxon, but he didn't because he believed that unconsciously every Englishman would feel the weight of surrender as a word that would import and subtly offend their very Englishness. Of course, the French had already surrendered.

This is unconscious psychological cuing at its very best and it is thought that Churchill was completely aware of what he was doing. He explicitly and consciously understood the import of these linguistic subtleties. A lawyer emphasized this unconscious cuing by stating that a friend of his-who was a judge-confirmed for him that in a court room when someone stops speaking in the simple, direct wording and tries to 'flower up their speech', it is a sure indication that they are covering up something. *("No officer… that was not a place I would ever have gone to"* or Bon Jovi's *On a steel horse I ride.* Sounds artificial and Yoda like, because the structure and feel of the sentence-to an American speaker- have an Old English word arrangement.) Not only are the face and the eyes the window to the soul, language and speech patterns are also embedded in our physiological responses, and even some parts of our language can belie deeper unconscious sub-structures that we are unaware of (black snakes). Just saying the word pain can be painful and doctors treating patients should avoid discussing pain levels for too long. Watch 'reality' TV shows now and you can easily see when someone wants to look smart for the camera, we all live vicariously through them.

Mirror neurons are mostly located in the relatively older parts of the brain. They may be in other parts of the brain doing other jobs as well – I don't know. But what I see here is that there is a unity in the way we understand gesture, motion, language, and their accompanying emotions. This is the right brain and limbic system ensemble form of communication that later migrated into a more explicit left brain linguistic declarative form, which was further removed into symbolic representation with the rise and further development, and spreading of the written word. And this now helps me to see why music can set off a flood of neurons firing all over the brain. When we watch rock bands jumping around or we see Yo Yo Ma completely entranced in his performance, we can totally empathize with him. If we can play an instrument as well, this engagement is reinforced at an even finer level. So when we just listen to music on a stereo, we are reacting to the portrayal of emotions and feelings that occur inside of us through their portrayal of the harmonics of sound and this is incredible enough. But when we watch music being played, we are in some sense playing along with the musicians we are watching in front of us. This goes a long way toward explaining why rock bands started to move around on stage so much, as opposed to classical musicians who sit down. I believe this can allow classical music to be pushed into a more abstracted and cerebral realm where it did not start.

It explains why the guitar has become the instrument of choice for rock bands. You can jump around with a guitar strapped around your shoulder, but you can't jump very far when you are behind a piano or cello. With a guitar you have the ability to portray your emotional engagement explicitly and on a bigger scale through your overt actions. This is a very attractive option, if your audience have difficulty staying engaged over long periods of time. (Sound bite culture) It also explains why events like a massive festival concert are so appealing. When you collect thousands of people together and everyone is running through the same set of experiences-as they watch them together- it really is amazing, and it must be quite addictive for the performers as well, which I am assured is so. (As Hitler realized, emotions are contagious.) This collective and emotionally engaged aspect of music and dance is part of our evolutionary-selected religious make up and is evident in our willingness to participate in everything from large music festivals to theatre or small jazz gigs. One of the rudimentary essences of the collective religious experience is the induction of the individual into a trance-like state that occurs as a result of collective and emotionally engaged synchronized rhythmic movement. (Ding! -The long string of big words bell)

Not only are we unconsciously performing along with the band, but we are reveling in some very old emotional centers within our brain that are quite literally pre-linguistic. This is where the trance aspect of things starts to happen and it seems that all cultures have instinctively understood the power of this type of – lowering of consciousness experiences. Along with enjoying the music and our lowered explicit consciousness into trance, we can also consciously appreciate things like the lyrical content of a song on an individual intellectual level. (Though not so much in most pop music) We become absorbed in the unconscious rhythmic structure and appreciate the linguistic cadence of the poetry itself, which is indicative of right and left brain integration. (It is Dave Grohl from *Foo Fighters* 'contention that white people dance to the lead hook in lyrics, regardless of the overall message.)

We will discuss the nature of poetry and how it is more easily memorize a little later, but I will note quickly that this ability to remember melody and rhyming is the reason that books like the *Odyssey* or the *Gilgamesh* epics were written and presumably told to others in a poetic form, and this is also why the early Vedic writings from India are so repetitive. The writers of these epics were trying to establish repeatable sound bites, which they wired straight into the brain in a way that the brain became most adapted to. Through the use of rhythmic and melodic repetition, you can establish lasting memory across different sections of the brain simultaneously and load it more easily into the long-term memory structures in the right side of the brain.

By binding words-or anything else like math-to the physicality of rhythm and melody, you can create a double coded brain worm. When we tie any type of learning experience to a musical expression, we reinforce the 'emotional' import of the message. This helps to firmly establish the lessons outside of the temporary holding areas, which tend to be in the left hemisphere. Who doesn't remember happy birthday? All mathematical learning by rote should be tied to songs and sung to children to engage them. We will see a beautiful example of how this type of learning can be implemented when we discuss Indian music and how it is so skillfully taught to others through embedding it in the body with singing.

Rhythmic trance seems to create a lower threshold of consciousness (participation mystique).and there are similarities in the brainwave patterns and the resulting psychological environment when one is completely engaged in dance and certain aspects of meditation. The actual brain mechanics of trance and altered states of mind is something I don't have much to say about, because I know almost nothing about it. Though, I now suspect that it works by shutting down the parts of the brain involved in self-inspection, where as schizophrenia works the opposite way by ramping self- inspection up too far. It seems that the practice of meditation encourages synchronized brainwave functioning that seems to reduce the ego's overt intrusion (read *Left Brain*) into the field of consciousness. I do know what it is like to be immersed in music both from an emotional point of view and to be completely engaged while performing it. This will be addressed in the next chapter much more fully.

What I will say is that trance and collectively induced trancelike states of mind and the use of psychoactive drugs to achieve engagement is a fundamental and worldwide phenomenon with an ancient pedigree. (From Tunguska shaman to uptight British Quakers and on down into Patagonia) The key experience seems to be an opening of the mind to the empathetic oceanic feeling of immersion into the collective unconscious and/or shutting off the ego's vigilant inspection. Any eastern or western mystic can elaborate-however obtusely-this state of mind for you (unscientifically). Read into that what you will. We will touch on this again later, because it is a key element in the evolution of our psychological makeup and dammed interesting.

A lot of the revelations we are witnessing in neuroscience have occurred as a result of the use of various brain imaging techniques, which include fMRI's and PET's. An fMRI is a giant machine that can observe the blood flow inside of your head through functional Magnetic Resonance Imaging. It does this by reading the subtle magnetic polarization of your blood. The presumption is that your brain is most active where the blood is flowing. So if we tickle your feet and a certain part of your brain receives a rush of blood flow, this part of the brain- more than likely-has to do with your feet. The brain itself has something like 20 billion to 100 billion neurons and each neuron can be either directly or indirectly connected to about 20 thousand more neurons. This level of interconnectedness is staggeringly more complex than the whole of the worldwide internet, and the inter-connection between various neurons occurs in more than one way.

When we watch blood flow in an fMRI, there is not a great degree of accuracy going on. I have heard an analogy that seemed to sum this up well: fMRI's are like dropping a microphone into a stadium of one million neurons. We can tell that the neurons are cheering about something, but we are not even close to being able to listen into a single conversation much less really understand who scored a goal, or if it is a music concert going on. We only can observe the relatively large movements of blood flow, which indicate only the *above average* flow. The whole of the brain doesn't stop working when one or more parts start to get extra blood flow. We are only witnessing and trying to interpret fluctuations above a median.

Scientists have put electrodes directly into the brain to pinpoint fairly specific groupings of neurons by sending weak electric currents directly into those places. This is mostly done in animals, because it is very intrusive, but quite a lot of this has been done in humans as well. Sometimes the doctor needs to have a very accurate understanding of where a disturbance is in the patient's mind. By probing the brain with electrodes, scientists have discovered that many aspects of the working brain are highly localized. Like the specific region in the brain that tells us we are inside our body or not.

The discovery of the phenomena of mirror neurons is indicative of the brain's vast interconnectedness, as well as its relative localization. It was realized that a monkey that had an electrode stimulating the mirror neuron region could not help but copy the actions of a lab assistant as she puts away the surgical tools in front of the monkey. The monkey would copy every hand motion as though it was also putting away the tools that it was watching being put away. The neuronal connections to the frontal lobes that stops us from automatically acting out our every thought was severed in this monkey and it could not help itself. The ability to mimic these observed gestures is intimately bound to the enactment of the gestures themselves. From this simple observation comes a flood of new understanding, so much so that many books have been written on this subject alone. Some of them debate whether there is actually an area of mirror neurons or whether this is all a reflection of a higher order of interconnectedness.

fMRI's and other brain mapping techniques have allowed scientists to have a fairly accurate understanding of the location and underlying structure of integration that ties together the various parts of the brain. But what is really exciting-to me-about neuroscience is that neuroscience is by its very nature multidisciplinary. It seems to me that everybody should be aware of this field of inquiry from evolutionary psychologists to artists and philosophers, because it has much to say to all fields of human understanding, and it is in turn benefiting from its ongoing connections to all aspects of human endeavor. Being able to trace what the various parts of the brain are doing, and how these parts are interconnected, has led to some surprising discoveries that have sweeping ramifications beyond our rudimentary understanding of how we think. The connection between language and motion mentioned earlier, and the recognition of the importance of the unconscious processes involved in emotions and with the amygdale specifically-which is very concerned with values-are two major philosophical paradigm shifts that may even have implications in the legal system. The recognition that the body is so closely linked to the brain should not be so surprising and I would now like to take a look at some of the implications of this.

A Body of Work

It appears that people with eating disorders or severe body image issues like anorexia actually see their bodies in a mirror as overweight, although they are severely underweight. The body map or the actual mental self-image of these people is so distorted that they actually experience and see their bodies as being overweight. When they look at themselves they see fat. I wish to dovetail a number of anecdotes together to make a much larger point, so bare with me. (See *The Mind Has a Body of its Own* by Sandra & Matthew Blakeslee)

Mr. Grunwald, a professor of neurobiology at the University of Leipzig, was doing experiments on the way that the brain registers touch by blindfolding people and getting them to feel simple embossed patterns like an X. Then he would remove the blindfold and most of them could draw the shape accurately after having only felt the patterns with their fingers - except for an anorexic woman who could not draw what she felt with her finger tips at all. Her brain had become-or was-wired in such a way that she could only discern the embossed letter under her fingertips. Her ability to resolve the figure or the acuity in her finger tips was very poor. This professor went on to theorize that anorexic women may have a poor relationship to the body map inside their brains.

He continued his experiments with another anorexic woman, who was also willing to participate. He dressed her up in a very tight fitting latex body suit that she could wear under her regular clothing. When she wore the suit, she was forced to be constantly aware of the feel of her skin and the movement of her body inside the suit. The woman very quickly began to gain weight. It is thought that she had begun to explicitly remap her body into a more accurate assessment of its volume due to her awareness of her body by constantly touching it herself. This mismatched body image seems to stem from an underdeveloped or atrophying of the right parietal lobe, which specializes in the spatial mapping of the body mandala. What the aetiology of this deficiency is questionable. It is probably the result of a collusion of different things. Whether this map/brain function has atrophied as a result of under use, or its atrophy gave the individual an incorrect assessment to begin with is a chicken and egg (nature vs. nurture) discussion. Because of the brain's ability to remap itself (neuroplasticity), it is also a somewhat redundant question, because it is more important to help the person move forward.

There is a Jungian psychologist who lives in Toronto called Marian Woodman who told this story on the CBC about a trip to India she made in the sixties. At the time of her trip, she was suffering from what would now be diagnosed as anorexia. She was sitting in a hotel lobby in India one morning, writing in her journal and a very fat woman sat down right beside her. So Ms. Woodman moved down the couch to give the woman more room, but the fat woman moved with her so that she was always touching Ms. Woodman. Ms. Woodman moved again and so did the fat woman until she had her pinned at the end of the couch. The next morning Ms. Woodman came down to write in her journal and the same scenario played out, but it seems that she sat with this fat woman for a longer time rubbing up against her. This went on for at least a week and Ms. Woodman was spending a longer and longer time sitting beside this woman not saying anything. Then one day, she came down stairs and the fat woman wasn't there. She began to look around for her corpulent friend, but she was gone. Another man walked up to Ms. Woodman who she did not recognize and this man told her directly that the fat woman was not coming to sit with her that day. This man informed Ms. Woodman that she had been sick and did not enjoy the feeling of her own body so he had hired her to sit beside Ms. Woodman every day until she felt better about herself.

This is the exact same idea as the latex suit except that it is not an abstract latex suit. It is a healthy real woman touching an uptight westerner with an eating disorder to help her understand that her body became quite divorced from her. The most amazing thing about this story is that the Indian gentleman immediately saw that Woodman was sick and intuitively or quite consciously understood what she needed to have happen in order for her to begin healing herself. He actually paid someone to make it happen and never told Woodman until he saw that she was getting better. She actually did get better and this was in fact a life changing experience for any number of reasons. My intuition is that well adjusted corpulent people should help anorexics, if they become hospitalized and the main body of the treatment should simply be motherly touching. I'm sure that a lawyer could find a way to construct a lawsuit out of this scenario and sue the fat woman for something or other.

This is the deep wisdom of yoga, which is again the re-linking of your body to your mind. You actually yoke yourself directly back into your body. We are a body-mind continuum and the body contains the desire toward the wisdom of health. Happiness cannot be manufactured or purchased. It arrives unbidden and this is the grace of joy. The surest route to joy is through the body and past the left brain. But of course, we need to create a special committee of egghead male specialists to compile data that reflect a 50 percent increase of the healing power of touching, 19 out of 20 times. We put ourselves right back into the box of our left brain thinking and we can't get out unless we actually do.

I wish to be explicit here: I see the overarching question in all of this discussion as, what the aetiology of this type of disease? Or what is the root cause of a radical body image problem like anorexia? Is it that the brain's body map is underdeveloped and the person simply cannot correctly asses their relative body weight or has the body map atrophied due to some poor life habits, possibly as a result of psychological abuse from others? Ballet dancers, for instance, live in a culture where they are constantly tormented into keeping their weight down. On top of that, they have such short professional careers that addiction to painkillers is very common as they try to squeeze everything out of their bodies in the few short years they have to actually perform. These eating disorders that we are bearing witness to are probably a combination of many things that lead people to this blindingly poor body assessment, including cultural pressures. These are western post industrial problems. What I have been led to understand is that we can change the way we 'think' about these things–largely by stop thinking about them all together-and through engaging in a process of work and a reconnection to our body/world, we can actually affect the way that the brain perceives our body map. By developing better body mapping through engagement in both physical and mental work, we can change our physical appearance and then actually reintegrate the unconscious wiring of the brain that is affecting the self-image. Bulimic models take note! In a very real sense it doesn't matter how you got here, it is how you are going to move forward that counts.

It seems that even doing simple things like walking on cobble stones or sand in our bare feet can help us to regain our consciousness of the body map, and this in turn, can lead us to losing or gaining weight.

Riding around on a four wheel rascal is the final coup de gras for a severely overweight person. They have completely divorced themselves from their body and integrated a mechanical device into themselves. Ironically, bodybuilders-to a certain extent-also divorce themselves from a realistic perception of their bodies. In some body builders' minds their muscles don't ever look big enough. They have the same body assessment issues as anorexic people, but in reverse. (They seem to be always looking at themselves in mirrors in the gym.) For overweight people, simple balancing exercise like walking on cobble stones in bear feet helps them to develop or re-establish the wiring involved in body mapping, by forcing the body to actively balance itself from the bottom up again. (Again with the yoga) It also seems that simply pretending to be doing the motions involved in exercise-in our mind's eye-can also help to re-establish and reintegrate the body mandala. The brain, to a certain extent, fails to distinguish between thinking of an action and actually doing the action. It strives to build up the connections between the neurons involved in the performance of the action you are thinking about anyway. By working the brain in this way, we are actually also firing the muscles involved in the action-to a very low extent-it is a start. Video games aren't all bad, but they are not good for us either. We are very good at distinguishing between real people and video avatars at the unconscious level, so we are not getting the benefits of running by watching our avatar run.

    It seems that with *sustained effort*, this remapping can become fairly permanent, but if not maintained, this system will atrophy again. If we remap the body mentally, we gain a more accurate picture of the body as the body actually changes. It is thought that people who lose weight too quickly, haven't had time to readjust their body's mandala to their actual size and they still feel themselves to be overweight-like a ghost limb. So, simply getting the weight off doesn't help, though it's a good start. This level of remapping can take years. A conscious re-envisioning of the body shape needs to happen to really have weight loss take hold. (Does my fat ass, look fat in this?) We will discuss the various aspects of the brain's inherent plasticity later. What I wish to highlight here is the importance of body mapping and the way that the brain perceives and then actually *is* the body.

Later on I will be discussing muscle memory as it relates to learning in sports and music, but I would like to make a quick note on what I mean, as it bears some relationship to the discussion above. Muscle memory, also known as procedural memory, implies that there is learning going on in the body, which may be true, but really there are many different parts of the brain that are taking care of all of these different spatial relations and movements. This type of muscular learning and body mapping goes on in the striatum cerebellum and amygdale areas of the brain specifically, though in a largely unconscious way. The term muscle memory is used in the sports world and is a bit misleading, and it has become a short form or catchall term like *emotion.*

There doesn't seem to be any real learning going on in the muscles themselves and we don't lose weight or learn complicated body movements in the muscles. It does seem that these complicated patterns of movement are downloaded or are linked with older parts of the brain where we are able to re-enact them unconsciously. Complicated muscular movements–like playing piano-take a long time to integrate and they are never performed completely unconsciously. This is the idea of 'patterning' where you repeat physical activities over and over like a free throw in basketball or a corner kick in soccer, or playing swing time on a cymbal or scales on a guitar. The pathways that we develop to connect these parts of the brain together-as we learn complicated patterning-will, to a certain extent, get unconnected if we don't keep using them, but they do come back quickly if we re-engage with them (myelination of the axons). This is why my guitar player doesn't know the cord progression, because it is irrelevant to the physical pattern he was playing.

This illustrates nicely how much of our life is unconscious. If we are driving our car to work along a roadway that we have driven many times before, we don't need to pay very much attention to any aspect of the drive. We don't consciously register the scenery or our physical motions as we control our vehicle. But, if we are driving in a foreign country in a different car, we can become very conscious of every aspect of the trip, which is very taxing on the brain's energy, because it involves so many different functions simultaneously, like mapmaking, observation of our surroundings and the muscle control involved in driving.

Reading the second chapter, I talk about Arthur Koestler and his analogy of the desktop computer and the guy who was kicking it. We are in a position to illuminate just how far forward or inward the science of the mind has taken us. Arthur Koestler came out of the enlightenment milieu when it was believed that reason was king. His concept of the brain accepted the narrow premise of the triune brain, which sought to explain that the neocortex of the human brain evolved over and around the reptilian brain. This model led him to believe that we have developed a supercomputer that more or less got stuck on top of an old piece of junk (the amygdale and limbic system). He also was led to believe this extremely misleading thought that we only use 10 percent of our brain. We don't we use all of it all the time. This limbic system seems intent on constantly getting us into fights by short cutting us into our emotional responses. I have seen film footage of people with almost no emotions and they are strangely ghostlike. There was the thought that the neocortex or new cortex suddenly exploded-in a relatively short evolutionary sense-inside our heads. While it did seem to grow quite rapidly in an evolutionary sense, it doesn't seem to be a brand new part of the brain at all. It is actually quite like the stuff that we already have. The way that Mr. Koestler saw things, was that we should strive to act reasonably at all times and we should always strive to gain mastery over our base emotions, which we obviously should do. What I have repeatedly sought to point out is that there is a very subtle patriarchal spin to this form of argument and this spin is shot through all of our notions of the primacy of logic and reason, which is in turn a reflection of our left brain dominated culture. (Read books by Antonio Damsio or Joseph LeDoux to understand the value of emotions.)

Obviously we do need to control our emotions, because we can't just punch everyone who presses our buttons. What is now being realized is that emotions are the building blocks of understanding and reason itself. The clean delineation between raw emotions and enlightened reason-that Koestler saw reflected in the brain's structure-is not so obvious or even desirable. It is certainly not how the real brain works. I won't go into it, but Arthur Koestler had some trouble controlling his own emotional outbursts. These outbursts are well documented in any of his biographies and so we can see that this was an aspect of his own personal shadow as well. The interesting thing about the shadow is that you can usually see it quite clearly in everybody else or even look for it in the structure of the brain, if this is your ongoing agenda which-one more time-the left brain supplies us. In Koestler's case, he displaced elements of his own shadow on to the wider sweep of emotional humanity. (We must be careful when we psychoanalyze.)

The Sea of Emotions

While we are dipping our toes into the emotional realm, I should like to explore some of the differences between the female and male brains now. What I will be talking about is largely from an author called Louann Brizendine who wrote a book aptly called, *The Female Brain*. Also see BSP#20.

As I mentioned earlier, young women spend an inordinate amount of time watching other people's faces when they are growing up. This makes sense from an evolutionary standpoint, because women historically spent more time looking after children and you need to know, if a baby was in stress. Women seem to be inherently much better at trying to gauge other people's emotional situations. As mentioned earlier, scientists have witnessed female chimpanzees prying stone weapons out of male chimpanzees' hands in an effort to reduce the escalation of injury amongst all of the parties that are in a fight. This emotional engagement of women has probably been *the critical aspect* in building intelligence in our children and a key element in the evolution of our species in general. (You can matronize that.)

In the book *The First Idea*, the authors build up the thesis that our recent spectacular evolutionary advancement-over the last 30,000 to 80,000 years- is quite possibly based on our ability to engage in emotional interplay. We became a smarter species as a direct result of more empathetic and engaged parenting -right brain. This thought seems to be backed up by the specific evolution of our color vision, which as mentioned earlier, is most accurate in the human flesh tone range. I will get back to this, but my big point that I am hammering home is that it's not our ability to rationally abstract that makes us smart, it's the whole of the integrated package. It is the reintegration of our rational that is important.

Men don't seem to be as hardwired for this emotional interplay and I'm not sure why, but I have my suspicions. Men seem to have a natural inclination toward more abstract topographical and spatial awareness, which of course, would be reinforced from the get go as they wandered about in the world hunting. I don't think anyone will argue with the thought that men traditionally do the hunting, sometimes with tools.

One of the points the Ms. Brizendine makes is that a woman has to move to extreme crying before a man will really take note that there is something wrong in the emotional environment. Men seem to need a catastrophic emotional display to simply get them out of their own self-absorption and see someone else's emotions. If a man wishes to know how successful his relationship to his wife is, he need only look at *her face* and it will tell him everything. Women display their emotions much more openly on their faces and women do cry a lot more than men for all sorts of reasons. It's just a fact. Read into it what you will. This seems to be part of what is behind Jung's reasoning that women are feelers (the redundancy of nature versus the nurture argument).

This difference is due-in part-to a different set of hormones that start changing the brain and body in our infancy. Women produce a lot more of a hormone called oxytocin, which does a number of things such as helping the womb to contract in child birth. Surges of oxytocin also stimulate the flow of milk in the breast. The aspect of oxytocin that I wish to highlight here is that oxytocin also encourages empathy, probably in tandem with our old friends the mirror neurons. As a result of this hormonal difference, women's brains are actually different and for a number of reasons - you can take it to the bank. This does not imply that men's brains are better or anything like that, it just means that evolution has seen fit to create two genders and hemispheres with very different agendas. Nature always seems to hedge her bets and she doesn't get stuck in either or scenarios. She always leaves room for ongoing adaptive change.

Doctor Brizendine highlighted the difference between men and women-in the BSP Podcast-with an example that I really loved. She was saying that she put a sticker on her husband's computer that said: *"I know exactly how you feel."* When she came home from a tough day at the hospital or wherever she worked and was venting about some problem, she noticed that her husband's first inclination was to analyze the situation and go into problem solving mode. This is not what women want. They want you to justify and acknowledge their feelings about what is going on. A definitive solution is somewhat inconsequential. She then went on to say that even though her husband had learned to repeat this handy phrase (I know exactly how you feel), and they both knew that there was a certain amount of insincerity in his using the phrase, she still felt better after hearing it. She could then allow her husband to go into his fix it mode. Husbands of the world take note! Because, I know exactly how *you* feel.

Nature has also seen fit to increase the amount of oxytocin in men when their partner is pregnant or when they are in love, as well as literally flood the female system with it at this same time. This might explain some of the reasons why we form an immediate attachment to our children when they are born, because our empathy is so ramped up from all the oxytocin in our system at this time. (Men also tend to stick their bellies out slightly when talking to pregnant women.) The whole process of child birth was truly a mystical experience for me. My male friends also commented on the timeless aspect of this environment. The interesting thing for me was that even the explicit recognition of this altered consciousness I was experiencing didn't bring me out of the experience itself. If you wish to experience this slowed down aspect of the mind, the other intense life experience is the marriage ceremony. Witnessing birth and getting married are truly life altering archetypal situations and it seems that your hormones enjoy forcing you into an explicit recognition of this fact. I had a dream about being in a grave yard the night before I got married. My old self was dying and my new partnership needed room. It is quite common to dream of marriage just before you die.

Human intelligence is attached to or chosen from the X chromosome and women have two sets of X chromosomes, so they have a much better chance of evening out any random mutation that may occur in the intellectual sphere. In men, intelligence has more of an 'all or nothing' feel to it. Men might be spectacular at math (the idiot savant) or physics, but completely inept at dressing themselves with a sense of style or interacting comfortably with anybody else (the great geometer coxeter). Women are rarely this lopsided in their intellectual development. This is not an indication of overall intelligence which, as we have discussed over and over, is contingent upon a vast number of interconnected things and I would always throw relative empathy into an estimate of intelligence.

One of the things that will make you smarter is pretending to be smart and hanging out with smart people. When we separate the perceived slower kids off into separate class rooms, we actually help to make them more stupid by association and we reinforce the constant unintelligent feedback loop through our conscious or unconscious cuing. Conversely, we don't make smart people dumb by having them mix with dumb people. We do our children-who are perceived to be stupid-a great injustice by reinforcing their stupidity when we move them into an environment of stupidity. Just looking at pictures of smart people can make you think you are smarter, and guess what? If you think you are smarter, you will actually do better on tests. If everyone around you is stupid and you think that you are stupid, guess what? (Placebos are real) Part of a meditation technique intending to help you develop a closer union with God is to explicitly imagine yourself as identical with your savior. By trying to envision and integrate the various aspects of Christ or Buddha, or Krishna you actually become those very aspects of the deity you are meditating on. I should think that Christ is thought of as being fairly smart.

Steven Pinker also tackles this belief that there is no difference between the genders in his book, *The Blank Slate*. The view that there is no real biological difference in the sexes became prevalent in the sixties and on through to the nineties as a result of the dominance of a scientific outlook called the 'Social Science Model'. This is the model that brought us, or backed heavily by, behaviorism which I will take a lot more shots at later. The three main tenets of this social science model theory are: 1. We are born as a blank slate 2. There is really such a thing as a noble savage, and 3. There is some type of ghost in the machine of our brains. The blank slate I have briefly discussed-and to some extent-the ghost in the machine as well, which is the implication that thinking or a soul exists beyond or separate from the brain (Epiphenomena). The noble savage is the thought that people in their natural habitats are benignly peaceful.

I will quickly demolish this as well. The idea of the noble savage seems to be proffered originally by Jean-Jacques Rousseau after a brief discussion he had with someone returning from Tahiti. Suffice to say people living in their natural environment are much more likely to be a victim of homicide or rape than anyone living in a modern western society, something like ten time more likely. The per capita murder rate in primitive societies, especially among men, is higher than our modern 20th century murder rate by almost double. This little eye opening fact includes all of the slaughter in all of the wars, including the two great world wars in the twentieth century.

But I digress. What I wish to stress yet again is that women are indeed different from men and this difference starts in the first 10 weeks after inception when the male's testicles start to form inside the womb and start to flood his bodily systems with testosterone. If you think this doesn't affect young boys, try raising some of your own. Only a person who has never raised children could think there was no difference between the genders, or someone that is so blindly fanatical about their viewpoint that they really are not looking at the real world at all. But no one in our great tradition of western science gets this type of ideological imbalance, do they?

Boys seem endlessly fascinated by trucks and cars, and tools and girls really aren't. They seem to be much more interested in role playing, like being the mommy or the teacher and things like that. There are always exceptions so please put back your knives. This makes sense from an evolutionary stand point. Female/male roles-to a certain extent-are the roles genders have embodied over history. Testosterone also predisposes men to seek multiple sexual partners so that their genes are spread more widely. This is how nature has arranged us, and along with our desire to procreate, she has put us in other conflicting situations where these 'primitive' urges must and should be contained.

From an evolutionary standpoint, women have a vested interest in finding a partner that will stick around and help with childrearing. Oxytocin and the accompanying skill of reading emotional situations help women suss out the best long-term partner. Of course, modern society is so completely different from the environment we evolved. These observations sound trite and they are. What I am driving at is that just because men have testosterone, it doesn't mean that they have a license to commit adultery. We are not just our hormones or the evolutionary heritage of our brains, and we cannot use these things as excuses for our bad behavior even though our alcoholic recovery coach tells us this is the truth. We are a socially integrated ensemble and there are prices to pay for fooling around or getting drunk all the time. The legal argument, that my hormones made me do it; will not fly in a courtroom. Women can and do choose to have multiple partners if they wish and it seems that nature has developed many "so called natural" situations where females find advantage by playing the field as well. There is one tribe in India in which the women have multiple male partners. (See Phantoms Pg. 183 from *The Thodas Tribe of South India*)

The thought that homosexuals are somehow unnatural has been fostered by people who have no real understanding of how nature works. Nature creates a wide range of beings constantly, and like our trying to express exactly what an impressionist painting is saying, what is normal in human behavior can lead you into a bunch of intellectual foolishness. It's better to have actually met some homosexuals and talk to them than try to define them in your tiny brain.

It is also important for boys to participate in rough and tumble play, which girls don't seem so inclined to get into. Boys learn a great deal about socialization and body mapping through this type of rough activity and they also learn a lot about their body's strength by punching each other. It has been proven that a lack of play can lead to a-social behavior in men, and this rough and tumble contact is an important part of male play. (Quickly: it seems that the one unifying personality trait in serial killers and sociopaths is that they weren't allowed to play at all as children.) We do our children a great disservice when we don't allow free, unstructured play out of fear they will get hurt. The world is a far less violent place than the 6 o'clock news makes it out to be and children need to have unsupervised rough and tumble play to develop their own boundaries. Breaking an arm can be a learning experience. I did it. If rough play were such a severe evolutionary disadvantage Mother Nature would have stopped it in many species. She obviously hasn't and it seems that the advantages to our cognitive ability outweigh the potential of accidentally hurting ourselves. Play engaged in willingly, is crucial for our ongoing brain development. The world doesn't come pre-wrapped in bubbles to keep us safe.

Early learning experiences in empathy and body mapping are extremely important to young developing minds. As I am now hammering into you, the importance of emotional engagement in learning is discussed extensively in the book, *The First Idea*. One of the authors worked closely with autistic children and their inability to engage emotionally seems to be the main functionally relevant symptom of autism. This inability may ironically happen, because autistic children have a heightened awareness of the emotions that they are surrounded in; and they cannot tone down or properly contextualize the experience of other people's emotions so they avoid looking at other's emotional displays. Overt emotions seem to cause stress in autistic children or they seem to be overwhelmed by emotions of their own and others. Autistic children have difficulty building symbolic meaning in the world and within themselves, because they lack or avoid the ability to engage emotionally. I will give an example: I heard about a doctor who was showing an autistic person a movie and tracking their eye movements. In the middle of a very emotional scene, the autistic viewer moved his concentration to a light switch. He was already fascinated with light switches, but the point of the story is that the emotional portrayal in the movie was inconsequential or perhaps simply overwhelming and so he looked to light switches. Autistic children tend to function largely out of the left brain

If a baby has autism, their inability to properly contextualize emotions can have serious effects later on. (Autistic babies don't seem to smile at all.) The first three years of life (while we function largely out of our right brain) are the crucial period for learning to read emotions and engage in emotional interplay with other people. The building of a symbolic representation in the world is needed to move on to higher forms of symbolic intelligence; symbols are being built by being double coded. *"In this way, complex regulated emotional signaling leads to more and more differentiation between the symbol and its external points of reference, allowing for greater and greater interiorized operations."* - *The First Idea* Pg. 286

Symbolic representation allows us to build a more coherent picture of reality, both inside our heads and in the outside world. Symbols point beyond one-to-one correlations and allow us to be involved in a deeper integration with things. We can then more clearly understand, or conversely, we can more easily interpret the world with using interconnected reference points linking us to the outside through our ongoing symbolic representation. The first step of symbolic abstraction/integration occurs when we are young, which seamlessly transitions into our language development; which is symbolic representation at the next level, and to a great extent, a repurposing or hijacking of the brain.

I will explain the ramifications of this thought and providing examples of symbolic integration, using an example from this book *The First Thought*. One of the authors Stuart G. Shanker worked with a woman in the United States called Sue Savage-Rumbaugh who is quite famous for her primate work. Rumbaugh has been working with great apes for decades, but this book concentrates on a species of great ape called 'Bonobos'. She has two star pupils that she is teaching to 'talk'. Their names are Kanzi and Panbanisha.

One day Panbanisha was walking around the forest with Mr. Shanker and she took him by the hand and then stopped and pointed to a fungus, then pointed to a board with symbols on it that she uses to speak. She pointed to the symbol for bad and after some time, Mr. Shanker realized that Panbanisha was telling him that this fungus in front of her was bad to eat. Mr. Shanker then went around the forest with Panbanisha for another hour and she pointed out all of the things that were good and bad to eat in the forest. After each lesson or example of something that was good or bad to eat, Panbanisha scanned the doctor's face to make sure he understood what she was saying.

These apes can articulate well beyond simple words like good or bad, but what is important here is that Panbanisha not only understood the symbolic relationship between good and bad things, she was also very concerned with telling this to Mr. Shanker, who she presumed did not know any of this information. After she showed him this first fungus and realized that he had no concept of what he could and could not eat, she felt compelled to teach him and then verify by looking at him in his face that he understood her. The important observation is that the ape scanned the doctor's face to make sure that he understood. The ape knew how to understand the expressions on another person's face and could also understand-through engaged empathy-the implications of the signaling that the other face expressed. This event happened only after the ape was very comfortable with Dr. Shanker and had become 'friends' with him. These bonobo apes also have the same range of color acuity in their eyes that we posses and they can understand the import of the subtle changes in skin tone or emotional expressions that occur on the doctor's face.

The above example really lays out quite beautifully how the mind works as an ensemble of the body/mind. Panbanisha has a very sophisticated map of her environment and one of the ways that she can explain it to you is by tying things in her environment to the symbolic/emotional concepts of being either good or bad. She can empathize with you by watching the emotional display on your face and she also gains understanding by watching you through the implication of your expressions, whether you understand her or not. The emotional display is occurring through both faces and in the associated body language of both partners that are involved, and this is the key to learning. It is the physical hook that symbolic or abstracted understanding hangs on, because it raises the overall energetic level of the input stimuli that causes it to be established as multi-valence memory. Without this physical engagement in the world and the attachment to an underlying symbolic layer (right brain), the world is simply an unanalyzed and fairly random, passive collection of facts. We have to fall down to learn how to stand up. If I went to Africa and watched bonobos in the wild for a month or so, I would probably miss all of the ongoing subtlety of their understanding of the world. The social cuing of this species is very subtle, and to really understand them, we have to integrate ourselves into the troop over a number of years.

There is a radio show called *Age of Persuasion* on the CBC and the host made the point once on the show that the way that you sell products is by connecting them with emotions. How do I sell bricks was the question. The answer is that you don't sell bricks, but you can sell the concept of a warm safe house with a fireplace and good food, and you imply that the bricks on the outside of the house are the best choice of building materials that will allow this inner harmony to happen. That is: you sell the symbolic and largely emotional representation of bricks. Also, it is easier to sell stuff, if you can hook it on to a set of emotional and unconscious, personal and largely sentimental reminisces (Jeep Patriot). Through this type of emotional engagement, you may help the client to understand that bricks are really the superior building material and-by implication-they are being cheap or uncaring to their family by choosing otherwise. Rational arguments can only drive sales so far, because they force the discussion into the intellectual abstract and you are not selling abstract bricks you are selling homeland security, and you want that blank check with the sentimental feeling it brings.

It seems that raw emotions are more diffuse and less rigorous, and they can also be a reflection of relative intelligence. They are linked more closely to the metaphoric and illogical unconscious side of our brains, which is the domain of the personal and collective shadow. A crafty sales man can enter the conversation through this back door and encourage us to open our wallets more easily. (Hitler sold us one huge war and George Bush sold us two others, and the blank cheque of homeland security. The NRA's answer to gun violence is more guns, but there is obviously no conflict of interest there. How about an armed guard at every school in America no matter what the cost, except for the poor ones?) The HBO series, *Mad Men*–about Madison Avenue advertising men in the sixties-drives this point home over and over. (The Kodak slide tray is called a carousel-arousing Disneyland sentimental childhood memories- not a slide wheel or spin do-dad)

Back to the great apes: another story in *The First Idea* was one day Mrs. Savage-Rumbaugh came into work after having only had three or four hours sleep, due to a heavy workload. The other ape that learned to talk is Kanzi, who when he saw Mrs. Savage-Rumbaugh, became very concerned with her emotional state. Kanzi went to great lengths to figure out if she was first upset with him or with some of the other chimps. *"In a flash his mood changed completely. He rushed over to Sue and, very gently, began to poke and prod her to make sure that she was alright. After she had passed this physical, he began to explore other possible problems. He pointed at the lexigram for bad and then stared intently in her eyes. He appeared to be asking Sue whether she was angry with him, and certainly Sue interpreted it in this way, because she quickly assured him that she wasn't. Then Kanzi hit the key for Panbanisha: was he asking whether Sue was angry with one of the other bonobos?"* Pg.178

Exactly like a mother with her child, Mrs. Savage –Rumbaugh is communicating at a very sophisticated and integrated level with Kanzi and most of the communication is in the form of non-verbal facial perceptions and is embedded in their associated context along with the implicit recognition of this by both partners. This ensemble conveys depth of meaning to any of the words that are being used. The words themselves are only a small part of the communication. She can sit with this ape and engage in very long complicated discussions about what they should do that day, where they should go and why. If you raise a child or fall in love with someone, you will understand this type of communication intimately.

One day, Kanzi kept insisting that they go to a specific place in the forest, which no one else wanted to go, and when they finally got there, it was realized that Kanzi had left a toy there he wanted to retrieve. This bonobo most certainly can envision the past and future, and this one ape in particular can move himself into a future environment to retrieve a toy from the past. In a nut shell: the ape is very intelligent.

There are a number of problems in trying to teach apes to speak. The first is that they don't have a voice box that can create the sounds needed to articulate words. This is actually a much larger problem, because along with a voice box, you need to develop the related brain architecture. A voice box won't simply evolve independently without a whole series of integrated elements within the brain that are both a reflection of its existence and the drivers of its creation; mirror neurons-which apes have, though fewer-and the associated creation of empathy and probably the ability to sing itself. Singing and drumming merge into a larger narrative; from that we both create and express (probably still relatively unconsciously), and from this, we can peek into an explicit sense of ourselves as separate individuals. This leads to the exteriorization of our understanding, which could gift us the ability to use an explicit denotative language. Learning to speak isn't like turning a light on to a blank canvas as in *Planet of the Apes*, and suddenly all the apes in the world self-organize. The canvas is blank, because its blank and it needs at least 50,000 years of evolution to build it up.

You could counter by saying, well the ability of humans to speak has been hijacked into areas of our brain that actually did other things before, and that maybe the monkeys are the same and we can simply hijack in the same way into their heads. They do have the same abilities, but in certain key areas we actually have quite a lot more. What I am trying to show is that there are an entire suite of things that need to evolve over time in confluence with each other and the denotative one- to-one aspect of our speaking, and the subsequent ability to write is only a very small sub-section that has become overly confused by its own sense of importance – because it does the talking.

So if we set up experiments where we put monkeys in a room alone with a ragdoll mother and a wire mesh mother that feeds them, and we try to determine if the monkey wants the affection of the ragdoll or the food from the wire mesh, we have completely missed all of the nuance that could be gleaned from the situation. These were the type of experiments that behaviorists performed in the 50's. (Harold Harlow in particular) I can imagine a nurse cuddling this baby monkey after the experiment and gaining far more information from looking at the monkeys face than any disconnected *facts* the ridiculous doctors gleaned. Though, in some footage of this experiment that I recently watched, the nurse was as detached as the doctor. Such is the power of indoctrination to authority.

Real understanding comes from emotional engagement and a relationship that is built over time, The ability of these bonobos to talk at all is a reflection of the whole situation, not only their ability to point to lexigrams on a board, but the ability of the researchers to pay attention and seek to understand the meaningful connections between the speech symbol and what is being talked about. (Of course, this is exactly where too much personal interpretation can enter into the process and we tip into the narrative based ologies that behaviorism sought to rid us of) All of this understanding is a result of the whole situation that the bonobos are in. They are talking because they have learned to study the faces of the researchers and this is crucial in that they are constantly inferring intent. Like us, they understand our emotions through understanding their own and this is the crucial step in higher cognition. This type of interplay is statistically irrelevant and not easily quantifiable. Thank God women are studying in this field. Incidentally, it seems that Kanzi very quietly mouths his words (talks) as he reads a sign (Embodiment).

I saw a show about chimpanzees that were rehabilitated after having been experimented on for years. The chimps were put into a nice habitat together and are allowed to live their days out in peace. On this show, one of the doctors who had done some really nasty experiments on them came to visit and the chimpanzees immediately recognized the doctor after having not seen him for 10 years. They were quite obviously livid. Why do we persist in thinking animals are stupid? What do we gain?

I want to quickly point out that B.F. Skinner, the founder of behaviorism, earnestly believed that a small cadre of dedicated scientists, in collusion with the federal government, should implement his behavioral methods directly on to our society for our own betterment. Behaviorism is the left brain's position in the world in a nutshell. (It would take a lot to fully back this up and I will explore it in another upcoming essay, but for now it would take us way too far a field) If the left brain (the far right in politics) is left unattended, and it sincerely believes that it is in charge, this is the type of political system it will seek to create. Plato pushed for much the same agenda - that a small cadre of intellectual elites should run the show for the betterment of all of us. I would presume that, because Mr. Skinner was so narrowly focused on his tyrannical outlook, he never realized that *everyone knows what's best*. You can ask anyone in a bar anywhere in the world and they will all tell you what they would do, if they were in power, and that my friend is the real problem. The tyranny of opinion needs to be spread out.

Only Change is Constant

I would like to take a brief look at neuroplasticity. It is now a proven fact that the brain can adapt itself over time, and by change I mean physically change – probably right up until the time we die. We don't stop playing when we get old; we get old when we stop playing. The brain can create new neural pathways and adapt itself to various problems that happen to us over time; for instance, adapting to the loss of a finger or our eye sight. The brain can also repair itself to a certain extent, even after such things as a major stroke, given an accurate assessment of the damage, and a timely program of mental and physical therapy. The brain cannot completely fix actual tears and ruptures, which resulted from concussion injuries, though some reintegration can happen by strengthening other axon pathways.

The mind seems to be its most flexible and its most physiologically changeable up until about the age of 25, but it never really stops being able to rewire and learn. Neuroplasticity was a concept that a few people had suspected to be true as far back as the fifties, but the dogma of science throughout the sixties was that the brain stopped developing in any real way shortly after birth. Much like the dogma of behaviorism or the social science model, or the circular motion of planets, or even the thought that a 10-pound stone would drop faster than a five-pound stone, this belief system effectively stopped all research in this area, until it was conclusively proven later against the myopic scientific blow back. The brain actually can and does constantly physically change.

In the *Brain Science* podcast, Ginger Campbell was talking about a book she read called *Train Your Mind, Change Your Brain* by Sharon Begley. The other book to read is *The Brain That Changes Itself* by Norman Doidge. These books both discuss neuroplasticity and I will get into this, but what really intrigued me about Sharon Begley's interview was the discussion about teams of scientists who went over to India to study the Tibetan monks living in exile in Daramsala, India. The teams were trying to find out if various meditation practices actually physically affected the structure of the brain, and it appears that they do in many beneficial ways, which I will get into. My lovely editor is also a meditation practitioner and she is wise indeed. The really interesting thing to me about all of this is that the Dalai Lama is actively encouraging the study of the sciences among the monks. The explicit stance by the Dalai Lama is that any Buddhist doctrine that is PROVEN incorrect by science must be acknowledged as incorrect. I just can't see the Ayatollah or the Pope, or Billy Graham (insert the name of any religious leader you wish to disparage. By doing so, you might gain a modicum of self-worth: HERE), going along with that truly enlightened stance. Who knows...miracles do happen.

In the treatment of both obsessive-compulsive behavior and depression, there have been great successes with mindfulness meditation practices. What seems to be going on in the brain-when people are suffering from these types of complexes-is that parts of the frontal cortex seems to be getting or garnering an overload of information from the emotional centers of the brain – primarily the amygdale. Obsessive-compulsive people, such as hoarders or compulsive hand-washers are continually thinking that something is wrong, and this seems to be due to a fixation on certain thoughts that they-on one level- understand are not correct, but on another level, are unable to stop thinking about. The particular aspect of these obsessive thoughts-hand washing, for instance-originate in the frontal cortex where most of our thinking and conscious planning occur. They will stimulate the amygdale where our emotions are activated. Or there is an almost constant vague feeling of fear in the form of hormonal signals etc., coming from the amygdale. (Yellow alert or let the eagles fly) These unspecified signals are grabbed on to by the neocortex and then given specific focuses. This feedback loop has been labeled a 'worry circuit' and obsessive-compulsive people have difficulty interrupting the ensuing feedback. As this circuit gets used more and more over time, the brain's ongoing ability to change itself, adapts its workload to this constant stream of information, and the connections–axons-multiply and also gets stronger (myelination). Neurons that fire together, wire together.

As an example in the real world (my favorite world), I may have the passing thought that I should buy a can of beans, even though I have 20 cans of beans already. This thought gets attached to some of the raw emotional anxiety that may be coming from my amygdale – concerning the future state of anything. I might then try to justify this emotion with thoughts like: what if they run out of beans in Mexico? Or I might eat a lot of beans this week and my daughter comes home and she want beans and I look foolish, if I don't have any on hand. They are so cheap anyway (in an effort to reduce cognitive dissonance). So the compulsive can't break the expression of this cycle of anxious feedback and over-thinking no matter how rational an argument is presented, because all these things might happen. What mindful meditation tries to achieve in these patients is teach them to detach themselves from their thoughts, and allow the thoughts to pass by without constantly feeling the compulsion to act on them, or even listen to them at all. In this instance, you are being taught that you are not your thoughts.

Behind obsessive hand-washing is the constant feeling that you are dirty, but what is really dirty is your own mind and your thoughts, since you cannot *not* think, and you cannot clean your mind. This inner dirtiness gets displaced outwardly and into things like hand-washing or two-hour showers. I saw a Qawwali singer called Nusrat Fateh Ali Khan and he was explaining to the crowd that you can wash your hands over and over, but you cannot make your heart clean by doing this. This is the essence of compulsive behavior. Excessive hand-washing is the physical manifestation of inward mental anguish or a refusal to admit unclean thoughts into your mind, or an inability to disengage from unclean thinking, or unclean reality. I believe true wisdom is a reflection of being able to allow ambiguity. In compulsion, you ritualize your actions in an effort to express them outwardly in an attempt to build a barrier between you and the world. This type of behavior is portrayed artfully in the movie, *The Aviator* with Leonardo de Caprio. Howe Mandel has recently admitted that he is obsessive-compulsive, especially about touching other people, which seems to be very common.

There is a tendency to ritualize your actions when you are confronted with feelings you cannot control. Most animals do this when they are uncomfortable. This drives the mental dissonance down into the body where it is somewhat pacified by repetitious movement. Yoga and making music is this process in reverse. You consciously ritualize motion to pacify distress in the mind through integration back into the body. The ritualization of movement is a founding element of religious practices worldwide. This subject is another essay.

Physiologically, obsessive thoughts seem to be magnified by an overactive left frontal lobe, which of course, is getting stimulated by all the worrying, and then we are in a chicken and the egg situation with an overt and vicious feedback loop. The frontal lobe actually gets physically larger, because of this over stimulation. This area tends to exercise more control over thinking patterns, because it is taking up more of the brain's energy. In other words, it is changing but not in a good way. Thankfully, patients can be led to understand that compulsive or even depressive thoughts they are constantly having, are part of the brain's own malfunction? People can be taught to stop over identifying themselves with obsessive thoughts or indeed over identifying themselves with themselves in general. It is a type of cascading malfunction or sickness, in that most *normal* brains don't have this enlarged area in their left frontal lobe or an overactive amygdale. Mindfulness tries to redress the balance in the mind by deflating the raging ego and allowing the more holistic right brain to slip in the back door. Yoga or any body work is an excellent way to encourage the right brain and or deflate the left, because the whole body map is the domain of the right brain. How many brainiac scientists actually do physical work?

What I am trying to illuminate here is really a huge thought and I wish to make it explicit in your mind. By the act of thinking with our minds, and actively being in the world, we are *physically* affecting the brain and the way that it works in the real world. By wishing or willing ourselves to change the way we engage in the world, we can actually change the way that our brain interprets the world. We can actually affect the physical construction of the brain itself. *We are the meaning in and of the world.*

The advantage that this type of treatment, over drug therapy, is that rewiring works from the top down by giving people the tools to change themselves, if they wish. Drug treatment works backward by suppressing the amygdale and/or the lower emotional limbic centers, and by also stimulating the frontal cortex or higher thinking "control centre". (Which seems logical, if you are attacking this problem with the thought to issue power over the environment? You would, of course, arrive at this conclusion, as I have hammered home repeatedly, if you are searching for an answer through the position of the left brain.) So drugs are suppressing the vague ill-defined anxiety of emotions and activating the conscious reasoning centers, but little or no learning will occur as a result of drug treatment. I presume that drug designers' thinking-in this type of drug therapy-is that the patient can and should be more reasonable, and eventually think their way out of this compulsive situation, if their emotional component is suppressed. (I am speculating, but this looks like yet another swipe at emotions.) This is more left brain for a situation that is caused by too much left brain. It's also possible that someone simply noticed that these drugs seemed to help people feel more at ease and that was the limit of their understanding (if it ain't broke, don't go fix'n it). There is no holistic attempt to search for an underlying aetiology as to why this specific patient has developed this specific disorder, because that takes time and money. (But hey we can afford a security guard in every school.)

Cognitive Therapy or meditation therapy focuses through mindfulness meditation to stimulate the lower limbic system (the emotional centers), while suppressing the tyranny of the thinking in the frontal cortex, or the more explicit aspects of the worry centers. This disassembling of the negative aspects of the ego happens through intentionally directing the thought processes away from the ego. I find this fascinating in that modern science is confirming the efficacy of a four thousand-year-old practice of meditation. I should think four thousand years of human study of meditation should count for some kind of proof. (Sublime western arrogance) If you wish to flip forward to the last chapter on Krishnamurti called, *No Guru,* you will see that his advice for becoming less hateful is to detach yourself from these types of thoughts as well. This is the mystic concept of self-annihilation, which allows the unarticulated and ambiguous ill-defined world to simply be. He advises that you fully acknowledge that hateful thoughts exist, but you allow them to move away and don't allow yourself to become attached to them. This is the essence of the Buddhist idea of non-attachment.

Thomas Metzinger sights the work of a number of researchers, Antoine Lutz and Ulrich Ott who have been studying meditation using EEG's. It seems that the sustained practice of meditation–over ten thousand hours-causes *"high-amplitude gamma-band oscillations and global phase-synchrony, visible in EEG recordings made while meditating."* Pg. 32 *The Ego Tunnel*- foot to A. Lutz. It is thought that the synchronous firing of a series of neurons is what creates the energetic threshold to be crossed that brings thoughts into our conscious attention. These types of synchronous wave patterns are associated with the perception of the various features of objects, length, texture and color, etc. Practitioners of meditation have long contended that there is a point where the ego or self-awareness drops off and you become immersed in an oceanic oneness (I excuse the poverty of language). What these studies seem to show is that the mind can achieve a form of synchronized integration in which the background of our integrated perception becomes the only perception. This is probably allowing the right brain its due or simply slowing down the areas involved in self-monitoring.

My admittedly weak understanding is that our conscious self-awareness is shown to be ultimately unimportant. This stepping aside of self-awareness emerges of its own accord through the ongoing development of a meditation technique. It cannot be forced into existence, because that act of force is a function of the left brain's egos desire to reassert by contextualizing, which is what you are trying to disassemble. You cannot attack your way to peace. I think that elements of this type of integrated brain organization are the key to understanding many so called mystic states, from the complete emersion into rhythmic dance and music, on to and including, the complete emersion in God-the ultimate paradox-of any mystic testimony. This is what I mean by grace allowing us access into happiness. As soon as you quantify, contextualize, analyze, measure etc., grace and or God-you remove them from experience and place them in the storage unit of the intellect where they immediately begin to die.

I think that this type of more integrated brain activity evolved as a result of and/or pleasant side effect of our long immersion in music. This engagement in music -among many things- has helped to promote an integrated sense of community through the production of empathetic hormones like oxytocin, which are known to be produced when engaged in both listening to and playing music. There is a whole cocktail of endorphins and hormones that are released when we enjoy ourselves and music. Some of this cocktail is even useful in the maintenance of the immune system (see *The World in Six Songs* by Daniel J. Levitin Pg. 98-99). Conversely, music may just induce positive actions within the brain and this was reveled in by our ancestors, simply because it feels good. Regardless, music and dance promoted social cohesion and personal wellbeing or even simply joy. These aspects of music allowed the opportunity for an evolutionary advantage to emerge. The suite of developments has been chosen over and over again and this advantage has worked its way into our DNA -if you will- to become an explicit genetic propensity. I personally believe that the Indian rishis in the Vedic time period of 3-2000 B.C. developed some of their explicit meditation techniques as the logical extension of their known hallucinogenic drug use and the rhythmic ritualization of the environment, which I'm fairly certain predates this period by tens of thousands of years. I will look a little more closely at this in the next chapter. I simply wish to show that there are, or can be found physiological and evolutionary underpinnings- left brain proof-to any number of so called flaky and or mystic phenomena, and that proof itself *is* an agenda of the left mindset.

This ability to consciously direct attention back toward better states of mind is -to my mind-the essence of psychotherapy by bringing various psychological problems to the surface or into your explicit consciousness, and become aware of the true nature of the situation by honest acknowledgement of the problem. Through this process of conscious acknowledgement, you learn to recognize that specific problems you have both are and are not the greater part of *you* or they are not part of your intrinsic self image. Ultimately, they don't exist separately from everything else, but they are enmeshed in your personal narrative. The meaning of this narrative is within your power to control.

Eastern philosophy would argue that we are all part of a seamless single entity.

This method of conscious recognition and expression are also how soldiers suffering with post traumatic stress disorder are being treated. If the terrible things that our troops have witnessed remain suppressed and locked below consciousness, they can continually manifest as a vague sense of distress just below the surface, and they can build up into emotional tidal waves. The real problem is not suppression. The real problem is our inability to actually suppress any truly awful experience. This idea of unconscious sublimation is one of the Freudian ideas that have gotten far too much purchase in the world. There is very little real science to back this up.

Thinking itself-for the most part-has nothing to do with what you would consider *you* both on an esoteric level and as a scientific observation. You may come realize that thinking goes on without you. By displacing your self-image, or putting yourself into a less self-centered context within the world, you learn to grow beyond your individual problems. A lot of what I consider to be the essence of creativity happens when you can teach yourself to get out of the way of the process of creativity. By learning to bring your problems fully into consciousness, you come to explicitly realize that the problems you are experiencing don't change at all, but you now see and experience the full dynamic of whatever it was that happened, and you grow to be less closely attached to it. There is very little in the world that hasn't been experienced by someone already.

There is no simple, quick solution to the really large problems in life. We must learn to grow beyond the problem itself, and if we adopt the correct attitude through conscious recognition, then these problems stop having a hold on us emotionally. In the world of science or religion, or any overtly constructed worldview, it will work out much better for you, if you don't cling too tightly to your ideas. They will let you down or get you killed, depending on how tightly you wish to hold on to and protect them. The first thing a 'proven' ideology does is kill somebody else.

As a caveat: any personal in-depth training, like cognitive therapy or psychoanalysis, is expensive and there is no shortage of suspicion (probably justified) within the heath care and insurance industry about the efficacy of psychotherapy or non-drug treatments in general. That which we cannot quantify, we have no power over. Unfortunately, there is infinite room for quackery and unprofessional misjudgment. Few people can afford a prolonged one-on-one treatment that involves anything other than a prescription for some drugs, especially under any personal insurance health plan, because the insurance company simply will not pay for them. Drug companies on one hand, are blessed with scientifically observable and therefore *provable* results.

As far as receiving a drug like Valium for depression, for instance, it is very hard to prove that people using it are *cured* in any real way. This is not just me rambling on about the world in a Pollyanna fashion. Even science agrees that anti-depressants don't cure you. They just help you to get some sleep. On the other hand, it appears that if people don't willfully seek to change their thought processes, they really do not change their thought process, no matter how much money or good-willed mindfulness meditation you throw at them. Mice that are forced to run on exercise wheels gain no beneficial effects to their overall cognitive ability. But mice that were allowed to run for pleasure and allowed to interact and play with other mice are appreciably smarter than other mice. There seems to be a direct quantifiable correlation between the brain's ability to physically change and improve and our intent or willfulness to actually engage in that change ourselves. We ironically must be taught how to learn, for instance. No one has perfect posture out of the womb. It must be worked on.

As an ongoing caveat to this caveat, in Saudi Arabia they rehabilitate fanatical suicide bombing jihadists with a combination of theological discussion and art therapy (primarily painting), which of course, is a program they can afford to run, because they are awash in money from selling us their oil. It seems to work. The number of incidence of recurring suicide bombers is very low. (For any number of potentially comic reasons)

So the essential realization that I wish to draw about neuroplasticity is that, if we learn to think properly, we can and are actually changing the physical structure of the brain. As we engage in learning new skills-like reading other people's faces with more accuracy-right brain again-allows more empathy to occur in us, which in turn helps us to better gauge other peoples' subtle emotional states. We are actually creating more and physically stronger neural pathways. The resulting build up of neuronal connections will stay with us-if we nurture them through our repeated usage-which allows us to get even better at these skills. There are a lot of different parts of the brain involved in this type of emotionally integrative interaction that needs to be inter-connected and a lot of the connections already exist, but need strengthening. (The brain allocates resources to heavily used axon connections through an ongoing firming process called 'myelination'. This is the building of a physical coating that strengthens the axon.)

It seems that musicians develop a physically observable mass of connections between the right and left hemispheres that non-musicians simply don't have. (The area between the hemispheres is called the 'corpus callosum'.) The buildup is suspected to be the integrative nature of music and it is also caused by things like using both hands simultaneously - that I have beaten to death just a little bit here. This development is also the result of the integration of the pre-existing division of labor between the different lobes of the brain that I won't get into right now. Einstein's brain had an abnormally large section where we know mathematical/abstract thinking is going on. Whether he was gifted this large part of grey matter or developed it as a result of his disciplined thinking is unknowable for his specific case. It is probably a combination of his inherent gifted ability (personality type) and his active nurturing of his own talent. (The gift of being able to do what you love.)

The down side of this is that, if a child is raised in an exceptionally stifled or abusive environment, such as orphanages from the communist era in Bulgaria/and Ukraine or the monkeys in the ragdoll experiments, try to affect any significant change, after certain various intellectual barriers have been established, is really fighting an uphill battle, because so many of the early opportunities (first 5 years) to establish this type of emotional engagement has been lost. There seems to be certain things that become fairly hardwired and more or less set at the neuronal level in the initial unfolding expression of brain structures that occur in early childhood.

The children in Bulgaria were strapped into chairs with a hole in the bottom to go to the washroom. They were 'trained' through severe under-stimulation to stop crying when they were hungry or uncomfortable, or whatever, because no one was coming to help them anyway. What psychologists look for in severe abuse cases is whether the children cry out for their parents, if they fall or hungry. If the children don't ever cry when they are distressed, they are probably being abused, because the children have been taught that crying leads to more pain and so they stop crying. This is suppression of emotions on a catastrophic level. These poor creatures from the orphanages are severely maladapted and socially inept, due to a complete lack of emotional engagement or even physical stimulation of any kind. What kind of body map could you develop, if you are strapped in a chair for these crucial developmental years?

The same guy who created the ragdoll monkey moms put baby chimps into a box for a year with no stimulation at all and some of these chimps didn't even have light for very long, and guess what? The poor chimps were psychotic and had to be destroyed. Thanks science. Check out what's going on in North Korea.

We in the west are initiating taboos all over the place so that caregivers can't touch children in case something inappropriate should happen. Scout leaders can't touch scouts or especially cubs or brownies. This is a sad situation. Children can't swing on swing sets, because other children might get hit. (University professors call these bubble wrapped children 'tea cups', because they shatter without the parents around to help them.) Thankfully, this is changing. The Ukraine is going through a similar problem as the Bulgarians have with their communist era orphans, due to the same type of ideological treatment. It has been found that when the kids become teenagers and released from the orphanages, they easily become drug addicts, which then leads them into prostitution so that they can supply their habits, etc. I would think that drugs have quite a lock on them, because street drugs do nothing but stimulate, which of course, is completely entrancing to you, if you have been literally starved for stimulation from birth. All of this mess seems to flow from an intentional lack of feeling relation as the communist government steamrolled its rational brave new ideology into everybody. It is overwhelmingly sad.

"Our ability to do science is rooted in our relationship with the universe, our nature as living beings. Our feelings and instincts are far more profound than our ideas. Our ideas allow us to imagine many things, but they can be unreliable, or misleading. It is the real world that

keeps us honest." – Neil Turok -CBC Massey Lecture: *The Universe Within* Pg. 14.

I am convinced that the deep and integrated teachings of authentic Yoga (not power yoga, yogersize or even simply Hatha/body yoga or any western commercial pulp fiction you wish to insert here) can benefit all aspects of the human condition. By becoming intimately aware of your body, you develop an excellent body map, and by doing integrated physical exercise along with breathing and meditation techniques, you slow down the brain's raging ego. This takes time, but it also allows you to gain insight into the simple truth that it's not all about you and your big Lincoln Escalade. My flaky contention would be that the universe/Atman/greater Self is inherently creative and lies in the background of our brain as an evolutionary result of what you might call the religious/musical instinct or the unconscious. We can all tap into this mindset by developing our skill at allowing the unconscious to come forward into our lives by simply getting out of the way.

Nothing More Than Memories

In psychology text books, you may find a quote to the effect that we can only remember seven things at one time. So the telephone companies in their infinite wisdom made a standard telephone number, seven digits long. This is the kind of erroneous, though relatively true notion that gets stuck in people's heads–like mine-and is accepted as a 'scientific fact' like we only use 10 percent of our brains. The real situation is that this idea of seven things in the memory refers to working or procedural short term memory only. I can quite easily remember my area code or the fact that I might be dialing a 1 800 number, as well as the number along with singing the melody to *Someone to Watch over Me*. This factoid sheds no light on the understanding that we remember things much more easily, if they are emotionally important. If a very sexy woman told you her cell phone number at a party, you would probably remember it quite easily and a lot about what she said and how she smelled, and moved etc. The reality with memory is that we remember things, if they have emotional import, but we don't subsequently remember the details as clearly or the wider reality of the situation as it unfolded; we only remember what carried the emotional value. If I tell you random numbers, you will probably only be able to remember seven of them in order, but what bearing does that have in the real world where nothing is a set of random numbers? You could train yourself to remember lots of random information for greater lengths of time by tying it to a melody. But what good is an ability to memorize random information or even PI to the 100th digit? It might make you better at jeopardy, but that is a pretty limited aspiration.

The brain runs at least two different types of memory systems simultaneously: declarative or explicit memory and procedural or implicit memory. Declarative memory is the various stories that we tell each other and the hippocampus seems to be the lynch pin in this type of memory. If the hippocampus is removed we don't remember anything longer than about 5 minutes earlier, and so all of our personal narrative after it is removed, is not set into our ongoing memory. Procedural memory is our ability to put on a hat, tie our shoes and walk to the store even though we may not know what the name of the store is, and we may be texting the whole time. Declarative memory can also have large elements of implicit/procedural content as well.

If the memory you resurrect contains strong emotional aspects, the ongoing remembrance of the experience can arouse any number of physiological responses beyond your control, like increased heart rate and fast breathing, etc. The ongoing storage of memory is reinforced by the initial and recent updated emotional impact, and if I have been through a trauma, the implicit emotional aspects of this memory will occur within us unbidden. This is because the various neurons have a tendency to fire in long and episodic cascades called 'entrainment'. The resulting emotional overload is coming largely from the amygdale, and if it is too overblown, you can have phenomena like post traumatic stress disorder or various phobias.

Long-term declarative memories are more gist-like and they tend to be episodic in quality. Every time we rummage through our memory, it's as if we pulled out the drawer or a series of draws all tied together to become what that *memory is*. We take a look at the storyline-that is the memory-then we put it back. What seems to be happening is that -in some sense-we are restoring into our brains a new interpretation of that old memory, because the memory is gestalt-like and metaphoric. We only really remember certain elements of the narrative explicitly, but we understand the import or temperature of the tale and we re-experience elements of the related emotional impact. In another sense, we are actually making a new memory every time. The memory we pull out and the one we put back, are not identical. The emotional impact is the same or maybe even slightly higher or lower, but the connections of the details have drifted one more generation away from the real thing. There is very likely reinforcement occurring from our inherited or ancestral memory systems as well, hence, the almost universal phobia toward snakes, spiders and the dark.

From an evolutionary perspective, we don't need to remember a lot of the details about a story. In many cases, the specific details really are extraneous. We need to remember the impact of stories and the abstracted symbolic import of things like dangerous situations. These types of experiences like being attacked by an animal contain an important loaded message in a condensed form that we can use and apply to other situations. (Stay away from tigers) The stories are abstracted and made into larger patterned frameworks and co-associated with symbols, like everything else. I believe elements of this process are in the background of our various religious narratives, but this would be a whole other book. Conversely, we need to remember how to drink water, but we don't need to consciously go through the process of remembering every time. If we encounter a very thick milk shake, we can access the drinking or eating procedural memories and combine them into a new milk shake procedural memory and immediately forget it as a conscious act.

An interesting thing about music is that people with severe memory loss -that resulted from diseases like Alzheimer's-can remember complete songs from their childhood. People who have no idea who they are or where they are can easily sing along with a song that they may not have heard for 30 years. They even know if you change a single note from within the melodic narrative. Declarative memory tends to be the first aspect of memory to deteriorate, and procedural memory tends to last much longer. You don't need to know who is helping you put your jacket on; you just automatically go through the motions and put it on. Memories are not stored in any one place. They are integrated across many areas of the brain simultaneously and I don't have a handy analogy to represent this aspect of storage, but music in particular, seems to resonate across so many interconnected structures and elicits such strong and integrated emotions, that it just doesn't wish to leave us alone. (See Oliver Sacks: *Musicophilia* or any Oliver Sacks for a lot more amazing anecdotes.)

It seems that the right brain is more geared towards novelty, exploration and bringing us new situations. The left side of the brain is more concerned with organizing and storing larger and more episodic/integrated memories and with overt comparison of larger patterns of stored information (the left loves what it has already). The right side of the brain is better at sussing out patterns and making or perceiving quick associative recognitions with new information. The left side of the brain has a higher concentration of physically longer and specifically dedicated neuro-circuitry, which probably reflects concentration on time-tested memories and the associated long range patterns that have become well established. These left brain pathways develop in strength through further memory usage and their initial long-term storage seems to be contingent upon our initial and subsequent emotional reinforcement. (See Elkhonon Goldberg's *The New Executive Brain or the Wisdom Paradox*)

"*If one had to encapsulate the principle differences in the experience mediated by the two hemispheres, their two modes of being, one could put it like this. The world of the left hemisphere, dependent on denotative language and abstraction, yields clarity and power to manipulate things that are known, fixed, static, isolated, decontextualized, explicit, disembodied, general in nature, but ultimately lifeless. The right hemisphere, by contrast, yields a world of individual, changing, evolving, interconnected, implicit, incarnate, living beings within the context of the lived world, but in the nature of things never fully graspable, always imperfectly known – and to this world it exists in a relationship of care. The knowledge that is mediated by the left hemisphere is knowledge within a closed system. It has the advantage of perfection, but such perfection is bought ultimately at the price of emptiness, of self-reference. It can mediate knowledge only in terms of a mechanical rearrangement of other things already known. It can never really 'break out' to know anything new, because its knowledge is of its own representations only. Where the thing itself is 'present' to the right hemisphere, it is only 're-presented' by the left hemisphere, now become an idea of a thing. Where the right hemisphere is conscious of the other, whatever it may be. The left hemispheres consciousness is of itself."* - Iain McGilchrist, *The Master and His Emissary* - Pg. 174-5

I will give a quick example of memory. If I went to lunch with my wife, there is very slim chance that I will remember what we ate, even 48 hours later, unless she told me she was pregnant or it was 9/11, or there was some reason that this whole ensemble was reinforced within that 48 hour window. Conversely, I may only realize that we were eating our lunch on 9/11 much later in the day and the memory of what I ate initially wasn't that important, but I may pick up on a detail of that specific lunch later so that I have a good story to tell. This detail may be only vaguely accurate (I was in a coffee shop when I first heard about the planes crashing in to the twin towers on 9/11), but subsequent emotional reinforcement occurs as I toddle out my constructed narrative, which may solidify the various aspects of the mundane things that were in my head. I go on to decide which of the relevant details are in the ongoing story line. After many repeated and emotional re-telling of this story, the formerly mundane aspect will become an explicit truth. (I had ironically just eaten a new maple jihad donut when I heard the news) This constructed truth would even pass a lie detector test unless a smart lawyer goes on to uncover an inherent ambiguity in my story. (No such donut exists)

It has been shown that if people are exposed to any kind of factoid, even though they know it to be false, a repeated exposure to this same fact will always seen to carry more truth. Our crazy former mayor Rob Ford convinced Torontonians that he is getting work done by repeating it over and over, even though every other councilor said he was the main impediment to getting work done. (Witness the incredible amount of gobbledegook that theosophy passed off as 'ancient wisdom.') We are inherently patternmakers and this probably has great evolutionary benefits, because we can establish patterns quickly (Right) and then download information and get it out of our explicit consciousness. Unfortunately for me, some of my narrative is constructed from long remembered stories in which I leavened my own relevant meanings. (The story about Marion Woodman in India leaps to mind) The story on its own doesn't carry as much weight as when it is allied with other relevant information, but it is the story that is remembered, not the discrete disembodied facts. (At least in my right-oriented mind) What would the universe look like, if the earth went around the sun?

Allied very closely with our memory, in terms of the accompanying architecture of the brain, is the sense of smell. Smell is the only sense that inputs information directly into memory regions for comparison. All the other senses go through a number of way stations before they are shuffled up and into any form of explicit memory. The sense of smell is wired into the older parts of the brain and is probably one of, if not, *the* most rudimentary or evolutionarily archaic way to sense our way in the environment. The part of the brain that deals with smells is based largely on a combinatory or integrative type of system. The sense of smell in humans is built through our ability to isolate particular smells; because we have a lock and key system we inherited on a molecular level, and then connect the smells to experiences or memories. This is another form of the double coding of our experience to emotions.

It is an open question as to whether we are hardwired to accept certain smells and reject others. Asian people find the smell of some cheese a bit repulsive and there are a lot of cheeses that smell like old socks or even quite a bit like vomit. In my humble opinion, they end up being the best cheeses to eat. But apparently, Asians have difficulty getting past the associations, unless they make an effort, which of course, they can do. Also, if they were not raised in an Asian country, they will not have this culturally associated bias. So this 'smell of cheese business' is cultural, but the aversion to the smell of feces, for instance, seems to be universal. But of course, it would be conditioned and not necessarily inherent.

So the brain remembers specific smells really well and then helps us to associate the smells with food that we want to eat or perhaps-on a more unconscious pheromone level-people we want to be with, etc. This is part of the reason that smells can trigger memories that are particularly intense. It unfortunately doesn't mean that smell-triggered memory system is completely accurate. You may remember your grandmother's perfume when you smell someone else's, but you don't necessarily remember exactly what the living room looked like and who was with you, even though you may seem to be flooded with all of the lovely details or your grandmother.

Marcel Proust wrote a book about Marcel Proust wrote a book etc.

Another aspect of this sense of smell is that we can learn to associate different smells with calming or meditation, but these associations are not intrinsic in the smells themselves. I once heard an interview with a yoga instructor who was saying that Sanskrit vowels such as Ohm resonated deeply within the human body and that the ancient Gurus knew this and made sacred utterings in such a way that they activated unconscious things from deep within the soul, etc. This is the same thing that aromatherapy is trying to do. It is really a chicken and an egg scenario and or right brain/ left brain scenario. Anyone that is experiencing aromatherapy or ancient Sanskrit sayings is already in a receptive environment and is willing to receive any association that comes along within the environment. Now, as I said earlier, it does not mean that there isn't an intellectual edifice that goes along with the Ohm chant or that the shape of these sounds doesn't resonate deeply within us or that the concepts aren't beautiful and full of meaning, because they most certainly are. I am simply saying that this contextual meaning is not a result of the inherent or intrinsic efficacy of this specific set of vowels in and of themselves. It is a result of the architecture of meaning that we bring to it. This is the same meaning that smells carry to us. You cannot disentangle these things from the context in which they exist. This conversely includes our belief that they are inherently inert – say… if you were a scientist. They are as inert as you believe them to be, or as full of wonder.

The particular vibrations that result from making the Ohm sound may cause a cascade of other properties to occur within the body that we don't understand, so I would advise suspending too strident a judgment here. There are many subconscious things going on in the world of smell that aren't clearly understood, such as how pheromones work in us. There may be certain physical properties that start to occur within the body when we vibrate at such and such a frequency… I don't know. My friend in India with the singing bowls certainly thought so. In terms of the way that a smell works in our brain and body-for the most part-I think we learn to associate things like lavender with relaxation. The smell of lavender is not inherently relaxing. We have learned to relax when we smell lavender, because we learned to relax when we smell lavender, and in fact, we do relax when we smell lavender. In the same way that we feel good when we force ourselves to smile. It is not an illusion and we are actually stimulating endorphins and a whole series of things start happening that lead us to feel better. People's faces don't become etched into a frown, because they are happy go lucky all of the time. If you think you're sick all the time, then you really are sick all the time, both physically and mentally. The mind expends much more energy in feedback than it does in feed forward mode, so it is constantly checking in with the body to find out how we feel. The body just goes ahead and feels and your body accurately represents the way you feel. If you are frowning all of time, your shoulders will slouch and you will lose energy and feel that the world is meaningless, etcetera. If you learn how to do standing back flips, they will definitely wake you up.

The way that smells affect us is a result of our evolution, in that we have come to accept many different things as edible. We determine what is edible by comparing it with our smell memory, which is excellent. As our species were spreading out of Africa and all over the planet about 70,000 years ago, we had to learn about a lot of different types of food. It was more advantageous for us to have a relatively clean slate in our olfactory sense, so that we could go on to develop our own associations about what was edible. It was also very advantageous for us to have a long and accurate memory of which smells were in fact related to edible foods. In fact, it was a matter of life and death. The vomit smell of some cheeses is a good example of the flexibility of this imprinting. We can learn to associate even this seemingly nauseating smell with something delicious. Like our ability to learn language, we are wired with a somewhat flexible strategy.

It seems that this highly combinatory aspect of the olfactory sense, may actually be a major contributor to how the rest of the brain developed. There is a thought that the brain's architectural development is more closely patterned after a combinatorial type of setup and that the ability to abstract and break things apart is a later aspect of our development. This ability to analyze has more to do with the advent of the cognitive capacities associated with the neocortex in the front of the head. Once again, even the most rudimentary living things can smell or sense chemical changes and react; so the most elemental thinking and earliest forms of decision making have always been associated with the architecture belonging to the sense of smell.

This combinatorial function within the brain makes a lot of sense when we start to think about how ideas occur to us. As Koestler showed us earlier, the real key to creativity and learning is the juxtaposition or bi-association of at least two different ideas (double coding). This combinatory ability seems to be the result of our ability to easily integrate left brain information and long term representational memory with the right brain's ability to rapidly associate and recognize/organize pattern along with deep connections into the older parts of the brain, including the olfactory systems. Nature does not stop at creating one way of solving a problem. She keeps on creating more and more, and then she saves them all.

Like our earlier association of the caduceus with the DNA strand or any number of blue sky scientific discoveries, we need this ability of hyper-integration to access and jostle long-term memories and facts. The discovery of the shape of the DNA strand is a reflection of our ability to connect real facts with other forms of information (unconsciously) into the right combinations, which creates a new representational metaphor, which must be recognized and tested consciously to asses if it is a correct representation of reality. An apt metaphor of this process could be the process of crystal formation in a saturated fluid. As mentioned earlier, Jung found that the shadow had an all or nothing feels to it and that it seemed to suddenly intrude into the conscious mind. The shadow is not necessarily negative, but it is underrepresented in consciousness. So if a scientist's main function is thinking, and the rational of the left brain's agenda, "sudden discoveries" in science would be an invasion of the under-represented right brain; and if you look at the discoveries I have been discussing, they all have a contextual penny drop aspect. The table of the elements only came about, because the guy who discovered it actually dismissed some of the atomic weights that he preferred for mathematical continuity. He was later proved correct and the weights he initially had were found to be wrong and his supposition was right.

The seeding of the environment is the collection of the real facts and observations that allows the molecules to skip over some of the random jostling and align more quickly. A lot of mental bi-associations happen below the threshold of full consciousness, much like thinking itself. I would lay my money that this type of unconscious collation is happening in parts of the brain that are closely associated to the olfactory senses. If only in the sense that hyper-interconnectedness is the over-riding principle in brain's organization. It seems that consciousness has risen as a result of our desire/need to instigate some form of CEO control over the various competing unconscious sub-systems (see the absolutely brilliant book *Incognito* by David Eagleman), possibly in tandem with our ability to abstract as a result of the development of the written word and its inherent abstraction of the world in the so called Axial age 500 B.C.E. This is the age of mankind when we literally emerged out of prehistory everywhere.

One of the hallmarks of dreams is this combinatorial aspect is that dreams seem to grab disparate aspects of your day. Sometimes the simplest gesture or some unobtrusive event of the day will come up in a dream, and then depending on your subsequent insight or interpretation, come to hold great importance. Sometimes the dream will connect these simple images to very remote and surprising memories. It is Jung's and my contention that the unconscious is trying to tell us something through our dreams and the dream images reflect the unconscious access to our unconscious understanding and our explicit consciousness, through this multi-layered mode of dream/speaking. I would be hesitant to think that any image in a dream is irrelevant. The really interesting thing is that this type of overt juxtaposition of images with seemingly unimportant information, and the heavily meaning laden metaphors that dreams seem to employ are accepted as a form of valid representation from within the dream world itself. (A very un-provable statement) This may also be why we are particularly susceptible (spellbound) by metaphors and fairytale type fantastic imagery in mythic storytelling art and music. They simply capture the non-explicit right brain welling up in the world through dreams. Poetic imagery resonates deeply with us, grabbing on to our archaic psyche below our ego, because it is a product of the very same deep and largely unconscious archaic understanding. Once again in Old Germanic a good story was called 'a spell'. You literally cast a spell out.

The earlier and more simplistic view of the brain that Koestler and others promoted was-amongst many other things- that the unconscious was a type of random jostling machine that throws ideas together, and if we are lucky, we have a good one popup like the discovery DNA. This is a simple representation of his ideas, but even as an analogy of a subsystem, it is wholly inaccurate and we have come a long way in our understanding of how much of our ongoing perception of reality is not consciously assessed. David Eagleman describes the unconscious as a 'team of rivals' in which each aspect of our unconscious is presenting a reflection of its perception and many of the mental constructions can even be opposed to each other. This is why the brain is so heavily invested in multiple layers of feedback and feed forward-nested hierarchies. Nature has loaded us up with many adaptations and competing systems of understanding, and each one is bidding for our consciousness. If another one starts to develop, she doesn't get rid of the old one. If the tension between competing visions is too much, the argument is shuffled upstairs for arbitration. A simple form of this arbitration is the vase and two faces trick in which an image flip flops between two faces, looking at each other with a white vase in between. One more time: we gain wisdom by embodying ambiguity.

Laughter, like smell, also seems to be an expression of our evolutionary advancement. It becomes more a more pronounced in the great apes with humans having developed the voice box and associated linguistic skills that allow us to really laugh. Koestler spends a great deal of time discussing laughter, because he smelled that it was important. Laughter-like music-fires the brain in a cascade that is the result of deep bi-association; and you need to be able to appreciate a joke by being able to gestalt (intuit below explicit consciousness) the many different aspects of the metaphor and implied drive of the narrative. Things like symbolic representation or mismatched linguistic tricks, or even the ability to release tension when being mocked in a tickle fight, are all indicative of our evolutionary advancement, in that they are understood in a non-explicit way and conscious analysis drains them of there being. Baboons laugh when they are stressed. What is the meaning of an Em7 chord? We cannot properly smile when asked-say by a dentist- when we actually grimace. A smile is a relatively unconscious action.

Pattern Makers

I think it is quite well understood that the unconscious does a lot of intrinsically creative work and that this is ultimately the reason why we have developed patterns of thinking and/or explicit concepts like the

Atman or God, or Homer's Odyssey of Athena. These metaphysical speculations and concepts have, in many instance, proved to be amongst our highest and most profound creations (like the hard nut of the sciences themselves), and I would be wary of psychoanalyzing these thoughts down into our 'nothing but' intellectual grist mill. Though the unconscious or at least our interpretation of it can be dead wrong, I would argue that the unconscious really is the ongoing ground of our belief systems and well of our ancient wisdom.

I don't know if God exists

I'm not competent to judge

I do know that what we believe

Can bring out the best and worst in us -Me

"Metaphysical speculation is music played by non musicians" - Stolen Byme

From my reading interviews with artists, and reflecting on my own experiences, I have started to realize that songs, books or paintings don't just pop out of thin air. There has usually been some sort of long or short unconscious brewing that has been going on before even the idea for a piece of art arrives for the artist to finally express; It rarely arrives fully done, though some contend that it does. This is also true of our explicit thinking and the real truth of the process is that we don't always completely direct our own thinking at all. This creates a real problem when we are trying to get to the bottom of the concept of freewill. As an example: I had been thinking about this book for over two years before I sat down and wrote any of it and then it just poured out of me, because I was ready to write it. The initial writing was very fast and extremely sloppy as I chased my ability to express ideas around. This seems to be a common experience with people who try to write books.

I had done a lot of research before I began writing. The first book I wrote was about 150 pages. I have since rewritten the entire book at least 13 times and parts of it (this part) many more times. I don't think this is the exception of how art and specifically writing happens. I would say that an ongoing assessment and reintegration of the piece you are working on is closer to the rule, depending on the chosen media. Poetry for instance, can happen very quickly. Many of my initial musings about how the brain really works were completely wrong and I had to correct many of the details of my thinking as I was confronted with accursed facts. The facts DO get in the way! It may seem that people are just creating art from scratch, but their creative acts are the culmination of much field plowing and weed pulling or even the clearing of whole forests of old growth hickory trees. Conversely, I have grown more comfortable speculating on what I understand now, for good or ill.

Artists or scientists, or students first become fascinated with something and then they start to explore this particular aspect of their world and they begin to learn about it (music or painting, letter writing, neuroscience or string theory). When they are sufficiently acquainted with the subject, they discover something new or start combining different aspects of their understanding in new ways, etc. This is how the creative act works. It seems to brew below our conscious realm of intention and it is a result of an ongoing meditation and fascination or attraction to something, hence, its close analogy with romantic love. Because we are fascinated, we willfully study and fill our consciousness with details about the subject, which gains in its emotional investment. We then become attached to our understanding and wish to protect it. This is the power drive, which we cast around ourselves. We may even come to believe that we are the thoughts we have created. This is an aspect of the grasping ego, which can only see itself reflected in its own history or constructed narrative by being objectified (tools, stats, philosophical systems, etc.) The ego seeks to convince us that we invented or even grasped-as in control or manipulate-the theory of whatever. In *The Ego Tunnel,* Thomas Metzinger argues that there is no definable property within the brain that is the self, because the brain is an expert at creating this illusion of self or ego-hood. It is also an expert at supplying a narrative to back up its ongoing creation. If you can be honest with your introspection, you will come to realize that ideas pop into your head despite any desire to control or initiate them. Of course, there is a directed spotlight of attention, but this is a very specific aspect of the intentional act of concentration.

In the next chapter, I will explore more explicitly our relationship with our conscious and unconscious perception and its relationship to the arts. I wish to point out that what neuroscience is discovering can be seen as a stunning confirmation of the root and essential message behind much of Indian philosophy, if you wish to see it this way. The East has constantly asserted that the ego is an illusion and that there is no 'I' at all. We are deeply connected to everything and our concept of ourselves as an ego is fairly arbitrary and deeply problematic. This is essentially, the difficulty of meaning. I came to his work way too late to talk about it in anyway other than V.S. Ramachandran is in absolutely in harmony with much of what I have come to understand. He has the advantage of actually being a scientist, but he is open and un-dogmatic, and probably a poet at heart.

I would add that the unconscious seems to prepare us for creative realizations; for instance, in the psychoanalytic situation, you will be presented with dreams even though you contend that you never regularly remember any of them. If you consciously take the time to go into the process of understanding your dreams and then actually see an analyst, you may unconsciously or quite consciously begin to meditate on your various situations. The fact that you start to dream at the beginning of an analysis and your dreams are concerned with your present situation, or they reflect a large component of your personal narrative, should come as no surprise. What is surprising is the depth or scope of insight that the unconscious brings into this situation. (The first dreams of an analytic situation usually foretell the whole subsequent arc of the analysis, but they are so 'symbolically dense' that they are very difficult to understand. Subsequent analysis is needed to fill in the details, and bring to the dreams and you the dreamer, a richer understanding.)

There are great similarities with the creative act and when you are actually working on creative projects. It is quiet astounding what happens spontaneously. As many authors will tell you, the words sometimes seem to write themselves; some say that they just have to let their characters speak for themselves, etc. and some explicitly say that this is not true. This wallowing in the unconscious (and passive right brain), is part of the addictive aspect of creating and being creative. Michelangelo said that the statues were already inside of the block of marble and all he had to do was clear away the rubble around them. This is not an exceptional or disingenuous attitude. And I don't think he was being snobby or intentionally obscure. I think he really believed this, or knew it to be true. He recognized that ownership of creativity is being dishonest. You can also see this clearing away of the excess rubble as the work of the left brain, as it tries to establish the specific form of what the right brain already understands is implicit in the unformed. This is how the left brain looks into the right when it stops saying no.

Why people become fascinated with certain aspects of their environment and not others, is what I don't understand, but how they become fascinated probably has something to do with their inborn temperament. I have learned to just go along with anything that really interests me. In fact, I have to consciously narrow the field all the time, and if I allow this fascination with a subject to go on long enough, or the reason why I followed this one route as opposed to another, will become apparent. Or conversely, I will read my own meaning back into my fascination later, and it really doesn't matter in the long run. It is still meaningful. Some scientists can do math all day long, where as others like Jane Goodall can spend years in Africa alone with apes; musicians have to play with other musicians and other people need to do sports, or dance. All of these activities can become creative explorations of the larger Self, but the key to being creative is to get out of the way of what is happening and allow it to take its course.

One of the intrinsic aspects of the mind is that it is creative or combinatory and we stop it from being so by enforcing our rational explicit egos on to it. Or we try to force ourselves down certain pathways due to our own egotistical drives. (This is my leading problem with overt and militant fundamentalism, which is to express the unforgiving desire for certainty. I think behind it is a desire to reign in the unconscious which always has a dark or at least very fluid and ambiguous way of being.) In a very big picture way I see it as the left brain seeking to impose order on to the fluid and ambiguous right brain with the left's ability to say no to information coming from the right. It would take a great deal of discussion to show why I think this, but the more I read about bilateralization the more I am convinced that this is so, and that I'm not alone in this understanding of the situation. There are any numbers of reasons for not doing the creative things you feel inclined to do. My personal feeling is that the journey itself is important. You may never do a great painting or write a hit pop song, but what you learn along the way about the world and yourself is the point. As my yoga teacher loves to remind me: all the obstacles that occur along the way are to be embraced as another aspect of the unfolding of the process itself. At the very least, you will have the knowledge and experience of having tried.

Art reintroduces you to life by lifting life out of our unconscious reality and displacing it into the symbolic realm, which can be quite ambiguous. For instance, we see flowers all the time, but we may not really look at them (due to a poor sensate function), then we see a painting of flowers by Van Gogh, and because it is art, we actually spend time looking at it. There is an Arabic thought that music resonates within us, because God has put all of the emotional states inside of us, waiting to be experienced and listened to. Music taps into the work that God has prepared. (Archetypes) This is true from the right brain's perspective, but it smacks of those dammed un-provable metaphysics. Another way to think of music is when listening to it, you slowly become more and more adept at experiencing the finer and more subtle emotional experiences through real engagement. This is true with all of the arts, although music specifically resonates at a very deep and largely unconscious level.

Because the right brain brings the world to us, and then hands it over to the left, there is a feeling that we already have an understanding of things like music, which in a very real sense we do. The right brain intuits music unconsciously and the left creates a narrative to convince us that we understand it so that it can be taken in by the ego. The right gives everything to the left to be represented and compared or analyzed so we have the feeling of it being familiar, and once it has been driven through the intellectual grist mill, it is returned to the right. This is how art reintroduces us to the world.

More simply put: you gain understanding by making an effort to really experience the world. So you build up or reinforce connections between different parts of your brain and this extra connecting and integrative mapping feels good and allows more to happen. Ironically, by displacing the world that we are discovering through art or creating symbols, we can actually experience the real world in a deeper and more integrated way. We invest the world with meaning through our symbolic displacement of it. (How's that for an egghead statement?) Art establishes-explicitly in us-the connection between life and a symbol, so that we can better understand the symbolic nature of reality. Art doesn't imitate life. It is life. Life is already symbolic; art and life are in bed together always. Art programs are the first thing to get cut in a recessionary budget. Thanks. I'll just re-count those beans.

If you wish to search for a creative outlet, you would do well to look back into your childhood and try to find something that you did that made you happy, like cooking or stamp collecting or whatever, and then follow your intuition and the excitement of feeling. Jung spent whole days and weeks on end-in his latter life-building elaborate sand castles with stones on the beach at Kusnacht. Through this type of play (immersion in the right), he deflated his conscious control, which allowed his unconscious to come forward. Play is an essentially pointless activity and that is the point. Much of the drugs taking by artists is done in the naive belief that they need to do this to create-or more explicitly-to tame their egos. The truth is that they learned to create in a drug-induced state and they can-if they wish-learn another way without the drugs. (Be careful not to throw your devil away though; you may throw out the best part of yourself.)

Let's say that you decided that you should take up diary writing. The first substantial benefit to you is that you sit down and decompress for an allotted time period each day. You could call this a meditation - I would. Secondly, you begin to consciously think about your day and the other people and things that are involved in your life, and by thinking about them, you displace them or actively move them into the symbolic realm of your diary. The third benefit is that through the continual process of writing, you simply get better at the craft of writing itself. You learn how to communicate through the written form-which it seems anyone who has ever written a school textbook-has never learned to do, so you have that going for you.

You may also learn to simply enjoy the act of turning a good phrase, which will start to happen despite yourself. Ironically, you learn to understand the world that is all about you and your place within it, by expressing your thoughts outside of yourself. When you write stuff down, you stop the thoughts from rattling around in your head unbidden. And best of all, diary writing is virtually free. You may start to suddenly experience your own clever turn of phrase or wonder at an insight into someone else's personality. This can be the unconscious coming to the fore and it feels like someone else is participating in your activity. One of the first things that Jung made his very busy and usually rich patients do was sit down and paint out their dreams for him. One of the main benefits was that they were forced to decompress, if they took this process at all seriously. If they didn't do this and/or take the process seriously, he would send them home.

I am not saying that your intuitive artistic mind is always right and that it will always lead you to the right answer within yourself. This is most certainly not the case. In fact, sometimes our intuitions can be completely wrong as we have seen with Kepler's harmonies of spheres and possibly the world of string theory. This intuitive/subconscious ability of the mind to juxtapose ideas in creative ways is part of its intrinsic spontaneous state, and the interesting thing is, that it *is right* about its intimations of the world and your inner self, a surprising amount of the time. (The periodic table) When it is right, and you feel certain that it is, it probably is. The proof of reality unfolding over time, and your own subjective feeling of whether you are right or not, is the best criterion that you have for assessing the correct path you have set out on, whether the path is dream interpretation, or stamp collecting, or character assassination in your diary writing. Reality or introspection will let us know, if this is really the best use of our time.

Life is to a great extent a self-fulfilling prophecy. If we believe that the sacred Ohm can bring our mind into a more meditative state, then we actually will train ourselves to enter a more meditative state. In some studies, it has been determined that people who watch videos of smart people, will do better on tests, and if you take the same people and bombard them with videos of dumb people doing dumb things, say most of the footage on Jack Ass (our evolution in action), they will actually score worse. Over the long haul, it will do you good to hang out with or be exposed to smart people, or be involved in a creative enterprise with creative people, or simply have the naive belief that you are clever. This is probably why self-assertive people seem to succeed, or why the smallest amount of praise can light a fire in someone. We believe something is true and we make it true, and we make something true by believing it is true. (Didn't you hear God telling you to get out of the way?) But of course, reality gets in the way of this Pollyanna worldview, but not necessarily within our minds. You cannot change fate but you can change your attitude toward it. It is also quite interesting to witness how some people around you will protest at your striving toward your own betterment.

Because of the mind's own neuroplasticity, you can actually teach your brain to work better, and affect the way it works on a physiological level. This makes perfect sense and goes a long way in explaining why psychotherapy works on someone who is willing to believe that it will work. If they happen to be working with a good doctor; their view of the world can really change. Conversely, if you are exposed to meditation or eastern philosophy/religion and you have an excellent teacher, you really are fixing yourself. (This is why the Dalai Lama IS the Dalai Lama) This also explains why a Nobel Prize winning scientist can teach some students and an inordinate amount of them will become Nobel scientists. A good teacher helps you to understand how to learn and be brave in your learning, and when you learn to learn, your brain can actually apply itself to anything. Or I should say: you learn to approach anything with an open mind and sense of wonder, which helps you to see through preconceived notions into the quanta-like essence of the situation. Same water different vessel. The desire to learn is both an inborn drive and something that we nurture within ourselves.

I have been practicing Anusara yoga recently. Anu means to hold or go after and Sara refers to the midpoint or centre of being or the heart. So Anusara refers to holding on to that which is important or trying to contain or express the essence properly. As discussed in Chapter One, there is a belief that if you can bring the body into balanced order, the mind will follow. This idea flows out of the belief that the universe is trying to get you into proper alignment and you are resisting this, because of your own ignorance – that is a result of ego attachment. If through your own will, you can integrate proper physical postures, and the resulting balanced harmonious thinking practices that go along with them, you can prepare yourself for a radical transformation called 'enlightenment'. The explicit intent of tantric/yoga practices is to allow and/or create an emersion in ecstasy. Be that as it may, I think this is essentially positive and I would say not a naive worldview, and one worth trying to experience. We in the west are too focused on thinking as the ultimate tool. We have put all of our eggs into this basket of thinking, and the basket leaks or is logically paradoxical. *See footnote at end of book.

I would like to expand this argument about the perceived meaning and associative meaning, and the relationship that they have to smells one step farther. This is really one of the main drives of this book. I was listening to a gospel recording yesterday and the singers were singing about how Jesus helped them to see clearly, and how they were healed by Jesus. This is kind of like aromatherapy in that the singers have externalized the source of their understanding of Jesus. They have come to realize greater meaning in their own lives through an external realization that was delivered to them through the writings or sayings of Jesus. I could argue that the singers have actually changed themselves through a paradigm shift and I don't think that many of them would be overly concerned with my intellectual analysis. I think other parts of the Jesus gospel would emphasize the belief that Jesus is within you anyway and you only need to discover this fact to be healed. (The kingdom of God is spread out all around us.) What I wish to emphasize is the thought that it is important to externalize this aspect of your new understanding to a certain extent. This should be done so that you don't begin to identify too closely with the process you have undergone.

If you become completely identified with your own healing or the healing power of Jesus/ Mohammed or Vishnu etc., and you believe that this essential shift in understanding was entirely a result of your own willpower, or that *you* have caused your own change or healing, then there is a very great temptation to believe that you have achieved some form of unique Godsend knowledge. (This is one of the great temptations of Christ and the Buddha; also why Prometheus was punished by the Gods, and also how the ego seeks to regain control). If it is true that you have received God-given wisdom through merits of your own, there is the probability of mistakenly believe that you should be able to proselytize to others and heal them all as well. This can lead to the belief that you are some form of a new prophet with a mission of your own. Jung called this type of mental trap 'inflation' and this is why Mohammed (in my opinion) declared that he was the last prophet. He was warning people of this inflationary spiral. Even trying to heal other people can be a reflection of your own selfish power drive and an underlying desire to control them. It is not necessarily a reflection of love. You cannot heal other people. You can help to create an environment in which people can heal themselves. You can lead them to grace.

Hitler is a very good example of where a severe inflation can lead you. Hitler always believed that his intuition was correct and thank heavens he made some serious blunders as a result of not listening to his generals. He always insisted on trusting his divine intuition. Hitler seemed to have been extremely intuitive-and also a left hander-and he was a master at reading the temperature of the crowd he was addressing. This consistent over-assessment of his intuition was possibly a reflection of an excessive right brain–left hand-attachment? His main blunder was in believing that retreat was cowardly and he lost his army in Russia, because he refused to retreat and regroup repeatedly.

I would love to know what the executives of GM, Chrysler, all the banks and especially Lehman Brothers, were dreaming about (I mean the actual dreams they had while asleep), just before the government stepped in and bailed them out, or in the case of Lehman Brothers collapsing? Because these companies are also a perfect example of an indestructible inflationary left brain-power-drive-hubris, which leads to a fall (too big to fail). It seems everyone else in the world was making small cars along with the egotistical lunacy of giant SUV's. A snake extended these executives a nice juicy SUV (bank swap, predatory lending, etc.) apple of greed and they just had to bite. And they believed that they were doing the right thing right up until it all crashed around them, and when they all got bailed out, the banks went right back into the shit pile. (Mistakes were made, but not by me) This ever-so-human folly is largely due to our ability to retroactively and selectively create a left brain self-referential narrative that we feel fits best for us. The banks showed that they were indeed naked and ashamed, but meaningless in the face of a raging billion dollar ego, and our inability to punish them. (Pompous crocodile tears, Lance Armstrong and Rob Ford). My larger point is on the nature of meaning and how it is important to understand how we achieve meaning or embody meaning. However, if there is temptation to completely identify with that understanding of meaning, then this is not a good path to enter into. We have the right to work. Work only exists now.

Our brains are highly adaptive meaning machines and the largest part of the way that we consciously interact in the world is through the presumption and recognition of consensual meaning that we accept as explicit and true. Most of the time this is enough to get us through, but sometimes it is not. True wisdom lies in being able to distinguish the difference.

"True wisdom lies in conceding to ignorance that which is its due." - Author, *Proof and the...* Pg. 312

"A passionate public debate recently took place in Germany on freedom of the will-a failed debate, in my view, because it created more confusion than clarity. Here is the first of the two silliest arguments for the freedom of the will: "But I know that I am free, because I experience myself as free!" Well, you also experience the world as inhabited by colored objects, and we know that out there in front of your eyes are only wavelength mixtures of various sorts. That something appears to you in conscious experience and in a certain way is not an argument for anything." Thomas Metzinger, *The Ego Tunnel* - Pg.130.

This quote is a great example of scientism. Do we all know that *everything is only wavelengths*?

Break My Heart Again and Again

This all leads me up to a very interesting aspect of our human psychology that I would like to briefly explore called 'cognitive dissonance'. The underlying idea behind cognitive dissonance is that humans have a very hard time holding conflicting viewpoints within their mind, and they will usually choose to believe one viewpoint and then consciously or unconsciously seek out ways to reinforce their initial conclusion. This is a reflection of the left brain's narrative agenda and its obsession with what it already knows. As an example in the real world: (from *Mistakes Were Made*) if I wished to join a fraternity to bolster my social mobility, I may need to undergo some form of hazing ritual. This will undoubtedly be humiliating and I may seek to later justify this humiliation by convincing myself that this really is an excellent fraternity and this 'temporary suffering' is worth a lot more than it really is.

Physical hazing and humiliation are key ingredients in any brainwashing regime. I will defend the administering of the hazing ritual and its results as a form of justification to myself so that I don't have to admit that I was a fool to participate in the first place.

No one wishes to have their belief system undercut and so most people will seek out ways to reinforce their existing position instead of jettisoning their ongoing intellectual and emotional investment. This is the phantom limb pain, caused by a right brain stroke in a nutshell. This type of reinforcement of a non-rational opinion (that's not my hand beside me), is at the heart of what is now understood as cognitive dissonance or the opposition of conflicting views of reality. George W. Bush and Bill Clinton firmly believes that taking the leash off of mortgage restrictions, and allowing unrestricted and unmonitored banking practices in general, was the right thing to do against a subsequent landslide of evidence to the contrary in 2008, but of course, George W. Bush in particular, will and is still defending his position. The position of intellectual rigor is always right. The world messes everything up against your will. If logical rigor is the agenda, everything must take a backseat, including reality.

Another example: if I was given the choice of getting a free jar of jam by choosing between one that I knew and two other unfamiliar types, I will choose one of the other two instead of the familiar well-known brand. But, if I was offered to choose between 20 different types of jam, I will gravitate toward the brand I know already, because I have been presented with too many choices, or too much dissonance. I will default to my comfort zone. The left brain loves what it already knows and it has the power to say no to 19 other types of jam.

There is a creationist argument that runs something like: God has placed the skeletons of dinosaurs all around the world as a test to the faithful, so that on the day of judgment, He will be able to sort out the non-believers from the people of the Bible. God created everything six-and-a-half-thousand years ago and so God must have created the dinosaur bones. This is a feeble attempt to find a reason for God's doings. I would call this magical thinking and it is an extension of participating in mystic and an obvious result of left brain's narrative default against ongoing cognitive dissonance. This example is at the extreme end of this type of phenomenon, but very similar attitudes prevail in all aspects of life.

I have been listening to the Ricky Gervais's podcasts with Karl Pilkington and Pilkington practices magical thinking all of the time, as he develops scenarios to justify his understanding of nature. He constantly refers to his brain in the third person. He posits that his legs are doing something else in his sleep or that two other flies are ganging up on a third, because they are mean and he feels compelled to break it up, because the fight is unfair to the third fly. Ants seem to be lost and confused, if their ant hill is ruined or any manner of anthropomorphism is enlisted to explain his observations. The interesting aspect is that Pilkington develops a story to contextualize his observation and will not be convince otherwise. This is a simple aspect of cognitive dissonance. I think that in his mind he is thinking deeply about nature, but he lacks the scientific structure to see through his own ongoing projected self-deception. This is how the medieval mind worked before the rational and explicit logic of science swamped us.

What we read into a situation, and what is intrinsically there to be exposed is one of the main problems in modern psychology. In the eighties, there was a wave of patients who became convinced that their ongoing problems were caused by childhood sexual abuse and they were completely unconscious of this abuse, because of their ongoing repression (a now disproved belief that humans have a natural ability to not remember terrible things: the ocular Freud). Various analysts became convinced–because everyone else believed it-that unconscious active repression was the root cause of many of their patients' psychological problems. It seemed that those being analyzed had 'come to' the realization that they had been sexually abused in early childhood, and they had repressed this information. The difficulty with this diagnosis is that it is almost impossible to prove if the sexual abuse really happened, because it happened so far in the past. The belief-within certain parts of the psychology community-was that patients regularly repressed their terrible memories and they genuinely were unconscious of them. Like the alcoholic Kennedy story and our train wreck of a mayor, Rob Ford. It is convenient to blame someone else for your problems and come to believe this is true.

Since the eighties, it was realized that very few people are completely unconscious of traumatic experiences. The real problem with traumatic experiences is that people have great difficulty actually forgetting them and now-after a number of devastating legal cases-it was determined that in many instances the specific charges of child abuse were either completely un-provable or simply untrue. But of course, what analyst could 'afford' to relinquish this position retroactively? They believed they were right and invested in this belief up to the hilt. Would they be in serious legal difficulties, if this phantasm is exposed? They would also have to acknowledge the fact that they were not helping people understand themselves, but in fact, caused a great deal of harm, by literally tearing families apart – accusing a member of the most heinous and unforgivable crime. (This is *power* or the *wish* to heal, trumping humility and love.)

We all seek to create a unified understanding of ourselves in the world and this can mean leaving out, or glossing over other aspects which disagree with our viewpoint (the brain does this all of the time), even or sometimes in the face of the most well-reasoned argument, or when presented with simple and easily verifiable facts. People with a really terrible mother will, ironically, defend their mother stridently when confronted with the facts of abuse. This was at the heart of the soupers vs. sparker's debate we saw earlier and also the ongoing belief in string theory, or my understanding of Jung's work etc. This is also at the very heart of the book that you are now reading: we all create some form of meaningful world view and I would contend that this aspect of our thinking is a reflection of the way the brain has evolved, but *we seek to see through the negative aspects of this*. A state of unending mental dissonance is stressful and probably at the heart of most mental anguish. Unfortunately, the left brain's ego seeks to resolve tension through the assertion of will. Hitler thought that there would be a sudden turnaround in the war, right up until he shot himself.

There would not be much dissonance in my ongoing religious belief system, if I was born a Hindu in Varanasi, India or an Anglican in early Victorian England or if I surrounded myself with (Tea Party/occupy Wall Street/subprime mortgage) like minded activists. All the people and the larger social environment that surrounds me would reinforce my understanding of a God-infused world, and I would easily discount any opposing views that did not accord with this idea. This ability to relentlessly dig for actual facts is at the heart of the scientific approach. It is a process that must be rigorously learned and the process itself is counterintuitive to us at a very basic psychological level. That the world is counterintuitive is the underlying problem with explaining or deeply understanding the mysteries of Quantum mechanics and is at the heart of the intellectual disconnect between what makes *sense* in our world and what is really going on at the subatomic level, or apart from any form of representation that we construct.

Most mythologies are seen as an attempt to resolve cognitive dissonance or at least display it. Things like seeing astrological beings in the sky or the universal occurrence of creation stories and their related mythological genealogies. Mythologies can also be understood as a representation of the texture of the poetic mind (right brain), and as we try to impose logic or analyze this way of understanding the world, we seek to kill it. (Frankenstein chained to a rock) On the other hand, the fact that we dream may have evolved as a result of our unconscious nature trying to resolve this same internal dissonance, in that dreams try to project us forward into the future instead of leaving us in the sentimental past: dreams offer us a way forward and beyond our present problems. Dreaming presents us with a multilayered and symbolic 'answer' to our unresolved and largely unconscious issues. I believe that the unconscious can connect us-through dreaming and other inherently creative methods-with more archaic strategies of dissonance resolution, or put us in touch with wider and more ancient evolutionary aspects of the human experience. (I believe this is the essence of the belief in past lives.) The template of the same basic human psychological problems has arisen in us over and over again, and in some sense, we as humans are a temporary manifestation of a rich and ongoing process. World mythology or deep religious insight is the collective, outward manifestation of the individual and an inward observation of the unconscious dream world.

I was watching a travel show about India and the host went to Darjeeling. He met with a fellow who grew tea by fertilizing his plants with diluted cow dung that had been aged inside of a cow's horn and buried for some amount of time under the ground. (On a symbolic level, the cow's horn is associated with lunar and feminine aspects, which I'm sure played into this belief system.) This fellow happens to grow the most expensive tea in the world, which is raffled off every year to the highest bidder. I'm sure that some clever scientist could prove that burying the manure inside of a cow's horn was a pointless exercise and he may seek to prove it by setting up experiments where separate batches of tea were grown in similar hill side areas without cow horn manure in double blind conditions etc., but I am also sure that this experiment would not convince this fellow that the cow horn dung was irrelevant. (Metaphysics by non-musicians) The long and short of it is that regardless of which farming practices this fellow chooses to use, or which belief system he functions under, he has gotten himself into a position imbedded context-where he is growing the most expensive tea in the world. And like our proving that homeopathy doesn't work, trying to dislodge this cow horn belief system would be difficult and ultimately pointless. Everything in this fellow's life reinforces his belief in cow horn manure, because he actually grows the most expensive tea in the world and you can take it to the bank.

Because we believe that homeopathy makes us feel better, we actually feel better or grow the world's most expensive tea. For many people, the severity of a headache can be reduced by simply telling them that they just received a shot of morphine. Conversely, you can give them a shot of morphine and convince them that you haven't given it to them, and they will feel no pain reduction at all. We seek to understand the world in the terms we have chosen to believe and we disallow information that contradicts our cherished understanding. The job of science is to build our understanding of the world by using methods that can be verified independently, and by constructing experiments that don't allow the ever-present human bias to enter into the results. Science as a project takes a certain amount of humility, in that any ongoing belief system you construct will certainly be undercut at some point. Conversely, some scientists seem to arrogantly believe that they have the right to convince us that God is dead. I'm still waiting for the corpse.

I am completely prepared to acknowledge that we have constructed God as an extension of our wish to resolve our earthly desires or whatever, but I still don't see this argument as the nail in the coffin that ends God's existence. I think we should relish and actively participate in the fact that we have created such an incredible idea, or articulated so many profound religious worldviews. To my mind, this concept of God is the pinnacle of human speculation and it is reflected back to us constantly in an infinite and wonderfully-manifold enterprise that is the world's mythology and religions. I also would add that God is in the deepest and most paradoxical layers of scientific thought. We can experience this truth by diving deep into our own psyche. I would also add that this type of revealed introspection is the essential *experience* – not simply a thought process-that is sought in ritualized drug use or the inducement of trance states in all so-called primitive societies, which drive us into the arms of the metaphorical right brain through disassembling the strictures imposed by the left. You've got to get in, to get out and get back in again.

Free Ketchup

There is a raging debate in the neuroscience community about whether we are deterministic or whether we embody freewill. Michael S. Gazzaniga in his book, *Who's in Charge* develops some of the best arguments I have heard yet, and I would like to summarize them quickly. The main argument against freewill comes from a number of studies that imply that our motor control commands occur inside the brain unconsciously before we are aware of doing something like moving our limbs. Scientists found that there is electromagnetic information rattling around inside our heads a micro second before we consciously decide to do anything. So the supposition is that we actually don't have freewill and that everything that happens to us is causally determined by electrochemical processes proceeding or, *outside of* our explicit conscious control. Or that our unconscious is actually directing everything and we effortlessly construct an ongoing narrative that enables us to believe that we have willed things to happen, like moving our arms. There are a number of reasons that this argument is wrong and I will unpack them for a little bit, because I find it fascinating and it's my book.

First: because it can be proven that motor commands occur before our overt conscious and directed will to move them, does not mean we don't have free choice to do anything. Many people choose not to commit crimes all of the time. We could all engage in illegal activity all day long, but we don't, because we are embedded in a society that frowns upon this behavior. Evolution has formed us with some elements of a self-evident pre-existing moral code-like our consensual agreement that the world exists, or words mean something etc.-and these ideas run very deep. Almost everyone would never even consider having an incestuous relationship and we don't have to ponder whether we should be worrying about a bottle neck in the genetic code. We just feel morally outraged at the thought of incest. And so we choose not to have an incestuous relationship over and over again. Now, you may counter that our desire not to have incest is unconsciously generated by unconscious evolutionary pressures, as in Freud's Oedipus complex, and in fact, we still have no freewill in this situation. But it seems to me that our ability to decide not to do something is as relevant as our unconscious drives seek to stop us. Again, nature only instills a propensity to act in certain ways we decide by not doing something or by saying no to not doing it.

The second element in this argument is an extension of a metaphor that Mr. Gazzaniga developed that I think is brilliant and has really hit home with me. Mr. Gazzaniga compares consciousness and or freewill to a metaphor about the nature of traffic. Traffic cannot be understood, if you study it from the level of a single car's individual parts – say... the steering wheel, nor can it be understood from studying an individual car as a whole. Traffic can only be understood when you look at the way thousands of cars self-organize and follow rules that have been learned or 'imposed' by naturally occurring or consciously observed constraints (traffic lights and passing lanes, etc.). In this same way, you cannot understand our freewill by studying the electrochemical interactions of a single neuron or even by completely understanding the interactions of all the major components of the brain. Freewill and our ability to be law-abiding citizens can only emerge at the level of a collective society and our freedom is imbedded within the larger context. To speak of a single individual alone in the universe as being law-abiding makes no sense and so freewill does not occur until you are set within that context of various constraints that are the essence of a collective society. This is known as emergent behavior and I will discuss it later.

If you only studied the universe at the quantum particle level, you would never be able to predict the world of Newtonian physics, because it is in no way implied by the behavior of quanta. So if we search for freewill at the level of causal interactions between individual neurons, we will completely fail to understand the meta-level of human interactions that are involved in our social relationships. I also realize that Evolution is a meta-level phenomenon. To say that giraffes have longer necks to reach better food is a far too simplistic statement, because they also have long legs, which are an advantage to avoid being eaten. The long neck may be the result of these animals having to overcome the difficulty of drinking with their unusually longish legs, etc. The real story is that with any of the single examples-out of context- which we try to establish as a driver or retroactive form of causation in evolution is only a single aspect. We impose it as a drive when we reverse engineer, and nature doesn't reverse engineer anything. Giraffes have developed all of the things that go into being a giraffe as a result of evolutionary pressers acting within the complete ensemble of the world in which it exists.

The real key to a deep understanding is having the proper metaphor and I see this as religion's strongest suit – at its deepest level. Religion has always supplied us with metaphors that hold a completely separate truth and I think science has quite often been forced to develop the same tangential type of thinking in order to explain its confrontation with unending complexity. Chaos theory and fractals are an excellent example that I won't get into here. It is my belief that scientists are chasing metaphors and that the meta-nature of metaphors is what religion-at its best-always strives to supply, and science is now playing a game of catch-up or return. I would also argue that the concept of God emerges at a higher level of complexity just like the phenomenon of traffic and we still have no proof, but we do have another metaphor.

Embedded in this neuronal conception of our 'absence of freewill' is the idea that consciousness and freewill are synonymous. The meta-view (thanks to Iain McGilchrist for this), is that only the left brain seeks to posit itself through explicit ego-driven consciousness. Just because we are not conscious of every single detailed minutia in our world doesn't mean we are automatons. Being unconscious of various elements of ourselves (like the firing of neurons before we act), doesn't strictly imply a loss of overall control. It only implies it if we seek to establish ego-driven consciousness as the controlling entity, or in fact, if we think that control is the point or to be even more redundant, we only see it this way, because we feel compelled to establish a point at all. Being and consciousness exist in all shades of relative ego-driven awareness and we are both free and not free depending on how you wish to evaluate the situation and I would argue that you are both wrong and right to say we aren't free. When someone murders someone else, we feel in our bones that they have taken on the mantle of divinity, in that they have decided to arbitrate between life and death.

> *"It's not that we don't have freewill; it's that we do not have it."*
> *"Freewill doesn't exist when we look at it from nowhere."* PS

To sum up: we have freewill, even if it is an elaborate illusion created by alien overlords who would seek to enslave us by creating the illusion of freewill. This seems in my mind pretty much proven and I don't care if it isn't. There is a movement that is trying to force our recognition that there seems to be no identifiable source of freewill. This is because they are trying to explain everything as though our brains were the centre of a maniacal universe of self-righteous introspection, created by analytical reverse engineering. To a certain extent, I simply choose to believe, place value and love my right brain, in the illusion of freewill, because I seem to be the sum of many of my own reasoned choices. Fate's hand is always looming at the back of my head. Maybe I was always going to write this book, but after having spent so much time on it, I firmly think that it was my doing. The Dalai Lama is after all the Dalai Lama not Bob the Michelin man. I'm going with jerk school on this one.

The brain can to a certain extent create new neural pathways and teach itself new tricks. The exact extent of the brain's ability to do this is still being looked at, but it seems as though some pretty radical changes can and do occur. We teach ourselves to become what we teach ourselves to become. Different parts of the brain can change from their regularly associated tasks and take over new ones. For instance, if you lose your sight, parts of the brain that is regularly associated with sight, will start to take over other functions. At a certain point though, things are less flexible, for example, you may never be able to speak a foreign language without your native accent, if you begin to learn that new language after the age of 25. Though, I am convinced that you could learn to fake the accent, if you really tried, and thereby, convince listeners that you were fluent in the language. Actors seem to learn to do it regularly.

Meditation is not some eastern mystic mumbo jumbo. It actually encourages the brain and the person to be more relaxed, receptive and empathetic. Meditation creates and nourishes neural pathways that help the brain to remain that way. Simply not talking for some time every day helps the right brain to engage with us. Whether the particular Buddhist or Hindu tradition you approach meditation from is correct, must be judged from the overall actions of each practitioner and teacher. Buddhist monks don't seem to get into a lot of barroom fights, and Buddhist's are pretty low on the killing and crusading end of things. Of course, the Crusades weren't the fault of religion, right? Meditation also encourages us not to hold on to negative thinking, because it realizes that we embody what we think. People who act out their aggression are actually aggressive. The distinction between acting and being is somewhat arbitrary and you don't control aggression by pretending to act it out. You control it by controlling it. If you swear all the time, you are the torrent of swearing.

What is the meaning of life is a dumb question asked by egg heads that don't go outside enough and play in the sunlight with other people. It is the question itself that seems to be reasonable, and above all, logically constructed. It obeys syntactical rules, but it is actually not a question. It is a joke. Representational language itself tricks us into accepting the question as reasonable. Life is meaning, is the answer. You go into life. You do not observe it from your armchair. Things get ugly and you deal with them. Life is beautiful and you revel in the bedazzling awe of it. You participate in the grand play and I do mean play.

The psyche is life – deep and endless. There are many layers and we should not be content to flit about the surface. We will not heal ourselves in a passive state of ignorance. A new Dolce and Gabbana handbag will not heal us. We really do make ourselves healthier by engaging in life. Play seems to be the key in that it leads directly to joy and the opposite of play is not work, it is depression.

"I cannot run, but I can walk much faster than this." – Paul Simon

There seems to be actual inborn elements of ancestral memory or archetypal templates. I personally believe this is the root cause of people believing that they have encountered past lives, though the Buddhists and Hindus contend that some element of individual souls actually migrate. I certainly don't know the answer to that one, though I would be inclined to have a look into it a little more closely without a prejudiced attitude. But I like flaky left wing ESP type science.

Lastly, don't trust anything I have said up to this point. Take it from me, I wouldn't.

Oh yeah and *just say NO to negativity*. I want that on a T-shirt.

Along with, *"Don't chase the light alone."* And *"I am definitely here."*

6 THIS WAY UP

"The river is not only passing across the landscape, but entering into it and changing it too, as the landscape has 'changed' and yet not changed the water. The landscape cannot make the river. It does not try to put a river together. It does not even say 'yes' to the river. It merely says 'no' to the water – or does not say 'no' to the water, and, by its not saying 'no' to the water, wherever it is that it does so, it allows the river to come into being. The river does not exist before the encounter. Only water exists before the encounter, and the river actually comes into being in the process of encountering the landscape, with its power to say 'no' or not say 'no'." –The Master and His Emissary Pg. 231

In this next chapter I will be looking at the world of modern music and creativity within the arts in general, with a view towards gaining a deeper understanding of the nature of these paradigms and how they relate to the rest of the book. We will focus a lot more on music, which is the most immediate of the arts, the most difficult to render into words and my personal favorite.

It seems that musicians have actually caused change in their brains, which has resulted in it functioning in an observable and more integrated way. Music involves so many different types of information all happening simultaneously, and a musician's brain tends to be more highly or at least differently integrated then a non-musician's, especially the linkage between the left and right lobes. Music involves the development of a lot of different cognitive skills that allow you to appreciate the lyrics, emotions, cadence, rhythm, both large and small pattern recognition and/or the elements of explicit and regimented musical composition, along with eye-hand coordination across both hands.

Music is embodied and that is its strength. We are truly robbing our children of an amazing opportunity at brain growth when we don't expose them to music. Gutting music programs in the educational system are denying our children the chances at better brains and children that are good at music have proven to be better at math. The arts do not lead directly to jobs like computer programming or bean counting, or door hinge greasing. It is unfortunate there is the thinking that the arts do not deserve the extra money and time to give our children. I would counter that we as a society ultimately want people with flexible minds in the world, not people who punch in computer codes all day long and are profoundly bored when they are doing it. Music and the arts actually create a better brain, not just in my flaky left wing Pollyanna idea of what a better brain might be. Science -despite itself- is finding hard evidence that this is actually so. You can literally take it to the bank - just not right away. You will have to wait a few years for its liberal flowering.

"Perhaps this going 'through' a thing to find it's opposite is an aspect of the right-hemisphere world, in which 'opposites' are not complete, an aspect of its roundedness, rather than linearity. However, I would say, at the risk of pushing language to or beyond its proper limits, that time itself is(what the left hemisphere would call) paradoxical in nature, and that music does not so much free time from temporality as bring out an aspect that is always present within time, its intersection with a moment which partakes of eternity. Similarly it does not so much use the physical to transcend physicality, or use particularity to transcend the particular, as bring out the universal that is, as Goethe spent a lifetime trying to express, always latent in the particular. It is also a feature of music in every known culture that it is used to communicate with the super natural, with whatever is by definition above, beyond, 'Other than' ourselves." - Iain McGilchrist, *The Master and His Emissary* Pg. 77

Music at its best absorbs you completely while you are engaged in the process of listening to or playing music. The linguistic aspects of the brain are engaged while listening to lyrics and the emotional centers in the brain are triggered by the overall ensemble of harmonies within a piece. The emotional feel of certain cord structures and the way that these deep emotions can overwhelm us seems to be music's deep inherent power. Though, how the individual timber and feel of certain combinations of notes reaches us so deeply is a bit of a mystery. Music certainly disassembles the ego in that we are usually unaware of ourselves when we are listening to it. This absence of the explicit ego and the embodied reveling in the ability of music to contact/represent/be our emotions is probably one of the basic reasons music is enjoyable. You and your brain simply enjoy being engaged, integrated and multitasked in real time in these different ways. Music as an art form cannot escape the linear nature of time. Music must occur over and within time and therefore you must become engaged in it - to *listen to* it.

Certain chord progressions and melodies do imply very resonant emotional responses; at the simplest level minor chords are more sad or melancholy than major chords. You would not write a triumphant military march in minor chords (though reveille ironically is in a major key). There is a paradigm common among musicians in which each key or individual chord of a progression, or in fact each single note, can be related directly to a single specific color. I have heard Joni Mitchell (who is largely untrained in terms of musical theory, which is obviously no impediment to making good music), talking about why she liked working with the saxophonist Wayne Shorter so much. She said it was because she could tell him to play some orange over a certain movement and he understood what she meant. Joni also has the luxury of being a fine painter as well. From within my own universe, and through my conversations with painter friends, I realized when talking to them about painting that we are really talking about the same types of elemental things (on the deeper levels) when discussing music with musicians. I would say art is 'a sensitive articulation of a vague inner dialogue' except that this is not nearly enough verbiage to sensitively articulate my own vague inner dialogue.

"Art is a sensitive articulation of a vague inner dialogue."- I am pretentious or tweet that shit.

I recently heard an interview on the CBC, discussing synaesthesia, which is rewiring or perhaps more subtle integration of the brain where people hear colors or taste sounds, or associate various geometric shapes with certain colors. For instance, the letter A may be distinctly pink and seven may be blue. This is the most common form of synaesthesia. In another form Em7 will be seen as a predominantly blue or mauve chord with the other harmonious colors and shades also mixed in. It seems that many composers over history have had this rewiring to a greater or lesser extent, and many people have it right now (Stevie Wonder, Billy Joel, Rachmaninov and Eddie Van Halen were all mentioned). This ability seems to occur more frequently in artistic people. Or conversely, allows them to embrace the arts or actually drives them into an artistic life, because the arts are so much more intense or multi-dimensional to them. (Billy Joel wrote a piece of music for his daughter in hunter green. I just think that is wonderful and magical.) My understanding is that ability like this allows or prepares the individual for the ability to understand music, or indeed, many sensory experiences, in this multi-leveled way. I would also presume that anyone with this ability would become especially sensitive to external stimulation, because all sensual stimulation would be multi-leveled.

Whether all people with this gene would see an Em7 chord as distinctly blue or other notes as specifically orange doesn't seem to be the case. Some people have written down their own approximate color associations and other musicians have elaborated their associations into their own system. Other synesthetes seem to be able to relate to these associations, but it's not a lock fit. The Em7 chord being blue may be something like aromatherapy, where the artist has learned to associate blue with this specific musical harmony, but it doesn't seem to be entirely this way. All people with synaesthesia do not explicitly see the Em7 chord as predominantly blue. This is probably because few people with this ability even understand that they have an extra ability until it has already become an explicit or individually understood talent. I think that more sensitive musicians/artists who don't have this ability could also be taught an associative process involving direct color matching to individual notes and chords. This associative ability is interesting in that it is not some random rewiring. The brain seems to easily embrace the world in this multi-leveled way.

* *See footnote at the end.*

There is also the thought that this is the initial state of the brain in younger pre-linguistic children and that we all start with this way of undifferentiated perception. As we grow older, we further delineate our perception of different aspects of the environment, probably as a result of our brain growth, which is a result of the pruning that happens around the age of three to five years (this is probably un-provable). It seems that the different sensory sections are usually physically close together in the brain and synaesthesia seems to be a type of spill over between sections. The subsequent growth of the brain is not under the chaffing rule of some uber-comptroller with a sensory agenda. Some individuals develop a more fluid sensory integration.

My personal belief is that many people could be taught to listen to music with their eyes or listen with a greater sensitivity of the other senses; for example, people can learn to feel certain chord progressions with more emotional intensity and this *ability* to cross-wire is always inside of us, as with the ability to grasp metaphors. Who will thrive with this teaching is still probably a matter of inborn temperament or early childhood exposure, which is what I am driving at here. Temperament is a result of an ambiguous correlation between what has been given to you genetically (through ancestral reinforcement), and what you grow up to accept as culturally normal or what you discover on your own as you follow your inner daemon or not.

This somewhat selfish will to follow your own inner urge is what separates the expert from the hobbyist, and also what drives someone to put in the time needed to be either good or excellent at what they do. For instance, Ustad Ali Akbar Khan describes the moods of raga Mian-ki Todi, which is a morning raga. The mood in the piece is one of devotion, a little pathos and heroism. These ways of describing music would have more impact on you, if you grew up with an intimate understanding of Indian classical music in India. But again, I believe that we all could participate in deeper understanding if the will to understand was somehow lit within us as we were growing up. We could all be culturally conditioned to be more accepting of this more metaphorical feeling/right brain mode of understanding. I love the thought of a heroic mood in music.

This way of expressing the mood of a raga is culturally explicit and totally accepted in India (if Rachmaninoff tells you this piece is blue, then it is blue). At the very least these musicians use and learn to understand these metaphorical ways of discussing music as they seek to articulate what they know and feel to be true. Also, artists and musicians have-through practicing their craft-literally developed more of these integrative pathways in their neural network between the literal and metaphorical aspects of their brain because they think about music and use both hands to play it. Written Chinese characters use similar pathways. This may explain the constant head-butting between science and religion. They are both wired to misunderstand each other at very elemental levels, as a result of their different specific trainings and neural orientations.

The other interesting thing about hearing someone talk about synaethstesia is that this whole metaphorical correlation between music and color -that I had heard about years ago and had thought was simply a quaint idea- instantly became explicit and real. Instead of a metaphorical poetic connection, I now understand explicitly that this is the way that some people experience the world they live in (like chimpanzees cupping each other's balls or auras). This connection had been an interesting analogy for me but something I couldn't find a way to directly apply. This is another aspect of Koestler's bi-association, which is an intrinsic aspect in the *Act of Creation*.

This idea of bi-association has been rattling around in my brain for 25 years or so and like so much else in this book, I have found some explicit and less than explicit reasons for how we allow the creation of new ideas in our mind or why we find humor funny. In the *Act of Creation*, Koestler discusses his ideas over hundreds of pages, all in an effort to round out his metaphor of bi-association. I read his book and tucked this idea away for many years, and then I heard an interview with someone talking about brain evolution and how the combinatory aspect of the olfactory sense may be a blueprint for much of the brain's subsequent architecture. All of a sudden this whole metaphorical paradigm becomes explicit and rooted in the real world. Instead of being an analogy that I exploit within a poetic idiom, there is now some tenuous, though real, connection to the hard sciences here.

This is where the human mind will constantly outshine computers. Computers cannot make this leap between storing the metaphorical idea for 25 years and then re-envisioning and connecting it to a set of scientific facts, or indeed another metaphorical representation. The integrated brain can flip flop easily between the implicit and explicit or Sukshma and Sthula. It is only because Koestler made such an impression upon me in my youth that I have been compelled to read into any neurobiology; and, of course, I could be very wrong in my assumptions here because of an explicit will on my part to build up my own somewhat coherent world vision. Time will tell.

I Don't Mind

    I will now shift gears completely. I read an interview with Thelonious Monk's son and he was talking about how modern jazz musicians were going to school and learning jazz theory and technique. In other words, they go to school to learn how to play jazz. Well, of course Thelonious Monk's son grew up in a house with the best jazz musicians all around him and he was saying that he never heard them discussing theory. They were more concerned with their emotional portrayal of the piece or what the spirit of the composition was, or the price of good weed to smoke, or whatever. To be playing at their level implies that you already understand theory and technique or that your chops are together; but at the higher levels of musicianship chops are superfluous. When children learn how to play music or paint, a lot of their time is spent just getting their chops together, i.e. learning their technique, embodying procedural memory. This is largely a matter of physical patterning and memorization, much like an excellent skier or skate boarder. They become involved in learning to relegate complex physical patterns into their procedural memory by repetition.

    The intellectual aspect of learning music specifically involves understanding the mathematical aspects of musical structure, things like stable harmonic relationships, which are learned largely by rote like multiplications, except that scales have an emotional connection that multiplications should have. (Interestingly, there is a section of the brain fairly dedicated to math, but multiplication does not reside there.) This is the more explicit or declarative aspect of music, which like everything else that is important, is double coded in that individual notes and chords also contain emotional tones. Single notes don't embody a strict emotional value: on a one-to-one or in a denotative way. The same note can have its overall emotional tone changed by placing it within different surrounding harmonies, in the same way red looks different when put next to blue or green. As I mentioned earlier, the chord Em7 has a certain overall feel to it when played alone on a piano, but it would feel different coming from a string or brass section.

That feeling tone is embedded in all music and is an excellent example of how the mind is embodied. If we contain our discussion to the physical patterning and procedural memory of music, we have implied that there is an explicit distinction between the body and the mind and that this distinction we have sought to create then implies a separation of what is being learned or how we should teach it. There is, in fact, no such strict separation and I will attempt to dispense with this type of terminology from here on in as in my world it is another assertion of the left brain's desire to control. I would say that, for the individual absorbed in a performance, the less you consciously think about the mechanics of what you are doing, the better. This is the Zen aspect of golf or the essence of the Nike slogan: *Just Do It*. Music is also like this and there really is very little explicit or declarative thinking going on while playing it.

I will give a very quick example. A woman phoned me at my music store once who had won $2,000 worth of CD box sets; but she had a problem because she didn't like music that much and she didn't know what to buy. She told me that she definitely didn't like Miles Davis so I suggested a Thelonious Monk box that was just released. She thought she liked jazz music in a quaint way and asked me what Mr. Monk's music was like and I told her that I found his music quite funny. She came into the store the next day and tracked me down, because 'I am such a nice fellow on the phone', and I played her Thelonious Monk. She didn't think his music was funny at all and it dawned on me that she had absolutely no references or bearing to bring into the conversation. I was at a loss to explain exactly how his music is funny, but I could say, 'it's not exactly funny like slap stick'. To make a long story short, I convinced her to buy a complete Mozart box set and give it to someone else in her family that eventually might realize the stunning gift they had just received. Artists have a very real feeling for their work that defies articulation, or at least my ability to articulate succinctly.

I will stick to talking about the mechanics of music for a while, but the nebulous and inarticulate will trail us like clouds of glory. For a piano or saxophone player, the finger coordination that is needed to play the instrument will most likely start with the practice of scales. Each key has a scale of notes and there are also some other scales or assembly of notes that have come to denote certain types of music. There are gypsies' scales that greatly influenced eastern European and Jewish klezmer music or vice versa, as well as scales that sound uniquely Spanish or Islamic (minor pentatonic with half and quarter notes), and Chinese (pentatonic). These scales were discovered over history and, like mathematics, they seemed to already exist in nature. Interestingly, elements of a musical culture can be identified by listening for the combination of scales and/or rhythmic structure being used, if you are an expert listener. (Chinese use of pentatonic or the Cuban clave are obvious examples.) Twyla Tharp talks about engaging in ritual as a precursor to creativity; this type of practice is ritual and ritual drives out too much explicit thinking which negatively effects the welling up of creativity.

 For a drummer this bodily patterning takes an even more literal form and to learn drumming involves teaching your body to perform complex rhythmic movements like polyrhythms. A polyrhythm is a rhythm in which two or three time signatures are identifiable. Polyrhythms are all throughout African music and its step children, Jazz, Blues and Afro Latin music. To begin with, you must learn some strictly physical techniques to acquire the body patterning involved in playing a polyrhythm, but along with this patterning you will begin to understand the relevance of the feel of the groove as it works within the larger ensemble of the music that is being played. I will discuss Indian music later and somewhat separately and we will see how Indian musicians have taken some of very technical aspects of musical education and developed a very different approach to the way that they are taught to unclouded minds.

 What I have noticed is that immature players have a tendency to be entranced with technique, usually speed. It is one of the more mundane aspects of music that can be easily identified by a young listener. Conversely, I have been taking some lessons again and I really need to brush up on exactly these simple elements of technique. Though I would like to submit myself for the world's slowest drummer, I intend to hit a drum only once a year for two years or so. It's all about what's in between the notes.

 One of a drummer's main concerns is keeping steady time for the rest of the band. There is great discipline involved for the drummer when they are backing up a singer. The job of the rhythm section is to serve the singer (whom most people are listening to anyway), and this active restraint and servitude can be delicate and profound. Jim Keltner and Steve Gadd are excellent examples of this delicious restraint within the pop realm. Paul Motian is another brilliant example from the middle period Bill Evans recordings. To play music well, you have to learn to play the music, which is to say you should serve the music you are playing, which also implies that the music you are playing is worth serving (essentially a religious stance). Truly great musicians listen really hard to what they are playing and what is being played around them. Technique then is a means to an end, not an end in itself. You have the right to work, but you do not have a right to the fruits of your labor. So what Thelonious Monk's son was saying was that music lessons should involve musical sensitivity or focusing on listening, not just playing and technical wizardry. It really is about what you don't play; but these are the greater lessons of life.

Part of the way that the mind becomes engaged in music can be explained by elaborating on this idea of polyrhythms. If a drummer is playing a polyrhythm, he is doing at least two things at once - much like patting your head and rubbing your stomach. The most common root of western polyrhythms is 3 against 4. I will write it out only because with some variations it has become the cornerstone idea behind all Latin music and all swing time in jazz.

I was watching a show about the Baku peoples in the rainforests of West Africa and two men were smoking out a termite hill, and they were playing two against three on the ground as they fanned the smoke with their newspapers. The same type of cross rhythm is used in U2's *Beautiful Day*. As soon as Bono sings the line it's a beautiful day, the drummer plays across the 4/4 pulse in a triplet starting on the y of Day.

In all Blues by Miles Davis -from the *Kind of Blue* album- the band is playing in 4/4 and the melody is played in a 6/8 rhythm across it. The 6/8 time can be counted as 4 beats or two sets of 3. *Kashmir* by Led Zeppelin is another example where John Bonham the drummer is playing 4/4 and the string section is moving across in a 6/8 pattern. It's hard to explain music in words. What I am trying to explain is very easily grasped with examples and I will try to reference enough genres so that you might have heard of one.

As a drummer is learning to play a polyrhythm, she must learn to split her brain into two camps, controlling each hand separately. This is only a temporary situation as the mind learns to integrate the body's independence, or possibly the brain becomes accustomed to reinforcing this integrated division. The drummer can then sit back and intellectually observe the flow of each rhythm separately. I used to practice Latin rhythms with two or sometimes three other percussionists and, once you get your parts together, it is quite amazing to let your mind wander around the room and listen to how all of the other parts work against each other and together. In Latin music all of the different rhythmic parts are subservient to the clave, which is in itself a broken form of 3 against 4. The wooden bars (called 'clave') that they use to play this beat have an excellent tone that cuts through the sound of the other percussion instruments. I was playing the drum kit in these situations, and to some extent, I was leading the rhythm for the Conga players. What is interesting is that, if I made the slightest misstep or lost concentration, the whole ensemble blew apart and immediately stopped. The drum patterns for me were so difficult that I could not re-enter the pattern again as the music was playing, and we had to start all over again with me leading.

Polyrhythms can be much more complicated than 3 against 4, though, when you bring in odd numbers like 5 and 7, but this is irrelevant to what I am saying. What musicians are doing when they are learning things like this is dividing the brain so that it is integrated once again at a 'higher' level. This is yet another aspect of double coding and possibly why musicians have observably stronger connections between their right and left lobes. On a more symbolic and physical level, they are integrating the body with the brain.

It seems that after the strain of paying attention to a song, or concentrating very hard to learn a new and difficult piece of music, the mind of a musician or we as the listeners enjoy the subsequent release that results from having forced our minds to hold on to this new way of understanding. It is like straining to suss out the dialogue in a Shakespearean play as it unravels before you. Though in music, this type of tensioned integration can be achieved in many ways and musicians are adept at exploiting all forms of them. There is a great joy or release of tension created by exploiting various forms of dissonance within a melody. This can be done by using notes that fall on the periphery of the established or obvious resolve of the harmony. (Handel does this with great effect in the last amen of the Messiah)

Within a song, some writers will establish a melodic pattern then mutate, invert or do any number of things to this established pattern in your mind, before bringing it back to the pay-off, as it were. Wynton Marsalis calls it the 'gut bucket' - with a resolution or even a restatement of the main motif, which will usually contain the melodic resolve. Pete Townsend of *The Who* and Neil Finn, *Crowded House*, constantly insert a few extra bars after the bridge or last verse of a song so that the final chorus is not in the same place that you expected it to be. This extra section tends to have a suspended feel and your mind starts searching for the melody again. I was listening to Ein Kline Nact's music and I noticed that Mozart structured the leading melody so that the resolve note or tonic passed over and over very quickly before pressing into the melody again. This literally leaves you feeling unresolved and you mentally anticipate the pay-off somewhere, but he doesn't give it you. I'm convinced that the more you listen to music, the more you become accustomed to melodic ambiguity.

"The left brain constantly searches for that which it already knows; novelty is largely the purview of the right." – Tweet that shit.

This tension release can also be done with lyrics where the artist will explore different meanings within a phrase, disassembling and reassembling the concept in your mind. Elvis Costello uses this idea in a song called *Man out of Time,* where he exploits the double usage of the word '*out*' in the title phrase, amongst other things. A lot of Elvis

Costello's and Lennon/ McCartney's early work was really playing with lyrics and not necessarily trying to say anything particularly meaningful (*Eight Days a Week*). I heard an interview with Elvis Costello in which he mentioned that he saw a sign in America for the Quisling Clinic and he wanted desperately to use this name in a song. Not only is it an interesting set of phonemes, Mr. Quisling has gone down in history as a member of the French government who colluded with Hitler.

The mind constantly seeks to grasp or construct meaning, be it within harmony, pattern or the cracking of a metaphor. An artist can exploit this by implying order or meaning and then pulling it just out of reach so that you have to take one more step to get it, or by implying or explicitly stating multiple and even conflicting meanings simultaneously, or, simply implying meaning where there is none at all.

When I was young, there was a whole bunch of young jazz musicians who were being called the young lions; these were people like Roy Hargrove, Wallace Roney and Joshua Redman. (Wallace Roney went on to become Miles Davis' protégé, one of the few people to ever play trumpet on stage with him; and, just before Miles died, he gave Wallace one of his trumpets.) When you listen to jazz music on a recording, it can have a tendency to appear a little stale and intellectual. I think this is what stops most people from liking it. You have to make an effort to grasp the flavor of each artist. When you experience it live, you get the real feel of it. There is an excitement that occurs when you are watching someone solo at the edge of their ability, which is palpable and everyone becomes part of this experience as it unfolds.

The truly great players can play the entire spectrum of colors on the palate and bring their soul directly into what they are playing, which is to say that they can tap into the immediacy of the emotional environment. This is because great players have set up or learned to approximate the resonance of these different emotional environments within themselves and they can dip into this well, which they embody over and over again.

What I have noticed is that young players have difficulty playing ballads. You cannot fill a ballad with notes and it is actually more difficult to play slowly than it is to develop speed and technique. When playing slowly, an overt effort will be noticeable, because there is so much more room for you to make a mistake and any poorly presented or slightly mistimed note is left naked and exposed for our inspection. I happened to have been at a concert of the jazz piano player Geri Allen, with Wallace Roney accompanying her on trumpet, the night after Miles Davis died. I had not seen Wallace Roney play before but I did know that Miles had passed on his mantle to him. During the whole first set, every time Wallace Roney soloed, it was not very good and I thought, well he is having a bad night, which is understandable. When the band opened the second set, they played a ballad and Wallace Roney poured his soul out onto the floor. It really was something spectacular. And this is my larger point: it takes emotional depth to do art well. At that moment, Wallace Roney was the ballad he was playing. He was fully connected. Like actors that can cry on demand, you must know where that emotion resides. This is a crucial thought and I will come back to it. This is the opposite of the passive nature of abstracted sentimentality. No amount of chops makes you feel deeply attached to music.

"Does one need to love? Don't ask-feel it." – Pascal, *"On the Passion of Love"*

I have noticed that some artists identify themselves too closely with their role as an artist. This is the great trap that actors especially seem to fall into and you can see quite clearly how it can happen, because everyone around them is always telling them how great they are and they believe it (insert any number of recent or past train wrecks here). If the artist gets pulled along by their own success without actively participating in their career, they can get what is called 'type casting'. They are caught in a certain genre or too closely associated with their perceived screen persona. Obviously, a lot of actors are just happy to work and they don't really care. In my opinion the human personality is wave-like and varying. I would add that the idea of a renaissance artist as someone who is dabbling in all sorts of different forms of expression would probably be more common if our present society was more amenable to it. We-as a consuming public-have some difficulty accepting a multi-layered character, because understanding nuances takes time and effort and wide angled passivity. It is easier to become and/or portray a one dimensional persona in this our desperate sound bite, twitter culture, because it takes time to elaborate and establish any amount of depth. There is even a sound bite that would have us believe that you can only really do one thing well in your life. For a long time, it was thought that you should dedicate yourself to one career path, but I think this is changing and people are simply bored with one single career. Never underestimate the power of boredom.

Creativity is like peace. You cannot wage peace, you must allow it. Part of the reason I am writing about art is that I believe art is largely the process of art; and, by discussing the process that artists are involved in, I am trying to illustrate what it means to be creative. I believe that the beauty of art is that *it drives you* and, like religion, you don't get lost in your own self-reflective absorption. In art you are constantly realizing ways to experience life and art by exteriorizing yourself from within, through the act of self expression. Expression is the outward flow, which constantly reattaches us to the world because we are participating in all aspects of it. I believe that many artists have been deeply troubled individuals, but they have mustered on by immersing themselves in art. Andy Warhol is one of the greatest and most prodigious of this century.

One of my greatest heroes -among many-is Pat Metheny, whom I have seen live at least eight times. I have also had the great pleasure to meet him, if only briefly (he was particularly articulate, warm and genuinely humble with a soft mid-west accent). The first time I saw him live and in concert was literally a revelation. He was touring on the *Still Life Talking* album, which is one of his best, by the way. What got to me about this particular concert was that he was constantly juxtaposing radically different emotional environments. The band would play some crazy dissonant explosion and then Pat would immediately sit down and play a solo ballad on acoustic guitar. What I most remembered about this night was that the band didn't slowly work the audience up to a fever pitch and then climb back down again. They presented the music in a series of quick ruptures. Each song was different and this forced you to change emotional gears quickly along with the band. The other thing that blew me away was that Pat Metheny doesn't just stand on stage and present his music as a disengaged intellectual. He achieves the greatest of balances between all forms of music and emotions while remaining passionate (I can't think of a less cliché word).

The thing that I have learned from people like Pat Metheny, and I will use his career as an analogy (you could easily insert many other names in here: Miles Davis, Meryl Streep, Brad Pitt, David Bowie, Pablo Picasso or Paul Simon would all do) is that these artists have constantly sought to reinvent themselves. Or they have been unafraid to evolve a new viewpoint and incorporate it into themselves. They have been living their lives outside of the context of what people expect them to be, or they have become unattached to their own self image and they participate in their own becoming. This is more of a soft listening for inspiration than an active gutting of your self-image. Andy Warhol would start to work, as he waited around for his next inspiration. The only constant is change.

Pat Metheny has explored a vast number of styles over his career and there are many peaks that are quite different. He has done a whole album of guitar feedback, which was quite *avant-garde* (and received by the public very poorly), and he has done fully charted orchestral work, along with exceptional trio and quartet jazz albums, as well as his hugely successful group albums. During the five years that I have been writing this book, he has produced at least eight recordings and I would say that at least five of them are amongst his greatest works. He is truly firing on all pistons. The most interesting aspect of this work is its incredible diversity. I believe that he is one of the most financially successful jazz artists of all time (Miles Davis or Diana Krall might be other candidates), and this is why the critics have been hard on his music: you can't be both good and successful at the same time.

One of Pat Metheny's later recordings is called *The Way Up* and there is an extended interview with him on the live DVD, discussing the process of writing this album. He talks about getting together with Lyle Mays, his collaborator on the 'group' recordings, and discussing the idea of doing a long single piece of music. Before they wrote anything, they spent a week just talking about what it was they really wanted to do. These two people had been working together for about 30 years at this point and I wish to point out their commitment to exploration. I attended a talk that Pat Metheny gave at the CBC where he discussed bringing Lyle Mays a recording he had made of three notes played on a guitar. This was presented as a possible song idea and Lyle Mays recognized the value of these three notes and agreed that they could compose a song out of them. Yup, those are three good notes. (This is not unlike the first notes of Beethoven's *Fifth Symphony*.) What is amazing to me is that after 30 years of working together, they were both willing to sit down and reassess some of their cores values; and, in my opinion, write one of their best albums to date.

This relates back to my earlier point about Brian Eno. What Pat Metheny has done throughout his career is that he is willing to redefine the chess board. *The Way Up* combines classical composition ideals with the freedom of jazz. In large sections it has a bass drum keeping a pulse that a DJ can use to mix for a dance club. My niece spent a wacky night clubbing around in Paris, ending up at the Buddha Bar, which is one of the premier dance clubs in the world. She recognized Pat Metheny's record when I played it for her, because she had heard it at this club. This is how you bring this complicated music to people. You bring it to them, because you don't expect them to come to you. Why would they? Jazz is for snobs. What Pat Metheny has accomplished with this album is really quite a fresh hybrid of much of his past knowledge and skills in composition; but he has also allowed into his vision aspects of popular present day culture. You can easily despise what is going on in the world of culture and reject it. This will make your petty ego feel good like buying a new Gucci bag (mount a guard at the tomb's entrance), or you can engage in the real world and search for what you like, embrace it and use it to reinvent yourself.

Since I initially wrote this section, Pat Metheny has trumped even this amazing piece of work with a recording called *Orchestrion*. At the time of making my final edits, he has done three more CDs. Very briefly: he has said that he felt that jazz musicians weren't holding up their innovative end in the ongoing process of music. He has collected and had built for himself a vast amount of servo-driven automated instruments. With this collection of stuff, he has invented a single person improvisational -midi operated- mechanical orchestra. By using electronic interfaces (midi technology), he has fashioned an automated mechanical beast that can be programmed 'on the fly' and he can also play complicated set creations. (There is a fascinating DVD out now and I was privileged to have seen this tour.) He contacted some people who have been inventing new types of instruments and commissioned them to create a number of interesting gadgets just for this project. So there are many acoustically generated sounds and instruments on the piece (*Orchestrion*) that are completely new. This would all be mildly interesting at best, if he wasn't able to create beautiful music with this machine; but, of course, he has created an incredible CD, which has also garnered critical acclaim simply because it's good.

I was listening to the CBC classical station and wondering why there are no more Mozarts or Beethovens. Classical music has become almost completely self-referential along with classical ballet. They have created a pantheon of accepted composers that is god-bedazzled and unassailable. How could any modern composer live up to these airy ideals? I worked with some young classical musicians and they agonized about their technique, because they were forced to agonize about their technique by the establishment that surrounds them; having said that, the level of technique among classical musicians is truly astounding. The preoccupation with their technique leaves them little time to think about composing and improvising; and I believe the whole classical edifice beats out of you the idea that you shouldn't even try to compose. To be young is to agonize. No one is ever going to be able to live up to Mozart's talent and it seems to me that no one is really trying anymore, although I personally love Arvo Part, who is one of a handful of popular living composers.

As I was listening to the radio, I wanted to pick up the phone to call the CBC and tell them that there are Mozarts and Beethovens all around us right now. They just aren't making classical music and why would they? You wouldn't like it anyway. People composing in that style of orchestral arrangement are all doing soundtrack work and they are consistently patronized, because they have *lowered* themselves by doing soundtrack work. This context of a soundtrack doesn't make classical music any less beautiful. The *Lord of the Rings* soundtrack could certainly stand on its own as a composition, not to mention the works of Ennio Morricone who I think was allowed to peek through the door of the classical pantheon once for the *Mission* soundtrack. These pieces of music are edited and formatted for the movie soundtrack, they are not written to be performed as a single symphonic concert, which would be a completely different compositional mindset. Writing to a specified set of parameters can either be a constraint to be embraced or a limit to be rejected, but to a great extent all compositions have a program or set of parameters. We can't move the king into the fridge. I believe it is a reflex of naive sentimental idealism that would continue to think that compositions are simply given to us wholly formed out of the blue (the ever so angst-filled Trent Reznor of Nine Inch Nails has done a haunting soundtrack for the movie *Social Media* and won an Oscar so maybe it's cool to compose after all).

All compositions are work. Mozart and Beethoven spent hours composing and so do modern soundtrack composers. Obviously, some are better than others at creating stunning melodies, etc. But this type of composition work truly is 90 percent perspiration and I refuse to believe that Mozart's 10 percent of inspiration is so astonishing that it completely negates or overwhelms a conversation about living composers. I would add that this mindset - it's all been done, etc. - is powerful fuel for people who would search for reasons not to try to be creative. On the other hand, Mozart or Shakespeare really is something spectacular in the world of creative endeavors and their 10 percent are that much better. I would argue that Ali Akbar Khan and Ravi Shankar, and any number of recent jazz and pop musicians are of equal, though completely different stature to any of these classical composers. But of course, they have dedicated their talent to a different set of musical skills that bear little resemblance to classical music composition.

Parting the waves of those few feint friends
  Fingers once offered are now too heavy to extend -Elvis Costello, *When I Was Cruel No 2*

I recently had a fascinating conversation with a fellow who played classical piano. The essence of his viewpoint was that when he was playing, Bartok specifically, he was captured in an environment that was completely unique and indicative of that composer's living spirit. These specific piano works resonated very deeply within him on an obviously rich emotional level. I should like to think that this is really the true essence of what classical composition is. The musician/artist has developed writing skills and also found a way to communicate their rich and personal sound environment, which has been communicated to us through time by the written medium. We can participate in this piece of art by allowing the blowing together of ourselves with the piece in the conspiracy of music. Music is such a rich experience that you are afforded the opportunity to really touch an essential aspect of the composer and no amount of verbal gymnastics on my part can describe the fullness of that experience. Music can tap directly into a complete nonverbal emotional resonant environment and we can also press it into serving our intellectual distraction, but it definitely has the tendency to escape or transcend beyond our intellectual foolishness, especially when we are directly engaged with it.

I recently found out that the reclining voluptuous nudes associated with Titian were to some extent 'simply' pictures of naked women for the bedrooms of rich renaissance Italian merchants. Of course, anything like pornography would have been much more difficult to get a hold of in renaissance Italy and it seems that these fellows who bought these pieces where quite shy about the purchasing of these paintings and some buyers sought them out anonymously through discreet dealers. But of course, Titian had found a corner of the market that no one else was exploiting and he was getting paid quite well for these paintings, which was something. The word 'simply' is so loaded.

Benvenuto Cellini (a master gold smith and bronze caster), complains in his autobiography how hard it was to actually get paid at the end of a contracted gig. It was easy to get patrons, but not as easy to actually get his share of the money after the completion of a piece. Benvenuto had excellent and well moneyed patrons, such as the King of France, who seemed to have been entirely satisfied with the work he produced. Any number of things could be said about Titian and his maverick painting of nude women. It seems, to a certain extent, he painted pictures for a certain clientele so that he could get paid for his work. (See *Worldly Goods* by Lisa Jardine for a fascinating discussion of renaissance finance and worldly acquisitions in the non-nobility of the nouveau riche protestant Dutch. It seems bling is as old as wealth.)

We sometimes put art on a pedestal where it doesn't wish to be. Nothing is ever 'nothing but,' and if I wish to reduce Titian to a pornographer, I eliminate a great swath of depth from the conversation. To relegate these painting to being 'simply pornography' cheapens both them and me. You can never have a concept so firmly in your back pocket that it can be relegated into 'nothing but'.

I remember hearing an interview with Neil Peart, the drummer from *Rush*, (God bless him), when drum machines were first becoming part of the pop music scene in the eighties. He said something to the effect that the problem with drum machines was the programmers were programming things into them that a drummer couldn't do. I'm sure he subsequently recanted this statement. What he misunderstood at the time was that drum machines were a separate instrument. A drum machine didn't have to be a drummer. Most of the people programming drum machines were not drummers and this was both a good and bad thing. Drummers are 'hopefully' experts in rhythm and feel etc., but the record producers who were programming these machines had other agendas. When Moby first started making records, lots of people said he wasn't a musician at all, because everything that he did was 'just' editing together samples of other musicians work.

The contextual error here was in not understanding the nature of Moby's instrument. For Moby, the whole studio is an instrument. He plays the modern recording studio and the entire western music library as he feels it. This was a new paradigm and we have no choice, but to accept it because the kids that are listening to music don't care what I would like to call an instrument. They just want good music to dance to: two turntables and a microphone will do. Modern composers don't necessarily have to compose for an orchestra or a piano, or whatever. They compose with the instruments in their environment, because they are embedded within the broader context they live in. It might just be that the orchestra itself is the problem or, better yet, the skill needed to chart an orchestra may be the main impediment in modern composing. Composing for an orchestra has a very specific skill set, which has been left behind in a sound bite world that doesn't particularly care about skill and craft. David Byrne hammers home the thought that music is always a product of context from the high notes that birds sing to be heard in a forest to building a special concert hall for Wagner so that his extended brass section would sound better. I became a champion of craft, because it is an excellent form of ritual that brings you into the work.

"Logic is like the poetry of fridge magnets."- Ambiguous quips by the author.

An example of the embedded and time-bound nature of such skill sets can be illustrated by taking a look at the evolution of dance music and the recording arts. In the world of dance music, it is impossible to say whether current technology is driving innovation or if it is the artists embracing new technology, and the subsequent musical innovation that is driving the hunger for even newer technologies. We certainly wouldn't have dance music without sequencers or pitch and phase electronics, and especially the Pro Tools home computer recording systems. The whole development of modern dance music has moved in lock step with the technology that is both driving and being driven by it. Also, innovators are excellent at finding unintended ways to exploit technologies: garage bands led directly to pod casting, which the Apple people never saw coming. The conversation about which came first in electronics is redundant and overly intellectual. I would argue that this is really the great lesson that I am trying to expose about how the evolution of everything works. Looking too closely and then trying to tease out the string of causal relations -alá Newton, or driving the wish to establish the ideal moment of inception, is ultimately self defeating, like endlessly ransacking your top ten lists.

Mozart might be mixing dance tracks in Ibiza as we speak and he could care less about trying to organize a whole room full of classically trained musicians. He would be experimenting with Pro Tools, cocaine and ecstasy, and his music would in many ways be a reflection of this environment, along with a healthy dose of his own genius. If he were alive today, he would have learned a completely different skill set within a completely different set of cultural parameters, and he would be fully committed to them.

Genius is a confluence of that rare personal ability to become completely engaged and committed to your skill, along with the good fortune to have the fates gift you the environment in which to achieve the full expression of your genius. I would argue that the main impediment that any number of modern artists has in becoming hailed as a genius is two hundred years. We can see these living artists on YouTube every day and they are all too human. To be held in high esteem as a genius they need to be displaced into that sentimental backward looking realm of intellectual abstraction.

I do not wish to bandy the term 'genius' around too flippantly, but I will say that we are surrounded by them in all fields of human endeavor right now. The ultimate etymology of the term genius is that you are both a reflection of and the embodiment of the divine spirit of the age in which you live. Caesar was the genius of his age, because he looms so large in the historical record. We can only see the whole of the 'spirit of the times' ensemble in the rear view mirror, through our highly connective and meaning-generating brains. Our affinity towards sentimentality, as reflected by the left brain's penchant, seems to get stuck on this historical record. I personally would argue that Jesus does not become tarnished by committing to be human.

Back in the sixties and on through the seventies and eighties, the jazz and classical fields were both a little redundant and, as a result of this, the composers of the time got pretty far out there – almost relishing their intellectual obscurity. Or possibly this obscurity was the result of climate and their accumulative aesthetic choices; composers both reinforced and brought about their own navel gazing obscurity. This type of hyper reflective self-absorption was all around the art world and it created a culture of possibly drug-fuelled arrogance. This time period was at the height of experimental 'free jazz' and the era of the dreaded 20th century composer caught within the extent of post modernism. It seems that if you were to be taken seriously, you had to be dissonant, abstract, pretentious and militantly serious about it. I think that music was working through the intellectual ruptures that occurred in the other fields of art. Music was passing through the intellectual grist mill that modernist/ cubist etc., painters had gone through. Music seemed to have embraced the DADA 'stream of consciousness' experimentation.

In many ways this was a reaction to the stuffy climate that musicians were in; for example, 20th century composers wrote a streaky line on the score that represented someone bowing the music stand (apparently this helped the classical musicians break their preconceived notions of what music was. Yea, thanks for that). A lot of jazz musicians stopped composing all together. They just got behind their instrument and a microphone and played. John Cage 'wrote' a piece of music that he didn't play at all. He sat in front of the piano and the music happened all around him. This is an intellectual observation, but by any definition of music I would care to offer, it would not qualify. And of course that is the point. I am of two seriously conflicted minds with this kind of stuff. The *avant-garde* has a tendency to produce great musicians, because these fellows know where the edge is. They have been there, had a look over into the abyss and probably jumped, then came back to tell about the freedom of flight. The *avant-garde* tends to become the norm, given enough time as it absorbs into the perpetual hunger of society. Examples like the Talking Heads, Beethoven or Brian Eno leap to mind, or Picasso,

Turner, Basqiuat or Warhol in the art world.

It is just painful for me to listen to 20th century *avant-garde* stuff and I like to consider myself pretty tolerant. This is how I really feel. I can handle a lot more dissonance than most people I know. I just find free jazz indulgent and unforgiving to the listener. It may be fun to play when you are tapping into the unconscious directly like this, but to my ear it lacks organization and polish. It is deeply immersed in the tyranny of freedom. Dreams tend to be unorganized as well as they come forth from the unconscious. If you can remember them clearly, and if you can honestly commit them to paper, you will see that, without some form of editing on your part, the time lines will tend to be mixed up. Usually the act of writing dreams down on paper involves organizing and editing them to some very great extent. This is not cheating. It's just editing and your waking mind does this without much effort because the chaos of dreams or your unbridled unconscious, or even an unrestricted hyper-consciousness (as in a schizophrenic episode), is very difficult to translate directly. I would contend that great stories and myths of the past came to us in a polished way, but the original seed was from this associative unconscious well. This wild seed constantly peeks through in great art as in Shakespeare's *Light Thickens,* but it never suffers from becoming properly set. The primary job of the human mind is to organize reality with a healthy dose of implied meaning. The etymology of edit is that the editor was the fellow who matched opponents in the gladiatorial ring in Rome.

Well written prose doesn't flow from your mind and directly onto the page. It has to be worked at. Eloquence is not a natural flow of spoken language. The mind doesn't form thoughts eloquently in the language we speak, though it is influenced by each language's inherent structure. A word-for-word written transcript of a conversation between two people is almost impossible to understand, especially if you don't first understand the underlying context. Much of what is going on between the listener and the speaker is implied by the context and is understood to be so by both participants. The cadence is broken up with many stops and starts as the speakers try to formulate the words. Next time you listen to an interview on the radio or TV, add up the number of times you hear ah and um. It will start to drive you crazy. What some modern art had sought to capture was a more direct access to the unconscious flow *as if* this were more real or honest. This was what Dada poetry and free jazz were all about. You would write down or play whatever came to your mind directly without editing or consideration to rewrite. Part of the problem with this abstracted intellectual wankery is that it exists only in recorded/written form. On the other hand, the corner stone of modern jazz is improvisation, which is what I love about it.

    Dada is French baby talk for 'hobby horse', meaning the concept is so simple, a baby can get it. (A Shaman's drum is also known as a horse.)The French now call baby talk mommynaise. I like that.

DADA SONG

An elevator's song

That had dada in its heart

And overtaxed motor

That had dada in its heart

The elevator

Was carrying a king

Heavy breakable autonomous

He cut off his big right arm

Which is why

The elevator

No longer had dada in its heart

Eat some chocolate

Wash your brain

dada

dada

Drink some water

From Dawn to Decadence Pg. 720 – The single best book I ever read seven times.

I was inspired by this discussion on Dada and wrote my own poem, but I could not help myself and tweaked one of the lines after the fact. It was moderately better as a result of my tweaking. This automatic or direct type of artwork has finally worked its way through our culture. Collectively, artists have stripped everything down to the bottom, and to my mind this process has left us a little barren, naked and lost – like endlessly being ironic. For an absolutely fascinating insight into, and critique of, the parallels between schizophrenia and the modern and post modern art movements, I would highly suggest *Madness and Modernism* by Louis Sass. I came onto this book too late to incorporate its wisdom. And as a side note, I personally get to perform John Gage's non-piano piece several times a day – though few people appreciate my technical and compositional ability.

One of the things that I love about art is a finished product. I love the craft and implied intent of artwork. This type of automatic art is interesting and some fun if, like Jim Morrison, you are in need of breaking through to the other side. But to me it smacks of too much intellectualization or possibly not really caring to think this through to the final conclusion. If you listen to 12-tone music (a composition in which all of the notes in an octave are considered as equally valid, and it is therefore, stuffed full of dissonance), it doesn't engage you in any emotional way. It is a stuffy intellectual wanking and you only have to watch the person playing it to get the joke, because their body gives it away. Watch an early interview with Andy Warhol. He is such a smart ass that there is nothing of him left, because he has developed a public persona of disengagement and is so completely drenched in self-absorbed irony. Ironically, he was meant to be incredibly engaging, if he liked you.

The real gist of my much bigger dig at modern conceptual art is that I don't understand it. I could nod my head at a show and talk about how freeing the experience was etc., maybe wave my hand like the Queen or something. But it just seems like one moldy intellectual breakthrough, beaten to death. I think conceptual art-by its very nature-has to be snobbish, exclusive and cynical or we will see that it stands naked and embarrassed by its excessive self-referentiality. It is ultimately an intellectual joke that must put all of its weight into pretending that it is serious with the implication that you simply do not understand it. Its stance is hyper-irony that is so ironic that it's not sure where the truth is anymore. This-to my simple mind- is exclusionist and indicative of a weakness in communication. We, the artists and collected snobs at the plastic-encased vacuum cleaner showing, are IN and you the uneducated or poorly indoctrinated, non-massive-rimmed-glasses-wearing viewer are out. You should pay us to be IN while we laugh at you from behind our well-moneyed navel gazing façade. I have come to realize that Andy Warhol worked his way through these contradictions and simply created art for money in the seventies by embracing portraiture almost as a trade

    This is the tyranny of the disengaged intellect: the self-reflective, hyper-aware intellect seeks to create a coherent narrative, regardless of its truth when compared to the rest of the world. The worst aspects of modern and post modern art -in my opinion- have gotten trapped in the abstract expression of the over-weaned intellect. It doesn't seek to reintroduce you to the real world through displacing the real world into creativity. It displaces everything into the emotionless intellectual gristmill of the haloed idea then stridently asserts its implied validity. This is its tyranny. It is the essence of abstraction divorced from the mediation of irony or even sarcasm. It is naked and embarrassingly intellectual. All of these emotionally vacant snobs now nurture a form of the distant Andy Warhol look as if it's embarrassing to get excited about stuff. Abstract art does not illicit depth of feeling; it does not seek to wash you in a new appreciation of pain or love, and it is a brazen affront to the question, *"what am I looking at?"* Like those bastards on Wall Street, bad art should be punished for its arrogance. This art reflects the same intellectual divorce from the world that Wall Street has shown us, by not caring at all about people's lives that have been ruined here in the real world; not in the abstract.

    "The last weapon of desperation is ridicule."- Witty quips to self-inflate.

    I think Marcel Duchamp was very aware of his ironic poking when he hung a toilet urinal on the wall and to some-or probably to a great extent- he was also serious about the urinal being an object of art. If I hang a toilet seat or a hunk of meat, or a piece of shit on the wall and claim that I am anything but a charlatan, to my mind, this is a pathetic stance. The intellectual barrier between readymade and artist-formed has been crossed. Let's move on. I fully accept that everything can be art, or indeed God, but I cannot, or will not, throw out all of my discernment. I am not engaged by a toilet seat no matter how profound you think it is (see Marla Olmstead, *My Kid Could Paint That*). Brian Eno tried to do something wonderful. He snuck a long thin hose and a bottle of urine into an exhibit of the famed Duchamp urinal and tried to piss in it. I'm not sure if he got away with it, but it was valiant nonetheless. He brought real urine in the real world, to a real urinal on the wall. Get it? If you are too art bedazzled to laugh, poke your left eye back into action.

My wife, son and I went to the MoMA museum in New York, which was probably a bad idea. After traipsing through four floors of 'art', and getting myself in a thoroughly foul mood, which in itself was psychologically interesting, I came off of the escalator and was confronted with Henri Rousseau's *The Sleeping Gypsy 1897*. A young woman was standing to the right side of the painting talking about it to 30 very young school children and I burst into tears. I'm not sure why. I'm far too metro-sexual. All of the metaphors within this work are heavy with my internal meaning and it is just plain beautiful, and art is like that. It can just take you over and make you cry in a public place. Ultimately, there really is a depth in that painting that I don't see in a pile of wool on the floor, with a sign beside it that says, *"Don't Touch"*. Fuck that! Wool is for touching, urinals are for pissing, art is for crying!

As I mentioned earlier Pat Metheny released a recording of guitar feedback called *Zero Tolerance for Silence,* saying something to the effect that within this noise was implied all of the melodies. This is-to a certain extent-how musicians can hear music, because within a single chord played on an instrument, any number of melodies can imply them. This occurs because, as you vibrate things together, a harmonic overtone series happens. The sympathetic tones happen inside the instrument as a result of the natural resonance of the instrument itself and also the collusion of the artist's own unconscious that is always trying to construct pattern out of the randomness of noise.

This is the method Beethoven used to compose when he was deaf. He would feel the piano vibrating through a piece of wood placed in his mouth and he could feel in his jaw and eardrums, and read the various implied secondary harmonics, etc. I have nothing but respect for Pat Metheny and my personal feeling is that he was being honest in his defense of this piece and that he genuinely loved this work. I also believe that it is a result of his genuine engagement in the feel of it. It's music after all, not urinals. Pat Metheny was willing to publicly defend his feedback recording and he did try to explain to people his vague inner dialog. What irks me is when a modern conceptual artist hides behind the ambiguity of their intention and I believe that if they opened their mouths, we would see the emperor without clothes. We are back in the area of proof.

My good friend Michael and I went to see Brian Eno speak at the Art Gallery of Ontario here in Toronto, Canada and because my friend Michael had worked with Brian, I figured I would finally get to meet him. Sadly, it was not to be. I have on the other hand never read an interview or book of Brian Eno's without being totally entranced. At the end of this fascinating talk, Brian Eno took some questions from the audience and one fellow stood up and said he had a great idea: you could create a collection of artists and each one would be allowed to use their special talents to create integrated video/music/performance art. I think this fellow expected Brian Eno to get excited and throw money at him or something. Eno then said something to the effect that it could be a great idea, if you could make it work.

Great art or even great commercial ad campaigns are not created by committees. Actually, getting together with a bunch of musicians enough times a week to create music is difficult enough; finding money to record and then trying to sell your recording etc., is very hard work. Like composing, *this is work* and it has to be committed to and done, and it is made a lot more difficult if everyone is equal in a collective. You have to patiently listen to everybody's opinion, even if you think they are talking out their asshole. Reality gets in the way of great ideas. Committees have too much reality. Look in all the parks in all the cities and you will never find a statue to a committee. Thankfully, some artists possess tremendous soul force and fate colludes to allow them to drive their great ideas all the way into the world. Tim Booth of *James* said that some people think that getting a record contract is the end of your problems as a musician, but he added the caveat that it was only the beginning. Like it or not, you are part of a larger whole.

"We tried making movies from a handful of stills." - Peter Gabriel

You've got to get in to get out and then back in.
Now again my problem with conceptual art is that someone has gotten themselves into a position where they can have a wingy idea and then they can hire a whole bunch of peons to make it real for them. I will beat a concrete example to death here: some guy (I won't name him, because I refuse to promote him and the story is better as a metaphor) in Toronto hired a bricklayer to build a thick low wall of bricks, something like 50 bricks at a time over a three-week period. The 'bracketed artist' said it was great, because people could interact with the building process and see the fellow construct a wonderful piece of art. What stops people from standing in front of any number of construction sites all over the city and watch someone lay bricks? I guess they just don't feel the wonder that this great artist has for art, even though his art happens to be this interactive brick wall. Actually, it is a bricklayer building a brick wall and it happens all over the city all the time, and people are rightly blasé about it. But this 'artist' didn't even bother to come to Toronto to do this installation. He hired a brick layer to do it; he probably searched endlessly to find an artist bricklayer who really understood the meaning of what he was doing. But the artist/bricklayer only got paid scale and the conceptual artist got paid 50,000 dollars for coming up with this mind blowing idea. I guess he came to Toronto to see his vision realized in all its interactive glory, or maybe not. It doesn't matter. It was conceptual and he could envision the process in his god-bedazzled fertile mind's eye. This is all a bad joke and I refuse to pay any money for it, but somehow this art has pushed the envelope or some such intellectual hogwash. Again, this is indicative of the left brain's fascination with concepts over process, where the left brain is entranced by the displaced object, and for this (bracketed) artist, the real physical object is actually unimportant, and as a side effect, it is also completely useless. Ok I'm done. I got that out so let's move on. I was starting to spit all over the page; I was in such a rabid frenzy. Sarcasm is truly the tool of the weak. Alive is God's name that is most inclusive.

There is a cabinetmaker that I have become quite enamored with recently by the name of James Krenov. He is considered-within the cabinetmaking world-to be one of the main artisans that have led a resurgence of people making hand-crafted cabinetry over the last 20 years (both professionals and hobbyists). This commitment to a craft is not the type of job that will make you rich, but Krenov's contention is that the work itself is the reward. Art really is process. This fellow uses hand tools almost exclusively and never sands his work with sandpaper. Reading his talk about his work is very much like reading a dissertation from a Zen master.

In his books, you might read a long discussion about collecting and looking at pieces of wood. He tells us we should always be inspecting and tending to the wood. This is where you will find inspiration and this helps us develop a relationship to real things. This is the ongoing search for inspiration through the act of ritual. A certain piece may inspire you to create a cabinet, as you suddenly realize this piece in its context. Or Mr. Krenov might have a lengthy discussion about how you could align various grain patterns to create the appearance of lift or motion, say on a door or side panel. You allow the wood to influence your construction, because you are the human part of the process, not a machine. Jack White makes a similar point. How can you be pretentious, if you allow the wood and or piece of music itself to dictate its terms to you? All you have to do is pay attention and let it create itself. Mr. Krenov's work is very contemporary and clean in its design. There is no attempt on his part to uphold any past design ethic. My larger point is that this is about as far away from conceptual art as I can get, and I find that within this type of considered craftsmanship, there is a nobility of the soul at the human scale that has been deserted by the airy world of vapid conceptual art.

I will digress here yet again. It's what I do and what I want to do in this book. What I realized about criticism in general (I love to dig at music critics, because I have opinions too), is that a good critic like Northrop Fry or Jacques Barzun helps you to understand culture and its works of art from within a broadened context. A piece of music can be simple and either you love it or you don't. But sometimes you need to see a piece of art set into a proper frame and I would argue that a critic's main job is to help you set art within a wider cultural ensemble that is indicative or not of each piece. Artists aren't simply the result of their cultural influences. An artist can be something wholly new or they can be completely set against the cultural tide that surrounds them. Only the greater context of meaning means anything.

I will give you two examples of what I mean by my understanding of a larger cultural setting. One of my favorite musical artists is a Brazilian fellow called Carlinhos Brown. When I heard his first recording, *Alfagamabetizado,* I was completely blown away so I started buying his new records as he released them. His second record was very different from the first (*Omelette Man*), and I really didn't like it, but I loaned it to a friend of mine who really liked it and he convinced me to listen to it again. I will honestly tell you that, with the release of each subsequent record by Carlinhos, I felt at first let down by it, but I now press on through and give it a real chance. I realized that Carlinhos Brown just gets better and better with every recording. The only context I can receive his albums is my own. I know very little about the whole Brazilian scene in which he functions and with every new recording, he is progressing and changing as an artist. I have also realized that I have to play catch-up with him, or at least I must be willing to expand my inner frame of reference to allow in his wide angle. This is the essence of what is behind prejudice or pre-justice. I may have an unwillingness to adjust my own framework and a critic can help me to contextualize a piece of work that will then lead me into this new frame. It helps if you can leave your baggage at the door. We get stuck in a moment.

The other recording that helped me to understand this idea was called *The Spirits of Our Ancestors* by Randy Weston. This recording was quite heavily arranged (in a big band sense) by a woman named Melba Liston and there is no shortage of great players on it: Dizzy Gillespie and Pharaoh Sanders to mention only two. But, when I first listened to this record, all I heard was something like a Duke Ellington record and I am not a big fan of the early big band swing era. In fact, I was not really that thrilled about any type of large jazz ensemble arranging. I liked to consider myself more progressive than all of that. In my mind, this type of large band music was antiquated and better left alone in the sentimental dust bin. Well, you must be careful about what you invest hate energy in, because you set yourself up for a nasty conversion. Everyone I was working with at the time kept hammering this recording into my brain and I eventually allowed it in. I have subsequently come to consider it one of my favorite Jazz recordings of all time. I have gotten a lot of my friends to buy it, (like St. Paul who wrote a bunch of letters and became an evangelist, no not really). I did eventually come to understand that arranging for big bands is an amazing talent. We don't gain wider consciousness by simply imagining beams of light. We gain it by diving into the darkness of what we don't understand. Maybe I will eventually become a full blown conceptual artist – probably not.

The thing about art is that it flexes its muscles best in the world of metaphor, and this world, like the inner world of archetypes, can be somewhat ambiguous. If I explain away the metaphor, it doesn't really have that much punch, like someone inadvertently telling you the punch line to a joke. If I tell you the joke, I have also limited your participation and possibly consigned the metaphor to a singular view, which is itself limiting. The advantage of metaphor is that you must come to it. The metaphor of sowing seeds on different types of soil seems to be one that has been used worldwide and is apt in terms of how a metaphor needs to find fertile soil to be understood. We as westerners may have been led to believe that Jesus was the one who proffered this metaphor properly or that he was at least the first to use it. (The Buddha also liked this one.)

If a person is engaged in the conversation or engaged in what they are reading, a metaphor allows them to become part of the creative act. This is why Rap music falls dead on me. Don't get me wrong, there is some good Rap music (Jay Z for instance), but for the most part, they are just telling me or really drilling their message at me. They don't invite me in for a drink at the well; they just yell about how the well got dirty. Ok... I get it: some mother fucker dirtied the well. How do we move forward? As mentioned earlier, metaphors and/or an excellent aphorism can hold a number of conflicting truths simultaneously. They are still truths, just not logic-driven.

The biggest advantage of metaphor is that it is concise or condensed. *"Surly thou dost protest too much"*, reveals a whole ensemble about the nature of lying. You have a hard time lying to someone with the same confidence with which you could tell the truth. Shakespeare obviously understood this embodied aspect of lying quite clearly and reduced this whole concept into one, tight handy quip. An alternate example of a very succinct quip is one that I cannot stop thinking about from the pop group Iron and Wine: *"Godless brother. As far as I can tell, the night won't compensate the blind."* This one line could contain a whole story, if you wish to expand it. One great master of this type of condensed word play is Elvis Costello. You really get what he put into his work.

This set of lyrics is from the *Imperial Bedroom* and the song is called: *Man Out of Time*

There's a tupenny halfpenny millionaire

Looking for a four penny one

With a tight grip on the short hairs

Of the public imagination

For his wife and kids some how

Real life becomes a rumor

Days of Dutch courage

Just three French letters

And a German sense of humor

He's got a mind like a sewer

And a heart like a fridge

He loves to be insulted

And he pays for the privilege

And now I will proceed to drain this of its blood. I believe the short hairs refers to the public's attention span, which is not very long; but also I think it is a British colloquialism for pubic hair, which could also represent a man's sexual attention span, which is also not very long. This tuppence halfpenny thing is British colloquial for money-two pennies a half a penny etc.-and I believe he is saying that this individual has a high opinion of himself. It also seems he is looking for a prostitute or a cheap date - a four penny one. These words simply sound great as they spill out. He seems to be living his life largely outside of the scope of his family, and for them, real life is just a rumor. They only hear about real life through telling them about his experience of it - if only in his mind.

Dutch courage is drinking heavily so that you can do something when you are drunk that you don't want to do. French letters are the condoms the British supplied to the soldiers when they liberated France in the Second World War. Germans are known for both their bawdy and extremely dry sense of humor, and it's a bit of a backhander, in that Germans-in Europe's eyes- take themselves a bit too seriously(Germans tend to be not that funny, really). These are all countries near England, but across the channel in the real life rumor. When we do jobs we really hate, we love to be insulted and pay for the privilege. In other words, we take the shit we are dealt with to get the cheque. Or even worse, we have such a low value of ourselves that we pay someone to insult us. The fellow in the song is pondering to himself about killing his wife or committing a crime, and as the record unfolds, you realize that he does something and ends up in jail or becomes a *Man Out of Time* i.e., outside of the normal world. I have by no means exhausted this unpacking and I have to a certain extent only allowed you to see my perspective of it. Elvis Costello would probably have a whole bunch of different things to say about it and you could probably add a thing or two as well. In many ways he could simply be playing with words and allowing us to imply our narrative back into his word play. This is the whole point: all of these things can be or are true in some way and the metaphorical style allows us all to participate.

   The eighties music and culture thrived on metaphorical ambiguity, both sexually and lyrically. It became a bit of a mania that artists could and should be very ambiguous. They all seemed to suggest that they didn't have to define themselves, because they were artists and somehow were elevated above such trite and explicit matters as justifying their ambiguous verbiage. They probably adopted this attitude from the 12th century painters and composers, or the ever-elusive jazz musicians that were ahead of them. On the other hand, any explanation that is offered can limit what can be understood, and it tends to shut down the listener's engagement. This is part of the downside of metaphors, as well as exegesis. Metaphors are open to multiple interpretations and the real world of business, law and diplomacy cannot function in this way. Neither can Facebook by the way. Metaphors are not the language of law or government, or science. Religion is the flexible language of seeking to express the eternal ideal. Communism and science for that matter have created almost no music.

Some younger artists also have a tendency to hide behind this type of metaphorical ambiguity, because it disguises the fact that they don't have anything really substantial to say. Van Morrison or Bob Dylan can speak to us directly, because they know who they are and what they want to say.

"Enlightenment still don't know what it is"- Van Morrison's *Enlightenment*

"It is true that sometimes, you can see it that way"- Bob Dylan's *Oh Mercy*

We in the west have become enamored with youth culture (we are a young continent), but when you look at it, what is Brittney Spears telling us that we really need to know? Or what is American Idol telling us? These kids can't even sing their own songs. It is glorified Karaoke and we take it *way* to seriously. Brittney Spears is intent on telling us she is young and sexy and we become fascinated with the subsequent train wreck that is her life. We all know that a young woman can be sexy, but again we are entranced with the illusion.

"Every generation throws a hero up the pop charts."- Paul Simon

And we all watch them fall back down again with equal relish.

Like Joni Mitchell said, she was a long distance runner in a short distance race. I personally like the brutal endurance of the marathon more than the flash of 100 meters. This is also why soccer has a hard time gaining traction in America. If you commit suicide how can you ever find out if you could have fulfilled your purpose if such a thing exists? Staying vital as an artist is not a riddle to be solved, but a process to be involved in and *experienced* right through to the bitter end.

What's a Meta Phor

Lord Krishna was sitting in a field one day and he developed the desire to gain an understanding of the true nature of Maya or the nature of self-generated illusion, and along with this, how the great cycle of time worked. Brahma the great lord of creation heard his questioning and came to help him understand the nature of long time. He said: *"My child I will tell you all about Maya, but first you must get me a glass of water from that meandering river just over there."* This seemed like a small price to pay, so Krishna went off to fetch the glass of water. As he was walking along a wooded path to the river, he spotted a lovely young maiden with swelling bosoms who seemed to be demurely beckoning him into her hut. 'Brahma will wait for his water', he thought 'this lovely maiden needs my attention now.' After many days of lovemaking this maiden felt the need to introduce Krishna to her father who immediately liked the boy and proposed a marriage. This seemed like a good idea, and after many years, Krishna and his wife had all kinds of lovely children. They built an excellent farm and were truly leading an exemplary life together.

One day it began to rain very hard and the river by their farm began to swell. Krishna ran towards his house to alert his wife and children and bring them to safety, but it was too late. He arrived just in time to see all the people he loved swept away down the swelling river and smashed against the rocks farther down. He also-in an effort to save his family-got caught up in this raging torrent and was swept downstream. After struggling for some time, he managed only just enough strength to swim to the shore and drag himself up on to the riverbank to safety. As he stood up, he noticed that Brahma was sitting right in front of him and Brahma immediately asked him if he had the glass of water. Anymore questions?

Ecstasy

As you may have noticed, most of this book has to do with the mind and the various ways in which we view the world through our intellectual lens. I did briefly discuss the way that women experience ecstasy in religious engagement and that is where we shall go now.

The early sixties saw an explosion of British guitar players who were all experiencing the emotional power of the blues: Eric Clapton, Jimmy Page and Jeff Beck are among some of the ones who built lasting careers out of this initial explosion. England was probably a suitable place for this conversion. Because of the uptight nature of post Victorian mores, overt emotions were not encouraged (stiff upper lip), and also the two great wars had leveled parts of the social playing field. The feminist movement, the social parity of blacks, and the arts in general gained a lot of traction from this post war social leveling.

What caught the young guitar players was the emotional directness of the Blues, not an intellectual process. It was more the feeling. This feel is what would become Rock and Roll, which is truly the child of the Blues. What the kids are connecting to is the intensity and emotional directness. If you seriously look at the history of modern American music, it is tough not to concede that most of the great new ideas came from Black musicians. Miles Davis liked to call all of this new music in the west 'black American music' and he was right, although jazz did borrow heavily from the classical music that preceded it. The irony is that most black music was made popular by white people adopting it and selling it to other white people. Vanilla Ice is one of the more extreme examples of a white guy obviously using black ideas and getting huge commercial success, but Chet Baker and Gerry Mulligan, Benny Goodman, Bix Biderbeck, Elvis Presley and the Back Street Boys could all be thrown on to the pile. I will be speaking in very broad generalizations here, which unfortunately is the imprecise language of psychology, anthropology and sociology.

What popular black music contains so well is the immediacy of the emotions. That's why it's called soul music. This may be a reflection of centuries of pain coming through their cultural consciousness, but what is represented or embodied so well in soul music is capturing the expressed emotional moment, which sucks you, the listener into participating in the engagement. I have always said, if you don't like Bob Marley or seventies Funk music, you have a serious tight ass problem.

This idea of emotional engagement is really the essence of great musical performances. When an artist doesn't have the will or strength to become totally engaged in a performance, they can at least portray this engagement outwardly, if they are good. I would also add that this isn't necessarily an intentional deception on the artist's part, not like lip syncing. No one can be on their game all of the time. To portray this type of engagement in a live situation-to my mind-includes the knowledge of what musical engagement is in the first place. And the act of portraying engagement can and does actually force you to become engaged, much like smiling makes you happy. I should think that Beyoncé knows exactly what this feels like. She always seems to be absolutely present. This is probably the essence of what good acting is, which is to become the role that you wish to portray. Engagement is really the key to becoming and/or being good at anything. And, like doing math with an abacus, soon enough you simply have to perform the motions and you become the math through the ritual of your body.

There is a state in music where you are simultaneously detached or really absorbed in the background of the music and fully complicit in the unfolding of the event. Pat Metheny talks about not playing, but listening really hard when you play, as if someone else was inside your head listening and telling you what you should play next, because it would sound good to them. When you become completely engaged in artwork the 'you' playing along is only the passive conduit through which the music is happening. Music is going on in and around you. Eastern philosophy has recognized this series of levels in our consciousness and has sought to express it directly in the hierarchy of gods. Krishna is a personal deity that we can worship as such, but he is also a temporal manifestation of Brahman who is the avatar of Vishnu, who Shiva allows to believe is the creator of the universe, which is then again an expression of that which cannot be easily expressed. This is encompassed by the divine creative essence of Atman: that which is both the ground of being and the inexpressible beyond the ground. The mind runs into paradox as it touches the edges. There is another level of engagement beyond being 'passively' absorbed in music in which your ego completely dissolves into the music. I once read an article in which a number of musicians discussed what this aspect of total engagement was like. At the time of the interview (eighties), Branford Marsalis said that he had been totally immersed in the music he was playing only a couple of times. These feelings of oceanic absorption are at the root of the experience that has given us the religious drive. Nusrat Fateh Ali Khan, the Sufi Qawwali singer from Pakistan, was asked if he had ever achieved this oceanic engagement or dissolution in music while he was performing. He said that he had this experience happen to him every night when he plays, and that this state was -for him- the whole point of playing. His expressed that his job was to try to get *everybody else in there with him*.

I was lucky enough to have seen Nusrat Fateh Ali Khan play twice and I should think that he knew how to become totally engaged. The point of Qawwali singing is to create this total absorption in the music between the singer and the audience so that together they are pushed into the trance of the religious realm. In the live performances I saw, Nusrat Fateh Ali Khan would start a song that the audience knew and he would get everybody involved, and after a while, he would start to improvise lyrics or start incorporating Persian poetry or Urdu religious verses, or any number of spontaneous things so that people would be listening really closely to hear what was being said. Sometimes these songs would go on for half an hour and, if the interest in the song seemed to flag in any way, he would either change something or simply end the song and start another one to draw the audience back in to reengage them. Singing along was definitely encouraged. I believe this absorption was what John Coltrane was experiencing at the end of his career when he would solo for 20 minutes.

The ancient Greek word for this engagement was 'tonus' and tonus is achieved when your physical ability was commensurate with your emotional attachment. The Sanskrit word for complete engagement in the moment is Sajhana or sadhana. Sajhana is my favourite word and my definition of it is: 'the act of being here now'. This idea also implies a disassembling of the ego, which will then allow complete engagement. This total engagement seems to come upon us unbidden, although it can be encouraged to occur in us by our active participation in art/music/dance/the body, etc. This, my friends, is one of the largest points of this whole book. We create and/or become meaning by engagement in the Now. Once again, this creates a problem for the ego, which then seeks to identify itself with this state of mind. We begin to think it is us doing this thing. There really is no 'us' to do it: *there is only it* - Krishna Brahman Atman.

An aside, it seems Eddie Vedder from Pearl Jam spent some time with Nusrat Fateh Ali Khan before Nusrat died, while Vedder was working on the *Dead Man Walking* soundtrack, and it seems that he was greatly influenced by this truly great religious man. I think Pearl Jam is now embodying this attitude of engagement by carving out a path in the world of pop, which is running alongside the corporate machinery. It seems they have taken the hint from the Grateful Dead and concentrated their energy on live performances. This is also why jazz records, for the most part, are recorded live on the floor. The artists are trying to capture that spontaneous engagement. Also, it's cheaper to record this way and jazz records almost never sell that much - certainly not millions of copies.

If you have ever seen a video of Jimi Hendrix playing guitar you understand what this elemental power of engagement is. What Hendrix had captured -that Miles so admired- was the combination of emotional directness and technical skill. This is one of the reasons why Hendrix is held in such high regard. I have seen interviews with numerous English musicians who have said that seeing Jimi Hendrix play was the single reason they went on to play music. One man *on fire* can change the world.

I was reading a book called the *Cultural Cannon* by Harold Bloom. In it he makes the point that one of the reasons Shakespeare is at the centre of the western cultural canon is because he can be performed and enjoyed by any level of society from the aesthetically adept, down to children. Shakespeare intentionally wrote to all levels of his audience without pandering to any of them. I would add that this is one of the reasons Led Zeppelin or Jimi Hendrix have such broad appeal as well. Even pretentious jazz musicians listen to Jimi Hendrix. In the sixties and early seventies, and again in the mid-eighties, people seemed to accept without hesitation a new and individual take on what music could be; and the best music was also the most popular. Joni Mitchell cites the early jazz period of Gershwin and Rogers and Hart-the so called American song book- as a comparable era where the best music was also the most popular. The disassembling of the music industry that has happened in the last 10 years will prove to be a massive boon to the art of music. It's all wide open now and everyone can make music fairly cheaply.

Oumwala Sajhana

In ancient Greece there was a whole side to their religious mythologies that we know very little about. These movements are now known collectively as the Greek mystery cults. They were the cults of Orpheus, Dionysus, Cybele, along with the highly evolved Isis of Egypt and later on, running somewhat parallel, were the precursors to Christianity: the cults of Mithraism and especially Sol Invinctus from the Far East, to name a few. They seem to reflect a continuation of elements of the older hunter-gatherer and 'matriarchal' religious ideals. All of these cults had some type of personal, and usually secret, initiation process. Some of them involved drugs similar to LSD. Argot, a mould that grows on rye, seems to have been one of the drugs of choice in the Eleusinian mystery cult, and the orphic cult seemed to have used opium. Opium poppies are quite common on the cult's relief that have come down to us. This may be symbolic. The priestesses at Ephesus used to hover over an open hole in the ground that was releasing intoxicating gases. This would get her high or help her commune with the gods, so that she could prophesize.

What was intrinsic to all of these ecstatic cults was the use of music and rhythmic dance or movement to induce trance-like states. The point of the initiation process was to help the initiate experience within themselves a state of ecstasy or trance, or at least participate collectively in a communal shift in consciousness. The use of music, dance and drugs was and is part of a whole religious ensemble that stretches back to the very beginnings of the religious urge in humans. The Indian Vedas (from at least 2000 BC, but probably 3500 BC and written down much later), discusses the preparation of the sacred Soma drug to be ritually taken by the Brahman and rishis. I have just found out that Soma was a combination of opium, marijuana and some other herb, possibly Ephedra or even magic mushrooms, with energizing properties like coffee that would help to counteract the slumbering effect of the other two drugs. The Greek mystery cults were among the last organized remnants of this Dionysian aspect of religion in the west and they kept infecting the Christian religion-especially in the Greek Middle East-until Christianity gained official status in Rome around 350 AD.

Gnothi Seauton: Know Thyself

Someone in Greece who had been through this religious *experience* was called an Epoptae or a seer - one who has witnessed for themselves the gods. This ecstatic aspect has become known in the west as the Dionysian side of religion as opposed to the arid intellectual or Apollonian aspect. Social anthropologists witnessed this ecstatic side of religion-in context-with the aborigines of Australia, the tribes in the Amazon and again when we established contact with the peoples of the South Sea Islands of Borneo, the Andaman islands in the late Victorian era and early 1900's respectively. These eastern peoples had ceremonies involving dance and chanting that would last all night long, and very frequently the men and women would achieve a state of divine trance. Also the various natives of the Brazilian rain forest, or the west coast of the Americas, have discovered many psychoactive drugs in their habitat (peyote, ayahuasca and magic mushrooms, to name a few), and have used them for the very same reasons.

What exactly is going on neurologically in a trance state is not clearly known, but this state seems to be induced in us by our uniquely human ability to synchronize ourselves (both our minds and bodies) with each other through the ecstatic engagement in music and dance. It seems that trance lowers the self-conscious ego-enforced reasoning threshold (possibly left brain), and allows the more fluid unconscious mind to come forward. It also seems to induce long-term collective empathy, which I suspect is another aspect of the gift of mimicry we inherited from the ensemble of mirror neurons and its associate hormone oxytocin. Much of this ritualized movement seems to come to us spontaneously from the phylogenetic – the older areas around the brain stem and animals constantly engage in ritual movement to reduce stress. These ecstatic rituals were always part of group behavior. We are, or were, all in a very real sense participating in the trance state we witness happening in others. From an evolutionary standpoint, this collective formation of empathy through mimicry is of great social and personal value, especially in a small hunter-gatherer tribe. It seemed to have survived and been refined in us by choosing to repeat throughout the ongoing miracle of evolution. It can quite safely be called a religious instinct in the same sense that birds have an instinct to fly south in winter. (Read Nicholas Wade's *The Faith Instinct*) This ability to become engaged in the present resides in us all, right now. This is the whole idea of the inner archetype writ large.

Humans have developed at least two ways of experiencing the world: first the analytic and second the more integrative and fluid symbolic. The right brain, in cahoots with our beautiful frontal lobes, sees a woman on the street or a woman in a Picasso painting, or Athena on the Acropolis, or an interesting rock in a river bed and connects this individual sighting with the symbolic super structure of all women. There is a central hub to which the image of women is attached, but all manifestations are *spokes of difference.* The analytic seeks to differentiate and isolate each woman/spoke in order to compare. The symbolic seeks to integrate similarity and recognize each place inside of the wider context of the wheel. I think this is the main intellectual problem with the concept of the archetype in that it is not an intellectual concept at all. It represents everything that cannot be pushed cleanly into an intellectual box. Archetypes are a whirlpool in the stream (they are a higher or meta-state of organization, caused by the constriction of moving through an environment), and it is pointless to break the stream down into its individual drops of water. Archetypes are both pushed by the water behind them and pulled forward by the gravity of our intellect, and they coalesce into a whirlpool (increase in their implicit meaning) when a blockage occurs (we get stressed). They are the ever-so-human sign posts created by thousands of years of observing sign posts. They are a reflection of our unique ability to think symbolically.

An archetype could be something simple like our ability to become enraged. This impetus to become enraged happens very low down in the oldest parts of our brain. But the urge can be modified by our environment and subsequently built upon by our ongoing commitment to it. We can then actually plan out a crime over time while, all the while, being absorbed in the remembrance of our primal rage. The initial stance of rage has been canalized and modified by our ongoing commitment to it. Rage itself has an evolutionary purpose, but it was bumped up through the brain from the spine through the hypothalamus then into the amygdale and up into the neo cortex, if need be. As the initial reflex evolved, each step of the ladder has gained a little more control. And so the original archetype pushes its way up from this primary stance to be *filled in* finally by elements of consciousness and intent.

I can't resist this: the human mind processes all tools used through the left brain, because tools are an abstraction of work in the environment, but we don't approach musical instruments as tools. The right brain is so in love with music that it treats musical instruments as a human being. The right brain doesn't treat them 'as if' they were human. Like all symbolic thought, they are human. We become one with them in the same sense that a metaphor is not a representation of similarity; it is recognition of being identical/at one with/engaged in, that other. In some very real ways, we don't make music. We become one with it like having a lover. The metaphors are not strained; they *are* the/a truth.

It came to my attention that the human body has developed a system that kicks in after extreme physical exertion. The endocannabinoid system releases chemicals that react with receptors in the brain that get us high after extended physical exertion. This is the physiological reason for the runner's high. These largely dopamine receptors, are also involved in the act of getting high from marijuana and other drugs, and creating the accompanying euphoric sense of empathy. People have been selected for the ability to endure long distance running, probably as a result of their ability to catch big game through endurance hunting, which is the act of running an animal into a state of heat exhaustion (thought to be the oldest form of hunting big game). Humans can practice endurance hunting, because we have the ability to carry water and we don't over heat as easily as large animals, like an antelope. So we, as a species, have retained/acquired/embodied this endocannabinoid system to help us persist in the hunt. We have repurposed or simultaneously developed it (co-evolved) to experience religious ecstasy and trance-like states of mind through collective rhythmic dance. It would be interesting to know how long our species have been smoking pot (at least 5000 years in the historical record), and whether this ability to get high developed as part of the same reward system. Drugs and visions are old and rationally explicit thinking is the new kid on the block.

We don't seek to understand (displace ourselves from) the animal we are hunting so that we can imagine ourselves finding them. Hunters *are* the animal that they chase and this is their advantage. This is probably the appeal of modern big game hunting, though I see guns as a pathetic disengaged super advantage.

Participant: *"Couldn't one call this knowledge also mystical knowledge?"*

Professor Jung: *"That would be a metaphysical term. We view this question, however, from the psychological standpoint. Then we understand that there is still another way of gaining knowledge that is simultaneously a life process. Naturally, these things are alien to us, but become more understandable if we make ourselves acquainted with the psyche of eastern man. In the east, the intellectual thinking processes recede very much into the background. The whole philosophy of the Upanishads and classical Chinese philosophy, for instance, stem from life processes whose nature 'is' and at the same time a process of gaining knowledge. This stands in contrast to the academic intellect that is often empty and, as we know, doesn't always do us any good. For women particularly, it's something destructive, for what basically concerns her is not the intellect. What concerns her is gnosis. That's why so many women are most deeply disappointed by their university studies, in particular philosophy, because nowadays (1940) philosophy is treated intellectually, in contrast to antiquity when it was still a life process. Then it was gnosis – a drive, a fact of nature, an inner need. It was like water seeping into dry ground. Gnosis is knowledge stemming from blood. Thus, the alchemists say of the stone: 'Invenitur in vena, sanguine plena,' That is, the stone or lapis is found in blood-filled veins. That's why it is also called sanguineus, or carbuncle, or ruby."* - Carl Jung: *Children's Dreams* Seminar - Pg. 260

Tantric yoga-from Kashmir-is thought to be a reflection of a number of self-realized women teachers, re-initiating their male students back into the secrets of the immediacy of sex. The Apollonian intellect of men has a tendency to displace us and then seek to reject the maternal world, by focusing primarily on abstracted representation it has created. This is somewhat safer for intellectuals. Men fly around in the air of intellectual thinking. They feel safe in it (computer nerds' outward reflection of this inward intellectual safety net is an underlying *suspicion* that there will be an apocalyptic conspiracy theory in the world, etc. (Outward shadow) When you can't disassemble your thinking through a confrontation in the real world, you tend to presume that your thinking *is* the real world. Women are the real world (Maya) and they can bring men back into their bodies, which is more profound and integrated wisdom. (This rejection of the flesh is the root problem that the Catholic faith has grappled with as it organized itself. Diocletian tried to enact laws prohibiting men from self-castration in the fourth century.) Tantric sexual practices are a reflection of a higher integration of the real wisdom of being in ecstasy now. It also seems that an inordinate number of contemporary yoga teachers -mine for instance- and the majority of the initial Jungian analysts were and are women - surprise! Women are already here now. Do you have that glass of water?

Younger people, who would seek to have yet another intense experience, are naturally drawn to the immediacy of the drug experience. Also, the fact that drugs are taboo in our North American culture, lends them some of their mystique. What we in the west have done is eliminate any cultural polish, or larger contextual religious polish, that the collective and organized aspect of these oceanic experiences might have had, or *can have for us now*. In the past, people would not take drugs alone. The essence of this experience is instructional/collective and societal. This continual yearning for the Dionysian is probably evolutionarily hard-wired and has manifested, yet again, in the modern Rave scene, which has their drug of choice: the aptly name, 'Ecstasy'. My larger point is that this same inherent Dionysian urge, is what drove young white kids in Britain into the arms of the Blues and also got so many people to the Woodstock festival. The sixties, in essence, was a massive reassertion of the Dionysian aspect of the collective psyche as it continually seeks to redress an overt Apollonian stance. As all of the hippies have grown older, they are doing what aged wisdom in society always does to the Dionysian urge: seek to shut it down with an Apollonian conservative backlash. They would wish to help their children avoid the promiscuous "mistakes" of their own youth. Witness the resurgence of Fundamentalist Republican Tea Party ideology in the United States and the vicious anti-intellectual stance of this movement, which is completely absurd. This is the tyranny of the vocal minority.

This Dionysian aspect is better known and moderately more accepted in India-and the various eastern religions-as the left-hand path (read right brain). Tantric practices, and the huge devotional resurgences of Hinduism, have occurred partially as a reflex against the mogul Muslim insurgence in the medieval period, specifically. Overtly devotional practices tend to embody this aspect of understanding. The more militant aspects of Islam in India have been disassembled in part by the ongoing acceptance of Dionysus within the Indian culture and the fact that Indian religious practices simply overwhelm daily life. This unending wave of Hindu devotion has resulted in long eras of exceptional religious tolerance. This tolerance is also reflected in the various Sufi cults that arose from within Islam itself. These cults have a tendency toward disrespect for strict doctrinal purity and far greater acceptance of music. The political suspicion of the left-hand path of Sufi cults, and/ or the rise of right-wing orthodoxy within the political machinery, is partially what is responsible for Islam's failure to capitalize on the undoubted technological and mathematical advantages it possessed from the 12th to 15th centuries.

I am disappointed, but can understand why modern western society has felt the need to endlessly crush this type of personal experience. These types of experiences are uncontrollable and they lead to-in extreme cases-new prophets popping up all over the place. The Protestant Quakers initially embraced this type of immediate experience of God (quaking with the Holy Spirit), but they also helped to set us on the Lutheran anti- aesthetic path by downplaying all forms of external adornment or representation. This is also part of the reason Muhammad is the seal of the saints or the last prophet. In the Greek mystery cults-or at least in the ancient cult of Isis-there was a lengthy training period before you were allowed to enter the inner sanctum and go through the ceremony that allowed you to witness the godhead for yourself. The priests would canalize this process by preparing the initiate for their experience and, for the most part, the initiates were forbidden to divulge the divine essence of the understanding, even if they could articulate it (an early form of Masonic Scientology?). The process of ritual is the displacement or expression of the symbolic into the real world.

In *The Golden Ass of Apuleius* by Marie Louise von France, she discusses the golden ass, which is an obliquely written account, reflecting Apuleius initiation into the Isis cult around 300-400 AD. She explains that these mystery cults were reasserting the feminine Eros or feeling aspect into the very Apollonian patriarchal society of Roman-dominated Greece. Ibn Arabi had an ecstatic vision of Sofia/Eros as he perambulated the Ka'aba in Mecca. This is the same thing. If you missed it, this is one of the largest points of this whole book. Feeling, Eros,

Dionysius, Isis, Kali, Mary, Shakti, right-brain etc., this is the other half of reality that the west seems intent on burying through self-mortification of the body. The former Pope Benedict told us that it might be OK for male prostitutes to use condoms to help curb the spread of Aids (really…that's the best you got? How many male prostitutes could there possible be in the world? By implication, a woman prostitute is bad no matter what. Men have used forms of this absolutely idiotic argument against women for eons. Women should cover their hair up, lest they tempt men while in church. Benedict also thought to apply his ocular wisdom towards yoga and he once said that yoga shouldn't be practiced by good Christians. Such is the weak will of everyone who needs the Pope to keep us on track and out of our bodies. At least he was smart enough to retire.)

There always seems to be a societal urge for balance between Logos and Eros, and these types of ecstatic practices have continually re-manifested themselves and confounded the explicit western patriarch. This experiential urge has been the cause of most of the western religious upheavals. She was behind the Albigensian and Cathar heresies of the 1300's. Elements of Protestantism and the ecstatic Quaker movement specifically sought to redress the balance, but were swallowed in an Apollonian backlash almost immediately. The vicious suppression of women in the witch hunts in America and Europe are more of the same. The sixties sexual revolution was a fairly successful manifestation of Dionysus, which is now experiencing more backlash.

Most of the Catholic saints in Europe, including Hildegard von Bingen, Brother Clause of Switzerland or even Thomas Aquinas, were people who initially had heretical and or ecstatic visions, and they persisted in holding on and developing their heretical views, though this perseverance was later accepted, and then canonized back into the fold. If the Catholic Church doesn't kill them, it seems they make it stronger. An aside, I personally believe the reason that the Taliban can induce so much suicidal frenzy amongst its adherents is because within their unbelievably strict ideology there is absolutely no room for the experience of ecstasy (no singing, no dance, no women, etc.) and so this primal urge toward ecstasy manifests itself in the build up and execution of ecstasy through a suicide. There is virtually no other outlet to truly experience God when the tap is so tightly closed. Afghanistan is a quagmire we would do well to leave alone.

In my loose Pollyanna world I would say that on the whole, the modern rave scene has proved to be largely harmless: a bunch of kids get really high and dance all night, go home and have sex. I honestly think this is what some of them would be doing anyway, but at least at a rave they are not getting violent and they are contained. I'm quite sure that the incidence of fighting is extremely low at raves. Ecstasy (the drug and the attitude), doesn't seem to encourage acts of violence. Although, I have recently heard that the suicide rate is higher amongst Ecstasy users than even hardcore cocaine users, and that can't be good (possible urban myth). Life is inherently dangerous and there are some swing sets that shouldn't be removed from the playground even if little Johnny got kicked in the head.

Most of what I remember from my sordid adolescence (in the late seventies and eighties), was getting drunk, dancing and waiting to watch who would start fighting – no, not really true. I'm a lover not a fighter. Does it still sound cliché? The fact they are a forbidden trance, and ecstasy gained a dark forbidden aura, makes kids want to experience them. Like homosexuality, these ways of being are a fact and a very old fact - probably older than prostitution. We must build a bulwark against the black mud of occultism (see Dr. Freud). Drug use and rhythmic trance are common to all of the so-called primitive cultures, and seeking this divine engagement is the single largest component in the making of a Shaman, which is also a worldwide phenomena. Whether these shamans are good or evil (right or left hand), seems to be a matter of their own personal temperament or integration into a wider social morality. Of course, the dark under belly of drug use is addiction, which is never far away.

For the kids of my generation and beyond, it has been this elemental Dionysian aspect of rock music that 'turned us on'. All you have to say is 'fuck the man' and everybody starts cheering (see *Trapeze Swinger* by Iron & Wine). When Pete Townsend smashed his guitar, there was nothing left to say except that he had to get a new guitar to play a show the next night, so I guess there was something else to say? This effort to control the Dionysian is why rock music has become the voice of rebellion and also some of the reasons why we have this bad boy rebel image at all. India has gone down a very different road from us. They talk about the left and right hand paths with a sense of resigned ambiguity. We wish people to stay on the right hand path of canalized devotion, but a certain amount will take the left hand no matter what. As just mentioned, tantric practices probably started with female yogis and some of the men then turned this type of practice into a written document – go figure. The left hand always seems to regenerate the orthodox right hand and then elements of the left hand become stale, formalized and orthodox too, needing to be disassembled and regenerated. The *'times they are a changing'* by Bob Dylan has been used in a bank advertisement.

There is no strict right way to see the world and we must allow room for the push and pull. A great mind can allow the opposites to play within itself, while moving to transcend the tension.

Divine Raga

I will be talking about Indian classical music in this next section so that we can fire up another well developed and completely different cultural canon. In the Indian tradition, the drive of musical training is toward instilling the ability to improvise. They nurture the desire to function from within the moment not the ability to portray 'what that moment should be like'. Indian classical music recognizes its kinship with western jazz, but they have developed their own idea of what improvisation is.

The basis of Indian classical music is the raga, raaga or rag, at its most elemental level. A Raga is a scale with a distinct emotional value placed on certain keynotes within the progression. The progression can be played forward in a certain order and then reversed, possibly with some changed notes as you move back toward the root or the resolving tonic note. There is never a key change in Indian classical, because the instruments have so many passive resonating strings that cannot be tuned on the fly. This eliminates the possibility of changing key. The resonating strings are drone notes like the extra pipes on Scottish bag pipes and they restrict the key that you can play the instrument in. For the musicians reading this: the ability to change key within a song has to do with the western development of the piano and harpsichord, and the realization associated with tempered tuning. (Hence Bach's well tempered Clavier). Indian classical music has not developed some of our forms of polyphony, which is multi-voiced harmonizing. They prefer to emphasize the unique solo voice and they have sought to bring value into the unique texture and emotional expression of each note instead of exploring something like a multi-textured orchestra. Of course, they have embraced these things now, but they were not a large part of the Indian musical environment until the late Victorian era.

What Indian musicians did develop among many things was a range of far more subtle notes within each of these scales. The Indian musical system has developed half and quarter tones. These are the notes that would fall in between the notes represented by the keys on the piano. For instance, there could be a note in between F and F sharp and this would represent a quarter tone. Some of these notes strike the western listener as dissonant and your listening palate must become accustomed to these harmonies. Hendrix chose the most dissonant interval in western music to open Purple Haze. This interval (the flattened fifth) was known in medieval music as the devil's interval and it is the same interval that fire engines use to get your attention, but it now passes relatively unnoticed in the west as being dissonant. (The devil does have the best tunes.) So, we in the west can become accustomed to dissonance and quarter tone intervals through paying attention, because they are certainly accustomed to them in India.

When Ravi Shankar was studying with his guru Allauladin Khansahib, he would only be allowed to learn a new raga after he had completely mastered the one that he was currently working on. He said this usually took about a month or two (again, a single melody of a raga would rarely be longer than 40 notes total). What his teacher was trying to instill in him was an appreciation of the inherent value of each note. (You may ask: how long would it take to become a great sitar player? It seems to be about 10,000 hours required to become proficient at anything. I would think more like 10 years to become a master, if you averaged five to eight hours a day, 300 days a year. That is a little more than 20,000 hours.)

A friend of mine told me a story about a fellow who wished to learn from a master sarod player. He finally got to meet the teacher and the teacher asked this fellow to sing a scale. After singing a full eight note scale, the teacher told him to sing only five notes then three and finally only sing one note. The teacher then told this prospective pupil that the first lesson was over and he should go home and practice that one note for a week and then they could move on again to a second note. The teacher possibly just didn't like this fellow, but I also believe he was trying to teach him the value of a single note expressed with engagement. Or an understanding of the tone and color of a single note, and how that note should resonate within your being. Would you like fries with that?

I am a drummer and I studied the tabla. I have played music since I was 16. In my early thirties, I became completely immersed in Indian classical music and the world seemed to conspire to help me in this. In Indian classical music, there is no written notation to learn. Everything is sung to you. They have rightly understood that singing locks the patterns you are learning into the mind much better than having to retranslate into the mind from a written score. With the act of reading notation, you must first learn to recognize written music and then you must constantly convert the musical phrase back into a melody or rhythm from the page. Of course, this can be done with little effort by someone well trained. When a pattern is sung to you, this extra conversion step is taken out and it simply is a melody, and a rhythm. The other advantage to this way of working is that a tabla player can sing a phrase to the sitar player or a dancer and they can all understand what is going on, and relate the phrase directly into their individual spheres of expertise. It is the same vocal notation for all aspects of Indian music and dance. We don't have to chew the piece in our mind's eye and then regurgitate it through the intellect. Conversely, this technique creates difficulties when passing information on to future generations. India is very big on personal transmission through the guru lineage (Eròs). Truth is a pathless land.

When learning an instrument in the Indian system, the first things you are taught is pattern and the very next thing you do with any pattern is learn how to invert and expand on this pattern. Or, you immediately start to learn the rudiments of further improvisational possibilities. I will get a little technical now, but I feel that it is an important point. One of the standard Indian turnarounds or signals that a song is coming to an end is a 32-beat measure played three times in a row. This measure is divided into three groups of seven, and a phrase of eleven (7+7+7+11=32) this is repeated three times always ending on the one of the next bar not the 32nd beat of the last. So if the tabla player is playing a pattern in 4/4 time, he must be able to break this already established pattern apart and convert it to a seven-beat pattern and an eleven-beat pattern. This 32-beat pattern is learned almost immediately, because everyone recognizes it. Where this type of improvisation gets crazy is when someone is soloing. I have seen Indian percussion solos that are well over a half hour long and involved two percussionists (I will tell you as a drummer I have very little tolerance for drum solos, I find them indulgent and usually quite nonmusical. They either quickly get too technical or they are dummied down for the white folks.) Indian soloing on the other hand, has a pace and composure that is not as overt as it is in the west. Indian musicians are trained for improvised and structured soloing from the beginning and they seem to be unconcerned with how long it takes to flesh out and properly display an idea (very difficult to format for MTV).

Part of the Indian classical bag of tricks is that the soloist will begin with a phrase; this can be a Raga melody or the accompanying rhythmic pattern. They can adapt this root phrase into different time signatures against the original time signature. (Thelonious Monk used this trick of inversion a lot; the head to *Straight No Chaser* being a good example. He exploited this type of triplet inversion in his solos all the time, so did Jimmy Page of Led Zeppelin in *Black Dog.*) For instance, if the raga is in Tintal or a 16-beat phrase in 4/4 time, the soloist may play the melody in a five or seven, or 11-beat time signature against this 16-beat phrase. If you are playing in a five-beat phrase, you will have to play at least five full 16-bar phrases to match up with the one beat again. 5x16= 80 beats, or 16/ 5 beat phrases. This may sound like simple math, but all of the 5-beat phrases you play, except the first, are played against the original implied pulse of the time signature; then the soloist may go on to play the same thing in half or double time. Suffice to say, the Indians have developed some sweet alchemy in the realm of their classical music.

My good friend, Ravi Niampally, who I only seem to run into at Ravi Shankar or John McLaughlin concerts, was telling me that he followed Ali Akbar Khan around for five consecutive concerts in India. This master musician played the same four or five ragas at each concert but each time he played them they were completely different. Each raga is the same melody played for usually a half an hour or so – some times an hour. So Ali Akbar Khan played this same set of melodies for at least two and a half hours all together over five nights and had not rung his creativity dry. Musical construction is epigenetic as well, meaning that any change or nuance can lead to more change until the melody or rhythm is significantly different. This can happen because of any number of choices an artist makes as they play within their medium. The whole point is that the artist's skill is commensurate with their ability to open themselves up to the inherent creative nature of their own being. This involves both listening and playing.

"Astrology presupposes that we are identical with time. It expresses the quality of the moment at which we were born. Insofar as the reconstructions of character in astrology are correct, we evidently have to be identical with the moment of birth, or with time. My view on this is that time is a psychological function, identical with living as such. Such a view cannot be proved, but is extremely valuable heuristically."
C.G.Jung -*Children's Dreams* - Pg. 102

Also Indian classical music is tied to the time of day that it is being played. There are morning ragas, evening ragas and even late night and pre-sunrise ragas. A music concert can go on for five or six hours, or sometimes all day as the musicians play through the different moods associated with the times of the day. India though, has always had an explicit connection with the larger celestial happenings, so to tie music to the moods of the day is quite natural. Each raga will have a different feel to it; morning ragas tend to be expansive and mellow. I saw Ravi Shankar play an afternoon gig once and he was playing a raga that was melodically very difficult for me. Maybe the brain can't take a challenge at three o'clock in the afternoon? I have discussed Indian music because it allows us to peek outside of our own cultural box. Like the Chinese qualitative aspect of numbers, there are other ways of approaching anything and a radically different paradigm can be most enlightening. Indian philosophy has been a real eye opener for me and I look forward to diving more deeply into Chinese thought and music as the translations of more work happens. Unfortunately/fortunately, China is in the process of rediscovering her cultural heritage herself after the lunacy of the Cultural Revolution. Who knows what was lost to us as a result of the invasion of Tibet.

Part of what I am driving at is the recognition of how the mind works when engaged in playing music. The mind seems to thrive on patterning, but the patterning is not explicit; it is flexible. Again, there is no hard wiring going on here. In terms of the physical arranging of ideas within a song, I have noticed that, allowing for some significant variations, the same types of broad patterns emerge time and again. These patterns can be applied to many creative situations and the most common is based around four parts. I will relate it first to pop music. First: you introduce a theme or motif working toward the main idea as stated in the chorus. Second: you restate this whole section, possibly with minor variations, to solidify the main motif and establish a resolution in the listeners' mind. The third section is a bridge. This can be totally unrelated to the main theme and in literature this would be the section of the book where the hero experiences his darkest night. This section is setting you up for the final lysis, which is the restatement of the main theme at another level.

This idea of the third is talked about by Joni Mitchell in relation to her lyric writing and I will show one of my favorite examples, which is from Jeff Buckley. In the song the *Last Goodbye*, Jeff Buckley explores the feeling of a young man as he leaves his girlfriend. The boy knows in his head that he is too young to settle down and that he will hurt her feelings; however, he also loves this unique girl. As they part for the last time, he asks her to kiss him 'out of desire not consolation'. So the main dynamic tension is established through elaborating on the unresolved feelings in the song: the desire for love and the inability to commit, the thirst for experience in the now, and the recognition of the larger flow around you, etc. Instead of resolving this tension, he introduces a seemingly unrelated image when he gets to the bridge, which he very cleverly puts at the end of the song and it displaces us from this otherwise fairly tight narrative. The bridge/ending has an image of a bell that rings in a church tower – straight into his heart. This bell could be an inkling of weddings or any number of things, but the theme is distinct because of the introduction of a new melody. Symbolically, bells represent conscious and spiritual awakening. Jeff Buckley doesn't elaborate on this image within the song, but allows it to remain a beautiful epiphany and you are left to imply meaning into it or not. This is the third. And this third element usually occurs lyrically or melodically in the bridge, which is where an overt dynamic change can occur as well. Joni Mitchell can be more difficult to analyze in this way because she is such an idiosyncratic songwriter and she tends to work in cyclic forms a lot, but these ideas are in her work as well – most often in the lyrics.

There are also four stages of a classic drama and they can be related directly to the interpretation of a dream as well. The sections are: first, the locale which is the exposition or introduction of the theme, 'once upon a time', etc. Second: is the dramatis persona or exposition, which is the introduction of the characters' problems and why they have them. This is where the introduction of tension through duality/conflict occurs. Third: is peripeteia, or the ups and downs of the story. This is where the dramatic element is usually played out. The fourth section is either a lysis or catastrophe, depending on whether it is tragic or romantic.

In dream interpretation, you would first identify the sections and then associate other material to the images to fill out the exposition. For example, when I was much younger, I had a dream where I was forced to crawl toward my girlfriend's house in extreme winds, across very slippery black ice. This happened at the corner of two main streets here in Toronto named College and University. This is a pretty typical anxiety dream and I was telling someone about it later, and they pointed out that I never went to either university or college for a secondary education. I was obviously concerned about this at the time and it seems that my dreams were trying to alert me to this fact. But dreams tend to be oblique like the oracle at Delphi. I cannot remember the lysis to this dream though, as a narrative event. It may simply have been the emotional environment that the dream presented to me. I can remember very clearly the frustrating tension of crawling on black ice. Oh those teenage years! This is like Aristotle's methodology in which you collect the various elements and analyze them or categorize them to gain an explicit intellectual understanding.

This is the same quaternary dynamic structure that we see reflected in the sacred Ohm of the Hindu religion. And I would argue that it is the same dynamic that is reflected in all narratives from our own dreams or Grimm's fairytales, or even *War and Peace*. This is the natural rhythm of the human psyche, which is both reflected in our creations and imposed backward into them by our efforts to uncover or impose a pattern in them. Everything seems to arise out of nothingness and this is the great mystery. How does consciousness arise out of matter, etc? The quaternary Ohm is the single best example of, and indicator pointing towards, this divine mystery. But, I digress.

One of the most important aspects of dream analysis is the overall feeling of the dream. Did you wake up scared or calm, or crying? Everything in the dream must be related to the overall feeling tone. This schema of breaking down a dream into four different sections can be very helpful when you are trying to get behind your own dreams. This is analysis, where you pull apart the various aspects and seek to illuminate the symbols so that they can be recognized. The tricky part in dream analysis is to reduce the whole dream into one sentence and realize explicitly the overall meaning of it – much like trying to identify the main character's reasoning within a play or the overall point or meaning for their being. This is an analytic tool that can be used to format and look more deeply into art. What I find interesting is that most artists are probably unfamiliar with this basic schema but follow it nonetheless – as do our dreams. This is what Jung is driving at with the idea of an archetype. Whether we are aware of it or not, we follow intrinsic behavioral patterns and elements of our growing consciousness, which are more or less explicit recognition of these structures.

"Why must we dream in metaphors, and try to hold on to something we couldn't understand."- Seal

We know that when people are in love everything seems great and they don't get as upset about things in their partner. In my own Pollyanna universe, I like to think that this is the way we were born to be, or that when we are in love we have glimpsed the way our brains and personality were supposed to function in the world. As an extension of this idea, I also have a hard time envisioning sudden creative solutions popping out of the mouth of the guy in the office who is just plain miserable all of the time.

My contention is that Buddhist/Hindu/Sufi etc., training or a deep analytical and practical understanding of many of the world's less dogmatic religious traditions should at the very least instill in the practitioners a more positive outlook - or provide an alternate perspective into the world, reflected from a wisdom tradition. If you consider science to be a wisdom tradition, then this is also the main goal of the sciences. If we can achieve a more positive and integrated outlook or window clean the soul, or even if we come to believe that such an integrated outlook is possible, we are in many ways better positioned to respond to the real world in a creative way. I think one of the essential drives behind psychoanalysis is to clear out the warehouse so that we can then receive the new spring collection. We will then be looking good as the world takes on creativity. Creativity, or at least a more positive outlook, is better for everybody: your relationship with yourself and everybody else will be better or more forgiving, and hence more productive.

Krishnamurti's main contention would be that we should try to look deeply into problems through analysis, but no amount of belief in illusory thought constructions will change facts. It is of some comfort to believe that we will not die after death, but this really doesn't change the fact that we will die. What is most interesting is trying to understand why we are afraid to die, which is really more about our fear of living, etc.

If you wish to skip to the last chapter you will find a stunning quote by Krishnamurti on love. What he is saying in a nutshell is that we learn to love by letting go of hate. Love is a mystery and it will happen by itself, as long as we stop dwelling on hate and let it go. This is not some naive Pollyanna view of the world. It is, to my mind, the underlying truth, if we can nurture or uncover a better attitude toward everything. Hate is a fact. It is part of our consciousness, but we don't have to nurture it. We don't clean house by imagining what it will be like when it is finally clean. We clean house by taking out the trash, right now.

Now it seems that science will back me up on this very point in that the mind seems to function better when it is happy. This insight is a very strong support for the recent trends in child psychology and psychology in general. You cannot give people too much love (which is not to say that you can't spoil them. Gifts can be a substitute for real love, hence African aid, which can also be viewed as an extension of a power drive). Genuine affection and love will encourage a secure feeling in the world and encourage children to explore and grow within their environment.

In the *Evolution of God,* it is Robert Wright's contention that mankind's moral compass (reflected in our western religious traditions writings), becomes wider when people are forced or encouraged to cooperate with their neighbors. War is rarely a good thing for anyone involved. Although those good folks at Halliburton may disagree, war is not good for business in the long run. In Jungian terms this means that we should work toward embracing our collective shadow. We can work toward what I think is a foundational understanding of ourselves, which is when we focus our hate on somebody else, we are really rejecting a part of our own larger self. Through this externalizing of our shadow on to our enemies, we actually create a way to absolve ourselves from being responsible for what we dislike. We then get to bandy about a spicy hint of self-righteous indignation. The path toward this realization is nurtured by a religious attitude toward the world, and I mean *religious* in the widest possible sense of the term. Whether you believe in God/gods or not, is largely irrelevant.

I have tried to show, however obliquely, that scientists function under this same type of religious or awe-inspired attitude as they work to uncover the mysteries of the universe. But, some of them go to great lengths not to drag God into it. God is an element of science's shadow. When you throw the religious/emotional/value etc., attitude out completely it will crawl through the back door in some very subtle ways. You may then have people become religious fanatics for String theory or rabid dogmatic atheists, or you might call the Higgs boson the God particle, etc. Modern cosmology is the next turn of this unending spiral of insight, and any theorizing about how it will all end is another form of metaphysics dressed up or expressed as higher mathematics.

Metaphysics in the ancient world was closely allied with the concept of physics; and in the Middle Ages there was very little attempt to separate astrology from astronomy or indeed to separate God from his celestial residence. The Arabic philosophers were very concerned with creating an understanding of the cosmos. They carefully read through the only written authorities they had, which were the newly translated books by Aristotle and Plotinus. They proceeded to weave fantastic, though logical, webs of angelic hierarchies, first and second intellects, and all manner of gradations, cast about the heavens until humans finally make an appearance in the tenth sphere down from heaven, hopefully trying to gain an intellect. They tried to create or express unity between Islam, science and aspects of the older Persian religions that were all around them.

Hamid al-Din al Kirmani advises us that God can only be conceived in a double negative. Any thought that we might have concerning God is mistaken. A double negative would run like this: we assert that God is not in the universe, but the double would be that he is not, not in the universe. We don't know where God might be, because our minds are in no way prepared to understand this and we must negate all mental and physical images. God is simply beyond our ability to understand – sounds strangely like the universe itself. *"But what of standard, religiously-based discourse about God? Al Kirmani's answer is that what humans speak about when they talk of God is actually the intellect at its highest and ultimate first level. It is not really God and should never be confused with the true Lord Creator, but it is as close as humans can come. It suggests God, but is not him."* - Paul E. Walker: *The Cambridge Companion to Arabic Philosophy* Pg. 85.

"Faith is an island in the setting sun, but proof yea, proof is the bottom line for everyone." - Paul Simon

This quote from Paul Simon, dear reader, is really the whole impetus for this book. I suspect that this line just popped into his wonderful brain and caused me 15 years of hard meditation. In fact, I know that he wrote this record largely "on the microphone" from pre-recorded ensemble drum tracks. Such is the profound wonder of creative people. This simple line from a song holds all of the beautiful ambiguity about everything and it has taken me 350 pages to untangle it in my own mind. The atheist agenda would seek to assert a negative (God does not exist). They issue this assertion as an act of cleaning up extraneous theories in the manner of Ockham's razor. The logical fallacy is that they assert the elimination as though it were a positive assertion, or a necessary operation. It is somehow more correct to take this particle away. My viewpoint is to sidestep this completely, and assert the psychological FACT of the concept of God, and/ or the psychological fact that a lot of people have expended a lot of time constructing a coherent string theory or end of the universe theory, or conspiracy theory. This is how our brain works. It is part of our brain's inherently creative wiring diagram, but we become fascinated with our theories as they come out of our ass. And just because our theory has the polish of cosmology, doesn't mean it's not metaphysics all dressed up. We are metaphysics and no amount of logic will keep us safe from that.

Richard Dawkins has expended what I consider a phenomenal amount of energy and verbiage trying to first delineate and then actively foist his atheism. To my mind, he is in the same place as the man who hates God. God presses at his jugular with every waking breath. (See *A Universe from Nothing* with Lawrence Krauss on YouTube to witness someone dancing around God. At around 49 min, he quotes Einstein who specifically said God and Mr. Krauss tells us, Einstein didn't mean God. Oh that stupid Einstein, he doesn't know what he's talking about!) These guys all seem to know what I mean when I use the term God (some anthropomorphic man with a long grey beard comes to mind), and then they go out of their way to tell me I don't know what I'm talking about. It is the obsession with, and the poverty of, their conception of God that I wish to expose. We are mirrors and when I look at Mr. Krauss specifically, I realize the poverty of my understanding of the physical sciences. It's not the belief system-and atheism is a belief system-that offends me, it is the overt militancy of the position. Near the end of the video, Mr. Krauss tries to express his humility, wonder and awe as he contemplates the universe. This is quite clearly his religion and it's all over his face and posture, but he can't resist a snipe at God.

I just listened to Lawrence Krauss again on *Quirks and Quarks* 22/01/2012. He can't resist taking a swipe at religion and it seems I can't resist a swipe back. He was talking about the origins of the universe and how it came from nothing. He went on to say that as we discover more about the origins of the universe, and more about modern cosmology in general, *"The mystery is far more interesting than the myths or fairytales that people have come up with."* He is being intentionally patronizing by using the term 'fairytale' to describe origin myths. Obviously, he means religion and I think he is seeking to drive the last spike in the atheist's argument by eliminating God from the creation of the universe in the first minute, by showing that something from nothing isn't impossible. I'm not so sure cosmology has a better story. I will say that modern science is the newest interpretation of the story, but to imply that science is completely made up of pristine and non-interpreted facts is simply wrong. I only seek to expose the fact that science is trapped within linguistic confines like everything else and I would go on to argue that Lawrence Krauss's God-drained universe is a mirror image of the literal-minded fundamentalist viewing of the Bible. Each view seeks to drain the depth out of the world that we may be left with only certainties and facts like severe Asperger's. You cannot completely remove humans from any of this discussion and all of the human-created stories ultimately say more about *us* than the universe. Really, we are the most interesting part of the universe. Like it or not-in my mind-what better word (human) sums up the feeling of awe and wonder? It's our word, we invented it. Yes! Yes, it's got baggage, but don't we all?

Who's a Happy Man?

Wittgenstein was a fairly depressive and quite frankly compulsive type of character; but he did find some reward in thinking deeply and developing his own philosophy. And it seems as if he felt that he had come to grips with whatever demons were set against him. Wittgenstein is an example of someone who put the world through his own intellectual grist mill. He tried to come up with a set of basic statements that reflected a real truth: *"I believe this world of a happy man being better"* was one of them. Even though he approached the world from a very intellectual angle, he felt that he had arrived at some of the same basic truths that other people have found as they too followed their different paths, be it in religion or science. In essence, he returned to the fundamental grounding of metaphor (right brain), by following logic (left brain) to its final end and conclusion, which is a contradiction. He believed that thinking was the sickness from which he was trying to cure himself and that questions themselves are actually the problem.

I should like to make a confession and admit that much of my argument in this book is a reflection of Wittgenstein's profound anti-philosophy; and I have recently realized how deeply it worked its way into my thinking without me having explicitly realized it. I have also realized that I am far from alone in my viewpoint and this has been humbling. Nonetheless, I will still call this my book even though I clearly realize that it is an amalgamation of many other peoples' more brilliant thinking.

What I am driving at is that the happy man statement seems to be true on many levels within the human being. If you are happy, your body seems to fight disease better and you seem to be engulfed in a larger swath of the actual reality that you are. You are probably observing the flow of that reality more accurately than other people who are pissed off all of the time. You will probably get along better with everybody else, because they will be drawn to your 'good vibes', and I would also add that I think the world will-to a certain extent-conspire to agree with your rose colored outlook. Of course, the world will also conspire to fulfill your attitude if you are an asshole, or seek to correct you if you are too Pollyanna-like. I will paraphrase the chimerical Buckminster Fuller: if your only tool is a hammer, you will tend to treat everything as if it was a nail and the world always has a bigger hammer.

On a biological level, your body will generate depressing chemicals if you are depressed and happy chemicals (endorphins and dopamine's) if you are not, and/or shut you down completely with a nervous breakdown if you persist in disobeying its efforts to adjust your attitude. My admittedly weak understanding of neuro-chemicals leads me to believe that the production of depressing chemicals is not necessarily a life sentence and that through your own effort and observant hard won realizations you can turn that biological ship around. This is the chicken egg thing again. To my mind it is an endless dance between all of these things but nothing is written in stone from beginning to end. We have centers in the brain that can unleash rage but we can also control this primal urge. Some very stable/creative people have come out of really bad situations and in some sense the World, simply is a bad situation. Five thousand years of eastern philosophy-and one of its most recent exponents J. Krishnamurti-would contend that there is a foundational shift in consciousness that is available to us through our effort, which is not simply a belief system but an experiential way of being.

Even in situations as seemingly simple and straightforward as trying to build something, an even temper will help you out. I work with a lot of carpenters and I will tell you from experience that for the most part the older guys don't get upset about the work at hand. They know that anger causes mistakes and mistakes cost fingers, and that anger ultimately is counterproductive. Truly great craftsmen nurture, or have come to embody, an even temper, because they need to be able to think clearly. They recognize that everything is a process and reflection of experience. They can arrive at creative solutions through their work and trust me there is a lot of creative thinking and problem solving involved in construction. Construction is ritual expressed in the world. How many times have you seen an interview with a pissed off jazz musician? I know, never. As far as long term strategies go, anger is not a good one to try to sustain. Being an asshole seems to shorten your career arch in the music business (but stunningly not in the business world, though Lehman brothers got the axe). Tiger Woods is inconceivably an angry young man, because you cannot play golf well and still be brooding and angry. You may be able to drive a ball down the fairway when you are mad, but you will eventually have to put it into a hole, and anger or distraction is not conducive to good putting.

After all, aren't all the things we do a form of game that we play, and aren't all games played better without anger? Well… excluding professional wrestling or maybe hockey, or monster truck racing, but I could find non-anger wiggle room in all of these sports as well. Geopolitics certainly can't be sustained for a very long time from a position of vengeful anger. Even the United States can't spend money on the war in Iraq forever. (They are now suing Al-Qaeda for $6 billion. Good luck with that.) Sustained anger seems to be the position of the disenfranchised, and the disenfranchised over the long term become enfranchised or die. It's like Ghandi said: *"An eye for an eye makes the whole world blind."* An endless cycle of vendetta drains the system over the long term and eventually, in a large integrated society, some form of law will come to prevail.

Nataraj

It has long been presumed that the first crafted instrument was the drum, which would have been made out of perishable material like wood and animal skin. We don't have any ancient drums to confirm this, but archaeologists have found flutes made of bone that are extremely old. I don't have a date for you, because it doesn't matter (actually I do: 36,000 years old, found in Germany). The presumption is that man was using flutes also made of perishable material such as reeds before this date, but I would add that the human voice is obviously a musical instrument and was used as such for a much longer time than any of these crafted instruments. Birds were probably singing millions of years ago, and it seems that they sing just because it feels good. Witness the dawn chorus of birds as the sun comes up. This is the prayer of the heliotrope and why wouldn't they sing? The sun is coming up. Incidentally, the air is calmest early in the morning and the bird song carries much better. Some wise ass scientist will come up with a theory as to why birds sing in the morning, but they don't have one yet and the birds couldn't care less what intellectual box we construct.

If you analyze or even just listen closely to someone's speech pattern, you will realize that within a simple conversation there is a musical cadence and that, within ordinary speech, each person is using various notes to express themselves (this is the ribbon of changing pitches). It was Pythagoras who first apprehended the rules of harmony for the west. The story goes that he was walking by a metal workers shop and heard a man beating a length of metal and that depending on where the metal was placed on the anvil the blacksmith would get a different note; the longer the piece of metal, the lower the note. The difference between a professional musician and an amateur is one of refinement and learning. A professional knows about the relationships that exist between the frequencies of the notes that she is using. The big question is why does the universe obey or in any way reflect mathematics? Incidentally, the planets fall into the exact same spacing as the notes in our western seven-note scale with Jupiter sitting on the fifth, etc.

Now this fellow Pythagoras was a Greek mystic and he recognized that, like math, nature had given us-in music-a whole ensemble that was inherent in nature, but that these inherent relationships could be expressed or further articulated with observable rules. The Pythagorean brotherhood's credo was "all things are number" they were pretty big on number. The various relationships that exist between these naturally occurring notes are captured on the modern keyboard, but the piano is-to some extent-a bad instrument with which to express these formal harmonic rules. We in the west have tampered with the strict mathematics of harmony. This tampering allows us to change key within a piece of music and I will explain this further as we go along. Also, the east has chosen to include other notes in between the ones that we are accustomed to using.

When you hit a note in the centre octave of a piano, for example, the note A which vibrates at a very specific frequency of 440 beats per minute. It also starts other notes within the piano vibrating. These notes are called the harmony or harmonic overtone series notes-the strongest resonating notes are on the octave-that is the two A notes which are physically closest to the A that you struck, which are the same note an octave higher A 880 and the octave lower A 220. The other A's within the piano will vibrate as well. These other A notes are eight whole tones, but twelve individual piano keys away from each other hence the term octave. The next most sympathetic notes are the ones five-hole tones away. Going up the scale, these are the fifth which is the E note then the third is the next most resonant, which is C, then the fourth and seventh and ninth, etc. The notes of the first, third and fifth harmonic are called a major tri-tone and they represent the root notes of any major chord. The Three Stooges sang this tri-tone at the start of every episode. *Hello! Hello! Hello!* And it is the harmony that the Beatles used in *Twist and Shout,* as they build into the chorus: *Ah Ah Ah, well shake it up baby now, twist and shout.* These perfect mathematical harmonies can be heard by the Le Mystere des Voix Bulgares. These women sing largely unaccompanied and in what is known as 'just intonation', as opposed to tempered tuning. You will rarely find music on this earth that allows you, even on a recording, to glimpse such beauty and profound sadness (the best kind of sadness). I believe most Gregorian chants are also in mathematically perfect pitch.

Tempered tuning came around the time of Bach (yet another mystic type), and what tempering a piano means is that you slightly bend the notes as you move away from the centre octave so instead of A880, you have something like A884 then A1770 is next up. This tempered tuning occurred as a result of the development of the layout of the keyboard itself – initially the harpsichord, but later the piano. Tempering developed as a result of the technical challenges that became apparent as people tried to integrate this new keyboard instrument within the existing elements of an orchestra and this influenced the subsequent development of music, and the orchestra itself. Tempering a piano is why you have to hire a piano tuner and you can't do it yourself at home with an electronic device. The strict mathematic harmony of a piano has been fiddled with, but it is a very subtle fiddling, one best expressed through the majesty of a real human being; listening with real ears. (Apparently, the marvel of modern technology now allows us to tune our pianos with a machine so I stand corrected, though I would still hire a tuner, as would any self-respecting orchestra. An inordinate amount of tuners are or were blind, because their listening acuity is so refined. They have a tendency to develop perfect pitch.)

Now what I am getting at with all of this is that, as you go into your understanding of music, the mathematic beauty can become quite astounding, but it is not an obvious A B C beauty. It is very subtle and nuanced and yet it does bow down to rules, but all of these rules are vaguely flexible in the face of personal opinion. Like mathematics and geometry, the rules in music have been discovered; they are simply there, supplied for our uncovering, in nature. By listening, we have established which harmonies are pleasant and stable, but like aromatherapy, we can be taught to appreciate less stable harmonies or we can learn to accept and genuinely enjoy, less and less obvious structure. Lester Bowie who is a fairly *avant-garde* trumpet player is reputed to have approached Roy Hargrove after a gig in Japan and said something to the effect of, *"Damn Roy; that's some nice playing, but I didn't hear any bad notes."* Miles Davis said that if you accidentally played a bad note, you should play it again so that the audience wouldn't know. Miles had a knack of playing notes that were just on the edge of being bad, but he would hold that note longer so that you could feel it in all its badness. I have heard many people complain about Chet Baker singing out of tune, but I personally am convinced he is intentionally singing in flattened quartertones. This same type of flattened note is common in Brazilian singing and is called the 'Brazilian blue note'. This is not to say there is no such a thing as out of tune and that we should simply accept the twelve-tone pandemonium of 20th century composers.

"The legendary Danish physicist Niels Bohr distinguished two kinds of truth. An ordinary truth is a statement whose opposite is a falsehood. A profound truth is a statement whose opposite is also a profound truth."– *The Lightness of Being*, Frank Wilczek - Pg.11

There's no mercy in a live wire
No rest at all in freedom

Choices we are given

It's no choice at all

The proof is in the fire

You touch it before it moves away Yeah

But you must always know

How long to stay and when to go - Fly written by Patty Griffin performed by the Dixie Chicks

So again we have structure and flexibility and the larger point I was driving at was that we achieve freedom through discipline. First, we learn the rules, the law, how harmony works; we become technically proficient, we read the Bible and associate various nouns to individual things in our environment, etc. We are a camel loaded in the desert. But, we have a very long journey ahead of us and if we have a teacher whose main concern is with establishing adherence to rules, we will never be a lion much less a baby at play. There are rules of composition and rules for playing the blues and you have to be quite comfortable with the rules before you can go throwing them out the window. Some of this throwing out is good, but as Jung liked to say about modern art, they have forsaken beauty. Free jazz just completely pitched the rule book, and I'm not so sure that this is the way to go. I personally like to see the rule book artfully toyed with.

The price of freedom is eternal vigilance, but I would add that it is also the acceptance of responsibility and discipline. Vigilance to my mind does not mean military intervention or any type of guarding of your freedom. It means that you should be vigilant to not deny others the same respect or amount of freedom that you would garner for yourself. This means that you allow difference of opinion as a natural reflex of your own freedom of opinion. Foucault believed that we were so trapped in our self-referencing intellect and our endless search through ourselves that we had actually fallen asleep to the real world and that we have mistaken our deep self-referential gazing sleep for a type of vigilance.

Jesus saw a man working in his field on the Sabbath and one of the disciples asked if this man was not breaking the law. Jesus said: "*Man, if indeed thou knowest what thou doest, thou art blessed: but if thou knowest not, thou art accursed, and a transgressor of the law.*" (Luke: 6) This quote seems to say the opposite of what I am saying. Jesus is trying to help his disciples understand the relevance of consciousness; freedom is an extension of wisdom. Just breaking the rules without taking responsibility is childish or ignorant, and the law should rightly punish you. It is your moral responsibility to try to become conscious and if you reject this path you really are cursed. When Hammurabi codified the law, it was so that everyone would clearly see for themselves what the law was; there was now no excuse for not knowing.

I was thinking about the idea of divine punishment and how it is continually cited as the inherent beginnings of religion. Organized religion is said to have begun as a way for the systematic patriarch to garner control over large masses of people through brain-washing them into believing that God or the gods would punish them, if they went against the rule book the organizers wished to promote. This is the Atheists initial, and I would say childish, argument. The very next argument I hear regularly is how could a good God create evil in the world? First, of all I would say that the whole idea of self-denial (dietary restrictions, etc.) or divine punishment could be seen as a form of consciousness rising but it is also ritualized, because it has been determined by that individual society to be valuable. By becoming aware of the proscriptions against doing something, you become more aware of that thing which you are not doing, and hence more self observing. God will be very close to a Muslim's thoughts if he or she is confronted with western alcohol and culture on a regular basis. These proscriptions can become more flexible for the "enlightened". The previous Aga Khan told his followers with some self-irony that wine turned into water the moment that it hit his tongue. Tantric practices can seek to break the barrier between you and any perceived taboo. The tantric ideal is that all of the world can be seen as a tool that should be used by you to help promote your greater understanding. This type of cultural taboo-breaking should be pursued under the guidance of a teacher or it can degenerate into narcissism and infantile self-indulgence.

Benjamin Franklin turned around his hatred for one of his acquaintances by asking that person to lend him a rare and expensive book. This act of asking to borrow something sets up a state of cognitive dissonance in the other person. It would be very rude on the other person's part to refuse to lend you something, and it is also incongruous of that person to lend something to someone that they hate. So the other person will then seek to resolve this inner mental dissonance by trying to justify their actions by actively downgrading their dislike of you. By borrowing something from your enemy, you have created a relationship of mutual indebtedness and you have also forced that other person into your relationship with them as an equal. Benjamin Franklin became lifelong friends with this fellow. (Iraq/Iran) Israel could ask to borrow some plutonium from Iran?

This type of behavior is also done mentally in some meditation practices, in which you seek to embrace your shadow by nurturing the idea that people you dislike have been gifted to you. By practicing this ritual, you try to gain a better understanding of both them and yourself. It is the actual enacting of the ritual and the religious practice that is important; nothing happens in the real world by simply acknowledging that an idea is sound in a detached philosophical way. Religion seeks to activate both symbols and the will through ritual practice in the real world.

I am-in my less tolerant moments-quite sick of hearing American Fundamentalists spouting off about Christian family values. Jesus had no such political agenda: *"Do not suppose that I have come to bring peace to the earth. I did not come to bring peace, but a sword. For I have come to turn a man against his father, a daughter against her mother, a daughter-in-law against her mother-in-law. A man's enemies will be the members of his own household. Anyone who loves his father or mother more than me is not worthy of me; anyone who loves his son or daughter more than me is not worthy of me; and anyone who does not take his cross and follow me is not worthy of me."* -Matthew 34-37

So much for family values: the Prince of Peace knew that the bonds of family are the strongest psychological bonds in a human being, and if the person was to accept a radical altering of their viewpoint, and was going to embrace an ensuing change in society itself, family values was the first place to start the attack and/or consciousness-raising.

You can think of the Sword as a metaphor for understanding and war as an elevation of psychological tension in order to bring about radical change. (The war on boredom) I would like to hear a literal fundamentalist explain this quote: Evil and pain are here to help us learn. Adam and Eve in the garden were profoundly bored. The apple seems to have actually been a pomegranate, which is the most sensual of fruits. Eve probably wanted to shake things up a bit with that ever so sensual pomegranate. God bless Maya. Consciousness is intimately bound to pain. If Eve gives you a delicious pomegranate in the garden alone you may suddenly realize that you too are naked in the world. Come join the lovers in the pomegranate trees.

The beginnings of religion lay in the human ability to experience a transcendent state of mind through rhythmic movement, music and communal ritual; the elements of organization and systematic repression came later with society. Organized religion shuts off the direct tap to God, because transcendent wisdom is liberating and dangerous; women and joy seek to embody this eternal wisdom. What are you thinking about when you are singing or dancing, or having great sex or making art? You are not thinking about anything, if you are doing it for real. You *are* the singing, dancing or the great sex itself. This is the transcendent and symbolic. To transcend is to get out of the flow of time and to be here now, if you are here now, then nowhere else matters. God put evil in the world, because evil is real; without evil we have no tension and without tension, there is no transcending of tension. I could argue that only eternal boredom is inherently evil.

You could actually make a good argument that boredom is a result of our intellectual detachment from the world itself. I think that this is the essence of existentialism in that-as a philosophical position-it sought to elevate the intellectual displacement of the world into a central abstract tenant of being. It sought to explain why we are depressed or un-free or whatever, through pushing it farther into the intellectual grist mill. The weird thing about all of this existential navel gazing is that it gets really boring. I recently found out that Sartre was a speed addict (the drug) in the later part of his life, probably not a good place to be when building a philosophy of life. You cannot-even for one second-not do something, even making a decision not to do something is doing something. My contention would be that the decisions to do things should flow out of 'being there' at the time you are making the decision; although, in our imperfect understanding of the world, a reasoned and thoughtful consideration is probably the next best thing.

The great healing God from Greece, Asclepius, is customarily drawn or carved with a dog at his side. This dog was a symbolic representation of the intuitive aspect of healing. Healing could only be truly accomplished, if the doctor grasped the whole ensemble of the situation, which took a bit of intuition. Dogs can smell things – unseen things that doctors can't.

It seems that dogs are actually being trained to detect some forms of cancer in a patient well before it can be seen in an x-ray or MRI. So artists tend to smell themselves into the future. They sense which way the collective psyche is going, largely because they are already bored with where it is. Smell is the most associative sense and a very fitting word/metaphor/etymology/right brain etc., for the ability to allow the random jostling needed to create your way out of boredom. Whether great artists drag culture forward with them or arrive where it is going before everyone else, is an intellectual chicken and egg discussion. If their vision becomes popular, it is impossible to tell if they have struck a chord in the public psyche or caused the public psyche to come and resonate along with their vision.

Bono from U2 once said something that I thought was quite insightful. U2 came out of the eighties anti- establishment era and they had to deal with the ambiguity of selling massive amounts of records without seeming to collude with the very establishment that allowed this. Bono was saying that Rap music was in some sense a more honest stance, in that they didn't pretend they didn't want your money; they would sell you the sun glasses, T-shirt and your sneakers, whatever it took to be a 'playa'. The art of advertising went through a similar disingenuous phase in the eighties in that it was considered bad taste for a serious actor to appear in a commercial promoting any type of product. If you did this as an actor, it was generally accepted that your serious career was over. Now, it seems that you can re-establish an ailing career by being a TV spokesperson. Valerie Bertinelli will probably be doing movies soon, now that she is such a fit bird. I stand corrected she has her own TV show now. My friend Michael was bemoaning the fact that artists stop making pop songs when they get to the later more serious part of their career.

This is the exact trap that Curt Cobain found himself in. He had set himself up as the ultimate anti-establishment by writing a song that was a discussion of exactly this problem, which ironically became a massive establishment hit: "*Smells like Teen Spirit.*" The story goes that he saw an ad for an underarm deodorant with the catch phrase 'smells like teen spirit', which struck him as ironic or let's just say it struck him. Being an artist, he took this little nugget and spun it into a whole ensemble that represented the way we are sold a dream by the establishment. If we all smell like teen spirit, we will get laid all the time because teens are full of pheromones that make you horny, etc. The chorus of the song is, *"I feel stupid and contagious; here we are, now entertain us"*. He was contagious and he penned probably the greatest song to come out of the nineties; all other pop songs from this era were measured against this yardstick. Now it seems that Michael Stipe from *REM* was a friend of Curt Cobain and suspected that he was suicidal or at least realized he was quite depressed, and was trying to help him. Out of this whole cultural ensemble (which is the story of coming of age, which is also learning to deal with paradox), came the other great song of the nineties: *"Losing My Religion."*

Life is bigger, bigger than you and you are not me

The lengths that I must go to the distance in your eye

Oh no I've said too much I've set it up

That's me in the corner that's me in the spotlight

Losing my Religion

Trying to keep an eye on you

And I don't know if I can do it

Like a hurt lost and blinded fool

Oh no I've said too much.

Michael Stipe writes in a very dense style and he moves from idea to idea very quickly. He was personally quite shy: *"that's me in the corner, that's me in the spot-light"*. And his religion is-among other things-Pop music itself – the lengths that I must go to the distance in your eye. (May the mote (speck) in your eye be from the Bible?) What you have to give up or sell out, or collude with to keep yourself in the public eye. If the author is being truly honest, he has 'said too much'. This in a nutshell, is the artist's dilemma: I want to make art, but I have to eat and so I have to sell my art to people who don't understand my art or me, just so that I can do art (*If I could stick a knife in my heart, suicide right on stage, would it be enough for your teenage lust? It's only rock and roll -*

Rolling Stones). This whole dilemma only exists in the hyper-reflective ever searching intellect. Art is actually a progression outward and away from this stifling intellection.

Don't tell me what the poets are doing

Those Himalayas of the mind

Don't tell me what the poets are doing

On the street and the epitome of vague

Don't tell how the universe is altered

When you find out how he gets paid, all right

    Gordon Downie - *The Tragically Hip*

  Van Morrison simply refuses to play this game at all and everyone thinks that he is cantankerous. Van Morrison has rightly sussed that fame is a collective projection and he rightly says that he is not famous, at least in his own mind. Fame is ultimately irrelevant; living life and playing music are relevant to him.

  And after all of this, I will say again that the truly great problems in life are insoluble and ultimately paradoxical. You constantly create a new paradigm or artistic vision, and when you are committed to it, it might become culturally relevant and propel you into stardom. The paradigm itself can then lose energy and become a cliché or parody of itself and this will be the rope that strangles you. But what doesn't kill you makes you stronger and, it seems that by illuminating the problem (or bringing it to consciousness and making explicit what it is), you can move beyond it and back into nakedness. You can re-bite the apple. Andy Warhol committed to being a business.

  The overriding cultural propellant of the eighties was boredom and angst (the result of unemployment) and the punks gave us the idea that anarchy was better than boredom. Eventually, we realized that this doesn't work and we tried to change things through positive engagement (Live Aid, etc.). The nineties saw the promotion of an extremely self-righteous political correctness within our culture. This was a painful growing experience as well, because it creates a hyper-awareness of everyone else's misdemeanors. This is all flowing out of an extroverted will to power which is a natural reflex against self-introspection. The Grunge movement was a backlash against this over weaning self-righteousness, which could not sustain its own tight-laced contradictions. I think there is a softer more introverted feel working its way back into our culture (bands like Iron & Wine, Fleet Foxes or Bon Iver), which will, over time, burn itself out again as it butt heads with the Tea Party, and so we go on and on. The thing is to live the cultural movement through to its logical conclusion and then *let it go*.

I would add that within culture the real dilemmas are created by the artists themselves. In essence, they create tension as a means of propelling themselves out of their own boredom. This is why the original revolutionaries (Trotsky, etc.) had no compunction about killing people for the revolution. In their minds, the world has to be brought down to zero again and then it could be built up into a brave new post-revolutionary world. If the means justify the end, then the problem that the communists encountered became the difficulty of keeping the end untainted by the means. The regime becomes far too busy simply covering up its own guilty bloody mess. The revolution goes completely off the rails as the guilt builds up from having witnessed the murder. (Iraq again)The double-think way to avoid the burden of this guilt is to displace the ends beyond your own lifetime (cognitive dissonance or the second coming of Jesus, etc.). Then it does not matter if a lot of people get killed, tomorrow they will all thank us, especially if we control the subsequent narrative.

Running Down the Voodoo

The eighties were particularly hard on jazz musicians and Miles Davis seemed to have avoided the whole cultural shift going on about him by just staying at home doing drugs and getting freaky with women. In my mind, Miles Davis best represents the ability to stay personally relevant. Miles re-emerged in 1986 with an incredible album called *Tutu* and didn't look back. There are only a handful of artists who have been able to create truly culture-changing records over more than three or four decades: Paul Simon, Madonna and Miles Davis are really the only ones that spring to mind easily: Sting, Paul McCartney, Van Morrison and a few others are hanging in there. Lots of other artists have had careers that where vital and spanned four decades but few have written and had relevant hit records so consistently, of course a hit record in the jazz world is not the same thing as selling a Graceland for instance, and hit records aren't the mark of a great career but they do show that an artist is in touch with the spirit of the times.

I was first introduced to Miles Davis when I read an interview in *Musician* magazine. This was the period of *Tutu* and *Amandala*. In my jazz naivety, I just accepted these records as representative of what Miles Davis did; of course, I knew he had been around for a long time, but I had no knowledge of either him or jazz. As I slowly gained a better understanding of the jazz world, I found that you will constantly keep coming back to Miles Davis. He has consistently been either the leader or as often one of the best representatives of each definable movement within jazz. (Picasso is the same type of figure in painting and both of these men were -by other people's accounts- assholes.)

Starting with the bebop style through the birth of the cool and into hard bop, then the controversial electric period -where we don't have handy genera tags- and then on to his even more controversial rap record, *Do-Bop*. (Trust me, *Do-Bop* took a vitriolic tongue lashing from the critics. The reality is that, excluding some poor quality lyrics, it is a pretty good record.) Pat Metheny once said that there really isn't a bad Miles Davis record. I would also add that there really isn't a bad Pat Metheny record either. Santana became culturally vital again by doing much the same thing as Miles did when he recorded his *Supernatural* album and that is working with other (usually younger artists) who are already functioning and immersed fully in the new cultural paradigm. Santana -by the way- is a huge Miles Davis fan. Go figure?

What Miles Davis has done throughout his career is actively search out young and talented musicians and helped develop them. The list of people who have worked with or for Miles Davis is quite literally a list of most of the greatest jazz musicians to date.

Jazz musicians in general tend to be more culturally flexible than pop musicians anyway because jazz music just doesn't pay that well and so these musicians tend to do a lot more recording and studio work. They get this type of work because they have such good technical ability and they are not as slavish to their particular cultural canon as say classical musicians tended to be. This co-opting of jazz musicians into the pop world started in the sixties with almost all of the Mo-town singles being played by jazz musicians. Sting took Miles Davis band over wholesale to launch his solo career with Dream of the Blue Turtles. Joni Mitchell worked with jazz musicians almost exclusively and guess what? She was a Miles Davis fan. Joni Mitchell worked with Wayne Shorter (play me some orange) who was in the Miles Davis quintet in the sixties and she also worked with Pat Metheny, and Jaco Pastorius among many others.

When I saw Miles Davis, he had a young fellow playing electronic percussion in the band. Miles found this kid in a club in New York playing in some type of hip hop band and asked him to join his band. The kid told him that he didn't know anything about musical theory and didn't know if he could play jazz. Miles told him that he would teach him theory, but that what this kid had was hip and that was enough. One of Miles Davis's drummers-Omar Hakim-talked about being in the band and how he was afraid to really open up when he was playing. The other musicians told him that he wouldn't even be in the band if he wasn't good enough. In other words, he had already 'made it' so relax and enjoy the ride. John Scofield also talked about playing in the band and he was saying that if the band was cooking, you wouldn't even know that Miles was on stage. But, as soon as things got boring or stale, Miles would be all over everybody, changing key or assigning new roles to everybody or ending the song, or whatever it took to get everybody playing well again. What mattered was the music. I could ream off a lot of anecdotes, but I think you get the picture. Much like Nusrat Fateh Ali Khan, Miles Davis is listening to what is going on, and because of the nature of jazz composition, he could enter into the piece and direct it from within. This is one of the advantages of allowing elements of improvisation into the work over more strictly formatted pieces. This is also a reflection of what I would consider the defining advantage music has over other arts: music happens in real time and can be affected directly. Once the cooperative juggernaut of a multi-million dollar film is headed in one direction, it is very hard to turn it around.

I will also add that there are a number of artists that I desperately admire who are completely irrelevant as far as cultural impact. These are artists that are hell-bent on pursuing their own vision regardless of the consequences. Rickie Lee Jones was almost mortified when she had a huge hit with *"Chuck E's in Love"*. She had envisioned her career as a slow climb into a position where she would have artistic control and could do anything she wanted. So on her second and third albums, in an effort to slow her career; she intentionally arranged the songs so there could be no single. Oh to have such problems. I have bought a lot of her records throughout the years and she has done some excellent work that few people seem to have bought. (*Flying Cowboys* was quite successful; *Traffic from Paradise*, *Ghostyhead*, and *The Evening of my Best Day* are all excellent records).

   Steve Tibbetts is another good example of somebody who no one knows anything about. He has recorded two of my favorite albums, which are called *The Fall of Us* and *A*. These recordings are deliciously irrelevant. But my all time hero in the profoundly irrelevant department is Mark Hollis from *Talk Talk* fame. His solo record, *Mark Hollis* is one of the undiscovered great records of all time. That's all I will say. Also, see *Laughing Stock* and *Spirit of Eden* by *Talk Talk*.

   On the other hand, James is a band that is culturally relevant, but the fates and fickle America seem to have conspired to ruin their career. After they released their best record to date, *Millionaires*, the president of PolyGram USA, their American record label changed. It seemed for some illogical reason that the new president of PolyGram USA hated their guts; and this spiteful fellow almost single-handedly ruined their career-certainly in the States anyway-by refusing to release *Millionaires* in America, despite the fact it was the number one imported CD at the time, at least in Canada. James have produced yet another great new album, one of their best (and they do have some stinkers in there), which is *Hey Ma*, that is also bound for the American dustbin by the looks of it. Such is the spiteful nature of pop music and culture in general.

It's about the work

   One last artist I should like to prattle on about is Bjork. She, for me, embodies this hungry search and flexibility of vision, and she is the embodiment of 'methods of work'. I will largely talk about *Vespertine*, which to my mind, is her greatest work yet.

   Bjork is really good at juxtaposing different paradigms and resolving them into a higher unity. She really likes the dry staccato sound of square wave drum machines stuck together with extremely lush string sections. She knows her way around classical music and she has a very good vocabulary when it comes to discussing the nuances of it. Bjork can identify string sounds or approaches to string sections in relation to various composers and she can communicate or articulate her vision or the specific sound she is after to other people. This ability to communicate music to others, tend to be the ability to develop relevant metaphors or analogies. (I want the drums to sound like ripping paper.) Music is almost always a collaborative effort; so having a vision only means something, if you are able to articulate and then actually give birth to that thing you wish to create.

On the *Vespertine* album Bjork assembled a very interesting group of musicians. The first part of the team was a couple of *avant-garde* soundscape artists called 'Matmos'. These fellows make music with dentist drills and bird cages, along with visually triggered Theremins, decks of cards and handsaws. Clearly they are used to thinking outside the box. When they got the call to work with Bjork they were quite excited, and at their first meeting, Bjork explained to them that she wanted to capture the sound of pussy willows opening so that she could trigger this sound with some electronics. These poor fellows phoned all around to various botanical societies to try to find someone who had pussy willows that were at the point where they were going to seed. My point is that even though these guys were clearly on the fringe, Bjork could *out fringe* them. They were put in a position where they had to take her request for pussy willows seriously. This may have been a method that Bjork used to set the tone of their ongoing collaboration. Upon meeting Daniel Lanois for the first time, Brian Eno had Daniel record him while he wandered around the studio floor for a half hour with some chains strapped on to him so that Daniel had no idea what was coming next.

On the recording, Matmos did some very interesting things like walking rhythmically through gravel or shuffling a deck of cards to establish a rhythm. Juxtaposed to this are Vince Mendoza's orchestral and choir arrangements, along with a stand up harp player named Zeena Parkins. The harp is not exactly one of pop music's centerpiece instruments, but it is a credit to both Zeena's and Bjork's ability to adapt it into this environment. In the live concert settings they reworked the other pre-*Vespertine* material so that the harp was also incorporated into the material being played on that tour.

When Bjork was putting a touring band together for *Vespertine*, she was having great difficulty finding a choir that sounded the way she wanted and it seemed that about two weeks before the tour was to start, this issue of having a choir to tour with was still not been resolved. The production team decided to hire a separate orchestra in each city; such is the ability of classically trained musicians that they can learn the music pretty much on the spot. The choir element on the other hand, would be a stable unit and would travel with the band. Bjork was getting a little stressed out about this issue so she ran away to Greenland on the spur of the moment (I can imagine her manager's response when he found out she was in Greenland). By some coincidence, Greenland was having an Inuit choir singing festival, and of course, Bjork went and found exactly what she had needed.

Over the course of the tour, she worked some of the Inuit singing styles back into her other music. She makes the point that sometimes you have to completely change everything to get the right answer. I would add that Bjork is willing to let the right answer come to her and be the right answer. This is, to my mind, the willingness to allow the unconscious flow of the world to come forward or to stop pressing the issue with your precious ego's wish to exercise control over your environment. It seems that the environment –unconscious whatever- colludes with your passivity to achieve an equitable solution. (Atman)

I will explain my meager understanding of some of Bjork's methods of work, which is really the larger point I am making: how do creative people function in the world? Bjork says that she likes to create a whole new persona for herself. The exploration of this persona then becomes the new record that she is working on. She allows herself to function from within this ongoing construction. (Beyoncé has another name for her sexy persona others have a stage name, etc.) This is a very important point in that these 'constructed personalities' are a part of us already, and through them, we explore different aspects of who we are – both immersing in and reflecting back the world around us through the lens of our own creativity. (Bono toured as the devil in an effort to dismantle his overt self-righteousness) When you actively create a persona, you have allowed an aspect of yourself to come forward from the unconscious and the ongoing truth of your artistic creativity is in trying to represent this truth.

One of the threads running throughout the *Vespertine* recording is an exploration of the sensuality of domestic bliss. This theme only came to me slowly, but I did know that an original title for the album was Domestica. Bjork is getting to that age where you settle down a bit, but instead of fighting her age, she explored the experience. I see this recording as a way she can develop an external metaphor through which she can explore and embrace this new phase of her life. Also, some of the record is quite sexually explicit, which she quite bravely embraced on this recording. She uses this overt sexuality as an image that she can juxtapose against other pictures of simple domesticity to create dynamic tension. Much of the explicit meaning of the recording-if there is any-is probably only realized by us and the artist much later. The artwork is like the creative archaeology of a dream that can only really be understood against the wider back drop of history. (We endeavor to organize the chaos by extending meaning.) Joni Mitchell went on a very long road trip for inspiration after a bad breakup and gave birth to *Hejira*, my personal favorite. Bjork looked inside; Joni went on a walk-about.

Bjork is someone who is really exploring her own psyche quite openly within her work and artists that are this brave always fascinate me. She once mentioned that if she woke up one morning with a dream, she could have a piece of music finished by the end of the day that represents the dream. Her song *Hyper-ballad* is a great representation of the fluid nature of her creative process. I heard that she wrote this song for Madonna (urban myth). Real creativity is the process of bringing anything into the world, capturing messages from the unconscious is only the tiny beginning.

On *Vespertine*, Bjork explores her cultural ancestry on a song called *Pagan Poetry*.

Paddling through the dark currents

I find an accurate copy

A blueprint

Of the pleasure in me

Swirling black lilies totally ripe

He offers a handshake

Crooked five fingers

Form a pattern

Yet to be matched

A secret code carve

In a palm of fingers

Form a pattern

Yet to be matched

Morse coding signals

Pulsate

Wake me up

From hibernate

On the surface simplicity

But the darkest pit in me

Is pagan poetry

Pagan poetry

    Of course, Bjork is originally from Iceland and so this song is recognition of her cultural heritage, but I would also add that it is uncovering aspects of her collective unconscious. The darkest pit is the Christian culture's shadow element, and in this pit is pagan poetry. Norse people are in the culturally advantageous position to have written down and retained a lot of their mythological stories, unlike the Druids, Picts or Celts. Because of Iceland's remoteness, they were converted to Christianity quite late (around 1000 AD). Iceland is one of the few western cultures to have written down and pass on to us a large collection of sagas or stories of their pagan past. Europe's Celtic heritage, or mythology or collective dream, is almost completely lost, because the Celts intentionally refused to write down these legends.

When Bjork observes her inner creative being, she both is and finds a linking back into her cultural past and her own unique heritage. (Religion)

On another song called *Joga* she talks about being pushed out of the normal world to a higher state of consciousness, a state of emergency… how beautiful to be. She wishes that she could live her life at that level of engagement. This is the essence of what NOW is. This is Sajhana or sadhana, which is the ecstasy that yoga is trying to connect you to. Bjork has isolated the essence of the yoga experience, which is the ecstasy of the body in the world. Or in another song called *It's Not Up to You*, Bjork talks about trying to master a perfect day with six glasses of water and seven phone calls. By consciously observing and/or actively ritualizing her environment (compulsion), she can allow the ego to relax so that the greater world can come forward. This is how the right brain is witnessed, and this song could be a hymn to the passive right brain.

If you leave it alone

It might just happen,

Anyway

It's not up to you

Well it never really was.

Just lean into the crack

And it will tremble ever so nicely

Notice how it sparkles down there

I can decide what I give

But it's not up to me

What I get given

Unthinkable surprises about to happen

But what they are

It's not up to you

You have the right to work, but you do not have the RIGHT to the fruits of your labor. Bjork is out swimming in a deep sea and I personally find her work to be somewhat uneven. There is some of her music that I am really not that enthusiastic about, but I am the kind of listener that will forgive a lot from an artist that I like. This is the price of trying to follow the work of someone who is really exploring deeply. Great artists who are trying really hard can make spectacular failures (Paul McCartney, has a collection of *bad* Picassos). I would rather waste my money on five bad David Bowie records, hoping to find yet another gem from him, than suffer through 10 minutes of another cliché blues old time white boy record. With Bjork you take the good with the bad, because her good is so much better than other people's and I will say *Vespertine* is the first full album by Bjork where I felt she really nailed it from beginning to end. Joseph Campbell once said in an interview that you should read great books-we all know which ones they are-but also read everything by an author that you like, because when you read everything, you can see how an intellect has evolved over time. This slows down our tendency to elevate people up into hero status. When you become intimately familiar with a full body of work, the whole ensemble and context of a human life is understood more clearly. The good and bad in a body of work can be a reflex of our own infantile judging, but of course, I do it all the time. No bad Miles Davis records.

 I also realize that writing about Bjork is a bit futile, because it is very hard to express what it is about her that resonates within me without getting abstract and rambling on about what a visionary she is or how you, the reader, should somehow understand what I mean by visionary. I cannot pull you into my intellectual ensemble, nor do you necessarily want to come along. What I have tried to do is pull out the bits that tie into some of the themes of this book, but of course, Bjork has a totally different agenda. What I have found in her music is more reinforcement of the key ideas that I have come to believe and maybe that is just what I have been saying all along. I look for meaning/beauty and I find it. I quite possibly misrepresented the arc and intent of Bjork's career. On the other hand, I don't think I am an irrational observer. What we are left with at the end of the day is that, for me, her music holds great meaning-and I could say this about all of these artists not just Bjork-and my presumption is that she has also poured/explored her version of meaning within her artwork. I bring my own meaning with me and together we conspire or blow together to create, and this conspiracy brings art/religion etc., into life again and again.

"It was rarely noticed that when nothing is revered, irreverence ceases to indicate critical thought." -Jacques Barzun

A Fish Rots from the Head

I believe that what these artists have found is meaning and that their real or self-constructed meaning is what drives them to create art in the first place. This meaning flows from the ability to become engaged with the world-which to my mind-involves letting the ego or your own willed self-image recede into the background. Ironically, you can become more engaged and have a better self-image by nurturing a more passive attitude toward this drive for self-image. This was the essence of Jung's work and it has direct relevance to all aspects of life. The ego looks at itself through other things (creating a Frankenstein). The world/culture more or less agrees with the ego's assessment as witnessed in its power and bling, and this feedback loop is reinforced because we don't stop until we have a nervous breakdown.

"By accomplishing nothing, everything is accomplished." -Lao Tzu

Collecting power is not as simple as all that, but these are the main elements in the equation. Confucius hammers this point home. I have only ever had very limited power in my life, and as a result, I find it a deep mystery. The thing I least understand is, why do people who are rich-beyond ever being able to spend what they have-continue to drive themselves to collect more power and wealth. The phenomenal culture of greed that has recently been displayed by Wall Street seems mind-boggling at best. Is there some point when these people stop to think to themselves what the point of this drive is? (This is the type of speculation that a total outsider to power-like me-would make) I think that these are the types of questions, if really asked, lead to nervous breakdowns or a financial collapse on Wall Street. They are avoided like the plague, because they smack of left wing navel gazing. Read *Fooled by Randomness* or *The Black Swan* by Nassim Nicholas Taleb, for an insider's view of the world of greed and ruin; or watch any of the recent slew of documentaries about the 2008 collapse of Wall Street. They hold a stunning portrait of the paradoxes inherent in left brain egotistical greed in action.

Great teachers hold their students up to the mirror, but it is our task to look. Behind this world of Maya or ego collecting, is the wider and more ambiguous ocean of un-interpreted reality, where ethics and morality become a little greyer. The real world eludes our human desire for the clean relief of black and white. (Why did Jesus curse the fig tree?) This natural state of moral ambiguity is well evidenced in the collected folk and fairytales from around the world. (But they're just fairytales) This image of nature's eternal ambiguity is represented in the archetype of the trickster figure. This figure also participates in a more completed God image. The trickster is also the divine messenger and truth speaker (Khadir/Mercury). They reflect symbols back at us and a great example is David Bowie as a clown on the *Scary Monsters* album. Prometheus/Frankenstein is another example of this message. Many of the folktales with a trickster strive to reveal to us a higher sense of resolution through exposing the tension behind our apparent moral ambiguity. Nature has her own agenda that is essentially vacant of morality. We are forced to bear witness to ambiguity when we suspend our intellectual power drive.

The persecution of Job in the Old Testament Bible explores this suspended moral tension and illustrates this ambiguity by telling us a 'story' about the collusion of God with the devil as they engage in a bet for Job's soul. Job tries to adhere to a meaningful relationship with God throughout his tribulations in this world. And the real question is why has God allowed this torture? Even Jesus on the cross asks why he has been forsaken. The moment of greatest faith is intimately bound together with the moment of our greatest doubt and suffering. And this is really what is behind our question about evil in the world: why does God allow it? Kali, the Hindu goddess of destruction, is so fierce that she can swallow time itself, but she is also a great boon bestower and a font of wisdom, if properly understood. Kali is nature represented symbolically, never permanent and always ready to take everything away. Science strips her of her symbolism to expose the lie.

Jung's main realization for me was that, whether implied or explicit, meaning can lead to an essentially religious attitude toward life. Jung sought to engage people with their own dream world (private myth) so they would be able to see that their ego is only a part of their entire being. Through looking at the unconscious, people could reconnect with the larger Self that extends out and beyond us. This larger Self is the wellspring of creativity, where all manner of art and religion germinate.

"There is nothing for it but to recognize the irrational as a necessary- ever-present- psychological function, and to take its contents not as concrete realities that would be a regression, but as psychic realties, real because they WORK. The collective unconscious, being the repository of man's experience, is an image of the world that has taken aeons to form. In this image certain features, the archetypes or dominants, have crystallized out of time. They are the ruling powers, the gods, images of the dominant laws and principles, and of typical, regularly occurring events in the soul's cycle of experience." Jung – Two Essays - Pg.95

Come to the orchard in Spring.

There is light and wine, and sweethearts

In the pomegranate flowers.

If you do not come, these do not matter.

If you do come, these do not matter.

    Jalal al-Din Rumi: Translated by Coleman Banks with John Moyne

"Skepticism is the chastity of the intellect" -George Santayana

    I will slide down the pole into one more philosophical tirade and critique the penchant to create 'what if' scenarios like the so called ticking bomb scenario. Is it moral to torture someone or their children or wives, etc., if they know where a ticking bomb is and you could save American lives? The Bush administration practiced this type of "philosophical exploration" and it ultimately led to torturing people or having them tortured elsewhere for any number of reasons. The argument itself seeks to quantify moral ambiguity by displacing it into a 'what if' situation, where we can pretend that this situation isn't real and seek to arrive at a logical conclusion to it by lending it the sheen of our rationality. The whole thought process behind the "exercise" is dangerous and illusory, but its "rational conclusions" create real suffering in the real world and the logic of the decision must then be held on to because it's logical. This ticking bomb scenario has never happened in the real world, but the torture that is supposed to stop it from happening, has and is really happening. The real problem is in our believing that the intellectual exercise is valid. "What if" does not exist in any tangible way. This is the ambiguity of Kali the destroyer.

Jean Chrétien (former Prime Minister of Canada) recently talked about the phenomenal amount of pressure George Bush put on Canada to join in the war on Iraq. He refused on moral grounds, because there was no proof of W of MD, but mostly because it was such an arbitrary invasion of another sovereign country. This was the first time Canada didn't back a war with either Britain or America. You can say a lot of things about politicians, but we had one that stood up for a belief and was right. When the man at the top is corrupt, the signal that trickles down is that corruption is OK, which manifests in any number of bad decisions in the real world. Or a fish rots from its head. *"We're in the de-reg. business."*- George Bush Sr.

River Dogs

I have debated with myself endlessly about performing an exegesis on one of my own poems. I realize that it is somewhat pretentious to do this. On the other hand, I do know my own private language better than anyone else and it may prove of interest to someone. Jay Z has just done this type of decoding in his autobiography and it is fascinating to hear him pick apart his own lyrics: *"Like a couple of bras get 'em right up in there"*.

This first poem is a piece I have rewritten many times. It was originally written to the tune of an acappella song called *Blomstertid* or summertime by a Swedish band that I love called Frifot from their record called *Sluring*. These musicians play Norse folk music and some of the compositions are over 300 years old. They arrange and update them to a certain extent (regenerating the past for inspiration). I went through a phase in my private intellectual world where I became immersed in the

Viking culture. I read through the Icelandic Sagas, and from some of my further reading, the Byzantine Empire, I realized that the Vikings travelled all over the earth. In fact it seems that they were trading well into northern Pakistan and China a very long time ago (800 CE), and every once in a while someone in the wilds of northern Pakistan will have a blond haired blue eyed baby. Eastern Vikings also contain Mongol DNA.

This all inspired me to write over 300 pages of a fictional novel in which one of the two main characters are named Ungar who also travels into the Far East. (The character is loosely based on Harald Hardrada) Ungar is an archetypal Norse poet or bard. I would suggest *The Hammer and the Cross* by Robert Ferguson to any reader interested in pagan poetry.

In Norse mythology the main god, Odin is strung up on the world tree, Yasdrigall, which represents the centre of being and is a parallel symbol of the cross, or a symbolic uniting of the opposites. (Christ was crucified between two other people one of whom went to heaven and one who didn't.) Through this willing crucifixion, Odin seeks to meet the gods and go to heaven, and as a reward for his commitment to transcend, he gains the ability to sing and compose poetry, amongst other things. What a surprise. The ability to sing sagas was very highly prized in Viking culture. The Vikings put great store in a clever analogy like grim skull for a balding man. This is the level of unconscious ancestral heritage that Bjork is talking about when she sings about pagan poetry. Odin is also the god of berserking, or blood frenzy. Hitler unleashed this god or tapped into this archetypal layer in the Germanic peoples in the Second World War. Odin is a much more ambiguous/natural type of character than Christ and is more representative of the pagan and archaic layers of the northern pre-Christian unconscious. He is more closely allied with the chthonic or nature spirit of the world. Poetry and berserking both represent an immersion into the primal undifferentiated natural psyche where creativity happens of its own accord.

This poem was originally written as a lament that spontaneously arises inside Ungar as he bemoans his fortune. He has been chased out of his homeland and is forced to do some soul-searching. He is forced to endure an outward journey of discovery that, in turn, represents his inner search.

River Dogs

Let us sing now of things older than winds strong

Let us climb up among great trees to see clearly

Let us sing this new ship off this cold seastrand

Gods come and grace our wayward path

I have sighed by this river, dogs foul wending

I can see in my dark heart rot

For it's this love that I must chase unending

Come in then bleeding, this poor new thought

If then a loosened tear shall fall

All grim and dream soaked

Darkened from this river's bottom

To grace, this our lonely road

Lord, give us strength to sing this our endless song

And leave hope for our returning

For when at last I'm bathing in my lover's solemn arms

I will set my life and spirit burning.

Singing of things older than the winds is an allusion to allow the unconscious to come forward or to be immersed in creating poetry. God created Adam by breathing into him and we recreate our inspiration by blowing together like the wind. Shamans in the Siberian north have to string a rope between two trees and climb up these trees to have their souls elevated into the spiritual plain. They would climb up and play their drum into the wind; their drum is called their horse and they ride, and sing themselves into the spiritual realm or out of mental sickness. They literally ride their horse out of this world to recapture the lost souls of the sick or to reattach their own spiritual beings. (I am a drummer so this image fits me well) A ship obviously is no good stranded on a strand, but this could be an initiation ceremony where you compose a song for a new ship or a new leader on a ship. In my mind it is indicative of Ungar's commitment to the journey itself in that he is willing to perform the ceremonies that will begin his quest. Or he is willing to put himself in the proper psychological state or get himself in tune with the larger flow before asserting his will and ego.

Ungar is forced to leave his homeland, because of a decree by the king issued from the bow of a ship. Psychologically, a ship is a feminine container, so Ungar has been removed from the feminine, because he has been condemned to leave his homeland which is the result of a judgment that was issued from the bow of a ship by a man, and so his ship is physically stranded. His life has stopped flowing and so he is out of the Tao, which is right beside him in the water. He instigates a ritual to re-establish movement and allow him to enter back into the feminine flow. He is in a serious dilemma and he then seeks to put himself into proper relationship with both the world and his inner being through composing a song. He is Odin on the tree seeking the gift of tales. When we reject ritual as a superstition, we also deny ourselves the ability to enter into a process that has much deeper psychological roots than we are consciously aware of. This is especially true when you witness people's utter bewilderment around a sudden death. In some ways there is only process left to reattach ourselves to flow.

The *Viking Sagas* from Iceland came about as a result of Viking kings wishing to convert the Norse. The conversions began by Hakon the Good in 936 AD and finished brutally by King Olaf. These kings were solidifying their power base and also attempted to convert the whole of the Viking population to Christianity around 1000 AD. If you weren't with the King and Christ, you were against him, and you had to leave and exist *outside the law*. King Olaf also went that extra mile and sent missionaries to Iceland ostensibly to convert the heathens, but really he was trying to unify the various outlying tribes under a single power base signified by both the power of religion and its entwinement within the state, through his divine kingship. King Olaf might have learned this trick from Charlemagne, but these types of political solutions seem to occur over and over fairly spontaneously. I will not draw the parallel to our own times again – even I know it's tedious.

Before this larger conversion of the Vikings came about, each man was allowed to decide for himself if he would support the new king or not. Many who did not wish to support the king avoided persecution (specifically being outlawed) by leaving Norway and going to Iceland. Others continued the tradition of raiding all around the world and helped sustain the image of the blood-thirsty Vikings. Still, others travelled to places like Constantinople and served the emperor. The Iceland sagas are the stories of all of the peoples who left Norway to set up an independent and free pagan state in Iceland, and their various travels around the world as well.

I came up with this idea of a river dog and will be honest it is two words that have no special meaning together other than that I love the way they seem to imply something. I love it so much that I named a whole collection of writings from this period, *River Dogs*. The foul-wending is the cruel twist of fate that has befallen the hero. Wending is an old English term referring to the curve of a river. I believe it is also a weaving term and possibly a bent wood-boat-making term. I usually avoid these kinds of old colloquial sayings, but the poem is trying to reflect a medieval Norse bard and the word sounds good in the line. This heart-dark-rot bit was an attempt to portray the hard angular sound of the Norse tongue. It is very difficult to sing this cleanly, because of the harshness of the phonemes themselves. Norse is only moderately more beautiful than German, which is also very hard and angular, and really not that pretty to sing. To a certain extent, I was matching the actual phonemes that occurred in the melody of the song itself. I was stealing. These words that I have written and the sound of the phonemes within the song match very closely some of the lyrics that are being sung by Lena Willemark on the *Frifot* record.

Come in then bleeding is an allusion to the pain that must be suffered to gain any amount of wisdom, and in the song, Ungar is welcoming this understanding (break my heart again and again). It is a poor new thought, because it must be assimilated and you must bring your wealth of experience to give it meaning. It must be brought into the world. We are given a symbol and we bring it into reality by re-linking it both to ourselves and trying it out in the world before it comes back to us fully. The loosened tear all grim etc., is the dark message that he must accept from the river's bottom or the unconscious. Grim and dream-soaked matches the cadence of the Norse lyrics that existed in the song already, but I was particularly pleased with this image, because dream-soaked seems to imply that this message can also propel you forward in the way that dreams have multiple meanings. It's heavy and wet. There are literally dreams that you have while you are asleep, but we call our aspirations our dreams. Being dream-soaked seems to imply a certain weight and heavy engagement, possibly being still half way in the dream itself. Ungar then prays to his deity for guidance and understanding. He does not confuse his ego with this message and places himself into a proper relationship with his unconscious, or the gods. He wishes that he can return 'with hope' so that he can *will* this message back into the world. I have never been happy with these two last lines so I later got rid of them. They seem trite and smacked of convenience.

    I can't tell you why I originally became so entranced with Norse culture, but I can tell you how it has affected me. Well before I started to write this novel, I had a series of dreams that seemed to reflect my personal ancient heritage. First, I had a dream about an old used shipyard in the south of England-I might have known this-but I subsequently verified that my great-grandfather worked in the ship-building trades in southern England while he was trying to get enough money to bring his family back to Canada after having lost his first wife to the great plague in Saskatchewan. Some of my ancestors on both sides of my family came from southern England, though a few were builders in Manchester as well. The Vikings made a large cultural impact in England and Scotland around the coastal regions especially in the far north and west midlands. The Norman invasion was a north man or Viking invasion and obviously the English coast was their access point. The second dream was about a group of Norse warriors caught out on an ice flow. In this dream, the warriors had very large spears that were highly polished and quite broad at the blade more like a Islamic sword. They used these blades as mirrors to reflect the sun back into my eyes as I tried to either get to them or help them get off the ice. I suspect, but cannot prove that there is Norse blood in my veins. In a lot of ways I don't really care at all. I am proud to be a mutt.

    I have heard a Norse ballad that has the exact same melody as the Irish ballad *She Moved Through the Fair*. The Norse ballad predates the Irish one and apparently the cultural influence moved from Scandinavia to

Ireland. In fact, the bagpipes are a Middle Eastern instrument (called a 'swarm'), that the Vikings brought to Scotland and Ireland probably from the Visigoth kingdoms in Spain. The Norse is also big on fiddle music as well. The kings of Leon were the last grasp of this great southern kingdom of Norse who was pitted against Islam in the defense of Europe in the high medieval period. This is not to downplay the massive influence of the Celts on Irish/British heritage. They were also great travelers whose influence has been extensive throughout the world. All of these various races have been mixed up everywhere by now, and none of us are racially pure in any real way. Racial purity is the dream of idiots. For some reason I have been having a series of dreams about Krishna/Shiva lately, so much for the archetypes and inborn cultural heritage.

Cultural Drift

I have become enamored with the idea of what I call cultural drift. For instance, in the Bible, Jesus curses a fig tree on the way to overthrow the tables of the money changers. On the way back, the apostles see that the very tree that he has cursed has withered and died. Obviously, these two images are meant to reinforce each other (the literary devise is called a 'frame') but what I find fascinating is the very specific image of a fig tree. Why would Jesus kill something that had nothing to do with him? This probably was a very easily understandable allusion to the people that were living at that time, and of course, we do not have fig trees in our northern climate, so the image becomes a bit more of a mystery to me, as are great swaths of the *Book of Revelation*. Fig trees are to this day considered very special and sacred in India. I apologize for going on about this fig tree image, but it was the image that started my understanding of cultural drift. Jung discusses this very same passage in one of his books and I have been unable to locate it.

"A great teacher was once asked to explain one of the most seemingly mysterious actions recorded in the Gospels, Christ's cursing of the barren fig tree. "Become a Christ, he replied smilingly, "and then you will know why he did that." How to Know God: The Yoga Aphorisms of Pantajali; by Swami Prabhavananda and Christopher Isherwood

"Allegory is rather like a haunted house: the greatest danger is in one's own imagination. Visual images from the past can deceive us twice over. They may do so in the way an artist intended, but they will also deceive us when we are out of tune with the thought of the period in which the image was created." The Ambassador's Secret – John North preface. The two quotes found me long after writing this section.

Another example of this drift is Moses' dream of the seven fat cows that were delivered to the pharaoh as presaging a famine that he believed was coming to Egypt. Moses' dreamed of seven fat cows and seven starving cows that represented seven years of surpluses and seven years of famine. I recently found out that in the Egyptian *Book of the Dead*, seven cows refer specifically to the cult of Hathor and it would appear that Moses used this image, or was given it, in a dream that reflected the culture he lived in. This was a very specific image that the Egyptians would immediately recognize or conversely, Moses was so immersed in Egyptian culture that his unconscious produced images from Egyptian mythology. I have a hard time believing that the Jews living in Egypt at this time would be totally unacquainted with Egyptian religion. If Moses really had the ear of the pharaoh, this image of seven cows would have been a very clear and concise reference to the Egyptian *Book of the Dead*, which I can say quite comfortably, predates the Bible (as does the concept of the soul and bodily resurrection).

We do not possess an understanding of the complete cultural matrix this message either sprang from or was directed into. The biblical spin is only one of the ways that we can understand this image and I suspect that this image encompassed much more culturally relevant material to the people of that era. This is what I have come to call 'cultural drift' which is the metaphor's own willingness to become completely divorced from its original context. So what I have done in my own writing is taken an image like river dogs and put it into a setting so that *you* the reader will assume that it is a metaphor with a wider meaning or possibly a long cultural lineage. I have implied meaning into the image so that the meaning will attach itself to the image. You are invited to struggle with the metaphor to try to understand it and hopefully put some of your own meaning into it. Conversely, these images have meaning within my work simply because I say so – and they do. I speak my own private language to myself and I slowly unpack my own meaning. These things get stuck on your fingers.

"Stop making sense, Stop making sense" –David Byrne from *Speaking in Tongues*

What Jung did was work on a way to break these archaic images down into their archetypal basics from which he could reorient or retranslate them back into our modern language, and time period. Jung then developed his own private language that related to his ongoing psychological outlook and proceeded to relate these types of images into this constructed frame of reference. He created a way for us to perform cultural drift in reverse. He applied this technique to the personal dream world of his patients and to things like the arcane writings of the medieval alchemists, who had also developed their own very complicated private language. Joseph Campbell was inspired by Jung's approach and helped to give birth to the burgeoning field of comparative mythology. Trees are one of the great archetypal images and I could write pages and pages on trees alone, and in fact, I have written pages on just this one single fig tree image.

Of course, I borrowed heavily from Jung's approach throughout this book, but what I got very interested in was the abstract question left by the specific image; for example, a 'lilac bleeding star', which I will discuss shortly. Who could write such an image? Well it seems that a poetic mind regularly practices this type of free association and in fact all human minds seem to use elements of this poesy. (This is the caduceus, DNA connection.) Schizophrenia may be reflecting a somewhat manic element of free association and its patients seem to get caught in hyper-associating and juxtaposing linguistic elements out of *normal* contexts or into non-normal ones. It has been speculated that schizophrenia may be the result of not limiting the flow of possibilities, which is what the unconscious does for us. It pre-chooses words based on implied context, i.e., baseball bat, not flying bat. In a way, this is one of the real keys to creativity, which is that we allow the unconscious to more freely associate without falling apart into infinite freedom.

So in my own writing, I intentionally introduce abstract images or allow them to remain, if they come to me on their own, because in my mind, it allows the reader to pour in their own meaning-aside from or instead of-having to understand my private language. I do not wish to advocate intentional obscurity in writing and I'm not trying to create an intellectual barrier of pretension. To some extent, I try to flesh out inner connections if the image is too oblique, even though they are my own. But, I do allow these images to stay with the implied intent that they carry meaning and I imply that I am reflecting some type of cultural drift. In some cases the cultural drift that exists is only between my unconscious and the written work that I have produced. This is not me being obscure or pretentious-to my thinking-I am allowing the reader and me to participate in the work and pour in their meanings. This is now an intentional strategy that I slowly came to accept, and these types of images now occur despite my bidding, because I both nurture and allow this associative mindset. The biggest reason I allow some forms of obscurity in is because I enjoy it in other people's work. (Faith is an island; I will play the swan and die in music.) This type of approach was also influenced by the sublime ee cummings. I have actually gone even a bit farther to embrace nonsense sometimes. What I have realized is that even nonsense hangs together of its own accord as we struggle to collect meaning. Just ask John Lennon.

"You wave your attention like an autograph" is a line that recently came to me. It is nonsense, but I see it this way: a very pretty girl chooses to pay attention only to the things that she can use as cultural leverage; an autograph is proof that you have met someone important, and therefore, you gain in your importance, because you have got it as your proof. (My neighbor was at a bar in NY with Jay Z.) You-through this autograph-have gained a little cultural leverage and so you wave this proof (autograph) around until people get tired of it. Then you turn your attention to something else that will draw people back and look to see how pretty you are. You wave your attention like an autograph is really a very concise way of saying a number of things, but you have to do some work. A burned out boat called 'trial by fire'.

I recently found a kindred spirit in my loose and wiggly world of metaphors. This is the song writer Sam Bean from Iron and Wine. This is a lyric from a song called *Pagan Angel and a Borrowed Car.*

Love was a promise made of smoke in a frozen copse of trees

A bone cold and older than our bodies slowly floating in the sea

Every morning there were planes

The shiny blades of pagan angels in our father's sky

Every evening I would watch her hold the pillow

Tight against her hollows, her unholy child

I was a beggar shaking out my stolen coat

Among the angry cemetery leaves

When they caught the king beneath a borrowed car

Righteous drunk and fumbling for the royal keys

Love was our father's flag

And sewn like a shank in a cake on our leather boots

A beautiful feather floating down to where

The birds had shit our empty chapel pews

Every morning we found one more machine

To mock our ever waning patience at the well

Every evening she'd descend the mountains stealing socks

And singing something good where all their horses fell

Like a snake within the wilted garden wall

I'd hint to her every possibility

While with his gun, the pagan angel rose to say

My love is one made to break every bended knee.

   Outside of his beautiful sense of cadence, each line is a complete vignette on its own.

I especially like the machines that mock our patience at the well and the righteous king fumbling around drunk. What is the overall message – the aftermath of the wars? I have my own conception of his work, but I don't *really* know, or it would take a lot of pages to explain each line. Better to say it's just beautiful and I love it for that.

This is River Dogs significantly re-written and altered to accord more strictly with the vocal phrasing of the recording. I did this so that my band mates would be able to learn the song more easily and sing it by using the existing melody exactly. It matches the phonemes of the song almost identically and was written two years after the original. I had to drop all of the conjunctions like, 'if, and or, but' and I realized that by doing this you allow some more ambiguity to creep in, but also the metaphors get much denser. It is a very interesting prospect to revisit something of such personal import and really work at changing it.

River Dogs

Let's sing into all that's verdant

Look back on these green lands

Heave onto all man's burdens

They'll sing in our new strong hands

I'll not fall this river dogs foul wending

And quell this bleeding storm

Lord gives us strength to sing endless

And youthful hope our return

If a lilac bleeding star should fall

Its form loosed and dream soaked true

Darkened from this rivers bottom

To grace our long sea strand

Then bleed our soul to ever more

Our blood turned hard, but this heard

To drowned all streams seek endings

Leave this for new found love

 Singing to all that verdant is an allusion to Khadir or Jack in the green, or as Paul Simon says so well: *"the urge to push like spring."* Ungar is forced to look back upon his childhood or his own spring, because he is in the depths of winter or the dark night of the soul. But he will do the work or heave unto all man's burden. Bob Dylan has a line: *"I'll buy shoes for everyone even you, while I'll still walk barefoot."* This is the Christ figure taking on punishment for everyone and his hands gain in strength through this work, and so he sings praise for them again, giving thanks to align himself properly with the universe. Again the river dogs carry his fate that he cannot avoid, but he will not fall or curse them as they are the greater order that must be lived in. (What doesn't kill you) The river has always been seen as an image of fate and I intentionally avoid the ocean, because it is such an obvious image of the unconscious, if only in my mind. All water images can represent the unconscious and in some sense they can all be seen as equivalent, but rivers flow and all of these images are not exactly equivalent. Frodo looks into the future after seeing his own future mirrored in an image in a small bowl of water poured by the elf queen. The future in *Lord of the Rings* is dominated by the singular/Cyclops eye of power that foretells his fate. This eye also sees him. This image of the elf queen pouring water is an exact copy of Aquarius the water carrier. So deep, so wide.

 The lilac bleeding star business is a very specific image I came across recently. If you are born under a lilac bleeding star you are cursed or compelled to travel. I believe it is an image from the Far Middle East (Uzbekistan one of the cultural cradles of the Indo European world) and might be a well known allusion there, like a fig tree, but what I like is the angular dissonance of the words themselves and the dense 'three-word metaphor', Lilac bleeding star. Who could have put those three words together? Maybe in Persian or Urdu all of these words have a common sound or they are a more sonorous fit; but if you give this image a little cultural drift, it becomes something beautiful and it's mine now. (I would gladly accept an offer from the BBC to make a travel documentary film that would search out the underlying cultural matrix of lilac-bleeding star. We could search out the roots of Indo-European language and culture in Georgia/Turkmenistan and/or Kashmir: call me?

So now the truth is bound to Ungar's recognition that he could not escape his wandering. The lilac's form is dream-soaked and true, and he must accept this and wander until fate allows him to stop. Again, the truth is darkened from the river's bottom or the unconscious, but the truth has been allowed to come up and it is now a fact. It now graces the boundary between water and land, which is a sea strand. This is the boundary between his first understanding and his complete integration or acceptance. This knowledge is the art of becoming conscious. His blood has turned hard or he has become, or had become rigid, but he now accepts this fate of having to travel after having heard this message for himself. *"All rivers end up in the sea"* is a line I first heard from Pete Townsend. I paraphrased this thought into: drowned all streams seek endings. In other words all life must end and that end is a final dissolution into the great unconscious or ocean (thought must return into the right hemisphere). But Ungar, and me the writer, leave behind us this token or song so that people in love or people who are open to experience can gain some wisdom from his/my writings. This is the desire to be remembered in art and also it is a call across the ages so that someone else may recognize their own humanity in yours. People's experience of life can be very similar and Ungar is trying to point out that he stopped and listened for the greater voice to help him find his way. What else can we really do when we are at a crisis? The apostles went fishing and Christ *came to them*. (I will spell it out: fishing on the water. Engage in something passive to allow life to approach you. It is a beautiful metaphor.)

Ungar, like all literary and dream characters, is to a certain extent a personification of me and to a certain extent he is a product that is beyond my personal interference. Writing is a very strange blend of willful direction and subsequent editing and also simply allowing the story to occur in spite of you.

Now, I will tell you that a lot of this explanation about the poem is my reading backward into what I have written and I will explain what I mean in my long-winded way. I was listening to Randy Bachman's Vinyl Tap last night on CBC Radio and he was talking about a literary idea called a 'mondegreen'. This occurs when somebody is listening to a song and they hear the lyrics incorrectly. The example they used was: *"excuse me while I kiss this guy"*, instead of *"excuse me while I kiss the sky"*, which is a lyric from Jimi Hendrix. When I am listening to music, I intentionally don't listen to the real lyrics very closely, because I like the way things sound and I can play with these sounds to make my own lyrics. There was a long period in my life when I was only listening to music in other languages, because for the most part, lyrics in pop music are terrible. I have written some of my favorite lines of my own poetry from misperceived mondegreens. Love is in love with your dark glasses is one that I am going to use somehow. I believe it was from hearing a line in a Neil Finn song incorrectly, but I honestly can't tell you which one now. Also, *"I couldn't buy an ass full of steam"* is from an *Audioslave* recording, but it's such a stupid image I doubt that I can use it, although I find it quite funny.

The dark glasses line is about how people can't see each other's eyes anymore and they fall in love with the appearance of the person or the bling that they display, instead of reading their soul through the window of their eyes. Stars seem to wear sunglasses all of the time, because their eyes are so blood shot or they are high, or they just wish to retain some form of privacy in their public life, etc. Their glasses allow us to project on to them, because we can't get a good look at their expressions. (It is an accurate, though cynical metaphor for our times) But I wrote or misheard the line first and I explain or expand, or infuse the meaning into it later. This is how my mind works and I have learned to accept it. *Smells Like Teen Spirit* probably happened this way, in that it is a very ambiguous line and Kurt Cobain spun it out until it represented what he wanted to say, or maybe he had no idea what he wanted to say. Or… maybe he knew exactly what he wanted to say and recognized the aptness of the metaphor immediately. Art can be very ambiguous and ingenious. The job of artists is to follow what attracts them and let the critics sort out the process.

For me, I have found that I go through waves of interest that stretch over very long periods of time and ultimately I circle around similar ideas repeatedly or I collect similar types of lyrics despite myself. I constantly write down anything I find interesting and I collect these things in a series of notebooks that I have been writing in for some 30 years now. In the back of the books, are dream journals that I have collected for just as long. Some of the other things that I collect are wicked quotes from my reading and it is always easy to rephrase something I have found into a lyric, because I am accustomed to playing with language. Also, I have tried to reduce larger thoughts into tight aphorisms, so writing in a dense style is something I have practiced for some time. We don't create in a vacuum. If I feel like writing or I begin to expand on an idea, and I don't feel it to be complete yet, or I am in need of inspiration, I simply troll through these books; they are all loose and wiggly. But, as I was saying, I tend to come back to or unconsciously circle around certain themes anyway, because they are a concern to me or my inner daemon; so trolling through my wiggly books isn't as haphazard as it might seem.

"The dreamer held no fragrant rose, tangible and public, with which to demonstrate to all the truth of his dream." -Richard Tarnas

Some of what I consider my best poems is the direct result of copying down a dream into a poetic structure. These poems are very powerful, because the images are already dense and interesting. Like, 'without the court so late at night, in through the open window crept insight', which again was handed to me ready-made, all I had to do was fill out the message. Things like mondegreens-I would like to think-are also participating in this same intrusion of the unconscious into consciousness in that you are hearing something that isn't there, and because the unconscious has no language, it is forced to attach itself to whatever floats by. So in some sense your unconscious is allowed to fall with you into the process, but most of the time we pass this over as a mistake, like pointing to the left, but saying right. Da Vinci used to un-focus his eyes and look at water stains on his walls for inspiration; this willful deconstruction of the overt consciousness is not new.

When John Lennon was asked about George Harrison being successfully sued for copyright infringement for *My Sweet Lord*, he immediately said that George should have changed the song more and he would have gotten away with it. George Harrison defended himself by saying that he had unconsciously stolen the song and was not aware that these songs were so similar and they are. John Lennon could be a little too brutally honest and possibly wrong.

Within the blues genre, most of the lyric writing seems to be shuffling around different set pieces: 'Bring my pay check home every day' 'caught my woman messing with another man' 'heard my back door slam' 'a little John the conquer root and a black cat bone'. If you know the code you can write blues songs forever. Rush had a lyric something to the effect that you cannot create in a vacuum, but I can't remember the exact lyric and so I will paraphrase and let the editor figure out if I have to seek permission to reprint in whole or in part, etc. What exactly do we own? Napster has uncovered the obvious truth about copyright.

What I am saying is that if you are going to rip stuff off you have to be a little bit clever. Better if you trust your own instincts; out of this trust, you will develop a more unique voice that reflects your inner vessel. This involves listening and being willing to start with nothing. Quite often I have no idea what I am writing and I allow the editing process to establish order for me after the fact or I re-read and edit meaning back into what I have been writing. I suspect Bjork works in this way as well. Bjork has of late become enamored with ee cummings and I suspect that he works this way as well. How do you explain a line like: *"nobody not even the rain has such small hands"*? Or to give this ongoing ramble of mine some sense of coherence, this lyric from *Medulla* by Bjork springs to mind.

And these teeth are a ladder up to the mouth

These teeth are a ladder that I walk

That you can walk to if you want

If you want up to the mouth

The mouth's cradle

The production of the *Medulla* CD is almost completely vocals. There are only a few other instruments on it, and so the whole recording quite literally comes from the mouth's cradle. The medulla is located in the older limbic area of the brain that deals with the brain's interface of the unconscious and speech, and poetry specifically. I am quite sure that Bjork is driving at the same thing I am, which is: get your ego out of the way. The mouth's cradle is an analogy for the unconscious in that you allow your mouth to talk without your mind being in the way .This is the highly prized ability to create poetry or tell a story. You put a spell on everyone. The Atman (the inherent creative essence of being) is both within and without us.

I will write out two more of my poems: one is very light to show you that I am not some brooding intellectual dissident, while the other was an attempt to write a series of terse aphorisms and collect them under a loose theme. *Meander*, the second poem contains my epitaph. How's that for dower?

She was a pretty young sprig

Full of all of her life and spring time

Taking on the tiered world

And that sort of thing

Summer danced us out of Eden

Apply our hands to work and freedom

Autumn wonder at the splendor

Taking pictures to remember

Winter has arrived at last

Settle in and let it pass

Summers hands bled into winter's evenings

One moment dressing the next one leaving

Meander

Give up our dead

Lift up our life

Though we may lie with broken things

Forget our fate

Ring in this love

And end our life's meandering

Cast not your eye upon this corpse

But witness what's alive in thee

Sing alive in freedom

Set the witness free

We run like water in to this dream

I'll be younger when I'm older

Is this the world I'm meant to shoulder?

Without you the valley is wide

When you're standing on one side

It's better to travel hopefully

Than it is to arrive

Sing alive in freedom

Set the witness free

We run like water into this dream

We run like water into this dream

Into this loving.

   This second poem was actually recorded as a full song by a lovely singer named Stephanie Belding, on an album I worked on with her called *Lustre*. The producer of this record was my good friend, Michael Kulas, who is one of the people who has helped me to understand Brian Eno better. I believe Yeats wrote: *'cast a cold eye on life and on death'*. My line: *'cast not your eye…'* is about not letting death have a hold on you. I had thought that having to go through something like being a witness at a particularly gruesome trial would have to affect you in some way, or just having seen something terrible can have great aftershocks and so the line: *'set the witness free'* seemed to sum this up. Post-traumatic stress disorder is the result of being witness; we all must carry our lives with us. We are all left to carry ourselves back into life through the depression that comes with the passing of a loved one. I have always felt very odd about how quickly everything else goes on living after someone dies, but the fact is that if we cling too tightly to our sadness, it will kill us as well. What's interesting to me in this song is that after Stephanie set it to music, and played it for me, she said that she knew some people who were going through a similar situation to this song and I never found out what she meant by this. She must have read this poem very differently from me, as is my wish.

"Sometimes it's tougher to look than to leap" – Stranglers, Skin Deep

I don't think I can avoid a minor detour into *The Stolen Child* by W.B. Yeats. I do not read poetry very often, but I have a recording by the Waterboys that is a musical adaption of this poem and my wife and I are reduced to tears every time we hear it, much like the last page of *Ulysses* by James Joyce. I'm not sad when I hear it. I just simply can't control my metro-sexual crying. This is really the cathartic power of art and I can think of few other things that can elicit such profound feelings. Flamenco music and dance are definitely one.

Where dips the rocky highland

Of Sleuth Wood in the lake

There lies a leafy island

Where flapping herons wake

The drowsy water rats;

There we've hid our faery vats

Full of berry's

And of reddest stolen cherries

Come away, o human child!

To the waters and the wild

With a faery, hand in hand

For the world's more full of weeping than you can understand

Where the wave of moonlight glosses

The dim grey sands with light,

Far off by furthest Roses

We foot it all the night,

Weaving older dances

Mingling hands and mingling glances

Till the moon has taken flight;

To and fro we leap

And chasing the frothy bubbles

While the world is full of troubles

And anxious in its sleep

Come away, o human child!

To the waters and the wild

With a faery, hand in hand

For the world's more full of weeping than you can understand

Where the wandering water gushes

From the hills above Glen-Car,

In pools among the rushes

That scarce could bathe a star

We seek for slumbering trout

And whisper in their ears

Give them unquiet dreams;

Leaning softly out

From ferns that drop their tears

Over the young streams,

Come away, O human child

To the waters and the wilt

With a faery hand in hand,

For the world's more full of weeping than you can understand

Away with us he's going

The solemn-eyed:

He'll hear no more the lowing

Of the calves on the warm hillside

Or the kettle on the hob

Sing peace into his breast

Or see the brown mice bob

Round and round the oatmeal chest.

For he comes, the human child

To the waters and the wild

With a faery hand in hand,

For the world's more full of weeping than he can understand

 The second stanza seems to imply some form of pagan ritual involving the faery vats full of stolen cherries. I should think this is a reference to intoxication, and he seems to be juxtaposing this care-free ritual with all of the troubles in the world that cause it to be anxious in its sleep. This ritual is taking place at night so it has a dream quality to it as well. This is indicative of the unconscious in that there is no sense of moral judgment both in a dream and in this ritual, both dreams and rituals occur outside of time. Much like Shakespeare's underlying political views or some of the *Old Testament* or nature herself, who has given us the personal unconscious, there seems to be no easily discernible moral agenda here. Yeats then takes great pains to fix us in the real place where this is occurring by constantly reiterating the natural setting using specific place names and images of water and animals. Then in the third stanza he again fixes the place by mentioning the water from Glen-Car, but explodes the specific image by bringing in the image of a star being bathed in this pool and he tells us that they are whispering into nature's (the trout) ear and causing it unquiet dreams. This is man's unique consciousness speaking back into the silence of the unconscious waters of nature. And man does cause nature to have unquiet dreams. We are the problem.

In the final stanza, he pulls the whole poem together and gives you the key to understanding what is being said. This is the world of judgment or the world of the Buddha's sword where discernment is needed. This child must come into the world of today not the fairy world, and this world will divorce him from nature. Things that he now takes for granted, like the sound of cattle or water boiling in a kettle, will not cause wonder or suspend his aimless thinking without his deeper awareness of them. Although deep in his cultural heritage, which is behind the screen of the natural world, these faeries still wait and this dream and ritual have already taken place, and are always taking place. This is another way of describing a drug experience. You may have wonderful insights into the nature of reality, but you still have to come back into the world; it truly does continue on after we die.

If you are sensitive, you can regain his wonder where ferns drop their tears. And this poem is trying to give you that same sense of wonder. Throughout this poem, Yeats seems to be both saying yes and no. You are both going away from nature and you are also always with the fairy, although as you gain consciousness, you will also understand why the world is weeping. Much like the experience of the first broken heart: we all know it is coming for our children and you could try to warn them about the consequences of their actions, but it won't help them a bit. You must remind them afterwards to re-join you with the lovers in the pomegranate trees. This poem is to my mind another reflection of the moral ambiguity of nature, in that she must be both elevated into a life-giving symbolic realm and experienced as real earthy dung-filled mire.

The gold is always in the dung heap.

"Didn't I come to bring you a sense of wonder?" - Van Morrison

Yes.

1 ARIADNE'S STRING

I personally believe that much of dynamic that results in various philosophical discussions and that ensuing construction of a world of thought (religious, scientific or artistic) is the result of an inherent and or constructed individual temperament or the unfolding of an inborn personality type as opposed to the recognition of some singular 'fact' that exists separate from our perception of it. I am suspicious of the assertion of an unvarnished truth that has been uncovered by one side of an argument or the other. Possession of 'the truth' sometimes smacks of the egotistical self justification of a view point that is recognized after the fact. In my humble opinion there is no single unadulterated truth that lasts for eternity (although there might be and it might also embrace a contradiction within itself); there is only our transitory understanding of our limited world view as it reflected back to us in the here and now.

One of the people who greatly influenced the way I think about the world, and the way that I came to think in general is the psychologist Carl Jung. (The book to begin with for the interested reader is *Psychoanalysis* by Marie Louise Von Franz) Jung was largely responsible for the development of the idea of personality types. This idea is based on what he understood to be the only ways in which the world could be perceived or apprehended. I don't think I can avoid a somewhat lengthy sketch of this idea and some of Jung's other ideas. It will become clear as we move through the book that these Jungian ideas are some of the elemental building blocks of my ongoing theses and that a relatively clear understanding of them now will allow us to move beyond them or conversely more deeply into them. You can think of this section as an attempt to define some of my terms so that we can actually discuss these things later on. I have leavened this section with many anecdotes in order to entertain you as we move along.

The benefit of the Jungian approach to understanding the human condition is that it is an open system and it embraces all manner of contradictory human endeavor. It is a reflection of Love/Eros not power. By taking a look at Jung's elemental ideas of personality types and by exploring the possibility of inherent archetypal structures of the psyche such as the Shadow and Self, we will begin to develop an understanding of the different ways in which the world can be framed and then understood as we build up conscious understanding. This will also-to a certain extent-help us to see how we are in turn influence by unconscious paradigms or analogies in our thoughts and how these thought paradigms are further consciously influenced by us.

Some of the elements of this argument will become cornerstone ideas that we will greatly expand on and then further dissect. If after reading this chapter I hope that we can agree that every individual doesn't perceive the world in the same way as every other, if we can concede this we will have gained some ongoing traction. This single thought shall put us much farther ahead in our understanding as we attempt to grasp on to the other various world views, which we will encounter. I have come to realize-and will attempt to illuminate-that much of the temperamental differences we encounter in all areas of human endeavor are a result of the bilateralization of the human brain.

It is also my contention that there really are underlying and relatively constant motifs of thought, but that they are expressed in a unique fashion as they pass through each individual. If I were desperately interested in being politically correct, I would say that all brains are equal. What I am saying is that all brains are not the same and that these underlying thought motifs express themselves differently in us for a vast number of reasons: things like culture, depth and breathe of learning, the time period you exist in and inborn individual temperament and relative mental health. (Same water, different vessel)

Jung came to understand that there was a general division of people into introverted and extroverted biases, based on the way that people react to being in the world. The introvert relates to the world through his/her own inner perception of the environment, while the extrovert perceives their inner self through their relationship toward the outward environment, or with a more outward looking stance. Once again, an introvert understands the exterior world through an understanding of her interior self. The extrovert understands herself or develops her image through a relationship with the exterior world. Put very simply, an introvert might try to explain to you who they are or why they did something and an extrovert might ask you to tell them what they should do, and by collecting a lot of opinions from other people, they would plot a course forward. In an introvert, an internal understanding is the primary understanding in an extrovert an understanding of the external situation or a representation of facts is the most important aspect. Reality is a subtle blending of these two primary stances and no one can function competently with only one viewpoint. But, people do have a tendency to favor one of these two elemental positions over the other and this may be a result of their inborn-possibly genetic- temperament, or it may be sociologically/culturally reinforced, but more than likely it is a beautiful combination of both.

There are four more sub-groups related more directly to the means in which we can and do build up our perception of the world. (There is a reference glossary in the back of the book) They are SENSATE, which is mostly concerned with facts and corresponds largely to the scientific method (Geology, Archaeology, Accounting etc.) in their extroverted form. THINKING has to do with abstraction, rational assessments and the general perceiving and representation of an object or model. INTUITION is primarily concerned with the future, and to a certain extent, with the past, or what has or can be done. And FEELING is concerned with the relational or value laden aspect of things, i.e., I love cookies. They make me feel good.

So the sensate function lends weight to the world by giving it a form of substance. It is concerned with facts. Thinking helps us to understand what the thing is by lending it a conceptual framework. Thinking gives us the names of objects, which is a subtle symbolic abstraction. This is largely a left brain function, which incidentally controls the linguistic representation of concepts as well. Intuition can help you realize what can be done with the thing once it is apprehended. Intuition is usually a casting forward or backward; gaining and assessing of information, more or less unconsciously. Feeling tells you whether anything means anything to you. You don't need to figure out why you love your mother. She is the sum of a long relationship and she and her image carries great relation for you. You feel this in your bones. Broadly speaking, women tend to be feelers and men tend to be thinkers. This is a large source of the endless problems that occur in the communication between the sexes, because thinking and feeling are diametrically opposed functions. Feeling is more the function of the right brain, which has a tendency to be more integrative or context driven. If people are too far apart in their temperament, it's like the conversation they are engaged in is at completely separate tables and in different languages with a poor translation.

Jung developed this conception of four sub-types as a result of his understanding that there were only four ways to experience reality: sensate is the fact of the world; thinking is an abstraction or collation of that raw fact. Feeling is a relational quality of the world, and intuition can plot a course into the future or is a more unconscious integrated holistic assessment of the situation. These four concepts will become more and more explicit as we proceed. The current thinking in the world of evolutionary biology is asserting that there are inherent differences between the sexes possibly as a result of the influence of hormones, and that these differences start to manifest almost immediately after conception. So there is an ongoing biological root to our different orientations. Also, the orientation of the sensation and intuition functions -when tied closely to thinking- represents a fundamental division in the sciences. Theoretical physics is a result of the intuitive or relatively associative expression of that type of thinking and the ongoing testing of theoretical ideas against reality is the more sensate expression of the sciences.

Jung highlighted his understanding of the different types by showing that different nations and cultures tended to have their own expression of these general typologies as well. This could be inborn or culturally (i.e., nurtured verses nature) conditioned or more probably it is a combination of both. The Germanic nations tended to be thinkers, as any perusal of Schopenhauer, Hegel or indeed the beautiful infrastructure of the country itself should confirm. The French on the other hand, tend to be feelers. Jung sited the abundance of subtle words in the French language related to feeling (esprit de corps representing collective feeling or ennui being an example of a subtle feeling of mild depression), and I believe there are about 15 individual words in French, each denoting the very subtle gradations in feeling tone that you may wish to express; whereas Germans are said to have two words to describe feelings: 'gemutlic' being one. (This lack of German feeling words may participate in the realm of urban myth, but I will use this possibly insulting example to highlight a larger point. I personally love Germany, if that means anything.)

Most German words used to describe feelings are related more closely to emotional states as opposed to accurate feeling tones. (More about this distinction later) In German, if you ask someone who they are, a more literal translation of the question you are asking them is: *"what do they do"?* This is the extroverted thinking aspect whereby you tie the person to another real concept – in this case, their job. Paris on the other, hand is considered by our ad agencies as the city of romance/love and light. Most people feel this to be true and Paris is then idealized as such for the American public. Paris happened to be a lover in mythology also. It seems the French can't get away from it.

The Italians or at least there political acumen has a tendency to be Intuitive. Hence their rapid changes in parliament, the next one may finally do some good. A stable good government is just around the corner and we should give them a try. The English and Dutch round us out by being largely sensate, this is they embody a willingness to deal with the world as a series of facts. The British ethos was to forge on in the face of the world and do your duty while the Dutch mastered double entry bookkeeping and many of the subtle aspects of mercantile trade. (Numbers don't lie.) Americans are overwhelmingly extroverted and largely sensate thinkers as well.

All western European nations have a decidedly extroverted leaning while the East Asians (India, China, etc.) have preponderance towards to the introverted. The west wishes to change the world through political action or action of any kind. While the Eastern religious ideal wishes the individual to seek change within him first and thereby effect change in the world around them through aligning with a higher ideal. Of course, we must be careful when we make these broad generalizations, but this brings us to one of the running threads of this book: is there any provable truth in this concept of personality types at all? Or stated differently, do we have a valid view of reality when we generalize? Have we just succumb; to trying to further rationalize some foolish folk psychology?

This type of generalization about race, etc. is very common in the real world and is excellent fodder for humorists, but if it enters into the political or scientific realm it is explosive. If there is a truth in 'racial' generalizations what kind of sliding truth can it really be?

I will try to show that the pragmatic approach or radically skeptical outlook is the best means that we have to discern and apply concepts. This means that if we must judge any concept or accepted set of truths by their advantage or efficacy to us, or by the proven usefulness of the paradigm that they represent - more on this later. All generalized knowledge should probably come with a caveat of some sort. This does not mean that we must reject generalizations wholesale. And I have intentionally generalized above so that I can now issue my ongoing caveat, which will get fleshed out as we move along. For now I would point out that the current-overly politically correct-mentality can also lead us into all sorts of foolishness when it runs into a generalization like racial customs, etc. This is why comedians love making us uncomfortable by poking fun at these types of stereotypes. Labels like retarded or vertically challenged are important and the words themselves can come to symbolize and firmly hold on to some powerful psychic magic, like the current media fever over the N word. Comedians on the other hand can get great laughs out of twisting us into our personal discomfort (cognitive dissonance), which flows from juxtaposing our unconscious assumptions against our overt and consciously nurtured, political correctness.

I have found that Jung's framework of personality types can be very useful and seems to reflect a generalized and sometimes very specific and accurate viewing of reality. This understanding can be very helpful when dealing with and trying to understand other people. Big business has gone in for this concept of personality types in a big way, because it helps to disassemble some of the confusion inherent in discussions between the different personalities involved in trade (discussions with the Chinese and Indians about having all of our industry, for example). Or an understanding of personality types helps to make you more aware that everyone doesn't necessarily think like you. Business and trade has been a great force for promoting peaceful understanding. War and conflict, in the long run, is bad for wider business.

One of the more interesting aspects of Jung's exploration of the unconscious is the concept of the shadow. Most people have a preponderance to embody one of the major personality types with a second type functioning as an auxiliary or support in which they are also relatively comfortable. It's best to conceive of the four personality types in a wheel format.

Thinking

Sensate   -|-   Intuition

Feeling

If your most prominent function is thinking, you will most likely be comfortable with either intuition or sensate as an auxiliary. Feeling will most likely be an aspect of your shadow function or the aspect of your personality in which you are the least comfortable. Or in psycho babble this is the part of your personality that lies largely undeveloped and so it is-for you-the most unconscious. This shadow aspect of yourself is a part of your potential personality that is now the least developed. This shadow orientation has been left behind while you have continued growing and adapting yourself to your environment through the ongoing reinforcement of your major function. Because it has been left behind by you, but still exists in potential, you will have a tendency to project it or externalize it on to other people. You will usually project it or see it most clearly in people you don't like. Conversely, in its positive aspect, it will also play a large part in the personality of the person or people that you fall in love with. Truly opposites do attract. The unconscious shadow retains a certain amount of psychic energy, which can then lead you towards a fascination with this aspect of yourself that you don't understand. If you are predominantly an introverted thinker you will have a tendency to demonize and be fascinated with other people's faults as you witness them being exposed in the extraverted feeling part of your personality.

The tendency to demonize shows up in the real world in this way: say we have an introverted thinker maybe a professor of philosophy at a university. This man is very comfortable with his internal monologue and can entertain very complicated thinking dialogues within him. He may run into a woman who happens to be an extroverted feeler. In other words, she is very good at sensing the tone of the room she is in. She understands herself through sensing and embodying the feelings of others. Extroverted feelers are very sensitive to the emotional tone of their friends. These types of people are good at parties, because they are comfortable with this area of interpersonal understanding and they embody and gain control over the tone of the environment, and help to steer it into a better feeling. The professor may be largely un-aware of this woman, because he's involved in his own thoughts for the most part. Then, one day, he asks this woman some simple question and is taken by surprise by the warmth of her answer. She, for her part has always been impressed by this man who mysteriously seems to be able to live inside of his head. The woman's warmth stirs this man with feelings that he is unused to; she seems to be talking directly to him, very straightforwardly. Let's cut to the chase and for the sake of simplicity call this feeling and attraction the stirrings of love. The professor's blind side or underdeveloped feeling side can now be projected on to this women and it can be quite exciting to begin experiencing this rush of emotion that is tied to this unknown. There is always a certain amount of fascination built up around the shadow and it can unleash great stores of psychic energy.

I am not implying that this fellow's feelings are a vacant illusion created by his blind-sided ignorance or that they are somehow not true. This is how we distance ourselves from reality by psychoanalyzing it into intellectual safety. My point is that his feelings are less developed or less acute and somewhat unwieldy. Love is an intoxication wherein you embrace that which is completely other and seek to become one with it. The shadow or undeveloped aspects of the personality-when they first intrude into consciousness-have a tendency to be all or nothing. They can give you a completely accurate assessment of the world or you can miss the mark entirely, because of the explosion of the latent energetic value- what we might call passions or emotions-and you may be equally certain that you are correct when you are in fact dead wrong.

Now, if we spin this scenario out for a couple of years and let our cynicism creep in, the professor may come to hate exactly those aspects of her which he fell in love with in the first place. Her love for him is always touchy feely and never logical. She always wants to go out and surround herself in the warmth of people who she has feelings for. Her family is important while his doesn't understand him and he makes little attempt to let them into his interior kingdom of thought. When he was in love, he enjoyed these distractions (of being immersed in another environment, because he was experiencing these things through and with the woman), but if he retracts back into his dominant typology again, the external environment that he associates and enjoys with her becomes an annoyance to him and ultimately she will embody that annoyance. He begins to demonize his own underdeveloped shadow aspects and this takes the exterior form of simply hating this woman, who perfectly represents this shadow in and outside of him. She both is and is not his shadow. The real problem is their mutual projected unconsciousness, as they both seek power.

This goes a long way to explain the bitterness involved in divorce; that which made the thinking man whole or the most unconscious aspect of him was brought into a relationship with the rest of his personality through his love. If this feeling part of him does not develop over the course of the relationship, and remains entangled in the unconscious, it will then remain projected on to her instead of being integrated and realized more or less consciously by him. Love is the bridge to greater understanding. What we don't understand about ourselves, we can't understand about the larger world or other people around us. We tend to leave it in the unconscious where it causes no end of trouble through our ongoing projection. We project or externalize on to the world that which we do not understand consciously. These unconscious aspects of us are never inert. They hold potential or latent energy. To really integrate these submerged parts of the personality is very hard work, involving a lot of soul searching, honesty and sensitivity, but above all, they should be uncovered in an atmosphere of forgiveness. If you nurture hate for these demons you will fight them everywhere, in both yourself and others.

I once worked with a fellow who immediately didn't like me. It took me two years to realize that he didn't like me. He hid it very well from me. I found out accidentally at a party when someone told me that this fellow really couldn't stand me and the way I did things. I was astounded, because I just thought that this guy was shy and quiet, but what I understood immediately was that we were firmly in each other's shadow. He disliked me and I could not pick up on it, because he was such a different type than me. What I then realized was that this was a great opportunity for me to take a look at my own shadow through him. I was very careful with everything that I said to him and I tried very hard to be clear and concise when I addressed him so that there was less room for any misunderstanding between us. Jung called this approach, 'bush manners'. It's when two strangers meet in the forest, they are very careful and the meeting must be ritualized at a very slow pace, because sometimes there is no way to understand what the other's intentions are. Both partners must progress with utmost circumspect to determine if the other has evil intentions. The real breakthrough with my friend came, when we got together and played music a couple of times. We were both quite good musicians and through this love of music we shared a common language in which we could communicate without any preconceived notions about each other. Ironically, through playing music we were forced to listen to each other. The real difficulty with the unconscious aspects of our self is the fact that they are not conscious. We must carefully move around them to slowly let them grow into our explicit consciousness of their own accord, such as trying to sleep. You cannot force yourself to understand.

I will add one more dimension to this brief sketch of typology that was made known to me from the internet: this is from the Jung, Briggs, and Meyers personality tests that are used a lot in the business world. In addition to the eight main types, they add two more subdivisions: judging and perceiving. The judging type is just that. They resist the belief that the world is morally neutral. There should always be a call made as to whether an aspect is right or wrong. This is a very North American -left brain- ideal. The perceiving function is more comfortable with a grey wash; morality tends to be tied to specific situations and is constantly in flux-the more context-driven right brain. Neither attitude is entirely correct. The art of living, I believe, is to be in balance using each tool in accordance with the situation. If George W. Bush (poor explicit thinking) had used a little more perceiving, we may have avoided Iraq, conversely if the British had shown better judgment with Hitler and listened to Churchill (stunning extroverted intuition) more closely, the Second World War may have been much shorter. Of course, the world is far more complicated than these brief sketches and we shall endeavor to avoid 'what if' scenarios as much as we can.

One of the main initial drives in a Jungian analysis is the integration of the shadow or the highlighting of the unconscious aspects of you. Jung liked to posit a larger and more whole personality that encompassed not only all aspects of *you* but also included elements of the larger exterior environment. An understanding and integration of this Whole potential self is the ultimate goal of an analysis.

The shadow aspects of the personality-when unrealized-will tend to be confused with the other archetypes or it will be harder to disentangle and delineate the shadow from other unconscious aspects of you. When the shadow is unrealized it will have a tendency to carry a greater undefined emotional charge. This is the initial all or nothing phase of coming into contact with this aspect of yourself that I mentioned earlier, and also the reason that anger and rage are blind. Through disentangling or bringing forth into your consciousness the unrealized aspects of your personal self, you can be led to an understanding of this extended and greater Self.

For example, if you were an introverted feeler, your auxiliary function may be intuition, which is also introverted. An introverted feeler always understands what is important to them. They view the world though the litmus tests of how they value to things. They don't need to analyze what they like or dislike about people or things, they feel all of this directly in their guts, especially if they are intuitive. The next part of your personality that you could build a relationship with is the sensate. This would be a relationship with some more factual information in your life, say the various specs and accessories involved in buying electronics that you enjoy, or an appreciation for a well made car, or possibly taking more responsibility for your finances. It could also manifest in your accepting elements of the judgments of others as factual instead of always going with your gut.

The hardest part of your personality to integrate and utilize in the world, if you are this type is extroverted thinking. To truly integrate this aspect might involve really going through the facts and agendas of various political parties and candidates in an earnest attempt to vote impartially. Or coming up with a workable written plan to plant crops in the third world, involving a realistic trajectory and timeline for delivery of seeds and planting schedules. Wars always come down to specific battles, but they are actually won by the army that is the best supplied and well rested. This ability to deliver an army to the battle field is extroverted thinking in the sensate realm of action - the so called field Marshall. So an introverted feeler can understand perfectly well how people are suffering in Africa. The difficulty for them is marshalling the external world into correct action and communicating this reasoned action plan into a reality that can be adapted and followed over a long committed time scale. Also, the introverted intuitive aspect will desire to get on with the next project, so sticking to a long term project involving constant intellectual reassessment of facts is quite a challenge for the ever-searching and shortened attention span of an intuitive.

I will give one more example of someone whose shadow is in the sensate realm.

A relationship with money is a part of the sensate realm of a personality. Money has to do with facts. You only have so much money and your bills are X amount. These things are stark facts. When you don't want to deal with facts like money, you can safely assume that this is part of your own shadow and not dealing with your shadow, the world will conspire to bite you on the ass. You may develop a resigned philosophical attitude toward your negligent money position by saying to yourself that you are 'content to live in the present' or that you always spend your way through all of your money and that the future is really an illusion. Then, you start to develop an aversion for people who are carefully planning for the future, because for you–intellectually-the future doesn't exist. You search for like-minded philosophers and come to embody this intellectual/existential sheen to further convince yourself that you are right. On the other hand, it becomes exceedingly difficult for you to borrow money and initiate any long range planning like buying a house. This will become a problem in any long-term relationship.

When dealing with your shadow, it's best to work in baby steps. For instance, don't try to do your taxes all of a sudden, if you have never dealt with money. It will simply be overwhelming and you will feel justified in not handling your finances in the future. I would suggest opening up your credit card statements and actually follow your spending habits instead of making the minimum payments and throwing the bill in the garbage, or actually try to disentangle an agenda from a political party's jargon on the national news. It will take five to ten years to become comfortable with your shadow, but if you don't, you will never understand how much of the problems that occur in your life are really of your own making. Fate is always in the mix as well and I am not saying that we live entirely in a world of our own conscious or unconscious psychic creation. This is a form of blaming the victim. But this type of introspection will help you to see that you are unconsciously sabotaging your own future.

The schema of the personality types above moves in an S shape as opposed to a cross. People are rarely comfortable with the diametrically opposed aspects of themselves and must grope their way around the wheel in this S like movement. So if you are an extroverted sensate, you might have an auxiliary function of thinking and a tenuous grasp on your extroverted feeling. The least developed function would be introverted intuition. This is the function where your shadow resides. A person with weak introverted intuition may constantly fear that the worst is going to happen -or the people they love in the future and so called facts will always back this up. You may develop morbid fears that they are going to be hit by a car or that they are constantly going to make some stupid mistake. People get killed this way all of the time on the news. Many compulsion disorders seem to be a reflection of a poor introverted intuition. A doctor can assure you repeatedly that you don't have cancer, but you could easily get it, and no amount of doctors can change this seeming statistical fact that cancer is always there in potential.

Extroverted sensate types are very aware of the facts in the outside world, but their intuition may constantly color their opinions of what these facts mean in a negative way. They may then develop a tendency to project their poor internal intuitions outside of themselves and quite often in a negative way, because this intuitive assessment of the world coming up in themselves is so unrealized that they don't even know that they are generating it. Or, they may project this negativity inward and develop a compulsive hand-washing ritual in an effort to try to stay mentally clean. Or they can become fixated on the thought that they are getting cancer or something like that. They may sense that this distress is coming from inside, but it must be attached to a fact, so it must be a cancer or liver disorder. Ritual hand-washing, for example, is an attempt at externalizing a vague inward mental attitude. No amount of hand-washing will clean your heart or dirty thoughts. This aspect of someone's shadow projection should be quite visible or identifiable to other people, because it will usually carry a strong and fairly irrational emotional charge. Some people are quite petulant about germs and even more petulant when you point out their unwarranted petulance. Yellow alert!

This poor intuition may also manifest in emotionally charged, overprotection of your children. You will not allow them to ride their bicycle too far away from the house or an extreme example would be: you just don't let them do anything without your protection, because they seem to be unaware of the facts of the situation as you see them. You have projected your poor intuition into the sensate realm as an overriding fear. This is the modern phenomenon of helicopter parents who feel they must supervise everything their children do. Somehow this has become an accepted social phenomenon, instead of the pathetic fringe behavior that it should be seen as. Of course, there are many other things involved in this sort of extreme behavior, but part of the problem when viewed through this personality paradigm is that the situation is an external manifestation of a poor relationship to your own introverted intuition in that you wish to control yourself and you exercise this control through externalizing your fear and casting it onto others.

Current media trends and government propaganda machines reinforce in us a constant nebulous fear of the outside world, even though statistically a fact the crime rate has steadily declined over the last 30 years. The actual statistic occurrence of random and unsolved child abduction is literally over a million to one or some 200 occurrences in the United States per year.

Your wandering soul

If you are unconscious of these aspects of your personality, your shadow will have a tendency to become confused with your Anima/Animus. This will be expressed as anxiety toward the opposite sex. The Anima/Animus is the aspect of your personality that corresponds to the opposite sex. In every woman is a wish, belief or image of the ideal male partner and it is the same for every man. You may not be able to articulate who that person is, but you sure know them when you meet them. Gay people tend to embody these images as well as projecting them. These archetypal images are delineated and refined in us over our childhood, through our interactions with the world. In childhood, these interactions are largely related to your parents. There are also some innate or intrinsic evolutionary aspects to these unconscious archetypal images.

For instance, the personal desire for beauty and seeming good health in a partner would be an obvious external indicator of the ability to successfully breed and sustain children, and therefore, mating with a healthy partner would help to propagating your genes. Personal fitness and or physical beauty or high social ranking should be an indicator of good health. So a somewhat idealized internal image of a partner would help us to more precisely focus our attention-from an evolutionary perspective-on to a proper healthy mate. Or, quite possibly, help us to gloss over some of the least obvious defects so that we can get on with the business of propagating the species. It seems we are hardwired to assume that people are attractive when we only get a glimpse of them.

An example of how this looks in the real world will require another politically incorrect thumbnail sketch. Let's say a man has a very overbearing mother and she is an extroverted sensate, judging with an auxiliary feeling function, this woman is concerned with the facts in the outside world and she doesn't take any shit. She is very certain of what is right and wrong. She has no time for mushy thoughts about how people should envision world peace. There are things to be done and she knows what they are. One of the interesting things about the concept of the 'types' in general is that within a family, there will usually be some kind of balance struck from within or into the extended community. Let's say that the father in this family is a mildly introverted thinking type with his intuition as an auxiliary; he is a business man in an office or someone working on the stock exchange. He uses his thinking to look at the stock market and analyze various trends in the world, and current thinking. However, his true strength is that he has a good nose for what is coming up in the trends of business, because of his intuition. Let's then imagine that these two people have one son who is terribly introverted and shy. He is gifted his intuition from his father with an auxiliary of feeling. He embodies the feeling tone, because of the domination of the sensate realm that his mother embodies. This has left feeling as the family shadow and nature may wish to balance out the equilibrium. The boy has no need to develop the other areas of his personality, because his parents do that for him.

The boy grows up to be a poet or musician or some such career that will guarantee his continued poverty. This boy has a tendency to try and find a partner that reflects the family situation he comes from: an overbearing wife who is like his mother. He is accustomed to this situation and will unconsciously gravitate towards it even though he dislikes it. If this situation stays unrealized in his own psyche, he will be drawn towards it repeatedly. The boy understands the parameters of a woman telling him what to do all the time and he gets to call her the 'old lady' when he's out drinking with his buddies. This is the unfortunate result of his unconsciousness of his situation in the world, and in an extreme situation, this internal blindness can be considered neurotic. When things go wrong, this person will be the first to blame others with an overt self-righteous indignation. He embodies the suffering artist.

Jung's definition of a neurosis is that you constantly expect new results from the same situation or constantly approaches new situations in the same way; then, expects to get new results. U2 said it perfectly: *"You've got stuck in a moment and you can't get out of it."* So this boy is looking for his mother, or as Freud said: *"He has an Oedipus complex"*. (I think these things are best taken on a symbolic level, because I think people really get steamy when they push Freud into the strictly literal meaning of statements like this.) So to a certain extent this boy is chasing his Anima, which is an internal image or symbol that is invested with meaning and has been built up in him as a result or reflection of his relationship with his mother. Mixed in with this are also aspects of his shadow, because of the relative unconsciousness of his relationship to his mother. Both of these internal images are unrealized aspects of his own underdeveloped personality. He does not need to bring these images into consciousness, because his mother has carried these aspects of dealing with the world for him throughout his whole childhood. Because she is so forceful and overbearing, she has denied him the ability to make his own mistakes and gain that painful insight into his own consciousness.

An extreme form of this type of introverted intuitive boy may manifest in reality with obvious character traits like being really bad with money, which is a sensate aspect of the world. So the wife always takes care of the bills, or you might hear things like: *"I have to go drinking on payday, because once the old lady gets the, check the money is gone."* Or, he dresses without much care, or in his late teens he would sit around his dormitory smoking cigarettes until two in the afternoon believing him to be above the world and the only person who really knows what's going on, but doing absolutely nothing about it. (I recently heard one of this naive type say: "*You can use drugs, but you don't let them use you.*" (Good luck with that.) He becomes full of ideas in a self-absorbed way, but lacks the connection to the world that would allow him to bring these things properly into birth. In this scenario of an over-sheltering mother, who inadvertently is denying the child life by being to over protective, the child has a tendency to develop a poor relationship with the sensate aspect of life. This unconsciousness will continually bite him. He then embodies the 'so hard done by attitude' and become cynical or be continually sarcastic, if he fails to confront it. Sound like anyone you know? (Too busy worrying about the future.) Also, the father is not blameless in this scenario. The father's job is to build a bridge for the boy into reality. If the father is too busy to engage the boy in life, it may be because the father is also functioning placidly within the same unconscious atmosphere. This is how you get an endless perpetuation of these types of problems (you could call it Karma).

Marriage is a good place to come to terms with these things and a good fair fight can clean the air. Of course, this implies listening to your partner and respecting their opinion. Love is the bridge. The archetypal mid-western Bible belter or fundamentalist Muslim keeps his daughter securely sheltered from life, and if she develops a rebellious streak, she may get out into the wide world, but be ill-equipped to deal with it. Apparently, there are a high proportion of mid-west girls in the porno industry, which is indicative of poor Anima relationship. If your father has refused you affectionate caring love your whole life, you will tend to try to find love wherever you can, but you may act in a somewhat indiscriminate way, or with poor judgment. It was noticed in the sixties that over-protected children were more likely to become Beatle maniacs, again as a way of rebelling, which was certainly in the air at that time. We have looked at some elements of dysfunction, but of course, most people grow up in loving homes and may have developed only minor forms of neurotic behavior. Over the course of this book, I will be building a picture of how the ongoing intricacies of nature verses nurture find expression, especially in the human animal.

I would like to digress here for a moment and discuss the nature of feeling. The feeling tone is probably the least well represented aspect of this perception model in modern western (especially North American) society. Throughout the book I will return to the interrelated concepts of feeling and emotion. As we weave in the other various themes of the book, it will become more apparent why this separation is important. For now, I will make a relatively explicit definition and elaboration of this idea.

In most of the nonfiction books that I have read you rarely find the term feeling or you will rarely encounter a discussion that is anything but quite rudimentary about how anyone feels about anything. Usually you will find the terms emotion and feeling being arbitrarily interchanged, for example: *"I became quite emotional at the baseball game when my daughter hit her first home run"* In my post-Jungian universe emotions have the connotation of undifferentiated. This means that a person describing their emotions can only vaguely articulate how they feel. What this person is describing as they become emotional about their daughter, is a sense of pride at their daughter's effort, etc., but implicit in all of this is the wider context of the feeling connection between the parent and the child. This isn't someone else's puppy dog running around home plate. It is a child that you have invested a staggering amount of work, attention and emotional effort. There is an implicit relational and value aspect to feelings that refuse quantification. There is no feeling without meaning.

The English term 'feeling' indicates the embedded nature of this aspect of understanding. In English feeling can denote a sense of touch, which is a very tactile experience or it, can also mean a premonition or vague emotion. This 'confusion' with a sense of touch may be where most of the imprecise connotations of the term come from. It may be the reason why the term emotion is more common in North American psych. I can think of no better English term than feeling because I wish to disentangle emotion and feeling, and I have no wish to introduce more arcane verbiage. I think feeling is the proper term, because in my mind, feeling implies an explicit connection to the body and you, and therefore, a real connection to the real world. This idea will play big as we move along and discuss the embodied nature of the mind. I think there is a tendency to discuss feeling as if it were something not relevant to the world at large, especially in the business world. For example, we might get sick of bleeding heart liberals. Feeling is explicitly relational and bleeding hearts just might be right, or they at least, can present us with another viewpoint. There is an absolutely perverse idea that feelings have no place in business and look where that has gotten us. Remote controlled weapons systems eliminate any form of feeling getting in the way of decisions to 'disrupt the enemy'. The history of war can be summed up by our ability to distance ourselves from our enemy and distance allows us to more easily abstract them into the enemy.

Poorly written TV shows rely on the music to help us understand the emotions that are being portrayed, which belies the embodied nature of feeling in that we cannot suspend our disbelief when the emotion being portrayed doesn't closely match the actors physical representation of it. We go with what we see the body doing every time. One of the most difficult things about writing and acting is to develop a way to imply the feelings into the characters without having to explicitly state them. Big business and the legal profession have more or less successfully eliminated feeling from their spheres of influence, but I would argue that it is to the detriment of both. On the other hand, science has moved forward at a phenomenal rate, largely due to the restriction of feeling or specifically for value judgment. But we will see that feeling enters in the back door -where angels fear to tread- when you refuse to shake its hand at the front door.

Jung's larger point is that all of the personality types are important if we wish to gain a whole or rounded view of any situation. It is Jung's belief that the greater Self, which we can become, is the result of the integration of all of these four/eight ways of understanding. If we wish to become more conscious, we need to first integrate these disparate or unrecognized aspects of our own personality. This means first confronting the shadow, which is almost always experienced as the least understood function, which in North American society, is usually feeling. The shadow, Anima, and various elements of our childhood and our inferior function can all be mixed together in to our emotional landscape, especially if we are particularly unconscious.

Jung called this mixture a 'complex', because it is exactly that – complex. What the analytical situation is trying to do is raise these complexes up into consciousness by disentangling them from each other and also from our Self-consciousness. By helping the analysand to see the larger context of their life story, they can then move beyond the rut-like patterns that they have fallen into, and hopefully, embrace a larger world understanding, through an expanded image of themselves in a meaningful relationship. There is no single recipe that an analyst can handout to someone to help them understand their own personal situation. Each individual is different and their greater Self will also be a unique, and hopefully, well-balanced expression of that greater individuality.

The analytical process can be very painful and you may begin to recognize that you may have wasted many years of your life chasing inappropriate sexual partners or you may realize that you were born into a very shitty home situation and that your parents really raised you poorly. Or you may have to come to grips with the realization that you are bad with money and you need to get out of dept. Such is the burden of greater consciousness. The real job then is to try to face these realties squarely and to find a way to move on and build up a future that encompasses this new understanding, without being narrowly defined by and therefore chained to, your past. Jung ultimately was trying to help people understand the greater meaning of their lives *now*, so that they would move ahead, and not wallow in self pity. It is difficult to love when you constantly drag all of your other junk along with you. (Robert Di Nero in *The Mission*)

Someone I know has seen a quack analyst and recently uncovered the "fact" that her father abused her. She had absolutely no memory of this and if it did or did not happen, she has no explicit memory of it, but now it seems to define everything she does. First: how could we prove that this ever happened, if she has no memories of this tragedy? And how can we ever find out if this-so called memory-wasn't supplied to her by to her the analyst? Second: Now she has a convenient excuse for her life being all fucked up. And this excuse is iron clad, because it's un-provable. Third: Whatever her relationship was with her father, it is now irreparably damaged. And finally: How does this information help her to move forward? This "uncovering" of childhood abuse is a very dangerous aspect of psychoanalysis and we must be very careful when making such accusations in the real world. Of course, that's not to say that childhood abuse doesn't happen. It most certainly does. The real point of understanding is to help you unhitch yourself from the past by becoming conscious of it so that you stop carrying it forward. Uncovering the past bears grave responsibility.

Lord of the Underworld

Where Jung has taken a lot of stick is with his theory of the archetypes, which has been scoffed at by some critics as a new version of Platonic mysticism. We shall be exploring this theme of archetypes throughout the book, but I should like to show you that Jung was always interested in, and continually sought to explore the fringe areas of the human situation. We will encounter many manifestations of archetypes as we move along and we shall have cause to discuss them in a lot more detail, as they appear in many different disguises throughout the various fields of human inquiry. For now, I would like to take a look over the fringy edge of reality and see if we can drop a rope down.

One of Jung's first papers was: *On the Psychology of So-Called Occult Phenomena*, written in 1902. The occult was an area that held great interest for him and the attitude that he developed toward such things was that the occult or any fringe areas of the human situation were all valid areas of inquiry for psychology; they were all manifestations of the human psyche in the real world. Obviously, religion is much older than the current scientific rationalism and some aspects of religion were the forerunner to the sciences themselves. Alchemy is the most obvious example. So by understanding and contextualizing these psychic things, we can have a look into the archaeology of the current mind. Humans have always endeavored to develop ways of understanding the world based on the tools or paradigms that were at hand. The Bible being one of the most well used paradigms within the western canon of understanding. So for Jung anything that has been produced or exerts an influence on the human psyche (all cultural phenomena like the occult), is worthy of study – at least from the psychological perspective.

In this spirit, Jung wrote a book about UFOs, which he was correct to do in that UFOs were, and still, are a massive phenomenon in much the same way that the *X Files* had such massive appeal in its day. People don't still watch that do they? (Apparently, three million Americans believe they have been abducted by aliens. (See *Mistakes were Made*,

Chapter 3) Here, one of the other main threads of this book has also been touched on. I will explore the psychological ramifications of belief in UFOs more tangentially later, but the explicit relevance to my main theme is that the UFO community has consistently failed to produce any real scientific proof, i.e., anything that can be verified by a repeatable experiment or validated by an objective scientific inquiry. We will see that supplying a coherent proof that aliens have in any impact on our world is very difficult. Jung's take on UFOs side-steps this issue of scientific proof completely and his thinking is that UFOs can or should be considered in a more psychological way as a psychic manifestation of an archetype of the human unconscious that is intruding into the world. A discussion of his view will help us to see how an archetype or symbol is "real" and effective in the world. It will also help us to further delineate the idea of proof.

"Theoretically, no limits can be set to the field of consciousness, since it is capable of indefinite extension. Empirically, however it always finds its limits when it comes up against the unknown. This consists of everything we do not know, which therefore, is not related to the ego as the centre of the field of consciousness. The unknown falls into two groups of objects: those which are outside and can be experienced by the senses, and those which are inside and are experienced immediately. The first group comprises the unknown in the outer world; the second the unknown in the inner world. We call this latter territory the unconscious." C.G. Jung –*Aion*, CW 9, ii, Pg. 3

When a person starts to explore their psyche through introspection or simply pay more attention to their dreams, they will see that the unconscious produces from time-to-time circular mandalas or images of wholeness. These are-in Jungian parlance-anticipatory inklings of the greater and more complete Self that we work towards. This image of a mandala is one of the richest and most fully encompassing of the world-wide archetypes that Jung discussed. The circular shape of a mandala is so primary and aesthetically perfect that it is an excellent vehicle to carry a symbolic representation of the wholeness of reality into consciousness. The UFO could be considered yet another projected form of this kind of anticipatory mandala. They can be thought of–symbolically-as a representation of the unification of things and UFOs specifically are also an expression of the ambiguity of a superior technology. UFOs can fly in ways that none of our aircraft can and the beings who fly them must have figured out how to travel at great speeds, possibly across the galaxies faster than light. In the fifties and sixties the general public were becoming dimly aware of what the ramifications of relativity and astrophysics were, because of the impact of Einstein's immensely popular persona. Interestingly though in the fifties and sixties there were constant sightings of UFOs on both sides of the iron curtain and it appears that the Russians were just as interested in this phenomena as we were. This UFO phenomenon can be thought of as an anticipatory symbol of political wholeness, as well as a personal mandala, or at least, as something that was politically neutral or trans-political.

"We put the shadow back into the boxes"- Radiohead: *Supercollider from King of Limbs*

I believe that what is partially behind this UFO phenomenon is a collective wish for some greater alien power to come down and save our ass. This is all ties in with the human proclivity to project our angst out and on to the world, if we perceive that things aren't going so well. We see-millennial Christ-end-of-world evidences-all around us and maybe aliens have an implicitly greater understanding of a higher technology that can help us out with our troublesome technology. I have heard both Barak Obama and Steven Hawking speak about technology saving us from our current technological problems. There is such a currency in this type of thinking. Aliens will actually save us from having to look inward and acknowledge our own culpable feelings and ongoing responsibility. Of course, human's created the Pandora's Box that is the technology that got us here in the first place. If you were living in the fifties and sixties, and you were under great stress; for example, from the threat of nuclear extinction at the time of the cold war, you may be inclined to look for a quick technological fix. An alien race that travels across the universe might just have answer you need. (If you look hard enough for anything, you are just likely to find what you were looking for. Weapons of mass destruction.)

So when the human psyche is put under stress, there is a tendency for it to produce an integrating or healing symbol. In this case, the symbol has become externalized or projected and is assumed to actually manifest in the outside world, much like the personal shadow. It is easier to assume that UFOs are something real and outside of us, than it is to focus our introspection inward and ask what their symbolic meaning is.

"As a matter of fact, life does surpass itself: it is always undoing itself, always creating a new day, a new generation. Well, it is always imperfect, but it is not necessarily imperfect from that power side. It must follow the law of enantiodromia: there must be destruction and creation, or it would not be at all. A thing that is absolutely static has no existence. It must be in a process or it would never be perceived. Therefore a truth is only a truth as much as it changes." C. G. Jung -Seminar on Nietzsche's Zarathustra Pg. 308

One of the ironies of a symbolic answer like UFO's or a mandala that has come from the unconscious is that they possess a multi-valence. This ambiguous multifaceted nature of symbols -in part- corresponds to what Jung called the tendency of things to become their opposite or they embody within themselves. Because they are a reflection of our psyche, a certain light and darkness is summed up with the term 'enantiodromia'. So these aliens may seem to want come to help us, but the evil aspect of the alien vision is that they may come to enslave us or subject us to some physical degradation - the so common butt probing. This butt probing is most certainly symbolic. I fail to see what information could be gained from a butt probe and if the aliens are halfway intelligent, they have the stick wrong - what do I know. In terms of people who have had an alien abduction, who are trying to resolve their psychic dissonance, this sexual humiliation might be turned around to their desire to be put into a privileged position of being chosen by the aliens. And they now have a message and implied purpose, etc. Things do become their opposite. This is the ambiguity of having a mission in life - that some smart arse like me will patronizingly psychoanalyze it for you.

This UFO vision, to my mind, was and still is a very powerful symbol that has snagged the collective consciousness. The proof of its lasting efficacy has been its endurance and the prolonged fascination that it has in many people's psyche. We can still have a conversation about it or make a show like the *X Files* and I don't have to try to explain to you what a UFO or an angel is. The more extreme end of this type of conspiracy phenomena is propounded by a number of writers. I will come back to this but I would like to discuss my ideas on why we develop and try to corroborate these extreme ideas about the world in the first place.

One of the hallmarks of schizophrenia is a tendency to associate meaning or infuse meaning into a lot of disparate things around you. This is a way to try to resolve some of the paradoxes that are inherent in this disposition. Schizophrenia is principally a modern, and largely, left brain phenomenon; this endless collection and collation of 'facts' and snips of information have been labeled a 'Meaning Fugue'. A fugue is a piece of music in which one melody is played by all of the voices in the ensemble. Some of the instruments invert the melody and play it backward or slower than the other voices. In a meaning fugue you create a vast tapestry of interconnected meanings associated with you either directly or indirectly. Schizophrenics have a tendency to swing from complete self-aggrandizement to feeling completely insignificant even within the same sentence. Both of these ways of being can and do exist within the mind of schizophrenics. Some will develop intricate visions of the world as a way to stave off a complete collapse.

For example, someone I know was convinced that the Yes recording, *90125* contained a secret message meant only for him, because there was some correlation between his birthday and the string of numbers in the title. I believe that to construct meaning out of the world in this way is a natural intuitive property of the brain, specifically, the left hemisphere. But, the problems start when this construction gains primacy over our experience of the real world and we start to expend energy in this hype-abstracted realm of introspection to the detriment of our ongoing engagement in the world. You are stuck in a neurotic moment. Conspiracy theorists have a tendency to build grand woven visions of interconnected self-referential meaning, though much of it is based on a series of ultimately un-provable assumptions. Amongst some of these *beliefs* are many of the various conspiracy theorems that are rampant on the internet. There is a group of people who secretly direct world finance (Hitler's Jewish conspiracy) or others who seek total world dominance, like the Rothschild's control of America through the U.S. treasury, etc. There is no gold in the U.S. treasury at all, because aliens need it. For some reason gold is absent in the rest of the universe so aliens come here in the droves to get it.

There are theories that the Queen of England and other members of the royal family are aliens who feed on human brains or something like that (I hope Lady Diana wasn't one of them. She seemed so nice). So we can weave a tapestry of information that seems to hold a proof by its endless interconnecting of self-referencing statements. We can pull all of the threads together and link them to each other by our own elaborate and quite consistent internal logic. This is the stunning problem with logic. What would our solar system look like, if the sun revolves around the earth?

I'm sure that delving into solving the world's problems creates the feeling that you might be a lone voice crying in the wilderness, but there are others who agree with you. The wilderness that is being cried into is better looked at as an internal and self-referential construction. I believe that this is the real essence of conspiracy theory: that it ultimately is a reflection of an inherently powerless and alienated stance in the world. This is both an individual problem and the individuals who propound this view are a reflection of our society, which has marginalized these very individuals. We are the set of psychic problems that occur in our society and it is very difficult to tease out any cause. I will discuss the limitations of overt scientific rationalism and causal reductionism later and how they are at root an extension of this same tendency toward over intellectualization and nurtured hyper-abstraction that has given us conspiracy theories, but for now I wish to show how intuition can sometimes run wildly astray.

It seems certain that our brains have been constructed by evolution to wish to explain our own personal narrative. The left side of the brain is fairly dedicated to creating distance for us so that we can form or abstract an interpretation of our world. The left brain has been dubbed the interpreter module (which doesn't exist as a separate entity in the brain). It is excellent at constructing a plausible, or even in a pinch, supporting an implausible explanation to everything that we are experiencing. Simply put: because an argument is complicated and shows a modicum of internal consistency or even rigidly and adheres to the most grueling logical construction, doesn't mean it's true. I am also certain that some smart ass scientist will eventually use a variant of this very argument to seek to convince us that God doesn't exist and that the concept of God is an illusion built up by our freaked-out interpreter module - good luck with that. If you wish to really understand the neuroscience and psychology of conspiracy theory, I would encourage you to read the chapter called *Rose Glass* at the very least. If you are content to be satisfied with a handy sound bite here it is.

> *"Conspiracy theory is a result of our left brains over active penchant to create a satisfactory narrative no matter how far-fetched, so that we can more easily resolve our inner psychic dissonance."* - Ucan Quotethat

When the Buddha was asked questions about metaphysics, he declined to answer, or he tried to steer the conversation back into the real world. (Richard Dawkins and Lawrence Krauss should take note.) Any answer that Buddha gave to a metaphysical question is ultimately un-provable, i.e. where does God keep his sneakers at night? Maybe beside his night stand? I am absolutely certain that to ask these questions about God is of the utmost importance to us as individuals. In fact, I think these types of questions are the most vital questions that we have to ask, and largely what this book is about. But there is a point where you have jumped off the page and have nothing to stand on. There is never a solid proof that can be given for any answer to a metaphysical question. That does not mean there is no truth or meaning. These truths have a texture all their own.

For both good and bad, we have a tendency to clutch at these dim threads of meaning in an effort to construct a worldview with meaning, but what kind of meaning do we construct and live with is a real question. If you go looking for meaning, you will find it. You may be looking for the reason why you are so angry at everyone and you may discover you were abused as a child. Problem solved. It's not your fault, it's everybody else's and you now have something else to be angry about. Where does it all stop?

> *"Truth is a pathless land"*- Jiddu Krishnamurti

Into the Underworld

In the psychoanalytic dialogue both people will be trying to articulate their positions in an effort to become more conscious of what is behind their beliefs. Slowly they are moving toward a larger truth or greater consciousness. There are many very subtle aspects to this continuous dialogue. The patient may see in the analyst as a type of father or mother figure and they may inflate their image of the analyst into some all-knowing, heavenly Guru with all of the answers. The analyst on the other hand, may have gotten into this profession in an effort to become a Guru and thereby wield power over others. When someone wishes to see the analyst as a Guru, the analyst may be especially susceptible to this type of psychic infection and then you can have all kinds of foolishness. This is what is known as transference. Each partner in the analytic situation projects (externalized personal unconscious, thoughts, wishes, etc.) on to the other person, and if this mutual unconsciousness continues, it can stall the ongoing process of the integration of consciousness.

This transference or the mutual projection of the unconscious in individuals lies at the very heart of the process of psychoanalysis itself. Transference is the great hinge on which the analysis will turn. We only expend an effort projecting our thoughts on to the environment around us if we are emotionally invested in these thoughts that we project. They must carry some meaning for us or represent things worth projecting or we would simply pass them by, because they have no value. You wouldn't want the analyst to have all of the answers for you, if you weren't concerned about trying to find the answers to the questions themselves. These mutually unconscious projections may produce the greatest source of tension between the doctor and patient. This tension, or the need to resolve it and move forward in the analysis, will hopefully push the partners to create a solution.

Jung liked to put people together-in the analytic situation-that had the same psychic blind spot, so that together they would get bored of saying the same things over and over, and together try to find a solution to their mutual ignorance. He would put two thinkers together and they would discuss their thoughts for months or years and then they would finally realize that they had stalled. They were simply running around the same intellectual rat track. Hopefully, this led them back to the dream world, which would also try to lift them out of this stagnation. This is the ongoing dialectic process seen from the psychological perspective. Marx saw this same process from a historical/sociological viewpoint. What Jung realized is that the only remotely objective stand point in this process was the unconscious of the two individuals involved. One way the unconscious articulates its position is through our dreams. This is the third creative aspect of the dialectic or ongoing two-way dialogue.

"The Unconscious does not look back. Despite the fact that it speaks the language of the past exclusively, it tries to foresee and portray the future. It is always several lengths ahead in the future, but speaking the language of the past." C. G. Jung- Visions Seminar Pg. 901

The unconscious seems to want to propel us toward greater understanding, or greater wholeness. Dreams are the voice of a thousand-year-old man. Looked at from an evolutionary angle, this makes sense. The right and more closely unconscious brain has an inherently wider perspective and its voice of metaphors are expressed through dreams. The unconscious seems to be concerned with trying to anticipate and supply answers for us to our problems through its more open integrated assessment of the world. What Jung also indicated was that the unconscious mind can also function in anticipatory ways, because of the multi-valence metaphorical nature of its expression. The contentious issue here is whether dreams actually have meaning.

It would also seem advantageous, to the species, to spread the different psychological functions-or different ways of perceiving the world-amongst the group. If a single individual could not easily contain all the ways of experiencing the world, it would be an advantage to spread understanding around the extended group. Some people are good builders (extroverted, thinking and sensate); some people might be better at easing the various tensions that occurs within the group (feelers-empathy), and some people are good at anticipating where to search for food (extraverted-intuitive). Others may develop their talent for healing people, shamans, for example (introverted-intuitive). Through an inner dialogue and/or an outer dialectic with other people, we slowly move forward into a greater understanding, if we wish. This can be thought of as the inherently creative aspect of reality. This idea of the unconscious trying to propel us forward also falls dangerously close to metaphysical speculation.

This thought that the unconscious has a will to push us forward is known in philosophy as a 'telos'. A telos is a system built specifically to pursue an end or goal. What that end or goal is seems to be greater understanding on our part, but this is my reading backward into the process and presuming a purposeful end. This is the classic teleological argument. It's like me saying wheat is so good to eat and God must have been very wise when he put it here for me. William Paley argued in this manner in an effort to prove the existence of God by using what is now known as the 'watchmaker' argument. It runs like this: the fact that there are watches or a universe, implies a watchmaker or universe builder. This was Paley's dim reflection of the infusion of classical Newtonian physics into the general psyche. Much like UFOs are a modern reflection of a dim Einsteinian understanding of relativity.

"Paley wasn't wrong to say that life is evidently functional. And he wasn't wrong to say that this functionality strongly suggested a designer. He was just wrong to assume that the designer was a being rather than a process. The eye was made for vision-it just wasn't handcrafted by God" Robert Wright-*Non Zero* Pg. 310.

This is the scientific rationalist ethic, which in turn, seems to imply a radical atheism. There just might be some wiggle room for telos.

So it might seem that the unconscious wants us to move forward. Why or where that forward is, is the difficult part. The east has developed the concept of the Atman, or Tao, which is ultimately the good energy of the universe that we have been born ignorant of – much more later. What I think is that it is inherent in human nature and the way the brain itself works to try to search out and construct meaning and/or read meaning back into things so that we can find comfort in chaos. How the brain constructs the world and how the brain is-in turn-constructed by feedback from the world was tackled more rigorously in chapter five, *Rose Glass*. We must be careful and seek to see clearly through some of the dangers inherent in making statements about where meaning lies, especially if our thinking about the world goes wrong. Let me illustrate in my circuitous manner.

There is some quite famous film footage of Carl Jung being interviewed by Richard I. Evans in 1957. In this interview, Jung is asked if he believes in God. Jung pauses for a second. I will paraphrase. He said: *"That it is a difficult question to answer. You see I know he exists. Not I believe that he exists."* Jung isn't trying to be intentionally provocative 'in the manner of recent rock stars'. He is stating what he believes is a bald fact. I think this statement is a result of his lengthy internal connection to the unconscious and being intimately involved in the unconscious processes of his patients. He conceived of the dialogue with the unconscious and the outer world as just that – a dialogue. Not a monologue based on your unconscious repression or wishes coming back at you from your dreams. He believed that the unconscious was a reflection of God/ Atman/ Nature in our own psyche with intent on trying to heal us.

If you addressed the unconscious or tried to decipher your dreams, you will see that the information that you received is sometimes in reference to things you would have never conceived of. Or the unconscious may be trying to tell you things that you really don't want to hear. I believe that a dialogue with the personal unconscious can ultimately lead us to a greater source of meaning for our lives. This is not mystical mumbo jumbo. It is a process that enters into an experience as real, like all true knowledge it is based on experience. What Jung has shown by this statement is that the truth-for an individual-is experiential. How can you tell Jung that he is wrong or that God doesn't exist? Jung is telling you point blank that he knows this as a fact. The presumption that Jung was not a madman would be implicit here. Conversely, Richard Dawkins seems as equally convinced that God doesn't exist. The Buddha simply sidestepped the argument and moved on.

Jung spent a lot of words emphasizing that he was an empiricist. His understanding was based on the information garnered by his senses not created by him dovetailing all manner of phenomena into some theory of knowledge that he wished to prove true. An empirical proof is one in which you derive your understanding of the world from the information collected from your senses. Jung spent endless hours with patients and in the latter years of his life he spent endless hours alone in quiet contemplation. Unfortunately, from an external scientific point of view, analytic or in-depth psychology or anthropology, and a number of other ologies cannot escape from a personal testimonial, or from this empirical type of proof. I can tell you I feel better, but I would have difficulty quantifying this feeling, or in fact, proving in any way that it's not *just* the result of a placebo effect. Do I feel better in eight out of 10 situations with an error of one in 20? (Though, neuroscience to a certain extent, seeks to quantify their understanding.) That does not mean that psychology does not hold a truth or that it cannot make you feel better. It's just that it cannot escape from the realm of the human mind from which it is born and the personal testimony that is a reflection of that very mind.

"At its core, therefore, science is a form of arrogance control." - Mistakes Were Made Pg. 108

Psychology is forced to build its truths through continued observation and comparative analogies with all manner of human endeavor, then it must continually test the perceived helpfulness of these assumptions against reality. For instance, if you dreamed of smoking a pipe, I might tell you that you desire the comfort of your mother's breast and that you smoke a pipe to satisfy some childish oral urges. Or, I may tell you that smoking tobacco is a thoughtful reflective pastime and that you express the need to engage in more thoughtful activity through pipe smoking. Or, I may indicate that the flame in the pipe bowl represents your need to kindle more desire or passion from within your straight laced daily life. If this pipe smoking happened in a dream, in a very public arena, there would be different connotations to its symbolic meaning than if you are smoking in a private smoking area. Or, you were terrified when you were smoking. That is very different than a passive or reflective smoke. All of these statements may be true, depending on the situation of the patient or the pipe may be a very common item in your daily life, or it may simply be part of the social milieu in which you live. So psychology is tied to individual humans and a static dictionary of symbols is no way out of this contextual dilemma.

The art of the analyst is to relate these personal images to the patient in a meaningful way without trying to force an inappropriate interpretation on to them. The analyst may be trying to tell the patient some very unwanted news and so there may be great resistance coming from the patient to a particular interpretation, and along with this the patient's own sense or feel for the situation must be appreciated. The patient should also be able to trust and know for themselves if the analyst has correctly sussed the situation. If the analyst seeks to convince you that you where abused as a child and you have no memory of these events but the analyst insists that you have repressed these memories. You have been caught in a circular self referential argument and I would argue that any presumption on either the analysts or analysand's part could be a reflection of a deeper unconscious power struggle. The analyst holds much of the responsibility for foisting an improper agenda in these situations, and I will discuss this in depth a little later. Even the analyst's overt desire to heal people can be seen as a possible reflection of their will to assert power over others and this will to heal must be guarded against on both sides.

We can see that psychology is on the far edge of being a hard science, and ultimately like all of the healing arts it is more akin to the arts than sciences. The scientific community has more than enough fodder to rebuke or deconstruct many types of psychological theory. For me, this is exactly where everything gets interesting. Jung did know that God exists, at least in his own mind, and in the long run, it's his mind that counts for him. Your own mind is the locus of all that you can really know, cogito ergo sum. *"I think therefore I am"* is an irreducible truth, but of course, not the final statement of this truth. We will come back to Descartes little cogito gem later.

Jung understood that someone whose mind was healthy, vigorous and engaged in the world had an intrinsically better quality of life, and a healthy mind was one that has a purpose or meaning-which in turn-leads to a purpose or vice versa. Jung felt that the best place to try to find meaning or a purpose to life was from within our own unconscious. His own experience had taught him that the unconscious seems to wish to propel us forward and that a truth won from this type of analysis was always a more powerful truth than one given to you by someone else – say... from a book. This is the main idea of this book and we will come back to it again and again. This is also the cornerstone idea behind the well articulated philosophy of Yoga and Tantra.

"The world of the happy is quite another than that of the unhappy."
Ludwig Wittgenstein -*Tractatus Logico-Philosophicus*

Jung understood too that religion was part of the human experience and that the world's religions discussed and articulated some of our highest ideals. An understanding of our religious urge could most certainly lend greater meaning to a life. He once talked about an atheist who was constantly challenging him about the concept of God, so Jung informed him that atheism is as much a belief system as atheism. Neither person could prove definitively that God existed or didn't exist and both people were caught in the same situation. This is the situation that the Buddha wished to avoid. I once saw Jon Stewart of *The Daily Show* telling his audience with some cynic disbelief that in a recent poll over 50 or 60 percent of Americans actually believed in God and angels, as if he knew this not to be true. What really counts is how your belief system affects your life and those around you. There is a Hindu thought that whether you believe in God or not doesn't really matter. What is important is the amount of energy you put into trying to figure it out, and ultimately, you will arrive at 'the truth' and the truth will be the same truth whether God is in that belief system or not. This anti-God stance is known as the path of hate. Or alternately, in the Sufi tradition of Islam, truth is said to be a crystal clear liquid poured out by God and it will take on the color of the vessel that receives it. Same truth different vessel: there is Islam's Truth, Hindu's Truth, and Christianity's Truth. You are the vessel that gets poured into.

"Who takes longer to reach perfection, the man who loves God or the man who hates him?" And the answer is: 'he who loves God takes seven reincarnations to reach perfection, and he who hates God takes only three, for he who hates God will think of him more than he who loves him.' Freedom from opposites presupposes their functional equivalence, and this offends our Christian feelings." C. G. Jung –*The Archetypes of the Collective Unconscious* - Pg. 36

The founder of Alcoholics Anonymous worked with Jung, who seemed to have cured him or at least helped him to understand what his life work would be. Jung believed that part of the alcoholic's drive, or indeed any addict's ongoing behavior, is a misdirected search for heightened awareness, or a misplaced search for meaning. Jung believed that the drug of choice starts by giving the individual a rush of excitement that is missing in their life. You could be the guy who gets pissed at a party and turns into the great entertainer, but when you are not drunk you may be quite shy and boring; and you quite naturally enjoy the boisterous aspect of yourself when you are drunk. When you drink, you are chasing that spirit. That is why booze was called 'spirits', or in some sense, you are looking for spirituality. Spirits are a distilled or refined essence, therefore, of a higher and more spiritual nature.

   Addiction is the downside of this search, where you are no longer in control. The first rush of a crack addict must be a tremendous feeling, but the reality of trying to get enough money to sustain that high, and the constant grinding obsession involved in pursuing that high, is far too much. There is no balance only an endless violent swinging back and forth between being high and doing all of the ugly things it takes to get you high again. You become what Tibetans call 'a hungry ghost' with a single unending hunger. This is another aspect of neurotic behavior. You wish a NEW answer would come from this situation, and like a neurosis, you start off seeking a resolution to whatever it is that is causing you pain in the first place. (Many addicts leave abusive situations.) In getting high, you found a shortcut that helps to numb you or you get high, literally to elevate yourself. You have inadvertently substituted one painful situation for an endless cycle of ups and downs. A lot of sustained drug use is really maintenance. You are simply trying to get to a relatively normal level of painlessness. Your addiction to the drugs, or the lack of them, becomes the generator of the pain that you seek to avoid. You are stuck in a moment and you can't get out of it.

   Here is one of the great ironies of life: all advancements in consciousness or knowledge seem to be bound up with pain - no pain, no gain. If you are going through a messy divorce, rightfully, you will feel depressed and it would be of small comfort when you are in the middle of it; for me to tell you that the depression is an opportunity to reassess some of your core values. In a relatively normal depressive state, your main function (thinking, feeling, etc.) or the usual way in which you deal with the world might be forced to take a backseat for a while. If you take the time to pry open the door to your dreams, the unconscious will try to supply you with a new path. In a depression, the main function is literally depressed or pushed down from conscious control or the total energy in the conscious psyche has been reduce and transferred into the unconscious. Your dream world can become quite active and intense in a depression as the total energy in the psyche tries to remain constant. The excess can become transferred away from consciousness and into the unconscious dream world. There is no magic bullet to get healed here. You must approach depression with patience and understanding. This will involve using bush manners, because you are out of your main function.

Unfortunately, it is very difficult to analyze your own dreams. It is not impossible, but you are at a great disadvantage on your own, because of a lack of an objective standpoint to disengage from the dream ensemble. It's easy to get caught up in a self-referential monologue. A humble attitude will help you greatly, and a willingness to accept the pain of self-realization. Of course, this is especially hard within a depression, because you are already in pain and the energy available to consciousness is lowered. The Sufi poet Jelaluddin Rumi asks God to break his heart again and again. He willingly accepts pain instead of running from it, because with pain comes knowledge. We are not talking about indulgent sadomasochistic physical pain here.

Depression is a main psychological function. The main function is the one most closely tied to your conscious personality, or your persona, which is the face that you present to the world. It is a larger component of yourself image that you have constructed or a large part of your understanding. The main function in which you usually navigate the world has been depressed and so the amount of energy that the rest of the psyche is supplying to it has been lowered. Jung called this psychic energy 'Libido', a term which Freud reserved for sexuality. Freud liked to push everything into the realm of sexuality. (Sometimes a pipe is just a pipe) As the conscious libido or energy is lowered, the unconscious libido is increased. There seems to be a constant amount of energy in the system at all time whether asleep or awake, or whatever. As stated earlier, the unconscious receives more energy in a depression and can become more active. In extreme situations such as a psychosis or schizophrenic outburst the unconscious can break through into your conscious world and overwhelm *you*. The distinction between attentive consciousness and fantasy becomes blurred in extreme psychotic episodes.

In a milder form of depression, you may find that you have a hard time in controlling your unconscious and you will do seemingly neurotic things. For example, you might become easily irritated with other people for no apparent reason, or uncharacteristically forgetful, etc. It is fairly easy to recognize this somewhat absent state of engagement in depressed people. The human consciousness can be thought of as an island that is surrounded by an ocean. The waves of this unconscious ocean are completely surrounding the individual island and lapping at the shore. The job of the attentive consciousness is to firm up the levies by establishing an ego or self image that you can identify with or conceive of yourself, which includes your persona or public face. Your persona allows you to know who you are and what you do; hence, the question of what you do as a way to find out who you are. The persona is the face that you address the world with and in many ways you are that face, but there is also a bigger Self behind it. In an extreme psychosis or schizoid episode the ocean can completely submerged the self-evident conscious personality and you can get lost in an endless set of introspective viewpoints like an endless hall of mirrors.

Depression is not to be taken lightly. It is my understanding that in a depression the brain starts producing chemicals that start the brain functioning differently, just as when you are excited, the brain produces endorphins like dopamine to make you feel good. This is why depression can be actively treated with drugs. Unfortunately, the drugs dampen the ability to form a conscious recognition of why you are depressed. The drugs also dampen your consciousness as it seeks to relate with the depression. This makes it even harder to gain any lasting understanding of the situation. If you wished to make that effort, anti-depression drugs seem to dampen the total amount of libido available to consciousness. I think in many cases these drugs may be necessary to get a person over the darkest part of their depression, but I also believe that they stop people from gaining any real insight into themselves. The pill-popping advocates wish to see depression as being caused by a chemical imbalance in the brain and this imbalance should be treatable with more chemicals, which sets the process into balance again.

"The makers of the drug always seem to say you're looking sick" – Iron and Wine

This is one of the other main themes of this book, which relates directly to the ambiguity of proof. Drug treatment in depression is partially a question of aetiology. Aetiology is the word used to describe the ultimate causal factor in a situation, or aetiology seeks to determine what the root cause of a depression or imbalance is. I could state that these chemical imbalances are brought about by the initial onset of the depression itself, not that the depression is caused by a chemical imbalance, but the argument then becomes a bit of the chicken or the egg. Ultimately, the body is just doing what it does not that it's necessarily right to do it. It may be creating depressing chemicals, because there is something wrong with you physically or it may be reacting to ongoing mental queuing, or it may be out of balance with itself and it is making inappropriate chemical responses. From inside of the depression you could think that the feedback loop has gotten stuck; a doctor may come into the middle of a process and -say for a mild depression- proscribe something to pick you up a bit. For the doctor, this route is an easy fix. Cynically speaking, the doctor gets paid and the patient is out of his office, end of problem. The drug companies are literally invested in this strategy and they spend a lot of money convincing doctors that this is the correct method of treatment.

The real complex of the problem is much bigger and it involves the whole person. The depressed person may dislike their job or their mate or any number of things, and they lack the understanding or will power to get around it. The root causes of all problems are ignorance or lack of understanding. If you can gain some perspective and understanding of a situation, you can then formulate a way forward and you will then feel that there is a point in investing energy or will power. In this attention deficit, quick fix culture, a pill can help you to ignore these deeper aspects of your life and they can help you just get through your day. I highly doubt that we were put here to 'just get through the day'. Another alternative to pills is expensive therapy, which is completely wasted on someone not interested in getting better. It would be great if everyone could go through a personal therapy, but we would have to have stacks of money and a slew of highly trained professionals. Everybody would have to be motivated to improve upon themselves and all of the analysts would be skilled, impartial and scrupulous. This is not going to happen.

I believe that Rydelin–along with regression therapy-will, in retrospect, be seen as one of the great gaffs in modern psychology, if only because so many people are being diagnosed with attention deficit disorders that are probably not quite that sick. When I grew up one of my best friends was someone who would now be diagnosed with attention deficit disorder. The reality was that he was extremely intelligent and profoundly bored with school. Had he been put on drugs from the get go, his brain could have become permanently wired to Rydelin output, or at least this part of his life would have been tied to middle level output.

It seems that the brain is constantly developing new wiring diagrams and I mean constantly, well into old age. When we put a young mind on these drugs, we are robbing the children of huge opportunities for cognitive development, or at the very least, these drugs are teaching young brains to wire up in ways we don't fully comprehend yet. How would drug companies know what the effects of 10 years of Rydelin use do to the human brain? It's not easy raising a child with ADD, but it's not easy raising children period. The fact is that you have children, so raise them; try to figure it out, go into the process and invest your time in solutions. Quick fixes are dangerous. I loathe pontificating so and I sometimes feel that I am a terrible dad, as well, but the fact is I am a dad. I would suggest cutting out all pop drinks for one, caffeine and sugar. They are a deadly combination on a young mind. I personally feel that most of the problem is dietary, but it is complicated. Bodywork like highly active and energy absorbing sports helps to dissipate excess mental energy, and helps the child develop some measure of control over an active mind.

I would add a caveat here: one of the members in my band just happens to be in the pharmaceutical industry (which I just found out), and he has been involved in the release of a new drug for ADD/ADHD. It is his contention that someone suffering from ADD really cannot function in the world. It seems that this problem is due to under-stimulation within the brain and so the child is constantly seeking external stimulation. (This is a very contentious viewpoint.) These drugs that treat ADD are actually stimulants or uppers, and you are trying to lift the child's mind up to a normal level of internal stimulation. There is more discussion of ADD later and the jury is out as to what is really going on inside the head. The point I'm trying to make is more a reflection of the propensity of doctors to prescribe drugs to children who are just overactive and their parents just don't want to deal with them, because it's inconvenient. Like schizophrenia and especially Alzheimer's, ADD has become a grab bag term that children get thrown into out of convenience. I have known a number of people with serious mental problems and it is no fun at all. There are no easy answers.

"A truly brave man can live with his enemies"- Aurangzeb

So again from a personal standpoint, a depression is an opportunity for greater consciousness. You are depressed for a reason; try to find what the reason is. This following passage is from Marie Louise Von Franz. She shows more clearly how the whole ensemble of a Jungian analysis takes form-in the world-and the artful way in which a talented doctor can help.

"I once analyzed an extraverted intuitive type, a businessman who had started a great many businesses in some faraway country and had also speculated a lot, and bought gold mines and the like. He always knew where possibilities were and made a large fortune in a very short time, absolutely honestly- quite decently- and simply because he just knew! He knew what was coming, what would happen in a few years, and he was always on the spot first and got the whole business in hand. His introverted sensation- he was rather a split personality- came up first in dreams as a very dirty, bad- tempered tramp who sat around in inns in a bad, nasty temper in dirty clothes. I induced the dreamer to talk to this tramp in active imagination and the tramp said that he had been responsible for some physical symptoms (psychogenic symptoms of a compulsory character), on account of which he had come to analysis, and that they had been sent because he, the tramp, did not get enough attention. So in his active imagination the man asked what he should do and the tramp said that once a week, dressed in clothes such as a tramp wore, he should go for a walk in the county with him and pay attention to what he had to say. I advised the dreamer to follow the advice precisely, with the result that he took long walks through many parts of Switzerland, staying in the simplest inns, unrecognized by anybody. He would wander along, and during this time he had a great number of overwhelming experiences which came through contact with nature: the sunrise and small things like seeing a certain flower in a corner of a

rock, and so on. It hit him right to the core of his personality. I can only describe it as experiencing, in a very primitive way, the Godhead in nature. He came back very silent and quieted down, and one had the feeling that something had moved in him which had not moved before. His compulsory symptoms disappeared completely during those weekly walks. Then he has to confront the problem of how he could keep this experience and avoid slipping back when he got home to his own country. So we consulted the tramp again, who said the he would let him off the symptoms if he would take an afternoon off each week and go alone into nature and continue his talk with him."

I thought that this was a good story to tell and wondered if I could find it so I picked up, *Psychotherapy* and started thumbing through it. There happened to be a book mark in the book so I went to that page and it happened to be the very story I was looking for.

In the story, we can see much of what I have been discussing all coming together in a condensed and articulated form. The inferior function has combined with the shadow in the unconscious to take the form of a tramp. Also, we see the part played by the unconscious in producing a healing symbol, which in this case, had to be acknowledged literally though the sensate function by this person having an actual discussion with his tramp figure. And we also glimpsed an intimation of the true effort that is involved in gaining more personal consciousness through the assimilation of the disparate parts of our personality. In this case, it was a specific task that needed to be done in the real world. This honest acknowledgement and acceptance of the burden can set us on the path to becoming whole or at least begin the process of assimilating and understanding our neurotic behavior. We don't gain consciousness by imagining beams of light. We gain consciousness by diving into the darkness.

"To overcome an obstacle or an enemy

To glide away from a razor or a knife

To overcome an obstacle or an enemy

To dominate the impossible in your life

Reach in the darkness

A reach in the dark

Reach in the darkness

A reach in the dark" - Paul Simon, The Rhythm of the Saints

There is a certain amount of consciousness to be gained by training your mind to concentrate on positive things; for example, picturing yourself on the Olympic medal podium with a gold medal or imagining a better job, or surrounding yourself with scented candles, etc. Yoga for instance, encourages surrendering to the heart and an opening up to Grace through real and lasting physical and mental training. In the strictly mental realm, the real and lasting deep therapeutic work also involves bravely facing in the other direction by understanding and accepting the darkness that stops you from getting where you want to go. One more time: *"You've got to get yourself together. You've got stuck in a moment and you can't get out of it. Oh love look at you now. You've got yourself stuck in a moment and you can't get out of it."* -U2. This stickiness also seems to be one of the main problems with too much left brain, which insists on the comparison with the familiar instead of engagement with the novel.

"The demands of rapid ongoing behavior typically do not allow organisms to await expected further information, or to sample the entire sensory environment. Based on a minimal amount of information sampled, the brain fills in the remainder in order to make a rapid response. This process of pattern completion is based on memory records of previous experience. Extrapolation based on incomplete information is one of the important rudiments of mental activity." – *Did My Neurons Make Me Do It* by Nancey Murphy & Warren S. Brown - Pg. 222-3

I will say that diving into the darkness is not a path to be taken lightly or alone. You can get yourself into some serious mental anguish that may overwhelm you, if you don't have the inner strength. Jung always said that his students were lucky, because they had Jung to teach them. He himself dove into his madness without the safety net of a Jung to guide him.

"If you bring what is within you, what you bring will save you. If you do not bring forth what is within you, what you do not bring forth will destroy you." - Jesus: Gospel of Thomas

Heal thyself

A deeper understanding of the inferior function can also shed light on some of the dynamic behind sudden religious conversion. A critical overheating of the shadow can be the cause of a sudden conversion or an about face of the personality. St. Paul was on the road to Damascus to persecute Christians when he fell off his donkey in some sort of epileptic fit. You could equate Christ at this point with St. Paul's shadow. The shadow doesn't have to be negative, and this episode can be understood as a symbolic internal analogy (unless you are a fundamentalist). From this perspective, we could say that St. Paul was really persecuting his own unrealized self-the Christ figure-and in one fell swoop, he has a revelation and heals himself. In *The Varieties of Religious Experience*, William James sites a large number of these kinds of radical conversions where people-seemingly overnight-turn a corner and never look back. (I would add that anti-depressants dampen a person's ability to achieve just this type of transformative insight.) Now, in St. Paul's case, it seems as though he never actually physically met Jesus Christ, so this conversion already has more of an internal psychological dimension to it. (Enantiodromia)

You can imagine the other apostles reaction when St. Paul comes knocking on the door. Here is a Gentile person who was sent to persecute this Jewish upstart, suddenly turning up and saying: *"No it is a mistake. It's all cool now. I'm on your side"*. It seems that the apostles were a little suspicious of St. Paul so they shipped him north to preach elsewhere to test his mettle. Of course, we now know that his conversion was genuine, in that he went on to write the largest and probably the only truly first-hand accounts that are extant in the *New Testament* (the various letters). The other gospels were written and formed to reflect the political agendas of the authors' years after Jesus' death. The earliest gospels were probably written by scribes from second-hand verbal accounts or an unfound common source called: 'The Q Gospel' – much more later.

Another interesting conversion from a psychological point of view is that of St. Augustine. It seems that he was quite a licentious young man, going to the forum to watch the various blood sports and sowing his seed with all and sundry. It seems that he got himself into a very over heated situation. His mother was a Christian and his father was a pagan so he was already in a split situation in terms of his family dynamic. Prior to his Christian conversion, it seems he flirted with Manichaeism, a more dualistic religion that was very popular at that time, which had been imported into Rome from the east. It seems that he sincerely wished to live a more chaste life, but lacked the will power to do so when he heard a voice in his garden telling him: *"sume lege"* (take and read). He opened up the Bible at random and read, *"Not in chambering and wantonness."* These words seemed to be sent directly to him. I will let the ever-articulate St. Augustine speak for himself:

"The new will, which I began to have was not yet strong enough to overcome the other will, strengthened by long indulgence. So these two, one old, one new, one carnal, the other spiritual, contended with each other and disturbed my soul. I understood by my own experience what I had read flesh lusteth against spirit, and spirit against flesh." It was me indeed in both wills, yet more myself in that which I approved in myself than in that which I disapproved in myself. Yet it was through myself that habit had attained so fierce a mastery over me, because I had willingly come whither I willed not. Still bound to earth, I refused, O God, to fight on thy side, as much afraid to be freed from all bonds, as I ought to have being trammeled by them.

"Thus the thoughts by which I meditated upon were like the efforts of one who would awake, but being overpowered with sleepiness is soon asleep again. Often does a man when heavy sleepiness is on his limbs defer to shake it off, and though not approving it, encourage it; even so I was sure it was better to surrender to thy love than to yield to my own lusts, ye, though the former course convinced me, the later pleased and held me bound. There was naught in me to answer thy call, 'Awake, thou sleeper,' but only drawling, drowsy words, 'Presently; yes, presently; wait a little while.' But the 'presently' had no 'present,' and the 'little while' grew long....For I was afraid thou wouldst hear me too soon, and heal me at once of my disease of lust, which I wished to satiate rather than see extinguished." -Confessions of St. Augustine as quoted in

William James -*The Varieties of Religious Experience*

This small quote really sheds so much light on us. It clearly shows how gaining consciousness has to do with exercising will power. St. Augustine knows the right thing to do, but shies from the commitment. Unfortunately, when you are within a depression, you really do not have access to the energy needed to exercise this will power. It has been drained away from the ego. Grace can be the small seed that turns this situation around. This lack of energy is the largest obstacle to getting better and a depressed person can suck the life out of the people trying to help them. There are two things I would say that are a small comfort when you are in a depression, but have proved to be very wise. You are not experiencing anything that millions of people all through history have not experienced. There are many pathways out of this forest and secondly all of the great problems in life are truly unsolvable. There is no final answer. The trick is to live long enough to see that you have grown beyond the dilemma itself. In retrospect you will see that there was no solution, but that the problem itself has now become unimportant. You have grown beyond it.

Some truly towering figures suffered from very serious depressions, Churchill being one of the most conspicuous. Had he given into the depressions that hounded him between the two world wars, he would not have been the leader of England in the Second World War. Fortunately, Churchill was a prolific and articulate writer and we have his own accounts to gain understanding from.

If I was to write a book, trying to explain all of the subtleties of Shakespeare, it would most certainly be longer than his collected works and would ultimately be a fairly pointless, and certainly arduous undertaking. Shakespeare can speak for himself quite well, thank you. That hasn't stopped many people from writing many volumes on him. This is because Shakespeare writes in a symbolic or poetic idiom. The symbolic or metaphorical idiom can contain many simultaneous meanings that in my estimation are reflections of our own inner complexity. There are two Sanskrit terms that illuminate a part of this dichotomy and they will be used frequently to highlight a running theme in this book. They are: Stula and Sukshma. The Stula aspect of things is the prosaic, ordinary or common, while the Sukshma is the spiritual or elevated. The third element is the Para or the transcendent aspect.

"The human personality is "ondoyant et divers" (wave-like and varying/undulating and divers) – Montaigne

The two aspects of being- the elevated and prosaic -were at war in our poor St. Augustine, and in reality, they are always opposed, but they can be resolved or transcended. It seems that creative solutions need to be instigated within us by allowing the dynamic tension to produce a healing symbol, Grace. St Augustine's resolution came to him through the collusion of a synchronistic event when he opened the Bible at random and found the passage that he needed to read. The symbol arrived from the outside world and fell on to the well prepared field of his thinking. There could have been any number of quotes that were fitting, but St. Augustine is telling us that this specific quote came to him. What I am trying to show is that we are always floating between these two opposed aspects of reality. Much of what is deeply understood turns out to be an intellectual paradox and this is the human condition.

In Canada, we had a prime minister named, Pierre Trudeau. The first thing he did when he came into office was to vote the opposition a salary raise so that all members of parliament were paid the same amount. It seems that for some time, the opposition party members in Canada received less money than the official government. Our current prime minister, Steven Harper, is trying to cut the funding to the opposition. Trudeau embraced the dialectic or the tension of opposites and the new Prime Minister is fighting it. This is a fight you cannot win and Mr. Harper has had to back down when the opposition caused such uproar that he almost lost his minority government. The thing that I have come to admire about Jung is that the more you gain an understanding of his work, the more you realize that he has created an open system of thought. Jung embraces the dynamic of opposition. This can seem to imply a more flexible conception of morality or a more flexible personal ethic. To embrace the opposition of the dialectic is to actively participate in allowing the creative third to unfold. It doesn't mean you are morally neutral.

The archetypes are the living sign posts of the unconscious. They are not distant ornamental aspects of a ridged dogma that must be adhered to. Jung tried to create a way of leading people into their own experience of living symbols. The proof, if you will, of the creative flexibility that

Jung nourished is shown to us by the vast amount of post Jungian writers. There are literally thousands of Jungian books as opposed to Freudian works or Marxist Leninist books. The Marxist paradigm especially, is one that is shut and only needs to be interpreted and implemented correctly. If communism didn't work in the Ukraine or China, it must have been implemented wrong. You must be interpreting this pristine manifesto incorrectly. If you don't agree with Freud's suggestion that sexually is at the root of your problem, you must have a resistance against the doctor due to repressed anger at your father, which you are projecting upon the doctor, which of course, manifests itself in a sexual neurosis that Freud can see quite clearly you are fighting him about. You should accept Freud's sexual interpretation and submit to his fount of wisdom. It must be you that is wrong. This is the kind of circular self-referential argument that I could put forward to represent Freud's view. This type of argument can be turned around on any person or ideology that I wish to disparage to prove my own agenda. Freudians, communist, regression therapists or committed ideologues of any stripe, are never wrong that their vision has been sullied or tainted as it moved into the real world.

Jung said many times that he was willing to throw out his theories, if they didn't work. Now, whether he was just saying this to be humble, I don't know, but at least he was smart enough to say it, which to my mind means he was smart enough to see through this trap of asserting ideological dogma as proof. This to my mind is the essence of a pragmatic empirical stance.

> *"Authority is the weakest proof"* - St. Augustine.

You cannot escape creating a paradigm through which to understand the world or yourself, but the danger in constructing such a vision is when you try to fiercely defend that paradigm. Surely thou dost protest too much. If you become a slave to your theories, you are not living through the changes that constantly assail you and these changes are a reflection of reality, which should be forcing you to reassess your vision. You've got stuck in a moment and to some extent you are dead. The only constant is change. Change arrives in the form of an unwanted guest. Let it in.

Don't Cry for Me Broadway

I worked in music stores for quite a while when I was younger and I remember people coming in and saying things like: *"I don't like the music of today"*. The last great recording was made in 1959 or 1969 or any date they wished to pick, depending on their age and the stiffness of their joints. These dates when 'Music ended', usually corresponded to that person's early to mid-twenties when they stopped actively pursuing music and got a job and kids, and responsible. This window after the teens, and before the age of 30, is a very important time in terms of brain development and neuroplasticity. We will return to this idea later. When you are young, you are more open to new experiences and you may gravitate to the music that your friends are listening to, or you may be a maverick and tell other people what is good to listen to. This is the point at which your personality is blossoming and music can be a significant part of your persona and your genuine emotional experiences. These days, music can define your style of dress and many other social triggers as well. If you are lucky, you may fall in love with all kinds of wonderful intense experiences that are also happening to you around this time. As time goes on though, you may drift away into your own private concerns and you might look back at that time of freedom etc., with a certain weepy nostalgia. This is the point at which you start to die, culturally anyway.

My wife and I went to a Betty Carter concert and someone in the audience requested one of her old songs and she simply said, I don't do that anymore. I'm doing this now. In other words, I'm not here to fulfill your sense of nostalgia. Miles Davis was the same way. He bravely moved on with his own concerns, while the uptight critics scorched him for going electric or hip hop, or hard bop or rap or whatever. This was not his problem. His job was to make music and be culturally relevant. Apparently, Bob Dylan had things thrown at him when he first plugged in an electric guitar at a live show in the sixties. Even freedom loving hippies it seems can be conservative nostalgic assholes.

"Sentimentality is feeling that shuts out action, real or potential. It is self-centered and a species of make-believe. William James gives the example of the woman who sheds tears at the heroine's plight on the stage while her coachman is freezing outside the theatre. So far is the

sentimentalist from being one whose emotions exceed the legal limit that he may be charged with deficient energy in what he feels; it does not propel him. That is why he finds pleasure in grief and when he is in love, never proposes. Sterne accurately entitled his story, A Sentimental Journey. The tears he shed over the death of a donkey and his preoccupation with the girl at the inn caused him no upset nerves, no faster pulse or quickened breath. He reveled in irresponsible grief and love. This condition explains why the sentimentalist and the cynic are two sides of the same coin. In such matters, the arts are transparent and the connoisseur can easily tell imitation feeling from the real thing." Jacques Barzun's *From Dawn to Decadence* Pg. 411 (The book to read and reread and read once again - truly a masterpiece.)

"The word sentimental is one of many euphemisms for the infantilism that is as noted, the besetting sin of an uncritical attachment to an ideology of any kind- in fact, it is the most dangerous form of original sin." Northrop Fry- Words with Power Pg. 140

When you start to vehemently defend your paradigm/ideology, you are approaching the future with sentimental nostalgia, or you are approaching the present dragging the past behind you. I think this is ultimately what is behind the extreme fundamentalists. *"Just give me that old time religion"*, to my mind is a statement that shows its true color. Religion only exists now. It carries a lot of baggage though, and that baggage can set you free or chain you to a rock. These so called religions, which cut people off from the world (Hare Krishna, Wako Texas, etc), are really all about power. Where love is lacking, power will surely rush to fill the vacuum. It sounds corny, but love does set you free.

If you are trying to get out of a relationship and the other person is threatening to kill themselves when you break up with them, you are stuck in a perverse situation that you have to walk away from. There is very little in the way of clear options for you and you have to call their bluff or alternately be willing to relinquish yourself to be-come the slave of their power. (All situations are never this black and white. I am illustrating a point) The person threatening suicide has shown quite clearly that power is their main concern by using the only bargaining chip they have left, which is their own life. The ideal solution would be to help this person see their error though patience and love, but you have to draw a line, when people take such an extreme position that they could also endanger your own life. These modern cults - Wako Texas, Jim Jones, Bagwan, Moonies, etc. - all function out of this type of control and fear. Unfortunately, power has been the bane of religious organizations from the start.

   The overarching irony I wish to expose here is that modern fundamentalist Islam is in the same boat as the western fundamentalist Christian movement. They both wish to save the world through a radical overhauling of personal freedoms in the name of bringing heaven down upon the earth. They are both preaching that we are near the end of the world. The conservative elements in the Catholic Church and the moderate elements within Islam itself have a tendency to dampen this type of fundamental extremism, but they don't react fast enough to the changing landscape for people. So some people feel they have to take the law into their own hands and bomb Iraq, or conversely, blow up the twin towers. This belief system can be summed up by saying: all evil is somewhere over there or outside of ourselves and we need to physically change the environment to make it better. This is projecting the shadow at its worst.

"The histories of Islamic fundamentalism and European imperialism have very often been closely, and dangerously, intertwined. In a curious but very concrete way, the fundamentalists of both faiths have needed each other to reinforce each other's prejudices and hatreds. The venom of one provides the lifeblood of the other." William Dalrymple: *The Last Mughal* - Pg. 84

The Iron hand crushed the tyrants head

  And became a tyrant in his stead

    -William Blake

American Fundamentalism and Radical Islamic Fundamentalism are two sides of the same coin. Both are striving to establish heaven on earth through imposing radical social change – piggy-backed into the world with fear. They are trying to force heaven down our throat by fiat.

Ultimately, when the United States looks at Islam, it sees its own shadow. I'm not sure what the civilian body count is in Iraq (over 80,000, I believe), but I am sure the Taliban, Bin Laden crazy jihadists/terrorists etc., would love to be able to match that body count man for man. To a detached observer with no ideological stake in this, who is the worst killer? Radical Islam is everything the extreme American fundamentalists don't want to admit that they are: over-controlling, sentimental ideologists. One of the first things an ideology does when it gets power is kill somebody, usually those who oppose it. Christians know this well from their more than sordid past. How many people have been killed in the name of the prince of peace? Fear stirs up emotions, as opposed to feelings; feelings are like looking down into the bottom of a clear well of water. Emotions are like stirring up all of the mud on the bottom with a stick. We will see how the brain has evolved its emotional response systems later, but for now, we are all on constant yellow or red, or bomb-the-shit-out-of-somebody alert.

The best lack conviction

Given some time to think

And the worst are full of passion

Without mercy

-W.B. Yeats touched up a little by Joni Mitchell from *Slouching Towards Bethlehem*

One of the last concepts I will tackle from Jung is the concept of Archetypes (next will be synchronicity, which will come up in the next chapter). Jung wrote a book that is now known as *Symbol of Transformation*. This was done while Freud was grooming him to be the leader in Freud's analytic movement. I will quote from *Memories Dreams and Reflections* where Jung sums up the situation nicely.

"While I was working on this book, I had dreams which presaged the forthcoming break with Freud. One of the most significant had its scene in a mountain region on the Swiss border. It was toward evening, and I saw an elderly man in the uniform of an Imperial Austrian customs

official. He walked past, somewhat stooped, without paying attention to me. His expression was peevish, rather melancholic and vexed. There were other persons present, and someone informed me that the old man was not really there, but was the ghost of a customs official who died years ago. "He is one of those who still couldn't die properly." That was the first part of the dream.

"I set about analyzing this dream. In connection with "customs", I at once thought of the word "censorship." In connection with "border" I thought of the border between consciousness and the unconscious on one hand, and between Freud's view and mine on the other. The extremely rigorous customs examination at the border seemed to me an allusion to analysis. At the border, suitcases are opened and examined for contraband. In the course of this examination, unconscious assumptions are discovered. As for the old customs official, his work had obviously brought him so little that was pleasurable and satisfactory that he took a sour view of the world. I could not refuse to see the analogy with Freud.

"At that time, Freud had lost much of his authority for me. But he still meant to me a superior personality, upon whom I projected the father, and at the time of the dream, this projection was still far from eliminated. Where such a projection occurs, we are no longer objective; we persist in a state of divided judgment. On the one hand, we are dependent, and on the other we have resistances. When the dream took place, I still thought highly of Freud, but at the same time I was still unconscious of the situation, and had not come to any resolution of it. This is characteristic of all projections. The dream urged upon me the necessity of clarifying this situation.

"Under the impress of Freud's personality, I had, as far as possible, cast aside my own judgments and repressed my criticisms. That was a prerequisite for collaborating with him. I had told myself, "Freud is wiser and more experienced than you. For the present, you must simply listen to what he says and learn from him." And then, to my own surprise, I found myself dreaming of him as a peevish official of the Imperial Austrian monarchy, as a defunct and still walking ghost of a customs inspector. Could that be the death-wish which Freud had insinuated I felt toward him? I could find no part of myself that normally might have had such a wish, for I wanted at all costs to be able to work with Freud, and, in a frankly egotistical manner, to partake of his wealth of experience. His friendship meant a great deal to me. I had no reason for wishing him dead, But it was possible that the dream could be regarded as a corrective, as a compensation or antidote for my conscious high opinion and admiration. There for the dream recommended a rather more critical attitude toward Freud. I was distinctly shocked by it, although the final sentence of the dream seemed to me an allusion to Freud's potential immortality."

The book Jung is talking about did bring the break with Freud. What Jung was saying in *Symbols of Transformation* was the conception of the archetypes and his own understanding of the deeper layers of the unconscious that he would go on to call the collective unconscious. In Jung's scheme of the unconscious, there are three levels to the mind. Number one: the ego, which is comprised of your persona and much of your overt consciousness. Number two: the personal unconscious, which is comprised of repressed material from your own life. The images you hold of your parents, your personal fears, etc. Number three is the collective unconscious, which is the collective heritage within the mind or the world soul, if you will. It is the thousand-year-old man that each of us could commune with and it is largely where the deeper and more elemental archetypes reside. There is constant interplay between these three parts, each mixing with the other in an undulating and diverse fashion.

I will now recount the dream, which led Jung to try to formulate an understanding of the collective unconscious. A house is a very common image of the personal psyche and if you repeatedly dream of being in the same house, you should take note. *"I was in a house I did not know, which had two stories. It was "my house." I found myself in the upper story, where there was a kind of salon furnished with fine old pieces in rococo style. On the walls hung a number of precious old paintings. I wondered if this should be my house, and thought, "Not bad." But then it occurred to me that I did not know what the lower floor looked like. Descending the stairs, I reached the ground floor. There, everything was much older and I realized that this part of the house must date back about the 15th or 16th century. The furnishings were medieval; the floors were of red brick. Everywhere it was rather dark. I went from one room to another, thinking, "Now I really must explore the whole house." I came upon a heavy door, and opened it. Beyond it, I discovered a stone stairway that led down into a cellar. Descending again, I found myself in a beautifully vaulted room, which looked exceedingly ancient. Examining the walls, I discovered layers of brick among the ordinary stone blocks and chips of brick in the mortar. As soon as I saw this I knew that the walls dated from Roman times, my interest by now was intense. I looked more closely at the floor. It was of stone slabs, and in one of them, I discovered a ring. When I tugged on it, the stone slab lifted, and again I saw a stairway of narrow stone steps leading down into the depths. These, too I descended and entered a low cave cut into the rock. Thick dust lay on the floor, and in the dust was scattered bones and broken pottery, like remains of a primitive culture. I discovered two human skulls, obviously old and half disintegrated. Then I awoke."*

*Please see footnote at the end of the book for a further comments on this.

"The concept of the archetype... is derived from the repeated observation that, for instance, the myths and fairytales of world literature contain definite motifs which crop up everywhere. We meet these same motifs in the fantasies, dreams, deliria and delusions of individuals living today. These typical images and associations are what I call archetypal ideas."- Civilization in Transition CW 10: Par. 847

"My thesis, then, is as follows: In addition to our immediate consciousness, which is of a thoroughly personal nature and which we believe to be the only empirical psyche (even if we tack on the personal unconscious as an appendix) there exists a second psychic system of a collective, universal, and impersonal nature which is identical in all individuals. This collective unconscious does not develop individually but is inherited. It consists of pre-existent forms, the archetypes, which give definite form to certain psychic contents." - C. G. Jung CW 9 Part 1 *Archetypes and the Collective Unconscious* - Pg.43

This concept of the archetypes brings us squarely into the realm of proof. How do we inherit such a thing as thoughts, or analogously, how do animals have an instinct? I will spend many pages trying to suss this one out. For now, here is an interesting story that has been well documented. It is a story about one of the men who helped discover DNA - a Mr. Francis Crick. He had been pondering the structure of a DNA molecule for some time. After a brief sleep, he awoke from a dream with the image of a Caduceus in his mind. That is two snakes intertwined as on the medical staff you see in doctor offices. The caduceus is the magic staff of Hermes the Greek messenger god who travelled between the two worlds - that of consciousness and the unconscious or the underworld of Hades and over world of the Gods. If Hermes touched you with his staff, you would fall asleep and enter the world of dreams. The staff itself represents the intertwining of the opposites, good and bad, Sthula and Suksma. The two intertwined snakes happen to be twisted into the shape of the DNA strand that we are now familiar with. This was the key image that led to the understanding of how the DNA strand made identical copies of itself, and therefore, how DNA passed genetic information on to other organisms.

    Another example of a specific archetype intruding into the world is through a fellow called Kekule or possibly Freiedrich von Stradonitz (see *In Pursuit of Elegance* by Matthew E. May. This fellow was pondering the structure of the benzene ring for a long time. While sitting in his chair one day, he had a waking dream in which he saw carbon and hydrogen atoms turning themselves into circles like snakes biting their own tails. This image of snakes biting their tails is also a very old symbol known as the uroboros. The snake eating its own tail is a symbol of among many things, disintegration and regeneration. The snake would eat itself into nothingness and reappear, i.e., shed its skin to regenerate. It also represents something that is complete unto itself in that the snake is self-perpetuating, because it has itself for food. Snakes, the world over, are seen as a representation-among many things-of self-regeneration, as it seems they never die.

    Now in both of these examples we have seen how a major scientific discovery has been brought to light in decidedly un-scientific fashion. Both individuals initiated a critical overheating of the unconscious by pondering specific problems and then they received a heavily loaded symbolic answer in a dream or semi-dream state. These symbols both happened to involve snakes, which have a decidedly ambiguous nature in world mythology. Both scientists understood that the symbols they received related directly to the problems they had been pondering. It's as if they both knew the answer and needed to relax their minds so they could bi-associate or allow a little jostling to occur in the data. This is much like when someone asks you someone's name and you can't think of it, then 20 minutes later it comes to you in the middle of a conversation. These types of insights have more to do with the brain being relaxed after a certain amount of exertion, although the disciplined and focused exertion is important. I also see this as an example of very strict sensate thinking being lowered, which allows more associative, intuitive unconscious to come to the fore. We will talk about the different roles of the right and left split brain later.

Both men in the above examples dreamt of very ancient symbols, which are heavily loaded with their own meanings. In the Garden of Eden, God chose the serpent to deliver the apple to Eve in order to lift humans from their state of unconsciousness. In India and elsewhere people kiss snakes in order to confront their darkest emotional fears; fear of snakes is justifiably deep rooted. To grasp the concept or flavor of archetypes takes a comparative and somewhat poetic mindset. One must become acquainted with world mythology and religious symbolism at a deep and extensive level. Kurt Vonnegut once said that if you wish to know what a great painting looked like, all you had to do was look at a million paintings and you would know a good one every time. There is no universal or statistical yard stick that we can use to prove that we have captured the meaning of an archetype. It is more of a gestalt that appears whole formed.

Once a symbol is delivered into consciousness, it is parceled into the multifaceted reality of good and evil - Suksma/Sthula etc., and we are left in the situation of the arbiters of will. The apple delivered to Eve was the same apple that hit Newton on the head and the Beatles named their record company after it, and some computer guy used it as well. Apples represent-amongst many things-forbidden wisdom and much like Pandora's Box. Once you accept this understanding, there is no going back. Are you looking for the perfect cherry blossom? They are all perfect. (John Lennon used to put an apple on a stand in his apartment and let it rot. This represented the apple record company for him. It started out great, but then turned into a continuous party that the Beatles paid for. Don't get me started on apples.)

So what Jung realized was that inside of everyone's psyche were ancient patterns of understanding that had evolved over the course of human history. These patterns were already in the mind, largely in the unconscious and they manifested themselves overtly in to various symbols in our dreams. He called the highly evolved symbolic representation of these patterns archetypes. Archetypes also manifest themselves in broader culture or in the collective psyche as the various threads of world mythology: a myth is a public dream and a dream is a private myth. (See Anthony Stevens, *Ariadne's Clue*). Archetypes probably have a great influence on the way in which we construct a view of the world and our own paradigms of thought. This was the point that Wolfgang Pauli would make in his book on Johannes Kepler, which he published with Jung. I will discuss Kepler's obsession with circles and his book by Pauli later when I talk about Arthur Koestler.

An example of an archetypal theme is the recurrent dynamic of unity within multiplicity: God is one, but manifests in Christianity as three. The multiplicity of nature can be represented accurately through mathematics. Scientists continually try to reduce their understanding into short beautiful equations. Like E=MC2, which is an equation that shows the underlying equivalency of matter and energy. Abstraction is the thought that things can be reduced into simpler constituents and thereby understood. E Pluribus Unum, or out of many come one. All of the various archetypes are in some sense a reflection of a single archetype, which splits into a multiplicity as it/they manifest in time. Hindus call this singular background totality. The Atman and all of the other gods in the Hindu pantheon could be seen as different manifestations of the actual underlying unity of the Atman. Our brain it seems can't handle the inherent unity of the world so we constantly divide it in our effort to create understanding. The holy grail of theoretical physics is a unified field theory or theory of everything.

The psyche can be thought of as an amalgam or unity of four personality types with introverted and extroverted aspects to make eight sub types. Taken all together, the separate modes of thinking represent the totality of the Self or a more unified personality that we can strive toward. The quaternary or the four aspects of the world that are resolved into one seems to be articulated specifically in a series of western archetypal concepts. Examples of this quaternary division are the four main-or three times four equals twelve apostles in the Bible, or God, Jesus, the Holy Ghost and the devil who represents the fourth as a shadow - the four points of the cross itself. The Arc of the Covenant carried four sacred objects: The tablets of Moses, a golden oil jar, a vessel containing manna, and Aaron's staff; the strong and weak nuclear forces, the electromagnetic forces and gravity, as the unruly shadow. All of these symbols represent unity in multiplicity. (See Marie-Louise Von Franz, *Archetypal Dimensions of the Psyche* Pg. 272.)

  Jung was partially led to his conception of the archetype by a patient in a clinic where he worked called the Burgholzli. This patient was telling him that the sun had a tube or penis hanging down and if the patient held his head the right way he could see the tube moving. Jung associated this symbol to one he had seen in an old Egyptian text that he had been reading, where the sun blows wind out of a tube. Why would this patient describe the same symbol as a three thousand year old text? It is a very specific image. I think Jung tried to discuss these things with Freud, but Freud proved somewhat resistant. It seemed Freud patronized Jung's dabbling in the occult and his attempt to come to grips with these types of synchronous events as childish.

  Jung did specifically talk to Freud about the dream in which he went into the basement that was an old Roman house. Freud discounted the rest of the dream and dwelled on the image of two skulls that Jung had found. Freud told Jung that he thought that Jung held an unconscious death wish toward him. Freud seemed to think that Jung wanted him out of the way; in the same way a teenager may want their father out of the way so that they can more fully express themselves. Jung felt that this specific image of the two skulls was not the whole meaning of the dream, but for the reasons Jung talked about earlier, he was uncomfortable going against Freud's analysis. After all, Freud may be right and you may just have resistances to his truth that just might then manifest as an unconscious death wish represented by two skulls in the basement of your dream. It seems that Freud knew a lot about Jung's very intimate personal history, especially Jung's various peccadillo's and affairs with other women. Also, it must be remembered that Freud had, at this point, chosen Jung as his worthy successor and probably expected him to play the dutiful son, but Jung finally became a heretic to Freud's dogma of sexual theory. (The books to read are *Jung: A Biography* by Gerard

Wehr or *Freud and Psychoanalysis* C.W. Vol 4- C.G. *Jung and Freud, A Life For Our Time* by Peter Gay) Much of this underlying tension surfaced when Freud and Jung went to America together by boat for the first time to lecture in 1909.

You see... it's all a tight circle: Jung has a dream of a customs official while he is writing a book that he suspects will bring about a break with Freud. Jung brings a dream that he believes is very important to Freud who insists that Jung has a death wish against him. Jung over time refuses the master's interpretation of the skulls and kills him metaphorically by writing the book that would force him to leave Freud's charmed circle. The dream that Freud is convinced holds a death wish (two skulls) is the dream most sighted by Jung as the one that lead him to the concept of a collective unconscious. This is the idea that eventually drives Jung away from Freud and so both of these men's interpretations are correct. Jung does have a symbolic death wish against Freud and this dream brings about the end of their relationship, from the Freudian perspective. From the Jungian perspective, the two skulls have nothing to do with Freud. They represent a more archaic layer of the psyche that Freud denied. We can only see this meaning or read into it the meanings that we see, because we now have the benefit of our historical hind sight. And this is the difficulty of meaning. Jung would later make efforts to get Freud and his sisters out of Austria during the Second World War, but I believe they never communicated directly after this break.

The very box that Freud wishes to keep closed (that of the occult), is the box that his star pupil must open. *"My dear Jung, promise me never to abandon the sexual theory. That is the most essential thing of all. You see, we must make a dogma of it, an unshakable bulwark. He (Freud) said that to me with great emotion, in the tone of a father saying, "And promise me this one thing, my dear son: that you will go to church every Sunday." In some astonishment I asked him, "A bulwark –against what?"* To which he replied, "*Against the black tide of mud*"- And here he hesitated for a moment, then added: *"of occultism"* as quoted by Jung in *Memories Dreams and Reflections* - Pg. 150. Of course, I have presented this argument largely from the Jungian perspective. When I was younger, I was quite invested in Jung, but I honestly do not feel a compulsion to defend him. The few examples seem to illustrate to me- quite accurately-the dynamic of their relationship.

The whole ensemble is an excellent illustration of dream symbolism and the way that it relates to the real world through the dynamic of our unconscious, conscious interplay. Both participants seem to be expressing, and therefore, rise into consciousness. Their unconscious desires and the dream world are being reflected back to them in the real world. We can also see the ambiguity of conscious dream interpretation and how each person could be emotionally invested in their own position. This was a crucial turning point in what proved to be an important relationship in both of these people's lives. The psychological underpinnings of this rift may have been deeply affected by, or invested in this situation. Freud was getting old and he was trying to establish a successor to continue on with his legacy, but his closest inner circle was breaking up. Jung was plagued by doubts about Freud's strict adherence to his system of thought. Freud's other star pupil Gerhard Adler would also leave soon after.

Jung mentioned a number of times that Freud never had the benefit of training in the scientific methodology. Jung also made the point that what he thought Freud had, in essence, done was to abolish any form of belief in God in his professional work and probably in his personal outlook as well. He then substituted an unwavering belief in his sexual theories. This is another theme we will come across again and again. This is the idea that if we abolish God or an external form of worship, there will be a tendency to enshrine our own thoughts or some alternative ideology as our source of meaning. This is the essence of hubris or the elevation of humans or human ideals into the role of Gods. We all have an inherent propensity to create meaning and this will be elaborated on in depth as we take a look at the current state of such diverse subjects as physics, linguistics, Icarus and the life of Johannes Kepler.

What I am really driving at here is, if we are responsible for how we construct a world view; for example, if we relate everything we experience to our pet ideology. Then how convoluted and ridiculous can our conception of the world become, if the base that we build our vision on is completely un-provable? Say, something like a conspiracy theory or belief in god. In some very real sense what we go looking for is being cast out in front of us by our own mind and we end up finding it. Conversely, we can spend our time dissecting the past with intellectual blinders on and then we only see what we wish to see in history as well.

The human mind is forever constructing a narrative. Be careful what you wish for.

One of the big questions I should like to address again is, if or why the human unconscious wants to sort things out for us. I believe if we think about the human unconscious or our ability to dream on the most prosaic level, it could be seen to be an evolutionary stratagem or an ongoing feedback adaptation to the environment. The prosaic level of things is the level I am least concerned with but, we shall have to slowly circle around this idea and develop a more metaphorical way of thinking before we tackle the implications of deep meaning within the unconscious.

The environment that humans are believed to have evolved in over the last two hundred thousand years seems to have been a fairly open savannah punctuated with trees, initially in Africa. This is debated and there is some thought that we evolved and adapted our behavior to exploit the boundary or dual habitats of savannah and relatively dense jungle. This is important, because we will see that the brain and our physiology – the ability to walk upright, etc. - has evolved to include many strategies that seem to be specifically tailored to this type of mixed grassland environment. One of the best ways to escape an attacking animal in these environments was to run fast and ideally climb up a tree. These two images of running to escape and being high up in trees are among the most common in the human dream inventory. Firstly, the feeling of being scared and of something chasing you is very common and the second associated image is the fear of falling or the sensation of falling in your dream; for example, out of a tree. I will also add that trees are a very common image in the mythological dream inventory.

Very young children have falling dreams even though they have never fallen. This would make sense on a most basic level. You should be wary of heights. Evolution would wish you to understand this basic element of your physical environment, if you have no experience of heights and so it could be embedded into the collective psyche. The Sthula aspect of this is a justifiable fear of heights; the Suksma or symbolic aspect is or can be interoperated as a warning against hubris or pride. If someone thinks too highly of themselves, they may also have a dream or series of dreams in which they are falling. The Greek legend of Icarus illustrates this nicely. Icarus fashioned wings for himself and his father out of feathers and wax, but Icarus flew too high and the wax melted and he fell to his death in the Aegean Sea. Icarus's father did not fly too high and seems to have made it to the next island. He had the proper cautionary attitude and lived to write the tale. It seems that the brain developed this strategy of an internal feedback loop through the unconscious and the use of dream imagery as a way of keeping people on track. We are right to look for, or indeed, create a deeper meaning.

In ancient Greece, people would go to the Oracle of Delphi to have their unconscious read by an expert. It seems that the priestesses there were in touch with the unconscious realm, or at the very least, they showed great intuition and insight into human personality. (This was somehow aided by the retaining of their virginity, though I doubt it made a difference. The important aspect was believed to be so.) You would tell the priestess your troubling dream or your current problems and the priestess would read the situation and come up with the appropriate answer or possibly give you an answer loaded with such ambiguity that you left to work out your problem. Though, I would say that the act of making the effort to go to the Oracle is in itself helpful by taking your problem seriously enough to want to consult with a professional. And a sufficiently ambiguous answer could again force you to focus your mind back to the problem, by making you function under the impression that you have been given the correct answer, but it is you that didn't grasp it correctly. If you believed that the priestess could truly see, you would be inclined to think that they gave you the correct answer. You read the correct conclusion backward into the situation, because of all of this mental heat that has been focused by you into your own unconscious. And of course, you could be completely wrong.

All of this attention may allow the mind/unconscious to go into its more associative or metaphorical pathways and you just may actually gain a better understanding of your problem. This process has its analogies all throughout history and is akin to the process of going on a pilgrimage in the Middle Ages. A pilgrimage would allow you time to reconsider your life or just simply experience some new scenery or get away from a bad situation. I think we are naive to believe that the collective unconscious cannot offer us valid insights in to ourselves or that some people cannot read clearly into other people's situations quickly and offer an accurate reflection of the problem they have been asked to solve. I think that some of these priestesses at Delphi were very good at intuiting correct answers to people's questions, but of course, there is already great ambiguity inherent in this type of situation. I have no statistics with which to quantify/verify anything.

The basic elements of the human condition have been evolving for a very long time and I should think many people have gone through the same range of emotional troubles and situations as we all have. Some people find answers and some don't. My presumption is that successful solutions would be an evolutionary advantage and propagated within our psychic inventory. Some people are intuitive or just plain observant and can read situations, either their own or other people's very quickly and accurately, and give wise advice they pretend to understand very well. This ability of the psyche is our collective heritage and we can all participate in the great inventory of collective wisdom that each of us receives at birth. Some people can learn to assess the archetypal matrix of a situation and come up with the right answer. I would also argue that the Bible/Koran/Bhagavad-Gita, etc. are excellent cultural templates for this type of wisdom.

> "Not in entire forgetfulness. And not in utter nakedness. But trailing clouds of glory do we come." -Wordsworth

Where things get interesting for me is in trying to frame some type of theory to describe the actual mechanics of how a specific image like this sun penis could get passed down through history. The idea that a specific image could move across two different people's minds independently or pass through different generations of people's unconscious is probably a mistaken notion, based on a naive belief in strict causality. I think that we will look in vain for some type of genetic device that passes on such particular aspects of information. Although I have heard an interview with a fellow who believes he is on the right track. This idea will continue to surface in a number of ways later and is part of the elaborate nugget of proof.

So the archetypes are elementary psychic units that manifest in the world in certain specific time-bound ways. The main Jungian archetypes are the Self, which is an anticipatory symbol of psychic wholeness or actually it is the process of psychic wholeness itself. In Sanskrit the Self or greater outward/inward continuum is called the Atman and can be associated in the external environment with either Shiva or Vishnu, etc. The symbol of the wise old man and the earth mother symbol are two more extensions of this. Various aspects of the wise old man will come up regularly as we move along. The Earth Mother or the inherent wisdom of Mother Nature has many faces from the evil Baba Yaga who lives in the forest in Russian fairytales and haunts children's dreams or the Hindu goddess Kali the divine Creatrix of life, and the destroyer of time itself. Or, in the west, as the all good Virgin Mary who is so rarefied as to be barely human. In current parlance we now have the Gaia movement in ecology.

The trickster is another very common archetype, which can be symbolized by a fox. In some Native American folklore, the fool or trickster was the only person who could speak the truth directly to the big chief and not face retribution. The court jester in medieval times served a similar function in that he could tell the truth as a joke to the king while the other people might just be telling the king whatever he wanted to hear. And of course, God is another archetype and by saying that God is an archetype, I in no way mean to imply that there is something 'only psychic' or 'nothing but' about this symbol. All of these archetypes live and breathe as a result of our engagement with them.

"I and I, in creation where one's nature neither honors, nor forgives; I and I, one said to the other no man sees my face and lives" -I and I by Bob Dylan from Infidels

It seems that in the unconscious, all symbols (archetypes) are really one symbol. This is the single one reality of Buddhism (Uma or One, hence Uma Thurman), but as the one undivided symbol enters the realm of time, it, of necessity, splits into this multifaceted universe. This single all encompassing unity is too much for the brain to deal with and must be unpacked or delineated. This is the art of understanding or the process of analysis. Vishnu sleeps on a cloud in the primordial ocean dreaming the dream that is our world and us. All is one in him, but he enters time in many different manifestations: sometimes Brahma, sometimes Krishna or Shiva, etc. Vishnu can adopt any of the various personified archetypes that might suit his needs, but his essential essence is profoundly detached from the world that *we might* understand as real. This is partly why polytheism isn't a problem for Hindus, because all of the Gods are the different manifestations of a single unified entity that is moving into the field of time only because of us. This divine background is the Atman, and the realization of this ultimate unity is the drive of meditation. This is also why some Hindu gods are portrayed with three faces, past present and future, left, right and centre; Shiva, Vishnu, Brahman. Suksma, Sthula, Para, etc. or one of the reasons why Christians divide God into a trinity that is not a trinity: God, the son and the Holy Ghost. It seems that the human mind needs a great deal of preparation to be able to absorb this underlying intrinsic unity. So the archetypes are multi-faceted in the realm of time and consciousness, but they point back to an inner/outer unity, which is also an archetypal symbol.

I personally believe that a breakthrough into an understanding of this fundamental unity within the world is the foundational aspect of enlightenment. Enlightenment is the grasping of the realization of the inherent unity of reality. (He, who says he knows, knows not.) This is the one of the great dangers involved in a full confrontation with the unconscious. The information coming to us from the unconscious is a tightly packed metaphorical truth and the interpretation and unfolding of this truth is the real art. Salman Rushdie knows the trouble of this multi-facetted interpretation all too well, as he was forced to grapple with his interpretation/poetic license involving the *Satanic Verses of Mohammad*. (The book to read is *Muhammad* by Karen Armstrong - Pgs. 110 to 117)

A person wishing to take on this challenge of unpacking the dense unconscious metaphors needs a guide to avoid the pitfalls that are inherent in interpretation. The main danger in a confrontation with the unconscious/archetypal realm is that you may begin to identify with the images and material yourself. Christ on the cross was offered dominion over the whole world/naked power. For example, you may have a dream vision of yourself presiding over a grand meeting of religious leaders and take it into your head that you too are a great unrecognized religious leader, or that, in fact, you have been specially chosen to lead the world religious leaders out of their errant ways. This is known as an inflation, where the ego literally gets puffed up and identifies with an archetype, in this case the healer/savior. This is also the lesson that is presented in the myth of Icarus. The dream may have been simply telling you to attend more church meetings or something much more prosaic. Without taking the whole ensemble of the dream and your ongoing relationship in the world at that specific time into consideration, it is very hard to come up with a definite interpretation of anything - dreams included. Science or various members of the scientific community are going through a form of this inflation right now as they rail against God and fundamentalism, etc. in an effort to assert that they now have the truth.

Compassion is not an abstract ideal to be striving for. We don't need to save the world. Sometimes it is enough to hold the door open for someone or forgive yourself for your ignorance. Practice will help you understand.

I was watching a show on TVO and they had a large number of religious leaders gathered together along with a psychologist. The details of this show are not so important and I will only try to capture my impression. There was an audience question segment and one fellow came up to the microphone and discussed a dream/vision he had while he was meditating in the wilderness. In this dream, he had seen the Earth Mother or Gaia elevated above the other Gods or religions. This dream was obviously of some importance to the dreamer and seemed to imply on a cultural level that we should be paying more attention to the environment. I don't wish to misrepresent this fellow, but it seemed to me that he was challenging the various religious leaders with his reassertion of the female/Earth Mother principle. Now, the psychologist on the panel was no dummy and he said to the fellow: *"The importance of this dream is what are YOU going to do with it?"* I believe that the psychologist had very quickly recognized that this fellow had identified himself with his message and became inflated. He had possibly been functioning under the assumption that this vision gave to him uniquely and he had a mission to bring it into the world. The psychologist-to my mind-read the situation beautifully and gently pricked the dreamer's balloon (inflation) by making his vision an individual responsibility not a cultural mandate. The dreamer now had a task that he was to perform and also he could go on to realize that this dream may not be a universal cultural message to be imposed on us. It may be a specific image for him to understand alone. On the other hand, I would say that this vision is indicative of what needs to happen and is culturally happening in the west. This individual has had a dream that does, to some extent, represent an aspect of the wider cultural spirit/sickness. The Gaia principle is related directly to the matriarchal/feeling relationship that is savagely under-represented in western culture (Public dream, private myth).

Buddhist and or Hindu Yogic training takes years, all in an effort to prepare you for the onslaught of internal and external unconscious, as does an in-depth analysis. In Zen Buddhism, it is believed that enlightenment can take the form of a sudden revelation - not to say that there is no training within Zen. My understanding is that a Zen awakening can cause a rudimentary change in your understanding, thereby allowing you to view reality more clearly. You aren't necessarily fully realized by one such breakthrough, but you are better prepared to move forward without being hindered by preconceived notions. You have tasted the honey.

William James discusses many sudden conversions within the Christian tradition in *The Varieties of Religious Experience*. The widespread use of psychedelic drugs is typical of the west's desire to short cut through this slow unfolding process and 'have it all now'. Drugs such as LSD and magic mushrooms push the mind out on to the ocean of the unconscious, but what is not understood is that if you are to raise a jewel from its great depths to the surface, you need to be able to first hold your breath, dive and then swim back to land, and then understand what the hell you have in your hand. With the raising of consciousness comes the moral/ethical responsibility of the knowledge that you have received. We can't start killing Muslims, because they aren't prepared to worship Gaia.

Oppenheimer worked at a fever pitch on the atomic bomb for many months. He, himself acknowledged that there was no stopping to grapple with the implications of what he was unleashing into the world. When they first detonated the bomb at Los Alamos he turned to one of the people he was with and quoted the Bhagavad-Gita: *"Now I am become death."* This was what was said by the Hindu lord Krishna to his pupil Arjuna. Arjuna was the leader of a great army that had assembled to do battle and Arjuna was expressing his doubt to Krishna as to whether he should enter into the savagery of war and slay his own countrymen. Some of the people he was about to fight were directly related to him and so there were questions about the wisdom of this battle. Krishna explained that the slayer and the slain are two aspects of the Atman or the great world soul and all of this surrounding battle is part of the great cosmic play in which we are immersed. We can never not act in the field of time. Deciding not to act is another form of action. After explaining this, Krishna turned to reveal his wrathful aspect to Arjuna. Now I am become death.

After delivering a long speech on the relativity of morals or the equivalency of the opposites that so offends our western sensibilities, Krishna enters the field of action and time as the slayer of men. Oppenheimer immediately recognizes in this symbol the parallel of what he had done in the world and realized that he too had unwittingly unleashed this wrathful aspect into the world. Though it seems he only became fully conscious of the jewel, he had brought into the world at this moment of detonation. As the mushroom cloud rose over the desert, Oppenheimer suddenly realized the full impact and moral ambiguity of what he had done and had been doing for some time. It seems this sudden flash focused his mind. Krishna also reveals to Arjuna a glimpse of his eternal and all encompassing wisdom, which is symbolized by a blinding and overwhelming light.

You may have a great insight into the affairs of the world or a stunning realization about yourself when you are taking drugs, but you still have to live in this world. How you bring this revelation you have had into reality is the difficult task. Jesus was crucified for his vision. This ambiguity involved in technology or creation as it moves into the world has become one of the great themes of modern movie making. This is partially the theme of technology rebelling against its creator. It is in fact one of the great themes of modern mankind as we grapple with our own consciousness. Mary Shelly explored it in *Frankenstein*, *The Terminator* and *Matrix* series are good examples of the ambiguousness of the theme. *The Terminator* actually changes sides: enantiodromia. And so bringing the jewel to the surface (creation) involves a moral responsibility, because when we open Pandora's Box (or a can of whoop ass) we may not get the lid closed again. War is hell with the lid ripped off. We are really discussing the wider theme of the loss of innocents, which brings me back to the quote on sentimentality and nostalgia for the past. Sentimentality is tied to inaction and nostalgia is tied to the past and both reflect a refusal to grow up, or the desire to wallow in the past and refuse the present. To my mind, they are two great sins. We will see that the left brain is more comfortable with representation and comparison because if it owns a concept it can exercise power over it. Not choosing to act is also action and Krishna avoids or transcends the dilemma of non-action and embraces action in the world by becoming the mystery of death itself.

We can't just willy-nilly go having babies all over the place. We have to raise them and that is real work

"Modest people induce boastfulness in others; so very sensitive people (who are always tremendous tyrants) bring out all the brutality in their surroundings. Sentimentalists bring out vulgarity and people who are afraid are attacked." – Marie Louise Von Franz

Jung considered symbolic thought or the realization of the meaning of symbols to be one of the most important aspects of being. To make explicit your understanding of external symbolic situations or to understand your own unconscious symbolic productions and projections on to the environment is a very important task. Producing and meditating on symbols or metaphors is what all of art does. Art is creating cultural sign posts that both reflect the artist interests and also mirror the wider spirit of the times. We shall briefly look at symbols and their relationship to us in order to round out this theme of archetypes. I wish to show here - and later on- how the poetic realm expresses itself through the ambiguity of metaphor and that it is exactly this ambiguity that is its greatest truth. I will come back to this theme over and over as we move along.

To begin with, we will look at the theme of innocence, lost because it is really about the weight of gaining consciousness. The poem, *The Stolen Child* by W.B. Yeats sums up this theme of the loss of innocence well.

Away with us he is going

The solemn eyed, he'll hear no more the lowing

Of the calves on the warm hill side

Or the kettle on the hob, sing peace into his breast

For he comes, the Human child to the water

For he comes the human child to the water and the wild

With the fairy hand in hand

From a world more full of weeping

Than he can understand

The water and the wild are both fitting symbols of the unconscious, the solemn eyed are those who have born the weight of understanding in the world. Tori Amos also plays with this theme in a song called, *Winter*.

He says when you gonna make up your mind

When you gonna love you as much as I do

When you gonna make up your mind

Cause things are gonna change so fast

All the white horses are still in bed

I tell you that I'll always want you near

You say that things change my dear

    I have used these poems to show you how a lot of information can be packed into a symbol or metaphor. This type of poetic metaphor is the same type of language that the unconscious speaks to us. It is our window into the way that information has been conveyed in pre-literate societies for a very long time. Where poetry and metaphor shine (essentially a right brain function) is in condensed images, like this image of white horses that are still in bed. I will unpack these poems a bit to show how I see the process working, but first I will say that whether you explicitly understand these images or not, is in some sense irrelevant. These images work their way into the fabric of your psyche in the same way music can reach in and tear your heart out. You have never said all that can be said, and like telling a joke, this type of analysis is an artificial representation of what is intrinsically a whole unto itself.

    White is an image of purity and chasteness. Milk is white and you drank it only when you were a small child and completely innocent. Wedding dresses are white to symbolize this state of purity as well. Most religious clothing is white; if you perform the Hajj, you would dress all in white upon arriving in Mecca. Horses and animals in general represent instincts; horses more specifically, represent virility and power within the instinctual realm. That is why you see Napoleon (in David's picture) riding a huge horse. Napoleon is seemingly unconcerned about this beasts' fierce raring underneath him. He is in control of this wild beast called 'the state of France' and also he is in control of his emotional/instinctual states as represented by this horse. Napoleon is calm and wise and unaffected by the contagious emotions that surround him – certainly an ideal in the frenetic head-chopping age of reason. Many other monarchs have been painted on horses or beside their favorite horses, though in far less dramatic ways. This image is an extension of the symbolism that comes from the age of knighthood where only the elite could afford to own a horse and armor. This ownership of horses became an indication of both wealth and power. A cavalier attitude (to be willfully reckless) is from the French word for horse, 'chevalier'.

   A bullfight in Spain follows this same type of thinking, where a single man is dominating the instincts of the bull, or Minotaur in the Greek myth of Ariadne. This ensemble was one of Picasso's favorite images; he painted himself obliquely as a Minotaur quite often. (Which I believe was him jousting about his sexuality. Also see Joseph Campbell's extended essay and references to Picasso's Guernica in *Creative Mythology*). Horses in the example of this poem specifically carry the shades of a girl's blossoming sexuality. The white horses are still in bed, because the girl in the song is still innocent. These horses and her innocence have not yet emerged from her dream world bed and into consciousness, but things are gonna change. She will experience life outside of her bed and she will conversely experience her sexuality in a bed. Her father is the speaker in this case and he would wish to protect her by saying he will always want her near, but of course, he cannot keep her with him. That can become a sick situation so he must let her go and he knows this, because he is the solemn eyed. He tells her he will have her around, but he is saying it only to comfort her.

   My wife and I were lucky enough to see Tori Amos in a very small venue in Toronto just before this song was released, and she exuded raw sexuality in a very powerful way. She would have been in her early 20's at the time and she was a force to be reckoned with. Also, on this same EP called: *Winter* is a version of *Smells Like Teen Spirit* by Kurt Cobain and Nirvana, which is an anthem of his generation that speaks directly to this theme of the loss of innocence. It seems Mrs. Amos was also concerned with this theme at the time, and of course, we have an archetype for that, called the 'Puer Aeternus' or eternal child. The Puer or female Puerela Aeternus is that individual who will not grow up. They don't seem to ever squarely face reality. Conversely, they can retain their childish fascination with the world for a long time, and they retain that divine ability to play. Mercury is the Greek god closest to this idea.

In this new world, things are changing. We are all in the water and the wild, but I believe we always were and always are anyway. I don't believe that anyone has not had the thought-at some point in their life-that the world they are living in was not out of control and that they weren't really facing an unprecedented sea of change around them. At least anyone that was awake enough too really look around them must, at some point, feel this way. Both the rise and collapse of the Roman Empire, the Black Death, any of the Crusades or the Renaissance; almost any point in history or a cursory look at anyone's personal life is sufficient to realize that all of life can be packed with exceptional events. Of course, we are in a uniquely explosive state of technological advance right now, but I would ask what good is fear to us? This is where we are. Let's all grow up bravely.

I watched Barak Obama sworn in as the 44th president of the United States and he quoted one of my favorite passages from the Bible: *"It is time to put away childish things."* He is right. In round two, Mitt Romney said: *"America doesn't apologize."* What a horse's ass he is.

Digression

I should like to end this chapter with what Jacques Barzun calls a small digression on a word. His digression was on the specific nature of pragmatism to which we shall have verbal recourse later. My digression is on the meaning of metaphor, symbols, and more generally, archetypes. In this book, I will be using the term 'metaphor' quite often and the explicit nature of the term was given to me by Joseph Campbell in an interview I heard with him. If you look up metaphor in the dictionary, at least mine, it seems to imply that it is an equivalent to a simile which is a term, used to compare two dissimilar things. For example, he raged on the battle field LIKE a lion. This use of 'like' is implicit in such statements that are *simile's,* specifically. Like is used in popular culture all of the time to denote the artist's poetic license, much to my chagrin. This is a *simile*, not a metaphor. A simile is where the use of 'like' raises a flag so that you get the artistic similarity. *"The wax rolled down like tears"*- Joni Mitchell

A metaphor is on one hand explicit in that you are actually stating the ambiguous fact that two separate ideas are the same. At least this is how I understand it. For example, you could say he was a lion on the battle field. The metaphor is Richard the Lion Heart; Coeur de Lion. Here you explicitly identify the person with a lion. This is the language or really the essence of prelinguistic thought that is reflected in religion and poetry, where a statement is made that doesn't imply the concepts you are relaying are similar. You allow the relationship to exist in its ambiguity.

The strength of a metaphor is that it can hold multiple meanings simultaneously. The unfolding of various ways of looking at the metaphor is really a personal understanding within the engaged listener. What is the sound of one hand clapping can be understood as an intentional affront to explicit rational thinking. You may be tempted to do an experiment to find out what hand clapping sounds like, instead of understanding that the phrase has no inherent meaning at all. Its purpose might be -amongst many things-to help you stop being so overly rational. Some modern poetry has left a sense of narrative completely out and is stringing metaphors together to create an overall environment of ambiguity. There is no point to the journey only the journey itself.

But what can I do with it?

On the way to the temple, Jesus curses a fig tree (Mark 11:12-26). When he gets to the temple, he overturns the tables of the money changers, which is probably the single act that upsets everybody and got him crucified. Outside the Jewish temple, there were people changing money into proper currency or gold, or a goat to donate to the temple. Jesus seemed to object to the fact that these fellows made a little profit from each transaction or possibly he objected to the whole thing. (Muslims now have a restriction on interest paid on savings as well. I'm not sure whether Mohammed got this idea from the Jews or the Christians, or came up with it himself. It seems Mohammed was well acquainted with aspects of both traditions.) On the way back from this episode at the money changers, Peter spots the fig tree that Jesus cursed and it is completely withered. Jesus uses this episode to help the disciples understand the power of faith saying: *"I tell you the truth, if anyone says to this mountain, 'Go throw yourself into the sea, and does not doubt in his heart but believes that what he says will happen, it will be done for him."* We don't normally see fig trees wither overnight and people get really hung up on this type of thing. On the other hand, when do mountains fall into the sea? To my mind, this is metaphorical teaching at its most excellent and whether these things happened in the strictest sense that the laws of science were temporarily overturned is irrelevant. What do we gain by insisting on the absolute fact of these examples? To my mind we miss what is really important about what is being said. This is that: metaphors point beyond themselves and back toward you, the reader, or indeed deep into the heart of a fig tree.

When someone gains enlightenment in the Hindu or Buddhist traditions, the whole world is showered in flowers. They don't write down that it was LIKE the whole world was showered in flowers. In their understanding, the whole world was literally showered in flowers. They blow the image right over the top so that it is understood to be a metaphor. What is partially behind this is an overt recognition that when someone gets their shit together, we all incrementally get our shit together, or we all enjoy a rain of flowers. Also, this is the language of our mind in prehistory before we believed everything could be pinned down and wrestled into submission.

Jesus also speaks in parables, but sometimes a parable and a very explicit statement are intertwined. When Jesus was handed a coin with Caesars head on it, he says: *"Render unto Caesar that which is his."* But there is a whole other level of implied understanding in this seemingly simple saying. First, is that you don't need money or any affiliation with this Roman regime so give Caesar his money back. You don't need it. Jesus was preaching a radical social program for those with the courage to follow. Or alternatively, you should be a dutiful citizen and pay your taxes, because the outer world is of little consequence, if you are spiritually developed. Pay your taxes and do your duty, but look beyond the confines of Roman culture. Both of these statements are true depending on where you are in your understanding of Jesus' message. Both messages are diametrically opposed to each other in terms of what you should do in your real life, whether you should collude with the Romans or buck the system completely. This also highlights more broadly your relationship to money, greed, etc. So both interpretations are true even though they contradict each other in terms of what your actions in the world should be, or how you bring this symbol into reality. I have a hard time understanding how a literal fundamentalist can reconcile such obvious ambiguity.

Nils Bohr called this paradoxical nature of truth a 'profound truth'. By lifting these passages out of context, I have perhaps implied meanings that aren't strictly applicable and some firebrand ministers might take exception to my foray into biblical interpretation. But to my mind, this is the strength and true nature of metaphor: it is flexible and ambiguous, for good or ill. I personally find it incongruous with Jesus' nature that he would kill a seemingly innocent fig tree to prove a point about anything, because I prefer to see Jesus as an eco-warrior, as is the youthful fashion nowadays. (Maybe he will be a hemp farmer when he comes back.) The interesting thing about this image is the specific symbolic puzzle that is the frame of fig tree tale itself. This fig tree is framing the money changer story and implying a relevance to it. And the overturning of the tables would become a very important episode in his life, depending on whom you wish to pin the crime of his crucifixion on to: Jews or Romans.

I think that possibly at the time of writing 70 AD, this fig tree metaphor had a much clearer, culturally relevant message. Possibly, it was not meant as a metaphor at all or the translation from Greek and or Aramaic may be loose. Fig trees are sacred to this day in India and apples don't exist in Israel at this time. It was really a pomegranate that Eve gave to Adam (the most sensual of fruits). I prefer to see and/or leave this image as a stunning and ambiguous metaphor and all is rosy in my Pollyanna world.

The other word that will come up often is analogy. Analogy comes from the same root as analysis, which is 'Analogos'. Logos is an idea, or possibly, the divine form or mother of all ideas in the sense of a Platonic idea. Ana is the connection or recognition of similarity. An analogy would be the example of explaining the inner workings of the mind by using a computer's wiring diagram. There is a sense that all analogies are pinned down and known unlike metaphors. There is a similarity, but there is no explicit sameness between these concepts. The analogy can be used, because it is the best paradigm of thought that we have at that time. What I am driving at in this book is the thought that these analogies can, and do, quite regularly become a mental straight jacket, because of their implications. We become trapped in an analogy and believe that it is an explicit and accurate representation of a phenomenon. All computer analogies of the brain are ultimately limiting.

For instance, the idea that the world was surrounded by a ring of oceans seemed to be quite common in ancient times. Who had the technical skill to dispel this thought? It seems that a Greek navigator called Pytheas was the first to travel around the top of the British Isle sometime around 400 BC where he encountered a dense fog on the cold sea that he presumed to be the end of the earth. It would be some thousand years until this was better understood. On one level, this image of an encompassing ring of water can be seen as an analogy for the enclosed self- conscious viewpoint of ancient peoples, as well as being a metaphor for the whole age of understanding. The metaphor can be expanded using analogies to explain it. The water contained within the uroboros (a snake eating its own tail), is a feminine image analogous to the amniotic fluid that surrounds a baby, so the image can represent the ancient mind, which was in its infancy and carefully enclosed by water. This surrounding water is itself also the symbol of the uroboros. Some ancient maps draw the known world encompassed by this snake eating its own tail. This is a very explicit historical idea, not just something I am making up in a flight of poetic fancy. Copernicus would explode this idea of a closed universe and also the relative uniqueness of human beings that went along with it. The ancient world was small enough to be understood much like the way a child thinks that the world revolves around them alone. Everything in a child's world is a relationship to their singular being. And so we use the analogy of the computer to represent the brain or a snake coiled around the earth to define a boundary until a better analogy comes along. A stricter mathematical analogy is, if: a=b and b=c than 'a' must =c. Math is so much cleaner than religion.

A symbol, on the other hand, is an image that points to another complex of ideas or is invested within an emotional complex. It is believed that the western writing system came from Mesopotamia. Somebody was putting soft clay tablets with an impression pressed into them (cuneiform) inside a paper sleeve to be stored. These soft tablets contained information that was used for accounting and people saw that the soft clay left an imprint or image on the paper envelope that was the same as the impression on the clay tablet inside of the envelop. Some shiny penny realized that the clay was irrelevant and that the image or impress could be used to represent the information in the same way as, and instead of, the clay tablets or the impression rendered on to them. This impression that was left on the paper is a symbolic representation and so later the Mesopotamians just drew the symbols directly on to paper. (Writing was invented at least three times–probably five times- independently in the world.)

A symbol or symbolic representation is considered a key element in consciousness in that it allows us to relate to the environment in an abstract way. This abstraction is not disconnected from the world; the impression on the paper in Mesopotamia related directly to an accounting of goods. The reason that the impression had meaning was that it represented a volume of barley or wheat that a farmer was storing at the temple. So this paper symbol represents the actual physical work of a person farming and an accounting of their labor that could enable tax collection, or payment back to the farmer, etc. For the farmer, this symbol on paper represented a considerable investment in his time, and therefore, carried a real and strong emotional value. Money carries this same energetic and symbolic value.

"Therefore, to create a meaningful symbol, the image must be invested with emotion. We don't have meaningful symbols (you can have imagery, but not symbols) unless they affect the image. Even seemingly impersonal objects, such as an apple or concepts such as numbers, we have found, require emotional investment, if they are to become meaningful symbols. As I will explain, an apple is not just red and round, it's something you give your teacher with pride and throw at your brother in anger. The

understanding of number concepts is based on how it feels to have a "lot" or a "little" of something. To a three-year-old, "a lot" is more than you want and "a little" is less than you expect. The second condition for creating meaningful symbols is the one that was a dramatic new insight for us. Yet, it was so basic in its simplicity that it also surprised us. This second condition is that a symbol emerges when a perception is separated from its action. The developmental process that enables a human being to separate perception from action provides the missing link in understanding symbol formation and higher levels of consciousness, thinking, and self-reflection." The First Idea - Pg. 25

Symbols emerge into our consciousness as a result of our human bodies being embedded in the world and our reactions to other people and the environment as we grow up. We will see later that this is an integrated functioning of our mind where the right brain presents the world to the left brain, which then re-presents the world in a symbolic fashion through analysis. This abstracted symbolic understanding is then reintegrated by the less explicit right brain again. When we encounter a new idea, we quite literally grasp the idea. We hold it in our hand and we can inspect it. To some degree, we now own and or have power over this new idea. This is an example of how the mind is embodied in the human being. We literally grasp with our right hand, read left brain regardless of which hand we use regularly and grasp ideas with our body/mind. Symbols then emerge out of this action/perception.

If a child stands at the door pointing and saying *"door"* you don't take the door off of the hinge and give it to the child. Both you and the child understand that the child wishes to go through the door to do something in another room. The child has made the symbolic connection with the word door and her ability to get into another room, but what has led to this symbolic exchange is the emotional intent involved in going to the other room. The child may ultimately want to grab a toy off of the couch and so the door is a frustrating barrier in accomplishing that action. The door exists beyond the denotation of a wooden thing with a knob, etc. So we build up our symbolic language through the physical/emotional engagement with and in the real world.

"We don't go to hell just our memories do

And if you go to hell I'll still remember you

But I thought you beat the inevitability of death to death just a little bit

I thought you beat to death the inevitability of death just a little bit."
-A wry Gordon Downie from The Tragically Hip

    I am going to beat this to death just a little bit, because it is an important point and it relates to our engagement with and emotional investment in archetypes. If I invite you over for a dram of scotch, how do I know how much a dram is? I have heard the size of a dram defined as an amount that is amenable to both the giver and receiver. So you see that the size of the shot of scotch that I pour for you is embedded in the extended context of the situation itself. A dram really depends upon many things, including my generosity, whether we both appreciate expensive/well-aged scotch and many other largely unconscious social cues. So the dram of scotch is a symbol of the whole situation with Scottish people who have intentionally left its measurement ambiguous. It is embedded in the social situation in which it occurs. (A friend of mine who is from Taiwan felt compelled to give me a bottle of scotch, saying that I had been very liberal with my collection, when of course, I was simply being polite. It is difficult to 'one up' Asians.)

    One last thing I would like to highlight is what I have come to call *symbolic drift*. An example of this is the symbol of an address. We use our address to represent the place or house that we live in, which of course, has much more meaning than the numerical designation that our numbered address is. Now, an email address doesn't exist in any kind of physical space that we recognize as anything, nonetheless, we all understand that the word 'address' leads people to you. The symbol of address has drifted even farther from its original designation and into the fairly abstract realm of computers, though it still points to a meaningful identification and representation of an emotional relationship. If in the future, people live in their cars like Paul Simon thinks, their address will still be a relevant designation, because of the way the term is used in the real world when we want to actually get in touch with someone. Like our feelings, the original etymology of the word is still discernible in the back ground of the symbol, but the explicit word now represents only a small part of the overall ensemble of meaning.

The word 'set' is the largest entry in the Oxford English dictionary. It has many different usages - all of them are contingent upon the specific setting in which they occur. A set of plates in which all are identical or Game Set Match, as in tennis, or chess set where many pieces are different or get, set, ready go, we don't get tripped up by words like this, because there are no a=b=c direct and logical wiring that exists in our language. All of our experiences are embedded in the world and they are loaded with our emotional and intellectual investment.

Part of what Jung was driving at when he discusses an archetype is that an archetype carries a lot of effect or emotional punch. You may have a dream in which an old man comes up to you inside of a decrepit church and tells you that there is gold buried in the floor. This is the archetype of the wise old man and it is very common all over the world. We encountered him earlier dressed up as a hobo in Marie Louise von Franz's story and we shall meet him again in the figure of Khadir in Arabic writing. By recognizing and/or relating this figure to the archetype of the wise old man you can align yourself with a much large understanding within the world. You then also have a wider symbolic matrix, which you can compare this fellow to other images.

Perhaps you will take his message seriously based on the presumption that he is indeed wise and take a second look at the decrepit state of organized religion within your own psyche or the larger world. In other words you might invest this symbol with meaning by taking it seriously, or conversely, it may be such a powerful dream that you have no choice but to try to understand the emotional import of the message. If you wake up crying, I would expect that you should take it seriously. You may then be compelled to go on and write a book called: *Proof and the Difficulty of Meaning*. So you then elevate this dream in to a symbolic understanding while recognizing that it is embedded in reality. I will point out archetypes as we move along so that we can get a feel for their slippery nature.

The last word I will discuss briefly is parable, which I don't use at all in this book, because a parable is explicit in that it does not try to hide the oblique reference. It is essentially an analogy, but again it is explicitly stated as such. Then, Jesus spoke in parables. I have a hard time understanding how fundamentalists can accept that Jesus uses parables explicitly, yet they cannot understand when the Bible is reflecting a larger metaphor like giving eyesight to the blind or raising Lazarus from the dead. It is one of the tenants of American fundamentalism that all of Jesus miracles really happened and that the Bible is literally and explicitly true. I think this is a reflection of the over-literalization of everything in the western mind, possibly as a result of our blind worship of the hard logic of science. Truth is a slippery fish.

2. IN SUCH MANNER DID I DREAM OF THE TRUTH

"Innovation is a twofold threat to academic mediocrities; it endangers their oracular authority, and it evokes the deeper fear that their whole, laboriously constructed intellectual edifice might collapse. The academic backwoodsmen have been the curse of genius from Aristarchus to Darwin and Freud; they stretch, a solid and hostile phalanx of pedantic mediocrities, across the centuries." A. Koestler – Sleepwalkers - Pg 434.

When I was in my late teens, and early 20's, I was quite a music addict and loved the album by The Police called *Ghost in the Machine*. This album was named after a book by Arthur Koestler. The title is an English translation of a Latin phrase: "Deux a Machenia", which is in reference to the secret spirit that the Greeks believed resided inside mechanical things or possibly all things. The ancients thought that most things were animated by spirits "Anima" is Latin for spirit or soul, hence animated. (When casting bronze statues, you build a clay or wooden piece in the main cavity so that the whole casting is not solid. This piece is called the Anima. Benvenuto Cellini discusses the Anima when he was casting his famous bronze Perseus that stood in the same square as Michael Angelo's David.) The next recording by the Police was *Synchronicity*, which was named after a book by Carl Jung. It seems that Mr. Sting was deeply immersed in these authors and I subsequently became deeply immersed in them as well, along with Colin Wilson, because I was my own man. I wasn't infatuated with Sting - I swear. Now I'm doing yoga, go figure. Choose your heroes wisely!

Arthur Koestler had a wide-ranging intellect and he wrote books about many subjects. The books that stood out for me in the formation of my thinking were his creative trilogy: *The Act of Creation, The Sleepwalkers* and *The Ghost in the Machine*. These books all deal broadly with the mystery of creativity and its relation to the arts, astrophysics, biology and the sciences respectively. They were a powerful trio when I read them and I always desired to write more on the subject of creativity myself. I will touch on Koestler's main themes, but there has been a lot that has happened in the world of science since he formulated his theories. And a lot has happened in my understanding of these themes as well, especially in the realm of creativity. This book you are now reading is largely the result of my constant meditation on these themes over the last 25 years and my slow realization that I could add more to this discussion. Koestler in many ways represented the spirit of the times. He wanted to embrace science and be someone who explained these things to others, but in many ways he existed outside of the strict scientific realm. He did correctly realize that Communism was a religion.

Koestler starts *Ghost in the Machine* with a long discussion on the triune brain or the three main sections of the brain. The oldest-evolutionarily speaking-part of the brain is the inner hypothalamus. This part of the brain unconsciously regulates our body temperature and the functioning of internal organs, like heartbeat, etc. and it actually extends down and is part of the spinal column. Koestler liked to refer to this as the older reptilian brain, which to his thinking was considered the seat of pure instincts or unreflective unconsciousness. Surrounding this is the cerebral cortex, which is the seat of some of the higher thinking that we see in various other animals. This is the mammalian brain where thinking starts to occur and then on top of, or in front of, is the neocortex or new brain, which is packed into the frontal lobes of our head. This is the area that is known to be involved in decision making, higher consciousness and possibly self-awareness or reflective consciousness.

Koestler envisioned this neocortex as a luxury item which has exceeded the owner's capacity to use properly. He uses the analogy of a simple shopkeeper who has found a computer and has realized that if he kicks it three times and then eight times, the computer spits out an answer of eleven. This is as much as the shopkeeper bothers to find out and he just uses the computer for this simple math. It is handy for him to do this kicking math, but of course, he could be figuring out the trajectory involved in shooting a rocket to the moon or surfing the internet. Computers in Koestler's time were much more rough and ready. The analogy is a little bit old and very misleading.

It seems that the neocortex (new brain) exploded on to the evolutionary scene some one hundred thousand years ago. However, it is hard to know exactly what our ancestors had inside their skull cavities. Relative skull cavity size is not a great indicator of intelligence. Apparently, Einstein's skull was quite small by modern standards. Koestler saw the neocortex as the basis of all rational thought, but this great tool was confounded to a certain extent - by being tied to the older more reptilian brain hardware that he believed was intent on generating our more base emotions and instincts. He was implying that man's aspirations to logical reason were foiled by his attachment to the more base emotions. (I am simplifying his thought, though this was certainly the import of his understanding of the brain structure.) I would say this triune stratification is just barely useful to us as a metaphor and most certainly is a far too simplified model of the brain in the light of modern neurological research. Much has been learned about the real mechanics of the brain since Koestler's writings and the main realization is that it is both far more integrated and nuanced than this simple triune outline. I have given this brief sketch so that we can grope forward in the same way, as the real understanding of the brain has evolved.

Subsequent fMRI (Functional Magnetic Resonance Imaging), and other brain imaging techniques (CAT and PET scans), have shown that certain tasks are taken up in different and sometimes very specific parts of the brain. The evolutionarily older parts of the brain seem to be organized in a more modular way, and the neocortex and prefrontal lobe interact and are highly integrated with all other parts of the brain simultaneously. The functioning of memory is analogous to the functioning of the neocortex. There is no single place where memories are stored. They are processed and then stored all over the brain and connected to the areas where they initially occur. If I have a memory that is associated to a certain smell, it will be retrieved and entrained with the areas associated with the olfactory sections. But I can see something and retrieve the smell memories even though these two senses (sight and smell) are relatively discreet entities within the structure of the brain, because the neocortex is in touch (through the long neuron's mostly running along the right hemisphere) with all sections all of the time and most of the other sections are in touch with most other sections. The neocortex functions more like a gatekeeper in the sense that its job is to say no or not no to information seeking consciousness. It's not that we do or don't have freewill: it's more like we *don't not have it*. Much more on this later, I just like this quote.

    An example of a traceable brain function that is indicative of our 'primitive' emotions is swearing. It occurs in the older parts of the brain, which would seem to imply that this type of emotional ejaculation is a very old feature of our instinctual language. Swearing is analogous to some forms of emotional alarm calls and can be-to a certain extent- automatic. People with Tourette syndrome are sometimes unable to control this type of speech and constantly swear. The age of reason and the subsequent existential philosophies constantly sought to denigrate this type of embodied emotion by implying that it was base or un-logical. Now we understand that the thinking brain and our emotional systems are so thoroughly integrated that if we attempt to section the brain off from its emotional underpinnings, in such a rigid manner, we will miss the more integrative aspects of our evolutionary development. This tepid dig–on my part-at explicit rational analysis will come up again and again as we move forward and we gain a marginally better understanding of thinking. Music is an example I will constantly return to too illustrate how the brain is completely integrated. For instance, listening to music seems to set off a flood of activity across many sections of the brain at once - from the oldest dark emotional underpinnings to elements of mathematical reasoning through to the 'highest' integrative poetic language and thought processing. A quick look at music immediately illuminates how the brain is hyper integrated. What I love about Koestler though, was that he was unafraid to write about all aspects of human situation the engaged him. He was unafraid of the chastisement of science. He tried to envision the full range of human endeavors on a sliding scale, with the arts at one end and science at the other, with psychology being somewhere in the middle. He uses the analogy of the spectrum of light; with the arts at the ultra-violet end and sciences at the infrared end, but that somehow both ends come around together and meet in the creative unveiling. Science historically has portrayed itself as a slow rational building of hard truths, based on meticulous research; each generation calmly building upon the existing edifice of the generation preceding it. The truth of the situation is that science is more like a series of sudden jumps, as one after another paradigm is broken through then integrated with other information, which is again discarded his is where science tips into the ultra violet and joins with the 'sudden' revelation of the arts.

The arts can be equally as obsessed with this rational or scientific idealism as the sciences are. Cezanne believed everything in nature could be conceptualized or expressed around the form of a cylinder. Braque used the form of a cube to break down nature. This is the essence of analysis which is the breaking down of things so that they can be put back together with new understanding. Musicians can become enslaved by the formal rules of harmony and yet still make great music. Bach is portrayed as a fellow who was entranced by the concept of mathematical perfection in his composing. But this -to my mind- also implies that he was unable to appreciate the beauty of a simple melody, which he clearly could do. He may have been quite slavish in terms of his composition, but this seems to have been his method of work and it obviously was very productive for him. He probably had no strict agenda and we are 'discovering/interpreting his method' after the fact. We all slide between the ultra violet and infrared and we sometimes jump across the gap. In some very real way, constraints create freedom instead of limiting it. In all things there is an element of the ultra-violet and the infrared. For example, the extreme left in politics (communism) easily tips into the extreme right, Stalin's total dictatorship.

Half Awake Half Asleep

In the book *The Sleepwalkers*, Koestler talks about the astronomer Copernicus, and how despite himself, he discovered the heliocentric system. For me this book helped me to understand that there might be chinks in the armor of scientific rationalism. This seemingly arcane discussion of early astronomy has much wider implications.

"The fool wants to turn the whole art of astronomy upside down"- Martin Luther on Copernicus

As the earth overtakes mars in its orbit, it literally speeds up from behind mars; because we are on an inside track. It seems as though mars- as seen from the earth's perspective-reverses in the sky. This is called a retrograde motion. This reversing of mars in the sky had been known for a very long time. There had been literally thousands of years of observation of the heavens that preceded Copernicus (1473-1543). But if Earth was the centre of the universe, why would this retrograde motion of Mars happen at all? Mars should travel around us in a nice even circle.

Copernicus was brave enough to enthrone the sun in to the centre of things in an effort to better understand this particular aspect of the Martian phenomena. On the other hand, he could not also jettison the idea that everything in the heavens was moving in nice perfect circles. He wrote a book-largely unread in his time-discussing it. It seems as though two of Greece's early philosophers had conceived of a heliocentric system: Heraclites had tried to launch a halfway house in which some planets went around the sun while others circled the earth. Aristarchus, on the other hand, did commit himself to a full-blown heliocentric system. It is quite hard to form a concept like that of the earth, tracing the heavens at what must be high speeds, simply because the earth we stand on seems so immobile, and if we are moving around the sun why don't we and everything else fly off into space? Not to mention the tandem realization that a day on earth must be the result of our spinning around an axis as well. The real problem with presenting a heliocentric system to anybody is that it is extremely counter intuitive, and seems to defy what our senses tell us and our simple common sense.

There was quite an inflexible dogma within the world of early astronomy - directly attributable to Aristotle. He believed that all planets must be moving in perfect circles. This idea became more entrenched during the dark and middle ages as active scholasticism was in some respects replaced by a blind belief in the wisdom of the ancients. Scholastic learning at that time was more concerned with the correct interpretation of wise men. Ptolemy and Aristotle dominated the arena of science. A better understanding of the world was further hamstrung, because accurate copies of these men's works or even complete copies of many books were virtually non-existent, especially Plato and the Roman historians. The main concern of pre renaissance knowledge was not the encouragement of independent comparative thinking. The enthronement of intellectual independence only began occurring in the west in the late 12th and early 13th century partially as a result of our more intimate contact with Islam and the subsequent invention of moveable type. As Copernicus set himself to really understand the motions of the planets he was compelled-by his entrenchment in this idea of perfect circles-to adopt an elaborate system of epicenters or wheels within wheels to try to save the illusion of perfectly circular motion. This idea of epicenters had been developed by Arabic astronomers and mathematicians and it seems Copernicus had these non-translated books, but with the relevant diagrams available to him in his study. Copernicus was also able to compare his own observations of the planets with the excellent and accurate observations of an Arab astronomer called Al Battani. Copernicus clearly understood the import of the mathematical drawings about epicenters without needing a translation out of Arabic. It seems he then applied this information directly into his heliocentric system and got all of the credit for its discovery.

So to account for the retrograde motion of Mars, Copernicus would add on several extra circles that had their centers fixed on to other places within the larger orbital circle of Mars to make the 'perfect' mathematical orbit somewhat nearer to the actual observed orbit of the planet. This idea of epicenters or extra orbital wheels got a little bit crazy-like drawing a circle with a series of straight lines-you need to keep adding more and shorter lines just to approximate a curve, but Copernicus was attempting to make his theory fit the observed data. It seems Copernicus stumbled upon the idea of the ellipse, which is the egg-shaped path that most of the planets actually move in. Then he abandoned the idea, due to his entrenched and prejudiced notion of perfect motion of the heavens. This less than perfect motion of an ellipse would be an offence to God's creation and also runs counter to Aristotle's teaching. This is an example of someone who is completely entranced with an archetype, in this case God's perfection mirrored in the perfect circles of his creation.

Ptolemy was the individual who gave us a crazy wheels-within-wheels universe and it seems even he was unsatisfied with this explanation. Ptolemy promoted the earth- centered view of things, but was compelled -because of the observation of the retrograde motions and other things -to displace the earth from the true centre of things. The theory just didn't fit the observed facts and Ptolemy knew it. He wanted an earth-centered universe, but couldn't put the earth at the true centre. Nonetheless, his concepts held sway until Arabic astronomers started doubting the accuracy of these ancient observations themselves, sometime around 800 AD. It seemed that the Arabic philosophers were less concerned with defending the Greeks than the west, probably because they had better and more complete translations of these Greek texts than the west had and Greek writers were pagans anyway - due to no fault of their own. The Arabic world had initiated the beginning of the crack in the presumed perfect wisdom of the ancients. If the ancients could be wrong or even just imprecise in their observations of the real universe, then maybe they were wrong about other things as well. Ptolemy had compiled what was considered the definitive astronomical text from the entire known Greek world and it had held sway over the west for 1500 years. It took the great insight of Copernicus, with the help of the patient observations and mathematical excellence of the Arabic world, to finally make the huge paradigm shift to the sun centered universe. The impact of this shift cannot be underestimated and we will see the ramifications of it again and again.

Enter Johannes Kepler, who accepted that the sun was at the centre of things. After obtaining even more accurate observations from a meticulous Tycho Brahe - he felt he could indeed supply proof. The interesting thing about all of this is how much useless conceptual baggage both Kepler and Copernicus had to jettison, and how much they could not bear to throw away. We were on the cusp of real science here and we must forgive these individuals for hanging on to their medieval minds. Through looking at their works, and trying to uncover their thought processes, we can peer into the window of this great transitional period of the Renaissance. In fact, we will start to see our own 'modern minds' and possibly grasp how little has changed in the world of science and dogma.

In mathematics there are five perfect solids - that is five regular solid shapes in which all of the sides of the shape are the same. They are: the cube (six squares), the three-sided pyramid or tetrahedron (four triangles), the octahedron (eight equilateral triangles), the dodecahedron (twelve Pentagons), and the icosahedrons (twenty equilateral triangles). Kepler was obsessed with the belief that the five planets in the sky (that he knew of) somehow fit into a relationship with these regular solids. God would not have created these five planets and five perfect solids unless there was some type of correlation. Kepler spent years trying to come up with the correct order of the shapes that would allow them to fit in between the planets. Quite frankly, he fudged numbers to make it work, and he seemed to have been conscious of the fact that he was lying, but he could not let go of this fixed idea throughout his life.

"If my false figures came near to the facts, this happened merely by chance.... These comments are not worth printing. Yet it gives me pleasure to remember how many detours I had to make along how many walls I had to grope in the darkness of my ignorance until I found the door which lets in the light of truth... In such manner did I dream of the truth?" – Johannes Kepler's *Letter to Herwart* - Pg. 266. *The Sleepwalkers*

This quote will end up being one of the cornerstones of this book as we move along and I will expand upon it a lot more. This is one of the best examples of someone 'intentionally' (half consciously) bending the truth to save the appearance of their theorem. You can imagine how much lonely work is involved in this research and Kepler wants to be right and show the world a beautiful new way of understanding. The math involved in his theory is so complicated that he assumes that most of his contemporaries will not be able to notice. A few slips and these mistakes probably won't matter over the long run, because Kepler is quite certain he is right about what he has developed. Kepler literally created a universe of meaning, which is built on a relationship between the planets and the five perfect solids, and he is absolutely invested in it. We will see this again and again (in Einstein's cosmological constant), and in such manner shall we dream the truth.

In the representational world of mathematics, everything is discovered in the sense of it being implicit in nature and we uncover or reveal its existence. It all exists somewhere in God's mind or in nature and we only uncover it. For example, the theorem for unending prime numbers is $1 \times 2 \times 3 \times 4 \times 5 \times 6 \times$. You can arbitrarily stop anywhere on the way toward infinity; then add 1. Therefore there must be a series of unending prime numbers, and there is. Arthur Koestler wrote out this equation on a wall in a Spanish prison, where he was held on death row, during his involvement in the Spanish Civil War in the late 30's. He seemed to have had a mystical experience of unity with all beings, as he contemplated this. The threat of death focuses the mind beautifully.

Numbers are "an archetype of order that has become conscious."
C.G. Jung *Psyche & Matter quoted* by M. Von Franz – Pg. 36.

It seems when we delve into mathematics or any of the sciences there is a suspicion that we are somehow cracking the mind of the creator, or truly peering into the essential substructure of things. This is some powerful Juju. This is one of the reasons why Pythagoras and his followers were mystics. Conversely, it boggles my mind to read how some modern physicists are trying so hard not to be mystics. When we are picking at the very fabric of the universe, it is alright to surrender to awe. When we make a discovery in the field of mathematics, we have discovered something that is 'just so' and yet we can gain confirmation of our discovery, because the theorem we have discovered can be directly applicable to the outside world, or it can be subsequently verified by anyone's independent testing. This is especially true in geometry, which was the Pythagorean specialty. Geometry seems to exist behind linguistic representation in the realm of form and occupies a special relationship to mathematics.

Kepler was born in 1564. The rigorous scientific method we have come to know had not yet been fully realized. One of the main themes Koestler tries to illuminate is how the pre enlightenment mind perceived science. However, Kepler refused to let go of concepts, such as the prefect solids being related to the planets, as their abandonment seemed to fly in the face of a perfect creation, and/or an idealized form behind the chaotic world. He was a divided individual who astride two worlds. To him mysticism, and especially astrology, seemed to be self- evident truths He made his money casting astrological charts all over Europe. I would contend that this dualism is really a keynote in the human intellectual journey. Sir Isaac Newton, who was born in 1642, might be considered as the first truly great scientist, and seemingly, a very rational individual. Yet he wrote at least as many treatises on alchemy as he did on science. It is convenient to perceive science as a constantly forward-facing venture, but in reality the ongoing enterprise of science-like everything else-is a construct and reflection of the human mind.

One of the other interesting stories in *The Sleepwalkers* is that of Galileo and his confrontation with the Catholic Church over his belief in the heliocentric system. This conflict is regularly portrayed as the titanic struggle of the truth of science against the mystic and dogmatic mumbo jumbo of the Church - the brave Galileo fighting the might of the Church with only his sling shot of truth. The wider angle of this picture is that- for the most part-the Church was fine with Galileo believing that the earth went around the sun. They wanted Galileo to restrict himself to acknowledging that it was merely a theory. The Church had some of their people on this issue as well, but it seems Galileo was a bit of a loud mouth and he really liked to press everyone's buttons. And even after being so antagonistic with the powers that be, Galileo was only confined to house arrest: not burned at the stake like Savonarola. He was free to receive visitors, mail, and more importantly, no one stopped him from doing science, if he wished.

Galileo, who truly was the father of modern science, was presumptuous enough to stand up in front of a court, convened by the Church and tell them that the burden of proof was laid on to them. He was saying that he knew the truth of planetary motion and that the Church must prove him wrong. The Church didn't seem to have objections to him holding the heliocentric system as a working hypothesis; they were much more wary of the theological implications. But as Galileo presented his case, he implied that the system that Copernicus had worked on was rigorously tested and in fact he was backing the Copernican system whole sale with its crazy wheels within wheels. *"For almost fifty years of his life, he (Galileo) had held his tongue about Copernicus, not out of fear to be burnt at the stake, but to avoid academic unpopularity. When carried away by sudden fame, he had at last committed himself. It became at once a matter of prestige to him. He had said Copernicus was right, and whoever said otherwise was belittling his authority as the foremost scholar of his time."*- Koestler *The Sleepwalkers* - Pg. 444

This discussion is not meant to belittle Galileo as one of the great men in science. (He undoubtedly was.) He did have the first telescopes and made many important and real observational discoveries through his patient scientific work. I use this example so that we can open the door to our understanding of the psychology of a proof. The FDA in the United

States allows the drug companies to argue with this same backward logic that Galileo used. In Europe, if there is the faintest whiff of controversy about a product being bad for the health of people they pull it off the shelves and the drug company has to again supply proof that it is safe. In the United States, the burden of proof can, to a certain extent, be put back on to the FDA, which has to prove that this product is not safe again. This form of proof, may not apply now, but it has been the practice that, after having passed through the FDA's testing once, that is enough. And of course, it is embarrassing for the FDA to have its shoddy work exposed. (Monsanto strong-arms a phenomenal amount of dubious things into our food chain), and of course, the drug companies have very well moneyed lobbyists to fight against any results that doesn't agree with their version of 'science'. (Again, Monsanto)

It seems that the Church's position in this scuffle with Galileo was that of cautious conservatism, which indeed it would and should be. Of course, this is the same position that the scientific community would take today. The Church would have allowed Galileo to publish his book, as long as he refrained from any theological augments over the implications of the Copernican system. Galileo was in the mood to fight and refused. It would be interesting to know how much Galileo understood about the sea change that the Copernican system subsequently initiated in the human psyche. It seems to me he was fighting a small battle with poor proof, but of course, and we will see this over and over - he was right.

The heliocentric system in the Suksma or spiritually elevated aspect was a huge revolution. If man and the earth on which he lives is not the centre of everything, and some blind force is moving the heavens and us, what then is God's role in creation? Are we a unique being put here by God and set to wonder at his creation spread about us like a glittering starry necklace? It would take a while for all of this to sink into the collective consciousness of humanity and it would also take a while for the heliocentric system to be proved definitively. But this was the beginning of the crack in the authority of the ancient Greek edifice: largely initiated by Islam, because they did not hold these pagans in such high esteem as we did. If these long understood truths/beliefs were wrong then what else might we be wrong about? Slowly, everything became open to investigation and doubt. This spirit of investigation- along with patient observation-has set us on the road to real science.

(How many fundamentalists does it take to re-screw a sun-centered universe?)

Science needed Newton to really nail down the concept of Gravity and the true laws of planetary motion. With Newton, it became evident that this was the way things actually were in the heavens and on earth. Newton would be able to develop the hypothesis of gravity and turn it into a true theory that fully encompassed all of the observed phenomena and through which we could make accurate predictions of all motion. His theory was only limited by the inaccuracy that existed in measurement. Largely due to technical limitations of the mechanical devices used for measuring anything in those times. Science needs both a build up and critical mass of accumulated data married to the conceptual leap into a proper theoretical framework. The development of printing allowed the collection and storage of identical referenced copies of information. This in turn, allowed someone like Newton to have access to that collected information, which allowed him to then put everything together. We will see this again in Einstein.

This idea of a theory is the wiggle room that some creationists use to argue against Darwin. Apparently, Darwin only gave us the theory of evolution, not the law. This is to misunderstand the meaning of a theory, and for that matter, a law. A theory is something that encompasses the observable data correctly as opposed to a hypothesis that is yet to be proven in any real way. A hypothesis is an attempt at a tentative, but working model. Both Darwin and Newton constructed correct ways of framing their understanding of the world, given the observable data that they had. Darwin didn't know about DNA and genetics. Newton only really represented gravity without actually understanding it.

Einstein also improved upon Newton's theory, but both Darwin and Newton were not wrong. They were both limited by technology. With these individuals we can observe the formation of the consciousness of a more rigorous scientific method. Newton's work gained much more attention at that time than Copernicus's work was verified independently many times and so was proven to be a correct model of planetary motion until the advent of an entirely new way of understanding the underlying structure of the universe was brought forward by Einstein. Darwin's theory of evolution is stunningly correct in almost all aspects and the subsequent understandings of genetics and DNA, etc. have only reinforced its usefulness.

Koestler's third book in his trilogy, *The Act of Creation*, deals more exclusively with the creative act itself as it occurs in science and the arts. This book made a lasting impression on me and rambled endlessly around my head. The creative act in an individual is not a plucking of something out of nothing. It is more a shuffling and rearranging or bi-associating of information within the psyche. It seems that creative people need a critical overheating of consciousness, along with an active engagement in the creative process itself. This allows the "reculer pour mieux sauter" or drawback and leap aspect of the unconscious to happen. This downloading and leaping forward ability of the conscious/unconscious can allow the metaphorical/analogist propensity of the unconscious brain to fuse a new paradigm or understanding into an expressible idea, which can be said to be a creative act.

This idea of draw back and leap is central to Koestler's understanding of the act of creation and will be one of the main themes that we will expand on as we move along. Later in the chapter on neuroscience, we will get down to some of the nuts and bolts of why this analogy is correct and how the brain creates our worldview. Creativity seems to centre on this type of tension and release. Tension can be generated in a human by external or internal sources. In the external world, the need to adapt to a new environment - politically, biologically, for example, seems to propel change. Internally it seems that boredom with the existing worldview or boredom with our own standpoint, and or, limited technique in whatever type of work we practice can be enough to initiate further change. Sex is a good metaphor or indeed a concrete example of the creative act in that it takes two people (until recently), to make a child. This need to resolve duality creates the tension that precedes the consummation of the creative act. In the teen years, just finding a partner can cause considerable tension. So constant brooding or meditation on a theme activates the lower strata of the unconscious, which jostles various information it has available. The unconscious strives to produce an answer to the dilemma and we might have a dream or simply a new idea occurs to us; we mistakenly believe that we thought of this idea ourselves. I will talk more about music specifically, because it is the field of the arts in which I am most comfortable, but these ramblings will relate to all of the arts, and in many ways, to the sciences as well.

PROOF AND THE DIFFICULTY OF MEANING

I have recently realized that my mind becomes more flexible when I drink coffee. I do most of my reading and writing in the morning while I drink coffee and I have heard that students who study for exams late at night while drinking coffee or taking caffeine should also drink coffee before they write the test. The part of the brain that has been downloading this knowledge is building these memories along with consuming coffee and the two are working synchronously. Neurons that fire together, wire together. I am also-what is called-a lark or early riser and so my mind is sharpest between 6-10 AM. People who constantly smoke dope when they play music have to relearn certain aspects of the way they perceive music. Sometimes they need to adjust their approach to playing their instrument as well, if they stop smoking dope. (I may have been in the room when this dope smoking thing had happened, but like Bill Clinton... I didn't inhale. I claim third party artistic licenses for this knowledge.) This is why some people think that the drugs are responsible for their creativity. It is largely because any creative activity is embedded in the environment that we learned its various skills, and the skills and the creative act are inseparable. If the drugs or caffeine is taken out of the equation, the brain seems to have some difficulty accessing these already learned artistic pathways with the same effortless fluidity. The mind entrains memories throughout the areas of the brain that are relevant and we subsequently retrieve them from the same places as ensembles. Although John Coltrane, Miles Davis, Peter Gabriel and Rickie Lee Jones all did great works after kicking an addiction to heroin. In fact, arguably, their best work. We will now take a look at how creativity works in the real world.

In to the Studio and Off the Page

One of the people that I greatly admire in the music/artistic world is Brian Eno. What Brian Eno is especially good at, when he is in the producer role, is focusing and generating interest in the work at hand. A chessboard only has 64 squares with which to play chess, but there are an infinite set of moves and games that can come out of this seemingly tight constriction; much like the ongoing creation of a melody from a piano that has only 88 keys. What Brian Eno likes to do is create a chess board, and leave it up to the artist to decide which move they should make. By doing this, he establishes implied direction. We cannot move the king over to the kitchen table for a discussion of metaphysics, or making a James pop record not the Eiffel Tower. There is a certain creative tyranny involved in having too many choices and I would add that true freedom is a result of constriction - more nay saying, than a field of infinite possibilities. Freedom is like a hole: it's what that is not there is important.

When Brian Eno was producing the James album *Laid,* the chessboard was that for each of the songs they decide to record, they were only allowed three tries at it, or three attempted takes, with the tape rolling. There would be discussions between takes about the 'feel' and 'groove' etc., but if the song could not be satisfactorily recorded by the third attempt, it was gone. (Arthur Koestler once said that death row was a religious hot box.)

The restriction of three attempts per song was the dynamic of the daily work. After the dinner break each evening, the band would stop work on *Laid* and start working on a second recording, which became known as, *Wah Wah*. This recording was completely improvised, but it was also organized around some structural guidelines especially as far as arranging ideas. The band might improvise around a palindrome for instance. A palindrome is a structure that ends the way it begins like the name ANNA. It is a mirrored word. One of the strengths that Brian Eno saw in the band, James was their ability to improvise and work out a lot of their musical ideas as opposed to other bands, which have a designated songwriter or song writing team. In the evening, the band were pretty much left alone in another studio with another engineer to work at the *Wah Wah* project, until the next morning when they started work on *Laid* again in the main studio with Eno.

Eno also did things like make the violin player Saul, play his violin with pencils. Eno developed all kinds of ploys to break these musician's from their habits and bring them into the present moment so that they would participate more fully in what was happening now. James held Brian Eno-quite rightly-in high regard and if he hands you pencils to play your violin, you give it a try. (Peter Gabriel took away his drummers cymbals.) It seems that Eno understands that musicians can become complacent or just plain rigid in their approach to things. They get caught up in their structural tendencies and continue to run down the same tracks and become bored. Boredom is the true enemy of good art work, just as a set of hardened arteries is the enemy of both science and religion - the heart for that matter.

While the band worked away on *Wah Wah*, Brian Eno was mixing parts of *Laid* or spreading his noufal dust, as my friend Michael likes to say. Now it seemed Brian Eno likes to work slowly and alone, but he prefers that other people work fast to keep them engaged. He created a situation for these two records in which he could have some time to work the way t he wanted. Near the end of the session Saul asked Eno what the *Wah Wah* record was all about and Eno admitted that it had been a decoy from the start. Eno felt that he could get a great performance out of the band by disciplining them to do only three takes of each song for the Laid record, even though those performances might be flawed in some way. The performance e heated up by this added pressure. But if the band were allowed to sit around in the evening and listen to these recordings they started to pick them apart and try to "improve" them by changing a note here or there, or re-sing parts, which Eno felt would impact the overall emotional truth of the songs. So he got rid of the band by engaging them in something else.

I have practiced this same three takes constriction while recording six songs for the *Fires of Second* CD and it works well. You are forced to pare down your performance and remove any extraneous frills you may have accumulated as you get closer to the last take. In the Pop world, this is probably a good thing.

This example of Eno illustrates what Koestler-to my mind-was driving at nicely. Eno forces many paradigms together, but not an infinite amount, so that things aren't left wide open. When you are trying to write a song you must focus on that song and flesh it out as it were. Casting about without an agenda or focus can be fun and exhilarating, but it rarely produces a good finished piece of work. *"Beauty is a function of truth; truth is a function of beauty. They can be separated by analysis, but in the lived experience of the creative act- and the re-creative echo in the beholder- they are inseparable, as thought is inseparable from emotion. They signal, one in the language of the brain, the other of the bowels, the moment of the Eureka cry, when 'The infinite is made to blend itself with the finite' – when eternity is looking through the window of time."* Arthur Koestler *The Act of Creation* - Pg. 333

A minor note Koestler has touched on is the function of analysis and I will again digress into a short look at this. Analysis is essentially an intellectual process where you break things apart in order to better understand their function. The word comes from the Greek root word "lysis", to unbind. Along with analysis-especially in science-is the belief that by taking something apart, you may have gained some mastery over it, or at least gained a better understanding or insight into the thing itself. Whereas, the world, or things in the world only exists as a whole unto itself within context; this is their quiddity.

So called primitive people use this type of analytic reasoning along with its related cousin sympathetic magic, to throw a curse on somebody. For instance, if you wish someone to fall in love with you, you must get a lock of their hair-an unbound piece or re-presentation of someone-and recite some sacred words to gain power over them. This act of spell-casting can occur, because of the hold that correlation has on the mind. Such is the power in our minds of the ongoing correlation between reality and words that signify it that 'the word' was God's first creation in the Bible and from God's divine words the entire world was unfolded. He was kind enough to let Adam in on some of this power trip and participate in this divine unfolding in that he allowed him to name the animals, or have dominion over them by naming them (this is the intellectual seed bed of our ongoing abuse of nature). We can see this mastery of concepts through naming in small children when they learn the name of a new object. For a child, an object that is named is part of their belongings or understanding. Once it has been named, that is enough, because the distinction between a small child and the greater external world is blurred. When they control the concept, they control the thing symbolized by it. (I will refer to this overall concept as Land Naming)

Now Brian Eno-I think-understands very well what the creative malaise of a pop band might be and this would be part of his intellectual analysis, which might be quite a brilliant observation in itself, but this observation doesn't create a great new recording. Eno's master stroke is in creating a path forward that is both flexible and open, but also creates or implies direction by restricting infinite freedom. The drummer for James (David Baynton-Power) mentions in an interview that if things are going well, Eno would just leave the band alone. But as soon as they got stuck, he would interfere with problem-solving strategies, or in severe cases, where no one could agree, he would impose a decision as the ultimate power broker and then move on. Ultimately, Brian Eno is a fairly hands-off producer, but this is only one style among many.

Look in the country and every city, you won't find a statue of a committee.

One of my favorite of problem-solving strategies was Eno's deck of cards. Written on his deck of some 80 cards, there were a series of ambiguous or sometimes very precise instructions. The idea is that you randomly pick a card and honor the instructions. One card might say, *"take something away"* or *"go back three steps"*. It was left up to you to determine how to interpret this information. Much like the Oracle at Delphi, the answers are not necessarily explicit, but they are to be obeyed as a way of moving forward. This card strategy is very reminiscent of the Chinese, I Ching. When you throw the I Ching, you are looking for an answer to a question and the process of throwing the I Ching, allows you to access the collective unconscious or the greater flow that is manifest within that specific moment; hopefully to obtain the correct answer or at least break the stalemate of your indecision. The unconscious we are talking about here is the unknown or objective third party that is unrealized and therefore not conscious. (I can feel you scientists getting steamy on my neck).

Koestler explores all manners of creative endeavor in his books in order to illustrate his understanding of how the human mind tries to perceive or represent truth/reality in various disciplines. In terms of language, Koestler illustrates how the different usage of words applies to the different creative disciplines. As explored in *Rose Glass* (Chapter 5) the correlations between language and thought. Koestler contends that language in science suffers from over precision, in that concepts like space or time seem to have an obvious meaning. Galileo thought that a planet left to itself would continue travelling in a circle, because to move in a straight line would allow it to travel in an infinite direction, which was unthinkable to him in that space-as a concept-must have a definable boundary somewhere. We now can see that space as a concept is much broader than subsequently thought. Space itself hasn't changed, but the meaning of the word space has changed greatly. The initial conception of space was married to an implied linguistic constriction. This constriction is partially a result of our sense of ownership over the concept behind the word. (This is largely the result of the fact that the left brain has dominion over linguistic representation or denotative language. I will stop entering in the narrative as much as possible, but I wish to explain that this bilateralization is at the root of much of this discussion and the whole idea will be explored in much greater depth as we move along. Bear with me.) There is now-floating about-an idea that space is actually filled up with dark matter and so it is actually not space at all but a very thinly populated medium.

Conversely, when writing a book or poetry, language suffers when not being specific enough, which is in fact, its strength Lit is very difficult to give fictional characters real feelings, because feelings are largely inarticulate, and hence nonverbal. They may or may not reside in the author's head. A writer must learn to explain or imply things indirectly through cunning and metaphors or by using the mirror of the environment in which the characters are situated. Film is particularly well-suited to display emotions, because so much can be implied visually by a good actor without saying anything. If the actor is good or she is just plain observant of the human situation, the language used gains in implied meaning by being embodied in context. The inability to accurately represent nuanced feelings has to do in part with the nature of the mind and body. What Koestler is driving at is that part of creative bi-association that happens when different ways of conceptualizing the world run into each other, creating tension. For example, we might become even more engaged in a book, because we have a desire to understand or pierce through the inherent ambiguity of an author's language. (ee cummings) Or we may need to understand some external process in the world simply because we are endlessly curious.

Koestler goes on to site Einstein's willingness to challenge the very roots of implied concepts, such as space and time in order to reorder the paradigm itself. Einstein once said there was no good reason not to assume that something dropped from our hand, couldn't fly up and away from the earth, even though everything prior to this instant, has been pulled toward earth by gravity. In essence, Einstein sought to take nothing for granted. No word has absolute sway over a concept.

In creative writing this ambiguous bi-association can occur by the juxtaposition of different metaphors. The simplest way is by using 'like' to spell it out for the reader where a simple description would be tedious. *"Her hair was like a shower of stars cast from God's open window."* As opposed to, *"She had nice hair. It was blond and looked very clean."* Poetry and religious writing, and for that matter, all early prehistoric written works, thrive on this more open linguistic ambiguity so that the reader is drawn into what they are reading. When the reader is engaged in metaphor, they are also participating in the creative act of re-constructing the metaphor itself. The inherent ambiguity and room for multiple interpretations remains, which then gives the reader room for ongoing participation or engagement. Wittgenstein, as we will see, has gained much philosophical traction from exploring the ambiguous nature of language and very much else.

What I am driving at-as it relates to my earlier discussion of Jung-is that this bi-associative aspect of the mind or the reshuffling of different methods of expression is a natural extension of the way in which the mind works (especially the unconscious). In dreams we see very clearly how the mind can grasp onto different apparently mundane images and reorganize them to express itself. Jung saw Freud as an antiquated Austrian customs official. Jung had to reinterpret this metaphor, although implicit in Jung's understanding of this dream was the assumption and/or constructed belief system, that there was a meaning to be uncovered in the unconscious. Science has an advantage over psychology in that it can test its hypothesis (even if it takes years to develop the technology to do so), explicitly in the world to arrive at a proof. However, it arrives at a proof through constricting its focus or narrowing its view of the world. Of course, we saw that Freud and Jung differed over what was the proper form of interpretation, or specifically, which interpretation of the image of the skulls in Jung's dream was the correct one. In the art/science of psychology there is only the unfolding of time itself to provide the efficacy of an interpretation or its pragmatic usefulness.

Jung felt that Freud had created a definite agenda in his dream interpretation method and that his agenda had ultimately become too narrow and somewhat dogmatic. Jung felt that Freud practiced an essentially reductive attitude toward dream interpretation (Freud always seemed to arrive at some sort of sexual explanation for everything. I do not wish to keep denigrating Freud I am using his perceived image and also Jung's views of him to illustrate a larger point.) Jung, to my mind correctly, saw sex as only a part of the human experience. Although, admittedly, a large part in the post Victorian area of the late 19th early 20th century when Freud was seeing his patients. Jung's method was much more integrative and sought to construct a way forward.

Just off the page

"Some people find psychic phenomena of no interest, which is fair enough. Most people are not very interested in the scientific study of the behavior of cuttlefish, or research into the genetics of mosses. Yet no one becomes emotionally antagonistic to cuttlefish or moss research." -Rupert Sheldrake, *The Sense of Being Stared At.* - Pg. 7

Koestler in his more mystic leaning was inclined to challenge inherent concepts as well and this brings me to the last book by Koestler that I would like to talk about. *The Roots of Coincidence* deals with ESP, synchronicity and the fringy boarders of modern physics. He starts the book by talking about the many scientific studies that occurred in the sixties on various para-psychological phenomena such as telepathy, etc., by Dr. J.B. Rhine and Professor H.J. Eysenck.

"Unless there is a gigantic conspiracy involving some thirty University departments all over the world and several highly respected scientists in various fields. Many of them originally hostile to the claims of the physical researchers, the only conclusion the unbiased observer can come to must be that there does exists a small number of people who obtain knowledge existing in other people's minds, or in the outer world, by means as yet unknown to science. This should not be interpreted as giving any support to such notions as survival after death, philosophical idealism, or anything else..." H. J. Eysenck, quoted by Koestler in *Roots* - Pg. 14. And here we have a real problem: all throughout history some people have believed that telepathy is real and many psychologists were also tempted to accept it as a real phenomenon. Freud begrudgingly gave it some wiggle room. In the thirty-odd years since *Roots of Coincidence* was published, we really haven't moved very far along in determining whether it actually exists or not. I will say that there are

significant cash prizes offered for anyone who can definitely prove ESP/telepathy, and no one has claimed these prizes.

One of the main problems seems to be the framing of a theory that, for science at least, explains the physical/causal mechanism by which ESP or telepathy could work. I will not make excuses, but it did take an Einstein to actually frame the explanation of how gravity worked. Newton could not come up with a rational mechanism for action at a distance, i.e., gravity. Newton just knew what the facts were. (It seems that Newton conceived of gravity as some kind of invisible whip.) But it seems telepathy can endlessly be discounted as a non-fact, or at least, can be quibbled over until an absolute proof seems to have vanished against the endless circumstantial evidence. Cigarette companies have been doing this type of shit-spreading for years. When people try to prove cigarettes cause cancer, they attack the evidence and drag it through the courts, but I think any reasonable person would concede that cigarettes cause cancer. Beyond a reasonable doubt is the best that we have now. Within the Hindu and Buddhist literature, it is taken for granted that a person can develop mind-reading abilities and some schools of religious teaching encourage these abilities, while others urge the pupil to move beyond these "tricks".

My biggest beef here is that if you listen to a skeptic talk about this type of thing they have already made up their mind about whether it is true or not. You will hear a lot of statements like: people want to believe there is another mysterious layer to the universe because they hold on to childishly unscientific modes of reasoning. ESP is-nothing but-a coincidence or a reflection of or intentional hoodwinking by very skilled observers of human nature etc. and the human mind has then supplied meaning backward into it. The more I listen to skeptics the more I am fascinated by the fact that they cannot definitively prove that ESP doesn't exist. They are in the same situation as rabid atheists and they have presumed that they have a scientifically unassailable and usually self-righteously antagonistic position and they presume that science completely backs them up. It's not their job to supply a proof it is sciences job to supply an active assertion in the negative. The way I see it is that they are making a negative metaphysical statement and because it is negative it is somehow 'more true' than a positive assertion of say, God or ESP. Conversely, like a creationist, I have only supplied a form of double negative in my argument, which is not a positive assertion of a proof which is what I'm ultimately here for.

On the other hand, science has to work in this way and someone seeking to prove that ESP exists must submit their proof to a qualified panel of peer review. You cannot prove that something like ESP exists while using poor scientific methods and defective reasoning. There are facts in the world and it is the art of science that seeks to construct a way of looking at the world that reflects a proper interpretation of the facts. But, the cornerstone of science is to definitively uncover the underlying causation. This highly successful way of working is based on our ability to deconstruct phenomena and express our understanding through the use of logic and is broadly known as scientific materialism. There are correct ways of collecting and interoperating data based upon double blind methods, etc. A collected panel of peer review will be able see through poor scientific reasoning and/or shoddy fact collection very easily.

The skeptic may go on to argue that humans have inside their heads an archaic way of thinking that would always seek to construct meaning out of mistaken causation. We might look into the heavens and imagine that there is a correlation between a celestial event and a situation that has occurred in our own lives. We then seek to tie these events together by constructing a worldview that satisfies our recognition of this observed correlation by retroactively implying some form of causation. We can construct a vast tapestry of observed correlation that may seem to gain weight by its very breath, but the reality is that we still don't have proof. Scientists, in turn, have sought to cast out this type of foolishness with such zealousness, that they have endeavored to convince themselves and us that no form of God could possibly exist. Yet they also have no proof with which to backup their ongoing claim. They also reason with weak arguments based on 'belief'. The main argument of science would seem to be a form of Ockham's razor. We should not multiply additional terms unnecessarily or choose the hypothesis with the fewest assumptions. Therefore, God is extraneous and there must be a unified field theory. I don't see that these two ideas are completely incompatible.

It is my contention (stated over and over again ad nauseam, in this book) that the will or urge, or delusion to seek meaning in the world is the inherited reflex of our evolutionary heritage. It is a psychological fact and we are that very meaning. The scientific ethos is very counterintuitive to our metaphoric mind and we are, to a very large degree, the product of our brain's inner workings, and the inner mystic seeps out all around us. We shall meet this inner mystic again as we explore the ethereal and abstract branches of theoretical physics. This doesn't mean that we have to embrace illogic or our non-rationality as if it were a poor step-cousin that we take under our coat with pity, because pity's dark side is arrogance. My contention is that this type of meaning, seeking illogic, is where a great swath of our creativity is and we would root it out of our mind to our own great impoverishment. Science might seek to demonize the irrational with the same fervor that fundamentalist lambaste Darwin, but this is again the rejection of their own shadow. The real trick is to create the ongoing structure of our mutual embrace and I would contend that God's hand will seek the backside of our head, for our impertinence.

"If God is dead, show me the corpse." - Me

Tell Me a Nice Story

In his book, *Freedom in Exile*, the Dalai Lama tells the story of his final moments before he escaped from Tibet. Obviously, he was under considerable strain at this point. He was uncertain, if he should remain and try to negotiate with the Chinese government or attempt to escape in order to consolidate his position elsewhere. I will quote him extensively here.

"It was at around this point that I consulted the Nechung oracle, which was hurriedly summoned. Should I stay or should I try to escape? What was I to do? The oracle made it clear that I should stay and keep open a dialogue with the Chinese."

The Dalai Lama was unsure of this advice and performed another form of divination called the Mo. This divination confirmed the previous oracle's decision that he should stay. He then consulted the oracle a second time, some days later and the answer to him was the same: stay and negotiate. Some of the people of Lhasa were starting to protest the Chinese invasion and things were getting quite tense. The Dalai Lama then received a letter from Chinese officials, telling him that they were preparing to "attack the crowd and shell the Norbulingka." This was the building that he was staying in at the time. The Chinese wished the Dalai

Lama to indicate on a map of the palace where he was so that they would not accidentally shell it and kill him. The Dalai Lama replied to the Chinese officials, trying to buy time, but he knew the situation was very bad and that many people could now be killed trying to protect him. "The following day, I again sought the council of the oracle. To my astonishment, he shouted, 'Go! Go! Tonight!' The medium, still in his trance, then staggered forward and, snatching up some paper and a pen, wrote down , quite clearly and explicitly, the route that I should take out of the Norbulingka, down to the last Tibetan town on the Indian border. That done, the medium, a young monk named Lobsang Jigme, collapsed in a faint, signifying that Dorje Drakden had left his body. Just then, as if to reinforce the oracle's instructions, two mortar shells exploded in the marsh outside the northern gate of the Jewel Park." The Dalai Lama then confirms the oracle's decision by performing the Mo divination again, which indeed, agrees with what the oracle has said. Forty eight hours after the Dalai Lama left the palace, the Chinese began to shell it and also machine gunned the defenseless crowd that was gathered about. At this point, the Dalai Lama realizes the impossibility of negotiation with these people.

I think we can quite comfortably say that the Dalai Lama believes in divination. I won't say that I have read all of his work, but I will say that he seems like a more than reasonable individual. There are a number of interesting things going on in this particular story: First: is the way that Tibetans talk about these types of phenomena, ESP, etc. The Tibetans approach them as a matter of fact. I will illustrate this with more stories later. Second: is that the decision to leave seemed to arrive at the last minute. The Dalai Lama had no preparations for this journey and he was unsure if he should leave at all. He seems to have left at just the right moment and obviously made good his escape. This is reading backward into history though and it is hard to discern what the oracle knew or didn't know in terms of the overall external situation. What is interesting is that the oracle changed his mind and the Dalai Lama's own divination confirmed this change. Of course, the Dalai Lama could be completely constructing this 'story' for our entertainment or tailoring the narrative consciously or unconsciously to fit his agenda. Or, if we concede that he is not bending the truth maybe he simply remembered it all wrong. But I would add that this is the type of heated memory experience that stays with you.

I personally am unsure as to the place given to oracles throughout Buddhist history, but in the Tibetan tradition, they are used regularly and accepted. When Buddhism came to Tibet, it displaced the older shamanic tradition called 'Bon' and, instead of killing off the older tradition, they absorbed some of it into the Tibetan Buddhist tradition. These oracles specifically are part of the much older Bon shamanic tradition, and shamanism was still a functioning religious tradition well into the communist era, all throughout northern Siberia and Mongolia, and presumably still is, although the Communists could be quite tenacious in their suppression of religion. This particular oracle seemed to forecast the future by accessing some unconscious persona/knowledge that the Dalai Lama calls Dorje Drakden. I would presume that this is the spirit associated with divination. We shall call it the collective unconscious in order to make it more antiseptic as is the patronizing western intellectual way. What is hard to know is how much intuition or real feeling for the situation this monk had while he was in a state of divination, but I would say that this truly was a life and death situation and any decision that came forth was to be taken very seriously. We are not dealing with party card tricks here. So we have the super heated consciousness that seems to activate the unconscious and propel it toward creative integration, we can quibble over representational details later.

The odds on the craps table are something like 49.5 for you and 50.5 for the casino. This means over the long haul the casino will win. Craps is the best odds you will get in a casino. Slot machines have much worse odds. Something like 80 percent of the money taken in at casinos is from slot machines, because the odds are electronically adjusted and quite obviously stacked against you. We constantly seek to construct a narrative that implies what we wish to see. Now, if people can control the dice throw through psycho kinesis, or somehow their minds can affect a physical change in the actual dice themselves, how the casino can set these odds at all? Casinos use accurate statistics that extend over very long periods of time. What I can also tell you is that gamblers certainly 'believe' that they can affect the odds. (Cognitive dissonance: our ability to discount that which disagrees with our opinion.)

I met a man driving a bus once who told me that he would meditate for hours before he went to the casino to throw dice. He also said he was quite rich from doing it. He was driving a bus, so I was a bit suspect, but he did say he blew the money living large. Such is the gambler's lifestyle. One of the things that Koestler points out is that when people are given dice to throw, they throw much better in the first five minutes of the experiment when they are emotionally engaged, than they do for the rest of the experiment. If you are asked to throw one thousand dice roles, you will get bored in such a situation. Casinos want you to stay a long time and drink their free booze, and suck in their over-oxygenated atmosphere, because over the long haul, you will become mentally tired, hopefully drunk and become disengaged, and lose your money. This is probably how the odds become even and come around to the casino's favor. More than that though, you *will* lose money over the long haul.

In *The Sense of Being Stared At*, Rupert Sheldrake offers up a vast amount of evidence from research that he and other scientists have been doing in the field of ESP over the last 15 years or so. I was unaware of this book when I began this book and just recently read it. He is making explicit what I have suspected for a very long time and that is, you *can* perform scientific research and gain quantifiable results when studying telepathy and ESP phenomena. In his book, he offers overwhelming anecdotal evidence that telepathy exists and that it is probably a natural evolutionary aspect of the mind itself not just in man, but in many creatures, I will have more opportunities to return to his thinking later on.

The bigger picture of these types of extra mental phenomena has been tackled by a number of people, including Carl Jung and noted physicist, Wolfgang Pauli whom published a book together called, *The Interpretation of Nature and the Psyche*. It was really two books: Jung's paper was *Synchronicity* and Pauli's was on *The Influence of Archetypal Ideas* on the Scientific Theories of Kepler - the same Kepler we touched on earlier. An attempt to treat this topic with any sense of decency always garners derogatory comments from the scientific community. Although, a scientific proof is difficult, it shouldn't be impossible. Most of the proof lies in anecdotal evidence, which of course, stands or falls on the reputation of the narrator. Science does not function on anecdotal evidence. Here's another story to whet your palate, as we sharpen our long rational knives.

In 1909, Jung went to visit Freud and he was curious to know Freud's opinion about ESP, which at that time seems he had rejected. Jung continues:

"While Freud was going on this way, I had a curious sensation. It was as if my diaphragm was made of iron and was becoming red-hot- a glowing vault. And at that moment, there was such a loud report in the bookcase, which stood next to us, that we both startled with alarm, fearing the thing was going to topple over us. I said to Freud: "There, that is an example of a so called catalytic exteriorization phenomenon." "Oh come," he exclaimed. "That is sheer bosh." "It is not," I replied. "You are mistaken, Herr Professor. And to prove my point I predict now that in a moment there will be another loud report!" Sure enough, no sooner had I said the words than the same detonation went off in the bookcase."

Jung had many experiences that fell astride this realm of psycho physical interaction, and being an open-minded scientist, he tried to frame a theory that could, in some way, explain these phenomena. The book that he wrote was, *Synchronicity An Acausal Connecting Principle*. Acausal means without apparent cause or not causally connected in a strictly A+B+C kind of way. Acausal events are relatively synchronous, not absolutely synchronized. Physical science is based on causality. This is the billiard ball way that things impart energy and connect to each other. (The book to begin with is *Psyche and Matter* again by Marie Louise von Franz. She is marginally easier to read than Jung.) In Darwinian terms causality is the arduous process by which we evolved from lower life forms, due to a combination of environmental pressures and random mutation. The process of evolution is seen as just that: a causal process whereby we slowly build upon variations through cause and effect.

Jung wishes to explore phenomena that are connected to each other by our observation or participation in the event, and our subsequent or implicit recognition of there being a meaningful connection. There is no strict causal connection only a correlation. I will discuss what synchronicity is not, for a few paragraphs, before we explore what it is more fully.

As science builds up our understanding of things, the corner stone on which it builds its scientific proof is the scientist ability to reproduce results. Experimentation ideally is a repeatable experience in order that it can be independently verified. If I show statistical proof that out of one hundred people who smoked heavily for twenty years, 60 of them got lung cancer that is something. If I can prove that out of a million people who smoked for 20 years, 600 thousand got lung cancer that is somewhat more impressive and seemingly more convincing. We can safely say that cigarette smoking for 20 years will give you a 60 percent chance of getting lung cancer. (I have made these stats up as an example. I quit smoking and I simply feel better. That's enough reason.) The wiggle room in the proof is in establishing the direct link between smoking cigarettes and getting lung cancer as a fact. Scientists need to establish the direct causal connection between cigarettes and lung cancer. It is difficult to prove conclusively that other various environmental substances weren't also involved. These other things include all of the car and industrial pollutants that we are exposed to every day. But to any reasonable judge, it seems that the cigarette companies were/are being extremely disingenuous, if they claim that smoking doesn't increase the risk of getting cancer.

Now I can prove that the half life of plutonium is ten thousand years through analyzing many different samples of plutonium, and establishing that half of the atoms in any sample of plutonium will break down making it less radioactive by half, after ten thousand years. I then have a scientific rule or theorem. This is the essence of statistical data. It represents a collection of verifiable facts. What is not encompassed in this set of facts is what happened to the other 40 percent of people who didn't get cancer or exactly why anyone person got cancer at all. The weight of the statistic is relatively mute on the *why* of things. This is where the strictness of a peer review becomes important, because there are a number of ways of interoperating conclusions out of raw data. For instance, it is very difficult to prove beyond a doubt that smoking alone has caused cancer in an individual. We also don't know why plutonium takes exactly that long to achieve half life and how the atoms know that they should be breaking down in such a well-timed sequence. In truth, why is a question that is unanswerable in a strictly scientific framework? We end up presenting endless chains of causality as an explanation and all of these chains must, out of necessity, restrict context to be represented at all. It seems that radioactive material tends to break down in cascades. In other words plutonium doesn't break down one atom every second. It will break down fifteen atoms in a second and none for fourteen more seconds, but it will achieve its half life target on time and on budget. How this happens is only vaguely understood (and not at all by me). This is where scientists use terms like quantum (which is to some extent understood), or instinct (which is almost not understood at all). It is like one hand clapping into a black box.

What synchronicity is trying to encompass is an acknowledgment of the singularity, or an explicit recognition of the unique event that is not flattened out by statistics. Synchronicity is elevating the unique event as perceived by an individual, or explicitly recognizing events that hold meaning, but would get smoothed out by statistical averages - the noise around the mean. Indirectly, this is the reassertion of the primacy of the individual experience, which science tries to remove from the equation when observing nature. We will see later that it is almost impossible to remove ourselves completely out of the causal chain, and so if synchronicity is infrared, and science is ultraviolet, they have or can come around and touch each other again in things like the uncertainty principle.

Science proceeds on the assumption that there is a perceivable order to everything and that this order can be framed in a language. The language of choice has been discovered to be primarily mathematical, especially in the realm of physics. So, physical phenomena can be framed within the field of mathematical formalism, or can be made to conform to a series of natural numbers i.e., a phenomenon analyzed and framed causally can be quantified and explored from within a mathematical framework. This translation of nature into language (math) is the guiding scientific paradigm, which seems to me to be an archetypal idea, in that it is a reflection of a construct of the human mind that has been discovered or perhaps metaphorically pried from the mind of God. This method has proven to be a very effective way to understand the world without God in it. It seems that there is an intrinsic mathematical truth.

An example of this perceived mathematical structure that we have uncovered is geometry. An even more spectacular and specific one is the periodic table in chemistry, which appears to be a particularly stunning example of the just-so nature of nature. By putting all of the elements on to pieces of paper, and endlessly arranging them on a wall, it was realized that there was an inherent order: the well known periodic table. The recognition of this underlying order also helped us to see how the inner structure of atoms affects the makeup of each of the elements. The periodic table is one of the best examples of the interconnection of intuitive and sensate reasoning. Another example would be in music: the explicitly realized harmonic relationship called, 'the circle of fifths', which is too convoluted to explain here. Musicians should be rightly dumbfounded by this naturally occurring relationship. I'm pretty sure Bach was. Instead, these profound underlying unities are simply taught in school as the way things are. My point is why are things this way and not any other? The question why is almost always an emotionally loaded question and reason usually leaves the room with its entrance.

To illustrate how synchronicity falls outside of this type of scientific formalism, I shall quote a story from M von Franz: "*I had a female analysand who was extremely suicidal. When I went off on my summer vacation, I was concerned over how she would get through this period without analysis. I did, however, take my vacation. I had made her solemnly promise that she would write to me if she had any kind of trouble.*

"*One morning, I was chopping wood and had these thoughts (I was able to reconstruct my thought process precisely later). This wood is still wet. I'll pile it up at the rear so that it won't be used first and will still have a chance to dry out. This was a rather long thought process that could be completely causally connected with my activity. Then suddenly, I saw this patient before me and thought about her. This completely disrupted the flow of my thoughts. I felt directly how this other thing broke in on my thoughts. I thought: What could that woman suddenly want from me? Why am I thinking about her? Then I asked myself if I could have somehow gotten to the thought of her from my preoccupation with the wood. There was no association path from the wood to her. I went back to the wood chopping and again her image was there- this time with a feeling of urgent danger. At that point, I put aside my axe, closed my eyes, and thought: Should I take my car and drive to her immediately? Then I got the quite definite feeling: no, it would be too late. Then I sent a telegram: "Don't do anything foolish," with my signature. Later it came out that the telegram reached her two hours later. At that moment she had just gone into the kitchen and turned on the gas valve. At that point the doorbell rang, the postman delivered the telegram, and she was naturally so struck by the coincidence that she turned the gas valve back off and is now -thank god- still among us."* Psyche and Matter - Pg. 24

There is a direct perceivable link between these events, but it is one of mental cohesion. We appreciate that the telegram saved this woman life, but in terms of causal connections there is none. There is only the 'psychic' connection between M. von Franz and the scene unfolding in the future. The easiest explanation is to say that this whole story is conveniently fudged or possibly that the narrative was unconsciously organized later to imply our desired implication. Or we can go right off the chart and say M. von Franz is some unhinged conspiracy theorist or something like that, but I honestly believe there is little to be gained from such hubris on our part. Thousands of yogis alive in India and throughout history are telling us that we can achieve a blissful state of union with God in our lifetime by doing yoga. And the whole Indian subcontinent has believed and endlessly elaborated on the collected wisdom of this manifold vision for well over four thousand years. Maybe they have something. There is no room in this story for some form of statistical justification. M von Franz didn't save one out of three analysands 50 percent of the time. It is a unique event that has meaning without a direct causal connection. We cannot abstract the human element out of the occurrence. This is the difficulty of meaning.

I will side rail the discussion for a second to point out, for me, one of the more interesting parts of Koestler's *Roots of Coincidence*. Koestler cannot resist sniping at Jung and his sniping will round out the picture that we are building just a bit: such is the delicious nature of Koestler's ego, or in such smallish manner, shall we dream the truth.

Koestler is referring here to Jung: *"He tried to get around the time paradox by saying that the unconscious mind functions outside of the physical framework of space-time. Thus precognitive experiences are 'evidently not synchronous, but are synchronistic since they are experienced as psychic images in the present as though the objective event already existed."* One wonders why Jung created these unnecessary complications by coining a term, which implies *simultaneity, and then explaining that it does not mean what it means. But this kind of obscurity combined with verbosity runs through much of Jung's writing."* Pg. 95 *"It is painful to watch how a great mind, trying to disentangle itself from the causal chain of materialistic science, gets entangled in its own verbiage."* Pg. 98 *"Like theologians who start from the premise that the mind of God is beyond human understanding and then proceed to explain how the mind of God works. They postulate an acausal principle, and proceeded to explain it in pseudo-causal terms."* - Pg. 98. Well you get the idea. I feel I have also babbled on in is this fashion.

I think what Jung's problem here was that it is very hard to try to proffer a proof or a confirmation of his theory without using a scientific framework, i.e., representing it in language. Jung did submit his statistical evidence in the book *Synchronicity*, to a mathematician for analysis, but one might presume that it was a like-minded mathematician. (I am also not aware of what state the rigors of statistical evidence were in 1952, but one would presume it was well worked out.) Jung repeatedly stated that he was an empiricist or that his knowledge was based on the senses, and therefore, was experiential (based on lived experience). As pointed out earlier by Sheldrake, the scientific community gets quite huffy about this type of research and I think Jung felt he really had no air tight and absolutely provable evidence to offer up to explain these occurrences, but on the other hand he was personally, absolutely convinced from his own experiences, that this type of telepathic phenomena exists.

I will say that reading *Synchronicity* is not an easy task. I read twice and it is very convoluted and dry (this is me struggling against my own typology). I found that Jung is a far more pleasurable read in most other works, especially his seminars that have been published in recent years. In a seminar he is free to meander and associate, and is less verbose in these formats. But a good understanding of his earlier work will greatly profit you when reading his later seminars. In the seminar format, he is talking largely to Jungians and there is a presumption that you are within his paradigm.

I think Jung coined the term synchronicity so that he did not have to drag in the baggage of other terms like synchronous with its causal implications. It is obvious from Koestler's snipe he was trying to intimate synchronization, but within a non-causal relationship. Throughout this book, I will highlight a lot of people talking about intuition and or sensate thinking, but almost all of them have a different frame of references or referents in terms of terminology. Sometimes you need to create a new term to help to delineate a new aspect of an older concept; for instance, I will constantly come back to the term intuition instead of saying right brain or preconscious recognition, for example. This whole area of acausal relationships is a very difficult subject to get at. Koestler does an admirable job and I have great respect for him, but he seems compelled to champion, on one hand, a more strict scientific reasoning. I think Koestler is sniping at Jung to bolster his own credentials in some way. After all, they are both writing books on, and about, what was at that time, considered fringe science, but Koestler is putting on a thicker veneer of scientific skepticism. Personally, I'm not so sure that constantly adhering to strict reason and/or scientific rationalism is the absolute beacon that we can use to peer into the darkness of nature.

Interestingly though after writing this line, I stopped writing for the day and went wandering about in my real life and I was troubled by my presumption. Later that afternoon I was listening to Canada's CBC Radio and they conveniently had an interview with Karen Armstrong who was talking about the Bible. Her immediate discussion was about how in the modern fundamentalist world, the *Book of Revelations* is being read as a literal ironclad blueprint of the end of times. (The book to read is, *The Bible a Biography*. Ms. Armstrong's simple, even handed humanity is profound.) The larger point that she was driving at was, in the west there has been two ways of attaining truth: mythos and logos. Logos is the scientific or rational method. Mythos is the intrusion of the eternal into everyday. If someone dies, it is just a fact that they are dead this is logos. Mythos would help you to link up this individual death with the eternal and recurring death of the human race, such as Christ's death. This wider perspective helps us to believe or realize that death is not the end. This realization may compel us to channel our energy into starting a foundation in our loved one's name, or work toward a cure for cancer, for instance.., By doing this, we give the individual's death greater and ongoing meaning, or simply to keep his or her memory alive. Mythos is intrinsically holistic and seeks to provide a larger structure of psychic truth to all aspects of life. Again, it is the collective voice of thousands of years of evolution coming from the human psyche. Mythos is the public dream, where as dreams are a private myth.

I was thinking that I had really over-stepped my boundary as a disinterested narrator by taking a swipe at Rationalism and Reason. After all, the rise of logos has been nothing less than spectacular over the last five hundred years. What I am driving at in my circuitous manner is that everything has at least two aspects. The Sthula or prosaic aspect of 'apparent' logos thinking has provided the literal-minded fundamentalist thinkers with the tools to side-rail the religious dialogue.

"I'll buy shoes for everyone, even you, and I'll still go barefoot"- Bob Dylan

Jung, in part, saw Christ as a symbol that participated in the archetype of the self, by which I mean the greater Self or the potential to which we can aspire. The Christ figure is the main western symbol of the wholly integrated personality, etc. Jung constantly reasserts: 'The Mythos' as psychologically meaningful. This is partially a reassertion of the feeling or relational aspect of life. We relate to and have feelings for, specific things and these things have meaning for you. So what I am driving at is that we can frame all of the writings about Christ in many different ways and all of these ways are an exploration of a very deep archetype that is ultimately a reflection of us. Consciousness is polishing a mirror. I would also add the caveat that we could always say more and any one interpretation must be recognized as tentative. This is the idea that we bear witness to our savior, which means we look inside and see it for ourselves and also we can tell other people, if we wish.

"Look under a rock and I am there, cleave unto a piece of wood and I am there" -Gospel of Thomas

My overall impression is that Mr. Koestler could not let go of the guideline of logos and to my mind he takes Jung to task for the same attitude that he is ultimately representing. Koestler doesn't want to be accused of obscurantism and yet he writes extensively about fringe science. I know exactly how he feels.

In the biography, *Living with Koestler*: (1950), his first wife Mamaine Paget took Koestler's handwriting to a mystic or analyst who said that Koestler's handwriting showed that he was, *"rather materialistic, but he is now becoming more religious."* – Pg. 125. It is interesting in itself, that his wife would do this. All of Koestler's scientific and non-political works were as yet to be written at this point, so he was a yet to be mystic. Koestler was a fairly ambiguous and conflicted man (aren't we all), who also had a very ambiguous relationship with his own Jewish heritage. He seemed to have rejected it completely-after some struggling-and of course, we can read all sorts of things into this if we wish. My ongoing contention is that if we throw out our relationship to God, we might just go on to write a book called, *Ghost in the Machine* or later a book about *The Thirteenth Tribe of Israel*, where we discuss a very arcane period in Jewish history. (His point in this book is that the thirteenth tribe of Israel are a tribe of Kazar's, who accepted the Jewish faith.) We may even join the very popular religious cult of communism and then go on to become its most strident critic and heretic. Who knows what antics we might get in to? The king of angst, Jean Paul Sartre, became a speed–the drug-addict, when he threw God out. Physician, heal thyself.

Jung was swimming in the mythological sea for long enough to know that we could only build up a mythos truth slowly by analogy and comparison. This is the key to an intellectual understanding of the concept of the archetypes, as opposed to an experience of them, in that they need to be realized through comparison (look at a million paintings you will know a good one every time). This is the type of symbolic representational thinking that the mind does so well. What Jung does throughout his work, and especially, in the seminars is endlessly circle around the same themes casting more and more light on them. This allows the reader to participate. This is the mythological method and it allows the individual to experience truth firsthand through an inner recognition of the analogy and their own individual comparison, strengthening the metaphor. Again, Jung's scientific outlook was based on empiricism, which can only hold a proof that is experiential. I would put Koestler's swipe down to temperament. It looks like a little scholarly backbiting to me. I can remember being quite precious about both of these authors, as I was growing up and it always irked me that Koestler took this swipe, so much so that I am still talking about it.

Well: How Did I Get Here

This brings us back to another aspect of psychoanalysis called 'transference', which in turn will lead us back to *Synchronicity*. In the analytic situation a person must be lead to their realizations. If the analyst just gives the patient all of the answers, there is no hard won truth and the analysand will probably just reject the handout of information anyway. The dragon must protect the jewels. There may be a tendency for some patients to start to see the analyst as the repository of all wisdom, especially with someone like Jung who in his later life, was quite a towering figure. This can create a discipleship where the analysand becomes far too dependent on the analyst. Or, the analysand will reject every bit of wisdom given to them as they struggle to assert their own independence. This specific aspect of analyses is known as transference, which is the result of a projection from the analysand to the analyst or vice versa. Mixed in with this projection can be a lot of personal baggage. For example, the patient may, more or less, unconsciously align the doctor with the image they have of their father or the father they wish they had, or the father they disliked. Or conversely, the projection may occur on the doctor's side of the relationship, because the analyst is having a hard time working with a physically ugly, astoundingly beautiful, extremely successful person and or annoying person. These projected unconscious illusions or genuine observational biases, need to be disentangled from the analytic conversation in order to clear a path toward real and engaged mutual understanding.

At the beginning of the analytic process, these personal effects are the bulk of the material the analysand must work through. This initial material is largely the result of a confrontation with their personal unconscious and looking over all of their life experience. Once they integrated their personal history (really took a good look at themselves), they can start digging in the collective dirt.

Jung tells a story about a female patient he was working with who dreamt that he was holding her like some pagan statue or God in a field of golden ripe wheat. Jung interpreted the ripe wheat as meaning that it was time for harvest and also that gold is always associated with a much valued object. Jung could now help the patient shed her projection on to him by explaining this image in its greater archetypal perspective. Jung helped her to realize that she had over inflated her image of him by associating him with a Pagan God. The ripe wheat that surrounded them- as a mythological image-has always been associated with death and renewal. In the Greek mystery cults, the initiate would hold a sheaf of wheat as a symbolic representation of their transcendent understanding. Once the initiate went through the sacred ritual, they accepted the death of their old self and the acceptance of a new understanding (this is considered a divine marriage). This is an image we shall return to later in the Demeter myth and this image has become associated with the Christian myth as well. In this specific dream, the woman's unconscious was expressing aspects of this much larger symbolic ensemble. If this dream is read in the strictly personal way, the woman could have missed an opportunity for expanding her consciousness. As a personal message, Jung informed the patient that she could now shed her infantile attachment to him or that aspect of her new personality was ready for harvest.

This is a big dream and the beauty of big dreams is that they are so multilayered. They contain both personal and wider cultural aspects, and they can help to establish our connection with a wider cultural heritage of which we are a part. This is the essence of a religious (or re-linking) attitude. This person may have overtly rejected her Christian heritage in which she was raised and is in need to seek or establish a connection with the more archaic pagan roots. These very pagan roots supply us with much of the underlying iconography of the subsequent Christian vision.

What the analytic situation provides is the critical over heating of the psyche. This can, when the moment is ripe, allow the patient to have an *Aha* moment of realization and experience a larger more metaphoric truth for themselves. This sense of ripeness is embedded or embodied in the situation itself and the language that we use to explain it. This is really the essence of analysis. It is the lysis point where the patient gains a personal understanding of the situation and grasps a truth that is experiential. What Jung also realized is that when the situation is ripe, there is a tendency for synchronistic things to happen. It's as though the outside world also conspires to bring about the inside world's transformation - a confluence between the outside and inside; the Sthula and Suksma become one in enlightenment. It seems that psychic phenomena are contingent upon the engagement of the mind and the analytic situation is nothing, if not engaging. This engagement can initiate a more unified perception of the world.

"It's so deep, it's so wide, step inside Spiritus Mundi" – Sting

Spiritus Mundi is a western term for the unified spirit world, the Uma in Buddhist jargon and the link between them is the Human mind. Copernicus was wrong. We are the centre of the universe.

"This self gives itself to that self, that self gives itself to this self. Thus they gain each other. In this form he gains the yonder world, in that form he experiences this world" – Aitarya Aranyaka, Anada K. Coormaraswamy from the *King and Corpse* by Mircea Eliade

Jung tells a famous story about a young woman he was treating, who at a critical moment in the analysis was given a dream of a golden Scarab: *"Suddenly, I heard a noise behind me, like a gentle tapping. I turned round and saw a flying insect knocking against the window pane from outside. I opened the window and caught the creature in the air, as it flew in. It was the nearest analogy to a golden scarab that one finds in our latitudes, a scarabaeidae beetle, and the common rose-chafer."* Synchronicity - Pg.33. This woman, who Jung was treating, had very strong Anima attachments or a very masculine consciousness, which manifest itself as tenacious, clinging to strictly rational Cartesian logic. In other words, she was very militant about the use of reason. She had studied philosophy, etc., and was very antagonistic about her stance. (Surely, thou doeth protest too much.) She seemed to be in need of a dose of non-rational in order to break her mental defenses. This scarab presented itself as an undeniable fact before her eyes, but the interesting thing is that in Egyptian mythology the scarab is a symbol of the rebirth of the sun. The scarab beetle rolling a dung ball is an analogy of the sun's journey across the sky. The beetle is pictured with a disc in its horns that is the solar disc. Because dung and the sun are so far apart, they can symbolize the same thing. Enantiodromia is the tendency of things to become there opposite. Gold is in the dung heap of astrophysics, I think.

Jung goes on to say that unfortunately, it is impossible to know if this woman was somehow remembering this symbolism of the scarab unconsciously in her dream. This is known as 'cryptomnesia'. But the symbol was very apt in a number of ways, the most impressive being it's historical legacy. Jung of course, would be able to fill out the various analogies behind this symbol so that the patient could gain further insight into its unique value, and be able to experience the richness. It is the patient's own dream and it came to them at just this time. This is a synchronistic event because there is no explicit, causal connection here outside of saying: *"it's a coincidence"*, which doesn't say much.

It took me a long time to realize that reason was not the be all and end all of philosophical inquiry. As I was wrestling with this debunking of reason many years ago, I awoke from a dream with golden letters moving across my inner eye that said: *"Without the court so late at night in through the open window crept insight."* This is a call for embracing irrationality. The court is the judging rational mind, and insight is a thief in the night. Now, I did know this scarab beetle story at the time of this dream/vision, but this same thought was formulated in such a completely different way as to be totally unrecognizable as an absolute equivalent. In fact I only realized the equivalency as I was writing this section. (I have no proof to offer you, which could substantiate the preceding statement. No fragrant rose.)

Jung continues by saying that these meaningful coincidences or synchronicities are recognizable, because of their archetypal character as opposed to dice throwing experiments, which can be represented in a purely statistical way. What statistics lack is any emotional or symbolic content, they have been analyzed and disentangled from reality. This is both their strength and weakness. In the analytic environment or indeed in all aspects of life, the surest way to tell if you have hit upon a complex-that reflects a lack of consciousness-in both your own life and others' is by gauging the emotional response that is attached to a thought or question. This highly charged area of the unconscious complex is the area that the analyst must slowly circle around and seek to illuminate, because it is most certainly 'complex' and therefore, much more emotionally charged.

"Surely thou doeth protest too much" – the Bard

Jung understood this idea of the complex. Through his work on association experiments very early in his career, this is a psychological thought that can be framed in a statistical manner and eventually, this method became the basis for our modern lie detector tests (the galvanic skin response). The premise is that a person cannot control the emotional charge associated with a complex. Say, if they have committed a murder, they cannot 'not' think about it, when asked a direct question. And if the analyst or lie detector operator runs through a list of words, and some of the words are associated with the crime, the person being tested cannot help but show an emotional response. For example, if you shot your best friend who you caught in bed with your husband and then thought that you had a reasonable chance of getting away with it and so actively denied the crime to the police, you would have a very hard time suppressing your emotions when someone said, "Gun" or "infidelity" or "best friend" from amongst a random sample of words. This is why poker players need to keep a straight face and not talk. Any emotional leakage could be indicative of the cards they are holding, especially if another player asks them a direct question. This is why poker players ask how much money the other player is playing with (it is considered bad form not to answer). This forces the other player to talk and you can listen for the strength or weakness in their voice when they answer. This is an explicit realization that emotions are embedded in our interactions, which in turn are reflected on our face. We are a body/mind.

Someone who is constantly giving lie detector tests or really anyone intent on being observant could develop their skill in reading people to such an extent that they could simply watch the person being tested. They would then be fairly certain that the subject was either lying or telling the truth by being very observant of micro facial expressions. And of course, these same people can build up observational biases or simply function under the assumption of guilt, which will make them believe that they can tell when someone is lying with 100% accuracy. This is how people who aren't guilty go to jail.

This type of observation is not a statistical or 'scientific' proof that can be brought into a court room. This is an aspect of the expert witness scenario, and the defense will, of course try, to discredit the validity of the expert. People who work in airport security are now being trained in lie detection methods, but of course, it is very contentions. It relies on a person's unique skill and focused ability to properly gauge emotional effect. It also relies on the officers not being blinded by, and therefore, unconsciously projecting their own prejudices and or personal biases outwardly. Do we really think that American airport security will give anyone that is obviously Muslim and carrying a Pakistani passport an unprejudiced once over? Conversely, the eyes truly are the window to the soul and no one can control all of their micro expressions perfectly, when they are lying.

The real question concerning the scarab beetle is how can a person's unconscious and the outside world collude in such a manner that a bug can tap a window, and if indeed they are colluding, what is the mechanism through which this occurs? The mechanism idea leads us back into the realm of causality. Synchronicity is defined as an acausal event and so the search for a mechanism/cause is wrong headed. We are in a loop that we can't get out of, but the loop has been created by our own wordplay and our in-grained and not unreasonable assumptions about the causal nature of reality. We will see later how these largely linguistic loops have side railed philosophy and scientific inquiry for decades. Synchronicity must be thought of as a unique act of creation in time. We cannot say that the archetype or the analysand brought about the event. The connection or recognition of meaning is strictly a mental construct.

Jung postulated four categories in which to perceive events: space, time, causality and synchronicity. The forth category is lying outside of the rational. We shall have to circle around this concept from many angles. It is not a simple thing to illuminate and I have no handy sound bite that I can feed in here. Well… maybe an imp and I do *"Can we do it, yes we can."*

Rupert Sheldrake has postulated the idea of a morphic field or morphic resonance to explain the apparent extension of the mind beyond the body. He uses the analogy of a magnetic field or the extension of gravity into space as a way of conceiving of this psychic field. He also created the term Morphic to separate his ideas from synchronicity, for example. We shall come back to this idea later, for now we will have a look at China.

China

The Chinese seem to have a very different view of numbers and causality than we do and this is a story that will illuminate this aspect. There were 12 generals on a battle field and they needed to decide whether to retreat or attack, so they put it to a vote. The vote resulted in seven generals wanting to attack and five wanting to retreat. They retreated, because five is a much stronger number than seven. I have been led to understand that the Chinese seem to have known about the other notes in the western musical octave, but they do not use them regularly. They have remained with the pentatonic or five-note scale, because of its internal stability. They aren't ambiguous notes in a major pentatonic scale. This is some of what gives Chinese music it's instantly recognizable quality. The Chinese also have developed a very intricate method of divination known as the I Ching. The point of the I Ching is that through a physical/mathematical operation, such as throwing a series of yarrow stalks or coins, you can arrive at a description of the just so-ness of the cosmic moment that you are in and therefore act accordingly. In other words… you can peer into the timeless unconscious to grasp at the uniqueness of the moment that you are in and then align yourself to it. Within this system is a presumption that there is a perceivable underlying flow that you can either be in tune with or not.

The full physical process of throwing yarrow sticks is quite long and convoluted and like the Japanese tea ceremony the process itself is meant to bring your roving consciousness into focus and back to this moment. The tea ceremony involves boiling the water and having the tea made in front of you through a series of whisking motions, which is a fairly drawn out affair. When the tea finally arrives, you are also there with it. There is no need to rush the tea ceremony. The tea ceremony is the point. Like yoga, which strives to calm the extraneous mind stuff, it is understood that if we become present in the moment, when we are seeking an answer through divination, we can actually pierce into the larger flow to gain a better understanding of that particular moment. If we constantly bring our past habits or future desires into our various actions in the world, there is no room for the creative NOW to emerge.

The four main characters of the I Ching (I believe there are 64 in total) can be seen on the South Korean flag. The main four represent diametrically opposed ideas, but taken as a whole they are a representation of a totality of stability - much like the eight or four main character types of Jung. This is another representation of the archetype of the self, or a different way of conceiving of a higher integration that has been developed within the Chinese cultural matrix. Eight is also a very strong number in China. The Chinese tend to see these characters of the I Ching as a representation of the archetypal flow of the world or the Tao as it moves through time. Time will move through these basic ensembles in a discernible order and the process of the I Ching can help you to understand explicitly where you are at that moment. This is much like Chinese astrology, which has twelve animal signs: Rat, Ox, Rooster, Snake, etc. You are born one of these animals as your personal totem, so you will reflect some characteristics of the animal of your birth year. This totem will interact in certain discernible ways with the other characters, as you move through the larger ensemble of the astrological signs. Astrology is very old Juju and very difficult to prove.

The three main religions in China are or were Confucianism, Buddhism and Taoism. They coexisted and commingled for a couple of thousand years at this point, and together, they represent a window into the Chinese psyche. These three religions have borrowed from and cross-fertilized each other in the same way as Buddhism, Islam, Hinduism and Jainism have cross-fertilized each other in India. In Taoism the Tao or Dao is the underlying order of reality, it has been called, "The Way". Like the Indian term "dharma", it means many things at once: the law, the way or the real underlying flow of the universe are some of the definitions. The job of the individual is to keep himself within the Tao not outside or against it. You can't push the river.

Jung told a story that he received from Richard Wilhelm, who was the author of one of the first books on the I Ching to reach the west: *The Secret of the Golden Flower*. Jung wrote a fairly long introduction for this particular translation. This story was a favorite of Jung's, and apparently, he repeated it so often that most of his acquaintances knew it by heart, and yet, he told it with such zest that they could still be drawn into it. I personally have read it at least five times in different works and I won't search out a direct quote.

When Richard Wilhelm was in China, he was in a village that was undergoing an extended drought. So the people of the village sought the help of a wise man from beyond the mountains. (Your own wise man will apparently not do in such situations. You need to bring out the big guns and the really powerful shaman are always far away.) After some time, this man arrived and he would not enter the village. He requested that they make him a hut to meditate in some distance place. After three or four days a torrent of rain was released on to the village and Richard Wilhelm decided that he must talk to this fellow to see how someone could make it rain. This fellow informed Mr. Wilhelm that when he had first come to the village, it was so out of the Tao, that it also pulled him out of the Tao. He had to remove himself from this situation to get back into the Tao. After some meditation, etc., he regained the Tao for himself and it rained. In his mind he had brought the village back into the Tao with him, or at least, established an aspect of the correct flow again. What is implied in this story that I loathe to make explicit, is that when you get yourself together the world incrementally gets itself together with you. You are the shower of flowers.

In the later nineties, I became entranced with a BBC documentary on China called, *"Beyond the Clouds"*. In this documentary, they followed the life of a number of people in a province in southern China. One of the characters was a doctor who had a young daughter of about 19 or 20. She came home one day and told her father that she had decided to study medicine. With tears of joy in his eyes, he tells her that she must never treat just the disease of a patient; she must always treat the whole patient. This-to my mind-is the great difference between East and West. Western medicine is all about the specific disease. Search for the specific problem and prescribe a specific drug to combat it. In fact, we constantly use military metaphors when describing our medical treatments. This use of aggressive jargon, in turn, belies our inherently aggressive stance toward creating better health. Even wishing to heal someone can be a reflection of power.

In this documentary, the doctor is telling his daughter that she must try to grasp the whole ensemble or view the whole situation in the round. Then you can see what has led this person out of the Tao and into sickness. I was watching a documentary on Ayruvedic medicine and one of the first things out of this Indian doctor's mouth was, *"I don't treat diseases. I treat people"*.

An example of this eastern approach might be in the treatment of a patient with cancer of the liver. It could be a great help to understand why the cancer is in the liver and not the kidneys and what has lead the individual's immune system into a situation where it cannot combat this specific problem. This specific cancer can be treated by helping the individual to strengthen their whole immune system. When we become sick, to some extent, we have lost the ability to effectively regenerate ourselves or effectively fight the specific problem. Each specific ailment can also be seen as a manifestation of a larger behavioral or environmental problem. In this case, severe drinking may have weakened the liver to such an extent, that it also gets cancer. Specific disease can be a full system problem, or the whole ensemble is not working correctly. A system-wide problem has manifested itself in a very specific cancer. And as an ongoing caveat, I am in no way denying the obvious benefits that western medicine has gained for us.

It is a fact that the body is always generating new cells and there is a thought that about every seven years all of the cells in your body have replaced themselves and somehow you are still there. The body wants to stay healthy, but sometimes, it needs specific and or general help. Attacking the specific disease alone is aggressive, arrogant, but overall it is convenient. It is much better to help the whole person to heal. Attacking problems is an effort to heal through enforcing power; could be seen–psychologically-as a projection of power. This ideology has developed within the healthcare system as a result of our having given doctors an almost "god-like" status throughout the fifties and sixties. The entrance of many more women into the field has greatly helped to disassemble the hubris behind this attitude. Healing is an art, which suffers when practiced with an overt agenda that seeks to control others through our healing powers. We may-to a certain extent-become an analyst or doctor in order to be smarter than other people, and thereby, gain some measure of control. We may wish to gain control over others, because we feel a lack of control over ourselves. Of course, we can psychoanalyze anything to death, but I feel there is a thread of truth to this.

In the east there is a much stronger herbal tradition which has yet to be stringently tested in the west for a more formal proof of efficacy. Although the western drug companies are securing patents in a frenzied-over-controlled-litigious fashion, as fast as they can. What the east does have is personal understanding expressed through lineage. They have very long written and oral traditions of the history and usage of herbs, which is a kind of proof. Of course, this leaves the usages open to an unscrupulous individual who wishes to exploit people, but that can and does happen in the west as well, just not as easily. (Drug companies would convince us -and the doctors treating us-that psychoactive drugs are the best way forward in treating mental health. They make a lot of money and they expend a great deal of energy spreading that money around the medical community. They have gained a lot of power through telling us this story.) Also, in Chinese medicine it discusses such things as Chi energy, which westerners would like to holdup as indicative of the fuzzy headedness of oriental thought, in that no one can find this Chi energy and quantify or sell it. These types of concepts, like Chi energy, Kundalini Yoga or the Dao, etc. - go back a long time and represent a vast and well articulated cultural ensemble. They have become-over time-an analogy or paradigm from which someone who is well trained can gain an understanding of the whole ensemble of the individual's health. But they fall over when abstracted and removed from their cultural settings.

    Interestingly, recent realizations in neuroscience have given us a better framework in which to understand this concept of Chi energy specifically. I will address this more fully later but briefly; the concept of Chi energy is an overt recognition of the brain's extension of the body into the space around the individual. This psychic extension of the mind beyond the body is real and is called the personal body map or peri-personal space. The mind-brain has evolved so that it doesn't absolutely distinguish the space outside of the skin as being separate from 'the distinct' you that is inside of your skin. The mind/body matrix is embedded in the world, not distinct from it and someone moving their hands just above your body directing Chi energy is not necessarily performing meaningless voodoo.

    Another paradigm along these lines is the system of chakras and Kundalini Yoga from Hindu philosophy, of which I will have more to say later. We might also throw into this bag of tricks the concept of gravity at around the time of Newton. The Chinese have developed a very different way of looking at the world and by trying to gain an understanding of their view of nature we can confront, and possibly, disassemble some of our own myopic cultural paradigms, hopefully to build a better understanding of reality itself. An honest investigator investigates. They do not begin with a supposition and then try to disprove anything that doesn't square with their premise.

"Incapacity to attain comprehension is itself comprehension"- Abu Bakr

The whole of western philosophy is built upon -to my mind- the acceptance and then disregarding, and then recycling again of various paradigms. (The book to read is *The Passion of the Western Mind* by Richard Tarnas or *The Structures of Scientific Revolutions* by T. S. Kuhn) Each philosopher is picking up some thread that another has developed or discarded. By giving it a new twist or viewing some subtly of it from a new angle, a new mind can develop a new understanding. We in the west are now in a position to take a look at a whole series of new paradigms coming from the east, but they have been born out of radically different matrices and context. If we barge in with blinders and arrogance we will wake the dragon and the gems will elude us. These eastern concepts much like many other articulated paradigms are subtle and nuanced. They need to be rounded out by an unprejudiced and contextual view of the whole cultural framework.

Fifteen years ago, there was no such a thing as World music. Now, I personally have a collection of 70 or 80 Indian classical recordings and a couple hundred other recordings from around the world. I can guess with some accuracy what part of Africa a recording is from that I have never heard before. Had I been born at any other time, I would have been very lucky indeed to have had any such exposure to these things. The down side of this is that there is such a glut of musical information out there that it takes great patience to pick through it all. I have heard lots of Indian classical music that-quite frankly-I could not understand, or just plain didn't like. But someone like Pandit Nikhil Banerjee is worth hours of bad listening to me. He is a true master and he resonates deeply with me. Again, the dragon protects his jewels. And so to really gain an insight into Chinese medicine or the I Ching, Hinduism, Aruvedic medicine or Indian classical music takes time and patience and an arrogant prejudice will certainly not help.

To sum up this meandering discussion is to say that in Arthur Koestler I found an author who had a wide-ranging, multidisciplinary intellect. I have read almost all of his books and through him I discovered that any subject can be interesting, if it is presented properly. Koestler wrote books on a very wide range of subjects, which included-as mentioned earlier-a book on the 13th or what he considered the lost tribe of the Jews from Kazakhstan. He started off his life as a communist and was one of the first hardliners to disassemble this entrancing paradigm, and ultimately, it is his thirst and drive toward understanding that is admirable, and as I said earlier, he pricked my ongoing interest in the creative act, and my subsequent weak understanding of science in general. Koestler was in touch with many of the leading intellects of his time and, was in earnest, at trying to popularize science and create larger conceptual frameworks for a vast range of subjects. To my mind his is a very admirable torch to carry.

He also proudly said that his books were burnt by the two worst regimes of his time: Stalin and Hitler ordered that his books should be removed from libraries and be burnt. He must have been on to something. Maybe the Taliban or some American Tea Party wing nut will honor me and torch this work, as long as they don't download it for free. I'm good with that. Bring the rain.

3 ASTROPHYSICS, ASTRONOMY, BIOLOGY AND BEYOND

"The supreme task of the physicist is the discovery of the most general elementary laws from which the world picture can be deduced logically. But there is no logical way to the discovery of these elemental laws. There is only the way of intuition, which is helped by a feeling for the order lying behind the appearance, and this Einfuhlung (literally, empathy or 'feeling one's way in') is developed by experience." – Albert Einstein in the preface to: *"Where is Science Going?"* By Max Planck

"The stars that decorate the sky, though we rightly regard them as the finest and most perfect of visible things, are far inferior, just because they are visible, to the true realities; that is, to the true relative velocities, in pure numbers and perfect figures, of the orbits and what they carry in them, which are perceptible to reason and thought but not visible to the eye... We shall therefore treat astronomy, like geometry, as setting us problems for solution, and ignore the visible heavens, if we want to make a genuine study of the subject..." - The Republic by Plato

When I first thought of writing this book I felt that a book on proof was quite an ambitious undertaking. I'm not from a scientific background, as you may have noticed. I like to use the narrow reductionist scientific outlook as a whipping boy. Fortunately, I have discovered that I am not alone. I have, from time to time read scientific works, mostly on astrophysics and quantum mechanics and I am very interested in this area, but I am no expert. My areas of expertise, if I can be so arrogant as to say such a thing are Eastern and Western mythology/philosophy, Jungian thought, western history and western music, pop and jazz. Ding!

"Mathematics is the language of the universe; it is not the sound that the universe makes." - M.E.

"The thing that is important about a hole, is that which it is not" – M.E.

"Science must above all divest itself of what will distort. Of course, to abandon ourselves to every personal whim or passion could never lead to any kind of shared truth. But achieving such lack of distortion is a much more subtle process than it may appear. *Objectivity* requires interpretation of what one finds, depends on imagination for its achievement. Detachment has a deeply ambiguous nature. The cool, detached stance of the scientific or bureaucratic mind ultimately may lead where we do not wish to follow. And the relationship implied by the left-hemisphere attention brought to bear through scientific method, with its implied materialism, is not no relationship – merely a disengaged relationship, implying, incorrectly, that the observer does not have an impact on the observed (and is not altered by what he or she observes). The betweenness is not absent, just denied, and therefore of a particular –particularly 'cold'- kind. We cannot know something without it being known to us – we cannot see what it would be like, if it were not we that were knowing it. Thus everything we apprehend is the way it is, because we see it in that way rather than another way. When science adopts a view of its object from which everything 'human' has as far as possible been removed, bringing a focused, but utterly detached attention to bear, it is merely exercising another human faculty, that of standing back from something and seeing it in this detached, in some important sense denatured, way. There is no reason to see that particular way as privileged, except that it enables us to do certain things more easily, to use things, to have power over things- the preoccupation of the left hemisphere." Iain McGilchrist, *The Master and his Emissary* - Pg. 166 (See end of book)

A Tackle for Reductionism

So a few years ago, I decided I should brush up on current scientific thinking and was lucky enough to have read some excellent works. This next chapter will be a discussion of a few of the authors that I came across as I was looking into things and preparing for this book. I have also done a flurry of reading while I was writing it and many of the ways in which I had presumed to understand things has been radically changed. This change in my thinking is mostly due to my overwhelming interest in neuroscience. Neuroscience will be seen-in retrospect-to have ushered in another fundamental sea of change in conception of ourselves and our place in the world. Physicists take note: Copernicus is an unwanted guest at the door and his day job is now working in a neuroscience lab.

The French philosopher Pascal discusses what he sees as two ways of looking into the world and he calls these ways the 'esprit geometric' and the 'esprit de finesse' or the geometric mind/spirit and the mind/spirit of the intuitive. Immanuel Kant came up with almost the exact same concept using the terms analytic or 'a priori' and synthetic or 'a posterior' (empirical, gathered by the senses). The geometric (analytic) mind can be taught to grasp the rules and definitions such as those that are inherent in mathematics, where a truth is easily verified and mistakes in reason are-with training-easily exposed. To question the truth of 2x2=4 is to misunderstand the whole of the field of mathematics. This statement cannot be false. The question of the truth of 2x2=4 is not a mathematical question at all. It is a matter of symbolic representation. The intuitive mind can also perceive a truth in which it is less easy to find verifiable consensus. Karl Marx believed that he had found a geometric truth within the realm of sociology and history. He thought that if all of the historical details of the world could be sufficiently analyzed, he could then build his vision of a brave new world which would become: a truth realized. This is the same mistake that Tea Party rapture-fundamentalist-apocalypse visionaries are making, which is essentially trying to fit a metaphor into the world. Or, mistaking geometric truth for finesse, which is like trying to make a curve with a set of smaller and smaller straight lines when a sweep of the hand could do it instantly.

Jacques Barzun, in my favorite book, *Dawn to Decadence*, delineates these belief systems for us and shows us that all of the various 'ologys', such as archaeology, psychology, sociology, creationismology, etc., cannot be separated from their inherently intuitive and non-geometric spirits. These various ologys contain a truth of a different order, but they might seek to convince you that they are, or participate in a scientific geometric truth, they are and do not. With all of these ologys come all of the people who hold these viewpoints and the ultimate proof of these viewpoints will be elusive. The devil is truly in the details and he has the best tunes.

Jacque Barzun calls this creation of ologys, Scientism. This attitude flows from the mistaken notion that reality can be encompassed or understood through abstraction. This does not mean that the same individual cannot comfortably live with both of these opposing views (an ology or scientism and science), as is clearly shown by painter/engineers like Da Vinci and others great thinkers in the Renaissance, and up to today. A truly great mind can hold many different and opposing viewpoints in balance, while understanding that they all reflect an aspect of the truth. We shall endeavor to explore the more geometric/sensate/left brain side of things in order that we might also expose the less than solid edges of this seemingly rock solid outlook.

A large impetus for this part of the book, specifically, was my resulting meditation on a conversation I had with a friend of mine who is a professor of entomology/biology at Trent University near Toronto in Peterborough, Ontario. His name is David Beresford and he is married to a friend of my wife's. We went to their farm for a visit one lovely summer's day. His area of expertise, among many things, is entomology or the study of bugs. The very first time I met him, we talked non-stop for two or three hours straight, much to the chagrin of the other people who were there with us, I should imagine. When we get together now, we usually talk non-stop and it seems to be more or less accepted that we will vent our brains in this way.

I was particularly interested in the Jungian concept of archetypes (surprise), and how that might be related to the instincts of animals. If humans can inherit ancestral memories, then a logical parallel to this would be the inherited instincts of animals. For example, how can the monarch butterflies that by the time they arrive in southern Mexico again, are a full four generations removed from the ones who left Mexico in the first place and find the same small area in Mexico not having been there before? (Luckily the continent narrows.)

There must be some information passed thought the genes or the cells or DNA that propels this insect to leave Canada and make a two thousand-mile trek. I have heard that these butterflies find the same place in Mexico by following air pressure zones or navigating by the stars, or wicked guess work. To my mind, this just begs more questions. If they travel by the stars, how do the butterflies know what the stars look like, and with the earth turning a third rotation over the eight hours of travel at night, which stars do they follow? Or if they travel by air presser zones or polar magnetic lines, how do they know to follow down the lines and not travel across them? Apparently, young birds staring at the stars from their nests are also studying the sky. Who knows how this becomes useful and what evolutionary mechanism compels them to do this. What Mr. Beresford said to me really floored me though. He said that instinct is a black box and anyone who says they know something about it is lying. The genetic underpinnings of this area of research in nature, is just not understood. Well, how can you not want to look at that? The serpent had extended me a juicy apple and asked: "Please… will you take a bite"?

"I would wish to dance my way out of Eden"-M.E.

I have found a few authors who are tackling this thorny problem and it seems that they are making some conceptual headway. The framework that seems most promising is an extension of the evolutionary framework proposed by Darwin. It would seem that the ability to exploit instincts would hold an evolutionary advantage to those who posses it. The actual mechanics of how this type of information is passed on could be a combination of our holding a neural propensity toward a learned skill or possibly an ability to access a type of field memory (Sheldrake). Or a direct passing of information and/or specific memory or a more nebulous memory ensemble passed generationally through genetic encoding on and into our brain as a fairly specific knowledge package. I have also heard proposals for memory being stored in the cell wall, which is then influenced by the properties of water. This is an element of the whole field of Homeopathy, which I know far too little about to comment at all, and in my mind, all of these proposals only beg for more receding questions.

Somebody who is trying to frame a hypothesis that would encompass some form of intergenerational transfer of information is Rupert Sheldrake. He wrote a book in the early eighties called, *A New Science of Life* in which he introduced a concept called 'Morphic Resonance'. The first thing that I have had people tell me is that information like instincts is passed through the genetic code, but exactly how is never explained. I'm not talking about how our genes know what parts of the brain they should be building so that we might be able to receive something like a language. Though, that is incredible enough and not very well understood at all. I would like to know how butterflies feel compelled to find Mexico and then actually do. Or, why humans almost universally believe in a form of deity, or why we fall in love. Most of this stuff gets explained by a reference to its evolutionary advantages and I would like to suggest that this simply displaces the question one step farther away. The expression of genes as they build something like our brain is a vaguely causal process and therefore the process is explainable as it unfolds. But instincts and or thought structures are much more nebulous in my mind.

I was introduced to Mr. Sheldrake's thinking when I saw an interview with him on a local public broadcaster in Ontario called TVO. I believe that in this interview he was talking about a newer book of his. I missed the beginning. In this interview, he discussed the difficulties involved in giving the scientific community a proof of some form of collective learning, but he did supply evidence of this very thing.

In England and Europe, before the Second World War, milk used to be delivered to people's doorsteps in a glass bottle. The bottles of milk had a paper stop on the top. When I was young, it was also sealed with a small piece of foil. In a bottle of real milk, you would have a small amount of cream that would separate and rise to the top, forming a layer of cream just below the paper stop. There is a bird in Europe called the 'tit' that had- before the war- learned to flip the top open and drink the cream from the surface. During the war, the milk delivery was suspended for at least five years. In England, it was closer to eight years. It was long enough that the entire population of 'tits' that learned this trick of flipping the top, were dead and only their offspring were alive. As milk delivery resumed after the war, it was noticed that the birds immediately resumed this behavior without having to relearn it. This is a very specific behavior that was passed on through generations. I cannot understand how such a specific task could be genetically coded and immediately resumed. But, of course, there are lots of these very specific behaviors.

Mr. Sheldrake designed an experiment that was very clever. He had a group of people (I believe it was in Cambridge), come together every day and work through the daily crossword puzzle. He would time how long it took the group to complete the crossword puzzles and he then arrived at an average duration, representing an average baseline. People would be working on the same crossword that had appeared in the *London Times* newspaper earlier that morning. The group in Cambridge would not have the opportunity to see or complete the same crossword, but many people in London would have already solved it. Sure enough, when the crossword had been completed in London that morning, the Cambridge group completed their crosswords quantifiably faster, and by implication, with more ease. What this implies is that, simply because someone else has learned something-even something very specific and mundane-it is easier for you to learn that same thing. Much like the Rhine ESP experiments in the sixties the collective hubris of the scientific community was more than willing to get out its big clubs and take them to Mr. Sheldrake. A good idea can only take hold when all of the people who vehemently oppose it are dead; that means it takes about 50 years for a true revolution in science to be accepted, Copernicus took much longer than that. Scientists know this.

Saint Augustine tells us that authority is the weakest proof. According to the sleeve of his books Rupert Sheldrake is a PhD, former research fellow of the Royal Society, a scholar of Clare College and a Frank Knox Fellow at Harvard University also former director of studies in biochemistry and cell biology at Cambridge University. He is probably not a chump and I should imagine that he knows how to run a proper experiment. Now I will say that it is the scientific community's job to weed out crack pots from making spurious theory's about what ever turns your crank and like me they probably have a prejudice when it comes to believing that the Queen of England is an Alien sent here to dominate the world economy while feasting on human brains, and rightfully so. But I do think Mr. Sheldrake has a hold of something, and his thinking is one of the main reasons I embarked upon this book. I am quite comfortable with Jung's concept of archetypes, which Mr. Sheldrake could not avoid discussing as a comparable analogy, although his hypothesis of Morphic Resonance is a different thing and I do not want to represent that it is simply an extension of the same idea.

    I will spend a bit of time building my notion of DNA before we look a bit more closely at Mr. Sheldrake. One of the current ways of thinking in the public mind about gene expression is that there is a lot of information that is being passed on through the genes or DNA. I hear a lot of things like: *"if my mother is an alcoholic, then I have a much greater chance of being an alcoholic"* and I have had people tell me with absolute assurance that scientists have found a set of gay genes and that no one can stop themselves from being gay, because it's in their genes. (Probably nice tight designer jeans) This is based on a misunderstanding of what DNA does. The same DNA code is in all of the cells of your body but all of the cells in your body are not the same, there is a very complex ballet being performed as the cells within your growing body diversify and react to the surrounding cells in their immediate and extended environment. Feedback from environmental cues-not only the cells next door but wider influences like the availability of food-is being registered constantly as gene expression unfolds. This subsequent or resulting unique expression of the genetic code is a result of many things being triggered in sequence, like the triggering and or eruption of certain hormones which then causes information feedback in the brain etc. The DNA that you have is only remotely like the blue print for a building and the ongoing ballet of the actual construction of everything is carried out by many other factors as they respond to the surrounding environment and the process itself and also refer back to the plan. This constant feedback from the surrounding environment creates an ongoing process that can radically change even genetically identical twins one could be gay the other not.

    As an example of this process of unfolding, if you take the cells from a frogs eye and implant them on the knee they may turn into functioning and integrated knee cells and continue to grow as a part of the leg; but there is a certain point at which they will continue grow into an eye on the frogs leg. The code in each cell is not hard wired from beginning to end; but at a certain point, triggers have been established that cannot then be turned off again. This is the essence of stem cell research; scientists are trying to harvest and or create stem cells because this is the stage of the cells genetic expression that is the most adaptable. These stem cells can then be used to help to mend or even re-grow new organs within or even outside of the body. Stem cells are cells that are in the infancy of their growth cycle which is the most flexible non diversified part. They are nothing but potential at this point.

I heard one of the Kennedy children saying that he was an alcoholic, because his father or grandfather was an alcoholic. Some doctor had told him he had the alcoholic gene. That's pretty convenient for both the doctor and Mr. Kennedy. He really can't help getting into his car driving to a liquor store, loading up a case of Jack Daniels and pouring shot after shot until he's blotto. You see my point: his drinking is a very organized activity, and if his genes made him do it, we will have to acknowledge that he has little or no free will, at least in terms of his drinking pattern. On the other hand the organized behavior of buying Jack Daniels could be seen to be a result of behavioral patterns that result from the expression of an overpowering urge. The further implication of this is that the genes have somehow initiated this complex behavioral action, and that this man's DNA somehow knows where the liquor store is, or compelled him to find a liquor store come hell or high water. The legal system would, and does, quite rightly- reject any scenario that negates our sense of free will and culpability for our actions. We will attempt to get to the bottom of this debate later. On the other hand, birds learned to flip the top of milk bottles off, which is-like finding a liquor store-a very specific behavior.

My weak understanding is that the genes are not like a rigid computer code and they do not dictate a set of specific and unchangeable behavior patterns. Though it is very tempting to use the analogy of computers when looking at the brain or other human properties, we should be wary of these types of analogies, and specifically, this mechanical reductionist analogy. The thought that my genes made me do it is essentially a mechanistic argument, which would like to present a relatively poorly understood and extremely complicated processes like the expression of DNA. Or, the electro chemical firing of neurons into simplistic terms that can be broken apart and analyzed into a form of linear causality. A-leads-to-B-leads-to-more-drinks-for-me-type scenario. This type of strictly mechanistic view would propose that everything can be explained or at least further illuminated (in terms of Physics and causality usually), by some sort of mathematical equation and/or a regressive analysis. Through an ongoing mental abstraction (by breaking things apart), we can then reduce and trace subsequent behaviors back through their causal antecedents and into a single identifiable moment and cause. An alternative to this reductive view according to Sheldrake is an integrationist's theory, more akin to the mind/body duality that I will proceed to hammer home.

The crux of the argument-as it relates specifically to the mind-is that you cannot reduce thinking down into strictly physical, electro chemical, set of causal interactions. Thoughts do not occur because my genes or a set of chemicals told me to think this or that. We are not simply passive recipients of the windy environment or completely unconscious and reactive creatures, and we cannot be profitably understood in this simple behaviorist way. This mode of thinking would seek to treat even thinking itself as a completely mind-bound entity that is forced to interact within the body in a strictly electro chemical or mechanical way. Conversely, there is another camp that would seek to imply that thinking is radically distinct from the biology that contains it and that it somehow sits – metaphysically- on top of everything directing the ship, but we will see later that thinking is not as simple as either of these ill-defined ideas would lead us to believe.

There is still a very common belief that thinking and the brain are somehow different. We will tackle this idea by entering into the question of sentience or self-consciousness, which if forced into a naive and strictly mechanistic outlook, can lead you into an endless regress as you try to pin down the beginning of thinking. This is called the *homuncular argument* and I will digress for a moment to explain. If there is someone inside my head directing consciousness, or my sentient representation of myself, a small being called a homunculus, then who is directing his consciousness and so on? Or if the world sits on a turtle's back, what is that turtle sitting on: another turtle, and is it then turtles all the way down? (See Terrence W. Deacon, *Incomplete Nature*)

The concept of sentience is the thought that our most essential self – the underlying true essence of our being- is that part of our thinking which is involved in watching ourselves as we perform tasks in the world. Or, the best part of what makes us human is our ability to section ourselves off from everything and abstract, and define the essence of both ourselves, and our environment. This way of representing ourselves is a reflection of the power of the scientific method itself. Sentience or our self-awareness when approached causally, and through self-observation, creates the impression that we are thinking about ourselves. For instance, we can have an image of ourselves thinking of how the concept of our own mind is different from the brain that contains it. Because we can represent this difference, it seems that the essential me is distinct from the observing mind that represents this thought. We can also think about our mind, thinking about ourselves; thinking about ourselves, thinking about our mind and so on. This concept of sentience has been framed as the act of self-perception or the abstraction of ourselves from the environment into the realm of thinking. This is really one of the beautiful illusions that our mind creates for us. The long and short of this speculative quagmire, is that *we are all* made up of this multi-layered thinking and our brain (especially the more denotative left hemisphere, but never entirely), artfully creates this illusion of our own thinking being distinct from a more abstract 'I', so that our explicit thinking can be expressed for us in this way. There are manifold advantages to this process.

Gene expression like thinking is the result of the genes travelling down the road of their ongoing expression, which in a perfect world, is the easiest route, unless environmental pressure (both exterior in the form of say, food shortages and/or internal pressures to change in the form of disease or stress), causes the subsequent unfolding to change or try to adapt. Nature is not maniacal in her approach. There is always room to flex. This is why you can have 'the cancer gene' and never get cancer. Genes express themselves in an *epigenetic fashion,* which I will define later and so the linear and/or too strictly causal way of thinking about this process is incorrect. Like evolution itself, we and the environment that we are in cannot be so cleanly disentangle from each other -which we can then clearly section off and identify specific root causes. That's not to say that it's not useful and informative to try, but this type of causal argument forces us to dissect, and essentially, kill the living embedded entity that we wish to explain. Everything in nature is moving in lock step with everything else. Mother Nature has supplied us with preponderances toward certain forms not locked in expressions of set pieces.

One of the other problems that comes up when we adhere to a completely mechanistic approach toward our understanding-especially toward the psyche-is that you are forced to use the very same psyche and its explicit linguistic representations, to explain itself. A strictly causal approach to everything will inevitably be a reflection of a prejudice within your own methodology. Which is: which part of the phenomena do you wish to study and where does that element begin and end? You need to have some form of external reference. You really cannot be sure that the chosen paradigm that you have framed is not a reflection of a ready-made paradigm being supplied to you by your own mind.

For instance, we feel convinced that thinking is a discrete aspect of our mind separate from everything else. Thinking-like the mind-cannot happen without a mind for it to happen in and a mind cannot exist without a body to supply it with blood and the raw sensate data with which to build-up a concept of its own being and a body cannot exist without the world to be in -and to beat it a bit more. We cannot have a brain that represents that world without all of the aspects of the world influencing our representation of, etc. We and our brains did not suddenly appear despite any creationist arguments asserting the opposite. We are the paradigm that we use to think about paradigms, and the way that we represent a paradigm, at the same time. We will later find our way out of this intellectual loop, do not lose hope. Modern Physics has had to deal with a variation of this same problem, of trying to disentangle the observer from the things that are being observed as well.

"In psychology… the problem of the relationship between mind and body can be avoided by ignoring the existence of mental states. This is the approach of the behaviorists' school, which confines its attention only to objectively observable behavior. But behaviorism is not a testable scientific hypothesis it is a methodology." A New Science of Life - Pg. 26

In other words, the psychology of B.F. Skinner's behaviorism avoided this whole self referential problem by developing a way of working that excluded the inconvenient suppositions of internal mental aspects of their observations. Everything had to be reflected in an abstracted statistic: my presumption is that this is a more "scientific" approach. With the behaviorist ideology, you can set up experiments and run them to get quantifiable results, like running rats through various mazes to find out how good or fast they are at learning or simply perceiving aspects of their environment. This seeks to drain animals and humans of any type of implied intention so that we can be studied with the implication that we are strictly reactive or mechanistic toward the world. This approach says precious little to us about how Muhammad received the Koran from God.

Behaviorism only sought to propose a reason or define a purpose for our actions. Its intent was to measure and quantify our response to situations, and if there were emotional underpinnings in all of these situations, they were irrelevant, because they could never be known in a scientific way. This allowed them to gain an understanding of the phenomena being observed by being able to represent that behavior using a set of scientific statistics that have been established and possibly proven to be true. This is abstraction and to my mind it is a double-edged sword. It is of necessity a very myopic and specific way of trying to gain understanding.

As an analogy: the early psychologists of the 19th and 20th century were fairly content to be able to assign a label to the afflictions they were dealing with. That was for some time, the extent of psychological understanding, and with exceptions, pretty much all that psychology had to offer for severe mental disorders. Behaviorism -in my mind- contained only marginally more insight into the human condition, but it was defended far more stridently in its time, much like the early Freudians or Marxists. I would argue that this type of strident defense is usually the result of the defender having unconsciously suspected that they were on shaky ground to begin with. The world is subtle and nuanced and a reductionist approach can only supply you with specific answers, or in the case of the early psychologists, handy names that seem to imply a mastery of the phenomena. This is both its strength and weakness. When the promoters of a reductionist viewpoint sought to explain and encompass the larger and more nuanced picture of the mind (or in a Marxist case: global economics or frustratingly ambiguous human nature, etc.), they may have a tendency to slip into dogmatic assertions like, "that's only, this" which is a reductionist reflex.

This may be the way that most science can create a real foundational understanding. I personally am a generalist so it is hard for me to view these reductionist paradigms without my own personal psychic attachments. To my mind the weakness in this method is the thought that you may feel that you really have an answer. You may tease out of the world -what seems to be a root cause of a phenomenon. In some sense, you really have, but to arrive at this specific insight (say: how mice develop or exploit their neural ability to locate food in a complex box), you have to eliminate other great swaths of context (the rest of the unrelated aspects of a real world environment like trees and predators and why the mice have evolved in this way as opposed to any other). The real problems in science arise when scientists become convinced that they have arrived at THE single correct answer. (I heard an interview recently with a female geologist who was saying that she has seen other geologist, almost come to blows while arguing over whether the origins of water were from either chemical or geologic processes that happened some two-and-a-half-billion years ago). (*The Quirks and Quarks* podcast 26-02-2011) We will see this narrow protection of ideas (land naming) over and over throughout this book. It is one of the main motifs of *Proof* and my contention is that it is another reflection of our inability to separate ourselves from our egotistical human nature.

Sheldrake continues on with a discussion of Jung's collective unconscious and how doubtful it is that anything like the Archetypal forms could be inherited chemically or through DNA, or by any other mechanistic agent. *"However, there is no a priory reason why psychological theories should be confined within the framework of the mechanistic theory. They may make better sense in the context of an integrationist theory. Mental phenomena need not necessarily depend on physical laws, but rather follow laws of their own."* - Pg. 27

The real problem here,-if you pitch the mechanistic approach,-is that it becomes difficult to create testable, quantifiable predictions when viewing the phenomena of the mind or many other things like rats. This is the cornerstone of the scientific methodology. Without causality you are forced into a situation where you have difficulty representing the world in a linear or abstract way. You may then seek to build up a convincing argument based around things like personal testimonials and comparative analogies, or even a descriptive narrative. To try to express an aspect of nature like the theory of evolution without also including a vast amount of context, is really the problem in a proof. We will see that reasoning by analogue is a very slippery fish as well and forms a very weak sense of proof. Most people aren't interested in vast swaths of context and some are simply suspicious of intellectuals all together.

As mentioned in the quote above, Sheldrake proposes the more integrative theory of morphogenesis in an attempt to tackle some of these problems. Sheldrake proposes the concept of a morphogenetic field that can influence form and can be thought of as something akin to an unconscious draftsman's plans for a house. I cannot think of another way to present this concept within the condensed framework of this chapter quickly, but I wish to help you understand that this idea will resonate-however obliquely-with us later on so here's a slippery analogous argument now.

Given the same set of materials and no plans, the carpenters could build many different structures, if they wished and even within the plans there is a certain amount of leeway allowed for each tradesman. For example, if you want wood frame windows, hard wired telecommunications or blue shingles on the roof, this can all be done without consulting the plans though, sometimes, it will be specifically mentioned. But the plans do call for this type of two story house to be built and not another one. They call for a human being not an oak tree. If you threw all of the material on to a building, the house will not spontaneously construct itself without an external source of work being applied. Although statistically improbable, physicists would seek to have us admit that it is not impossible that given enough time and an infinite number of building sights and material throwers, at some point a house will spontaneously appear, I remain unconvinced. I will have something to say about the emerging science of systems theory later that shows more clearly how complex systems like the brain can gain self-consciousness without having to resort to building sight material throwing magic.

So Sheldrake is proposing a type of field that can express preponderance to certain forms in time, analogous to gravity or a magnetic field. And before we get all preachy, let's just take a look. My main contention in this chapter is that particle physics has proposed and worked with hypothesis that are as nebulous and possibly of a more religious character than this idea-over the last hundred years-and we all now simply accept this state of quantum probability as being the way that it is, probably because we don't know-for the most part-what they are talking about. But the bravery and or hype abstraction that has worked its way through particle physics has not been accepted in biology and when someone tries to introduce a new and analogous concept into biology the long knives come out. I personally believe that bad and good people are psychologically contagious in many nebulous ways that don't fit easily into causal frameworks.

To get a flavor of how Sheldrake's field ideas express themselves, I will give a concrete example. If you saturate water with salt and hang a string in it, you will get salt crystals forming into their unique crystalline form. Salt, of course, is not the same molecular grid work as that of a diamond. The resulting crystalline form of salt is due to the inherent ability of salt molecules to bond due to the unique molecular structure of salt itself. The atoms in salt have only a certain set of limited ways in which these specific atomic particles can possibly align themselves (this is specifically their molecular chemistry). The atoms within a salt crystal will have a tendency to align in a structure that holds the most stable form, or forms that requires the lowest amount of energy to hold it together. The salt molecules are 'attracted to a state of lower energy or more stability'. This is why water turns to ice at a lower temperature; at higher temperatures, there is too much energy in the atoms of water for the bonding to occur and so the water remains liquid or gaseous.

The key to understanding how more organized structures occur is that there must have been an element of work and usually a constriction of some form. For example, we have poured too much salt into the beaker of water and saturated the mixture. We don't get gold deposits on the earth unless we have had the benefit of the super heating-under tremendous pressure- of simpler elements like helium and hydrogen within stars for billions of years. Or we don't get the intricate geometric forms of snowflakes happening without a very specific set of weather conditions occurring, as well that involve various temperatures and cloud formations, etc.

The complex structure of a snow flake is in no way implied by an observation of the structure of water. If the universe was only filled with hydrogen and helium, we could never predict that all of the other elements would emerge out of these two simple atomic structures. With the application of work, and the in the form of energy input, and some form of constriction placed on the constituents like the inherent form of the molecular structure of salt molecules. Higher orders of complexity start to emerge that are in no way implied by the 'simpler' lower energy forms.

What is interesting is that salt crystals do come together and form the same type of larger crystal structures. Really how can they not? It is known in science that crystallization can be speeded up by seeding a solution with an already existing crystalline form; a small piece of anything can be introduced into a saturated solution. This will help the molecules lock into their lowest energy positions more rapidly, it's 'as if' the solution is taught how to become a crystal faster, instead of having to go through the random molecule jostling that would eventually lead to the correct alignment that will form larger crystals. This is an analogy of a morphogeneic field at work; there is preponderance or lowest energy position within a salt solution that will form structurally more complicated crystals already but this formation is the result of restrictions.

In the biological realm, things have preponderance toward their final form, which is more of a generalization than a finished product seeking perfect completion. The attraction toward higher order stability is involved in the process of achieving final form through a relationship with the environmental queuing in both its restrictions and in the form of applied work. So a human being is shaped by the amount of food (Energy=ability to work) she/he is receiving as they grow up, and through the lack of food (restrictions), the person is a reflection of the whole environment.

I will use another example quickly. Our consciousness seems to be expressed more in what we don't allow into consciousness that simply allowing everything to come gushing out and into our minds. Our temporal lobes-in the front of our heads- work more as restrictors than expressers and consciousness emerges out of this limiting or nay saying. So this constriction of information is a form of work which by limiting the flow of information achieves expression in a focus of attention, the chess board analogy fits in here nicely. It's not that we don't have free will, it's that we don't have it; free will is a reflection of restrictions in our mental horizon not the ramifications of unlimited freedom that we embody. There is a terrifying aspect to unlimited freedom.

This idea of a morphogenetic field does not imply a morphogenetic field writer though, as in the case of the plans for a house. (The watchmaker's argument) These fields act on the environment in probabilistic terms, as in molecular physics. We know how many electrons surround a nucleus, but there is no way to pinpoint their exact location of a single molecule at any one time. You must describe an electron's location using probability calculus, *"Thus the morphogenetic fields of molecules 'restrict' the possible number of atomic configurations, which would be expected on the basis of calculations, which start from the probability structures of free atoms." Similarly, the morphogenetic fields of crystals restrict the large number of possible arrangements which would be permitted by the probability structures of their constituent molecules"* - Pg. 83

What he is saying is that it is possible that these morphogenetic fields are -or possibly influence-the underlying organizational structures of biological growth, which in turn, express themselves as a participant in the ongoing expression of the field as well; at all levels of complexity. The fields are not hardwired or God-written, but they seem to imply similar structure to individuals as things achieve more stability. A morphogenic field is analogous to the instincts-at this point in the sciences-and it is hard for us to know exactly what information the animal has been born with and what the animal could conceivably be learning from subsequent nurturing. Some animals are walking immediately after being born and some are moving inside the womb as though they are walking even before birth, so they must have some form of innate ability, and of course, migratory patterns in certain birds seem to be hardwired. Morphic resonance is an attempt to frame a hypothesis to encompass non causal information.

On a higher more abstract level there could be a morphogenetic field for elephants in which parts of the collected instinctual wisdom of elephants could reside or more concretely the probable pattern of elephant making, which will always make an elephant although some will be male some female, some slightly bigger or with a larger trunk. Similar past systems of learning and thought could influence the formation of subsequent systems as they are forming through Morphic resonance, the mechanics of this is not stated, because it is not a mechanistic model. He is proposing something that is analogous to fields of 'information' that also extends into the non biological realm. You could add in the analogy that schizophrenia is a modern decease that seems to be the result of our over urbanization, but how does a very specific brain disorder result from urbanization?

"In the morphogenetic field of an atom, a naked atomic nucleus surrounded by virtual orbital serves as a morphogenetic 'attractor' for electrons. Perhaps the so called electrical attraction between the nucleus and the electrons could be regarded as an aspect of this atomic morphogenetic field. When the final form of the atom has been actualized by the capture of electrons, it no longer acts as a morphogenetic 'attractor', and in electrical terminology it is neutral. So it is not inconceivable that electromagnetic fields could be derived from morphogenetic fields of atoms." - Pg.115. The Morphic field for hydrogen atoms should be an extremely strong attractor toward stability, it having been around for billions of years, and the pattern for hydrogen making having been worked out in the first few seconds after The Big Bang.

These fields can be subsequently influenced by nature's constant creativity or indeed pull creativity forward from the future, in the same sense as, or through this idea of a field. Random mutation can also continually effect change in nature by spontaneously tossing up new combinations, the field only creates/influences a propensity toward certain structures in the sense of a gestalt. Actually the field doesn't create anything *"Morphic resonance takes place through morphogenetic fields and indeed gives rise to their characteristic structures. Not only does a specific morphogenetic field influence the form of a system, but also the form of this system influences the morphogenetic field and through it becomes present to subsequent similar systems."* - Pg. 96. Exactly how the field acts through time and at a distance becomes even more speculative though, much like how thinking works in the mind or how instinct works. We are not at a point in our understanding of biology to start to assemble the really big picture yet. As Eric Kandel has expressed we have started these processes by viewing one molecule at a time and then we slowly build up the foundations of our understanding.

"It is not the literal past that rules us, save, possibly, in a biological sense. It is images of the past. These are often as highly structured and selective as myths. Images and symbolic constructs of the past are

imprinted, almost in the manner of genetic information, on our sensibility. Each new historical era mirrors itself in the picture and active mythology of its past." George Steiner *In Bluebeard's Castle.* Quoted on the first page of, *In Search of Memory* by Eric R Kandel

"*Machines are simplifications of the causal world. Abstractly conceived, a machine is finite, and all its features and future states are fully describable. They are essentially closed off from all physical variations except those that are consistent with a given externally determined function. Thus the whole notion of machine causality is predicated on a conception of causality that both excludes teleology from consideration and yet assumes it as the basis for distinguishing machines from generic mechanical interactions. The machine metaphor of the world implicitly begs for a watchmaker, even as it denies his or her existence.*" Terrence W. Deacon, *Incomplete Nature"* - Pg. 37

An important aspect of understanding causation is the realization that correlation is not causation, because if a scarab beetle taps on the window, it doesn't mean that my dream of a scarab caused the beetle to tap there. Or because I see a new dog on the street and then get sick it doesn't mean that the new dog made me sick. This is magical thinking and much of our ancient religious insight is based on this type of correlation = causation. It also doesn't mean that there is no confluence of meaning. The connection between these two physical events can still be psychic and meaningful, and to say that it is simply a coincidence, does not actually say anything. By constantly referring to coincidence you have in some sense just moved words around a page. The patronizing 'nothing but' implication of the word coincidence in this context is quite clear.

Complex biological systems can actually become self-conscious. We are the proof and we are a complex biological system. A final result of the complexity of a brain is the creation of self-consciousness, which is the culmination of billions of neurons functioning together in nested or multileveled and highly integrated hierarchies with feedback loops occurring simultaneously across all levels. (See *Did My Neurons Make Me Do I* - a great book with a dumb title and *A Universe of Consciousness*). The mind is not built up through a series of discreet causal chains. The brain is more like a web that allows waves of information to influence itself instead of a bunch of discreet packages all under the impress of an uber-comptroller. So identifying single neural pathways or even isolating off somewhat discreet sections of the brain does not really describe what is happening at all. I will explain this more fully later but the brain and nature are the same in that they can only be expressed using multiple and sometimes even contradicting analogies set with in a context.

My big point: if we approach the world like the behaviorist, we end up 'describing what is happening, usually in a linier way' and we then seek to construct larger theoretical frame works in which to support our detached causal observations. A lot of context must be passed over when we describe the liner unfolding of phenomena in it must of necessity be compressed into a simpler linguistic representation. The behaviorists sought to imply that our observed behaviors where 'just' more and more of this 'nothing but' causal chain. (A tiger is hunting, because he cannot reason into the future so he is 'simply' responding to his belly and he has initiated his hunting matrix of behavior etc. This is a behaviorists 'nothing but' scenario that only displaces our real understanding one level backward and in actual fact it is really only describing the actions. The question then becomes, where did the hunting matrix come from or how was it assembled into a matrix? We could say evolution supplied it but really, we are chasing homunculus.)

We may even come to gain an intimate understanding of the way that neurons fire in the brain and expand our search for various ways to represent consciousness among these atomic/chemical interactions etc. still adhering to a causal mechanistic approach. We can reduce thought/consciousness down to electro chemical reactions travelling along axons etc. and we could then seek to prove that *this* thought caused *that* reaction. This doesn't actually tell us why we enjoy something like music. This is the essence of scientific reductionism and abstraction, and there is much to be gained from this methodology but it's not the end. The reality of the situation is that complicated behaviors like memory or consciousness are out of the reach of physical science to strictly describe right now.

I will pursue this a bit farther, because it is a window into scientific methodology and in a broader sense the essence of or limits of proof. I have been reading through Eric Kandel's in search of memory and it seems that Mr. Kandel's contention is that once some form of chemical or electrical memory had been arrived at through evolution; it had proved to be so effective that it would be an obvious advantage, and was continually selected for. The real problem is crossing that narrow razors edge between inert matter and some form of living entity that could have developed a memory. But he also strives to show that this ability to 'remember' didn't necessarily have to wait for the development of a full blow human or animal brain or even the complicated system of axons and neurons that, we and even sea slugs now have in our heads.

Rudimentary learning and memory systems seem to have been quickly established in nature, the advantages are more than obvious and evolution is all about retaining advantages. Later we will hear about "thinking and memory" in single cell bacterium. Because nature retains and then modifies or hijacks systems, we can study simpler forms of life and simpler neurological systems to discover the more elementary aspects of more complex processes. Ontogeny: the developmental course of biological systems. When we gain an understanding of simple systems we can use this understanding of them to extrapolate how these processes impact on to the more complex biological systems.

One of the things about biology and the analysis of natural systems in general is that; it is not as easy to express biological processes by using mathematical models as it is to furnish the types of clean representations that physics seems to be able to supply. For instance, it is almost impossible to create a mathematical model that can quantifiably encompass or correctly express the delicacy of a growing organic form. Certain aspects can be captured like the underlying geometric forms– fractal geometry and the Fibonacci number series-but nature supplies us with unique biological expressions only.

For example, if a mathematical model could be created that could predict the final shape of an oak tree-or a unfolding of the solar system for that matter-the model would not only have to be detailed enough to extrapolate the interaction of all of the cells as they diversify into the various parts of the tree but it would also have to encompass the effects of the surrounding forest and various climate changes that would also effect the final shape and growth rates. This type of infinite and compounded complexity is known as epigenetic; plants and creatures increase in complexity as they grow larger. Stumps turn into hands or fins or heads for that matter. All cells in a body start from just two cells coming together but obviously the cells diversify to an unbelievable extent as the organism grows.

The concept of epigenesis provides a way to understand why there is an endless amount of melodies in music – melodies are also epigenetic. Each subsequent note in a melody allows many more options until the choices are recognized to be endless and infinite. Along with this infinite choice of notes, we can play the same two notes with different rhythms which allows for even more changes. If you add in the individual instruments distinct tone along with rhythm, tempo and note choice, you start to understand how infinite the choices really are. As stated earlier, mathematical models of music say nothing about how or why music can represent emotions and bring us to tears. But there are mathematic expressions within music that can be written down and certain stable and familiar harmonies are or seem to be implicit in nature itself and we have discovered them. This is more like generalized expression of fractal geometry. It can be used to artfully approximate visual aspects of our environment.

"Like words printed in ink on a page - which is one way to encode and store software for access by humans - any particular embodiment of this code is just a physical pattern. Its potential to organize the operations of a specially designed machine is what leads us to consider it to be something more than this. But this "something more" is not intrinsic to the software, nor to the machine, nor to the possibility of mapping software to machine operations. It is something more only, because we recognize this potential. In the same way that the printed text of a novel is just paper and ink without a human mind to interpret it, the software is just pattern except for being interpretable by an appropriate machine for an appropriate user. The question left unanswered is weather the existence of some determinate correspondence between this pattern and some pattern of machine dynamics constitutes an interpretation in the sense that a human reader provides. Is the reader of a novel herself also merely using the pattern of ink marks on the page to specify certain "machine operations" of her brain? Is the implementation of that

correspondence sufficient to constitute the meaning of the text? Or is there something more than these physical operations? Something they are both about?" Terrence W. Deacon, *Incomplete Nature.* - Pg. 99

Music is an even more complicated example of this thought, because we interpret various notes and cords as containing emotional values, as well as its being communicated through a written form. Like the novel example above, music makes very little impression (depending on your ability to interpret written music), unless you hear it performed. Music only exists as part of an ensemble that if dissected into bits ceases to exist in any meaningful way.

It was thought by some scientists in the 1700s, that if you knew the location and rate of motion of everything in the universe, you could the– by using math-accurately predict all of the subsequent unfolding of the universe to the end of time. This was a notion that resulted from (probably misunderstanding) Newton's clockwork idea of the cosmos. It was thought that you could even determine how many angels where dancing on any given pin head (not really). The reality of reality is much more nuanced; for example, even though cloned animals are genetically identical, the animals themselves are not literally identical and nature doesn't make clones. Every individual animal is the result of two sets of DNA. We have both a mother and father and this is one of the factors that allow for genetic drift in living things, along with genetic mutation in individuals, hence the slow march of evolution.

I think this idea that much of nature can be reduced into mathematical conceptions is a subtle extension of the ideal of the Platonic forms. I also think that at root this is an archetypal idea which takes over an investigators mind set and seeks to compress us in to a narrow view of reality that we can then express as if it were a tool. Geometry seems to thrive on simple and eloquent solutions to problems. Like the psychologists in the 19th century who where content with properly naming the affliction and this allowed them to exercise power over it. This type of insight into nature is very powerful and revelatory.

I will digress once more very quickly to discuss Platonic forms. Plato was the first philosopher to make explicit-for the west-the concept of eternal forms. Plato believed that all things in the universe had a corresponding ideal form in the mind of God, from which everything that we see in the real world was a somewhat imperfect expression. All oak trees correspond to the ideal form of an oak tree in the mind of God or analogously-from a scientific perspective-all phenomena can be expressed or represented to us using math. This is the essence of the idea behind the archetypes and it seems that even the archetypes themselves are an archetypal idea in that this type of Platonic thinking comes up in science and philosophy in different-though recurring-forms over and over. The archetype, as an idea, is an attempt to represent the thought that thinking itself seems to express itself or partake in some essentially stable and therefore recognizable forms. Evolution is an expression of this recognition of patterning, in that simple structures are retained and reworked into more complex individual expressions. A morphogeneic field is another more delicate extension of this Platonic type of thinking which is ultimately introverted and intuitive, associative or mythos oriented thought it seeks to present itself as scientific.

Though not explicitly stated in the sciences there is an underlying thought behind most physical research which is that; most physical phenomena can be expressed using mathematical language; especially in the realm of physics. I think that this-not unwarranted belief-is propelled by the innate inborn quality of the human mind to search for and construct meaning. And I would add that humans are quite good at finding meaning, many things discovered-initially by purely mathematical models especially in the field of physics-have been proved correct, and accord perfectly to both a mathematical conception or mathematical way of expression and the reality of the natural phenomena that is being expressed. This is why we can build computer models to predict physical phenomena. This type of mathematical representation or expression of nature has been discovered to be true; it is not strictly constructed by our mental exploration. This discovery of underlying mathematical harmony is the Platonic ideal. I will explain.

Using just the mathematics of physics you can predict things like; what would the maximum size of a star be before that star will collapse under its own weight. Or you might propose that objects like black holes exist (black holes are super dense objects that won't even let light escape there gravitational pull.) These types of things were first considered to be mathematically probable or they seemed to be reasonable propositions of how reality could be. They were then further analyzed using only mathematical models because we actually didn't know if -for instance-black holes actually existed. When later tested against the reality of the observable universe they were discovered to be true and largely accurate representations of the way things really are in nature. The centre of every universe seems to hold a super massive black hole. We can understand much about the way that our sun functions by building computer models of it, by exploiting our detailed understanding of the laws of physics.

The mathematical expression of phenomena is intrinsic in nature, and hence the appeal of the concept of eternal forms and or the underlying mathematical expression of reality through geometry (which is actually prelinguistic and representational in essence and math is used afterward to contextualize it), etc. The idea of a perfect and discernible *eternal form* beyond their specific expression in nature is essentially an introverted idea, whereas Plato's star student Aristotle was more extraverted in his outlook. Aristotle is considered to be one of the great forerunners of modern science and he went to great efforts to collect real samples of all types of things-especially in the field of biology-and he meticulously wrote down his various observations of the real world. He made attempts to categorize and organize the world around him in an intellectually satisfying way. The two opposing standpoints are at the root of western philosophy and science; each paradigm taking the lead at some point and then relinquishing the lead to the other viewpoint.

The abstraction of two specific personality types or approaches to the world became the basic idea from which Jung went on to express the concepts of introvert and extrovert. He used the two men specifically (Plato & Aristotle) in his book on personality types to introduce these elemental viewpoints, because most intellectuals would be somewhat familiar with these two personalities. Incidentally, great swaths of Arabic philosophy can be understood as an effort to reconcile the two great foundational thinkers and then further synthesize them with the revealed teachings of the Koran.

On another level, I believe that this dynamic-as it is reflected in science-is another reflection of the wavelike dynamic of the two competing types of perception: extraversion and introversion, Apollonian and Dionysian, which in turn, are also reflected in the inner workings of the brain itself. I believe at the heart of Mr. Sheldrake's conception of morphogenesis there is a subtle reassertion of the Platonic ideal, possibly as a counter to the overtly extraverted mode of thinking that dominated much of the sciences and particularly biology: behaviorism and it's frustrating bed partner, the social science model.

The hard sciences are dead set against any form of unsubstantiated introverted supposition and rightfully so, but that doesn't mean that the hard sciences own the complete picture of what truth is. This thought can be understood by looking at the theory of evolution, which is has been proved through the largely extraverted process of collecting endless examples from nature and then recognizing and comparing similarity through progressive analysis and endless categorization. Darwin's theory of ongoing natural selection is a reflection of an introverted hypothesis which is based on and corroborated by the detailed extraverted observation of nature itself.

Another very interesting example of underlying unity of nature was the discovery of the periodic table in chemistry. It was realized that there was an intrinsically deeper level of organization within the chemical universe itself which is profound, but by recognizing this stunning fact you still don't completely understand chemistry. The intellect likes to say things like: *"Oh that's just the periodic table, or just energy."* Energy is hand-pointing beyond itself and into a real mystery. My overarching wish here is to take a look at some of the deeper psychological aspects that creep their way into the ever so human nature of the sciences. I will throughout the remaining chapters seek to point out the ongoing and often petty rivalries that drive science forward.

Mr. Sheldrake has been kind enough to include at the end of his book some of the opinions of various scientists about his book. They range from the indignant to the sympathetic, it seems scientists in the field of astrophysics and quantum mechanics are more amenable to his hypothesis of a morphogeneic field than biologists are. Quantum mechanics has been wrestling with crazy hypotheses for some time now and some of these hypotheses have proved to be extremely helpful as a way to move forward. (As a quick example, listen to *Astronomy Cast: Episode 166*. This is a completely speculative and largely metaphysical, disguised as a physics discussion of multiple universes or multi-verses.) A hypothesis must be able to encompass the observable phenomena. In the realm of theoretical physics it seems that most of the vicious contemporary antagonists of Einstein or quantum mechanics are quite dead now and the larger community can get on with the business of trying to understand the universe. In fact, it seems that Einstein's view was so revolutionary that the most antagonistic of his contemporary scientist where simply slack jawed because they could not grasp the mathematical expression. Again, gravity was a physical hypothesis and its ultimate proof was its ability to encompass and predict how the planets really moved. Newton's representation was a better paradigm but not the final answer.

I feel I have poorly represented Mr. Sheldrake in that his hypothesis is much more nuanced and technical than I have time to represent. More than anything I should like to give you an inkling of the great difficulty involved in really understanding the root nature of something like inherited information. This would encompass the instincts and ancestral memories and the larger concept of the Archetypes themselves. Also, I have tried to present an inkling of the specific role that DNA and genetics hold in modern biology. This is one of the areas of personal interest that propelled me to write this book and I will circle around these concepts from another viewpoint as we discuss other things later on like the human compulsion toward religious behavior. For now I only wish to leave you with this thumbnail sketch of Rupert Sheldrake's ideas and along with this some inklings of the way that a proof is made and how science in general is done.

The Ghost in Darwin's Machine

Evolutionary psychology is a newer branch of the social sciences, which is using the theory of evolution to help explain both how our brain has evolved and how our social behavior and the resulting societies we have constructed -or found ourselves in- have been shaped by evolutionary pressure and conversely how we have shaped the ongoing evolution of our societies. The basic premise is that if all or most people in the human race show an inclination toward the same type of behavior: than this behavior has probably been selected and/or shaped in us by evolutionary forces. I will circle around the example of religion because I can't help myself and I like to poke my finger at the public face of the current scientific zeitgeist which is of a decidedly atheistic slant.

But first, this is a short example that will help to explain some aspects of evolutionary flexibility and how it is relevant over long and short terms. I recently listened to a show that was discussing the finch population on the Galapagos Islands. These are the very finches that Darwin used as an example of the dynamics of evolution. This quite diverse population was probably the result of one or two pair of finches being blown on to the islands and subsequently developed in isolation.

During the 1998 El Nino event in the southern hemisphere, the Galapagos Islands received seven times the amount of rain fall that occurs in a regular year and the finch population grew to a great extent. These extreme El Nino events are quite rare, but it seems that another one happened about two hundred years ago in 1780 as well. There are, on the Galapagos Islands, 13 different species of finch and the different species of finches occasionally interbreed. This interbreeding happens at a faster pace in times of plenty (the distinctly different species regularly inter breed at about the rate of 1 in 50 couplings), but the resulting offspring of these mixed breeding adventures cannot survive with their mixed adaptation tool box when the environment returns to a more regular pattern. The fossil record shows that this population of finches has been fairly stable, with these same 13 species of finch have been dominating for a very long time. It also shows that these mixed breeds do not go on to create yet another new species over the long haul.

If a finch that has a very strong beak used for eating large nuts, mates with another species that has a small beak used for smaller seeds, the chick will have a medium sized beak and medium beak strength, and/or other various blends of the genetic propensities. The beaks in this mixed bird are not strong enough for the larger seeds and mixes have the greatest tendency to be born during the corresponding explosion of breeding that is also happening in the regular species of finch that occurs with the El Nino event. This means that the supply of smaller seeds is being quickly devoured by the better adapted beaks of the already existing small seed eating breeds. The mixed breed finch is then left in a position where they are un-adapted to easily manipulate small seeds and not strong enough to regularly eat large ones and so they have difficulty competing with the more refined adaptations of the other stable species in the now post El Nino environment. The only reason they came into being is that nature created an exceptional bumper crop environment. In other words, the mixed breed cannot return to the 'specialized' or normal environment in which they must continue, because they have a hybrid mixed toolbox.

It would appear that the 13 finch species are best suited to the long-term environment of these islands, but it also appears that nature is always trying to fill in niches. (See *Darwin's Ghost* by Steve Jones) The relative size of the beaks in the stable population can potentially undergo changes quite quickly, due to the quick breeding cycle of the finches and ever-present pressure to adapt to environmental changes, if the need should arise. Sometimes nature jumps the slow queue and allows ongoing experimentation to occur. Nature seems to have a plan for sudden climate change at least amongst fast breeding animals. It should be no surprise that the global environment is always changing and that nature resists too much stability. So, evolution isn't this ridiculously slow moving process, especially when it comes to fast breeding animals; it is a somewhat flexible strategy. Even large animals will be ready to breed at younger ages in a stressful environment and this may explain why girls seem to be maturing faster in North America these days, although it is probably due to the staggering amount of estrogens in our environment.

Another example of the inherent flexibility of nature is seen in the moose population on the island of Labrador here in Canada. It is known that the entire population of moose on this island is the result of one breeding pair and one adolescent being brought into this environment by some hunters who wished to have an alternate meat source for themselves. The population is now in the thousands (may be tens of thousands), because it is an excellent environment for the moose. No natural predators and an endless supply of plant food. There is the thought that inbreeding amongst higher animals is detrimental to the genetic code and it is for a number of reasons, but this population seems to be doing just fine.

It is fairly well known that the Ptolemaic Dynasty in Egypt was almost totally inbred for 13 generations: probably two sets of new genes entered into this family around the 8th and 10th generation. It is also quite certain that some of the later rulers were showing definite signs of this inbred genetic strain, but at the very end of this line, nature threw up Cleopatra who seemed to have been a very intelligent woman, though perhaps not intelligent enough to have stayed out of Roman politics all together. My point is that Nature does not stick manically to any set pattern, but exploits situations through flexible approaches. All manner of tools are in the toolbox and some might be lying on the ground elsewhere.

Religion is without a doubt a worldwide and universal human activity. We need to have a fairly flexible definition of what religion is, but I should think this statement is self-evident. Religion at its most basic level seems to help bind communities together through reinforcing a common outlook or promoting a similar understanding of the world. (The cynic or 'realist' would say that it drives some communities apart and fair enough.) This common social bond is achieved through the practice of collective ritual, which usually involves music and rhythmic movement, which in turn, induces trance-like states that can lead the individual into a 'transcendent' state of mind. We will discuss the affects of this state of mind later, but suffice to say that if individuals have gone through this type of elemental collective process, they are more inclined to have empathy with the other members of their group and they will be inclined to help maintain the order of their group against the aggression of outsiders.

Two more quick examples of evolutionary-chosen activities are rough and tumble play and the ability to walk and or run immediately after being born. Most of the higher animals like chimps and lions participate in rough and tumble play. There is always the threat that this type of activity can result in the death of an individual, but nature doesn't really care about individuals. If this type of behavior was such a great disadvantage to a species, it would have been weeded out of our behavior patterns. There are so many advantages to our neurological development that result from participating in rough and tumble play-in terms of the development of the physical, mental and social integration of the individual- that it is worth the risk to lose some individuals. If we play rough, it's a good thing or at least it is evolutionarily sanctioned. Something in our 'nature' is being expressed through this type of action for a reason. The advantages of being able to walk immediately after being born are self-evident. Somehow nature sees fit to pass this ability on in the uterus, along with vastly more complicated modes of behavior that express themselves in the world, seemingly without having been learned. I will repeatedly come back to this.

In the area evolutionary psychology, I have greatly enjoyed the work of Robert Wright (*The Moral Animal, Non Zero* and *The Evolution of God* are excellent reads) Mr. Wright largely confines himself to the

Darwinian paradigm although greatly expanding upon it. This is not a knock on my part, but there is very little in his work to explain anything like an overheated consciousness receiving a vision of a flaming sword, or what a dream is, which seems to be my main concern at this point. This is more a reflection of the sciences in general in that very few people are willing to discuss the upper breathy reaches of complex systems, like why we have the concept of God in human societies. Ironically after I wrote this bit of foolishness, I found that this was exactly the subject Robert Wright tackled in his book: *The Evolution of God* and I have had to re-enter my narrative. What Roberts Wright's books represent to me is a very articulate look at the mechanics of Darwinian thought and the related subject of game theory and the ramifications of these two modes of thought. I have also subsequently found a number of authors who are very interested in the evolution of the religious endeavor and I will treat this subject more fully later on. For now I am pretending to write about the sciences.

I recently heard a person arguing that our behavior, and by extension our ethical or legal codes and/or the resulting moral stances of our society, should be a reflection of our underlying religious beliefs, because these beliefs are more naturally altruistic or they promote or enhance our altruism through our learning about our fellow humans. This implies that without the glue of religious moral authority, we start to degenerate into amoral thugs. This is wrong for a number of reasons. The fact that someone is an atheist or homosexual or drummer in a rock band doesn't mean that they go around killing people indiscriminately or committing petty crimes, because they have no fear of God. Every judge in the world could be a rabid atheist and we would still have a functioning legal system. Most people don't hurt other people, because they feel it's wrong or they can't bring themselves to do it, or it's simply not in their best interest. Conversely, many of the most Catholic of popes have initiated all manner of human butchery and cognitive dissonance and still believe that they are at heart really good people. *The New Testament* tells us that women shouldn't speak in church and the *Old Testament* gives us instructions about how to sell our children into slavery? There are many other pressures to socially conform in the world other than overt religious values. Ultimately, the problem with this thinking-in our specifically real world-is which religious vision would *you* choose to impose?

In *Non Zero*, Robert Wright articulates a new way of analyzing and expressing the underlying forms behind human interaction. The cornerstone idea is the theme of reciprocal altruism and its expression in game theory and how these ideas have become recognized as major forces in the dynamic of social interactions. Reciprocal altruism in its most elemental form is expressed in the tit for tat strategy, if I do something good for you, you in turn will do something good for me. Likewise if you cheat me in a deal, I will be less likely to enter into a deal with you again. The implication of this is that cheating as a long range social/personal strategy doesn't work well. Eventually, the cheater will be castigated within his own society.

Mr. Wright explores some other ramifications of evolutionary thought in terms of psychology and sociology, bearing witness to the fact that Darwin was stunningly correct in almost all aspects of his framework. Throughout most of the history of human society, individuals have lived in smaller collections of people than the society that we now find ourselves in. These small collections of hunter-gatherer societies have developed good collective memories and the ones that have been studied seem to spend an inordinate amount of time firming up the collective check sheets of their relative indebtedness to each other. Hunter-gatherer societies are very tight knit groups of between 20 and 100 people, and they cannot afford prolonged abhorrent behavior out of a member. Each member is in very close quarters to all of the others and social organization is constantly being monitored and reinforced either explicitly or unconsciously through our continued interaction within the group. Expressions of reciprocal altruism seemed to be hardwired into us, or it seems to constantly express itself unconsciously through us. As a result of the social engineering that went on in this very long hunter-gatherer stage (100 thousand years), in our evolution.

In terms of tit for tat strategy, Wright is not saying that cheaters never prosper, in fact over the short-term, and in a larger social setting, it can be a very effective strategy. His underlying thesis is that when viewed over longer periods of time, cheating will prove to be a less genetically productive strategy. Most people aren't cheaters and even the most repressive regimes in the world eventually come to an end, possibly to resurface again in different forms, but the weight of our collected history is proving too much for them right now. (The Soviets lasted less than 80 years; the Taliban and a whole slew of Islamic dictatorships are now up for grabs for a number of reasons: Arab spring.) We cannot go on cheating indefinitely, especially in smaller societies like the ones that our ancestors evolved in. There is no time to tolerate this behavior, because it negatively impacts the survival of the whole group and we are ultimately the end result of only those groups of people who have survived. The most severe form of chastisement is banishment and people who are banished would have a hard time reproducing. With globalization and current telecommunications, the world is becoming a very small place again and the only way a rogue state or an individual criminal can sustain an overtly petulant lifestyle is to go completely offline like Kim Jong Ill of North Korea. You could call this collective scrutiny an aspect of global Karma, if you want.

As societies grew larger, the pressure on each individual to conform to implied social rules has relaxed a bit. But the same strategies seek to find expression even across the societies themselves. For example, if I am the big man in a community of 100 people and I throw a big party and cook up a big pig, I would expect that you will be impressed and spread that information around in the village for some time. If you don't spend enough time talking about my party, I will make efforts to remind you. In this way, I can get invited to the next big cook up and reclaim some of my social debt. But the social aspect is what is important, not the amount of food I may or may not put in your belly. I have, by cooking up a pig, overtly stated my status to everyone around by throwing this big party. This is social 'Bling' as a form of advertising and display. It may also be viewed within a religious context, which doesn't have to have any sort of ulterior motive at all and will quite sternly elude this type of social calculus. This collective drive toward social effort can become a major creative force in large societies as we witness in all of the massive cultural sites (the pyramids included) all over the world.

A discussion of the forms of social strategies is applicable to evolution directly, because evolution is most certainly a long-range strategy, and over the long-ranges, the most adaptable or effective –social- strategy will tend to dominate a successful culture, and therefore, will be reflected in our evolution. So these tit for tat ways of living together have been constantly reinforced down through history. And by framing these phenomena in terms of social traction and reciprocal altruism, we gain an understanding of how societies form themselves and hopefully expose some of the mechanics behind the behaviors that we are now witness to.

If I may be so presumptuous as to sum up the aspect of Mr. Wright's work as it applies to this book. He seems to be saying that there is much in the world of sociology and psychology that can be profitably looked at from within the evolutionary framework. Game theory in general is an analytic stratagem, which seeks to eliminate value from social interaction. Game theory and evolutionary psychology seem to be framing all behavior in terms of utility and they stretch this point quite thinly. There are many things that seem to exist simply because they are beautiful things like music, art and the female orgasm, for instance. We can always create a system that will seek to validate these phenomena in terms of utility, but I ultimately think these aspects of culture exist beyond the narrow spotlight of utility.

Within the game theory/evolutionary framework, you rarely discuss purpose or value in this framework. Nature can have no over guiding plan. It has direction, but no purpose. Implying purpose into nature will lead us into the realm of anthropomorphism, which is where you add human characteristics to non-human objects. I see a subtle form of anthropomorphism in nature shows all of the time. The narrators lend human meanings to animal actions so that the audience can relate to these animals. *"Here, the tiger has searched out yet another female in an effort to spread his genes as widely as possible."* (I prefer to say that line with the voice of David Attenborough, although he resists Anthropomorphism heroically.) I highly doubt that the tiger has any inkling of spreading his genetic information. I think tigers quite rightly enjoy sex and sex is an excellent way to spread genetic information. This lack of purpose in nature seems to be one of the great stumbling blocks that some people have with evolution, in that Darwin has cast God out of the ongoing expression of the equation. Nature seems to have the purpose of passing on genetic information and she seems to employ a variety of strategies when trying to accomplish this. But just this simple statement of purpose is loaded with implied meaning. How can a tiger employ any evolutionary strategies? The tiger simply is those strategies embodied.

Evolution rightly shows that there are mechanisms that have been built up over time that allow change to occur through the retention of useful genes and behavior. Evolution then supplies the ability to adapt and pursue change through ongoing random mutation and creativity. Evolution also shows us that strategies that work get selected and these strategies continue on in the resulting gene pool. What we see -in our world now- are the result of the continual balance between random innovation and the time tested stability of the strategies that have proven to work properly. This appearance of meaningful direction in nature is a result of our perception of the results of complex systems, which move in lock step with the constant pressures to adapt to a changing environment and random mutation. Our wish to view nature as employing various strategies or as an inherently creative entity is largely due to our inability to encompass the whole of it in our minds. We witness a seeming stream of direction and then imply meaning backward. The writing of history itself suffers from this same endless attempt to suss out 'direction'.

There is much to be gained in terms of our understanding of human psychology and sociology when viewed from the evolutionary standpoint. Even the seemingly abstract realms of dreaming or religion can be dovetailed into a purely evolutionary context. On the more prosaic or personal level of the unconscious, I can see how dreaming could be an addendum to a busy day and a type of restful downloading or reshuffling of sensory information in order that the individual can challenge the next day renewed, and of a somewhat clearer mind. I will explore the mechanics of dreaming much more fully in the rose glass chapter. What Mr. Wright explains very well is that within biological or sociological systems, Darwinian evolution can be shown to be the most comprehensive theory to explain how sociological systems we live in are built up through interaction with ever larger and more complicated patterns.

Mr. Sheldrake goes on to explain in his book: *The Sense of Being Stared At* that ESP can also be seen as an excellent evolutionary adaptation and he supplies-to my mind-ample, if only anecdotal proof that Telepathy and ESP do, in fact, exist. How exactly they work is really a good question. His proof is built by a staggering amount of personal testimonials. It appears that many animals possess ESP and most humans could as well, to a greater or lesser extent. Hindu and Buddhist monks and Islamic mystics certainly believe in these things. Humans in a modern urban setting -it would seem-have stopped using this type of intuition, much like our radically decreased sense of smell, which is well below the level of a lot of animals. This sense of smell and taste can be sharpened by simply paying more attention to smells. (Neuroplasticity)

These acute sense abilities, like a really accurate and subtle smell sense, take up a lot of brain power and our heads are only so big. It seems evolution has seen fit to diminish our sense of smell, while increasing our higher cognitive abilities, and focusing on excellent bilateral eye sight, which presumably, is a worthy trade off. We have also developed the ability to use our reasoning skills to problem solve and we have become less dependent on our gut intuition, but like all aspects of the personality, these too can be nurtured and taught back into use. It seems that humans living in more 'natural' settings rely on this ability to intuit to a far greater extent than we do and only our western prejudice stops us from taking our intuition and or ESP more seriously. Conversely, primitive societies tend to presume many things due to overtly magical thinking as a result of there more total immersion in nature. (Participation mystique) Surprisingly, the scientific method didn't arise due to evolutionary pressures, and like good posture, it must be taught. (A bad joke, if you missed it.)

Interestingly, it is believed that European red foxes can see and use the earth's magnetic lines to orient themselves in space. (*Quirks and Quarks* podcast 29-01-2011) They first locate the mouse with their smell and hearing and then use the magnetic field around them to triangulate the exact location of sounds and smells, and then adjust themselves to be at the best distance to pounce on the prey. If the mouse or vole is hiding in the snow, or long grass, this ability to triangulate on the mouse's position allows them to pounce on a mouse from above. This scientist was saying that red foxes actually see the magnetic background of the environment in the same sense that raccoons can 'see' with their hands. The foxes have allocated brain power to this ability to discern magnetic field information as an evolutionary advantage. Migrating birds are probably using a version of the same ability.

As a related and analogous example, it has recently been realized that the whole idea of personal auras has an actual grounding in scientific proof. It has been supposed by flaky religious types for years that each individual is surrounded by a halo of color that reflects his or her spiritual achievement. Jesus was presumed to have a blue aura, which was later stylized in painting iconography into a golden color and rendered as a halo, then a crown. This is a stylized golden solar disc (borrowed from the Roman cult of the sol invinctus), and is not a reflection of his actual spiritual halo. It has been recently realized that people with a different brain wiring called 'synaesthesia' can actually see these colors around people. This effect is probably a reflection of the person with synaesthesia co-associating the emotions they are seeing/feeling intuitively in other people, with actual visual colors. (See Pg.327 for a lengthy discussion of synaesthesia.)

Briefly, people with this ability have a cross-wiring or more integration between their senses. They see colors or experience flavors when they listen to music or they see colors when they perceive emotions, etc. The interesting thing is that people who have this ability have great difficulty explaining it to other people. I can imagine someone possessing this ability, say… in Victorian England, and getting hooked up with spiritualists etc., and becoming a seer with an extra sense. They would have a hard time explaining the actual reality of auras to anyone, but they could convince you that these auras exist, because they are actually seeing them. In other words, they are not lying when they tell you that they see auras. You could become convinced of the reality of this situation, because you would not smell a lie. This phenomenon would then be explained by other people in a way that was relevant to the social climate of the believers. Or conversely, this particular phenomenon could be endlessly pooh-poohed by skeptical scientists, because they don't actually see the aura themselves.

This concept of auras was taken very seriously in the theosophy movement of Madam Blavatsky in the late Victorian era. Then of course, it was run out of town by our modern scientific rationalism and now we realize-as we step around through the back door again-that in fact this aspect of theosophy's flaky mumbo jumbo is actually a real effect of a rewiring of the brain and that it has a very 'rational' even scientific explanation. Some people may also have remnants of the ability to discern magnetic force or any number of things. I have never seen an electron, but I've been told they exist, but proof is the bottom line for everyone. So seeing Jesus with a blue halo was the best paradigm they had at the time: same halo, different intellectual context.

Let Us Sing Now Into Trees

This next story sums up most of what I have been discussing about evolution and puts it all into a wider context. There was a documentary that I saw on TVO called: *Ring of Fire*. It was about two young men: Lorne and Lawrence Blair who travelled in Borneo and Indonesia in the sixties. I watched the whole series, but the one I will discuss here is *Dream Wanderers of Borneo*.

Travel in Borneo is notoriously difficult, so much so that many of the last people on earth to have had the misfortune of making contact with westerners were living on this island. (The very last un-contacted people are now in Brazil). In this documentary, the Blair brothers hire a rhinoceros hunter and a number of other native men to take them into the interior of the island. In the era before GPS, they are literally travelling off of the map. The map they were using was literally blank in the section where they were travelling into. The rhinoceros hunter they hired had been in the area only once before when he was much younger. It appears -as things develop- that his memory of the earlier trip was a little sketchy. As these brothers moved inland, they remind the viewer of the dangers inherent in travel at this time. If one of them slipped and broke his ankle there is a very good chance that it would mean their death, in that there was no way to get them out again: no helicopter could airlift them out, and carrying an individual out of the bush on a stretcher was impractical. After a certain point, you would simply run out of food on the way back, because of the slow pace. They were also travelling up rivers that were too shallow to get their boats up. The bush around them was so dense that to make any more than three to five miles headway a day, was moving quickly. Carrying an individual out might be a death sentence to all.

There is an incredible scene where one brother explains to the camera that they are at least a seven-day walk out of the bush and they are eating the last of their food supplies. The camera pans around to the other native people who were hired to help them, and they are very calm and relaxed. In fact, many of the porters are washing themselves and doing their hair. The brother goes on to explain that the rhinoceros hunter had a dream that the tribe they are going to visit was not too far up the river. A runner has been sent up river-following the rhinoceros hunter's instructions-to find this tribe. All of the native people seem to take it for granted that this dream will turn out to be true. Incidentally, the tribe they are going to see are known head hunters. It does, in fact, turn out that the tribe is where the rhinoceros hunter said they would be and they do go on to meet them.

After some time with this tribe of people, it is decided that they should have a big party and a Shaman is sought to run the show. The cameraman (one of the brothers) dances with some vigor (in the free-form hippy way) at this party and they all have a good time. It is subsequently revealed that the whole point of the party was so that the Shaman could send a dream to the brothers. One brother (the dancing one), does have a dream that night and in the dream he meets the spirit of the forest, which is symbolized by a huge tree that extends all over the island. In the dream, they are allowed to travel without fear in the safety of the branches of this tree. The natives worship this deity, which manifests in the concrete world as the largest tree in their forest. They will not cut down the old large trees of the forest out of respect for the spirit of the forest in which they live. They also have an abstract symbol that represents this spirit. It is quite common to have this symbol tattooed on to their bodies and one brother gets this tattoo put on his upper right chest, with a needle on a stick, dipped in ink and tapped with a rock. He goes on to say that the whole trip out of the jungle was very relaxed. There was never a sense they were in the same danger, as they experienced going in.

Now, evolutionary psychology falters when it comes to offering an explanation for this type of anticipatory dream. I'm not sure that the onus is on evolutionary psychology to tackle this question. But I believe this is a part of the natural psyche and it is taken for granted by so called primitive people as such. There have always been people who have the big dreams that seem to reflect an understanding of the psychic texture of the times, or of the very specific events unfolding in their world. It seems that most of the dreams-or at least any that we can pry from so called primitive people-are collective dreams or indicative of the collective mindset of the group. These people are participating in a much more collective and relatively unconscious aspect of interconnected psychology than ego maniacal westerners. The dream that Moses tells the Pharaoh of seven fat and seven lean cows is an example of this type of anticipatory big collective dream.

All of the natives in the documentary take this anticipatory dream as a matter of fact. What I think is important to note is that in both of the cases of these dreams (the rhinoceros hunter's and the dream sent to the brothers), there was a certain amount of tension involved: the rhinoceros hunter would have known that they were running low on food and the shaman created an atmosphere (a big party) in which the brother's psyche could be focused or engaged. Incidentally, this idea of old trees that protect or enlighten people is a very old archetype and has gained much play again in James Cameron's *Avatar* film. I recently met someone who participated in an iawasca drug taking ceremony in Peru who experienced the forest talking to her. Paul Simon sings about this same participation mystic on rhythm of the saints. It is an extension of the same set of images or psychological archetypes that the Blair brothers experienced firsthand in Borneo. We will have an opportunity to discuss stress and received dreams later as well.

In the book, *Songlines* by Bruce Chatwin, he explains the Australian aborigine use of song lines as they navigate through their world. I will preface this story by saying that Jung understood that people in their natural environment didn't need to analyze their personal unconscious. It was spread out all around them; the stone was sacred, that fissure was a portal to the underworld, etc. So if you needed to experience your unconscious you would go to the place that was relevant to your situation. This is because so called primitive people are more a part of their environment. The external world is not perceived as a completely discreet and separate entity. This idea is known as participation mystic or a mystical participation in the exterior environment. Participation mystic implies a less explicit sense of detachment from the environment, or a devaluing of the creations of the ego or an easier acceptance of the metaphoric mindset.

"Buy the sky and sell the sky, these ideas are foreign to us" Chief Seattle & R.E.M

The sight of the Eleusinian mysteries in Greece was built on a deep fissure in the earth that was probably a very old and sacred Neolithic sight that embodied a lot of Manna (or psychic goo). As the Christians built their churches all over Europe, they understood this fact of Manna well, and they would usually build a church on to an already existing sacred sight to gain the efficacy of that sight, or to simply establish their new dominance over it. St Peters Basilica in Rome is built over a still existing shrine dedicated to Mithraism, which was a very common religion in Rome amongst the soldiers at the time. Mithraism subsequently influenced Christian doctrine and development. This pre-Christian shrine was recently uncovered in the bowels of the Basilica as a living testament to the Christian debt to Mithraism. Jung's dream of different levels of a house representing different levels of conscious growth is here, literally manifesting by one religious building growing over another. This is literally the west's psychic architecture, but I digress.

In Australia, if an aboriginal woman is pregnant, it is very important for her to consult a Shaman when she feels the first kick of her child in the womb. This is the point that the child is said to be, 'coming alive' and there is the thought that the 'child' actually may enter the womb at this time. When she feels this first kick, she needs to establish which song line she was travelling on, because that will become part of the child's totem. She needs to orient herself and her child in the world. (Re-linking) That child may have come alive while the mother was walking on a Cockatoo song line and the child may feel or be bred into an affinity for that song line his whole life, (this will be a part of his/her individual totem). And, of course, it will be well known by everyone that this child was born on a cockatoo song line. The tribe itself also has a totem that represents the whole tribal area or the inclination of the tribe itself, and that may be the Bandicoot totem with its own different song line. These song lines extend all over this and other tribes areas and they hold the key to maneuvering through these environments.

The elders of the tribe will take a large piece of bark off a tree and draw out this Bandicoot map, using the dotted style that has become associated with Australia in our minds. Along with this physical map is a corresponding song of the map, or the two artistic creations are representations in different media of the same thing. This Bandicoot song line song can be sung to travel and navigate within this area. Long slow notes are associated with flat areas and more staccato phrases will indicate changing terrain, etc. (Brian Eno met Bjork at a spa in London and he speculated that Bjork's use of large harmonic jumps in melody reflected her well travelled Viking heritage. I think she agreed with him). And so this map is just that: a visual representation of a song map of the area and it is common to trade these bark maps with your neighbors. You have then given them the right or privilege to be able to sing their way through your landscape. This is an excellent way to head off inter tribal tensions, because you have allowed your neighbor directly into your psyche. The song lines are the literal and spiritual map of Australia, because they are the manifestations of the songs that the original ancestors used when they sang the world into existence. Mr. Bandicoot and Mr. Cockatoo laid down their song lines long ago in the eternal dream time. The unconscious is spread all about you.

And God said, "Let there be light," Genesis 3

"*Each of the Ancients (now basking in the sunlight) put his left foot forward and called out a second name. He put his right foot forward and called out a third name. He named the waterhole, the reed beds, the gum trees-calling to right and left, calling all things into being and weaving their names into verses.*

The ancients sang their way all over the world. They sang the rivers and ranges, salt-pans and sand dunes. They hunted, ate, made love, danced and killed wherever their tracks led; they left a trail of music." - Pg. 73

So when you know your song lines, you not only have a very useful map of the environment, you are also psychically in tune with yourself and your psyche, in that your whole psyche is spread out around you in the environment of which you are now a wholly integrated part, and you have a map. You have both an individual song line that is part of you and a set of collective song lines in which to explore reality. This is the idea of re-linking you again in another way. And one more time: Yoga is yoking you up to the big picture. In, up, and out.

It has been conjectured-and I will discuss this at length-that language has evolved out of music that is embodied in the world and us. In 1982, Kate Bush released an album called, *The Dreaming*. It was her worst selling album to date and caused a crisis for her in that she was proving to be a commercial failure. There was great hope for her success in Britain when she first appeared and she initially had some huge pop singles. She was also very beautiful. For me, *The Dreaming* is one of her greatest works in that it was quite visionary and really experimental; usually a commercial death sentence. It seems that she was fascinated with Australian song lines as well, because the title *The Dreaming* refers to the aboriginal beginning of time when the song lines and the world was being sung into existence and also our ability to participate in that creation.

Sometimes aborigines will go on a walkabout, which means that they just set off walking. Needless to say, Australia is a very harsh environment, but some of these aborigines have gone walkabout across the whole continent. They have entered into *The Dreaming* and are spontaneously singing or following the song lines that have been laid down before them. By entering into the collective unconscious archetypal realm or the dreaming, or the morphic field, which is inside and all about them, they can know exactly where they are. The unconscious song lines contain information like where to get food, water, etc. You can think of it as a collected wisdom embedded into the Australian outback that also exists in potential in all natives and is a reflection of both their collective psyche and the land itself.

This information is linked to the psyche through song and rhythm, which induces the most integrative states of the brain. Most oral history is passed on through this method of rhyme, rhythm and melody, because the mind remembers information best in this multi-valence form in that-among many things-the different parts of the ensemble of the song or performance, or painted map reinforce each other. The entire Koran can be and is sung regularly even by the excessively repressive Taliban. Apparently, some yogis have memorized the entire Mahabharata, which are some three thousand pages of writing. And even very old people with severe Alzheimer who cannot remember anything about their personal narrative, will begin to sing along *in key* with songs from their distant youth. Poor Kate Bush needed a hit that could be easily remembered to reinforce her ailing career at this point, but it had to wait until *the Hounds of Love*. Ok kids, she seems to be fine.

But we still don't have a proof of this unconscious interface between us and the universe, or any kind of definitive scientific proof of the underlying validity of the concept of archetypes, etc. I am making an effort to build-up a thesis by circling around it, and obliquely reinforcing this concept of the underlying collective unconscious (Morphic Field/ Dreamtime/ Unas Mundi, etc). I feel a bit like a conspiracy theorist.

Jung referenced a quote in Latin that I have had difficulty locating in his work so that I could reflect the setting he uses. It is from Psalm 12: 8 in, *Circuitu Impii Ambulant*. The ungodly wander in a circle and/or the wicked walk round about or in Jung's interpretation the ignorant remain forever on the parameter going only around in a circle. His implication is that the wise literally spiral ever closer to the heart of truth. You can think of this circular movement in terms of the different psychological types in that the wise slowly explore all of the facets of their personality and eventually end up in the centre with a whole conception of the Self. Or that there is a central and un-revolving wisdom (an unmoving central axis) to be experience and by exploring all around, we can get closer to the centre or power spot (bindi), or the dreaming. By going on walkabouts (or engaging in play, etc.), we can experience the larger area of the collective unconscious and raise elements of it in to our consciousness. This type of inner meditation can take the visual form of a mandala that you slowly walk around until you literally end up in the centre. This is a literal exterior manifestation of in inner urge to be in the centre. This is why we bring a Christmas tree into our house, because this tree now represents the centre of the world. We adorn it with light as the sacred axis.

"Doubt is the crown of life because truth and error come together. Doubt is living; truth is sometimes death and stagnation."- C.G. Jung, Seminar on Dream Analysis Pg.89

For me, the most visionary book of the biblical era is the ones that the Church suppressed from the official canon. This is the Gospel of Thomas, the same Thomas who became known as, 'doubting Thomas'.

In the Gnostic tradition, his faith proved to be the strongest, because he doubted Christ. He did not blindly believe the message, but he tested it himself to find out its truth. This testing became an unshakable truth in that it was his truth, not a borrowed faith. This is our position again summed up in a myth or a metaphor, which is one of the psychological forms of truth as opposed to Logos, which is the scientific truth. All personal truth is experiential. It should accord with outer reality, but this accord may be oblique and I may need to resort to metaphors to represent it to someone else.

The Gospel of Thomas is a very early, if not the earliest Gospel. It is written in a very dense metaphorical style and so it lays open to multiple and sometimes contradictory interpretations. This is probably the main reason it was suppressed by the later Church fathers even though it carries what seem to be verifiable statements from the mouth of Jesus. It seems that what has become the Bible was being edited around or just after 200 AD and that the political landscape had changed somewhat by then. Jesus had promoted a radical vision of an apocalypse that would change the world for Jews specifically. t was slowly realized that this radical shift wasn't in the immediate offing.

In the Gospel of Thomas, Jesus is quoted, replying to some of the disciples who are asking him: *"When will the kingdom come?"* Jesus replies: *"It will not come by waiting for it. It will not be a matter of saying, 'here it is,' or 'there it is.' Rather, the kingdom of the Father is spread out upon the earth, and people do not see it."* Gospel of Thomas 3, in the Nag Hammadi Library 118. We cannot prove definitively that Thomas was ever alive or that he is actually quoting Jesus. It doesn't matter. The disciples needed a song line and Jesus pointed out that it was to spread all about them. They just needed to raise their voices and sing it back into existence.

A Blanket Full of Stars

I should now like to press bravely on into the wacky world of Astrophysics and Quantum mechanics. I am fairly out of my depth here and I will admit that the mathematical end of it totally eludes me. Nonetheless, I find it fascinating and have tried to read up on it as best as I could. I will restrict myself to some of the main concepts that bare a relationship to proof.

For a beginner in this field, I would suggest *The ABCs of Relativity* by Bertrand Russell. I greatly enjoyed this book many years ago or *A Brief History of Time* by Stephen Hawking. I will be borrowing heavily from *The Elegant Universe and the Fabric of the Cosmos* by Brian Greene, which are an excellent introduction, but not for the faint of will. If you are quite familiar with physics, there is little in the coming pages that you won't know already. If physics is not your forte, I will tell you there is no math coming up and this section of the book is important, because the world will appear less/more crazier to you after reading it, depending on your philosophical bent. The big point I will be making here is that physics, string theory and quantum theory are dabbling, if ever so obliquely in the realm of metaphysics. Some of the people working in these areas understand this and others refuse to admit it -in the same sense that communism was actually a religion- because it was so stridently atheistic.

Einstein had just put the finishing touches on his theory of general relativity when a man by the name of Schwarzschild used the calculations to hypothesize an area of space that was so collapsed that even light and time itself could not escape it. This subsequently became known or branded as a 'black hole'. This phenomenon is based on a mathematical model that seemed to coincide with reality. I don't believe that we actually have absolute proof of a black hole to date. Though, there seems to be little doubt that they do in fact exist. No one can go to a black hole or in fact actually see one, because there is no light coming from one for us to see. It seems fairly certain that at the centre of our own galaxy-and all others for that matter- there is a massive black hole around which we rotate. The centre of the galaxy looks bright, because there is an area above a black hole called 'the event horizon' where the light that we can see is circling around before it disappears into eternity. The subsequent Big Bang theory of the beginning of the universe is based on the idea of a black hole in reverse where everything comes out instead of being sucked in.

Most of Einstein's early work involved him thinking up scenarios in his mind about how the universe should be and then testing them later against mathematical formulas. Of course, I have greatly simplified. It seems that Einstein literally sat in a chair while at work in a patent office and ran thought experiments in his mind. These thought experiments involved people travelling in space or running beside light beams, etc. (I will sideline this very quickly to note that most people who have done significant work in many fields of endeavor have developed exception powers of concentration. This ability to focus the mind and keep it on track is crucial). Although Einstein's initial theories about gravity seem to have been a result of his recognizing that Riemannian geometry (a newer form of geometry dealing with curved surfaces), was directly applicable to the idea of a curved or bendable space. These ideas then became intrinsic to Einstein's conception of gravity. Many of the specific ideas that he conceived of in this (thought experiment) way were only much later verified in the world by actual experiments.

For example, it seems that Einstein speculated that light might be bending as it passes by large gravitational objects -like the gravity created by the mass of the sun- and it took some years to confirm this. This confirmation was held back largely because of the technical limitations involved in making such fine measurements of light trajectories and the need to do this actual measurement during a solar eclipse. The real master stroke of Einstein's thinking was in conceiving of space and time as an integrated and supple entity and not an even uniform and flat mat.

"The history of physics is filled with ideas that when first presented seemed completely untestable, but through various unforeseen developments were ultimately brought within the realm of experimental verifiability. The notion that matter is made of atoms, Pauli's hypothesis that there are ghostly neutrino particles, and the possibility that the heavens are dotted with neutrino stars and black holes are three prominent ideas of precisely this sort- ideas that we now embrace fully but that, at their inception seemed more like musings of science fiction than aspects of science fact." The Elegant Universe - Pg. 226

To give you an inkling of the mind-bending concepts that must be grappled within the newer conception of physics, only a few more examples will have to suffice. It seems as though the universe spontaneously erupted some 14 billion years ago in a single enormous event in which all matter and space were instantly unleashed. *"You don't have to search far to locate where the big bang occurred, for it took place where you are now as well as everywhere else; in the beginning, all locations we now see as separate where the same location."* Pg. 346

Even the very far edge of the universe as we know it, was the site of The Big Bang. In fact, there is no edge of the universe there. Only the universe as it expanded and to ask where the edge is, is like asking what ten miles is north of the North Pole. You start heading south again and the question is misleading (nicked from Stephen Hawking). Scientists seem to have an inkling of what it is that happened in the first few milliseconds after The Big Bang, or at least they can speculate about these first few milliseconds. From this they can construct models of the subsequent unfolding of space. But *why* The Big Bang happened or what caused it to happen at all is a complete mystery. It seems everything suddenly unfolded from nothing with tremendous force. It also appears that everything in the universe erupted from one extremely dense piece of matter that was about the size of a basketball. All of the known laws of physics start to break down the closer we get to representing the zero second point of The Big Bang, and there is no before. (Although Neil Turok of the perimeter institute is speculating that the expansion if the universe is a recurring cycle - more of a big wave than bang)

A lot of what has been going on in physics since Einstein's breakthrough has been an attempt to construct a unified field theory or a theory that can encompass all of the forces observed in the universe. (Einstein introduced two theories of relativity and spent much of his later career trying to reconcile them into a unified field theory.) This unified field would be a theory that could meld into one unified framework - the current understanding of the known forces in the universe that are: the force of gravity, the electromagnetic force and both the weak and strong atomic forces. The real nut of this problem is to construct a way of looking at the universe that can encompass both the force of gravity- which is fairly weak, but holds in place planets and universes-and is also relevant to the extremely small world of quantum mechanics.

Einstein's theory of relativity was a huge improvement on Newton's clockwork universe, not only in terms of the minute quantification of the observed data, but also, he ushered in a new way of conceptualizing the way that gravity actually affects things. This is the now famous image of a ball rolling on a rubber membrane causing the membrane to stretch or bend the space around where the ball is. This image explains (in a somewhat two dimensional way) the actual mechanics of how the force of gravity works and how objects affect each other in time and space, which are actually one and the same thing unified into space/time. An object's mass creates ruts or warps in the fabric of space/time.

As mentioned earlier, Newton didn't clearly understand the mechanics of how gravity worked, though he observed that it followed definable rules. These rules were absolute-given his ability to measure-and allowed Newton to frame his observations into a coherent mathematical theory, which could be used to make predictions about future events. This approach proved to be very accurate and is now considered to exemplify the classical or clockwork universe representation. We still use his methods and formulas to this day when we calculate the trajectory of a rocket or any number of things. Einstein created a more accurate metaphor to actually understand how gravity exerts a force at a distance, as well as supplying a more accurate mathematical model that represents the phenomena. So the larger paradigm change in understanding is in Einstein's explicit recognition that space and time represent aspects of a single integrated unit. Space and time are different manifestations of the same unified space/time fabric.

Einstein also further refined our ability to finely measure the real universe, by recognizing that objects actually bend the space around themselves. (Technical ability and theoretical understanding constantly move in relative lock step; each taking the lead and driving the other at certain points.) Objects get caught in the space/time ruts created by other objects, the bigger or more massive the object, the larger its rut will be. The affects of this space-bending or rut-making affects other objects at the speed of light. It is not instantaneous. So the effects of gravity are not instantaneous, but they are a reflection of the space/time continuum. So if a huge object entered our solar system, its gravity will only spread through space at the speed of light, which is the absolute speed limit of the universe-although this law may have been broken in the first few seconds of birth. So space-using a two dimensional analogy to represent three dimensions, with no objects in it, is thought of as being perfectly flat (though fluctuations occur at the quanta or extremely small level). The effects of time and the speed limit of light, influence the accuracy of our measurements in very interesting ways, on both the micro and macro levels.

There is very little overt mathematical difference between Einstein's conception of the way gravity works and Newton's in terms of calculating where objects will be at any given moment, but the devil is in the details. Einstein's special relativity is a major paradigm shift in our understanding of why objects do what they do as opposed to understanding simply where objects are. Einstein's conception of the universe brings into it such things as the effects of gravity on even 'mass-less' light. The mass of really heavy objects exerts a pull at photons of light that otherwise would move in a straight course. This can change the observed position of a star relative to an observer. In actual fact, it's not the light that's bending. It's the whole of space that is bent and light follows the shortest path through this warp in the medium of space.

Einstein gave us the theory of special relativity first in 1905. Special relativity, amongst many things, deals with the apparent paradoxical situations that arise from the relative motions of different observers. Einstein realized that if two observers were wearing identical wristwatches, but in motion through space at vastly different rates of speed, they will perceive that time moves at different rates for each observer. Also, different observers moving at different rates of speed with identical tape measures would arrive at different measurements, if they were attempting to measure the same object. If their speeds differed greatly they would each come up with a noticeably different length of the same object that they were trying to measure. There is no absolute pace of time or unit of measurement. These ideas are all relative to the observer. Except the speed of light, which seems to be the speed limit of everything, therefore you can measure distances in light years, which is the distance it takes light to travel in one year.

As an aside, it seems that moving backward in time is impossible at least for humans, Stephen Hawking said something very simple that thoroughly squashed this idea. If going backward in time were possible, how come no one from the future has come back to tell us about it? Argument over.

What I wish to draw from this is that the linier nature of time that we feel to be obvious is in fact not so self-evident. There is no single NOW that we all experience together as a seamless flow into the future. On the human scale, this inequality of time is largely irrelevant although you do get slightly younger than all your friends when you travel a lot in jets. It is the micro and macro levels of realities that prove to be the most confounding to our notions of how things really are. The relevant aspect of this conversation is that our common sense would not tell us anything about the real underlying principles of the universe. It is extremely counterintuitive.

The world of Quantum Mechanics is far wackier than this. Quantum Mechanics is the study of the very small atomic and sub-atomic microcosm. As mentioned earlier, what Einstein worked on for the last years of his life was a unified field theory. This is a theory that could reconcile his two theories of relativity with the emerging world of Quantum Mechanics. This brings us back to the world of Archetypes again. Einstein believed or worked toward the idea that there was a single set of mathematical equations that could represent or encompass all of the forces in the universe, or that there is a deep underlying unity of all of the forces - that we have 'so far' failed to express.

The four forces are again: the electromagnetic, gravitational and strong and weak atomic forces. This unified field theory is something akin to the idea of Unas Mundi or singular world, possibly singular in the mind of God. This idea was not a naive belief on Einstein's part, as it seems that working toward this assumption has proven to be extremely profitable. Scientists have recognized that at least three of these four elemental forces are directly related to each other, they are the electromagnetic forces and the weak atomic forces (the force which holds electrons in orbit) and it is believed that they will be able to provide a frame work that can encompass the strong atomic force as well. (This is the force that holds the atomic nucleus together.) It then seems that gravity is the odd man out, because it is such a relatively weak force when compared to the other three. You can easily rebel against gravity by jumping up into the air, but we need force to rip an electron from a stable orbit and even more to split the nucleus of an atom. There is a proposition that we exist in multi verses and this idea seems to be a result of our efforts to integrate gravity into a unified field theorem. Because gravity is such a weak force, it is thought that its effects might be spread amongst multiple universes that exist simultaneously. This smacks of metaphysics to my God bedazzled mind.

Einstein searched for this underlying unity, because he did find an equation that expressed the underlying unity between energy and matter. This is the now famous E=MC squared. Energy equals mass times the speed of light squared, or the amount of energy held within any unit of mass can be quantified, or in other words, everything in the universe can be expressed in terms of energy or mass. Energy and mass are different manifestations or different expressions of the exact same thing, linked to each other by a measurement that reflects the speed of light squared. This implies that an enormous amount of energy is contained in very small mass, hence the atomic bomb, which is only a small fraction (about one percent) of the amount of energy that could actually be released from plutonium. Nuclear reactors only release about 10 percent of the energy of uranium. (This is the thought that led to the conception of black holes, in that a black hole has an enormous mass, and therefore, the energy must be restricted to allow the mass to increase. All of the atoms in a black hole are very tightly packed together, so much so that even mass less light has trouble escaping this massive gravitational force.)

This theory of the equivalency of energy and mass was a result of Einstein's exploration of special relativity as it related to the microscopic realm of quantum mechanics. (This is a massive thought and you can see why he believed that he was truly cracking the code of God.) If all of the energy and matter in the universe can be expressed by one formula surly there was a great mystery at the root of the universe and Einstein called this mystery God. The robust atheists love to point out that Einstein didn't mean God and that he was using this term as a substitute for an implied mystery. I'm not so sure Einstein would intentionally muddy the water in this way. He used the term a lot.

A more detailed understanding of Quantum Mechanics proves to be a lot more complicated than grasping E=MC2. Conversely, this formula allows us to understand that mass or the real objects that we see and feel can be understood of as another manifestation of energy. If you pour enough energy into a particle by accelerating to or very near to the speed of light and then smash it into another particle, you can actually create more mass, this will be expressed in the appearance of extra particles. This is like smashing an orange and a grapefruit together and getting an orange, a grapefruit and a couple of avocadoes after the smash. This extra set of avocados is a result of the amount of energy that has been pushed into this interaction by us, inside accelerator. Energy and mass are interchangeable at the quantum level.

When I was a young lad in my 20's, a friend of mine loan me Fritjof Capra's *The Tao of Physics*. I will admit that at that time, very little of it made sense to me, but it did peek my interest and I have tried to keep abreast of the goings on in physics ever since. Apparently, this book is responsible for a lot of muddle-headed thinking amongst amateurs like me - a little knowledge.

Currently, the unified field theory has been revitalized by the development of string theory. I falter at the thought of trying to explain it, Brian Greene does an excellent job in *The Elegant Universe* and I will refer the interested reader to this book. A very quick sketch of the idea of string theory would be that the smallest ultimate constituents in the universe seem to be vibrating strings, instead of some hard atomic nugget like thing. The difference in the form of the matter that we witness has to do with the frequency at which each string vibrates. Different vibrational frequencies create different forms of matter or different atomic particles that makeup that matter. You throw in a shit load of very complicated mathematics and add in seven or nine or 11 extra dimensions, which no one has seen, and then compress some of the dimensions into extremely small packets called 'Calabi-Yau', then spend an unbelievable amount of time describing the shape of these packets. You then finally have something that approximates a mathematical version of aspects of microscopic reality.

It seems that initially there were five different string theories-back in the fashion disaster that was the eighties-that where all in play at the same time and aspects of each of these theories where at odds with each other until it was worked out that they were all different aspects of the same framework which has now been dubbed M-Theory. I will continue Mr. Greene's earlier quote: *"Quantum mechanics, even when only partially formulated, could make direct contact with experimental results. Even so, it took close to 30 years for the logical structure of quantum mechanics to be worked out, and about another 20 years to incorporate special relativity fully into the theory. We are now incorporating general relativity, a far more challenging task, and, moreover, one that makes contact with experiment much more difficult. Unlike those who worked out quantum theory, today's string theorists do not have the shining light of nature- through detailed experimental results- to guide them from one step to the next."* - Pg. 226

This is really a key philosophical problem in string theory, in that there now seems to be an infinite number of possible string theories. The string theorists have begun to argue that this is a new way in which science must be done, in that the theory itself if of prime importance and they do not seem to have the shining light of nature to guide them. I am no expert, but the essence of what is going on in my humble understanding is that. If I proved without a doubt that the moon is actually a giant bum, someone can create a string theory that will explain the flatulent orb we are witnessing. If they don't use the light of nature, whose light is guiding them then? The mathematics is so complicated that it is very easy for string theorists to baffle us or at least me with their bull shit. And didn't I hear Kepler calling out to me through the ages; in such manner did we dream the truth. I will return to this. I am sure the mathematics is elegant and profound but that doesn't mean it is a representation of reality. This, my dear reader is the real point of the book which is that when you indulge in this type of hyper abstraction (like string theory) you lose touch with the real world but the world you create is so satisfying and ultimately provable that there is no reason to doubt it's truth. At root I personally believe that this is a twentieth century sickness and I will prattle on about later.

This state of affairs represents two different aspects of the field of physics itself: the theoretical and experimental. I personally believe that these two aspects of looking at the universe represent different expressions of the human brain. Theorists express the integrative/intuitive right brain leanings while experimental physicists represent the sensate left brain expression. Real understanding in the world is the constant ballet between trying to develop and integrate a theoretical understanding of nature and then subsequently confirming that your speculation is in fact an accurate representation of nature. This is what the brain does all of the time and it is my contention that if you go looking for meaning you will find it.

"Faith is an Island in the setting sun" – Paul Simon

Now, if you remember I was saying that it seems to be impossible for humans to travel backward in time, well at the quantum level it seems there is a possibility that these types of things aren't impossible. Physicists have been smashing atoms in huge machines and observing the way in which they break apart and they have witnessed some phenomena that seem to be explainable by allowing the atoms to move backward in time. String theory also uses multi- dimensional escape hatches to explain events like this. Scientists have witnessed events that seem to be explainable by allowing an electron to briefly travel back in time reversing it for infinitesimally small periods.

Obviously, this presents us with a difficulty when we are trying to conceive of the universe as a causal chain unfolding over time. This gets a little complicated, but it seems that the way in which we observe quantum phenomena affects the outcome that we then perceive. Our relative motion and the device we use to look at the events and the recognition that these events can only be predicted within the realm of probability all seem to collude to interfere with the event that we are witnessing; in the same sense that you cannot describe the mind without using a mind to describe it. This is an aspect of the uncertainty principle which is the thought that quantum particles can only be described by their probable locations-not there absolute locations-at any single moment in time, because there is no absolute location and any real sense. To accurately represent nature you need to establish what has been dubbed by Thomas Nagel *"the view from nowhere"*, we can never have this view point because it must eliminate great swaths of context to try to achieve some form of pristine fact.

The universe at the quantum level is not an analogy of the mechanical clockwork world that Newton understood. Particles don't cleanly move from one place to another they seem to jump from one energy level to another without traversing the area in between, this is again due to the relationship between mass and energy. The idea that they are particles at all is misleading, but convenient. Everything is an expression of energy. This is where the term quantum comes from - as in quantum mechanics. This term quantum allows us to have a different linguistic paradigm-separate from the concept of causal particles-with which to conceive of this micro world.

On the quantum level it seems as though particle pairs (an electron and a positron and electron's evil twin brother), can spontaneously erupt from nothing and then annihilate each other, resolving back into nothing.

These linguistic analogies are always trying to express what we cannot actually see with our own eyes, and again, it seems that even our looking affects the way that we see. Scientists are forced to represent these phenomena by using models of mathematical probability, or they must translate these phenomena. They have looked into a mathematical language to represent it inside their minds. With these mathematical models, they can predict phenomena with an accuracy that is only limited by the machinery with which they measure and calculate-given a certain level of probability-although these phenomena are still very bizarre. Scientists proceed forward by witnessing thousands of interactions so they can build statistics that represent the probability of events occurring with some degree of accuracy. In this way, they can develop a picture of reality and confirm that it is accurate by measuring their expectations against reality: in other words they construct a form of proof. As stated earlier though, the odd man out in quantum mechanics is the force of gravity, which stops this theory from being a unified field theory and the unified field theory is the Holy Grail of science right now.

A Round a Gain

Light is the best example of the elusive nature of these slippery quantum fish, and I will give a quick thumbnail sketch of how we understand it, because it is and always has been the best metaphor for conscious understanding. In the realm of physics, light is best conceived of as both a wave and particle, depending on how you wish to measure or observe it. For a long time, light was thought to be a stream of particles that bounced off the eye and somehow brought reflected images into the brain. Some Greek philosophers thought that we sent ourselves-our Anima-out of our eyes to experience the world and that it brought the world back to us. In the 1800's a physicist called Thomas Young showed that light was better represented as a wave (more analogues to the way water moves), and it seemed to be predictable and measurable in this way as well. Einstein later resurrected parts of the particle theory again and we now use the term photon to represent a unit of light. There are two mutually exclusive ways of expressing the essence of light which is a reflection again of archetypal paradigms. We need a paradigm with which to squeeze light into out tiny brains.

Scientists have done experiments in which they would shoot what they thought was a single unit or photon of light through a hole. If they shot a series of single photons through a single hole, the light seemed to react as if it was a particle (it only lit up a single place), like taking shots with a BB gun. If they shot another single photon at a target on a wall with two holes in front for the photon to go through, they found that instead of one place being lit up the light reacted as though it was a wave and the single photon spread out across a photographic plate behind the holes into a series of valley's and peeks as thought the light where reacting like water coming through a break wall with two openings in it.

So if you shoot light through one slit, you get something that can be represented as though it was a particle called a photon. When you open up a second slit, the same light particles that were moving through the first slit will change their reaction and where they are going, so that the light particle is now going through two slits at once and will react more like a wave, and not like a particle. In other words, the light will change the way it travels depending on the type of experiment you set up, or the way in which you view it. Light will change so much so that it will actually go to different places depending on whether we shoot it at one slit or two slits. (Somehow the light knows we are aiming it at one slit and not two. This is a result of the way in which we are viewing the experiment.) Same light, different result depending on what we look for. The expression of the ultimate truth of light is beyond our conception right now. Like Newton's understanding of gravity, we can represent and express its properties.

The relevance of this so called double slit experiment is that it was recognized that our observation of light determined how light would behave. If we sought to actively quantify it, it would behave like a particle. If we only viewed the results of our experiment we would see the wave like qualities. This was the beginning of what has now been called quanta. Quanta is the recognition that the elementary stuff of the universe exist in multiple states simultaneously or that we can never put our finger on exactly what quanta is at any moment. Neil Turok described quanta in this way: if we throw a rubber ball at a wall Newtonian physics can very accurately describe and or predict the event. If you throw a quant at the wall, it's as if the quant knows that the wall is there already and will react differently, depending on our state of observation. Quantum mechanics puts human beings back into the universe again. We now know that we cannot be 'completely detached' observers or that we cannot represent the universe in a completely abstracted way. There is no view from nowhere.

My understanding of this paradox is that because the light is moving at light speed, there is no time involved in the light's path, or stated another way, time for the light beam does not exist, so somehow the light can determine which way it is to react, because there is no time unfolding. When you travel at the speed of light, time stops. Light does not need to decide which path to take. It can, and is already either or both paths at the same time, because there is no time occurring along the pathway of light. As far as the light is concerned, the moment of birth and death are simultaneous, and because light is moving at the speed of light, there is no causal time involved. Once more, as soon as a photon is created, say on the surface of the sun, the photon itself immediately arrives at its destination a billion miles away and is absorbed say… on your face. From the light's perspective, there is nothing only instantaneous creation and simultaneous dissolution. No matter how far the light beam travels there is still no time for it. So shooting a beam through one hole or two is irrelevant to light, because its creation in a light bulb and its arrival at its destination are exactly the same event. When you travel this fast (at the speed of light, which is impossible for everyone else), time slows down to a full stop for you. Sorry to beat this to death.

Now it seems that matter is also wave like. It is convenient to conceive of it as a solid collection of particles, but as soon as you try to put your finger on one particle, it becomes more elusive. *"In quantum theory we have come to recognize probability as a fundamental feature of the atomic reality… Subatomic particles do not exist, and atomic events do not occur with certainty at definite times and in definite ways, but rather show tendencies to occur."* Fritjof Capra *The Tao of Physics* - Pg. 68 Einstein at first could not accept this and uttered his now famous phrase to Niels Bohr: *"God does not play dice!"* (The actual quote was: "It *seems hard to sneak a look at God's cards. But that He plays dice and use 'telepathic methods… is something that I cannot believe for a single moment."*)

In the real world, at the scale in which we live, expressing the locations of objects is not such a problem, but in the world of Quantum mechanics the expression or prediction of subatomic particles qualities, requires a massive amount of mathematical formula that could only later be verified easily with the advent of computer models that could encompass this need for probability. Computers have allowed us to increase our accuracy in measurement simply because they can do so many more calculations quickly.

In fact, our ability to understand has moved lock step with the advancement of computers. To say it is a result of advancements in computers is to misunderstand how understanding evolves.

The proof of this increasingly complicated mathematical framework is the scientist's ability to predict what will happen to atomic particles in a meaning full way. Scientists can peer inside atoms to make these observations and predictions by whipping the atoms up to speeds nearing the speed of light and then smashing them together in particle accelerators. They are trying to break atomic particles down into their smallest constituents and assess the various masses of these particles and also try to figure out how all of these constituents work together. This is the world of hadrons or subatomic particles like mesons, gluons, quarks and antiquarks.

One of the reasons that it has taken the general public so long to gain any understanding of quantum mechanics is that it is extremely counter intuitive. Nothing is what it seems and nothing seems to make sense in the same way as the world that we can see with our eyes. The clockwork universe is not predictable from the scale of quanta, which exist with a different set of rules. I will give one more very interesting example, which is from Bill Bryson's book, *A Short History of Nearly Everything*.

Wolfgang Pauli postulated a theory called the 'exclusion principle' where certain subatomic particle pairs would somehow 'know' what the other was doing. *"It's as if in the words of the science writer Lawrence Joseph, you had two identical pool balls, one in Ohio and the other in Fiji, and the instant you sent one spinning the other would immediately spin in a contrary direction at precisely the same speed"* - Pg. 145. It seems that scientists in Geneva separated two photons by seven miles and demonstrated that by interfering with one, you did in fact instantly interfere with the other. Somehow the particles are linked, but in such a way that our concept of causality doesn't make sense.

These two particles must have initially come from a single larger particle to be linked in this way, and the connection between the two particles reactions is occurring across space at faster than light speed. Unlike gravity, it is literally instantaneous. Einstein refused to accept this phenomena's possibility and called this *"spooky action at a distance."* Somehow the history between the two particles keeps them in 'communication' or they are entangled, though this type of phenomena has only been achievable in a laboratory. (This is called 'entanglement'). Now, if particles can affect each other across space like this, maybe astrology is not completely off of our planet (just kidding). This, my dear reader is where a little knowledge is dangerous, and because of the compressed nature of time and space -at the extreme quantum level-these types of assumptions like astrology being an analogous or somehow valid expression of this aspect of quantum theory is just plain wrong. An analogy between large planets and the orbits of atoms or interconnected sub atomic particles is also way off track.

I have recently heard someone discussing these twined particles and they were speculating that this may be a way for us to communicate across vast distances. If I knew you had the other matched particle and you started to spin it counter clockwise my particle would immediately spin clockwise, no matter how far away you were from me. If we had enough of these particles we could develop a system of binary messaging like the language we use in computers. Although entangled quant have three different spin capabilities (up, down and 45 degrees, and they exist in these states simultaneously until we wish to view them. So they have vastly more computing possibilities than our current simple binary systems). We could then send people or robots way out into space and control, and or, discuss things with them in real time. Like Homer said: *"Even communism works, in theory"*.

We are witnessing the beginnings of quantum computing, which by all accounts will truly revolutionize the way we are in the universe. We will not use computers; we will be evolving along with them. It's like we will be able to ask a computer a question and the computer will not only know what our question is, but the computer will be involved in posing the next question back to us again. In the same sense that the quanta 'rubber ball' already knows where the wall is.

I wish to digress for a moment. It seems that scientists are well aware that they are teetering on the boundary of metaphysical speculations. God does seem to be playing dice sometimes. When a student approaches a Zen master, he is allowed to ask a question. For the Master, the question is the interesting aspect of the situation because it shows him where the student is, or what the student's mental puzzle is at that time. This question is a reflection of the way that the particular students mind is trying to conceive of the universe. Which I would argue is most likely a far too logical or representational outlook. For the master-who presumably has gained a measure of detached enlightenment-the question is an opportunity to assess the state of the mind of the student. The Zen master's job then is to confront the student with an enigma and he can choose or spontaneously arrive at an enigma, which is tailored to break into that student's habitual pattern of thought. Or, the master will approach the student from his shadow or weak side.

In 1992, I went to India and Nepal with my wife. While we were in Nepal, we went to a meeting with some Buddhists to see if we could meditate with them. I had hoped to meet someone that was wise and I knew that I might be able to ask my question. I spent some time formulating the question in advance. We were at a meeting with this nice English Buddhist fellow and he asked if there were any questions. I stood up with mine. I started by saying that I knew Jung and he cut in and asked if I could introduced him to Jung who was quite dead at this point. So I reframed my question amidst the laughter, asking if this white fellow from England could really adapt his psyche to the whole Buddhist archetypal situation or pantheon. My thinking was that both he and I, and our evolutionary heritage had come from fifteen hundred years of Christianity and that this was his personal unconscious psychological heritage, which of course-to my mind-ran deep in his blood (unbeknownst to me, a mildly racist attitude on my part). He also, without missing a beat, said that this is why the archetypes are called archetypes. Or, in other words, my thinking was much too narrow. I had created the terms of a paradigm in which I was comfortable, but it was more of a reflection of my own narrow understanding of the term, archetype. I was trapped inside the box of my meager understanding of what an archetype might be or how it can manifest. We got on quite well after that ego pricking.

What I am driving at is it seems that the universe is in the same situation as the Zen Master. It throws up answers to questions, but also supplies us with the phenomenon that seeks to confound our narrow need to construct logical questions. Nature forces us to confront the foundational paradigm with which we use to think of her. In some very real sense the questions are important matter for us. If we realize the importance and underlying context of the question, we can gain some insight into ourselves as we are reflected back at ourselves through the mirror of the universe. It helps to have a good teacher who can help us navigate through this stuff though. Quite often it's the question that is the problem not the answer. Nature has all of the answers. The answer to every question is ONE except when it is two or more, or something else entirely.

How this all relates to proof is this: what Einstein discovered was a new way of understanding how the natural world could be understood - same natural world, but a different way to conceive of the intellectual expression of its underlying principles. The way that we know that he was on the right track is that we have conducted experiments and made predictions based on his ideas. The theory that he uncovered, and the world that he applied the theory to, are in agreement. For example, Einstein theorized that gravity could bend the path of light and it was proven that this is indeed so. Also relativity predicted small abnormalities in mercury's orbit that the real orbit of mercury has. Bering's witness to this discrepancy in mercury's orbit was the actual moment that Einstein knew he was right.

I have been making my way through a book by Lee Smolin called: *The Trouble with Physics* and it is his contention that over the last 30 years no new advancement has occurred in the realm of theoretical particle physics (specifically due to string theory) that can be verified by experiment, and therefore, actually be called proper science. The nut of his argument is that almost all of the work being done in modern universities on particle physics is within the framework of string theory and that string theory is seemingly un-provable. There hasn't been any experiment performed as a result of a proposal of string theory that has given us anything like the bending of light as it passes by the sun. All of the people working on string theory, which is more than half of all of the people working in theoretical physics. Obviously, have a vested interest in the theory itself. It is their ongoing bread and butter. They are saying things like, *"Maybe we are on the cusp of a new way of doing science where we don't need to verify everything with scientific experiments. Or, if we continue with this theory it will eventually show us the correct answers."* This is Greene's quip about the light of nature. (Pg. 142) This is, in fact, a new way of doing science, except that I would actually call it a religion or deep metaphysics. Freud and many others have gone down this same path.

Mr. Smolin's major contention is that it is almost impossible for any new student of particle physics to work in any other area of theoretical physics outside of string theory. If you are a young scientist trained in physics and you want to work, you will probably have to work on string theory, especially if you are working in America. Brian Greene in the *Elegant Universe* gives the reader little inkling that there is any philosophical dissention aimed toward string theory, though he is not a fanatic. String theory is the new zeit geist.

String theorists seem to be able to pull a new theory out of their hats when they are confronted with a new phenomenon in the world, instead of predicting new phenomena that can subsequently be proven by experiment, which in turn would reinforce the case for string theory. The string theorists would lead us to believe that we may need to conceive of a new way of doing science, and of course, simple laymen like me are completely baffled by the mathematics. There is now a tool that should help to break this stalemate, and it is the Large Hadron Collider in Switzerland/France. This collider should allow scientists to peer into the very smallest of particles, Mesons, etc., and really have a good look. They have, in fact, confirmed the existence of the Higgs boson, which is beyond my brain's ability to explain. Then we will see if there are extra dimensions or maybe if strings even exist at all. It would be nice if they could take a shot at world hunger to.

The fact of the matter is that Nobel Prizes are given to physicists that have proven their theorem, and the simple reality is that there has been no Nobel Prize awarded to someone working strictly on string theory, because it is really more an exploration of complicated mathematics, than an accurate picture of the universe. I would refer the reader to Mr. Smolin's book for a more in depth look at this. What I wish to draw from this, is that it seems that these string theorists are entranced with the mathematical beauty of their theory and to my mind they have done the same thing that Freud did when he wished to install his sexual theory as a dogma. They have thrown out God and reinstated him in another form, and why I say this is that according to Mr. Smolin, it is actually hard to discuss any other theories with some string theorist and be taken seriously at all. Some of the people working in this area of theoretical physics are actually very hostile to any challenge to string theory. To my mind, it is always a sign of weakness. They are in the same position as the creationist who is forced to defend their stance by claiming to be doing science without submitting their work to the rigors of the accepted methods of science itself. To construct a method by which your theory can be tested experimentally, and then allow it to be subjected to peer review in the real world, in other words, by using the unflinching light of nature. I am by no means competent to judge this controversy either way, but I have found that the more research I do for this book, the more the prejudiced metaphysical underbelly of science/humanity has come forward. We will meet this obstinate behavior again. Surely thou doth protest too much. Such is the world of academia. See quote on Pg. 69.

Conversely, pure mathematics has given us many powerful tools to use in the real world. One quick example will suffice. The whole of our computer-generated 'natural worlds', the representation of fire, mountains and forests are all a direct result of the application of Fractal geometry. This is too big a discussion to dive into in depth, but initially it was thought that Fractal geometry was a beautiful, but useless mathematical concept somewhat analogous to the female orgasm I guess. (Sorry poor taste.)

Now back to my muddled physics lesson: in *Psyche & Matter*, one of the themes von Franz explores is that of trying to come up with a framework with which she can link physics with psychology or psyche and matter. Jung asserted that he would have no objection to regarding the psyche as a quality of matter and matter as a concrete aspect of the psyche, provided that the psyche was understood to be the collective unconscious or the largest most inclusive conception of the psyche. This is just simply nature, *"nature that contains everything, therefore, also unknown things…including matter."* P&M Pg. 40. The direct observable link between matter and psyche for Jung seems to be through synchronistic phenomena: the perceived link between the two events being a correlation of meaning.

When a synchronistic event occurs, it appears that the outside world has aligned itself with the inner psyche. This alignment as a confluence of meaning, also the mind seems to be able to catch glimmers of knowledge that still lie in the future. (Correlation is not causation) This may simply be a matter of our misunderstanding of the nature of the arrow of time as we constantly try to perceive the flow of time in terms of our presumption of causality. This linier causality is after all, the way the mind both understands and constructs its being in time and in the macro world in which we live it is a perfectly valid assumption. I don't wish to be misleading here so I will add that time only moves in one direction: forward.

Jung called this confluence between the mind and matter the absolute knowledge and he believed that the mind had temporarily tapped into a more unified world or that there was a confluence of meaning reflected both outwardly and inwardly. There are many terms from religion that try to articulate and encompass this way of thinking: Unas Mundi or singular world is from the Latin tradition. (The Dreamtime, or Atman even morphogenic fields are another stab at it, etc.) What Marie Louise Von Franz tries to explain in her book is that this Unas Mundi and the environment of the singularity or the environment where subatomic collisions take place are analogous concepts to this unified physical psyche, not identical concepts. This atomic environment is a place where the order of time and causality as we experience them in our mind and are not as strictly applicable. This is also an intimation of the concept of the collective unconscious where all symbols are a reflection of one symbol which becomes manifold or split up in the realm of time. This is how the right brain experiences the world before it is delivered to the left brain to be abstracted and represented with language and its tyrannical bed partner logic.

I'm going to beat this to death for just a moment. From nature's view point, light is just is and it is our rational delineating minds that cannot grasp its true paradoxical essence. A dream is the very same in that it is also a product of nature. A dream is its own interpretation. And like light or quanta, a dream symbol is in some ways all of the symbols/energies and still, it is only one aspect that manifests in time in a particular form or image. This is possibly why we feel that there is a unity behind the manifold aspects of the universe. The unconscious is forced to express itself in this way, because it is embedded in nature or *it simply is nature,* but we then try to express our understanding by representing it with language in a liner way. The brain cannot help sectioning off aspects for inspection and organizing it in order to simply express itself.

This feeling of unity underlying the manifold aspects of reality seems to be an archetypal idea on the grandest of scales whose various incarnations would be God/Atman; unified field theory and possibly the current string theory as its shot at the ultimate root of matter. Marie Louise Von Franz did analytic work with Wolfgang Pauli, which resulted in a number of books by both her and Jung. She was not a naive dabbler in physics like me. She had direct access to the best information available at that time.

As I hinted at earlier, time seems to be a somewhat elastic concept and I will go over it quickly from a different angle, because it is important. The main concept I would wish you to grasp here is that our mind constructs one version of time that we understand as reality. If I could travel very fast (near the speed of light), away from you, my concept of your now or the moment that you exist in. For me, it becomes much larger than your awareness of it. My now or the time I exist in as I move away from you actually encompasses a larger and larger chunk of your future, the farther away from you that I am. So my now stretches and is encompassing your now and your future. My now can stretch so much that it encompasses thousands of years into what you would call the future.

Now, I cannot tell you what your future is, because I am travelling away from you so that any message I send back to you will be arriving too late for you to read as it can only travel back to you at the speed of light. (This is where two entangled particles, which are communicating faster than the speed of light get really interesting) So this message that I send back to you will arrive on your doorstep well into your future, but probably not before the event that I could have theoretically witnessed. Also, because I am travelling away from you, I cannot witness your future, because I can't see it and will only know what your future is when I get back. So in some very real sense, the past and the future are all unfolding simultaneously, depending on your distance from an object, and your relative motion or whether you are accelerating. There is also a thought that we have completely missed the boat on what time really is especially in terms of causality. To separate time cleanly from *us* is a contextual error or a mistaken linguistic representation of it as a thing.

Synchronistic events-as postulated by Jung-exist outside of the causal chain and are contingent upon our observation of them, i.e., synchronistic events are unique and only understood by our implying meaning back into them. It seems to me to be a fact that these types of things occur and it is also a fact that time is a much less static thing than it appears in our limited view from earth. If (and this is a big if) particles can "communicate" with each other, I see no reason to deny flat out that there is no type of physic communication between either us and the environment or between two people. I realize fully that I am making an analogous argument and that it is weak. Another way to approach understanding is the introverted intuitive and or metaphorical way that the east has used for millennia. I would say that these eastern yogi's are the witnesses of the human soul and the breath of their vision is a scientifically valid area of research. The Hindu and Buddhist conception of enlightenment is that everything is really one thing and our minds need preparation to understand this fact. We, and everything else that we see, are a manifestation of one unity or Atman. Quantum mechanics seems to be peering over the edge and into this same stunning abyss and we also need training to grasp Quantum mechanics or indeed, to simply have good posture. Nature does not give us these things for free.

To my mind, the problem that I see in trying to understand synchronistic phenomena is essentially one of not being able to prove definitively (in a scientifically satisfying way) that they exist. I would add the caveat that if the scientific community at least took this type of study seriously as Rupert Sheldrake does, we could gain a clearer understanding and or, at least construct experiments to put it to bed once and for all. The feeling in science is that it has been put to bed and I am irked by my own pathetic special pleading.

Who would have guessed that physics would have turned out crazy? As we have seen, there are actually scientifically verifiable reasons for the completely flaky concept of auras, and we will see that aromatherapy also has a basis in reality. We must shift our arrogant paradigm completely and come back at these phenomena through the context of the brain and neuroscience to re-contextualize to really understand them. But some people actually see auras and they are not crazy or flaky. They have synathstesia; why not telepathy? By circling around, I would wish that these various themes will come into clearer relief.

What's the Matter?

When I was in my early 20's, I came to start my morning shift at the record shop I worked at and told my friend Steve about a dream I had that night, in which a good friend of mine Jill was coming back from Spain. She had actually been in Spain for some two months studying Spanish in Andalusia, where she got a crazy Andalusian accent. I had heard nothing from her for this whole period and was not in contact with anyone who knew when she was coming back, but I felt quite certain she was coming back to Canada on that day. (You will just have to take my word for it. I didn't 'remember' all of this after the fact.) I had woken up with this thought quite clearly in my head. As the day went on, I forgot all about my prediction, and then at five minutes to five, I received a call from Jill, who apologized for not having called me earlier. She had arrived around dinner time the day before and had spent the day with her family. I was actually wrong about the date of her arrival. I had the dream when she was already in Canada. Now, I can talk about Jung's theories about how the mind could perceive events outside of time or anticipate future events, and it is all just gingerly dancing around with words. For me, I have no need to build up a logical proof. I know for a fact that this event happened and that I had no prior knowledge of Jill's arrival. And I am not remembering this situation incorrectly or conveniently adjusting the truth to suite my agenda. I will say that Steve was pretty "blown away" when he realized I was right, and that I had predicted this event. That's what record stores were like in the eighties, man.

> *"So meditation has significance…in this process of meditation there are all kinds of powers that come into being; one becomes clairvoyant… all the occult powers become utterly irrelevant, and when you pursue those you are pursuing something that will ultimately lead to illusion."*
> Krishnamurti, *Truth and Actuality -1978*

I think that this quote from Krishnamurti really sums up the situation in that all of this discussion about telepathy, etc. On some level irrelevant, but fascinating and what Krishnamurti has pointed out is that if you are trying to harvest knowledge in an effort to bolster you position of power you are on the narrow egotistical path that is largely illusory and ill advised. But there are many pathways to wisdom and the strictly rational intellect can be one of them, and you have to get in to get out. When you arrive at the palace of knowledge, you must leave the strictly rational road behind.

I find it fascinating that physics, which is the most rigorous of intellectual pursuits, is constantly confronted with God - the most nebulous of concepts. In physics, we can construct a way of understanding the universe from just after the first billionth of a second, but we cannot grasp what happened just before that. This is to say, what caused this something that we call the universe to spontaneously unfold as opposed to there being nothing whatsoever? And more interestingly: the staunch refusal to allow any metaphysical speculation to muddy the field. String theory is proposing all manner of metaphysical hypothesis like Branes, which is short hand for different multi-verses and their colliding membranes. More to the point, why is there anything here at all, is not strictly a scientific question. It gets lost in the purview of metaphysical philosophy. All questions that begin with 'why' tend to slip into the feeling realm and out of the thinking realm where proof exists. In some sense, WHY is the ultimate question.

I was talking earlier about the way the Chinese conceive of numbers, more in terms of a qualitative value, as opposed to a strictly quantitative counting system. This paradigm shift of perceived value elevates the human interpretation of the flux of numbers or reinstates perceived meaning back into the universe. This is more of an analogous way of thinking, and this type of thought process is also the way that synchronicity, the archetypes and the arts in general must be thought of. Chinese people actually think neurologically different than westerners, if only in the terms of the way that language is fed into the mind. (More later)

Jungian and Freudian psychology both rely heavily on this type of analogous or comparative/value type of reasoning. This type of thinking can encompass the feeling or relational realm, and is not strictly wrong, only unscientific and different. The oriental view or eastern zeit geist has more to do with the stripping of the personal self out of the picture to reveal the meaning behind everything. We in the west approach reality the opposite way and we try to disassemble the world around us through analysis, and we end up seeing ourselves again or maybe we find God in physics. We quickly move on. The eastern orientation has to do with the inherent philosophical stance that your individual ego is-in a way-of an accurate understanding of the greater flow of nature that is beyond you. Conversely, it seems that the link back to nature is the individual psyche locked into a unique perception of individual events that we can then ascribe meaning to. The meaning that we feel is all around us -and of necessity- has a relational/value laden or feeling quality.

These unique psychic events or synchronicity also seem to affect the real world through an interfacing of energies. This is a bit of verbal mumbo jumbo. What I am saying is that, our psyche actually has a quantifiable effect in the outside world. When we are in a bad mood or afraid of something, these emotions can be contagious to other people or animals. This happens through our expression of our body through its ongoing and subtle cuing. Dogs pick up on fear extremely quickly. Or if we are mad all the time, and all we have is a hammer, we will tend to treat everything we encounter like a nail. (Buckminster Fuller) To express this in a very concrete way: everything that we see in the world that has been built by humans started as an idea in the mind of someone. The psyche has very direct effects *in the world*. Then, there is the more nebulous idea of a scarab beetle actually coming to the window or the idea that if you spend a lot of time hating someone you may actually be poisoning not only their psychic environment, but you are probably very adversely effecting your own mind and body as well - literally poisoning it with stress, etc. How the psyche affects the outside world is-from a strictly causal and physical aspect-a little speculative, nonetheless, it seems that there is an interface and psyche, and matter is part of a larger paradigm that we are only just groping toward. What is the sound of one hand clapping?

The reason that I have kept on this theme of intellectual paradigms is largely a reflection of my having read two books by Richard Tarnas and in his book Cosmos and Psyche there is a lengthy discussion of the major paradigm shift that occurred as a result of Copernicus realization of the heliocentric system, and the 'resulting' explosive flowering of the renaissance in general. I will elaborate on the nature of paradigms using the example of the writing of history specifically.

If you are discussing history or writing a book about an historical era or indeed making a documentary film you are always working with a certain agenda, you can only present the "Facts" in a narrative form as you have come to understand them. If you wrote a history book that was simply a collection of facts or small snippets of historical documents it would be intolerably boring and few people would be compelled to read it. We are and have been story tellers for millennia. One of the most enjoyable things about reading history especially, is the little gems of wisdom that the authors insert into the narrative. Those who don't read history are doomed to repeat it, springs to mind. (Afghanistan is a quagmire that is very difficult to get out of. Or, political revolutions rarely succeed unless there is collusion between the upper and lower classes. (Egypt Yemen, USA and Syria leap to mind.) These types of observations are really the distillation of years of reading history and the appreciation by the author that there is something to be distilled from sustained observation. All of these observations provide a context for us to understand what we are reading and these types of observations can also be a representation of the various biases that the author is trying to proffer-unconsciously or consciously-as a larger historical truth.

As mentioned earlier though, even the seemingly detached art of making documentaries is leavened with an agenda, usually a quite overt one. You would like to think that documentary filmmaking is simply a matter of turning on a camera and allowing reality to unfold before the viewer, or we would like to presume that the makers of the film have made an attempt to leverage the film with an equal or balanced viewpoint. An uninterrupted single camera shot for two hours of anything takes great patience. The reality is that documentary makers and film editors make thousands of judgment calls as to what is and isn't going into the final cut of the film. These choices usually are the result of an implied direction, or quite simply, as in the case of Michael Moore's film, an overt political agenda being elaborated on. For you, the viewer (Michael Moore has at least admitted openly that he has an agenda), it is a mistake to think that this is a bad thing. In fact, I would consider it one of the strengths of all of these processes. It is when someone is defending their position a little too stridently that we must take note, and of course, an active suppressing of known facts is simply being dishonest. (Weapons of Mass Destruction)

This active editing process is bound to our recognition that we cannot escape the limit of our own learning. We cannot help but seek to represent our own interpretation or understanding of that learning through our ongoing decisions. We create our own subjective paradigm either consciously or unconsciously, constantly. We can accept other ways of being in the world through digesting opposing viewpoints and I would say that true wisdom resides in being able to hold in balance two or more opposing viewpoints simultaneously, or quite possibly, by having no viewpoint at all. This is the thought that many arguments can be presented logically and justified in many ways. All arguments are based on an individual viewpoint from within the larger context of society and each viewpoint holds some form of truth. Therefore, each viewpoint can be recognized as tentatively valid. No one is really going to function in the world in this completely tentative non-positional way. The brain doesn't.

I heard Barak Obama on the radio addressing Notre Dame University the other day and some people in the audience were booing him, and he simply said, *"It's Ok"*. (They were upset about abortion or stem cells.) His noble position is that these people have a right to stridently disagree with him. This is the position of strength that Obama is trying to infuse into politics through his own profound example.

Richard Tarns discusses one of the current perspectives in the art of writing history, which is: there may be no patterning in history at all and that all writing about history is inevitably colored with human interpretation. We have projected all meaning and pattern backward into history, if we try to illuminate or discern, or extract movements and trends. (Edward Gibbon thought that the rein of Marcus Aurelia was probably the best time to be alive in the ancient world) In other words, we have misrepresented a bold series of facts as though there was a sense of cohesion or historical force within them. This artful misrepresentation -to my mind- is what writing history (and thinking in any way about anything for that matter) is all about and I quite frankly cannot envision doing it another way. Events in the world have all moved together and in lock step with the slim point of the present. And in constructing a narrative we seek to tease out causal connections using our hindsight. We constantly seek out correspondences in the world and we are right in the sense that our brains always do it for us anyway; hence, science being deeply counterintuitive.

Our alternative-in terms of our vision of the world and for ourselves-is to develop a skeptical understanding of everything while trying to deconstruct the paradigm within which we are functioning. Or, at least we should seek to be aware that we are constantly functioning within a tinted paradigm of thought. For example, if Michael Moore makes a documentary that takes to task corporate America or the deplorable state of the American healthcare system, we can all agree that he has an agenda. If you don't want to hear somebody taking the piss out of George W. Bush (and his naïve belief in the magical self-adjusting free market), there is a slim chance that you will be compelled to go and see one of Michael Moore's documentaries. We can see the paradigm he has presented to us and we can deconstruct it, but we can also recognize that Michael Moore has presented a coherent view of the state of America, possibly without much nuance, but there is a truth to be presented.

What Tarnas goes on to observe is that while we apply a skeptical outlook toward these films or a reading of history, we have, again adopted yet another paradigm. This one is the paradigm of radical skepticism. You cannot out-think thinking and you cannot, for one second, not do something. The reason that I have chosen to use the writing of history or documentary film making as an example of the nature of paradigms and agendas in thought, is that all of our thinking is largely a reflection of history in that our minds can only be absorbed in the present and can only reflect upon what has passed (i.e. history), either our own past or somebody else's. So then, all thought can quite easily slip into a frame or be subsumed and re-categorized by another paradigm.

Recognition of this does not leave us wandering about in a daze or lost to ourselves in a state of abstract navel gazing. We must act in the world. It is better to act in this world now, than in another one that you create in your mind. As I will discuss later there are no shortage of ways to try to be totally present in your thinking though being more firmly absorbed in this moment. Within the realm of action and reflection, we must accept that mistakes will be made and be prepared to learn from them. Again, the habitual inability to learn from mistakes or the problem of constantly approaching new situations with preconceived ideas is to my mind the definition of neurotic. Another elaboration of this point will come up later as we take a look at the writings of the Tibetan saint Tsong Khapa and the western saint Ludwig Wittgenstein. Then again from yet another related angle, as we look at the way the brain really works in view of the recent discoveries in neuroscience.

What the Hell or Hugging the Road

One bright lovely day, I was out with my wife and son and we were enjoying a camping trip in the great outdoors of northern Canada. We arrived in a town to get some supplies and what did I spy, but a musty book store! What is the best thing I could do while immersed in this great Ontario wilderness? How could I take this nature experience to the next level? (Oh, this game is on.) Well going into a dark dank bookstore and buying a book to read seemed to leap across the inner dankness of my mind. I saw a book on the front rack that looked intriguing. It was called, *Cosmos and Psyche* by Richard Tarnas. Well… I like astronomy and I like psychology and this seems like a good fit. I read the back page and it talked about his other book *The Passion of the Western Mind,* which is an historical overview of western philosophy and I thought well it might be hard going, but I'm up for it. As I read into the book I was very impressed with Mr. Tarnas's writing. He is clear and succinct and for about the first 50 pages, I was really excited, but as I read on I slowly realized that I had been duped. This was a book about astrology not astronomy.

Astrology is one of my personal pet peeves. I loved to run down astrology as a pseudo science, pretending that I knew astrology was trapped in the fuzzy-headed un-provable fringe of things. I love listening to astronomy cast, and they love to haul out the long knives and stab at this pseudo science. I also knew that Jung was a practitioner of astrology or at least acknowledged -throughout his career- that there was something to it. He addresses astrology quite extensively in *Synchronicity* and in a book that some Jungians would consider his greatest work: *Aion.* I was willing to overlook Jung's peccadillo, but I now had in my own hands a book that went deeply into aspects of astrology that I had not really thought out so well. I will be making a much larger point about the evolution of our understanding of the cosmos at the end of this chapter, so bear with me for a bit. I can see the glint of a blade.

Jung believed that one of the main reasons astrology had gotten such a bad name was that most of the people who believed in it or were working in this field were largely intuitive by temperament and that they were disinclined to do the real sensate work that was involved in framing a coherent hypothesis that could, in some way, lead to a scientific proof. This means that they were disinclined temperamentally to gather statistics and do the laborious mathematical sensate work of proof. This is the work that Rupert Sheldrake is now doing in the field of ESP. Tarnas sets you up in much the same way that I have so that you would realize that it is really a series of prejudices that keep you from even looking into astrology with any sense of seriousness. I personally am pretty far from being a convert, much less a missionary for this astrological outlook. I do have my academic career to look out for. But on the other hand I have already stepped off the deep end with ESP. I can also appreciate that Tarnas is building up a well written and quite stunning and coherent argument. He is certainly no fool.

What Tarnas does is lead the reader through the astrological cycles of the five outer most planets, which are the longest in terms of years so that you gain an understanding of how the planets affect the world zeit geist or world spirit. Because planets like Saturn and Pluto have such long orbits, it is easier to pick out extended patterns in their alignments and observe the way they that are reflected in their alignment with our earth. Mr. Tarnas concentrates only on the so called strong alignments: which is when Saturn, Pluto and the earth are in a straight line or form a 90 degree triangle to each other. The different forms of alignment are called conjunction, opposition and square - a square being a 90 degree alignment, a conjunction and opposition form a straight line in relation to the earth with either the earth on the end or in the middle. The beauty of his book is that he relates these heavenly movements to the major world events or directly to the lives of famous people's or major cultural movements in history. I was in the privileged position to have read extensively in all or most of the areas of history that he discussed and I had some familiarity with most of the people and all of the cultural events that he was discussing. I love reading history, so for me, this was like a thousand light bulbs of confluence repeatedly going off.

There is a lengthy discussion of the French Revolution (and I had just finished reading several books on that very subject)and some of the other major revolutions that occurred around the world, including the sexual revolution of the American sixties and how they see change tied in with the movements of Saturn and the other planets. Also, there are lengthy discussions about the lives of Freud and Jung. I am personally very familiar with the biographical details and minutia of both of their lives. I will pull some of the more easily chewed quotes from the book out in a second, but for an elaborate and very stimulating discussion this book is really on fire. It is a tour de force of associative thinking. I can't do all the work.

I will pick out what I thought was one of the most interesting examples in the book: it is about Herman Melville, the author of *Moby Dick*. Herman Melville was born in 1819 when Saturn and Pluto were in conjunction and also when Uranus and Pluto were in a square relationship. Karl Marx was born during this same conjunction. One of the archetypal themes of the Saturn/Pluto relationship is that of punitive retribution against nature and relentless obsession with projected evil. Karl Marx's evil was the capitalist system with a spicy hint of agnosticism thrown in.

Eleven days after Melville was born in August 1819, a whaling ship called the Essex departed from Nantucket and travelled to the South Pacific, where it was attacked by an eighty foot whale and sunk. The incident was written up by the first mate Owen Chase, who said that the whale rammed the ship repeatedly. The 20 surviving whalers spent 93 days in open row boats. Melville, in his early 20, signed on to a three-year whaling voyage, which took him to the same area in the South Pacific. While on that voyage, he happened to meet the son of Owen Chase who loaned him a copy of his father's original narrative. Exactly one full Saturn/Pluto cycle after Melville's birth in the next conjunction of these two planets, Melville went on to write and published *Moby Dick*. Just as he published this book in August 1851, another whaling ship, the Ann Alexander was rammed and sunk by an enraged sperm whale in the same area of the world. Melville was stunned when he heard of this coincidence.

"All these figures and events-Melville's life and creative imagination, the narrative and themes of Moby Dick, the titanic figure of Ahab, the killing of whales and whales that kill the killers of whales- profoundly reflect the character of the two archetypal complexes we have been examining here, Saturn-Pluto and Uranus-Pluto. I was considerably stuck by the extraordinary synchronistic patterning in which two of the events, Melville's birth and Moby Dick's publication coincided with the successive Saturn-Pluto and Uranus-Pluto alignments so precisely. These where the only two conjunctions of Saturn and Pluto in the first seventy years of the nineteenth century, and the only two hard-aspect alignments of Uranus and Pluto in the same period." - Pg. 240

    Moby Dick would, of course, go on to become a classic and Jung sights it numerous times in his work. We can write this whole story off as an eerie coincidence. For crying out loud this is the whole point of this book. We have only patted ourselves on the back, if we just write this off. We have congratulated ourselves for being myopic and quite frankly prejudiced. The only real proof that can be offered is the sheer weight of repeated testimony, and skeptics refuse to acknowledge this. I don't blame them, but is this rejection of testimony, a proof of their argument? (I will explore this much more later on.) The sword of reason cuts both on the downward and upward stroke.

    The larger picture of Mr. Tarnas's book is his excellent illumination of archetypal themes. Each planet is indicative of an ensemble and to really understand these themes takes a poetic and associative mindset. You cannot see any truth in this, if you approach it strictly with a logos thinking function. That is not to say that you must refuse to be rational or refuse to quantify, but how do you quantify Napoleon's career? History written in such a fashion is profoundly boring. You could add up the dead or check off the countries he invaded, but you would gain far more insight by understanding the whole ensemble of French history in that era and his unique and astounding career within the ensemble. This type of understanding takes time and a breath of learning. It won't greet you in the lab or at the bottom of a test tube or in a pile of statistics. I believe someone said that statistics are the greatest lie of the 20th century. They seem to present a rock solid proof, but in reality they are a loose and floppy fish that must be interpreted.

PROOF AND THE DIFFICULTY OF MEANING

Facts are simple and facts are straight

Facts are lazy and facts are late

Facts all come with points of view

Facts won't do what I want them to

-David Byrne from the Talking Heads

One of the main arguments against astrology is the thought that, historically, astrologers in the 15th century, for instance, didn't even know about the outer planets. They only knew about the five innermost planets. Tarnas gives the reader an extended look at the discovery and naming of the outer most planets: Pluto, Neptune and Uranus. With the exception of Uranus, these planets seem to represent their archetypal names well. Of course, they are all named after Greek gods, which in the west is the bedrock of our cultural/archetypal understanding. Once again, we create meaning, so let's have a look at what we have created.

Pluto was discovered in 1930, by Clyde Tombaugh after it was noticed that there were certain discrepancies in the orbits of Uranus and Neptune. Pluto is associated with the Greek underworld of Hades, where the goddess of vegetation 'Dionysus' was forced to spend the winter each year in order for her to be reborn in the spring. This is a worldwide mythic image, representing the death and rebirth associated with the annual cycle of sowing and reaping. (Being held in the arms of a pagan god) In the east, the Gods associated with this complex are the Hindu God, Shiva - the God of both destruction and creation, or the pair of Gods, Kali and Shakti. Kali is a bloody murderous individual from which Calcutta is named, while Shakti is the primal urge to vibration, rhythm and motion, which arises out of nothing. (The Big Bang) Kali seeks to send everything back in repose, while Shakti pulls everything out again. This is a representation of the ambiguous facts of nature being personified. *"Pluto is associated with the principle of elemental power, depth, and intensity; with that which compels, empowers, and intensifies whatever it touches, sometimes to overwhelming and catastrophic extremes; with the primordial instincts, libidinal and aggressive, destructive and regenerative, volcanic and cathartic...*"etc. Pg. 100 Synchronistic phenomena that happened around the time of the discovery of Pluto included the splitting of the atom, the rise of Fascism and the wider recognition of psychoanalysis.

Uranus seems to be the only misnamed planet and it would have been properly named after Prometheus, the being who stole fire from the gods, and gave it to man. His punishment for this act was to be chained to a rock and be visited each day by a bird and have his liver torn out only to have it grow back each night again. The archetypal aspect of Uranus would be, *"sudden liberating or awakening that which it touches, with unexpected innovative, disruptive and emancipatory consequences,"* Pg.166, so Uranus is associated with areas of enlightenment. Fire, of course, is consciousness and light.

The Uranus-Pluto Cycle

  15% orb   exact alignment to 1%

  1450-1461 conjunction 1455-56

  1533-1545 opposition   1538-40

  1592-1602 conjunction 1597-98

  1643-1654 opposition   1648-49

  1705-1716 conjunction 1710-11

  1787-1798 opposition   1792-94

  1845-1856 conjunction 1850-51

  1896-1907 opposition   1901-02

  1960-1972 conjunction 1965-66

Examples of significant events and societal changes that happened during these cycles are related, in an archetypal way, to the French revolutionary period (1787-98). Karl Marx and Friedrich Engel's published the communist manifesto in 1848. Lenin published: *What Is to*

Be Done? And along with Leon Trotsky found the Bolshevik party during 1896 to1907. 1960-72 saw many revolutionary leaders including Che Guevara, Ho Chi Minh, Moa Zedong, Fidel Castro and Jean Paul Sartre. This was the era of the sixties almost perfectly, which you older folks will remember well. Reaching back into history, the revolution of Spartacus happened in the conjunction of 74-65 BCE as did the rise of Julius Caesar in the next cycle, and still farther back to Alexander the Great whom established one of the largest states ever to exist during the conjunction of 328-318 BCE. We can also throw in Napoleon's career during the opposition of1787-98, Tamerlane 1390-1400 and Charlemagne 766-82. We can only dimly appreciate the tone of these earlier time periods, but for me, the sixties were still breathing as I grew up and you can get a better feel for the ensemble by thinking about that crazy time man.

In the realm of science and technology, the American and Russian space programs went all through the 1960-72 conjunction ending with the landing on the moon near the very end in 69. The Wright brothers achieved powered flight in 1903. The rise and proliferation of the telegraph, railroad and steamships during the conjunction of 1845-56, the invention of the cotton gin by Eli Whitney in1793 and the invention of movable type during the 1450-61 conjunction.

In the world of astronomy Copernicus's *De Revolutionibus* was published in1543 and Kepler finally embraced the heliocentric system during the next conjunction of 1592-1602. Special relativity theory was initiated in1905 by Einstein. The discovery of the new world all falls within an unusually long square alignment that extends from 1489 to1507. Along with the breathtaking creative explosion associated with the European Renaissance. Tarnas compiles a list that is much longer than this, just for these two planets and many more lists for the other planetary cycles of which I feel no need to rewrite. Suffice to say, given an open mind you will see that there is a pattern lying here.

I just read the back cover and there is a great quote by CBC radio host Mary Hynes: *"This is the closest my head has been to exploding while reading a book"*. In Canada, a lot of people are linked together throughout lovely leftist-leaning CBC radio. Much like the BBC, it is state run and quite liberal. Apparently, Liberal is a dirty word down in the United States. Anyway, I love Mary Hynes show called, *Tapestry*, which is a discussion of literature and religion at a very high level. I couldn't resist this quote, and it's my book, so what the hell. I did feel the same way that she did while I read his book, though. It was like someone had given you a master key to something you never suspected had any validity at all. This is really the essence of metaphorical truth, in that you are led to believe that you have gained an understanding, because it is so associative and interactive.

What Jung explores in *Aion* is the idea that the astrological aspect of the universe is a projection of the human psyche on to the heavens. The 12 astrological symbols represent a complete totality of the psyche, in the same way that the eight main I Ching symbols represent a melding of the opposites, with the ongoing flow of the Tao always holding the potential of all of the states. The 12 apostles also represent a totality of the understanding and unfolding of Jesus' message. So when we try to understand the 12 astrological symbols, we are trying to understand a reflection of all the personality types or a complete set of ways of understanding. I may not be very pushy, but if I studied astrology, I could learn to understand an analogy to pushy people through an archetypal connection to the sign of Taurus, etc.

You could define a projection as something the human mind would like to see in something else or we continue to project that which we believe holds a resemblance, for instance. When a person falls in love, a large part of that person's initial perception of their beloved could be considered projection, or the desire to see correlations between the various planetary arrangements. The person I fall in love with will probably carry a lot of the characteristics that I am looking for, though I may be largely unconscious of what those characteristics are. They will also be closer to the opposite of my personality type as discussed above. What I lack in terms of my Anima or soul's yearnings will most likely be project on to another and they will be perfect and I will fall in love. As ancient astrologers turned their gazed toward the skies, they obviously could not gain an understanding of the heavens in a detached analytic scientific manner. They not only lacked the equipment to properly see the planets, they would not have framed their questions about what they were looking at by using any of the modern scientific paradigm. This way of scientific thinking took years to properly frame into our consciousness.

As I was saying earlier, the so called primitive mind experiences their unconscious through projecting it onto the environment. An ancient Babylonian priest or Indian Rishi in 3000 BC was experiencing his unconscious through projecting it out and on to the cosmos - or later more inwardly as we collectively articulate the concept of our own soul. This set of stars, or that cloud of gas, represents a hunter or a water carrier, or some other set of projected archetypal referents. This is why God is somewhere out in the heavens. God is so completely 'other' that we initially cast God into a realm that is also completely other. As more and more people poured their minds into this task of understanding the heavens, the more a set of stable images started to emerge. A common language evolved that they all understood and they used this language to communicate amongst each other. Or possibly, certain unique individuals imprinted the heavens with their own deep vision, which subsequently became imprinted on to us as our collective cultural heritage, due to that individual's unique charisma. This type of top down cultural imprinting has lead to English being the dominant language of the world.

The political leader in many ancient societies was usually under the thumb of the religious leader. It seems that this set of specific astrological images was confirmed and more explicitly recognized-in a historical sense-with the advent of writing in Mesopotamia. Up until that time, the symbols were a little more flexible and dependent upon individual interpretation. This vision of the stars became the accepted cultural canon, which given enough time appears to be a "self-evident" truth. Like all cultural metaphors (religious and mythological), it was, and is, at no point completely static and always reflects the spirit of the culture. Writing really is the turning point in the establishment of cultural canon.

We have witnessed a form of this type of charismatic imprinting from an individual with the start of the ghost-dancing cult that emerged in the 18th century in the American west. One of the Lakota warriors believed or had a vision, or dreamt that if all of the warriors wore a white shirt, they would not be killed by white man's bullets. It seems that this whole movement came about as the result of one warrior's dream. Many people invested a great amount of time adorning these white shirts and developed rituals for the protection of the warriors. Ironically, there was an almost identical movement with bullet-stopping white shirts that appeared against the British in India. What I wish to emphasize is the power of the psychic contagion of this type of phenomena, not the misplaced trust in the bullet stopping shirts. I am not trying to imply that this type of psychic projection is a complete illusion. There is a feedback process involved when the person projecting their psyche is diligent. Although these types of intuitions can be dead wrong as the Lakota warriors found out. (White is a symbol for purity) Because of the desperation of the Lakota at this time, it seems that they were properly prepared to invest a great amount of energy into this visionary gambit.

    As Einstein sat in his chair, running through his mind games and exploring the way in which the universe worked, he was actually coming up with a real understanding that could be verified mathematically. I could say that he was projecting his unconscious desires to understand the universe out from his chair and on to the universe and we can leave it at that. But, of course, that is not the whole truth. I could also say that string theorists are projecting their desire to come up with a complete mathematical representation of the unified world and that they are caught in this same archetypal thinking that the ancient astrologers were caught in; just the next series of levels up in the spiral of understanding. But I would be foolish to say that String theorists could counter that fractal geometry, lead us to graphic design in the real world of movie making and a deeper understanding of coastlines, etc. Though, other examples like astrology must be carefully framed in terms of the amount of conscious and unconscious input they contain. Astrology obviously has a large unconscious and associative or metaphorical input, and the correct amount that should be acceptable is a very slippery fish to define. Conversely, I would add that astrology may just be giving us information or maybe participating in a larger unified psychic framework. (I offer no fragrant roses, as proof of my dream) Astrology may not be 'just' a strictly one-way projection.

    There is a temptation on the scientific side to see scientific progress as a rational movement forward, and of course, this is not unjustified. But, as I mentioned earlier, it can sometimes be anything but that. No matter how much of a geek you are and how much you abuse you body by only living within your hallowed intellect, you cannot escape the fact that your mind is embedded in a body, which is embedded within the world or at least your parent's basement. The difference between Einstein and an ancient Babylonian priest is the paradigm in which they have framed their discoveries (and the tools with which they quantify their observations). To a certain extent, this mythical Babylonian priest also had to test his theories. Of course, the actual dynamics of this society is lost to us in the ancient past and we know that powerful individual charisma can put forward idiotic agendas. (See Freakonomics radio: *The Folly of Prediction* 14/09/2011)

What is interesting is that as we project ourselves into the world, we can-if we are observant enough-properly negotiate nature and arrive at a form of truth. This truth can propel societies to construct pyramids or any number of things. Or, we can view all of this pyramid building as a manifestation of an overt power structure flexing its patriarchal muscle. There was a common belief that the pyramids were built by Jewish slaves toiling at the hands of their cruel Egyptian task masters. The truth appears to be more nuanced, if not completely different. It seems that most of the people who worked on the pyramids were not slaves at all. The builders were proud of their jobs and they were engaged in a massive cultural movement. It would be disingenuous of me to say that this work had no meaning for all of these people. For most people it was probably a pretty meaningful job. Let's be cynics and say that only a hand full of the ruling elite derived meaning from this huge building project. To my mind, we still have the pyramids and how much meaning has been poured into them over the last three or four millennia. The number of infamous historical figures who have stood in front of these same set of pyramids at Cheops is staggering. Who is the arbiter that would decide which set of meanings is valid or not? Be careful which facts you wish to look at.

Projecting ourselves out on to the heavens is the extroverted outward movement of the psyche. The introverted or introspective aspect is to look inward toward your dreams. Again, in both attitudes, if we are observant and humble, we can seek to negotiate our path ahead. We look out toward the heavens and find a mirror of our own inner archetypes looking back at us. In the ancient world, they didn't have the same understanding of psychology that we are uncovering. It was quite natural for them to project their unconscious on to or into nature. The raising of individual consciousness is aided to a great extent by understanding the nature of projections and seeking to withdraw or at least acknowledge them from a wider world. Jung was exploring another passionately articulated system of extroverted archetypal though, when he was studying alchemy.

Alchemy represents a massive collection of pre-scientific thought that stretches across more than a millennium, in which Jung could observe the evolution of the projected unconscious of hundreds of philosophers. Again, I will say Newton wrote far more on alchemy than on real science, almost three times as much and he implicitly believed that it was valuable. It was because he believed it. Alchemy is an extremely dense symbolic language, which Jung had to approach through painstaking comparative reading. It was like reading into someone's dream, but all of the cultural signposts have been changed into some other dense metaphor that is largely self-referential. Much of the early medieval writings on alchemy were Arabic in origin. Some Islamic authors had to hide their philosophical ideas inside of dense metaphors for reasons of their own personal safety. This is the same type of metaphorical reasoning that we see in astrology.

What alchemy was looking for was the philosopher's stone. This seems to be an image that represented completeness, or in Jungian terms, an image of the Self. In Hindu culture, this would be the Atman or great soul. The philosopher's stone was hidden in a dung heap or hidden in the last place that you would expect to look. The task of the alchemist was to find this stone from amongst the matter (mother, female, symbol, etc.) lying about him - because he thought too much. Or in other words, he was trying to take ordinary matter and change it into gold - the gold of wisdom. It seems as if some of the alchemists understood this as a metaphorical search and some were aware that it was, in fact, them that they were changing into gold. But of course, others were actually trying to create gold. The irony was that this dabbling with matter and chemicals, led to the beginnings of chemistry and inadvertently learning in the healing arts as well. We know for a fact that over the course of time, some of these fellows did actually discover many things that were directly applicable to the world. This is the Suksma, Sthula aspect again. In such a manner do we dream the truth? We explore the world through 'science' and we should realize that we are always looking at ourselves.

When we look out into the universe and cast our minds upon it, we do find meaning. What I am trying to show you is that this meaning we cast out is not necessarily an illusion. If the universe or the stars hold meaning, even though we supply it, we are better off if we pay attention to that meaning. There are great psychological lessons to be learned in this old pseudo science of astrology. A more nuanced airing and a recognition of the psychological basis of this 'foolishness' may in turn help us to nurture a more reverential attitude toward both the universe and ourselves, which on the whole is better for us.

We hold no dominion over the creatures: The King James Bible is wrong. (Hopefully, this is just a translation issue; better to think of our role as caretakers.) Icarus did fall into the sea and drown. He was trying to exploit nature and he got confused. Icarus tried to fly up into the realm of the Gods and become one of them -maybe he was a string theorist. Why should we pretend that we know more than him? Oppenheim and the Manhattan Project was another modern day version of Icarus and the Pandora's Box myth. If you can develop a reverential attitude toward nature, and the universe, you will be less likely to abuse it. You will - more than likely- develop a genuine feeling that you are a part of it. I would argue that this is self-evident. We are nature, but we need constant reminding.

These large articulated frames of reference like astrology or physics, hopefully, put our small ego back into perspective. In this chapter, I have tried to point out how much psychic goo gets stuck to everything, no matter how strident we are. The wider perspective emerging is that we are bound into nature and that seeking to extract ourselves from it is a bit of folly. This is the essence of the modern ecological movement. We respect the larger flow of our own environment by realizing more explicitly we are embedded in it. We are undulating and diverse, both wave and particle. We cannot stick manically to the profane aspect. It will impoverish us. Do we have a proof? It is all about us. More than likely buried in a reeking dung heap.

That's Not Science

This is an interesting curio that will show how the mind seeks to relate meaning into the universe and how the universe reciprocates. The original numeric correlations might have arisen in Babylon, but there is now mounting evidence that they originated a bit earlier in the original

Indo-European cultural matrix that came out of the Deniper and Don River Valley systems in southern Russia, possibly even earlier (4500-3500 BC?). It spread out into the world with the Aryan cultural juggernaut of India and Iran. The Babylonian priests were the first to fully commit this divine confluence into writing and they must have possessed a very full and satisfying vision of the universe around them. I envy their certainty. I have brought this anecdote into the narrative to illustrate the way that the pre-scientific mind collects and apprehends meaning. We are, to a larger extent, more than we wish to admit, this very same mindset. The ancient people did not delineate the mythos/poetic vision of the world from hard facts and reason, because they were both of these things - correlation et al. I have culled most of this from Joseph Campbell's: *The Masks of God* series and specifically the *Oriental Mythology* book, Pgs. 115-127.

In Hindu mythology, the great cycles of time are called a Yuga, which is 1,080,000 years and a Mahayuga, which is four times that sum: 4,320,000 years. One great year consists of 12,000 divine years, each comprising 360 ordinary years for a total of 4,320,000. Thousands of great years together are called a Kalpa and each one represents a day in the life of Brahma, who sits on the back of a divine serpent dreaming the dream that is our impoverished reality. Each of the four Yugas has a unique timber: the first is a golden age and then things get progressively worse. We live in the second one, I believe. At the end of a Mahayuga, the world returns to its original form to begin the process over again.

A resting yogi, who has achieved equipoise, has a heart rate of 60 beats per minute. Dance music in clubs is astonishingly twice that pace: 120 beats per minute. Actually, it is a little closer to 140 beats per minute now in the new frantic clubs. I would have loved it to have been 120. In such manner did I dream the truth? With the heart beating 60 BPM's, the heart will have beaten 43,200 times every twelve hours. If the yogi has achieved equipoise, he is truly in harmony with the universe.

As we proceed through the astrological constellations, there is a slight annual lag that pulls us out of alignment with the astrological signs. Every 72 years we move out of alignment by one degree so that means every 2160 years we have lagged behind by one full zodiacal sign or 30 degrees of an arc spread across the heavens that consist of 360 degrees. It is no coincidence that we have 360 degrees in a circle or 12 hours on the face of a clock. We have just moved out of Pisces and into Aquarius. Pisces corresponded loosely with the birth of Christ and he was known as Ichthys or the fish, and was symbolically represented as a fish for some time. (An aside note: I needed the spelling of Ichthys and I opened my copy of *Aion* by Jung directly to the page where he introduces the term (Pg. 73), if you wish to check. I can't prove this is so, you'll just have to *believe*.)

One complete procession through the zodiac would amount to 25,920 years. This is the great Plutonic year or cycle, which if you divide by an arbitrary or not so arbitrary 60, happens to give you 432. What is astounding, but hard to prove, is that it seems that the Babylonians and also the Vedic Rishis understood the retrograde processions of the equinoxes. This means that they had almost unbelievably accurate observations of the heavens with the naked eye. And to really understand this retrograde motion, you had to have accurate observations of the heavens over quite a long time - more than a few hundred years for sure.

A professor H. V. Hilprect tells us that all of the multiplication and division tables from Nippur and Sippar, from the library of Ashurbanipal, are based upon the number 12,960,000, which is to say 12,960 x 2 = 25,920, or one great Plutonic year. There is the thought that they did not come up with this number through astronomical observation, because the same number can be achieved through using 60 to the power of four, which will yield 12,960,000. The Babylonians made their calendars in such a way that they add up to 360 days in a year. That is 72 weeks of five days with an extra five days thrown in as a holiday. These extra days were considered sacred and most traditions adhered to these extra holy days. 5x72=360 and 360x72=25,920 - this is a happy coincidence. This is why we have 360 degrees in an arch; 60 seconds in a minute; 60 minutes in an hour and 12 hours in half a day, etc. It also seems that the Vedic Indians used a year of 360 days and that the year was based on a compromise between the solar and lunar years. The modern solar year is almost 365 days long and a lunar year is only 354 days long. The lunar year is twelve full cycles through the moon's different phases or twelve full moons (12 apostles, etc.) This is why Ramadan falls at different times every year. So 360 days in a year is a compromise position between the lunar and solar calendars, but it is much easier to work with mathematically.

In the Babylonian lists of kings, there are three different versions. We find that each sum of a king's individual life, adds up to a related number. The totals in years are as follows: 241,200 for the first list, 456,000 for the second and a later list were compiled by a fellow who was probably aware of the correspondences called, Berossos. In these, he gives us a number of 432,000 years. The Bible coincidently, gives a number of 1656 years for the first ten patriarchs. This is in the King James Version. All of these numbers are integers of the same number 1200, which to this day is the sum of divine years in a cosmic cycle in India, and again the number of hours on a clock's face 1200x201=241,200 1200x380=456,000 1200x360=432,000. Within the Jewish tradition, these same correspondences raise their ugly heads again. The Jewish calendar recognizes one year as 365 days, which in 23 years plus five more leap years amounts to 8400 days or 1200 seven day weeks. The later sum being multiplied by 72 gives us 1200x72=86,400. Multiply this number by five the amount of days in the Babylonian week and you get 432,000. Multiply 23 by 72 and you get 1656 - the number of years in the first ten patriarchs. There is a point for point correspondence between the calendar numbers. Even Iceland got into the spirit of the thing. In the Edda, we find that in Odin's heavenly warrior hall there are 540 doors. When the Gods battle the anti-Gods in the war with the wolf, 800 warriors will go through each door 540 x800=432,000. Bingo.

In Hindu, Buddhist and Jain mythologies, a complete prayer cycle is 108 prayers to the four corners of the world. One hundred and eight is a sacred number in India and is accepted as sacred throughout the Hindu, Jain, Sikhism and Buddhist reckoning systems. All of the bead-counting systems of these religions have 108 prayer beads and a complete cycle is always four times - 432, if you missed it. The interesting thing about these numbers is that most of them are divisible by nine, which you can take my word for it is a female number worldwide. (The interested reader could look into *The Great Mother* by Erich Neumann). You can tell if a number is divisible by nine, by simply adding up the numbers in the number; for instance, 1+6+5+6=18, 1+8=9 432=9, 108=9, 360=9, 2412=9, 864=18=9, etc. This is matter or the great mother, revealing herself through time. Nine is a feminine number possibly representing three times three. Three is a number that is heavily associated with the nature of the great mother who is the weaver of life. She weaves the tempo of creation: past, present and future, birth, life and death; beginning, middle and end; I, me and mine. What does it mean? I don't know, but it sure is interesting.

I can completely understand how someone who has been led to understand the correspondences would become entranced with the thought that there is a grand divine plan that is unfolding in front of and specifically for us. And you would not be completely wrong to think in this way, but this type of thinking also smacks of somewhat paranoid conspiracy theory in that you might begin to feel that you have cracked some great code in the universe that possibly only you can see or understand. In fact, the gaining of consciousness usually has elements of this personal attachment to it because, you as an individual, is realizing things that others around you haven't. If this wider perspective of your own consciousness is not balanced against an ongoing integration with the world, it can become an aspect of a personal inflation. This is why the east emphasizes or efforts to disassemble the ego structure and hold us to the transpersonal aspect of the Divine. Most religions speak to the ongoing necessity of mentorship and integration within a community as psychic safe guards.

It is -at this point- impossible to know whether these astrological correspondences were built up over time by excluding inconvenient "facts" (more than likely) or like the set of natural numbers themselves they reflect an inherent 'just so nature' of the universe.

Science has to draw the line at correlation and they are right to do so. I have sought to show that humans cannot be completely removed from the process of articulating truth all the way up to quantum physics. I am straining to show how our psychology gets stuck to everything for both good and ill and we see the ill version of this in the various rapture movements that are with us today. The end of the world is an aspect of tension projected out from within the collective psyche. It seems to raise its ugly head every time the world appears out of control and each culture imprints the end of the world with its own cultural signposts and or foibles. We are particularly entranced with UFOs and robots. You can 'have' a good idea or it can just 'occur' to you. You aren't necessarily that good idea. You can have a baby, but you don't own your baby. I like sugar, but I don't want to *be* sugar.

4 ALAM AL MITHAL

"Moreover, great styles in art do not evolve; they appear, as manifestations of intelligible insights, after which, as in the course of time the originating impulse fades, there is devolution to secondary interests, applications, and effects. Likewise in the history of any mythologically structured civilization (and there is none known that was not originally so structured), as the initiating metaphysical insight fades and the connotations of the metaphoric customs are forgotten, practical political and economic purposes take over, the integrative principal no longer holds, and the civilization goes to pieces." - Joseph Campbell: *Historical World Atlas* Vol. II Part 3 Pg. 265

"And to indulge in the study of the religions of others solely to understand their ideas and practices is equally untenable. Such an effort has no purpose other than the simple satisfaction we acquire when we learn something unfamiliar or exotic. The study of religion must be an investigation of possibilities of the human imagination, not simply the acquisition of data for their own sake. Without a theory, question, or paradigm that addresses some fundamental issue in the academic imagination and a method for correlating data, we have nothing at stake and no reason to care about our findings." - Douglas Renfrew Brooks: The *Secret of the Three Cities, an introduction to Hindu Sakta Tantrism.* Pg. 130-1

As I expanded my Jungian universe, I came across a writer by the name of Henry Corbin who was a professor of Islamic Religion at the Sorbonne in France. The book that had me interested was *Creative Imagination in the Sufism of Ibn Arabi*. With all of our collected western hatred being poured towards the Islamic world right now, I would like to start my discussion of religion by talking about a truly towering figure and Muslim Sufi mystic, Muhyiddin Ibn Arabi.

Ibn Arabi was born in Spanish Islam in1165. During the course of his life time, he travelled extensively through Islamic North Africa and much of the Middle East. He died in1240 in the city of Damascus – the oldest known city mentioned in the Bible. There are many themes that we shall develop as we encounter this great man, but I would like to quote-what for me-was one of the most powerful passages I have ever read. I will slowly unpack its meaning, as we go along.

"There is finally the shattering of all the self-evident truths concerning the historicity of history, of those truths which bear so heavily on our modern minds that failure to attach importance to the historical meaning or to the HISTORICAL reality of a religious phenomenon may seem equivalent to denying it ALL reality. Here we have tried to show that there is another "historicity." But the modern passion for material facts stops at nothing; it has fictions of its own, such as the supposed" eyewitness reports," which would have seemed blasphemous to a pious Gnostic reader of the Acts of St. John, well aware that on the evening of Good Friday the voice revealed the mystery of the Cross of Light to the disciple who had been drawn into the Grotto. "For the True Cross is not this wooden cross that you will see when you come down here again." And this is a truth, which was well known to Ismailian Gnosis. (Muslim wisdom tradition)

"If the cry "God is dead" had left many on the brink of the abyss, it is because the mystery of the Cross of Light was long ago done away with. Neither pious indignation nor cynical joy can alter the fact. There is only one answer, the words that Sofia, emerging from the night, murmured in the ear of the pensive pilgrim circumambulating the Ka'aba: "Can it be that you yourself are already dead?" The secret to which Ibn Arabi and his companions initiate us impels those whom that cry has shaken to the depths of their being to recognise WHAT God has died and WHO are dead. To recognise this is to understand the secret of the empty tomb. But the Angel must have removed the stone, and we must have the courage to look into the bottom of the tomb if we are to know that it is indeed empty and that we must look for Him elsewhere. The greatest misfortune that can befall the shrine is to become the sealed tomb before which men mount guard and do so only because there is a corpse in it. Accordingly,

it takes the greatest courage to proclaim that it is empty, the courage of those able to dispense with the evidence of reason and authority because the only secret they possess is the secret of love that has seen.

"Our meaning is expressed in the following anecdote which we owe to Semnani, the great Iranian Sufi; Jesus was sleeping with a brick for pillow. The accused demon came and stopped at his bedside. When Jesus sensed that the accursed one was there, he woke up and said: Why hast thou come to me, accursed one? - I have come to get my things.- And what things of thine are there here?- This brick that thou resteth thine head on.- Then Jesus (Ruh Allah, Spiritus Dei) seized the brick and flung it in his face." Henry Corbin - Pg. 96.

Ibn Arabi and this branch of Sufi's practice is what a Jungian would call 'active imagination'. This is allowing your rational-directed ego to let go or recede while, at the same time, allowing the unconscious to come forward and be the focus of your conscious mind. This is not a passive wistful daydreaming, but an active and sometimes terrifying dialogue or confrontation with the unconscious. In the Sufi terminology, they would call this an encounter with a vertical history as opposed to our regular horizontal history of dates, etc. In the vertical history or the Alam al Mithal, Ibn Arabi could meet Jesus or any number of beings, or things. He relates one such experience in which he meets with Sofia the Greek/western goddess of wisdom mentioned above. Ibn Arabi was in Mecca circumambulating the Ka'aba, which is the heart of Islam. All good Muslims should try to make the pilgrimage there at least once in their life.

"One night I was performing the ritual circumambulation of the Ka'aba. My spirit savoured a profound peace – a gentle emotion of which I was perfectly aware had taken hold of me. I left the paved surface, because of the pressing crowd and continued to circulate on the sand. Suddenly, a few lines came to my mind. I recited them loudly enough to be heard not only by myself, but by someone following me, if there had been anyone following me.*

Ah! To know if THEY know what heart THEY have possessed!

How my heart would like to know what mountain paths THEY have taken!

Ought you to suppose them safe and sound, or to suppose that THEY have perished?

The FEDELI D'AMORE remained perplexed in love, exposed to every peril.

No sooner had I recited these verses, I felt on my shoulder the touch of a hand softer than silk. I turned around and found myself in the presence of a young girl, a princess from among the daughters of the Greeks. Never had I seen a woman more beautiful of face, softer in speech, more tender of heart, more spiritual in her ideas more subtle in her symbolic allusions." Pg.140 -*Creative Imagination*

It would have been unlikely to have a real woman out on the central floor of the Ka'aba. This would be understood immediately by a Muslim. In this image, we can see a meeting with the Jungian archetype of the Anima. I am not trying to reduce these symbols to anything. My discussion is not meant to explain away or merely psychoanalyze and or reduce anything into a tiny box that we can say we understand. This woman is not "just a manifestation of Ibn Arabi's unconscious." That is our patronizing intellect. This is an event of great import in this mystic's life. We are witnessing a dialogue between this man and his soul. The anima figure here is understood by Ibn Arabi to be an incarnation of Sofia who, in the Greek Gnostic and Jewish traditions, is understood to be the personification of wisdom. She is the wisdom of the heart, the true wisdom, not the abstract intellectual reasoning of the mind. Sofia can also be partially encompassed in the archetype of the Virgin Mary, if that is the symbol closest to your understanding.

"A dream is its own interpretation" – Jewish proverb

Sophia starts coming to Ibn Arabi through a divine recitation of this enigmatic poem and then actually reveals herself to him as a beautiful Greek girl. The poem is a spontaneous manifestation of the unconscious, which has a tendency to speak in this dense and archaic metaphorical way. Ibn Arabi is touched by an actual woman and this whole experience becomes real. He is telling us that the inner world of visions is as real as the outer world of history and I wish to present this whole episode in a very wide context.

Ibn Arabi has-with this episode-broken through into at least Anahata or an experience of the heart wisdom. Or he is experiencing Gnosis in a very real way on the floor of the Ka'aba. He is explaining his path for us, that we might have a roadmap so that we can travel along with him. The writings of Ibn Arabi reflect the cultural setting in which he lived, and without a broad view of his work, and the cultural vessel that he was part of, we are a bit rootless. The beauty of reading Henry Corbin's work is that he uses a comparative method to translate this Islamic wisdom back into a western context for us.

I will choose a particular image that Mr. Corbin seized to expand on the wider historical context of this episode. *The Fedeli d'amore* is a reference by Henry Corbin to the troubadours of Europe. This particular image is a reflection of the heart of wisdom that is common to all religious insight. *Fedeli d'amore* is a French /Latin phrase meaning: 'fidelity in love' or a 'commitment to undying love for the chosen soul mate.' A troubadour would commit all of his deeds to the service of his loved one – this may be a woman whom the troubadour has only had a slender glimpse of. She then becomes-or already-is the unfolding of his anima. The commitment of the troubadour's soul to another in service was the highest ideal of the Pre-renaissance troubadours. This commitment could be seen as the literal western approach to externalize the personal soul, allowing it to manifest in the outside world as a commitment to an actual real woman. This is the western extroverted attitude that would literally be enacted in the world through deeds as a horizontal history.

Within the troubadour movement, this commitment could also be understood in other ways. In the vertical history or introverted aspect, this commitment of love was also understood by some as a commitment toward revealing your own soul. Because you don't have regular contact with this outward woman, the process becomes a meditation on an idealized inner version of that being. Really it becomes an inner meditation on your own female soul image or anima. This actual woman can manifest herself for you as a divine creature or the endless muse of your soul. You constantly re-experience her both symbolically and in reality through your continued service to her and meditation on your symbolic image of her. This can help you to create an expansion of your consciousness through the explicit and or metaphorical experience of Eros/Love and a willing surrender to continued service to her in the world. This movement was a reflection of both the positive and negative aspects of the subsequent Christian denial of the flesh. Dante's *Inferno* is a prime example of this dual nature of the Anima/Creatrix, in that he wrote the book for a woman that he claims to have only glimpsed once – the divine Beatrice. This is the service of the heart or an encounter with the Manipura Chakra, which we shall discuss later.

The idea of divine service has been even more fully expressed in the Hindu yogic tradition of Bhakti. In the Tantric tradition, a yogi dedicates himself to the service of a yogini or female master. It is thought that many of the original 13th and 14th century Tantric masters were women. This whole movement benefited from embracing a more balanced attitude toward women and, because of this they have a better attitude toward the body specifically. To accept a deity or teacher as a personal guru, involves a complete surrender and devotion to the service of love which is then directed toward the individual guru. This intense form of personal devotion is called 'Bhakti', which coincidently-as a spiritual movement-was most intensely practiced in southern India (the north had fallen to Islam) around the 11th to 14th centuries and is almost completely contemporary with the troubadour movement in the west. Along with this, was the real flowering of the worship of the God Krishna, of whom we shall have much more to say. The first and possibly greatest expression of a rich and artistic devotional movement in the west occurred as a result of the stunning personality of Eleanor of Aquitaine in the Bordeaux region of France. Through this relationship of devotion and service, we ironically receive within ourselves the love we wish to bestow upon others. We are-in the broadest sense -the 'other' that we wish to serve. This is again the essence of the transference in analysis and the deeper meaning of our encounter with our shadow.

> *"As we try to become more intelligent, we understand that the intelligence is not a satisfying end in itself; that it needs to bow to the heart, and that the only happiness possible for human nature is founded in self-sacrifice."* - Comte

The Sufis play fast and loose with history and that is what the first quote is really driving at. Any experience *is a* historical experience either vertical or horizontal, and the line becomes blurry in the world of a mystic. Henry Corbin introduces into this discussion an example from western philosophy of Nietzsche, whose philosophy tends to reflect the philosophy of power. Specifically, this is the famous statement that God is dead and we killed him. That may be true, but if God is dead, I should like to have some *proof*. Show me the corpse. The tomb that is sealed in the earlier quote is a reference to the church of one eye. A singular eye can only encompass a monolithic view like that of the extreme fundamentalist dogma or any inflexible ideologically-driven dogma. Or, in many ways, any church or organization that claims to know the single truth and would cultivate power to prove it. The proof of the ignorance of the singular vision-in Henry Corbin's analogy-is that there is a guard mounted at the door of the tomb. The guard represents the creation of an organization of people set on propagating and defending their version of truth. If you know the truth, what exactly are you defending? You do not own the truth. The truth is love and love is free; you cannot own it.

The corpse they defend in this case is the Bible. (In another case, it could be the Chicago School of Economics.) The words, and even more importantly, the message beyond the words are dead, if they do not resurrect themselves continually in a person's ongoing experience. It has been said that at a certain point in Hindu history, the Brahmin priests had to memorize the individual phonemes of the Vedas, but they had no idea what the phonemes meant. (These ancient words are still memorized in Carola southern India today.) They would go on performing the various sacrifices perfectly, but not knowing any of the contexts or meaning. How many times have you said the Lord's Prayer? Have you ever stopped to wonder why exactly the Lord would lead you into temptation? This seems a very odd thing for the Lord to do. It also implies that you should possibly question where exactly the Lord is leading you. Or, what does the Easter Bunny have to do with anything?

"I very much regret that his system-is a system. For myself I no longer believe in these various theories, which people keeps wanting to imprison the art of sound. Music is free; it does what it wants and without permission." – Berlioz, *Report to the French Institute (1866)*

Conversely, humans will pour meaning into the Bible and it's just the alternative or individual meanings that will irk the authority that has any stake in one interpretation of the meaning. This has been a large component of the intellectual history of religion, and the arts for that matter. Jung once said that anyone who followed a religion to its ultimate conclusion would of necessity become a heretic. This means that if you travel deeply into any system of thought you will always come into conflict with it.

St. Augustine was the single individual who probably most perfectly formulated the subsequent Catholic dogma, though he was very close to becoming a heretic in his lifetime. With the advance of time, and the solidification of the Catholic Church's power structure, Saint Augustine became one of the cornerstones of Catholic doctrine. St Augustine was one of the first western bishops to completely back the Nicene Creed, which was a doctrine that promoted the equivalency of the Father, Son and Holy Ghost. This was by no means the official doctrine of all of the churches in Christendom nor was it the majority's view in the world at this point in history. But largely through the skill of St. Augustine's writings, this single document became the official creed of the western Roman churches. (See *AD 381* by Charles Freeman for an excellent discussion of this).

St Augustine was writing at a time of great fear and trouble in the world. He was alive and writing shortly after the Sack of Rome in 410. The Sack of Rome was truly an unprecedented turning point in western culture. Romans had been living in their city almost entirely secure for 850 years. Thousands of people were killed, and of course, women were raped indiscriminately and this great city didn't recover completely from this sacking for another 700 years. Sack of Rome is one of the key ingredients-along with the fallout of Diocletian's sweeping reforms-that led to the entire western economic breakdown, which in turn, led us in the European west into the Dark Ages. It seems that Rome's loss of Carthage and the free African grain coming from there to feed the Roman citizens was the final spike in the coffin for the west. People at this time were quite rightly afraid and there was much discussion of the apocalypse. St. Augustine was a voice of power and clarity of vision. We will see other overt agendas and naked power-grabbing brought in on the back of apocalyptic fear soon enough. I would also add that Jesus was a heretic and propounded an apocalyptic vision in his lifetime, as well as all of the apostles and the Buddha, etc.

This is the danger of allowing anyone to look into the Bible or their own soul too closely. It was the Reformation's big problem as well. When you hand the Bible to everyone in the language they speak so that they can read it for themselves, you get the Church splitting into a thousand denominations. The Dali Llama said something to the effect that there are really four billion religions in the world – one for every person. With the advent of the printing press, the Catholic Church lost the ability to control the interpretations or the exegesis of the written document. When anyone could own and read their own copy of the Holy Scripture, they could easily look into it and debate about the meaning of the words for themselves. This is the double-edged sword of freedom and consciousness. The internet is yet another extension of this phenomenon. Conversely, the democratization of interpretation, forces regeneration from below and encourages debate within the monolithic superstructures of power - eventually.

> *"The depth of our Democracy is only as good as the voices of protest that she protects."* – Rickie Lee Jones

Jung's contention was that the Protestant movements weren't a religion. They were protesting against religion, hence Protestantism. What the Protestants specifically did was drain the Catholic religion of its ritual and mystery. The sacrament was not the real blood and the wafer was not the actual body of Christ anymore. It became merely a symbol of that; a more profane or Sthula image, signifying this mystery, but not explicitly participating in it. By taking the Catholic sermon out of Latin in the sixties, the Catholic Church eliminated what little mystery was left. (The Church's naive view on contraception, and the Pope's complete inability to handle the media, is proving to be another fatal blow to the Catholic faith in the west.)

The post-Renaissance period (from 1700 on) in history can be understood as a reflection of a larger ideological shift in the west toward self-perception and a slow-building toward the primacy of subjective understanding of the individual ego. I don't mean to imply any judgment as to whether this shift from a Catholic to a Protestant viewpoint is right or wrong. A detractor would point out that it is difficult to be engaged in a mystery when you are drinking wine and eating crackers with your friends. You are not nurturing an atmosphere that is wholly beyond you, but this to my mind, is largely a matter of insight and aesthetic. I personally think that people today have started to feel that the mystery of religion has been deflated from underneath them and they have just stopped going to church all together. This is why Nietzsche could announce that God is dead and we collectively did kill him. God has been brought down to a friendly guy who comes over to your house once a week and you develop a personal relationship with him, or we stick him on a coke bottle dressed up as Santa Claus.

What excited me so about Ibn Arabi is that I found an individual who was on fire with his religion. He also had a very powerful intellect and the ability and desire to articulate, and commit his vision in writing. Eventually, he settled in Damascus where the ruler of that time shared his more liberal views about religion and allowed him to follow his own path. I wish to point out that there has been no shortage of liberal rulers in the history of Islam. Unfortunately, media today sees to it that the wing nuts get all of our attention.

Ibn Arabi was alive at a period in Islam when aspects of Islamic dogma had not completely solidified. It never really does. The Islamic religion was still quite young and the mythos or mythological vision was still functioning. Like the Bible, the Quran is the word of God, but unlike the Bible, Islam has received the word of God through one single prophet. Muhammad received the Quran through a series of openings. He recited the word of God and copied down directly from his speech. (It is thought that Muhammad could not or did not write.) The Sufis could re-experience this divine breath by meditating on the words of God. This meditation process on the Quran is called 'Ham-Dami' or the breathing or blowing together of understanding. This is a divine (con)spiracy where the sacred and profane become one. It is quite common for Muslims to memorize the whole Quran. So we to can bring mythos back to life by allowing the spirit to re-enter the written word. This involves a double (con)spiracy. We blow in meaning with our breath and God in return blows his breath and wisdom into us, thereby animating (anima or soul invigorating), and our understanding. We are like Adam who was simply a piece of clay until God blew his soul into him.

Where things become tricky is when someone finds a meaning in the Quran or the Torah, or Bible that someone else doesn't agree with. The unpacking or elucidation of scripture is called 'exegesis.' This is the unfolding of truth and it is essentially a creative act where the reader and writer are both participating. I may read about Jesus overturning the tables of the money lenders and decide that I should punish the current banking system (or the Federal Reserve or Goldman Sacks, etc.) that caused the global credit meltdown. This seems like an entirely reasonable analogy and I might be able to convince myself and others that any manner of violent action was justifiable. I personally would caution that the litmus test of the opinion of your surrounding community should always be considered when you venture out on to this type of scriptural interpretation. You should seek out an external reference point with which to judge or mirror the correctness of your vision. The same holds true in dream interpretation, etc. (In this case of the money changers, not enough people understand that the CEO of Goldman Sacks is in fact in the training position for anti-Christ.) It seems that with our internet, even the Pope is not beyond communal chastisement. He doesn't have a clear understanding of spin. I digress and wallow in the profane.

We Have a Name for That

In Islam, God is conceived of as having 99 divine names. These names are set in stone around the door of the Taj Mahal. One of these names is Rabb or Lord.

> *"God can only be known in His capacity Of Rabb or Lord of something; the divine essence is by its very nature absolutely unknowable."* Claude Addas, *Quest for the Red Sulphur* - Pg.138

God can be known to us, according to Ibn Arabi in the things that have been created. Ibn Arabi traces his understanding of this knowledge back to two Hadith or sayings of Muhammad that are not in the Quran. These sayings are: *"He who knows himself knows all things"* and *"Things are veils in relation to God."* When they disappear, what is behind them is revealed. He who has revelation sees God in things just as the prophet saw what was going on behind his back. I myself experienced this station (maqam), Praise be to God! Furthermore, it is impossible to know God in things save through the manifestation of things and through the disappearance of their status. The eyes of the ordinary man stop at the status of things, whereas those who have the illumination of revelation see nothing in things, but God. Among them there are those who see God in things, and there are others who see things and God in them. *"The greatest illumination in this domain is when the vision of God is the very vision of the world."* Futuhat, quoted by Claude Addas.

Ibn Arabi is telling us that the road to knowledge of God is the same road that we must travel as we seek to understand ourselves and/or the world around us. God can only be correctly understood for us through the things that he has created, which is also us. This is his lordship. So the knowledge of things-for us-precedes the knowledge of God, but through our intimate knowledge of things we are led to an intimate knowledge of God. (Western science could take a page from this book. Science seeks to establish the name or status of things.) A higher station or ranking of knowledge is that in which a person has come to a halt in the divine presence and sees nothing around him but God. God is infused in everything. But there is one more station that is even higher than that, which is: *"The vision of God is the very vision of the world. The being who attains to this stage never ceases contemplating the multiple in the One and the One in the multiple."* Red Sulphur - Pg. 140

The beginning of real knowledge is the understanding of the symbolic representation of the world through the name that is assigned to it. You start to recognize the underlying unity of the world through having access to its greater symbolic understanding. You also gain an understanding of things in and of themselves. This is our recognition that things exist beyond our analytic or conceptual framework (name or status), and we are not the centre of the universe. Everything exists both absolutely and as a symbol, and so initially we experience it as a dichotomy through our discrimination. The next level of understanding is to realize that God is in all things and that all these things that God intrinsically is, includes us as well. So we begin to understand that all things are connected. The final 'intellectual breakthrough' is to BE that vision or to be completely immersed in God. Your eyes and God's eyes are the same. (There is a western pop song in which the chorus sings:

"God is watching us from a distance." I find this a very sad window and comment into our alienation. God presses at your jugular with every breath.)

To my mind, this is an example of how some people can get trapped in a dogmatic outlook. They may have gained some understanding of things, but they have stopped at one point in this process and cannot push onward into total dissolution. They stopped at one of the lower rankings and mistook it for the top station, and then they seek to defend the position they arrived at. They became lost in the beauty of a single vision instead of realizing that they could have all their visions be as beautiful. The highest vision of God is no vision at all. Nirvana is Samsara. If you see the Buddha on the road, kill him.

If I receive some knowledge at a lower station, I may feel an upsurge of love for my fellow man and wish to help them understand this intoxication that I have become. I may seek to help them by enforcing my vision through my various followers. Where love is lacking, power will surely rush in to fill the vacuum. This is another aspect of the power drive disguised as love. Sometimes even your desire to help other people is really an unconscious form of tyranny. There are many dangers on the road to complete understanding and if everyone is telling you, you are crazy, you just might be crazy. The hand that crushed the tyrant's head became the tyrant's hand instead!

All things are veiled. That is: all of reality is screened for us when we are unenlightened. Only God sees things clearly, but we can gain glimpses behind the veil, if God allows us (grace), just as Muhammad could see behind himself. All things are ranked in status as well. This is the intellectual process whereby we analyze and dissect. There is a lot of this type of analysis in any discussion of religion, but a true understanding shows us that the true status of all things is actually *One* with God. The underlying reality is singular, but split into multitudes, as it enters the field of time, intellect and space. God has made the world this way so that each of us can understand it in accordance with our own ability. We are locked in a vision of the world that accords with our own individual ability to discern. God's grace allows us to understand things with more subtlety. We must surrender to the service of God in order to gain or allow this grace to come to us.

We can see in the preceding paragraphs how the discussion of a single line can spread out endlessly. This is largely what exegesis is: the circling around an idea and the further expansion of a text. This is the same process that is used in psychoanalysis except that your own unconscious/dream is the text. One of the points of our expansion of a text or dream is to allow an increase in our conscious representation or to increase our explicit multifaceted understanding of things so that we can try to step beyond that limit of the discerning conscious understanding, and become alive in the experience of meaning.

All things that exist have been brought into existence by the divine command "BE!" (Kun). All of these things can be known by their name. But God can only be known by the names that he ascribes to himself: *"In terms of their ascription to Him. His names are conditional upon having come from Him. So He is not named except as He has named himself, even if it be known that a name designates Him, since conditionality in ascribing the names is to be preferred. God decreed all of this only so that the creatures would learn courtesy toward Him."* - Futuhat (II 232.28). *"Every name by which something is named and which expresses a meaning is God's name. However, it should not be ascribed to Him- and this either, because of the Law, or because of courtesy toward God."* (III 373.1) *"God has ninety nine names…These are "mothers" like the [360] degrees of the celestial sphere. Then every possible entity has a specific divine name, which gazes upon it. The name gives the entity its specific face, through which it becomes distinguished from every other entity. The possible things are infinite, so the names are infinite, since relationships come into temporal existence along with the temporal origination of the possible things. (IV 288.1) The names of God are infinite, since they become known from that which is engendered from them, and that is infinite, even though the names are reducible to finite roots which are the "Mothers of the Names" or the "presences of the names."*

"In reality one single Reality accepts all these relationships and attributions, which are alluded to as the divine names. Moreover, this reality demands that every name that becomes manifest ad infinitum, possess a reality that distinguishes it from every other name. This reality by which the name becomes distinguished is the name itself; that which is shared [with the other names] is not the name." (Fusus 65)

This is an example of the logic that Ibn Arabi develops. His writing is like a great fugue where he is playing many strings and themes at once, but all the melodies lead back to singular harmonies. When discussing the divine names (which can broadly be equated with the idea of the Platonic archetypes), he explains the rankings of the names; for instance, God can be a punisher, but God is also merciful. Mercy is a name ranked higher than punishment, as is knowing, because mercy and knowing are more inclusive. Alive being the highest ranking name of all, because all things participate in it. A'isha (the wife of the prophet) alluded to that way-station with her words: *"God has placed the people in their way-stations." The levels make known that which is ranked higher and that over which it is ranked."* (II469.11, 17) The names by which God is known are the ones that most commonly crop up in the Quran or have been specifically identified by Mohammed as names with which we can refer to God. Ibn Arabi is trying to establish a ranking in the legal sense here so that, if we should need to judge situations in the world, we can be with God and practice mercy as a higher station than punishment.

I somehow suspect that female saints don't bother with this hair-splitting logic. I also see that this attention to the minutia of the intellect-especially if we wish to commit our thought into writing-is also a path to God and that it is good to really challenge our thinking. There are many paths and intellectual discernment is one of them. The specific examples of Ibn Arabi's writing don't seem so obtuse once you gain an understanding of the technical terms being used and, like any author's work, once you are accustomed to their style, you can climb inside of the framework and become familiar with it. I also suspect that the extended translations-of this work specifically-were done by philosophy professors. I can understand the need for technical precision in that they do not want to misrepresent Ibn Arabi's thought, but it is very tiring reading.

I would also add that Ibn Arabi's meeting with Sofia becomes much more important when it is put into a larger context of Islam. This meeting can be seen as an indication of elevating his feeling function. Ibn Arabi is quite obviously a thinking man living in a very masculine society, but he spends a lot of his time writing about Eros and his heart. This, to my mind, is an indication of the wholeness or personal integration that he has achieved. Much the same thing could be said about the Persian poet Rumi, and in fact, it seems that the real undercurrent of Islam, as a religion, has always been a concern with the feeling tone. Overt thinkers especially need to establish this connection with Eros and Ibn Arabi is explicitly telling us about his inner journey toward understanding through his meeting with the archetype Sofia. Wisdom integrates everything.

It has been estimated that Ibn Arabi wrote 700 books in his lifetime - 400 of which are extensive. The main work that we are looking at is a book called the *Futuhat al-makkiyya*, or *The Meccan Openings*. A full translation is in progress and it is projected to fill 17,000 standard pages or 560 chapters. This translation may have been completed at the time of this writing. I don't know. The book I have is about 400 pages of translations from various sections of the Futuhat called: *The Sufi Path of Knowledge* by William C. Chittick. To really understand Ibn Arabi, or indeed any great thinker, you need to immerse yourself not only in them, but in all of their culture. In Ibn Arabi's case, he touches on many aspects of his known world. These things are reflected inside of his work and are very hard to understand without a cursory understanding of the time period, and a general understanding of Islamic thought.

Ibn Arabi's vision is a reflection of Islam, but he says things that an orthodox or modern fundamentalist Muslim would surely disagree with. As an example: the Islamic political world has not developed the rigid division between Church and state that the west has come to see as normal. The law in Islam is directly related to the Quran. This law is known as the Shari'a, and in Ibn Arabi's time his vast learning would have made him a doctor of the law. (In the Hindu and Buddhist world, they use the word Dharma, which also has the connotation of fate and duty, etc.) Anyone of great learning in Islam would have gained their education through the religious teachings in the madrasas, which are the centers of the education process. These madrasas are usually directly connected to-and sponsored by-a mosque and the teaching would reflect a certain branch of theological study with specific philosophical or legal leanings.

Within Islam there is a number of competing visions of what exactly is the law. The extreme end of this ideological bent would be a group like the Taliban, where their word is final and a woman might be stoned for not wearing the hijab, or I would be killed for listening to almost any western music, or music in any form, etc. Fundamentalist Christians attempt the same strict doctrinal interpretation and seek to impose their vision from outside in the same politically tyrannical way as well. And of course, like the west, there are many more humane visions within Islam. This is one of the reasons Ibn Arabi hammers home the thought that the names of God should be ranked according to their inclusiveness: Merciful being more inclusive and therefore ranked higher than punisher or wrathful. This can be seen as one of the ways in which he is using his religious understanding and teaching to make real functional legal distinctions in the real world. Judgments must be made in the world, but he is always cautioning toward understanding and mercy or forgiveness (Eros).

Within Ibn Arabi's conception of knowledge is a term called the alam al-mithal. This is: *"Where Active Imagination perceives events, figures, presences directly, unaided by the senses."* Corbin - Pg.43. This imaginary realm is a source of knowledge to be experienced and interpreted, and is definitely to be equated with the unconscious and the dream world. For Ibn Arabi, the Quran is the roadmap or template to which he can constantly re-orient himself, as he is experiencing the imaginary realm. The unconscious can be confusing and terrifying and for Ibn Arabi the Quran and Hadith are his Ariadne's string through the labyrinth, though he also claims to have been directed and helped by two specific inner spiritual guides. The first was Jesus and the latter was the figure, Khadir. These two figures are representations of the archetype of the wise old man, although Ibn Arabi knew that he had met Jesus specifically and not an archetype.

Khadir in Arabic literally means green. He is someone who can manifest himself many ways. If a traveller shows up at your door unannounced and unknown to you, it is incumbent upon you to serve her or him, because it is probably Khadir. All living plants can be a manifestation of Khadir who roughly accords with Mercury from the Greek tradition or Jack in the Green of English folklore. Khadir, like God, is a bit of a trickster figure.

On the one hand, Ibn Arabi comes quite close to walking on the edge of heresy, but on the other, in his mind, he strictly adheres to The Quran and the prophet-hood of Muhammad. Ibn Arabi is in some ways at the same point as St. Augustine. He is formulating the intellectual framework with which to see a revelation that occurred some 500 years earlier. Ibn Arabi is, in his own mind, firmly adhering to the Muslim tradition. This can be seen clearly in his discussion of the prophet-hood to follow. But also like all intellectuals, he is weighing and discussing openly all aspects of knowledge. The Christian Church initially engaged in this type of open discussion, but started systematically shutting these doors after the formation of the Nicene Creed. (Poor Constantine weighed in and out of this quagmire.) Ibn Arabi -as a result of Muslim scripture-is also forced to acknowledge the limit to which man's knowledge can take him and this limit is prescribed to us by the end of prophet-hood within the Muslim faith. This limit also creates the veils with which God screens off aspects of reality. God chooses to allow you to understand things through grace, but we can also make an effort through our will to convince him to allow us this further unfolding of grace.

Nothing remains for the friends today, because of the end of prophet-hood, but God's giving knowledge. The door to the divine commands and prohibitions has been shut. He who claims these doors after Muhammad has claimed that a Shari'a has been revealed to him, whether it conforms to our law or opposes it. However, in other than our time, before the Messenger of God, there was no such prohibition. That is why the righteous servant Khadir said: *"I did not act on my bidding"* (18:82) or his time allowed that he had a Shari'a from his Lord. God gave witness of that for him to Moses and to us, and He attested to his blamelessness. As for today, Elias and Khadir adhere to the Shari'a of Muhammad, either by way of conformity, or by way of following. In either case, they have that only by way of having been given the knowledge (ta'rif), not by way of prophecy. In the same way, when Jesus descends, he will only judge us by our Sunna. God will give him knowledge of it by way of knowledge-giving, not by way of prophecy, even though he is a prophet.

"So preserve yourselves, my brothers from the calamities of this place, for distinguishing it is extremely difficult! Souls find it sweet, and then within it they are duped, since they become completely enamoured of it." (III 38.23) Futuhat.

Ibn Arabi is saying that in the past, individuals like Jesus and Moses were allowed to proclaim the word of God directly through revelation, but that this form of assured knowledge through direct revelation ended with Mohammed's prophet-hood and the writing of the Koran. Mohammed is the seal of the saints and the final historical revelation to occur. Jesus will descend and judge us by our Sunna, which is the society we have created in the real world. And at that time Jesus will receive regular wisdom not prophetic wisdom even though he was a prophet before.

When Ibn Arabi was a young man, his father introduced him to the great Spanish philosopher that we in the west know as Averroes. Averroes is credited with helping to reintroduce Aristotle to the west and had a massive influence on the subsequent unfolding of Renaissance thought. I will let Ibn Arabi tell the story: *"And so, one fine day, I went to Cordova, to the house of Abu'l Walid Ibn Rushd (Averroes). He had expressed the desire to meet me personally, because he had heard of the revelation that God had accorded me in the course of my spiritual retirement, and he had made no secret of his astonishment at what he had been told. For this reason my father, who was one of his intimate friends, sent me to his house one day, pretexting some sort of errand, in reality to enable Averroes to have a talk with me. At that time, I was still a beardless youth when I entered. The master arose from his place, received me with signal marks of friendship and consideration, and finally embraced me, then he said: 'Yes.' And I in turn said: 'Yes.' His joy was great at noting that I had understood. But then taking cognizance of what had called forth his joy, I added: 'No'. Immediately Averroes winced, the colour went out of his checks. He seemed to doubt his own thought. He asked me this question: 'What manner of solution have you found through divine illumination and inspiration? Is it identical with that which we obtain from speculative reflection?' I replied: 'Yes and No'. Between the yes and the no, spirits take their flight from their matter, and heads are separated from their bodies.' Averroes turned pale, I saw him tremble. He murmured the ritual phrase: 'There is no power save God'- for he had understood my allusion"* Corbin - Pg.42.

Here we have a young beardless youth talking to the greatest philosopher of his time and telling him that scientific/intellectual philosophy does not contain the whole truth in a very short discussion, and according to Ibn Arabi, Averroes understood perfectly what was being said. Again, according to Ibn Arabi's biographer, Averroes later told Ibn Arabi's father that he was grateful to God who had *"let me live at a time distinguished by one of the masters of this experience – one of those who opened the locks of His gates."*

Ibn Arabi wished to see Averroes again and was allowed by God to see him in an ecstatic vision as though through a veil. Averroes did not know that Ibn Arabi was there as he was too absorbed in his meditation and Ibn Arabi said to himself: *"His thought does not guide him to the place where I myself am."* Ibn Arabi then goes on to discuss his last meeting with Averroes who, having recently died, was being buried. His body had been loaded onto one side of a donkey along with his various writings, which were being used as a counterweight on the other side. Ibn Arabi noticed the irony of the situation and said to his friend: *"On one side the master, on the other his works. Ah! How I wish I knew whether his hopes have been fulfilled."*

Here we have three layers of understanding: the first encounter is within the real world, the second in the imaginary realm and the third is an interface between the symbolic and real. None is explicit in its meaning, but taken together, they allow the reader to gain an understanding of the whole picture. Ibn Arabi is letting you know that from a very young age, he had broken through to a greater understanding beyond the intellect, and that this understanding was confirmed in the imaginary realm, and in reality by the greatest philosopher of his age, and that all of these images are a reflection of God's knowledge. To one with eyes that see, everything is both symbolic and real – YES and NO. Spirits take their flight from matter and heads are separated from their bodies. But within God, there is no dichotomy; there is only his absolute knowledge. This absolute knowledge is best explained through stories like the three metaphors, because it is almost impossible to understand directly. Ibn Arabi used Averroes as a symbolic representation of the scientific or speculative intellect.

Claude Addas discusses this same episode at great length in his book *Quest for the Red Sulphur*. His feeling is that this discussion of heads leaving bodies was about the resurrection after death. Mr Addas tries to pin down the length and specific dates involved in the retreat that Ibn Arabi mentions. It may have been a number of retreats and Addas shows that biographical details from this part of Ibn Arabi's life are sketchy and that there is only one written testimony from a disciple who actually talked with Ibn Arabi. This testimony is from a fellow called Ibn Sawdakin who also wrote a commentary on one of Ibn Arabi's books called the *Fusus al Hikam.*

It seems that after this early retreat, Ibn Arabi gave up owning anything. He gave all of his possessions to his father and said that he never even owned the clothes he wore for the rest of his life, always dressing in borrowed clothes. Through this act, he renounced anything that might have sovereignty over him. His only sovereign was God and that is who he must serve - no other. It also appears that at this time he had no human teacher. He asserts that Jesus was his first real teacher who was: *"Immensely kind towards me and does not neglect me even for an instant." Futuhat* Pg. 341.

Ibn Arabi talks about his state of mind during this crucial time period. It seems he was awarded a vision in which he saw himself under the protection of Jesus, Moses and Muhammad. During this vision, he explains, while Jesus urged him on yet again to asceticism, Moses announced to him that he would obtain a knowledge called 'Ladunni' – the very same knowledge, which the Qur'an (18:65) attributes to that interlocutor of Moses whom Islamic tradition calls by the name of Khadir. As for the prophet Muhammad, he advised Ibn Arabi to follow him step-by-step: *"Hold fast to me and you will be safe!"* Addas - Pg. 41

In this particular vision, Ibn Arabi was surrounded by enemies who wished to kill him and he was seeking refuge. When Muhammad announced that he should hold fast to him, all the enemies disappeared and Ibn Arabi started to study the Hadith or sayings of the Prophet at that time. This vision was related to us through a book Ibn Arabi wrote in which he tells people about his visions, but leaves out the various specific biographical details. In other words, he only deals with the archetypes, not the personal unconscious. What this implies is that within these dreams, there are also very personal messages related more directly to his individual life that he was also trying to understand. If you follow your dreams, you will see that this is so: the personal and collective are mixed. We can only imagine who these enemies were who surrounded him. Ibn Arabi is giving us a window into the larger collective nature of his personal journey. This is the collective wisdom or the greater mythology of it that is true. I would add that Muhammad is calling Ibn Arabi directly to the Muslim faith here, but also that Ibn Arabi is more than willing to listen to the teachings of Jesus. There are no strict doctrinal contradictions to be resolved in the imaginary realm.

Ibn Arabi was not at odds with scientific knowledge. Either he was not a fundamentalist firebrand who would have cursed Darwin. For him, knowledge could be acquired in three ways: through reflection or reasonable inquiry, through an unveiling in which God opens your heart directly, or through scripture (the Qur'an, which is the word of God). The two methods that you can understand are through reason or through an opening of the heart. They are not different-in essence-only in the mode of acquisition. Reason understands through acquisition and binding, while the heart knows through letting go of all restrictions and is in a state of constant flux as in keeping with God's never-repeating self-disclosures - *Chittick* Pg. 159. Reason or science is only one dimension of the world. It is not incorrect in any way. It is simply limited to the field of linear time or horizontal history and trapped within the intellect. The heart understands very differently.

"Know, O noble brother, that while the paths are many, the Way of Truth is single. The seekers of the Way of Truth are individuals. So, although the Way of Truth is one, the aspects it presents vary with the varying conditions of its seekers, with the balance or imbalance of the seekers constitution, the persistence or absence of his motivation, the strength or weakness of his spiritual nature, the straightness or deviation of his aspiration, the health or illness of his relation to his goal." - Ibn Arabi -*Journey to the Lord of Power*

How Did We Get Here?

Jung talked about the Sufis as one of the nourishing forces within Islam. They were constantly pushing at the boundary of what Islam was. Christianity has had many such figures throughout its history as well. In the early centuries of Christianity there were many competing visions of what this new religion was. One of the larger movements was Manichaeism that centered on a teacher called Mani. He conceived of the world in a much more dualistic form. He felt that God created both Jesus and Satan and that Jesus represented the right hand of God while Satan was the left. It was Satan who actually created the world, which was full of evil. Jesus was sent by God to redeem us from this imperfect dual creation. This seemed to accord to Satan quite a large hand in things and implied a duality of creation. This would not do and the heresy was stomped out so thoroughly that we actually know very little else about it. The early church fathers could be very vicious as they spread the word of love. It seems that the early Muslims and possibly Muhammad's own understanding of Christianity was the result of contact with two other 'heretical' sects called the Monopysite and Nestorian Church whose main tenet seemed to be that Christ was an actual human being. Go figure.

When Constantine made Christianity the official state religion of the Roman Empire, the whiff of power entered inexorably into the Church and they wasted little time in exercising this power. The first thing an ideology does is kill someone. Charlemagne had a very similar agenda in the 8th century, which was the imposition of political unification. He sought to establish a unity of Christian belief throughout Europe. He sought to control the only literate class in Europe -which at the time was the priesthood-and by controlling them, he could gain control over how people received information. Charlemagne controlled the only media source in his world. An absolute lock on media is the key to political suppression or indoctrination. It seems Ireland was out of the loop well into the 11th century and developed an eclectic mix of pagan and Christian thought, which Pope Adrian IV (1154-89) saw fit to rectify by putting pressure on English King Henry II. Henry was given the thumbs up to muster an invasion force so that he could "root out the weeds of vice from the Lord's field" and re-establish control of the media and the message.

"Kill them all, let God sort them out" was a phrase that the crusaders used as they successfully stomped out the Cathar heresy of southern France. They killed everybody in the region, who could not afford to buy their escape. Because this crusade was backed by the Catholic Church, it provided an easy way for a Christian to gain access to heaven by fighting heresy. They might get a little worldly wealth as well, without having to travel all the way to the Middle East, which was inconvenient after all. The Pope wished to deflect the incessant warring in Europe that was interfering with things inside Christendom at that time. This

manifestation of power in war is the vision of the Cyclops, which William Blake called indiscriminate evil or Orcs. I believe this is where J.R.R. Tolkien got the idea for the name. There is no reflective consciousness in an Orc or kill them all, and all the Cyclops could do in *The Odyssey* by Homer was swing around his big club. Odysseus confronts the Cyclops with the first known riddle to be written down. When the Cyclops asks him who he is, Odysseus replies that he is nobody and this confuses the Cyclops and Odysseus later escapes after blinding the poor beast. Singular vision is confused by duality, or in this case, ambiguity which is a metaphor or story. The blunt force of the Cyclops is useless in the realm of thought. I will stop hammering this point home. Actually, I might hammer some more later.

When I look at the Muslim world, I can see that it is a world of humans like ours, just as flawed and just as noble. The Muslims actually taught the west a lot and they were by far the more advanced society when the west confronted them at the time of the first crusades (1100's). They were much more advanced than the west in all of the sciences and treatment of women until well into the Renaissance. It is believed that the troubadour movement of courtly love in Europe was a result of westerners coming into contact with Islam through Spain, especially in the kingdom of Aragon. In fact, Islam had a lot to do with the Renaissance itself: the reintroduction and interpretation of Aristotle to the west by Averroes and the reintroduction of any kind of proper medical texts into the west, which was largely the work of Avicenna, another Andalusian Muslim. The medical writings of Avicenna had no small impact on thinking in renaissance Italy. His work was the definitive medical text for at least three hundred years and was still studied in England in the 18th century. Also, the final invasion and fall of Constantinople by Mohamed the conqueror in 1453, brought thousands of displaced Greek intellectuals into Italy and Europe along with many original Greek texts on philosophy and original Greek versions of the Bible. Such is the backward blessing of history.

Writers like Plato had only existed in Europe in poor and partial translations. Now, with the flood of Greek intellectuals to translate their books properly into Latin from originals, brought from their own libraries, the west had access to the proper and full originals. Many of the great Roman historians were known only in name in Europe. It was known that Livy wrote many books on history, but no one had a complete set of his works or the ability to bring all extended copies together to produce a complete work. Accurate translations and scholarly diligence finally put together complete translations of many such texts. The new art of printing then allowed the wide dispersal of identical copies of such works, so that intellectuals could reference page numbers and discuss certain passages over long distances in letters with each other. This gave Europe, and especially Italy, a new perspective of itself. In a very concrete way Europe rediscovered its Greek and Roman cultural heritage at this time (1500 AD). Europe didn't necessarily see it as a bonus. In fact, some felt the fall of Constantinople was the beginning of end of the world. Islam was undoubtedly on the ascendant at this time.

The west was also taught a lot about mathematics from Islam, hence the word Algebra. It is possible that Islam learned a lot about mathematics from its continual contact with India. As I discussed earlier, Copernicus seems to have cribbed much from Islam but along with this mathematical knowledge came a myriad of navigational devices that helped us to reach the new world.

The Muslim world was very concerned with such things as terrestrial geometry, because as Islam expanded, a good Muslim needed to know where Mecca was, so that he could face toward it when he prayed. The Muslims knew quite a bit about global positioning, in that there were Muslims both above and below the equator and a good 1200 to 2000 miles in either direction west or east from Mecca. The Muslim world had been studying the Greek texts on geometry and they had expanded on these ideas and had been applying them in the real world for some three or four hundred years before the west got access to them. The main reason that the west exploded with this reintegration of Islamic knowledge and Islam didn't seem to have been the difficulty of producing an Arabic script in a moveable type for the printing press. The west gained a distinct advantage over the east because of the ease of printing with our lettering and the democratic impetus of the printing press itself.

Christopher Columbus took a copy of Plutarch's *Almagest* and a copy of a mathematical treatise by a translator/mathematician called Regiomontanus with him to the new world in 1492. Many of these mathematical texts were only made available in the west after having been translated from Arabic and back into Latin again. My big point is that when we fight with Islam, in some sense, we are really fighting ourselves. We place our shadow on to their shoulders and lash out against our own fear. President Bush played this fear of the 'other' over and over, but of course, we underestimated him. He was the Cyclops swinging his big club about. Let's hope we can learn this lesson one more time. I was personally never so proud of my government in Canada and of our Prime Minister Jean Chrétien in particular, than when he refused to drag us into Iraq and it was interesting to see how quickly liberal became a bad word in the United States, as if we were some kind of surrender monkeys. This is the burden of multiculturalism: you are forced to accept other viewpoints and everyone doesn't necessarily want to jump into the melting pot.

I am trying to show that this discussion about an 11th century Arabic philosopher can have direct relevance to the world in which we live and I have chosen Ibn Arabi for a number of reasons: first, he writes in a meandering style that encompasses everything he puts his mind to. He is a rational hard-thinking individual unafraid of knowledge, especially science, and these two mindsets are not incompatible. And finally, because he tells us himself that he has broken through to the higher levels of consciousness and understanding.

Ibn Arabi had a vision in which he banged his head on a door, as he was ascending to heaven and so he realized that this was the door to prophet-hood. He then knew this door was shut. This was the final door that could lead an individual to sit beside God himself, and this would have been a clear indication to Ibn Arabi that he was indeed a prophet. This story, to me on an individual level, was a clear warning against hubris (but that's my agenda). Within the Muslim world, the idea of the last prophet has been interpreted quite literally. If you are a Muslim this presents no problem to you personally. It is simply within the realm of your doctrinal belief. I see it as an intellectual problem, because I am outside the frame of references. From within this worldview, there is no contradiction. Or, all true wisdom is bound to contradiction and this is simply one more.

In the Muslim world there can only be saints now. This probably wasn't much of an issue in Ibn Arabi's day, but not so long ago another prophet came into existence and started the Sikh religion. Then, after him came the founder of the Bahia faith and now in China, there is a new religion forming. If there are no more prophets and we wish to be good Muslims, how can we accept new leaders? This unfortunately is a great problem for fundamentalist Islam and they have been quite vicious in their persecution of Bahia's who, unfortunately for them, are mostly located in Iran - a country which has the great misfortune to be under an extremely repressive rightwing regime right now.

This is also a stumbling block for me. I can't help but see this as the same water, different vessel concept. Were I to become a Muslim, I should need a liberal Imam as a teacher, and of course, there are many of them. Truly religious people don't see everything as black and white as I have put forth here. In fact, I would say truly religious people are way beyond this type of childish idea. Of course, atheists or devoutly non-religious people love to cram religion into their own narrow box of understanding and then rail against it. Bill Moyers asked Joseph Campbell essentially this same question that I am circling around, *"Why had he not practiced some form of faith?"* He said that for him it was too late, in that he knew too much about all faiths to practice one exclusively. I feel this to be a copout, but I have no more courage than Mr. Campbell and certainly I have less book smarts. There is a Sufi saying that haunts me, *"why are you always window shopping? Go into a store and buy something."* Ouch.

"Do not worry, from morning to evening and from evening to morning, about what you are going to wear" Jesus - *Gospel of Thomas 36*

That Art Thou

All faiths can lead to the same palace of wisdom. In terms of their different dogma, I have no problem with the Buddhist contention that God doesn't exist, nor does it really irk me (at least this is what I tell myself) to read about physicists dancing about this very same issue as they stridently avoid the term God. The official Buddhist stance is that they are atheists and it's hard to imagine a Buddhist persecuting anyone for believing in God. I think these types of basic issues about conduct and dogma are the main stumbling blocks that most people have with religion. They mistake the medium for the message. Some people I have talked to refuse to believe in a God who would create such an evil world.

This is a handy excuse people use to become outraged at the Catholic Church or Islam, or whatever. By picking at these small elements of dogma, we can justify our anger with the Church, which again is an organization that is made by humans, much like democracy. I see this as the world of trials and we are caught in an imperfect understanding of it (this is not a call to inaction). Without the dynamic of the opposites, it would be impossible to gain further consciousness. Change thrives on tension: 1+1=3.

As the Romans were dealing with the early Christian movement, it was quite common for the early Christians to be accused of cannibalism or of partaking in ritual orgies. This was based on the Romans' sketchy knowledge or intentional misrepresentation of the Christian idea of accepting the host as the body of Christ. The Romans also misconstrued the Christian idea of brotherly love as some form of ritual orgy. These misconceptions occurred because Christianity was forced to be secretive and guarded in the first three centuries. Of course, the Romans envisioned the worst so that they could more easily justify their persecution. In a *New York Times* interview with John Friend (the head of the Anusara yoga movement), the *Times* writer intentionally inserted some lines into the article, saying that a large Anusara meeting turned into an orgy with people pressing their hotel keys into each other's hands. Of course, Mr. Friend denies this. But really, what if it did turn into an orgy? Is it illegal? This is such a loaded area (sexual abuse between gurus and disciples) that even a whiff of it has traction. This story will probably resurface in many subsequent articles. In fact, the Anusara movement has dissolved. Ghandi was accused of similar shenanigans with his niece near the end of his life. Such is the nature of urban myth making. Have we seen this happen anywhere else?

The Buddha is quite often depicted with a large flaming sword. He was depicted this way in the office of someone I knew. The woman had a very large Jade statue of the Buddha and I asked her why the Buddha would have a sword (obviously a martial weapon). She told me that the statue had come to her and that the sword was to cleave into the illusion of the world, or to discern the truth by rending apart the apparent opposites. It seems you must approach the world as a warrior and channel your aggression into discernment to gain enlightenment. (Love is War) I will excuse the poverty of my explanation as these images can be elaborated on endlessly. But to gain initial understanding, you must be prepared to fight and separate elements into discernment to gain wisdom. Or alternatively, if you see the Buddha walking down the road, you should kill him. This is not the real Buddha that you have seen, because the Buddha is not a god. He was definitely human. If you see him, you can be certain you have been caught in an illusion of your own making.

In yoga there is a suite of moves associated with being a warrior. To perform these moves correctly, you should seek to become the warrior in your mind as well as your body. Conversely, as you perform the moves, you do become the warrior in yourself. When the body is portraying these moves, we become the moves we portray, because we are a mind body duality. It takes courage to hold the postures as your limbs start to ache and your mind wanders to your pain. You will also find that you have a very difficult time not being happy, if you force yourself to smile all of the time. You do what you are and you are what you do. This duality is unified in us through our engagement in action in the world. This is the sword of discernment that the Buddha wields. We are in the world and so we should embrace our being without fear.

I think one of things that the west has missed about religion is the ongoing role of practice and ritual. Religion is something you do. When you do things, the things you do become you and religion seeks to establish patterns through reinforcing a moral agenda along with the ritual construction of an ideal. In India, religious practice is intimately bound with everyday life. Hindu religious festivals overwhelm everything, while we in the west get concerned about whether we are offending anyone by associating the Christmas holidays with Christ. We should change the word holiday itself, to simply 'Day'-lest we offend radical atheists by implying there could be something holy in the world.

A Buddhist does not worship the Buddha. They strive to become a Buddha and the Buddha is the one who has awakened. The east has never shied away from miracles or miraculous imagery. They never seem to get caught in this literalizing of imagery that the west now suffers. Krishna is customarily painted blue or the other Hindu gods are consistently rendered with multiple arms to emphasize their various powers or areas of expertise. All of the earth was showered in flowers when the Buddha gained enlightenment, because he did not gain it for himself. There wasn't anyone there to receive it. In a very real way though, the earth did change when the Buddha gained enlightenment: monasteries showed up thousands of miles away from where this happened and I am still discussing it with all of the flowers at my feet. This is-in some very real sense-what Rupert Sheldrake was talking about. When someone learns something, it is slightly easier for everyone else to learn it. So when the Buddha gains enlightenment, he gains it for everyone and the world is awash in flowers.

In the early iconography, the Buddha is signified by an empty seat. You should not get too caught up in his individual achievement, as this could lead you to stop trying to improve yourself, because you spend too much of your time concentrating on the Buddha. You will get caught being his follower, and when you strive to follow the Buddha, you will defend his ideals; by removing his image you cannot not defend something that never existed. If he wasn't depicted as an icon, you can't make this mistake. The idea behind not rendering his likeness is that he sits inside of you right now, so why look elsewhere? It seems that there was an explosion of the rendering of realistic human likenesses of gods for the purpose of worship that happened nearly simultaneously all over the west and into India around 200 or 300 AD. This is possibly a result of contact across the Silk Road.

The Buddhist stance on missionary work or evangelism is that if you are lucky enough to have heard the Buddhist teachings in your lifetime, good for you. They do not actively try to convert anybody (they may have in earlier times. I don't know). They certainly sent missionaries all over the world and they found fertile ground in China. If you are trying hard to convert people to your point of view, it can be a reflection of a power drive in that you may be trying to convince yourself of your faith, and you gain assurance that you are right by converting and convincing others.

One of the things that struck me in India was the unbelievable flexibility and creativity of the Indian religious mind. Hinduism encompasses-and for the most part- accepts an unbelievably wide range of experiences that are not considered strictly orthodox. In India's most enlightened periods, they have had no problem with Buddhism or Jainism, or later even Islam. They were all different manifestations of the same religious urge and each has cross-fertilized the other. Same water, different vessel. This enlightened stance was an intentional political agenda put forth and enforced by the ruling mogul elite. In fact, it seems that much of the most creative writing and analysis of Hindu yoga and philosophical thought was a reflection of the huge creative surge that also happened in Buddhism. The dynamic tension of this upstart Buddhist religion benefited both religions, which were both based around a profoundly gentle ideal at heart anyway. My wife and I saw a stone carver insetting Persian script along with Hindu verses at a temple in Agra. I asked him about it and he said we don't worry about such things here. Mind you, we came around a corner on to a street in Varanasi where there were hundreds of people milling about. The Muslims killed a cow in front of a Hindu temple in retaliation for the Hindus slaughtering a pig in their mosque. These are very grave insults. Such is the world of men.

The Buddha Shakyamuni (563-483 BC) was probably a Brahman or at least a warrior-ruler in northeast India, and his enlightenment was gained through or was seen to occur within and impact on to the socio-political environment of the times. Religion and politics are both part of the human experience and they cannot be disentangled from each other, though we would profess to live in a secular society. Separation of church and state is an important ideal, though the impact of religion in politics is evident everywhere for good or ill. This is especially true when you look at religion from a historical perspective. There is no clear boundary between what a religious attitude is and what a political outlook is. Both Muhammad and Jesus saw their message within a socio/political framework in that they wanted and expected to change the real world now.

Instant Karma is going to get you

Within Indian Hindu society there is a rigid class structure or caste system that involves four main classes with an endless series of subdivisions within these classes. The Brahman are at the top and their main responsibility in the world is to perform the Vedic rituals that keep the whole world and the humans in it, in alignment. While at the bottom are the untouchables who aren't allowed to do anything, but beg for their existence. This structure has been said to have evolved as the result of karma. If you are reborn as an untouchable, you must have done something in a past life to deserve this station. You have done better than those who are reborn as a goat and so you should fulfill your duty to the station that you find yourself in. You will slowly move up the queue. (Of course, this is greatly simplifying the idea of karma.)

The Buddha refused to acknowledge this class system and preached that enlightenment was for all who worked to obtain it. With his figurative sword in hand, he taught and spoke to all classes of people and one of his messages was that anyone could end the endless cycle of rebirth, if they worked at raising their own consciousness. Of course, some teachers in the Brahman class were outraged that other people from all of other classes felt that they could achieve enlightened understanding without performing intricate rituals, or indeed, that they could side-step the whole Hindu religious edifice. The Buddha was in part rebelling against this empty ritual mouthing of the Vedas that we talked about earlier. (Why defend a corpse?)

We must again place this caste system in context, in that India does not have, or has not encouraged, the cult of the individual. The ego in some senses has been seen to be an impediment to proper understanding. Nonetheless, this new message of the Buddha sought to undermine some of the very root social/political structures of India at that time. (Jesus promoted a very similar radical social message directed against Judaism some 500 years later.) The subsequent success of Buddhism caused a reaction within Hinduism, or this extremely creative period in world history caused a massive outpouring of religious yearning across the entire Indian subcontinent and beyond. Great religious teachers seem to come into the world in waves. The period of the birth of the Buddha also saw Heraclitus, Empedocles, Confucius and Lao Tse.

Ghandi fought against this same class structure with limited success. Historically it seems that the Brahman have continually sought to established themselves at the top of the heap over the last five or six thousand years of Indian history. They promoted the concept of ritual and racial purity, but the reality is that the Brahman caste is in no way racially pure, if such a thing exists anywhere. The Brahman caste has been growing and fluctuating for a long time as various parvenus move up and take their turn being top Vedic dog. There are still strong prejudices in India around the relative lightness of skin. The founder of the Sikh religion in 1699, Guru Gobind Singh, struck down this caste system yet again by inviting all members to be equal in a Sikh brotherhood. It seems that the Buddha was one of the most successful original templates for this type of radical social reorganization. It is an open question as to how much Jesus was influenced by these Indian teachings. Incidentally, fully realized Tibetan Lamas and Hindu rishis seek a good rebirth even though they could totally escape from the chain of karma. They do this in order to come back into the world endlessly and help all sentient beings gain enlightenment (quite a commitment).

Psychologically, the concept of karma has some very real effects: children of very liberal parents may develop a tendency to be stricter with their children, who will in turn be more liberal with their own, or conversely truly liberal and open parents will have liberal open children. Patterns of abuse propagate endlessly through people who have grown up in houses with abusive parents. Fathers may hit sons, who will probably use this same force to deal with their children, etc. These types of patterns become the short circuit template with which you begin to view and judge the world around, and you might be more likely to continue in this type of behavior. In other words, you have a propensity to get into or help create abusive relationships around yourself. No one is born a racist. Wisdom is a jewel that is very hard to find, while ignorance falls right into your lap.

The good news is that all of the cycles of neurosis and habit or karma are a reflection of our own ignorance or our not knowing any better. The Buddha comes to tell us that this chain of ignorance can be broken and the best path forward is the middle way between the radical opposites. This is the path of intellectual discernment tied to compassion - the active cleaving of the opposites so that they can be reintegrated into single unity. Emotional reaction or knee-jerk response is a very poor teacher. The root cause of ALL problems is ignorance and the path forward is a balanced learning.

Ireland for years had been a third world country within Europe. The British thought that the Irish were inherently lazy. That is how they became addicted to potatoes, which need almost no tending to grow. Of course, I am generalizing. Sometime in the eighties or early nineties, the Irish government decided to make post secondary education free for Irish citizens. Fairly soon after that, Dublin became the centre of the fastest growing economy in Europe, and also Dublin was one of the most expensive places to live in the world. They called Ireland the Celtic tiger.

Like the economic meltdown we are going through, it is hard to put your finger on the exact cause of Ireland's economic boom, but I would certainly put my money on this free secondary education structure. Like the great oceans, the world benefits from nourishment coming from the bottom. Conversely though, the arts never seem to suffer in impoverished societies. Cuba and Ireland are both good examples of culturally vital places that were financially poor. Ireland has let her artists live with very low taxes for a long time.

Sweden also has an extremely liberal attitude toward education. Anyone can go to school for as long as they want and subsequently the Swedes have the highest literacy rate in the world, but liberal is a very bad word. In fact, Sweden will allow anyone from anywhere in the world to finish their doctorate for free in a Swedish university. My thought as to why they would do this is that a certain percentage of the doctors will stay in Sweden, and if you wished to encourage people to come and live in your country, doctors would be good people to encourage. Education is really the key to solving problems, but it is a slow process and cannot be forced upon anyone. It seems to be well-known now that the way to help the third world is to educate women. Women don't seem to abuse power the way men do, or at the very least, they seem to use their education effectively. There is any number of good reasons to educate women, but again ignorance is the real problem. (It only takes one psychologist to change a light bulb, but the light bulb has to want to change.)

"Darkness; makes me fumble for a key to a door that's wide open"- The Police- *Ghost in the Machine*

If realization were all the Buddha gave us, it would have been a staggering achievement. But of course, he went way beyond this. I should like to dip our collective toes into another book that set me on fire not too long ago. This book is called *The Central Philosophy of Tibet* by Robert A. F. Thurman (Uma's dad). It consists of a prologue to, and translation of, a book by a very influential Tibetan monk called Tsong Khapa. The translated book is called the *Essence of True Eloquence*. This book is a very concise critique of the various aspects of the mind and our thinking, and it can help us to see more clearly what true understanding is.

Tsong Khapa is credited with bringing Tibetan Buddhism back out of a very decadent tantric-influenced phase and refocusing it on the real job of gaining enlightenment. Throughout the introduction, Mr. Thurman, contrasts this work of Tsong Khapa to Ludwig Wittgenstein's philosophy to show that Tsong Khapa's philosophical ideas are not alien to the western mind, though of course, they do predate them.

"Current notions of 'Meditation,' as dhyana, Samadhi, and so on, have been formed by popularized religious disciplines, such as Yoga, Vedantistic TM, the Americanized Vipassana, and pop Zen. The goals of these simplified disciplines must be considered somewhat escapist by Universal Vehicle standards. That is, whether they call it nirvikalpasamahi (thoughtless trance), nirgunabrahman (unqualified godhood), anupadhisesanirvana (remainderless nirvana), or satori, these disciplines seek permanent escape from the ills of existence in a transcendently altered, radically 'other' state of blissful peace. Thus "meditation" *for them is mainly content-less and one-pointed, since the ultimate contentlessness is their goal. The supreme anaesthetic their choice over present and future pains. The Universalists, including Unexcelled Yoga, rigorous nondualism, and real Zen, on the contrary, are critical of the notion of transcendence as a state, define "absolute" as "a-relationality," and thus consider that "entrance into the absolute" is a contradiction in terms. They affirm the terrible, wonderful insight of the nondualist transcendent Wisdom Scriptures, that there is nowhere to escape. Nirvana becomes apratisthita, "unlocated," "stateless," and Nagarjuna even insists that Nirvana is no different from samsara."* Thurman Pg. 131 (Nagarjuna is a very influential early Hindu philosopher).

You may ask where The Big Bang occurred. It occurred right where you are standing and everywhere else. This is a key insight for those who seek to escape from life on to a mountaintop and meditate. The inner world of meditation can be no less difficult than the outer world of strife and trial. And indeed they are the same thing. There is no escape. Nirvana is samsara; the sacred is the profane. Although many Hindu texts, and especially yoga texts from the third century onward, insist that the absorption into the absolute propels you into a state of bliss and ecstasy.

There was no Buddha to receive this enlightenment. From this key insight into nirvana comes the realization that the entire world and your individual striving consciousness are actually a greater unity, and therefore, everything should be dealt with in a compassionate manner. Do unto others as you would have them do unto you. This is indeed the golden rule. In fact, there is no other outside of you to do unto. There is only yourself, reflected back at you in everything else. It has been said that the entire study of the Talmud is but a footnote to this realization of the golden rule. (I've got my hammer out again) To my mind, this is not a discussion of arcane metaphysics. It is a realization of the intrinsic psychology and underlying reality of the human predicament in the world. This realization was for me another reinforcement of Jung's concept of the Shadow. He was not saying anything new, but he was putting the same unending message into a psychological framework, or retranslating it yet again for the west. We come back to paradigms. If the paradigm is open and functioning in a vital and dynamic way, it will get you where you want to go. Mercy is higher than judgment. The underlying truth that all religions seek is that everything is really one thing. If you choose to call that one thing God, that is fine.

What Mr. Thurman elaborates on in his book is that the central philosophy is not to be understood as a cornerstone or key to Tibetan thought. It is an illustration of the middle path, the central way, or the course that helps you to negotiate between the opposites. As an example, if we were to search rigorously for ourselves with honesty, we could come up with two ways of looking. We could assert that we are the sum of our parts, an aggregate of mind and body, or that we are totally different from this aggregate; our ultimate being is ephemeral and our body is just the vehicle that carries our individuality, or we are an intrinsically different mind/sentience. If we cannot with any certainty assert that either of these viewpoints captures the true essence of our being, neither a mind/body duality nor a singular unity, then we must logically assert that either we cannot find an essence, or that it is not there to be found at all. We should not introduce a third alternative that we are somehow there and not there, if we are to adhere to logic. Logic can do the job, but it must become subtle and nuanced. (Ondoyant ET divers) The stance here is that we will, if we try hard enough, look in vain for ourselves. We are a product of the mind that makes us believe that we are separate and distinct entities. And that very search for clarity is a reflex of our ongoing confusion that we cling to-out of a fear-that there is nothing else.

If we follow our thoughts closely, we will see that it is only to a certain extent that we actively guide the spotlight of our thoughts at all. As we saw earlier, it was a result of the intrusion of a dream of two snakes that allowed the structure of DNA to be realized. This intrusion of snakes into consciousness is a very real example of the divine creative urge that exists within the universe itself. If you wish to apologetically pull the divine out of the discussion, you can swap the word unconscious for universe and pat yourself on the back. Hindu rishis have been pounding this theme of the inherent creative genius in and behind everything for millennia. Yoga would advise that a little effort spent trying to find this inherent creativity will help you to realize the truth of this divine reflex for yourself. This is a discussion of that 'ambiguous fringe' of freewill again, and of course, we do have great control over directing our thought process as well, but the creative edge of our thinking seems to be a bit beyond our control. This is the intrusion of Grace.

In some sense, adhering to logic and building logical arguments is a commitment to the structures of language itself, and along with this commitment, is an acknowledgment of the binary or dualist structure that emerges from using language (explicit and metaphoric). Wittgenstein was one of the foremost explorers of the relationship of logic to language and he showed us that sometimes the usage of language can create the illusion that there is an absolute meaning behind statements. He conceived of language as having at least two different modes of employment: the first being the way that we all talk to each other all day long, which has an accepted meaning. This includes all the socially embedded and implied meanings along with extensive implied subtext. The meaning behind implied subtext is literally fleshed out when we use the various forms of physical interaction that occur as a result of being the body/mind ensemble. Much of our communication is received and correctly understood, because of the various gestures and intonations associated with the words. It is firmly placed within the overall environment in which a conversation is taking place. (I will come back to this later.) The other way to understand things was termed 'private language' by Wittgenstein, which means that all of the referents or names that we use refer back to contain a more strictly personal understanding that cannot be communicated concisely without an extensive elaboration, if at all.

The song *Winter* by Tori Amos, (which I just happened to hear on the radio recently) is a perfect example that probably has direct and explicit references to someone or some situation that she understands well and personally experienced. By making it into a song, she has already begun the process of lifting it out of literal context. I can now listen to it and break the song down using the context of psycho babble or any other number of culturally vogue paradigms, Marxist or Feminist, etc. and infer back into this work of art my own desperate attempt at meaning. All of these viewpoints are or can be correct, but for me to explain to you completely, my private poetic language would be a labor of some ridiculousness. (Though, I do take a shot at it later) this is my personal artillery of linguistic referents. My private language is a reflection of all of the various personal associations that I could draw into the conversation. (Like intentionally using 'desperate meaning', which strikes me as quite funny.) In some sense, this whole book is an effort to express and articulate my private language and we will see later that poetry tends to be a very condensed expression of private language. Again, the beauty and importance of Shakespeare is that his work can be interpreted in many different ways, according to temperament, psychological type, social setting or maybe even Marxist/feminist ideology. But the work itself still implies or allows much more than is simply written on the page.

Wittgenstein believed that a private language or a language of internal self-reference was a deception of the ego as it asserts its grasp upon the world and that we confuse our ego when we use this private language to reinforce the pronouncements we make, or we mistakenly believe that we have said something that is detached from its setting in the real world. If I say that this page is white with letters all across it, we can all agree that this is so, but if I tell you that God is an egocentric illusion, better put away as a childish construct of your own mind that is an entirely different thing. Or I may firmly believe that many crucial decisions of global import are being made by the Illuminati/Freemasons in secret somewhere. If we begin a conversation and I get dragged into this area, I will probably get quite emotional, which is a reflection of my own commitment to my private language in that I may have a barrage of internal referents that come spilling out, which in turn, are a reflection of too much of my time being spent on the internet chasing conspiracies that I can do very little about.

My possibly confused understanding of what Wittgenstein is saying is that behind all the talking that we generate, there is ultimately a private root assertion that I wish to foist upon someone else or simply try to prove to myself. I believe this is partially the 'nothing but' argument I was making earlier, which is the feeling that we own something when we can name it, but Wittgenstein has presented this at a much more subtle level. Also, behind this is the thought that we have actually said something true, because we can create a logically consistent argument to back it up. (See chapters *Golem's* and *Homunculus* in Terrence Deacon's *Incomplete Nature*)

Wittgenstein used word games to further illustrate this ambiguity of private language. If I tell you that I am a liar and that I lie all of the time, have I told you the truth? If I develop my private language, I can construct a vision of the universe, even as I adhere to the notions of logic. What Wittgenstein and some of other eastern philosophers are trying to show is that a better way forward is to say *"by never being satisfied with any supposedly analysis-proof element, and by sustaining the critical process itself as a valid mode of thought, cultivating a high tolerance of less than absolute security, the non-egocentric's attitude toward the empirical is thoroughly relativistic and conventionalistic. Having found that life goes on without any irreducible element, he works flexibly with what is consensually established and yet does not abdicate the task of refining the consensus."* Thurman - Pg 95. So real understanding is a constant unfolding of layer after layer of understanding itself and always being skeptical of the feeling that you now have gotten a hold of. Though, even this is not the final answer, because this radical detachment can create a hyper subjectivity that has its own neurotic pitfalls. The east believes that there is a final and complete dismantling of all of these critical thought patterns, which allows a real understanding to take over. This is called 'Nirvana'. You are a Chakravartin or a wheel rolling unto it.

Philosophy, as Wittgenstein conceived of it, is an ongoing therapy rather than an egocentric effort to explain the essence of life. By delving deeply and testing internal assumptions, you can gain an understanding of the way the mind works (what is the meaning of life? Life is meaning. It's not a question to ask, but a statement to make). And when you understand your own mind, then you can really try to look at the world unfettered. This is why the Buddhist asserts that there is no self with which to become attached. This concept of the self can be seen as an illusion that is supplied by the ego grasping for something to hold on to.

In the real world this means that you nurture an open attitude and seek to reassess your approach to situations, if only to confirm that you are not simply dragging your past behind you. A way to use your intuitive radar so that you can determine elements of your own personal neurotic behavior is by trying to suss out the emotional value that you put into any given situation. In a calm and detached way, you can seek to evaluate your emotional investment in what you are doing. Strong emotions can either cloud your rational judgment in a situation or they may also be an indication of your passionate engagement, which can be a very good thing. Wisdom is learning to discern which passions are the right ones.

Hit you Right on the Head

There was once a young Hindu boy who was learning philosophy at the hands of his master and the master had just illuminated his mind to an understanding of the unity of the world: *"My son, all is God; you are God; I am God; we are this entire universe and the universe is both within you and without you. That art thou."* Well, the boy was now full of God's love and was in a blissful God-intoxicated stupor as he made his way home. He made his way out on to the main road and he could see well up the road ahead of him. There was a Mahout yelling to him from high atop his fast moving elephant. The Mahout was in a great hurry and was driving his beast hard. The boy, who was full of God, thought to himself: *"I am God the Mahout is God and the Elephant is God. God cannot be in conflict with God. All is one."* Just as he finished this profound meditation, the elephant picked him up and threw him into a palm tree, breaking one of his legs and an arm. The poor boy wandered back to his master to tell him of this unfortunate meeting with God and the master said, *"My dear boy, why did you not listen to God telling you to get out of the way?"*

The Buddhists have a chant that even Lisa Simpson knows. It is Ohm Mani Padme Hum: *"All Hail the Jewel in the Lotus"*. Padme is a reference to the Lotus flower that grows out of filthy, shitty pond water. But it is Ohm or Aum that I wish to discuss. This is a sacred syllable. As you pronounce it, you must draw in a breath then breathe out while feeling this vowel as it vibrates throughout your body, resonating deeply within you and then you allow it to resolve itself back into silence (being a bit flaky might help you). Each of the letters has a mystical color and is analogues with a Hindu God. The three syllables are A U M. Brahma is the inhalation or A. Vishnu is the suspension of breath (the U) and Rudra is the exhalation (M where you close your lips). Rudra is known as the howler and is a God signifying destruction. There is also a large stringed instrument called a Rudra Vina. This AUM is the divine creation of the universe, which starts from nothing, slowly starts to vibrate with the creative Shakti or energy, until it comes into full flower and then resolves back into the nothing from which it came. This is also a reflection of the workings of your own mind. The real truth of the universe is both in the unfolding into being and the silence or the resolve that follows, as it moves back into nothing at either end. There is no point to the process only process. The yogi would practice this and other meditations, along with yogic exercises to burn off karma, or in western terms, eliminate sin. Slowly, through ever more subtle awareness, he transforms the universe into an ecstatic vision. He becomes that very ecstasy.

I slowly work myself up into a frenzy of writing as I try to elaborate and articulate an idea and then I feel that I've gotten to the nugget or heart of it. I compare it to some other ideas or simply recap everything, then I stop and I look at my book and I wonder what else I can write about. There is a feeling that I have really said enough about something, and that to elaborate further is patronizing to you, the reader, but - and there is always a 'but' – there are so many different aspects to all of the subjects and my ego is still firmly attached to its own fascination with ideas that I can't help myself. I believe this is what Wittgenstein was getting at when he talked about philosophy being a solution: if a philosopher followed the path of knowledge far enough, he could 'quiet' the mind stuff and just BE, or allow the silence to come forward. Out of the silence flows all the creative energy. It seems that Wittgenstein spent a great deal of time alone in a remote house in Scandinavia, which was a suitable location for such a melancholy philosopher.

The mind/ego constantly generates thought and is fascinated by its own capacity to do so. This is one of the key insights of yoga and meditation. The mind wants to wander around in the world of its own creation, endlessly playing in the field of time, much like Krishna playing with the cowherds or standing on the field of battle. Yoga seeks in some ways to constantly remind the yogi that they are in the world and yet not in it. They are firmly attached to a body that benefits from maintenance, but on the other hand, that body is only a temporary vehicle. It has been said that all of the physical exercises in yoga were really exercises developed so that yogis could sit still and meditate longer without becoming exhausted.

When you do yoga, the body itself helps you clear and still the mind of its extraneous mind goo. Actually, physical labor can be a similar meditation. Many of the postures and hand placements are highly symbolic representations of states of mind, and because we are a mind-body ensemble, we actually become that state of mind that we seek to represent in our physical postures. We yoke the body into ecstasy through a full expression of the body's ideal alignment and disciplined integration. Through our devotion to our practice—which is both an inward and outward commitment—we move toward a higher ideal. Tolstoy was also big on the idea of actual physical labor as a means to understanding and he was quite keen on working in the fields with the peasants. In fact, I believe he was one of a small handful of large estate owners in Russia that gave all of his serfs their freedom.

Whatever your action,

Food or worship;

Whatever you give to another;

Whatever you vow

To the work of the spirit;

Lay these also

As offerings before me. – Prayer to Ishwara (God) in the *Bhagavad Gita*

Exercise and physical labor or dance can help you to bring the mind back in to this moment, if the exercise is done with conscious intention. When Jung was chasing his madness hard, he would do yoga exercises to calm his mind down so that he could continue with his introspection. My personal understanding of Jung was that he had the distinct potential to have been quite crazy, but he went into his own madness quite courageously and raised his discord up into consciousness, or he created an integrated understanding of his particular demons. Jung's insight was an understanding from his own personal experience. He knew where the darkness was. He had challenged it directly and so he spoke from a position of strength and humility. When you are in great stress, someone may tell you to take a deep breath or you might spontaneously do this yourself. This will slow your heart rate and bring you closer to the now and an inner silence. Great musicians have learned the value of what not to play, and all melody is punctuated with pauses. I will talk about the physicality of music in upcoming chapters.

Does Your House Have Lions

There is a small footnote in this book by Mr. Thurman I wish to look at before we move on. After leading us through the main currents of Indian philosophy, Mr. Thurman gives us a brief outline of Jey Tsong Khapa's life and helps us to understand that Jey Tsong Khapa himself is telling us that he has achieved the state of a Bodhisattva, or possibly that he had become a fully realized Buddha. Jay Tsong Khapa took a retreat with some fellow practitioners for three or four years. In this retreat, he began a series of 35 sets of 100,000 prostrations, one for each of the 35 Buddhas of confession, along with many offerings and mantras, and he was also studying texts. Mr. Thurman adds up this practice in terms of time. Each prostration would be the equivalent of a combined deep knee bend and push up, which could be achieved at a rate of 10 per minute, or 6000 per 10-hour day. This astounding total could be achieved in slightly less than 600 days, along with the other things he was doing, three to four years is a reasonable time period. At this time, along with many other visions he received, a vision in which Manjushree extended the Bodhisattva's sword of wisdom from his own heart and the tip touched Tsong Khapa's heart: *"And the rainbow-coloured nectar of the five wisdoms flowed down the sword from heart to heart."* - Pg 83. He then received a prediction of his own Buddha-hood. Some few years later, he did achieve this great insight of Buddha-hood and what I wish to illuminate is the unbelievable commitment involved in this enterprse and the years of philosophical and physical training. The date of his enlightenment was 1398 and he was around 41 years old, having trained for this moment his whole life. Can I prove that this story is true? No, I cannot.

Nietzsche wrote an aphorism about the four stages of life that I quite liked. We are born as a child and then we turn into a camel. We must build up our strength as a camel, because the camel has to make a very long journey into the desert, carrying a lot of baggage. This baggage is all of the rules and training that a juvenile must go through, so the camel must be loaded down. If you are to follow any specific religious training or a scientific career, or you become a great athlete, there is a lot to learn. The Buddhist training is all about preparation of the mind so that it can actually accept the import of freedom or enlightenment. Yoga or the eastern and Brazilian martial arts are a similar discipline. Also, you can think of this baggage you must carry as your karma or your shitty, or excellent relationship to your parents or whatever binds you. In some sense, we must carry that baggage. To truly understand it, we must become intimately aware of it.

When we get out into the desert, we then turn into a lion. This is the freedom and the height of your power. It relates to the late 30's or early mid-life experience, excluding the crisis part. This is where you leave all of the baggage behind. You shed your baggage, because it is now useless and you need to be able to adopt the single-minded purpose of a natural animal. You need the strength and power, and passionate engagement of this great beast, but you also need the tools that the camel has brought for you through your discipline. Skills are a means to an end, not an end in themselves. Nietzsche was all about power so he would see this stage as a lion, but a badger would also be fitting. This is the age that Tsong Khapa takes on the task of performing all of the salutations and presses toward achieving enlightenment. Nietzsche never had any real power in his life so this becomes a running theme in his work. One wonders if Freud ever had good sex.

"Like the concept of God, we are bound by what we don't understand." - Author

The next stage is that you turn back into a child or a baby, but not the same child that you began life as. This child is not naïve. It is full of wonder and at play in the universe, but also contains the wisdom of this process and not bound to the process itself. Jesus tells us to: *"Come to me AS little children"*. Children don't judge as stridently as adults. They just accept the world as it is. Doubting Thomas gained understanding through doubting, but he wasn't completely identified with his doubting. Doubt is a tool of intellectual discernment that we pick up and put back down. The Buddha spent the years after his enlightenment gently teaching compassion and trying to help people understand his breakthrough. He did not pick up a sword and try to convert the world. You move beyond the lion.

In the *Bhagavad Gita,* there is the thought that everyone has the right to work, but everyone does not have the right to the fruits of their labor. Work done with the mindset on receiving the fruits of your labor is not good work. If you can renounce the fruits of your work, you will be freed from corruption. You can be freed from attachment to pain and suffering, but you will also regard others' pain and suffering as your own. You offer up your acts-or your work-as a sacrifice that must be accomplished so that cosmic order is maintained. (This is Christ on the cross.) You are in the world, but not of it and even confrontation on the battlefield between two armies is seen as a form of divine play. This is the message we encountered earlier from Lord Krishna and this is a large part of yoga. *"A man does not attain freedom from action merely by not engaging in action; nor does he attain perfection by mere renunciation,"* for *"nobody ever remains even for an instant without performing some action" Bhagavad Gita* (III, 4-5) It is incumbent upon us to perform our duties and fulfill our karma. We shall see later that attachment to the rewards of our duties is the main stumbling block to understanding.

In the early centuries of the Common Era in India, there was a great outpouring of religious feeling centered on Lord Krishna. Krishna is an incarnation of Vishnu who is one of the three great Gods that underlies reality. The others are Shiva and Brahman, or a much older Vedic version, is Rudra. The two devotional movements–Bhakti and Troubadours-are roughly analogous to each other in that there is a more feminine grace and acknowledgment of Eros to both.

There is a story that Krishna came into a village one night and all of the beautiful women or the Gopi Govinda (cow herds) came to see him as he played his flute, calling them to join him out in the forest. They all wished to make love to this blue black God. There were quite a number and so they all began to dance around him singing and clapping, and thus working themselves into a rhythmic frenzy. It becomes very erotic as the women place his hands and feet upon their breasts. Then, somewhat anti-climatically, Krishna helps them to understand that they are all his lovers in eternity or some such boring/enlightening philosophical message, and the women went home to their husbands.

What I wish to winnow from this story is a peek into the nature of music and dance. If you look at the history of religion, you will find that women didn't write manuals for retreat or suffer hair splitting dogma. Women experienced religion through ecstasy. They don't try to escape and/or describe the moment through abstraction. They experience the moment fully. This is dance and music, but for the western church, this intoxication became dangerous. You can't control ecstasy, because the experience is too immediate and volatile.

Music and dance both force you into *the moment*. You cannot dance a single beat ahead of the music, much less play it while thinking about how you took a shit-kicking on the stock market. Women are always portrayed in history as rending their shirts or crying piteously at the grave of someone, or just being too emotionally volatile to teach. This is thought to be their feminine weakness or their inability to control their emotions. I would say that it is also their strength in that they go into pain fully and then they are done with it, or at least they have truly experienced it.

In the east, women are portrayed as Maya the divine illusion of the world. In the episode related above, Lord Krishna flirts with Maya. In divine love play, she is personified as Radha his consort and they make music and love and experience life as play. This story is indicative of a great turning point in the collective consciousness in the east and west. If it had become more conscious, it might have propelled us in the west into the sexual revolution centuries ahead of now. It seems there were a number of women at the forefront of the troubadour movement in southern France. Unfortunately, this movement was aborted overtly in the west and we opted out for the extremely uptight dancing we associate with in this late medieval period, though you can never completely extinguish this Dionysian urge.

Witness the whole rave scene and their drug of choice Ecstasy. Maybe this overt flaunting of ecstasy is why gypsies have gotten such a bad rap throughout history. If you have ever seen a flamenco performance, you would understand what passion is all about. Gypsy music and flamenco music especially are openly erotic, but disciplined, refined and very intense. It is a display of controlled ecstasy. The women are always flipping their skirts up in a provocative manner, but it is stylized and controlled. Turkish belly dancing is a very similar erotic stylization. Young women always seem to be better dancers than young boys at the same age. They seem to feel it naturally in their bones. Dancing is not an abstract concept to be wrestled into submission. It is here and now and I think historically men can be seen as being terrified of this or at least they wish to subjugate, or control it. When a woman is dancing, there is an elemental power that men cannot escape, so men try to dominate or relegate it to the realm of illusion. Lord Krishna does not rail against this elemental power. He participates in the illusion, because it is an extension of him. He calls the tune if you will, or accepts the tune that's called. This is the same image or ensemble of images as the Lord of the Dance in Celtic mythology, not the Broadway production. Although, even in the Broadway style you still get a feeling for the power, even though the girls aren't allowed to move their upper bodies, arms or hips – such is the Catholic medieval/Irish aesthetic.

In Indian and Buddhist iconography, you are constantly reminded of the eternal duality of women and men, in that most of the gods are portrayed with their consort. This is especially true in tantric iconography where the consort is usually having sex with the god. The god and consort represent the opposites or dynamic nature of things as they enter the field of time. Each god is also absorbed in the other, in the creative sexual act. This is the same message that is encompassed in the

Song of Songs from the Bible. It is an openly erotic poem that only narrowly slipped through the censors, as the Bible was being compiled. This doctrinal editing was done largely by Greek Christians in the fourth century under the watchful eye of Theodosius in Byzantium. Subsequent exegesis had tried to abstract the *Song of Songs* into an entirely spiritual dialogue between God and Sofia or a man and his soul's yearning for God or whatever. The truth is that it can stand on its own as an erotic work. There is no shame in sex.

Your faith was strong but you needed proof

You saw her bathing on the roof

And her beauty in the moonlight overthrew you

She tied you to her kitchen chair

She broke your throne and cut your hair

And from your breath she drew a Hallelujah

I've seen your flag on the marble arch

And love is not a victory march

It's cold and it's a broken Hallelujah

    Leonard Cohen - *Hallelujah, Hallelujah*

The Bible leads us to understand that the first people that were down in the grotto, tending to Jesus' body-after the crucifixion-were women. They were the first people to bear witness to the resurrection. The two Mary's were there before any of the apostles. They were Mary the mother of James and Salome and Mary Magdalene the 'whore'. Mary Magdalene and Jesus' mother are both named Mary by no coincidence. In my opinion, they have the same name, because psychologically they are the same individual, split by the western patriarch – one all good and virginal and one all bad, but redeemed. There is an alternate tradition that was cast out of the Bible, but fortunately was later rediscovered at a place called Nag Hammadi in Egypt. In occurs in the Gospel of Philip where we hear that Jesus always walked with his mother Mary and Mary

Magdalene, and that Mary Magdalene, the whore, was actually Jesus' favorite disciple. *"The consort of the Saviour is Mary Magdalene. The Lord loved her more than all the disciples and used to kiss her often on her (mouth)."*- Logion 55 from *Jung and the Lost Gospels* Stephan A. Hoeller Pg.75

It seems that only Mary Magdalene truly understood Jesus' message of redemption. She came from the lowest rung of society to the highest level of discipleship. She received secret teachings that none of the other apostles were privy to or ready for, except maybe that other castoff – the doubting Thomas (my personal hero). The making of Mary Magdalene into a whore, is again the western Patriarch flexing its terrified muscle and that is why I say both Mary's are the same person, whether historically they were or not, is not my concern. This is an example of enantiodromia, the tendency of things to become their opposite. We condemn whores as the tempters of men and then we get TV evangelists (Jim Baker) who can't get enough of them. And we accept that Jesus' mother was a virgin and elevate her above Mary Magdalene. This is not a paradox. It is part of the natural flow of the universe. To my mind, it is much better to embrace the whore and raise her up to be the greatest of apostles. This is compassion, a flowing together of passions. There is great wisdom in these stories if we don't get trapped in the literal interpretation of symbols. Of course, this ennobling of Mary Magdalene was taken out of the Bible, because it was too hard to explain, much like the story of Job that apparently only just slipped through these same censors. The *Old Testament* was more comfortable with a certain amount of moral ambiguity within God. Or the morally ambiguous God of the *Old Testament* was closer to our understanding of God at that point in history. (See *The Evolution of God* by Robert Wright) In my world the Bible was written by humans; inspired humans, but humans nonetheless.

Jung noted that, as he became more famous, almost all of his closest admirers or compatriots were female and a lot of the subsequent literature associated with him was written by women. Women get it first and they come to the tomb first. Their truth is experiential. There is no compulsion to try to frame this understanding in a logically coherent philosophical doctrine. That is what men do. It seems that women also had a feel for Jung as they delved into the intellectual end of things. Of course, the Bible was written and edited by men and they were confronted with this awkward fact that women discovered the resurrection. So as this story was formed into its existing narrative by Mark, then later by Peter, etc., it becomes a story about an angel telling the women to keep quiet or the women become afraid, or Joseph of Aramethea takes care of the body of Jesus (this fellow seems to come out of nowhere). Women at that time were politically negligible so they simply went to the tomb and lamented while the male apostles did whatever they did, (it seems that they hid), but the women weren't spiritually negligible and their power is still peeking out of this story, if you look. Women are matter, men are nuclear physicists and they abstract matter into constituents and write on and on, and on about what women already are. This is why the anima is an archetype within men and it is the prayer of the heliotrope.

Plotinus (one of the last of the great Neo-Platonic thinkers), understood that flowers turn to face the sun as it travels across the sky. The flowers are in fact praying to the sun, singing the song of the universe. For an abstract thinker, this comes as a great revelation. This is essentially a recognition or poetic reinstatement of facts from the sensate realm. Think about our story from Marie von Franz of the hobo walking around the mountains of Switzerland. For women, this song of the heliotrope holds no such elemental wonder. Women have been planting gardens for millennia, they probably invented farming, which of course men took over. Women have no need to stop to listen for the divine song of the heliotrope. They are that song embodied.

Women probably invented weaving, as well as cultivation. Weaving became an art that was applied to many forms of prehistoric industry, from self-adornment to ship building. Weaving is yet another confluent image of Maya, the great female web of illusion. Witches weave a magic spell that entraps an abstract heart. The word 'spell' comes from a Germanic origin and means a story or tale that you become entranced by. The gospels are God's tales. The Medusa from Greek mythology is another fitting symbol of this type of entrapment. The Medusa's hair was a tangle of snakes, and if she caught your glance, you were turned into stone. Perseus cut off the Medusa's head by only looking at her through the reflection in his shield. This shield mirror is an image of his ability to use his reflective consciousness or his ability to abstract. (Much like the riddle of being nobody that fooled the Cyclops.) In terms of the evolution of our conscious understanding, this ability to reflect on our own consciousness or to abstract ourselves out of the moment has been a huge leap forward and has allowed us much in the way of cultural development. The hero is not caught in a spell and he can reflect on his passions and discern the truth.

"Dance for me Salome; weave me into your embrace" -Robert Palmer - *Pride 1983*

As an aside, I will point out that we have now moved into the Age of Aquarius, which is represented by a woman pouring water out of a large water jug. This is the water of wisdom or birth or the unconscious, or whatever aspect you wish to emphasize. The point I am making is that it is a woman holding the jug and it is my earnest, though possibly naive, belief that women will play a larger role in the next millennium. In the same way as Jesus or Ichthys the fish played a large role in the last two. We have just moved out of the Age of Pisces, symbolized initially by a single fish, then later around the turn of the first millennium, a second fish was added to the image. (Even the heavens change for us.) See *Aion* by Jung for an extended discussion on this collective symbolic matrix.

The west has a subjective thinking hangover. We look for logical explanations and place reason upon a pedestal and then run down the road of invention, fascinated with how intelligent we are. But it's women who suffer the consequences of our thinking. Women sing the dead bodies off into eternity.

Mother Teresa is such a powerful example. When my wife and I were in India, we met a girl who had gone to work with Mother Teresa. Of course, this girl was young and idealistic and wanted to save the world and good for her. These are all noble desires. The reality of the situation is that every day -without a break- Mother Teresa would help to feed and wash young children. India has an endless supply of unfortunate children. India is a filthy, wondrous place and the truth of the situation is that Mother Teresa burned these young ideal westerners out. They found that after a few weeks or months, they just couldn't take the endless squalor of Calcutta. Saving the world is noble, but the reality of saving individual children one at a time is very different.

Snakes

I wish to bring into this discussion one of the last great paradigms I will discuss. This is from Kundalini Yoga and I will be borrowing heavily from Jung's seminars on this, which of course, have a psychological slant. But Joseph Campbell, Deepak Chopra and Georg Feuerstein have much to say on this system, as well as many others. An excellent book to start with is Mircea Eliade's, *Yoga Immortality and Freedom*. We will have reason to discuss this work later.

Within the human body there are conceived to be seven chakras or discs; each disc psychologically representing a more refined stage of understanding. Chakra is an ancient Sanskrit word which seemed to originally refer to a throwing discus but also refers to a chariot wheel, or indeed any circular object. The first and lowest disc is located around the anus and the last or highest is located at the crown of the head or above it. They are in order: 1.Muladhara, 2.Svadhisthana, 3.Manipura, 4.Anahata, 5.Vishuddha, 6.Ajna 7.Sahasrara. In some other texts there appear to be 8 chakras, with the 6th Ajna the 7th Mana and the 8th Soma. The fourth chakra Anahata is located at the heart and is the beginning of true wisdom, bound with compassion. Tsong Khapa is telling us that he realized the seventh or full Buddha-hood. There are many Indian yogis who also try to tell us what full enlightenment is, but it seems that all analogies falter at a correct expression. The chakras represent many things, depending on your level of understanding. On a purely psychological level, they represent progressive levels of psychological insight. The Jewish Kabbalah system that Madonna is so nuts about is an analogous system that has also had vast amounts of meaning poured into, or extracted from it.

We gain glimpses of higher levels of understanding all the time, but to be completely immersed in a certain level, take persistence. Jung felt that it took about five years to be completely comfortable with the integration of a new personality type. It probably takes about the same amount of time to fully integrate the realizations of each chakra.

The first chakra, Muladhara, is the level of understanding in which everything is tied to fulfilling your immediate needs. This is the land of hungry ghosts (in Tibetan Buddhism), where all you want to do is stuff freedom fries into your mouth, and have sex. Freud called this the anal stage where you are fascinated with your own shit. On the radio, I heard an interview with a conceptual artist (who I will not name) who made a completely useless machine that generates shit. He elaborated that all art is useless and so his machine is art and we all participate in art through his shit. Of course, this shit is for sale presumably with a certificate of authenticity. This is Muladhara, not a very stunning revelation and this is where animals live, reptiles, especially. There is no reflective consciousness here. I personally feel conceptual art is an infantile indulgence. How many prostrations or how much devotion, or grace is involved in conceptual art? I'll tell you… none. So if you are living in Muladhara you are completely immersed in satisfying your immediate sensual needs: food, sex, and bowel movements. This is the ugly side of a crack addict. You cannot ever satisfy these needs so you are always hungry and your sentience or self-awareness is inconsequential, because you are a Hungry Ghost.

Svadhisthana is the level of baptism or second birth through water – a symbolic drowning. This is Christ being awakened by baptism in the Jordan. You peek your head out of complete animal unconsciousness and breathe the air for a while. This represents the level of the gut, where you may think to yourself 'I am hungry, I should get some food', etc. Manipura is at the level of the solar plexus and is the beginning of understanding. It is associated with the passions. You begin to understand and have a yearning for more understanding. But this stage burns with fire, and when you are at this level, you are still not in control of your emotions. You go up and down, because your feet are still in Muladhara, but you head has achieved some level of consciousness. However, very little control over your emotions. This reflects the double edge of being passionate: it propels you into action, but of course, you can get into trouble, because you haven't stopped to consider the consequences of your actions. All soap opera plots are based around this aspect. You have emotions, but no feelings. There is not the integrated accuracy of considered conscious understanding.

The great transformation occurs at Anahata. This is the level of the heart and this is where a self-reflective consciousness truly comes into being. If you can achieve integration at this level of understanding, you can be in a bad mood and stop and think to yourself: *"I am in a bad mood, why?"* You can then construct a path forward and garner the will to execute your desire. This is the state where the heart becomes an active organ in your interactions with yourself and with other people and you feel genuine compassion. This is the level where you can have an encounter with the larger Self that also encompasses others. Once the mind gets out of its persistent cycle of generating mind stuff, it can then reflect upon itself through a deep connection with the body and feeling. At this point, we begin true reflective understanding. Thinking needs to be tempered with feeling to be whole, and feeling will naturally temper the overt egotism or arrogance that can emerge as we gain understanding of ourselves and the world around us.

At this level of Anahata, we start to perceive our own small godhood and the danger here is that we identify ourselves with this god. We start to think: *"I have gotten to the level of Anahata, what a spiritually developed fellow am I? I am quite a bit more developed than everyone else I meet"*. When you think in this manner, you recede below the Anahata level once again. The moment you travel down this egotistical path, you slip backward to the bottom, because you have focused on acquisition like a hungry ghost. You have substituted intellectual and spiritual striving for food, but it is the same maniacal hunger.

The warning that Krishna delivers on the battlefield is...if you are attached to the fruits of your labor, you are not doing good work and your attachment will drag you backward, and you will begin to build bad karma again. These higher levels of understanding come to you through Grace. You can prepare yourself for the experience, but you cannot force yourself to gain the unfolding of understanding. One of the essential doctrines of yoga is that the universe conspires to gain understanding and it does this through us. It will bring this enlightenment to you, if you can get out of the way. Ironically, you can get out of the way through your own effort of discipline and by working toward your own understanding/surrender.

To reach and sustain Anahata, using the Jungian analogy, you must have truly integrated many of the disparate aspects of your personality, and as we saw earlier, the other aspects, like the shadow or the Anima/Animus or the persona, can be mixed up with the different orientations of understanding like extroverted thinking or introverted sensations. Most of us can quite easily achieve an integration of the first two levels of understanding and we regularly gain glimpses of the third, but the fourth is the true struggle. Joseph Campbell once mentioned that he felt Jung had truly achieved Anahata. This is the level of insight into another's situation where you can see the problem and you understand the correct method to help them. You have achieved a measure of compassionate empathy. You may address situations in your life now with genuine anger, but you do not become that anger. You use anger as you would use a tool. Anger is always tempered with compassionate insight and genuine engagement. So you become engaged in all aspects of the world, but you are not identified with them.

One small example: Jung once had a female patient who was very overbearing and physically quite large. This woman had gotten into the habit of slapping men on the face when she disagreed with them. Jung delivered her some very unwanted news about this aggressive habit of hers and she stood up and slapped him very hard. Jung immediately slapped her right back. Given the setting and the time period, this was a very risky thing to do on Jung's part. The woman settled down quite quickly and went on to realize that she didn't even know why she became angry like this and why she had been slapping men. Jung has many stories like this and my point is that Jung acted out of a deep connection to his self, not out of a preconceived plan to set up the environment to get slapped and then slap her back etc. Even this act of violence can be an extension of compassion.

Of the next three levels I have very little to say other than that they are a reflection of the first three in reverse and I hope further discussion may give both you and I a glimmer of understanding. I personally have had very little in the way of glimmer, and any extended discussion I could give on these other spheres of enlightenment would be merely an intellectual abstraction of my having read about them. I think my rant about conceptual art will show you that I can very easily slip back into the lower levels, and that I am quite comfortable being there.

"All of the time, I me mine, I me mine, I me mine." – George Harrison

In the east or India specifically, there are so many people and each has a role to play within the great chain of being. Because of the cultural leanings and the persistent religious teaching that individual experience is not the point, the Ego-in the east-seems to be able to be broken more easily. The west as gone down the path of the great individual and we all know who we are and what we are doing. For us, it is harder to disentangle our ego/persona from the things that we do. This is partially due to our confusion about the persona-or the face we show the world- and our ego, and our high tolerance of high profile assholes. Most people can disassociate themselves from their persona, but the ego is a little more subtle. We all know what we do and how we act in the world, but it's a little harder to know who we are without the prop of our outward face or career paths. Most young women will spontaneously point toward their bodies when asked who they are. This tends to be a female response in that they are more firmly attached to their physical being and men will usually sight the things that they have done.

The ego attachment makes it hard for us to truly absorb eastern philosophy. I recently heard that someone described the Tao by pointing out a window and indicating that everything that was in view was the Tao. For the west, Jesus was a unique individual who lived in Jerusalem and performed a series of historical acts at such and such a time and place, and we can prove he lived because we have a document showing that Pontius Pilate crucified him on such and such a date, and then went over to a wash basin and cleaned his hands of the whole ugly thing. Then someone made a snuff film called the *Passion of Christ,* showing him beaten up for an hour so that you can really get a feel for the historical truth of it. We are truly fascinated with our own shit. Westerner's have trouble understanding the Chinese concept of Tao or the subtleties of the polytheistic Hindu religion that lead up to the singularity of the Atman. Tao is not tied to anything that can be pointed to. It is everything all at once. How exactly do I measure and explain that?

I remember seeing a show about a fellow who worked at an institute for spiritual advancement. They were doing a lot of work in comparative mythology. One of his co-workers brought in a Sufi mystic to give them a talk and this guy was tapping away at his typewriter when this Sufi fellow walked by his open door. This other fellow immediately stopped typing and felt an aching pain in his heart. He understood that this Sufi mystic had a much larger heart than his and that this pain he suddenly felt was his heart trying to grow. This is a physical manifestation of a realization of Anahata. We are a mind/body duality.

Peter Gabriel was working on one of his recordings (US) and he found a fellow that played the Turkish Ney flute. This fellow was Kudsi Ergurner and while he was recording his flute parts, Ergurner mentioned to Gabriel that he should visit him at his institute in Paris. I'm sure Peter Gabriel was polite, but it seems he didn't give much thought to this offer. Soon after that, Gabriel was looking through a newspaper and he saw that all the world's great religious leaders were getting together for coffee. There was the Pope, the Dalai Lama and Peter Gabriel's flute player Kudsi Ergurner, whom was the head of the Turkish dervish order, all smiling to the camera. It's hard to imagine the Pope playing the piano on a pop record and no one even knowing that he was someone important. Maybe some nice chocolates around the studio and spruce it up a bit. This is at the very least Anahata.

The next level is Vishuddha. This level is where, *"the power of the elephant is lent to psychic realities, which our reason would like to consider mere abstractions." The abstraction, or the concept of God, has come out of experience. It is not your intellectual concept, though it can be intellectual too. But the main thing in such an experience is that it is a physical fact. And psychical facts are reality in Vishuddha."* –Jung - Pg. 56

I might be wrong, but I think this is something like Pope John Paul II going to Poland against the wishes of the communist government and shortly afterward 'in terms of historical time' the Berlin wall fell and communism collapsed. We can tally up any number of subtle arguments and all of them will show that this was not a result of the Pope's visit. But to deny the Pope's part in this truly astounding occurrence is naive. The elephant loan his power to psychic realities. There is no abstraction. Things flow from understanding.

Ganesh the elephant-headed God is now on your side. He is-among many things-the clearer of obstacles and you will find that reality might conspire to help you in your spiritual quest. You will realize that you have been lucky enough to have found a good teacher and it will seem to you that the universe is indeed helping you; and you are conversely helping the universe.

In Kundalini yoga, it is understood that a serpent lays curled up at the bottom of the spine, and as you begin your practice, you must first awaken this serpent. Some practitioners actually give it a physical bump to wake it up. You are trying, through your practice and self-realization, to bring the serpent up through the spinal cord and through the various chakras toward the thousand-petal light of wisdom and to full self-realization of higher consciousness. Jung had a patient who dreamed she had a serpent curled up at the base of her spine. She was a young European woman and it was unclear if she had ever encountered any form of specific Kundalini yoga teaching. In the forties and fifties this was pretty esoteric stuff, so it is doubtful that she could have known anything about this. Jung was struck by the fact that this woman dreamt about something so alien to her culture and yet so specific an image as this. The serpent represents the primordial energy or Shakti that lies dormant in all people, which we must awaken. It is also a good analogy for the older reptilian brain, which is directly connected to the spinal column.

I should like to quote Jung talking about Kundalini in another setting: the black Kundalini snake… *"That it wants to be recognized in the light, in consciousness, would be the psychological interpretation. Of course, in reality the thing is not so simple, because that process is connected with all sorts of mystical phenomena. People call me a mystic, but we really are chock full of mysticism; that word covers a large area of facts which we cannot understand. For instance, you heard this gentleman speak of immortality - that is such a regrettable piece of mysticism. But I must say that becoming conscious of the snake really has to do with the psychological problem of immortality. It has nothing to do with the question whether there is such a thing as immortality. It has only to do with the fact that people speak of immortality: that is simply a psychological necessity. And they always will talk about it, if only to try to disprove it, and that is what we are concerned with - the fact that they do talk about it, which is quite enough. For in the long run it is absolutely indifferent whether one has a sort of illusion or imagination, or whether it is a fact-it has ruled one's life in either case. Therefore, the fact that rules my life or that influences my life to a great extent is the psychological fact, whether it is true in an objective way or not; whether the vision one has had is an actuality, which can really be seen or whether it is a hallucination. That simply does not matter. The point that matters is that it matters psychologically. In the history of mankind, what could be called the most abstruse illusions, when looked at from a certain angle, have caused the greatest havoc and produced the greatest part of history? Think of the history of Islam, of Christianity, or of Buddhism. Those are historical facts, and one could say, brought about by illusions."* C.G. Jung *–Visions Seminars: Book 1* Pg. 296-7

I recently saw a quote from Richard Feynman about how the universe was so complicated that he could not see how God could have created it etc. God is truly at his jugular.

Jung went to India and maintained contact with a number of professors there, one of them told him that the Kundalini philosophy was associated strictly with physical medicine, implying that this spiritual aspect we are discussing is more or less irrelevant and that there is another side to Kundalini yoga that I personally know nothing about. I don't think Jung had any pretensions that he understood this system as an Indian practitioner might, but he was not afraid to relate it to his own understanding of psychology and I only bring it up to illustrate the point that there are other elaborate paradigms in existence, this being one that an individual could literally spend a life time understanding. The Chinese system of Chi energy is also fascinating and I believe there are direct correlations between it and Kundalini. Same water different vessel.

I met a friend of spirit

He drank and womanized

And sat before his sanity

I was holding back from crying

He saw my complications

And he mirrored me back simplified

And we laughed how our perfection

Would always be denied

"Heart of humour and humility"

He said "will lighten up your heavy load"

I left him then for the Refuge of the roads

-Joni Mitchell meeting Chogyam Trungpa in Refuge of the Roads Hejira

I should like to give the reader an inkling of the far end of religious practice and this is from the Buddhist Vajra or tantric path. In this tradition, the practitioner may set on the path of practicing lucid dreaming. This is where the dreamer concentrates his mental powers from within the dream state and controls the dream itself. One of the post Jungians, Anthony Stevens, talked about this method, but I will let Chogyam Trungpa Rinpoche explain how this can affect our real life. *"[This] is the dream that we have all the time in our lives, the fantasies and real experiences of our life during the day, the fantasies and the thought processes that make our life like it is happening in Disneyland. The search for entertainment is an important aspect of the dream activity. If you realize the dream as dream, then there is no entertainment...*

"If we realize dream as dream, the whole approach to life becomes less businesslike, but at the same time very practical. Relating with friends, relatives, the business world, enemies- all these experiences becomes more real... The point of this yoga is to free oneself from the Disneyland -like quality, which is our regular life, and replace that with dream experience, which is real life. From that point of view, if one could live completely in the dream world that would be much more real and pragmatic and efficient and complete than the so called non-dream world." -From *Secret of the Vajra World* by Reginald A. Ray - Pg. 246

I will quote Mr. Ray's book again: *"The trick here-and it is a challenge that every Vajrayana practitioner faces-is to stay with the journey. There is a temptation, when we feel inundated by the chaos of the ride, to indulge in emotional upheavals, become numb, or give up. When our neurosis is blatantly in our face- particularly as western practitioners-we may feel that we have made a mistake of some kind. We may go looking for absolution. Or we may feel that the practice is "not working" and stop meditating. Either one of these represents a 'wrongview'. It is precisely, because the practice is working and our karma is ripening so quickly that we find ourselves sailing in a very choppy sea. The antidote in such a situation is to stick with our practice.*

Emphasize emptiness, resting in open awareness, until the howl of the wind dies down a bit. Then hoist the sail again and get on with the voyage." Pg 252. This was the point that Jung was talking about when he had to do yoga exercises to calm back down and it seems that this tension is a necessary prelude to greater understanding. This is both the no pain no gain and the attachment to the fruits of our labor ideas.

Dear Prudence won't you come out to play

The sun is up, the sky is blue

It's beautiful and so are you

Dear Prudence won't you come out to play – John Lennon

I should like to come back to this world of Maya again and make a point, in fact one of the large points that this book is trying to make, if there is one to make. Two nights ago, I watched Barack Obama making an address to the nation. He was talking about the efficacy of his economic stimulus package of some eight billion dollars. He was saying that there are entrenched Republican ideologues who believe that the correct way forward is to do nothing, which somehow, the miracle of the free market economy will right itself. I don't know who but someone was even arguing that Roosevelt should not have interfered in the great depression with his make work programs. This is exactly the sentimental ideological do nothing attachment I am talking about: the world is going to hell in a hand basket and someone is arguing about the great depression and taking a dig at Roosevelt. President Obama handled this so well though, saying that every economist he had talked to, including economists that worked in both Bush administrations were convinced that a stimulus package was the only way forward. (There is also the thought that he was completely strong-armed into delivering this stimulus package, which in hindsight is proving almost suicidal.) Mr. Obama's job is to collect the best information he can get and make a decision. You were always left with the feeling that George W. was looking for someone to back up the decision he had already committed to i.e., find the weapons of mass destruction for me. Obama is treating the world as it is. He has to deal with an economic crisis, but he is also pressing forward. This is the hinge of the fine balance that must be achieved in leadership, you cannot spend all your time fire fighting or dealing with issues as they come up. You must be both driving the bus and looking in the rear-view mirror.

This is non-attachment in the field of time. You deal with reality as it is, not how you wish it to be, but you press into the future to make it better, however naive that may be – not clinging to the past as though it was some lost perfect template. It never was. There is no final answer only the process itself and your detached engagement in it. Let's make everything less Disneyland like. Disney thrives off our sentimental attachment to our idealized youth. For God knows what reason every child should go to Disneyland once.

Within most of the so called mystic traditions, clairvoyance and telepathy are taken for granted, and within Buddhism, it is believed that souls reincarnate regularly. An explanation of this phenomenon would be facile on my part, but I would like to briefly discuss the Dalai Lama. The Dalai Lama tells the story of his being discovered as the fourteenth incarnation of the Bodhisattva Avalokiteshvara, the Bodhisattva of Compassion. He was a small child of three living in a village in the province of Amdo in north eastern Tibet. After the thirteenth Dalai Lama had died, the body was left sitting in state and it was noticed that the head had turned from facing south to northeast, and a little later the then regent to the future Dalai Lama had a vision while looking into a sacred lake where he saw clearly the Tibetan letters 'Ah', 'Ka' and 'Ma'. These images were followed by the image of a three-storied monastery with a turquoise and gold roof, and a path running from it to a hill. And finally he saw a small house with strangely shaped guttering. He was sure Ah referred to Amdo and Ka must refer to Kumbum monastery, which indeed is or was a three-storied building with a turquoise roof. So a search party was sent out to look for the path up the hill and for the small house with strangely shaped guttering. The initial search party would find this house and a small boy living there who seemed to fit the bill, and so a second party was sent with a number of objects some of which belonged to the thirteenth Dalai Lama.

The 14TH Dalai Lama correctly recognized each of these objects and was subsequently brought to be trained as a monk, eventually being installed as the current Dalai Lama. Of course, he received the best education that could be offered in Tibet and was trained in many disciplines, including a firm belief in reincarnation, etc. But what interests me, and the Dalai Lama addresses this phenomena directly, is whether he was made into the Dalai Lama by his intensive training or whether he already was the Dalai Lama and his teachers only uncovered and polished up this innate aspect. His answer is that he is the Dalai Lama and that the discussion is redundant.

I heard a great story about the Dalai Lama visiting Mexico, I believe. Someone had hired some security to look after things while he was there, and it seems that these security guards happen to have been gang members, probably fairly tough individuals involved in lord knows what. When the Dalai Lama met these individuals, he simply accepted the situation, and eventually through his charm, won them over to such an extent that they were bringing their mothers in to meet him. He unmasked their pretensions and co-opted their underlying humanity. This is Ghandi's, Satya-gatha or soul force: you do not identify with it, you become it; you are both doing and not doing. Passionately engaged, but existentially detached. In the world, but not of it. This idea can extend through everything that we do from working in a car manufacturing plant to doing fine cabinet making or playing music, and acting or sitting on a mountain top and meditating.

I have noticed that whenever there is some kind of fundraiser going on musicians and artists are the first people that are called to help out, and by and large, artists respond to this appeal. It may have something to do with a guilty conscience, because artists get to do what they love to do all of the time, which is art. For whatever reason artists are fairly consistently on the left of the political axis and they are usually more concerned with social justice, etc. All of the artists that I know are either very poor or have been poor for a long time and I see this as a good analogy of non-attachment. If you ask artists if what they do matters, they will probably admit that in the grand scheme of things it does not matter at all, but to them it is a therapy and meditation. I am sure that very few of them could live contently without doing their art. It is sometimes quite astounding what artists will sacrifice to continue their work. This is our meditation in Chapter 6. First we shall peel back some of the shadows of the mind using the excellent unflinching light of science.

7 NO GURU

Discipline is a different beast. Disciple and discipline come from the same Latin root Disciplina, meaning instruction and knowledge. In India the disciple/guru relationship is very refined and is far more culturally entrenched. If you wish to become a disciple, you must strictly adhere to your guru's instructions, so you must choose a guru well. It is my weak understanding of the guru-disciple relationship that the disciple gains consciousness in this relationship through a loving subservient attachment to the guru. Your guru then directs your growth individually to help you develop your capacity to love by being both the repository and font of your Eros. The love for your guru grows and expands out and on to everything, because the guru is helping you to understand ecstasy.

Ravi Shankar's guru was Acharya Baba Allauddin Khansahib. Baba means father and sahib is an honorary title attached to his family name of Khan, which also means king or nobleman, hence Genghis Khan. Most of the really vital or well-developed skills and trades in India are passed on exclusively through the family line. If your father was a mason, you became a mason, and in this way, the refined knowledge specific to that guild is both guarded and nurtured, and possibly refined through ongoing genetic expression. Allauddin Khan had a son and a daughter. His son is the great Ali Akbar Khan who was a sarod player, an instrument that his father invented. His daughter became a sitar player who is reputed to be incredible, but very few recordings of her exist. Ravi Shankar married this daughter and thereby gained access into the family, which allowed him to become a disciple of Allauddin Khan.

Allauddin Khan was known to be quite a task master and I have been told that Ravi Shankar ran away at least twice, and was close to a nervous breakdown while he was his disciple. Allauddin Khan was so dedicated to his craft that he used to tie his own hair up to a roof beam so that if he nodded off while practicing, his hair would pull him awake, and like John Coltrane, he practiced for 10 to 14 hours a day. (You quickly get your 10,000 hours at this pace.) Ravi Shankar kept coming back to his guru, because he was one of a handful of individuals that knew Indian classical music at a mastery level. It seems Ravi Shankar had a great desire to become a great sitar player and it seems he was being crucified by this passion.

"And anyone who does not take the cross and follow me in not worthy of me." - Matthew 38.

"Come down off that cross we could sure use the wood." -Tom Waits, *Mule Variations*

The symbolic meaning of the crucifixion is that Christ's heart was in the centre of the cross. The cross represents all of the conflicting opposites held in dynamic unison and divine tension at the point of the heart. Therefore, Christ is the embodiment of the resolution of apparent opposites through his commitment to his passion, intersecting at his heart. Humans resolve nature's ambiguity in their heart through Eros/love and a commitment to continue.

A true disciple will be drawn into the tension of the opposites. These can be made explicit through opposition to the guru or opposition within yourself that the guru tries to help you understand. Confrontation with these opposites can be very painful. Maybe your guru shows you very explicitly that you really lack the discipline to continue learning a specific technique or you may lack the emotional depth to feel the moment properly. What are you to do? The guru is pushing through the seemingly unending series of projections by allowing them to collect in you or on to him and then slowly dispel them. There is more than enough room for abuse in a relationship like this, if the guru wishes.

The very first recording session I ever did was a miserable failure, and I got kicked out of a band that went on to record an album. I was probably 17 and it was my best friend's band, and I was out. This was very painful to me at the time and, of course, I reassessed whether I should even keep playing drums. I did keep playing and eventually got into a number of bands, and I am still playing now in a new band – playing original music. At the time of this writing, we are recording an album of original songs. We are called the *Fires Of*, with my patient, excellent friend, Michael Kulas at the production helm, yet again. Music is and has been my guru, and my most patient mistress. Because of my love for music, I can accept all of the misery she brings me.

When a number of people are involved in a creative act, it is a real pressure cooker environment and everyone is forced to assess who they are and what they are doing, sometimes to microscopic levels. I personally thrive in this type of situation, because it is so intense and everything becomes important. This is one of the reasons artists do art. At the time of creation, nothing else seems to matter that much, and of course, with distance each individual project feels less important. But the art that has been brought forward becomes a reflection or snapshot of that period of creation. It represents the various struggles you were going through. After a certain amount of time, the struggles become unimportant, because you have grown beyond them, but the growing process that allowed you to get beyond them was the art WORK itself. That process is reflected back to you in the piece of art, which helped to move you past the work itself and into a new consciousness, which starts the process all over again. Eve/Maya got us out of the Garden of Eden, because it was boring.

Jung said that all the truly great problems in your life are unsolvable, and you grow to a point where the problem is redundant, or you see the folly of the question that caused the false sense of opposition in the first place. An immediate example of this reintegration and opposition is men's desire to have a lot of different sexual experiences with different partners. But, there is also the recognition within men that they have to dedicate themselves to one person, which-strictly from an evolutionary or utility viewpoint is a huge advantage for raising children. It seems Mother Nature in her infinite ambiguity wants to see the genes of individual humans protected by two loving parents, but also spread wide by cheating husbands and wives. How people reconcile this is an ongoing problem that must be lived through in all its glorious ambiguity. You have to give up something to truly be a disciple. Love reflected in an unfolding consciousness will certainly help you to decide.

"The new principle is simple. It may be stated as a proposition: The more mentally active anyone is the less he is capable of pain… The half awake suffer most; the most intensely attentive are least aware of pain."
– Gerald Heard from *Pain, Sex, and Time*

In the same sense that dissonance rolls from the ears of an accustomed listener.

Idris Shah is a fellow who wrote a number of books on Sufism, and from him, I culled the great anecdote about disciples. He had this one fellow who seemed to be quite ardent in his desire to study Sufism and the teacher told him that he must be prepared to do anything the master asked him to do, no matter how crazy it might sound. Well, this fellow assured the teacher that he was excellent at following orders and he would follow any order with unmatched devotion. So the teacher told his pupil to jump through the window. The pupil slowly walked over to the window and opened it. As he put his leg out, he became very acutely aware that he was over five stories up. There was no ledge to crawl out on to, or anything to break his fall. He kept looking back towards the teacher, waiting for him to call him back from this fall. Finally, the teacher called him back into the room and explained that he couldn't follow orders at all. He told him specifically to jump *through the window*! He was trying to show this fellow that to obey any teacher blindly is a mistake and this is part of the guru-disciple relationship. The guru should be functioning in a relatively open system of dialogue. The guru can simply be creating slaves out of an overt power drive.

In the analytic situation, it was always stressed by Jung that both of the participants are always learning. If one of the people is sure that he has all the answers, the whole relationship becomes open to abuse. There have been a number of abusive religious figures in our time, some worse than others. The surest measure of whether a relationship is abusive is to test the compassion and freedom (love) of the situation. Most repressive modern cults seek to actively limit personal freedom, always under the guise of being for your own good: *"we are only thinking of your well being"*, etc. I do not wish to dwell on the negative aspects of modern cults, but I would like to discuss Gurdjieff for a moment. This fellow was quite influential in the sixties, due largely to the writings of Colin Wilson and Gurdjieff's own star pupil, P.D. Ouspensky. Gurdjieff was first introduced to me through Kate Bush, who mentions him on her first album on a song called *"Roll in the Ball"*, which she performed to my slackened jaw on Saturday Night Live. I subsequently found out that Gurdjieff had been an influence on Robert Fripp and most probably on Keith Jarrett – two artists I greatly admire.

PROOF AND THE DIFFICULTY OF MEANING

I will give a very short and probably unfair summation of his paradigm. What Gurdjieff believed, and he is probably right, that people spend most of their lives in a type of waking sleep, doing things automatically. We see this in the automatic reflexive responses that we constantly give all day: *"How are you? Fine."* When someone gives you a non-cliché answer, and you get a laugh, it wakes you up a bit. So the pathway to higher realizations is constantly refocusing the mind through 'severe' intention. Gurdjieff woke his pupils up in the middle of their sleep and got them to do complicated yoga exercises without warning them. There is a story of him driving around London-in the 1930's-refusing to use the brakes of the car, and when you read the works of P.D. Ouspensky and Gurdjieff, there is a propensity in them to emphasize the miraculous and occult aspect of their understanding. The two of them seem to slip into telepathic states quite often and I am sure that this is a true reflection of their state of mind.

When I was in my 30's, I went to a meeting of people who practiced Gurdjieff's methods. My initial impression was that they all seemed geeky. They waved their hands every time a certain word was spoken. What they were doing was acknowledging that they were intimately aware of the conversation, and every time a word like HE was said, they moved their hands. By doing this, they further acknowledged that they were all awake, if you will. Some of what they were doing was reinforcing what they called the watcher or the reflective sentient consciousness. In this practice, they were constantly trying to bring this observing mental aspect into the foreground. If you were to read Tibetan Buddhist writings or Hindu philosophy, and some yoga texts, you might find that they go out of their way to emphasize that these states of telepathy or even the watcher aspect of consciousness can be a stumbling block or by-product of the quest for true enlightenment. I would also argue that this watcher consciousness can become a way to self-referential and that this is a problem in, and of, itself.

I have a friend of mine called Ron Bock, whose parents were with the Beatles when they went to India to study with the Maharishi. Ron spent a lot of time with the Maharishi as he was growing up, and the Maharishi told him that the people who had studied the Gurdjieff method were the hardest to work with (I just recently went to Rishikesh and saw this very ashram). Transcendental Meditation on the other hand, is a slow unfolding of the deeper integrated unconscious through going into the mind and allowing it to supply its own wisdom. Gurdjieff is working the other way around. I am not competent to say which way is the right way, but I will say that it seems both Gurdjieff and P.D. Ouspensky got cynical and pessimistic in their old age and it seems P.D. Ouspensky started to drink quite hard. I cannot verify the truth of this, but Colin Wilson mentions the impression of sadness that surrounded Gurdjieff's final years in *Beyond the Occult*. I can see no other more valid barometer with which to asses this belief system.

Colin Wilson wrote a book on Gurdjieff called *War on Sleep* and also a book on Jung called *Lord of the Underworld*. Colin Wilson was hugely influential in my later 20's and I was led farther into Gurdjieff after having read the *Outsiders* and *Beyond the Outsiders*. Like Arthur Koestler, Colin Wilson was unafraid of exploring all aspects of the human condition. In one of Marie Louise Von Franz's books, she calls Arthur Koestler 'the person who most closely represents the spirit of the age of the sixties. I would say Colin Wilson most closely represents the seventies/eighties for me. There are plenty of books by, and about Gurdjieff for the interested reader, and I only bring his work up so that I can delineate some of the various pitfalls that someone can encounter when becoming a disciple and alternately show by example, what a great teacher is like. (An excellent book to read about discipleship is *Feet of Clay* by Anthony Storr.)

In the book *Yoga Immortality and Freedom* by Mircea Eliade, he mentions a Sanskrit term, which is the technical term used to denote the state of being in the moment. This term is 'Sajhana' and it means the art of remaining completely immersed in the now and also a willingness to submit. (I should like to humbly submit this word for the O.E.D, if it is not there now.) The term is alternately spelled 'Sadhana' and also implies-among many things-spiritual discipleship. Over my years of reading, I found one writer who, to me, seems to hit the nail right on the head and has been a huge influence on all of the points that I have been emphasizing in this book. He is Jiddu Krishnamurti. The corner stone of his teachings is very simple and yet extremely difficult. The mind has a tendency to relate everything to the past or it tries to project itself into the future, because that is all the ego has. All knowledge is in some sense historical. *"You've got stuck in a moment and you can't get out of it."*

Conversely, the mind has a propensity to look forward to the future and imagine what everything will be like. Some people who are health nuts or body builders get caught in this; if I can just lose 30 pounds then I will be able to do such and such, or if I can just get my abs all rippled then chicks will dig me. In other words, if I can accomplish some specific thing, then I will be in a position to actually live life to the fullest. Jung called this attitude, 'living the provisional life'. Provided that this set of things happens, I will be able to live my life. If you look hard or not even that hard, you will see this way of thinking happens to people all the time. It is an illusion. There is no white picket fence, no perfect wife or perfectly constructed wedding; no amount of flat tummy will help you to have better sex. There is only this moment, right here right now. Everything else is mind stuff to be stepped outside of, or go deeper inside into. As Nagarjuna has stated *"Nirvana is Samsara"*, or Jesus said, *"The kingdom of God is spread out all about us, but none have eyes to see it."*

No method

There was a woman in the late Victorian/Edwardian era who spearheaded a large movement that was trying to combine theology and philosophy into a true world religion. This movement was called the 'Theosophy Movement', and the woman's name was Madam Blavatsky. I know almost nothing about this movement except for the titles of some of the books associated with it and that they were actively searching the world for a messiah to lead us into a new age of enlightenment. In certain circles in the late Victorian era, this Movement was enormously popular and they came to believe that they had found this world's messiah. The Theosophy Movement gave their messiah an excellent education at Oxford and created a whole subdivision within the theosophy movement for him called the 'Order of the Star in the East'. At a certain point, this great world messiah called all the main people in the Theosophy Movement together in India for a jamboree or something (they probably had real steamed hot dogs). This new messiah mounted the podium amid great expectation and told the waiting crowd this story.

The Devil and a friend were walking down the road together. There was one other fellow a little farther up ahead of them. The devil's friend noticed that the other fellow bent down to pick something up off the road and he looked at it, and put it in his pocket. The devil's friend turns to the Devil and asks: *"What did that man pick up?" "He picked up a piece of the truth,"* said the Devil. *"That is a very bad business for you, then,"* said his friend. *"Oh not at all,"* the Devil replied. *"I am going to let him organize it."* And with that, Jiddu Krishnamurti informed the audience that he would no longer lead any organization. Any leader would have followers and followers are too tempted to follow. *"I maintain that truth is a pathless land and you cannot approach it by any path whatsoever, by any religion, by any sect. That is my point of view and I adhere to that absolutely and unconditionally. Truth, being limitless, unconditioned, unapproachable by any path whatsoever, cannot be organized; nor should any organization be formed to lead or to coerce people along any particular path."*-Krishnamurti 100 Years by Evelyne Blau - Pg. 85 (I told you to jump through the window.)

   He never again formed anything like this type of structured organization. He did continue touring the world and having discussions with people, and giving talks. He sought to engage the members of the audience to help them to see clearly what was behind the questions they had asked, and tried to focus them into the mental structure of that moment. Like the Buddha he refuses to be drawn into metaphysical discussions, because they are ultimately irrelevant to you and your true understanding of what the now is. Krishnamurti always talked in a very clear and concise manner. He never buried anything under the weight of excess technical jargon. This is an art that I feel I have not mastered. His assertion is that these types of elaborate verbal paradigms are ultimately constructed to hide behind ideas. It is a form of intellectual arrogance and webs of meaning are one of the pitfalls of the higher chakras, specifically in terms of the intellect. Obtuse technical jargon is the cornerstone of the great deception of mystic teachings, such as the Masons or Scientology, etc. I could go on and tell you more about his life and elaborate on his philosophy, but in truth, I have decided not to. Krishnamurti's books are all very easy to read and I would suggest the *Essential Krishnamurti* as the only one you really need to buy. This book will make your heart ache.

Words

"Question: I am full of hate. Will you please teach me how to love?"
"No one can teach you how to love. If people could be taught how to love, the world's problems would be simple, would it not? If we could learn how to love from a book as we learn mathematics, this would be a marvelous world. There would be no hate, no exploitation, no wars, no division of rich and poor, and we would all be really friendly with each other. But love is not so easily to come by. It is easy to hate and hate brings people together after a fashion. It creates all kinds of fantasies; it brings about various types of co-operation, as in war. But love is much more difficult. You cannot learn how to love, but what you can do is observe hate and put it gently aside. Don't battle against hate, don't say how terrible it is to hate people, but see hate for what it is, and let it drop away. Brush it aside, it is not important. What is important is not to let hate take root in your mind. Do you understand? Your mind is like rich soil, and if given sufficient time, any problem that comes along takes root like a weed, and then you have the trouble of pulling it out. But if you do not give the problem sufficient time to take root, then it has no place to grow and it will wither away. If you encourage hate, give it time to take root, to grow, to mature, it becomes an enormous problem. But if each time hate arises, you let it go by, then you will find that your mind becomes very sensitive without being sentimental; therefore, it will know love.

"The mind can pursue sensations, desires, but it cannot pursue love. Love must come to the mind. And, once love is there, it has no division as sensuous and divine: it is love. That is the extraordinary thing about love: it is the only quality that brings a total comprehension of the whole existence." –Think on These Things 1964

"Truth or God is something totally unknown. You may imagine, you may speculate about it, but it is still the unknown. The mind must come to it completely stripped of the past, free of all the things it has known, and the known is the accumulated memories and problems of everyday existence. So, if there is really to be a radical change, a fundamental transformation, the mind must move away from the known. For love is not something which you experience yesterday and are able to recapture at will tomorrow. It is totally new, unknown." –Athens Talks - 1956

"True education is to learn how to think, not what to think. If you know how to think, if you really have the capacity, then you are a free human being - free of dogmas, superstitions, ceremonies, and therefore, you can find out what religion is." -Think on These Things - 1964

"We are trying to find out what it means to die, while living – not committing suicide. I am not talking about that kind of nonsense. I want to find out for myself what it means to die, which means, can I be totally free from everything that man has created, including myself?

"What does it mean to die, to give up everything? Death cuts you off with a very sharp razor from your attachments, from your gods, from your superstitions, from your desire for comfort, next life and so on, and on. I am going to find out what death means, because it is as important as living. So how can I find out, actually, not theoretically, what it means to die? I actually want to find out, as you want to find out. What does it mean to die? Put that question to yourself. While we are young, or when you are very old, this question is always there. It means to be totally free, to be totally unattached to everything that man has put together, or what you have put together – totally free. No attachments, no gods, no future, no past; see the beauty of it, the greatness of it, the extraordinary strength of it, while living to be dying, so that throughout life you are not attached to anything. That is what death means.

"So living is dying. You understand? Living means that every day you are abandoning everything that you are attached to. Can you do this? A very simple fact, but it has tremendous implications – so that each day is a new day. Each day you are dying and incarnating. There is tremendous vitality, energy there, because there is nothing you are afraid of. There is nothing that can hurt – being hurt doesn't exist." -Madras January 1, 1986.

I will refuse to say anything more on this. In fact, I should have said nothing, and will leave you with a question mark instead of an answer.

Van Morrison sums up the situation so well on one of my favorite recordings of all time. He said that this was one of the best songs he ever recorded and I would not contradict him. The album is *No guru, No method No teacher*; and the title track was written for Krishnamurti.

The chorus is, *"No guru, no method, no teacher, just you and I and nature in the garden."*

A YEAR WITH A SWOLLEN APPENDIX

Part of what I was trying to do in this book was a direct result of reading *From Dawn to Decadence* by Jacque Barzun. Instead of giving you a bibliography at the end of the book, he cited books from within the narrative, which he felt were excellent and worthwhile reading. As I was reading his book, I made long lists of his suggested reading on the various subjects he was discussing and ones I was also interested in. I subsequently bought many of the books that he suggested (about 20). One example of his suggestions was *The World of Yesterday* by Stefan Zweig, which is an autobiographical account of post Victorian Vienna and Austria. This fellow Zweig became a librettist for Richard Strauss, one of the greatest living German composers of the period. It seems Hitler took great offence to a Jew writing with Mr. Strauss and there was a lot of trouble for Mr. Zweig after Hitler moved into Austria. It seems that the Austrians were particularly virulent anti-Semites. This same Stefan Zweig wrote an excellent biography of Marie Antoinette. He subsequently moved to South America where he killed himself, presumably as a result of Hitler's maniacal hatred of him. It seems Hitler was really insulted by this particular Jew. My point being that this fellow Stefan Zweig was a writer who I might never have encountered had Jacque Barzun not literally hammered his love of him home to me repeatedly. Stefan Zweig was an excellent writer who wrote a1000 pages on a subject and then reduced it to 300. The final resulting books are the essence of terse, crafted, and succinct writing - really a great pleasure to read. And he represents the strict task master that I wish I had the restraint to emulate, but I am enamored with meander.

So I would like to write out a hit list of my favorite things. Of course, I leave myself open to the accusation of being pretentious or full of myself, or whatever. It is my contention that art is an indulgence anyway and that pretensions should be avoided, but the whole situation is, in its very essence, pretentious. Please don't bother reading any further, if this is your feeling. On the other hand, you toughed it out this far. I have seen in print that Jacques Barzun was accused of being a style Nazi, but I would say that he was probably the single best example of prose writing that I know of, and I have had his prose in the back of my head the whole time I have been writing. You can literally open *From Dawn to Decadence* on any page and read a paragraph and be completely satisfied with his thought. I wish that I could write as well as him. I may be in the gutter, but at least I'm looking at the stars.

As mentioned earlier, I enjoy reading history, but I would add that I only read history that is readable: academic history is for academics and quite frankly is written by people who can't write. Barbara Tuchman is one of my favorites: *The Guns of August,* deservedly won a Pulitzer, but not for history. She won the prize for excellence in her writing (Pulitzers for history are only given for American history). The rest of her books are all good, with *The Proud Tower* being exceptional as well. Along with Tuchman, you may want to read *Paris1919* by Margaret MacMillan, a lovely Canadian author who is an admitted Barbara Tuchman fan.

In ancient history, anything by Peter Green is exceptionally readable (especially *Alexander the Great* and his book on the Hellenistic era *Alexander to Actium*), or Michael Grant (*The Roman Era*).

I really enjoyed *The History of the Ancient World* by Susan Wise Bauer, as well. It seems women are some of the best historians.

The two books on the *Victorian era* by A. N. Wilson: *The Victorians, After the Victorians* and also *London: A Short History* are excellent, though his book on Queen Elizabeth was sadly unreadable.

Norman Davies's books on Europe are a great introduction to good narrative history: *Europe a History, The Isles and Microcosm* all bear multiple readings. As are the Will and Ariel Durant series: *The Story of Civilisation*. He is a great writer and this series is truly a monumental effort. His book on Oriental heritage was the first history book that I ever read. This was some 30 years ago and I just finished the full series last year. I wanted to know if the series was as good as I remembered it being, and it is.

All of Adrian Goldsworthy's books on Rome are excellent.

Michael White is also very fun to read: *Leonardo*, *Machiavelli* and *The Pope and the Heretic* are all great books on the renaissance period.

William Manchester (*The Last Lion*, Winston Churchill's biography is excellent. Simon Winchester (the two books on the writing of the Oxford English dictionary *The Meaning of Everything and the Professor and the Madman*. I have also read at least four others by this author and they are all good. Simon Schama, especially on Britain, you can read anything by all of them and like Miles Davis all of them are good. *Citizens* is a particularly excellent read about the French revolution.

A history of *Medieval Islam* by J.J. Saunders and *The Arab Peoples and the Middle East* by Bernard Lewis are a good place to start, if you wish to understand the history of Islam better. I personally loved reading the travel log called *The Adventures of Ibn Battuta*, By Ross E Dunn. It is an excellent window into all of Islam in the 14th century. This fellow Ibn Battuta traveled at least twice as far as Marco Polo did over his life time and a full century before him. Ibn Battuta traveled the whole of the Islamic world and seemed to have gotten well into China and India.

One of my favorite books is *Mehmed the Conqueror* by Franz Babinger. It is a great look at medieval Islam in Turkey and at the fall of Constantinople, specifically.

Constantine's Sword by James Carroll is a very good look at the beginnings of power in the church, as is *AD 381* by Charles Freeman. Power is a great lure and it is important to understand.

Mark Kurlansky, *Salt, Cod and the Basque History of the World* are all fun (and I mean fun) and easy to read.

A good general history of India is difficult to find. These few are all good:

A History of India by John Keay is probably the best introduction and the easiest to read.

A Cultural History of India edited by A.L.Basham and *The Wonder that was India* by the same author.

Ancient India by D.D. Kosambi is a little old, but a good read.

Gem in the Lotus by Abraham Eraly is particularly good.

Tournament of shadows by Karl Meyer & Sharren Brysac is an excellent look at the Raj and there are also some interesting things said about Madam Blavatsky and her political agenda.

A real eye opener and reassessment of the whole arc of Indian history is *In Search of the Cradle of Civilization* by Georg Feuerstein, Subhash Kak & David Frawley

I will also suggest any other book by Georg Feuerstein. I have read *The Yoga Tradition* and I am currently immersed in *Tantra: The Path of Ecstasy* and *Sacred Sexuality*. These books are the single best introduction to Indian philosophy that I have found and I only wish I had discovered them earlier.

Jungian Psychology

Psychological Types

Two Essays on Analytical Psychology

Symbols of Transformation

The Practice of Psychotherapy, are the best place to start, if you wish to read Jung himself

Along with his seminars, as mentioned earlier I have constantly returned to his autobiography, *Memories, Dreams and Reflections*. It becomes a better book every time you read it (I think I'm at six times now) and I am much older and more ready to receive his very inclusive wisdom.

All of Marie Louise Von France's books are excellent pick any one, along with Anthony Storr, Erich Neumann and Anthony Stevens - although Erich Neumann is a little tough going.

Joseph Campbell is a great read especially *The Masks of God* I don't know where to put them, but anything by Arthur Koestler or Colin Wilson will certainly provoke your thinking.

Both of Louis A Sass's books *The Paradox of Delusion* and *Madness and Modernism* supply an in depth reading into schizophrenia and modern art, and they both retroactively shaped my ongoing understanding of many aspects of this book. They both have nothing to do with Jungian psychology, but they do have the benefit of being excellent and readable works.

Religion

Karen Armstrong has been a huge influence on my thinking and she has proven to be extremely even handed with all faiths.

John Dominic Crossan has been a huge influence on how I perceive the formation of the Bible and the Gnostic gospels. And he also has an excellent analysis of how epic poems are recited in the real world. Also Northrop Frye*The Great Code* and *Words with Power*.

Henry Corbin has helped me greatly in understanding Islam.

Michel Chodkiewicz, William C. Chittick and Claude Addas can all be looked at, if you desire to know more about Ibn Arabi specifically.

Mircea Eliade has great insight into the religious mindset. His book on yoga and another on Shamanism has had a massive impact on my thinking. Both of these fellows Corbin and Eliade were acquainted with Jung personally through the *Eranos* lecture series, which Jung often participated in as a keynote speaker. Joseph Campbell was the editor of the various yearbooks that came out of these meetings.

Elaine Pagels books on *The Gnostic Gospels,* etc. are all worth reading and have also been a great influence on my understanding of the early church.

As far as Hindu philosophy goes, it is a massive field. I started with *A Sourcebook in Indian Philosophy* by Sarvepalli Radhakrishnan and Charles A. Moore. Also, *The Principal Upanishads* by Radhakrishnan.

As mentioned above, start with Georg Feuerstein- *The Yoga Tradition*. You will not dip your toe in a better book than this deep well.

Ananda Coomaraswamy might also be a place to start. He has written books on the Buddha.

Buddhist thought is obviously well represented by the Dali Llama, but Chogyam Trungpa is very fun and easy to read. Robert A.E. Thurman is an excellent author on Tibetan Buddhism as is W.Y. Evans Wentz

I really enjoyed *Secret of the Vajra World* by Reginald A. Ray. It is one of the best books to read, if you wish to gain an understanding of Buddhist Tantra.

Daisetz T Suzuki's books are great to read, if you wish to gain a perspective on Zen Buddhism. I also really enjoyed a book called *The Wheel of Life* by John Blofeld from Shambhala Press. It is an autobiography of a western Buddhist living in China in the forties and fifties, and it is surprisingly candid.

Richard Tarnas's *The Passion of the Western Mind* is in my opinion the best introduction to western philosophy you can get and as mentioned earlier in the book, *Cosmos and Psyche* is a truly mind blowing read.

I have been reading through a very profound book this year that I highly suggest called, *How to Know God: The Yoga Aphorisms of Pantajali* by Swami Prabhavananda and Christopher Isherwood. Pantajali and Shankra are two of the cornerstone philosophers of India from around 600 Common Area.

Science

The Elegant Universe and *The Fabric of the Universe* by Brian Greene

ABC's of Relativity by Bertrand Russell

The Trouble with Physics by Lee Smolin is an excellent critic of String theory.

The Lightness of Being by Frank Wilczek is an excellent, easy book to read about the state of physics and dark matter research today.

A Brief History of Time by Stephen W. Hawking

A Short History of Everything by Bill Bryson is a great place to start with – well everything.

Anything by Rupert Sheldrake in the field of Biology

Robert Wright's *Nonzero*, *The Evolution of God* and the *Moral Animal* are excellent books on neo-Darwinian thought and game theory.

The Universe Within by Neil Turok is an excellent introduction to the history of and the current state of astro/quantum physics by a really wonderful human being. I was privileged to have seen is Massy Hall lecture in person with my son.

Incomplete Nature by Terrence W. Deacon – an excellent though difficult book about systems theory and much more – very inspiring.

Jared Diamond's *Collapse* and *Guns, Germs and Steel* are both excellent reads about anthropology/sociology/history/etc.

Darwin's Ghost by Steven Jones is excellent introduction to Darwin and the ongoing understanding of genetics as it relates to evolution.

Neuroscience

The Emotional Brain by Joseph LeDoux is an excellent introduction to the emotional underpinnings of neuroscience. It is well written and easy to understand.

The Ego Tunnel by Thomas Metzinger is an excellent place to start, if you wish tackle some of the underlying philosophical arguments that have both occurred and further propelled neuroscience.

Incognito: The Secret Lives of the Brain by David Eagleman is an exceptionally easy read that will give you a real insight into just how much we don't know at all.

In Search of Memory by Eric R. Kandel is simply a wonderful and very human book by one of the founding fathers of neuroscience. I was surprised at how much I enjoyed this touching and well written book.

Mirroring People by Marco Jacoboni is a good introduction to mirror neurons.

The First Idea by Stanley I. Greenspan, MD and Stuart G. Shanker is an excellent book on language and symbols and has caused me to reassess many of my ideas. This is where the emotional and embodied mind was nailed down for me. I was groping toward an understanding of this and they really brought it home.

Did My Neurons Make Me Do It? By Nancy Murphy & Warren S. Brown is a difficult read, but a very important look at the structure and modes of functioning in the mind. It combines both the philosophical implications of neuroscience and grounding in the reality of how the mind really works along with much systems analysis. This is probably one of the single most influential books in my understanding of neuroscience, but it has a dumb title.

The Master and His Emissary by Iain McGilchrist is probably one of the 10 best books I have ever read – full stop on any subject. If you read my book, you will have an idea of what he is driving at in his (bi-lateralization of the brain), except that he will paint for you such a rich canvas that the poverty of mine will become all the more apparent. The feel of this book is similar to Karen Armstrong and Oliver Sack's work, which is very human and inclusive and overall right brain. With a smoking page-turning narrative, it's a book like *Dawn to Decadence* that leaves you hungry to explore everything in the world, especially the romantic era.

Oliver Sacks and Elkhonon Goldberg have greatly influenced my continued reading in neuroscience and are dimly reflected in the later writing of the book. I have endlessly debated whether I should intrude into the existing narrative, or whether I should cut my losses and write another book strictly about neuroscience. It is already a very large subject with a lot of excellent writers already in the mix. I will say that these two are excellent with Mr. Goldberg being somewhat technical, while Mr. Sacks seems to approach the whole subject from a much more feeling toned and empathetic stance – very refreshing to read. *Musicophilia* by Oliver Sacks could have forced me to completely rewrite *The Way Up,* because there are so many amazing revelations, but in the end, I have decided not muddy my original narrative with even more digressions.

Mr. Goldberg's views on right and left brain division are profound, and being a left-handed person myself, I found much to chew on in terms of my own proclivity to constantly associate different paradigms – right brain activity. But Iain McGilchrist, drawing on Goldberg and others, showed me what it really means in terms of culture in the broadest most inclusive sense.

V.S. Ramachandran and Sandra Blakeslee's *Phantoms in the Brain* is a very readable account of one of the experts in the field of neuroscience. I came to this book very late and referenced it for instances of blind sight, because it is so readable. Also, this book confirmed that many of my speculations were not the long shots. I began to think they were, because Mr. Ramachandran comes very close to some of my speculations about right and left brain issues. The book was written in 1998.

I cannot say enough about the *Brain Science* Podcast. Ginger Campbell is the type of person that I really respect and admire. She seems to grasp the importance of her reading and subject matter and is genuinely concerned with giving it away.

All of the Steven Pinker's books are great, especially *How the Mind Works*. I was forced to reassess much of his thinking while writing this book. It is interesting when a seemingly full paradigm gets swallowed by a much larger perspective. In this case, neurobiology has swallowed linguistics wholesale by reassessing the root contentions.

And I love Wade Davis books. He is an ethnobotanist and overall an adventurer. Brian Eno once said how he loved hearing stories about people, who went to the North Pole and did extreme things, but that he had little desire to do those things himself. I'm like that as well. Wade Davis is one of those guys who goes to crazy places and tells us about it. Malcolm Gladwell was a massive influence on me and was a large impetus for me trying to write a book at all. *Blink* and *the Tipping Point* don't need me to say anything. Their success speaks volumes. After finishing my third rewrite of this book, I bought a copy of *Outliers,* which I intended on writing into this book in some way. Again, *Malcolm Gladwell* is a more than worthwhile read.

I would add *Fooled by Randomness* by Nassim Nicholas Taleb and Freakonomics by Steven D. Levitt and Stephen J. Dubner were very influential in my weak and habitually derogatory understanding of Stats. I have also become a *Freakonomics* podcast junkie. I drive a lot.

Something Novel

As far as novelists go, I have not read too extensively in nonfiction in the last 15 years, but I was fanatical about Tolstoy and Dostoyevsky when I was younger, and have read *The Brothers Karamazov* at least seven times. I reread it last year and would gladly read it again. One of my best friends Michael Kulas read *The Brothers Karamazov* six times and I just had to get a leg up on him. I have also greatly enjoyed Salman Rushdie, John Irving, Robertson Davies and Kurt Vonnegut.

The Book of Laughter and Forgetting, Unbearable Lightness of Being and especially *Immortality* by Milan Kundera hold a special place in my heart and I would say all of his works are well worth reading. His critical essays are fascinating: *The Art on the Novel* and *The Curtain and Testaments Betrayed.*

Music

I am a music junkie and I worked in the music industry for far too many years. When it comes to trivia in the pop music realm, I am pretty hard to stump, but of course, I have my weak areas.

For me, good music is largely about good writing (I have a low tolerance for poor lyrics). Composition in the widest sense of the word is my current mania. Someone once told me you can't shine shit and it's true. Disney should take note. They have been shining shit for years.

Indian Classical

Obviously, Ravi Shankar is a master on sitar and I had the distinct honor to have seen him play live twice with his lovely daughter Anouska, but I found his recordings to be uneven. My personal favorite is Live at the Monterey Pop Festival, though I don't own a lot of his work. On the other hand, Nikhil Banerjee can do no wrong. These four recordings are sublime:

Classical Heritage of India on BMG # *DSAV1054* and *DSAV 1039;*

Traditions classiques de l'orient vol 16 & 1 on sono disc. Volume 1 is one of my favorite recordings of all time. His version of Rag Manj Khammaj is so delicate and heart achingly beautiful. Good luck trying to find these.
If you can't find them, you can hear Nikhil Banerjee playing *Manj Khammaj* in a duet with Ustad Ali Akbar Khan on Mr. Khan's own label *AMMP Vol. 4* (cat. AMMPCD9405)
All of Ali Akbar Khan's work is amazing, but for the beginner I would suggest *Morning Visions and Vol. 3* (cat. AMMPCD9406 & AMMPCD9404 respectively)
Also, the group called GHAZAL with Kayhan Kalhor (from Iran, playing spike fiddle) and Shujaat Hussain Khan (sitar and vocals) is a cross of Indian classical with Persian classical music. All of the recordings are excellent, but I particularly enjoy *Swapan Chuadruri* the tabla player who is not on all of them.

Pop Music

I will avoid the obviously great bands like Led Zeppelin, Pink Floyd and the Beatles etc., but I will add The Police, Sting, Kate Bush, Peter Gabriel, Jethro Tull, The Tragically Hip, Tom Waits, U2 and XTC for good measure.

One of my heroes Carlinhos Brown is almost unknown in North America. I love all of his records, but if you feel the urge to buy one, I would suggest *Omelete Man*. Carlinhos Brown, along with Marisa Monte, are huge stars in the Brazilian pop world, but because they sing largely in Portuguese, they cannot break into the American market.

Two of the greatest pop writers to emerge in the last 15 years are Neil Finn of *Crowded House* and Elvis Costello. I would like to say that both of Neil Finn's solo records (*One All* and *Try Whistling This*), might be his best work and they have received limited exposure in North America. Elvis Costello can pretty much do no wrong, although he can go all over the road.

The other great songwriter to emerge recently is Patty Griffin. She has consistently turned up on the Dixie Chicks records and also worked with Emmylou Harris, but her solo records are unbelievably beautiful (anyone of them).

James Millionaires is probably one of the greatest lost pop albums of all time. It really should have been huge. Of course *Laid* and *Hey Ma* are great records as well.

Joni Mitchell and Van Morrison have been mainstays of my listening for years. All of their recordings are fairly good (Van less so than Joni), but I constantly come back to *Hejira* by Joni Mitchell and *No Guru* by Van Morrison. I try not to be sentimental, but both of these albums are part of the fabric of my DNA now and they draw me like a magnet.

Radiohead are the gods of progressive music and you cannot do better than *OK Computer, Amnesiac and Kid A*. Also, *King of Limbs Live from the Basement* is way better (more real, if that makes sense), than the studio version and you get a free full-length video. Their recordings are truly master pieces, and they prove that there is always something new to be uncovered.

I am a fan of Soundgarden and Chris Cornell has had a great career outside of the band (in Audioslave and solo records), largely because he is a great songwriter. This is a talent/skill that will help you to endure. The rest is all trim work.

I was a huge David Sylvian fan when I was younger and I recently bought *Blemish* an album from 2003, and I am afraid, he has tried very hard to become irrelevant. The later Japanese records are great and the first five solo records are all excellent.

Finally *Talk Talk, The Laughing Stock* and *Spirit of Eden* are truly unrecognized master pieces, along with Mark Hollis solo record (which is really a master piece of deep understatement). These are not fun or simple records, but if you like Radiohead you will understand the brave depth of these records.

Rickie Lee Jones is someone who never seems to fall off of the top of her game. Her later works have the depth of a life lived in the arts. She is really trying hard to be excellent, and for so many reasons, her work is good. The *Evening of the Best Day of My Life* rarely leaves my car. Brian Eno's work speaks for itself. I really don't know where to start: *Ambient 1, Music for Airports*.

Jazz

Obviously Miles Davis and John Coltrane, etc.

I have really enjoyed all of the later Jan Garbarek records, pretty much from 1989 on. They are all good with *Twelve Moons* and *I Took up the Runes,* being stand out favorites.

Keith Jarrett is truly a towering figure in modern music and there is something good to say about everything he has recorded. Some recordings are not for the average listener. His recording of *Shostakovich* was way too much for me, but I do keep coming back to his work over and over again. My personal favorites are: *The Koln Concert, Dark Intervals, Radiance* and *The Melody at Night with You* (probably his most assessable recording). As far at his group work: *The Blue Note* recordings, *The Cure* and my personal favorite *Changeless,* which is a series of modal improvisations with Gary Peacock on bass, and the incomparable Jack DeJohnette on drums.

John McLaughlin is another great artist and all of the Shakti recordings are excellent. The later live ones are marginally better recordings. I've have had the privilege to see Shakti twice. Their profound joy is infectious.

And my hero Vince Mendoza is well worth the money. *Sketches* is marginally better than the rest, but as mentioned earlier, *Vespertine by Bjork* is really good and you can also hear his arranging on Elvis Costello's *My Flame Burns Blue*, and the later Joni Mitchell works where she redoes her earlier songs.

Pat Metheny is the other towering figure and I would suggest *Still Life Talking*, *Letter from Home*, *Secret Story*, either of the Metheny Mehldau recordings and especially *The Way Up*. *Orchestrion* has proven to be an enduring listen and his new *Unity Band* is a great quartet record, but again they are all good.

You would be hard pressed to find anything as beautiful as *Arvo Part* on this earth. *Te Deum* is one of a handful of classical recordings to sell over a million copies. My personal favorite is *Miserere*.

I was lucky enough to see *Nusrat Fateh Ali Khan* twice before he died. He was truly an incredible artist and anything is good. All of the Real World recordings are worth owning, and also the *Dead Man Walking* soundtrack for you Pearl Jam/ Ry Cooder fans.

One of my personal peccadilloes is a Nordic band called *Frifot*. Most of the recordings are the same three people: Per Gudmundson, Ale Moller, and Lena Willemark. Some earlier recordings like *Nordan* on ECM featured other jazz players. *Sluring* is the best recording so far, but again they are all good (*Nordan* standing out among the early works). This is largely Swedish folk and medieval music, but they are not antiquarians trying to preserve anything. This music is alive and well, thank you. I don't know why I love *Frifot* so much, but it is best not to question these things, just follow your heart.

There are so many other little nooks and crannies of music that I love.

Again thank you very much for your indulgence in my indulgence.

GLOSSARY

A priory: Knowledge before the fact.

Acuity: In reference to fine delicate motor skills from the same root as acumen which means coming to a point or being refined.

Aetiology: The search for a first cause or primary reason behind a phenomenon.

Altruism: The 'natural' inclination in humans to get along.

Analysand: A person who has engaged in psychoanalysis with an analyst – a patient.

Enantiodromia: The tendency of things to become their opposite.

Empirical: Knowledge-based on experience in the real world.

Epigenetic: The way that systems increase in complexity, from say an acorn to a tree.

Extrovert: Perceives themselves through the outside world.

Feeling: Rational, concerned with a worldview built on relation. What does this mean to me?

Gnosis: With the wisdom of God, as opposed to Agnostic: without the wisdom of God.

Gordian Knot: Alexander responded to a prophecy that he who un-tied the Gordian knot would rule Asia. This Gordian knot was literally a knot of rope that secured some kind of cart to a post. Alexander simply raised his sword and cut the knot in two, and of course, went on to rule Asia.

Introvert: Perceives the outside world through the lens of themselves.

Intuition: Intuition is the result of our largely unconscious perception of our environment. We may notice the smallest movement in someone's facial expression and think, I want to get away from this person and moments later they are in a fight with someone else. This is not magic or ESP. It is the result of our brain's constant assessment of the environment below the level of consciousness, hence non-rational

Intuitive: Non-rational and concerned with a view of the world that has to do with the future of events.

Ismailian Gnosis: An Arabic wisdom tradition with links to western and eastern philosophies and religions. The Aga Khan is an admirable world leader of the Ismailian faith at present.

Land Naming or Land Nama: When in a strange environment, you seek to see the familiar around you or ascribe names, places that you know to this new environment. (New Amsterdam became New York, for instance.) Also, an extension of this attitude is the astrological symbols in the heavens where we seek to infuse meaning on to the unknown.

Meta Level: Existing at a level of complexity that is not implied by lower levels of understanding, or existing at a level of complexity that cannot be understood through reduction into constituents. Traffic is my favorite example-metaphor for the mind/brain-of a gestalt that eludes strict analysis.

Metaphor: See Pg. 62 for an extended look at metaphor, simile and analogy.

Metaphysical: Meta means more than or in addition to, or beyond. So metaphysical is anything that is beyond the physical or provable world. Science is physical, religion or God is metaphysical

Para: Transcendent or supreme. Prajnaparamita is the transcendent knowledge of the other shore: Pra is before, Jna is wisdom or thought; Para is transcendent or beyond; mita is shore.

Participation Mystique: A term coined by Lucien Levy-Bruhl, which was meant to indicate the more archaic level of consciousness where the individual identifies more completely with their environment. It could be argued that this is a representation of the right brains being in the world. People in a state of participation mystique are magically participating in the world around them, for example, that stone is special or women might not be allowed to see something sacred at a certain times of the year, but no one knows exactly why. Jung uses this term extensively in his writings and I should have as well, because it sums up so many concepts.

Polyrhythms: Rhythms that partake in two or more time signatures at the same time.

Procedural Memory: The largely unconscious ability to use your muscles; for instance, the ability to tie your shoe, or indeed, walk out the door without thinking about it at all.

Projection: The preponderance of people to externalize unconscious aspects of themselves on to their environment and or other people. Pop stars may train-wreck when they can't fully separate themselves from what is being projected on to them by their adoring public.

Sensate: Non-rational and concerned with a view of the world that is only interested in facts. Where the McDonald's is the only relevant aspect of the environment, not why the hell should we settle for McDonald's.

Solipsism: A theory, which I do not subscribe to: that only the self can be known and verified – an essentially narcissistic view of reality.

Sthula: Gross or physical.

Suksma: Subtle or refined. See Para

Teleology: Good luck. A belief that naturally designed things functions primarily as a reflection of ongoing utility.

Thinking: Rational and concerned with a worldview based on intellectual assessments – much maligned in this book unfairly. Has a tendency to displace reality away from the object being contemplated.

What's Being Said

"Finally a single volume in which Greg Heard has masterfully deconstructed Dan Brown and his conspiratorial fantasy. This is the book that the public has long been waiting for."

-Author

"This book reads like a Chinese menu." – A person who's been to New York

"A Pulitzer Prize would certainly be in the offing for this one. Too bad the author is a foreigner."

"I've read a lot of deep and rich books and I will tell you that this is definitely the first book that Greg Heard has ever published, whether he will be enjoined into the celestial pantheon of wordsmiths or be congratulated into the intellectual nebula of psychic explorers is yet to be determined, but he has certainly written this book!!!" – Italics Aremine

"Its shitastic; I was bejazzeled" -Ponderous Hyperbolae

"Reading takes a lot of time…someone should help me with that." – Thisare Mine

"I wish he would just shut up, but he can't help himself." Rave on John Dunn

* Footnote to Pg.103

I didn't want footnotes, but I began reading *The Master and His Emissary* after I had "completed" this book. I realized that this single book was probably one of the three greatest books I have ever read, along with *Madness and Modernism* by Louis Sass. Iain McGilchrist is a profound thinker/psychologist who demystified the western culture. I realized so many things about my own narrative that were actually the result of the divergence of right brain and left brain. Jung's separation of feeling and thinking are largely the result of right brain (feeling, values etc.) and the left brain (rationalism abstraction etc.). The title of the book *Proof* (left) *and the difficulty of meaning* (right) is based on the opposition, and hopefully integration of these two antithetical viewpoints. Page after page of this book led me into stupefied wonder, and also largely confirm where I had gotten to in my own thinking, to the point that I felt I might look like I lifted much of my work directly out of McGilchrist. As you will see, by the next footnote, this started to happen a lot as I neared the end of my writing. Ultimately, I have re-entered my narrative and tweaked some of the salient arguments here and there, but I didn't have the will to engage in a complete rewrite. Mostly I culled some spectacular quotes and I would say to the interested reader that if you enjoyed my book, Iain McGilchrist will take you well beyond my humble offering. I have subsequently read through both of these books since this footnote and these works have been the locus of my next work of essays probably called *Private Concerns*.

*Foot note Pg. 311 17/09/2012

I just watched *A Dangerous Method* by David Cronenberg and I was both surprised and delighted to see that his read on this whole episode was almost exactly the same as mine. I felt compelled to say that I in no way plagiarized his material or comments for this section of my book. Even the comment about Freud needing to have a good fuck was inserted by Cronenberg without my knowing. I shouldn't say that this 'fuck' comment was a particularly stunning piece of writing on my part, but nonetheless, I was quite struck by the similarities of our narratives. Of course, most of our stories were culled from memories dreams and reflections, but still it was quite uncanny. Keera Knightly is utterly captivating in this film and I highly recommend it, if you wish to dip your toe into Jung's world.

PROOF AND THE DIFFICULTY OF MEANING

*Footnote Pg. 319

There recently has been a great scandal in the Anusara community and there are many accusations flying around of mad sexual practices and Wicca Covens, etc. I think this whole scandal is a result of Americans forcing their prudish sense of purity on to the whole yoga world. These are real people doing what real people do, which is fuck and mess around with religions. It has nothing and everything to do with the actual practice of the body. Anusara yoga is a business model and businesses become corrupted in many ways. The saddest thing is that Anusara teachers tend to have the most rigorous training of any brand of yoga. I recently did some yoga in Rishikesh and the teacher was terrible.

*Footnote Pg. 323

   The interested reader should defiantly read *V.S. Ramachandran.*

I recently started my second book by him, but he has been studying synaesthesia longer than anyone else and he is so wonderfully balanced. I have also been greatly relieved to find that Mr. Ramachandran found confirmation for many of my more tenuous speculations and I am trying to contact him to suss out his feelings about auras.

*Footnote Pg. 359

Neil Turok takes on both Richard Dawkins and Laurence Krauss as well in *The Universe Within* Pg 246-7. Also see *Mind and Cosmos* by Thomas Nagle for a much nuanced viewing of this atheist agenda, especially as it relates to evolution.

ABOUT THE AUTHOR

Greg Heard's ongoing studies for the past 40 years in all manner of books include Iceland sagas, eastern philosophy, early biblical studies, world history, mythology and the sciences. As someone who lives his life in the creative realms: first, as a carpenter on film sets to support my family, to creating and playing music with his band, to writing poetry and fantasy fiction for the sheer enjoyment, there has always been a yearning to know life's meaning through the lens of left-brain practical and mundane sciences. Most artists do. There always seems to be a need to understand where the spark of inspiration comes from in order to create the masterpiece.

Made in the USA
Charleston, SC
29 May 2015